Luminos is the Open Access monograph publishing program from UC Press. Luminos provides a framework for preserving and reinvigorating monograph publishing for the future and increases the reach and visibility of important scholarly work. Titles published in the UC Press Luminos model are published with the same high standards for selection, peer review, production, and marketing as those in our traditional program. www.luminosoa.org

D1522390

The Persianate World

The Persianate World

The Frontiers of a Eurasian Lingua Franca

Edited by

Nile Green

UNIVERSITY OF CALIFORNIA PRESS

University of California Press, one of the most distinguished university presses in the United States, enriches lives around the world by advancing scholarship in the humanities, social sciences, and natural sciences. Its activities are supported by the UC Press Foundation and by philanthropic contributions from individuals and institutions. For more information, visit www.ucpress.edu.

University of California Press
Oakland, California

Suggested citation: Green, Nile (ed.). *The Persianate World: The Frontiers of a Eurasian Lingua Franca*. Oakland: University of California Press, 2019. DOI: https://doi.org/10.1525/luminos.64

Library of Congress Cataloging-in-Publication Data

Names: Green, Nile, editor.
Title: The Persianate world : the frontiers of a Eurasian lingua franca / edited by Nile Green.
Description: Oakland, California : University of California Press, [2019] | Includes bibliographical references and index. | This work is licensed under a Creative Commons [CC-BY-NC-ND] license. To view a copy of the license, visit http://creativecommons.org/licenses. |
Identifiers: LCCN 2018044520 (print) | LCCN 2018050251 (ebook) | ISBN 9780520972100 () | ISBN 9780520300927 (pbk. : alk. paper)
Subjects: LCSH: Persian language—History. | Lingua francas—Eurasia.
Classification: LCC PK6225 (ebook) | LCC PK6225 .P48 2019 (print) | DDC 491/.5509—dc23
LC record available at https://lccn.loc.gov/2018044520

27 26 25 24 23 22 21 20 19
10 9 8 7 6 5 4 3 2 1

Dedicated to the memory of
Marshall G. S. Hodgson (1922–68)
on the fiftieth anniversary of his death

CONTENTS

ILLUSTRATIONS

MAPS

FIGURES

A NOTE ON TRANSLITERATION

For Persian, Arabic, and Chaghatai Turkish, the chapters in this volume adopt a slightly modified version of the transliteration scheme of the *International Journal of Middle East Studies*, simplified without recourse to macrons and underdots, though preserving the ʿ*ayn*. For the sake of consistency, for both Arabic and Persian w has been used, rather than both w and v, to designate *waw/vav*. Chapter 1 similarly follows *IJMES* guidelines in using modern Turkish orthography to transliterate names, source materials, and terms from Ottoman Turkish, alongside *IJMES* Persian transliteration for the names of Persian texts and their authors.

Two reasons influenced the decision not to use the now widespread "Persian" system adopted by such journals as *Iranian Studies* and the *Journal of Persianate Studies*. Firstly, the anachronistic implications of adopting modern Iranian vocalization of Farsi. Secondly, the consequent overriding of variations of Persian pronunciation in various other regions of Eurasia. While the standardized system adopted here does likely better reflect Central and South Asian pronunciations of Persian, it is no universal panacea, and it raises issues of its own. The guiding attitude has ultimately been a pragmatic one to render words recognizable to specialists while avoiding the more blatant assumptions of Iranian normativity and centrality regarding the broader Eurasian history of the Persian language.

Through their coverage of Ming and Qing China, chapters 3 and 6 use the Hanyu Pinyin system for their romanization of Chinese words.

In the half century since Marshall Hodgson coined the term "Persianate" for his three-volume work *The Venture of Islam: Conscience and History in a World Civilization*, his neologism has been widely adopted by scholars of the Middle East, Central and South Asia, and even further afield. In studies of the medieval and early modern eras, and increasingly beyond, the term has become something of a leitmotif. Yet despite the general embrace of Hodgson's vocabulary—and the expansion, even reification, of his original "Persianate zone" into a "Persianate world"—there has been very little attempt to further define and delineate the concept, still less to test the hypothesis that lay hidden in this terminology. The validity of what we might call the "Persianate hypothesis"—of the long-term dominance *qua* influence of Persian over the other languages and cultures of the eastern Islamic world—has been widely taken for granted. Indeed, in an increasingly celebratory literature that has championed the "cosmopolitan" profile of Persian literature and Persianate culture at large, questions that concern cultural hegemony, let alone the role of Persian in the implementation of imperial power, have largely been sidelined. Altogether, this makes for poor history, because it avoids key questions of process: of how Persian gained its hegemonic "Persianate" status; how it subsequently maintained it for so many centuries; how (and indeed whether) it did so differently in the various regions where the language was used; and, crucially, how and in what forms Persian came to stamp its "Persianate" profile onto other languages and literatures.

To address these basic questions of the Persianate as process requires that Persian be examined in its various relational profiles; that is, in relation to those other languages and literatures now routinely categorized as "Persianate." That is, in order to examine the expansion, continuance, and eventual contraction of Persian's influence over various peoples and their own languages it is necessary to study Persian in direct relation to those sundry other languages. Hodgson coined the term "Persianate" precisely to point to these procedures of linguistic and wider cultural contact. Yet despite this, few studies have developed the relational and comparative approach required to scrutinize Persian's struggle for hegemony, even for plain and harmless "influence," over Eurasia's other linguistic and literary cultures. It is here that the present volume makes its intervention by drawing together linguistic and area-based expertise to document the multiplicity of interactions that created and maintained the much-vaunted "Persianate world" that stretched unevenly from the Balkans to Bengal, or even China. The methodology brought to bear in this volume's twelve case-study chapters is therefore a comparatist one of tracing how Persian related to its various linguistic interlocutors, whether literary Chinese or vernacular Turkic. For neither the Persianate as process, nor the Persianate world it created, can be understood through Persian sources alone.

In addition to developing this comparatist method for unpacking the processes implicit in the term "Persianate," this book takes seriously, if critically, the very notion of a "Persianate world." Perusing much scholarship, readers might be forgiven for mistaking this term as another way of saying "India and Iran," perhaps with a quiet nod to Afghanistan. But however rich their literary heritage, those few regions are insufficient to comprise a "world" in any meaningful sense, particularly a world located amid the continuously intersecting geographies of Eurasia. For this reason, the present volume seeks to de-provincialize the Persianate world from its familiarly Indo-Iranian moorings by making a more robust case for a "world" that encompassed the greater part of the Eurasian continent. *The Persianate World* therefore brings into conversation scholars working on Persian texts that circulated as far apart as China and Britain—the far axes of the Eurasian continent—with researchers of Persian's more familiar homes in India and Iran. The introduction and subsequent chapters reach from western Europe and the Balkans through the Volga-Ural region to Siberia, thence down to China, with a limited outreach to Southeast Asia before making a fuller arc back into the Indian subcontinent, and thence to the wide and varied territories of Central Asia, the Caucasus, and, of course, Iran.

This terminal placement of Iran is deliberate, because to situate Iran at the perennial "center" of a Persianate world is not merely an expression of methodological nationalism. It is also a plain anachronism that negates the historicity of the Persianate world in all its capacity for dynamism, multiplicity and evolution. As the introduction to this volume makes clear, there is no doubting the importance of parts of Iran (and no less of parts of today's Afghanistan and Uzbekistan) to the early history of written Persian, and to the literary and bureaucratic forms with which the language became associated there. But to recognize this is emphatically not the same as situating either Iran or even a more capacious "Khurasan" at the perpetual center of the Persianate past. To do so would be to render the Persianate world no more than a magnified "greater Iran," or alternatively a "greater India," as it can sometimes seem. To avoid perpetuating this mischaracterization, and to make a more credible case for the existence of something deserving the heuristic title of "world," the following chapters consider Iran as only one contributing region of the Persianate world. In a work of world history, this decentering of Iran is justified for two further reasons. Firstly, because in different periods and regions, Iran was not necessarily regarded as the primary point of reference for Persian. For the many Muslims who dwelt from the Volga basin up to Siberia and down into Eastern Turkistan, it was Transoxiana (specifically Bukhara) that was long seen as the *fons et origo* of Persian learning. Similarly, Timurid Herat and Samarqand were the most influential Persianate role models of the elites of the Ottoman and arguably also Mughal empires. Secondly, the decentering of Iran is also justified by this volume's main focus on the Timurid period onwards, on the centuries during which a multiplicity of Persian literary traditions and hubs of Persianate culture came to dilute the sweet clarion call of Shiraz.

It is in the hope of promoting this more mutable and protean picture of the Persianate world that this book's adopts the rubric of "frontiers." As various world historians have shown, to use the model of frontiers is to suggest spaces of cultural *métissage*, of the linguistic fusions and literary syntheses inherent in Hodgson's foundational conception of the Persianate. And finally, to speak of a world of frontiers in the plural is expressly not to speak of a world with a "center" in the singular. It is the making and unmaking of this more pluralistic and permutable Persianate world that the following pages seek to explore.

ف

The Persianate World is the outcome of a lengthy research and conference project funded by the William Andrews Clark Memorial Library and the UCLA Center for 17th- & 18th-Century Studies. Additional funding was supplied by the UCLA Program on Central Asia and the Irving and Jean Stone Chair in Social Sciences. Together, these sources of financial and administrative help made possible the three international conferences and supplementary seminars that brought to Los Angeles scholars from France, Russia, Turkey, China, Australia, and the United States so as to lend initial shape to the essays in this volume. I would therefore first like to thank the program committee of the Clark Memorial Library and the UCLA Center for 17th- & 18th-Century Studies for awarding me the William Andrews Clark endowed chair for 2015–16, which funded the three international conferences at UCLA. I am especially grateful to the erstwhile Clark Library director, Barbara Fuchs, her successor Helen Deutsch, and the staff of the Center for 17th- & 18th-Century Studies, particularly Erich Bollmann, Jeanette LeVere, Kathy Sanchez, and Candis Snoddy. At the UCLA Program on Central Asia, I would like to thank Bin Wong, Elizabeth Leicester, Nick Menzies, and Aaron Miller for their years of support for the Program on Central Asia under my directorship in 2008–16. And I am grateful to Sanjay Subrahmanyam for releasing funds from the Irving and Jean Stone Endowed Chair to invite several additional speakers. For enabling my access to the varied materials cited in the introduction, I also thank the Charles E. Young Research Library at UCLA (especially David Hirsch) and my graduate student Sohaib Baig, who helped copyedit several of the chapters under my supervision and created the three maps. I am finally grateful to Eric Schmidt, my editor at the University of California Press, for his enthusiastic support of the book project, to Peter Dreyer for his careful copyediting and to Manju Khanna for preparing the index.

For a variety of reasons, not all of the more than thirty presentations at the "Frontiers of Persian Learning" conferences and seminars ultimately found a place in this volume. More than a question of quality, this was ultimately a matter of trying to ensure an even regional and temporal distribution of contributions to the book, an agenda that lay somewhat at odds with the far greater abundance of expertise on the history of Persian in India and Iran. Yet regardless of these ultimately editorial matters, these other presenters and discussants played an essential role in the intellectual evolution of this book. I am therefore extremely grateful to Janet Afary, Muzaffar Alam, Ali Anooshahr, Subah Dayal, Walter Hakala, Kevan Harris, Domenico Ingenito, Arash Khazeni, Mana Kia, Rajeev Kinra, Hajnalka Kovacs, Paul Losensky, Ryan Perkins, John R. Perry, James Pickett, Ron Sela, Rahim Shayegan, Sanjay Subrahmanyam, Audrey Truschke, Paul Wormser, and Liu Yingsheng. I hope that the following pages will provide these and other friends and colleagues with some small measure of the stimulation and inspiration I have gained from their work.

Nile Green
Los Angeles, June 2018

MAP 1. Sites of Persian use in Persianate Eurasia

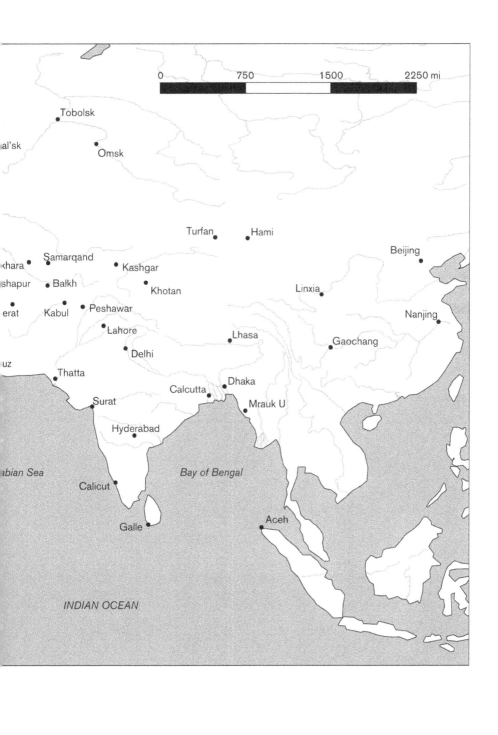

0   750   1500   2250 mi

Tobolsk

al'sk

Omsk

Turfan   Hami

Beijing

Samarqand   Kashgar

khara   Linxia

shapur   Balkh   Khotan

erat   Kabul   Peshawar   Nanjing

Lahore   Lhasa   Gaochang

Delhi

uz

Thatta   Dhaka

Calcutta   Mrauk U

Surat

Hyderabad

abian Sea   Bay of Bengal

Calicut

Galle   Aceh

INDIAN OCEAN

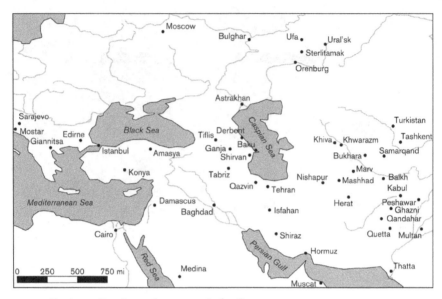

MAP 2. Persianate Eurasia, northern sector in detail

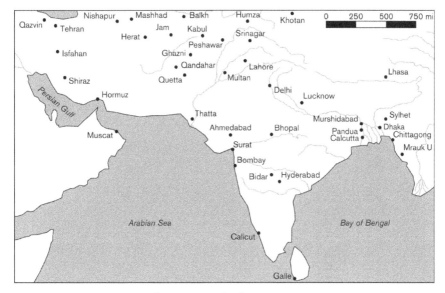

MAP 3. Persianate Eurasia, southern sector in detail

Introduction

The Frontiers of the Persianate World (ca. 800–1900)

Nile Green

DEFINING THE "PERSIANATE"

By the fifteenth century, having gained written form as a fashionable patois of the court poets of tenth-century Bukhara, Persian had become a language of governance or learning in a region that stretched from China to the Balkans, and from Siberia to southern India.[1] As a lingua franca promoted by multi-ethnic and multi-religious states, and aided further by education and diplomacy, Persian reached the zenith of its geographical and social reach between the sixteenth and eighteenth centuries. Then, from the early nineteenth century on, it was undermined by the rise of new imperial and vernacular languages. By around 1900, the language, which had once served to connect much of Eurasia, had retreated to Iran and neighboring pockets of Afghanistan and Central Asia, where it was refashioned into the national languages of Farsi, Dari, and Tajiki. The period between 1400 and 1900, then, marks an era defined by the maximal expansion then rapid contraction of one of history's most important languages of global exchange.

By focusing its case-study chapters on these five centuries, *The Persianate World* aims to understand the reasons behind both this expansion and contraction of Persian by identifying what functions the language was able and unable to serve in the transformative early modern and modern eras of intensifying interactions across Eurasia. By looking at the various "frontiers" of Persian—in the linguistic, geographical, and social senses of the term—the following pages chart the limits of exchange and understanding between the diverse communities brought into contact by this language. In geographical terms, this book moves beyond a static model of Persian's linguistic geography to trace the mobility of texts and text producers as far away as the British Isles and China, as well as the localization of Persian in Central Asia and India. By focusing on "horizontal" geographical frontiers and "vertical" social frontiers, on routes and roots, this book seeks to identify the limits—indeed, the breaking points—of Persian's usefulness as a medium of information, understanding, and affinity. If scholars now take for granted the notion that Persian was a shared lingua franca, it is important to identify more precisely who shared it, and for what (and indeed whose) purposes they did so. In focusing on the five centuries that most densely marked both the making and unmaking of one

1

of Eurasia's greatest lingua francas, *The Persianate World* is an exercise in tracing the contours and constraints of the cosmopolitan.

As an exercise in world history, the aim is to decouple the study of Persian from both explicit and implicit methodological nationalisms. In recent years the promotion of the "Persianate world" based implicitly around competing cultural centers in India or Iran has at times carried the ideological baggage of formerly dominant secular nationalisms, whether Iranian emphases on a "cosmopolitan worldliness" distinct from the Islamic Republic or Indian emphases on a "composite culture" distinct from Hindutva. Yet however politically appealing or morally commendable such approaches may be, they are a methodological stumbling block for world historians. For this reason, the approach developed here is neither one of teleology nor unity, but rather one that emphasizes contingency and fault lines. The purpose is neither to promote Persian nor to champion its Persianate offspring, but rather to analyze them as a field of sociolinguistic contact, and in doing so recognize the roles of hegemony and competition that are easily downplayed in celebrations of "Persianate cosmopolitanism." By decoupling the language from the exclusive heritage of any particular people or place, the aim of this book is therefore to denationalize the study of Persian in order to recognize more fully the shifting social profiles of its users and the changing spatial contours of its locales. To this end, the selection of case studies aims to accentuate the non-Iranian spaces of Persian, while in no way depreciating Iran's already well-mapped contributions to the language. In order to lay a historical framework for this world-historical approach to Persian, Iran's contributions are contextualized in the historical survey that follows below.

In recent years, Persian has been rightly celebrated for its inclusiveness, bringing together Muslims, Christians, Jews, Hindus, Sikhs, and even Confucians in a collective if disjointed conversation. Against this apparently cosmopolitan backdrop, this book identifies the spatial edges, social limits, and linguistic breaking points of Persian's usage and usefulness. By asking whether in its connecting of different communities, Persian served more as a language of coercive governance, educational opportunity, or literary humanism, we can assess the limits of the "cosmopolitanism" that has been much celebrated in recent scholarship. Over the past few decades, the expansion in Persian studies has seen scholars focus on previously neglected regions of its usage (particularly India and Central Asia) and previously overlooked genres (particularly lexicography and travel writing). While collectively such scholarship has made a strong case for the humanistic and administrative achievements of Persian, we have far less sense of its functional limitations and social fractures. It is a rule of thumb that the reach of learned lingua francas is geographically broad but socially shallow: one might speak Persian (or Latin) with a fellow scholar from afar, but not with the cobbler next door. Many core questions arise from this basic problematic. Was the wide expansion of Persian enabled but ultimately disabled by its close but constraining ties to the political geographies of ruling states? How did the Islamic affiliations of Persian shape the frontiers of its republic (or empire) of letters? What forms of social interaction or organization could Persian not cope with? At the same time as pointing to the bridge-building achievements of Persian, this book therefore traces the political, social, and semantic fault lines that the language was unable to bridge, and which explain why so successful a lingua franca could dissolve so rapidly in the nineteenth century.

In conceptual terms, the discussion of Persian's scope and impact has been framed by the terminology of the "Persianate." Before proceeding further, it is therefore necessary to scrutinize this concept and its various derivatives. The term "Persianate" was first coined in the 1960s by the world historian Marshall Hodgson in his *Venture of Islam*. Hodgson explained and defined the term as follows: "The rise of Persian had more than purely literary consequences: it served to carry a new overall cultural orientation within Islamdom. . . . Most of the more local languages of high culture that later emerged among Muslims likewise depended upon Persian wholly or in part for their prime literary inspiration. We may call all these cultural traditions, carried in Persian or reflecting Persian inspiration, 'Persianate' by extension."[2]

This foundational definition has two core implications. Firstly, the "rise of Persian" was a direct cultural consequence of the rise of Islamic "civilization" (another key Hodgsonian term; he also called it "Islamdom"). Secondly, this had subsequent consequences for the development of other "more local languages of high culture." As a historian, Hodgson thus thought of the "Persianate" as a linguistic and literary process based on cultural imitation, and thereby, if only implicitly, on power. Other scholars might have spoken more plainly in terms of hegemony: Bruce B. Lawrence has noted of the concept that in it, "two elements are paramount: hierarchy . . . [and] deference."[3] After a considerable lull of a decade or two, Hodgson's neologism (along with its counterpart "Islamicate") began to have impact as other scholars adopted the term, particularly since the late 1990s.[4] Yet despite its widespread adoption, "Persianate" has rarely been more fully defined, let alone problematized as a concept or demonstrated as a process. In order to lay clearer conceptual parameters for the term, the chapters in this volume take on the empirical task of investigating the Persianate as process.

Because Hodgson's foundational definition conceives of Persianate culture as a product of contact between Persian and "more local languages," it is clear that the concept cannot be tested empirically by looking at Persian, or Persianate texts in other languages, in isolation. For this reason, the case studies brought together in this book share the basic methodology of looking at languages in contact. In different chapters, this linguistic contact is between Persian and a spoken vernacular, such as Punjabi; between Persian and an emergent written vernacular, such as Turki; between Persian and an established literary language, such as Chinese; and between Persian and an ascendant imperial language, such as English. These inter-Eurasian as distinct from inter-Islamic contacts were not what Hodgson had in mind. For his Persianate model assumed two things: an Islamic (or at least culturally "Islamicate") context in which Persian (and Islam) were in a position of cultural and political dominance; and, by extension, a geography confined to what used to be called the eastern Islamic world (or, as Hodgson himself preferred, the "Persian zone"). By contrast, this volume not only reflects the wider historical geography of Persian's usage that reached ultimately from China to Britain. The studies of language contact presented here also show how Persian interacted with literary and linguistic cultures that both were and were not under the cultural or political dominance of Persian or Islam. It is only by questioning the two core assumptions of Hodgson's model that we are able to examine the actual workings of scribal literary and sociolinguistic exchange, and in so doing trace the Persianate as process.

After Hodgson's momentous venture in rethinking Islamic civilization in world-historical terms, several other scholars have since the late 1990s proposed amendments or alternatives to his concept of the "Persianate." The first was Bert Fragner, who put forward a model of *Persophonie,* or "Persophonia," based on the regions connected through a shared language, in which the basic conceptual distinction is between Persian as a "mother tongue" (*Muttersprache*) and as a "second language" (*Zweitsprache*).[5] Traced in its evolution over several centuries, this carefully demonstrated distinction allowed Fragner to distinguish his wider arena of *Persophonie* from Iran and Iranians, both in their earlier manifestations as the Shuʿubiyya movement of the ʿAbbasid period and in their later manifestations in modern Iranian nationalism.[6] This basic but key distinction allowed Fragner to place emphasis on the Asian traditions of multilingualism among which Persian served as a "transregional contact language" (*transregionale Kontaktsprache*) between a variety of different peoples and their own local languages.[7]

The approach developed in this book accepts Fragner's emphasis on Persian's role as a transregional contact language. Through the aggregation of skills that collaboration affords, the following chapters subject that sociolinguistic contact to closer scrutiny. However, *The Persianate World* differs from Fragner's implicit emphasis on spoken Persian by instead emphasizing the importance of written Persian so as to develop a model of "Persographia" in place of "Persophonia." For as shown in more detail below, the scribal practices and manuscript-based exchanges that expanded and sustained the Persianate world across the length of Eurasia did not necessarily require the ability to *speak* Persian.

The approach developed here also differs from Fragner, and Hodgson before him, in terms of chronology. Fragner closed his conspectus in the late seventeenth century, which he saw as marking the "decline" (*Niedergang*) of *Persophonie* through "the emancipation of the Islamized daughter-languages [*Tochtersprachen*] from the Persian foundational pattern [*Grundmuster*]," devoting only five pages to the language's subsequent three hundred years of history.[8] By contrast, many of the case studies in this book focus precisely on this neglected period between

1600 and 1900, the period when Persian is usually assumed to have passed its high-water mark. This shift of temporal focus allows us to show instead how the language both continued and ceased to function as a *Kontaktsprache*. As noted earlier in relation to Hodgson's assumption of Islamic political power, this later focus also allows us to analytically separate Persian's role as a transregional contact language from conditions of Muslim political supremacy, thus allowing us to question their correlation. In spatial rather than temporal terms, the attention given here to Persian in the Chinese, British, and Russian empires performs a similar purpose.

Published thirteen years after Fragner's *Die Persophonie,* the next major reassessment of Hodgson's model was provided by Brian Spooner and William L. Hanaway's edited volume, *Literacy in the Persianate World.*[9] As anthropologist and linguist respectively, Spooner and Hanaway developed a conception of Persian as a social practice and cultural technology that was, crucially, "anchored in stable forms of writing."[10] This emphasis on written Persian as distinct from a spoken lingua franca was based on a core hypothesis that "written language has had a dynamic that is distinct from that of spoken language—essentially a culture of its own."[11] From this starting point, Spooner and Hanaway developed a conception of Persian as a stable written koine used by specific professional groups, which should be analytically distinguished from the more linguistically protean and socially diffuse spheres of spoken language.[12] This book's model of Persographia follows Spooner and Hanaway's focus on Persian as a *written* contact language. As such, the conception of the "Persianate" developed here is not that of an intangible cultural *Geist.* Rather, it is conceived as a set of specific skills and practices belonging to small, often professionalized, groups of people who were not connected by an immaterial common language or "culture," but whose contact and communication was based on tangible written documents and often limited to specific topics. An emphasis on the practice and material of writing and on the social and spatial locations of writers (whether literati, bureaucrats, or plain scribes) are therefore key constituents of such an approach.

Another recent vision of the Persianate world (or rather, an "Iranian world") is articulated in Hamid Dabashi's *The World of Persian Literary Humanism.*[13] In contrast to Spooner and Hanaway's focus on material writing practices, Dabashi's emphasis is on literature as a transhistorical medium of "literary humanism." Dabashi proposes that the "subversive" and "flamboyant" profile of Persianate literary culture (*adab*), which had "an effectively feminine disposition," was always distinct from "the commanding doctrinal beliefs, strict juridical injunctions, expansive metaphysical mandates" of Islam.[14] This is quite contrary, then, to Hodgson. Although he devotes parts of two chapters to the Mongols and Mughals, for Dabashi, the geography or "world" of Persian literary humanism remained focused on Iran as its "epicenter."[15] Beginning and ending in the geography of modern Iran, Dabashi's survey charts the history of the Persianate world as a nationalist teleology.[16] Ever since Hodgson coined the term "Persianate," world historians have struggled with the legacy of earlier nation-based frameworks of the kind that Dabashi monumentally resurrects. The richness of its textual readings, notwithstanding, Dabashi's Iranocentric conception of Persian literary humanism therefore stands in stark contrast to the approach adopted here.

In contrast to this downplaying of the connection between Persian and Islam, the next major work of relevance is Shahab Ahmed's *What Is Islam? The Importance of Being Islamic.*[17] In his discussion of the Persianate world, Ahmed reasonably questions the concept on the grounds that it "assumptively privilege[s] linguistic and 'ethnic' elements" and so risks "falling into service of the ever-recrudescent appeal of conceptualizing Islamic history in terms of 'Persian' and 'Arab' nationalist readings."[18] Instead, Ahmed proposes what he calls a "Balkans-to-Bengal complex," which was "locally polyglot," but whose "producers of high culture, in particular, were, above all, 'polyphone.'"[19] This emphasis on multilingualism, to put it more plainly, is important. As noted earlier, this is the key but often missing link in the cultural process Hodgson originally defined as "Persianate." Yet for present purposes, Ahmed's approach is ultimately unhelpful, given the foundational emphasis signaled in the subtitle of his book. As Ahmed defines it, his Balkans-to-Bengal area is "most meaningfully conceptualized not in terms of the Persianate, Turkic, or Perso-Islamic, but of *Islam.*"[20] This is to reject nationalist particularism only to favor Islamic particularism, even if it is Ahmed's appealing version of Islam.

While Ahmed's model creates conceptual openings for the study of Islam, it forecloses the remit of the Persianate by that very emphasis. Because for world historians at least, the "Balkans-to-Bengal" region is a religiously pluralistic space, a pluralism that is even more prominent when we turn to the larger Eurasian spaces across which Persian was used. In trying to take seriously the Persianate world as process through Fragner's notion of "language contact" (*Sprachkontakt*), non-Muslims become an important part of the enquiry. To reduce the "Persianate world," or "Balkans-to-Bengal complex," to a rebranded version of the "eastern Islamic world" is therefore to sidestep the crucial questions about cultural contact and exchange that make the concept of the Persianate worth investigating in the first place. As with nationalist models, this brings us again to the heuristic importance of recognizing and examining "frontiers," whether they be linguistic, spatial, social, or, in this case, religious in form. For to test the limits of Persian is to trace its fortunes in the interstitial space of these various types of boundaries.

This brings us to the final major recent work of relevance which is Stefano Pellò's *Ṭūṭiyān-i Hind: specchi identitari e proiezioni cosmopolite indo-persiane* (The Parrots of India: Mirrors of Identity and Indo-Persian Cosmopolitan Projections).[21] Together with scholarship on Judeo-Persian, Pellò's monograph allows us to factor Eurasia's religious pluralism into our understanding of the Persianate world and thereby its socio-religious frontiers. More than any study to date, Pellò's makes an evidence-based case for conceiving of Persian (more specifically, Indo-Persian) as a "pluralistic literary culture [*cultura letteraria plurale*]."[22] He makes this argument through a case study of Persian texts written by Hindus who were exposed to the language through their service in the Mughal imperial bureaucracy. As a result, he argues, Persian acquired functional social effects through serving as a "tool of intercultural communication [*strumento di comunicazione transculturale*]," with the poetic anthology (*tazkira*) in particular acting as a kind of virtual space for what he terms "literary interaction [*interazione letteraria*]."[23] Pellò has identified around a hundred and fifty Hindu Persian authors (mainly but by no means exclusively poets), whose number peaked in the late eighteenth and early nineteenth century.[24] However, the broad historical survey below suggests that we should be wary of generalizing Pellò's carefully contextualized findings into a broader picture of Persianate "cosmopolitanism" in all times and places, or assuming that literary interaction was capable of automatically producing sociopolitical harmony. This is a question to which we will return in connection with Jewish, Sikh, and Christian producers and consumers of Persian texts. Rather than generalize from particular cosmopolitan contexts, then, we must scrutinize the fluctuating social reach and alternating political functions of Persian through attention to its multiple heuristic frontiers.

In order to trace connections and disconnections across Eurasia's many social, ethnic, and linguistic frontiers, then, we need to analytically denaturalize Persian's civilizational ties to Islam and denationalize its primordialist ties to Iran. After all, in religious terms, for many Jewish and Christian readers of Persian, it was Jami's treatment of the biblical figure of Joseph (Yusuf) that held greatest appeal, while for Sikh and Hindu readers, Persian was as much the repository of stories of gurus and gods, and of the secular pleasures of the good life, as it was of Islamic ethics. And in geographical terms, for the Ottomans, it was Timurid Herat that served as the primary model of Persianate culture, while for the Mughals it was Timurid Samarqand. For the Qing Empire, it was relations with frontier states like Badakhshan and Ladakh that drove their ventures into Persian-based diplomacy, while for the British Empire it was relations with the Mughal Empire and its successor states. For centuries, people from across India, Central Asia, and even Siberia looked to Balkh-i Bami (Balkh the Ancient), Bukhara-yi Sharif (Bukhara the Noble), or Hazrat-i Dilhi (Delhi the Sacred), as the center of Persian learning, rather than to anywhere in Iran. Indeed, the literary middleman who popularized Hafiz throughout the Ottoman Empire (and thereby Europe via the German translation of Joseph von Hammer-Purgstall) was the Bosnian commentator Ahmad Sudi Busnawi (d. ca. 1600), who had never travelled to Iran and relied instead on the Persian-reading savants of Istanbul and Baghdad to decipher Hafiz's more obscure verses.[25] Iran, then, was never the perpetual reference point, let alone the "epicenter," of the Persianate world, any more than Islam was the whole story.[26]

When focusing as this book's case study chapters do on the five centuries from around 1400 to 1900, there is even less reason to privilege Iran. With many of the people who produced written Persian moving between an inverted geographical triangle demarcating India, Central Asia, and China, Persianate culture in many ways flourished without direct contact with Iran. This is not to write Iran perversely out of such contacts—as discussed below, the Safavid era saw many "men-of-the-pen" migrate from Iran to India—but merely to question the perennial centrality of Iran to these Persian-based exchanges. Although medieval figures like Saʿdi of Shiraz (d. 1292) long retained their importance as poetic and pedagogic touch-stones, their writings had long been naturalized in their multiple spaces of reception and reproduction by the seventeenth century. The model of the Persianate world proposed here is therefore one in which the place (let alone the centrality) of Iran is less a given than a variable. Persian had no perpetual or primordial home-land, no *watan* to which it was destined inevitably to return, but instead charted a history that was contingent and contested across the multiple spaces that used and so claimed it.

In order to be an aid rather than an obstacle to exploring world history, the Persian language must similarly be understood as interacting with the other languages and writing systems of these areas of its use. In Fragner's formulation, Persian needs to be seen as a transregional contact language. Yet, crucially, it must also be recognized that such contact did not necessarily replace other languages, whether written or spoken, but rather connected their various users. And it is here that Spooner and Hanaway's emphasis on Persian as a spatially and tem-porally stable written language is important in pointing to the scribal practices, material implements, and trained personnel who were the agents responsible for creating and sustaining this contact. As a collaborative venture bringing together multiple linguistic skill sets, the focus of this book is therefore on written Persian in contact with other languages and, by extension, their own cultural or political frameworks; in short, it is a model of "Persian plus." By following Spooner and Hanaway's attention to the distinct profile of Persian as a written language, the following chapters deal with the deployment of writing skills and their associated forms of literate knowledge. This marks a much broader domain than literature, or even than literary culture, or *adab*. Rather, the domain of writing skills and literate knowledge also includes such functional expressions of literacy as bureaucracy, lexicography, and diplomacy, as well as the inscribing of public monuments and private talismans. Building on Jack Goody's pioneering work on the uses of litera-cy, the emphasis here is on Persian as a tool—often a closely guarded one—rather than an aesthetic.[27] In this sense, the literacy-based model here is analytically dis-tinct from Fragner's model of shared speech based on the *francophonie* of French-speaking Africa— it is a persographia rather than a persophonia. As a learned second (or third) language spread thinly across the wide regions it connected, in world-historical terms, Persian comprised a set of linguistic tools and practices that were adopted by many different peoples across the Eurasian continent. In this regard, its "frontiers" should be seen as not merely geographical, but also social, ethnic, and linguistic.

To this end, the case studies brought together in this book examine language contact in regions often presumed to be the edges of, or even entirely outside, the Persianate world. Unlike other studies that have emphasized either Iran or India as the core region of Persian or Persianate culture, the following chapters give equal attention to the Central Asian khanates and the Chinese, Ottoman, and British empires as spaces—and frontiers—of Persian. This in turn expands the spatial parameters of the Persianate world to the broader Eurasian geography of Persian-based language contact. The following sections of this Introduction provide a background and context for the subsequent case study chapters by outlining a general history for Persian that stresses the pluralistic and protean profile of its frontiers prior to the nationalizing reconception and retraction of Persian in the early twentieth century. This general history is based on a definition of the Persianate world as an interregional or "world" system generated by shared knowledge of religiosity, statecraft, diplomacy, trade, sociability, or subjectivity that was accessed and circulated through the common use of written Persian across interconnected nodal points of Eurasia.

FROM THE RISE OF "NEW PERSIAN" TO THE "TURKO-PERSIAN SYNTHESIS" (CA. 800–CA. 1200)

Developing in one of the most important crossroads of the Eurasian landmass, the Arabic-script Persian that underwrote the Persianate world emerged between the eastern edges of the Zagros Mountains in today's western Iran and the trading oases on the western edges of the Tang Empire.[28] The rapid collapse of the Sasanian Empire during the Umayyad Islamic conquests of 632 to 651 brought a new imperial language to the vast fallen domains of the Sasanians. That language was Arabic. The Sasanian Empire is routinely classified as "Persian"—though its centers of power were in Iraq rather than Fars—but it also reached as far east as what are now Afghanistan, Uzbekistan, Tajikistan, and parts of Pakistan (that is, Harey, Kushanshahr, and Sogdiana). For at least the next two hundred years, the prestige and power of written Arabic muffled the deposed literary Persian of the vanquished Sasanian order. Older literary and liturgical versions of Persian (known to specialists as Avestan and Pahlavi or "Old" and "Middle" Persian) survived chiefly as the language of the priesthood of a shrinking population of Zoroastrians. Through the migration of Arab settlers and the acculturation of local residents, Umayyad and then 'Abbasid imperial rule gave written Arabic two centuries in which to embed itself in the bureaucratic and literary spheres of the former Sasanian Empire. The degree to which even the eastern former Sasanian provinces embraced Arabic is seen in the influence exerted in the 'Abbasid capital of Baghdad by members of the formerly Buddhist Barmaki family of Balkh and in the compilation by the Central Asian scholar al-Bukhari (d. 870) of one of the canonical Hadith collections of the Prophet Muhammad.

Yet this picture of Umayyad- and 'Abbasid-driven linguistic rupture overlay a contextual canvas marked by considerable social continuity, albeit of the linguistic complexity of pre-Arabized Iranian languages. In the countryside, the old Sasanian landholding aristocracy (*dihqans*) remained largely in place, supporting praise singers and bards who used different versions of Persian, while gradually introducing new styles, meters, and vocabulary inspired by Umayyad and 'Abbasid court culture into their verses.[29] In the towns, members of the partially hereditary former Sasanian bureaucracy adapted their scribal skills to the new imperial dispensation, in the process introducing many formerly Middle Persian chancery genres into Arabic.[30] The literary traffic was therefore two-way. Albeit only surviving in Arabic works by later litterateurs such as al-Jahiz (d. 868) and al-Tabari (d. 923), the earliest known fragments of Persian written in Arabic script are attributed to Arab court poets of the early 'Abbasid era, such as Yazid al-Mufarrigh al-Himyari (d. 688), for whom Persian possessed a flavor that was at once exotic and demotic.[31] Whether by way of entertainers and courtiers, or of bureaucrats and scholars, the patronage of the upper and lower echelons of the state was crucial to the reemergence of written Persian through the borrowing from Arabic of a new script, vocabulary, rules of prosody, and repertoire of tropes and topics. Transformed through its encounter with Arabic, this emergent written vernacular is what linguists term "New" Persian (or up to the twelfth century "Early New Persian") as distinct from the Middle (Pahlavi) and Old (Avestan) Persian of the Sasanian and Achaemenian eras.[32]

Though accurate in outline, this picture of imported literary Arabic infusing local spoken Persian to produce written New Persian is a considerable simplification. By glossing over the various versions of spoken and written "Persian" that survived through the early centuries of Islamic rule over the former Sasanian domains, it ever tends toward a teleology. For the imperial, top-down drivers of change necessarily engaged with underlying social and linguistic conditions. The Persian that persisted through the first centuries after the Umayyad conquests was no single vernacular. Instead, the geography of Persian marked out a fragmented linguistic map of spoken and written dialects. It was this more complex linguistic landscape that Ibn al-Muqaffa (d. 757), who translated various Middle Persian works into Arabic, was attempting to comprehend when he described three languages—Pahlavi, Parsi, and Dari—as having been used under the Sasanians.[33] Of these (and other) regional dialects, only one would emerge as the dominant basis for the literary works in Arabic-script New Persian that appeared from the mid-ninth century on. This was a version of the vernacular Middle Persian (Dari) of the old Sasanian capital at Ctesiphon-Seleucia that had been exported east to Khurasan in the late Sasanian period and then consolidated by the Arab Umayyad conquests. The eventual ascent of this particular version of Persian was a highly contingent development.

FIGURE 1. The earliest New Persian text: Judeo-Persian inscription from Tang-i Azao, Afghanistan, 751–52 CE. Photograph courtesy of the Hertford-Wadham Afghanistan Expedition, 1956.

This linguistic map of multiple spoken Persian dialects was echoed in the orthographic pluralism of the eighth and ninth centuries. Prior to the emergence of this new Arabic-script Persian, both Dari and other regional dialects of Persian were written in the other scripts used by the various non-Muslim communities that still survived in number across the Umayyad-'Abbasid domains and even beyond into China. Hebrew-script Persian (known Judeo-Persian) predated the emergence of Arabic-script Persian and survived into the twentieth century. The earliest written records of New Persian are in fact in Hebrew rather than Arabic script. They comprise a rock inscription from 751–52 in the high mountain pass of Tang-i Azao some two hundred kilometers east of Herat in what is today central Afghanistan; and a letter from a Jewish merchant likely datable to 760 found in the Dandan-Öilïq oasis near Khotan along the Silk Road in what is today western China.[34]

Other early dialects of New Persian were written in Syriac and Manichaean scripts.[35] As late as 874, Middle Persian in Pahlavi script was still being used for funerary inscriptions in the Tang imperial capital of Xi'an, where families of the former Sasanian Zoroastrian elite had settled as refugees two centuries earlier.[36] The different dialects of New Persian that were written down in Arabic script by Muslims of the ninth and tenth centuries, such as the Sistan dialect interlinear commentary on the Quran, emerged in what was still a deeply pluralistic social context.[37] Yet what should be clear is that this social pluralism was expressed in an orthographic pluralism—the use of multiple writing systems—that prevented Persian from serving as a written lingua franca in the way that spoken Persian did.

As John Perry has noted, the "spoken Persian of the time served as a vernacular for Zoroastrians, Jews, Manichaeans, Christians and Muslim converts in Iran."[38] This was not yet true of Persian written in Arabic script, which would take several centuries—and several shifts across both geographical and social frontiers—to emerge as a written contact language for speakers of different languages and members of different religions.

Even so, in view of those later functions of written Persian, it is worth dwelling on the pluralist frontier rather than the national or even imperial geographies from which the particular forms of spoken Persian that were incrementally committed to writing and eventually to standardizing emerged. This highly pluralistic sociolinguistic landscape has led Bo Utas to claim a "multiethnic" origin for New Persian. Based on the "established fact that New Persian is a mixed language with regard to its vocabulary . . . [and] morpho-syntactic structure," Utas has argued that its linguistic development "may be taken to betray a mixed origin," such that "New Persian must be regarded as something of a multicultural construction."[39] Certainly, the world glimpsed in the fragmentary New Persian documents that have survived from the seventh to the ninth centuries points to the emergence of a new vernacular in complex symbiosis with the imperial literary and political culture of Arabic. If Utas is correct, then the development of New Persian might well be regarded as what Sheldon Pollock has, in a different context, conceptualized as a "cosmopolitan vernacular," which for many purposes eventually replaced its erstwhile Arabic model and rival.[40] As in other cases of literary vernacularization, local elites—the aforementioned *dihqans* and bureaucrats, but also breakaway dynasts—played the key role in the empowerment of their preferred dialect of New Persian. This forged a new pattern of patronizing New Persian literary texts, which were, crucially, written down in Arabic script, a development that took place in Khurasan and Transoxiana.[41] These were by no means Persian's linguistic homeland, but rather frontier regions where Persian had centuries earlier been imported and replaced the Soghdian language. Then, during the subsequent early centuries of Islamic rule, Persian had been reintroduced there by converted Muslim settlers. As Perry has explained, "Persian's geographical expansion was initially due to the rapid advance of the Arab armies eastward, where they and their converted Persian auxiliaries from Pars and western central Iran settled in Khurasan and Transoxiana."[42] As local governors of the eastern frontiers of the 'Abbasid caliphate formed their own breakaway polities by way of the Samanid (819–999) and Saffarid (861–1003) dynasties, it was here in Khurasan and Transoxiana that this particular transplanted then localized spoken dialect of New Persian began its rise to written prominence and, in time, dominance. Following the orthographic practices promoted by the chanceries of the Muslim-ruled Samanid and Saffarid states, this was New Persian in the Arabic script.[43]

Although the Arabic-script New Persian of the Samanid court emerged in a broader Central Asian context of orthographic pluralism in which different religious communities used different scripts (Hebrew, Manichaean, Zoroastrian Pahlavi), the sheer resources available to the Muslim-ruled court and chancery would eventually ensure that it was their Arabic-script Persian that would develop into a written lingua franca. Behind what Bo Utas has called the "panegyric argument" for New Persian's birth in the sophisticated court literary setting around the new Samanid and Saffarid dynasts, we should therefore recognize the operations of hegemony.

As clusters of material and symbolic capital, the tenth-century courts of the Samanids and Saffarids produced a series of literary works in the New Persian dialect of their Khurasani surroundings. Yet the Samanid and Saffarid court poets promoted and preserved rather than invented poetry in New Persian. An oral tradition of poetry had already been fostered in the petty courts of the *dihqans,* the local gentry, of the region. The compositions of this first generation of New Persian poets, such as Hanzala Badghisi (d. 835?) and Mahmud Warraq (d. 836), survive only as fragments collected by later anthologists.[44] The self-conscious dynastic ambitions of the Samanids attracted such poets to their capital at Bukhara. The most notable of these Samanid-sponsored figures was Abu 'Abdullah Rudaki (d. 941), court poet to the ruler Nasr II (r. 914–43) who, together with his patron, heralded a new era for Persian letters.[45]

It was not only Persian poetry that developed under Samanid patronage. Persian prose too began to expand its previously minimal repertoire of vernacular interlinear Quran renderings. Analytically if not necessarily spatially, this marked the emergence of the chancery as a second key site of written Persian along with the court. While both Persian and Arabic were used in the Samanid chancery, after a lengthy and complex contest between the rival promoters of these languages and skill sets, by the late tenth-century Persian seems to have become the dominant bureaucratic language, at least for internal purposes.[46] As we will see below for other eras and areas, Persian's role as a chancery language would have tremendous impact on the geographical and social expansion of Persographia, for this chancery and court model would subsequently be transferred from the Samanids to the Ghaznavids and their own successors. Here in the chancery the key figure was not the itinerant minstrel but the sedentary and often hereditary secretary known variously as the *dabir, katib,* or *munshi* . Such figures as the Saffarid secretary Muhammad ibn Wasif (d. 909) had also turned their training in Arabic epistolography and belles-lettres to composing poetry in the now fashionable written New Persian.[47]

For reasons that remain unclear, the Samanids took considerably more interest than their Tahirid or Saffarid predecessors in the promotion of Persian from a spoken vernacular to a literary language. Court and chancery resources, both material and symbolic, then generated a momentum. In 957, the Samanid governor of the Khurasani trading cities of Tus and Nishapur sponsored a New Persian translation of the Middle Persian *Xwaday-namag,* which detailed the heroic deeds of Iran's pre-Islamic rulers. Overseen by the Samanid secretary Abu Mansur Ma'mari (d. 961), this New Persian "Book of Kings" or *Shah-nama* included a prose introduction explaining how Abu Mansur had commissioned the work. Despite his presumed education in Arabic, the Samanid secretary made minimal use of Arabic loanwords.[48] Under the Samanids, then, New Persian was still very much a language in a state of ongoing transformation. When, at the end of the Samanid period, Abu al-Qasim Firdawsi (d. 1020) composed his more famous *Shah-nama* in epic verse, his lexicon still made only limited use of Arabic borrowings.[49]

Over the next few centuries, New Persian would absorb much more of Arabic vocabulary and prosody through the interactions of its creators—the secretariat especially—with the richer realm of Arabic letters. Such Arabization rendered New Persian an "Arabicate" language, so to speak, before it gained the prestige to foster its own "Persianate" offspring. However, the amount of Arabic vocabulary adopted by writers of New Persian during the tenth and eleventh centuries did not follow a simple chronological expansion and varied according to their sources, genres, and audiences. From the late Samanid period onwards, then, Persian prose writing began to be sponsored on a larger and more official scale, particularly by secretaries who were bilingual in Arabic—and now, crucially, biliterate—and New Persian.[50] The most important such figure was Amirak Bal'ami (d. 992–97), the vizier of the Samanid ruler Mansur ibn Nuh, for whom from 963 he made New Persian translations of al-Tabari's Arabic *Tarikh al-Rusul wa al-Muluk* (History of the Prophets and Kings). Such bilingual secretaries as Amirak Bal'ami, used to switching between Persian and Arabic in their day-to-day professional lives, were crucial to this initial expansion of Persian's written repertoire from poetic entertainments to prestigious prose histories of prophets and kings.[51] Around the time that Bal'ami's history was written, a Persian *Tafsir* (Quran Commentary) was undertaken by a group of 'ulama in the Samanid realms. Persian also began to be used for more formal translations of the Quran, figuring in interlinear glosses that appeared from the late tenth or eleventh century.[52]

The New Persian of Khurasan and Transoxiana was developed at the meeting point of several frontiers—ethnic and political, linguistic and orthographic—that would leave their permanent mark on the written language by way of the absorption of Arabic vocabulary, meters, and genres. New Persian also adopted from Arabic the system of numerical notation known as *siyaq*, in which the Arabic words for decimal numerals (rather than Indian-derived numerical symbols) were abbreviated into distinct graphemes.[53] By these means, as part of the package of secretarial education, numeracy became embedded in Arabic (and then in turn Persian) literacy.[54] The *siyaq* system of Persianate numeracy would prove durable: after being passed from Umayyad into Samanid usage, *siyaq* was in turn transmitted to the Safavids, Ottomans, and Mughals, and did not disappear entirely until the script and educational reforms of the 1920s and 1930s.[55] Yet despite the meteoric rise of Persian through so many dimensions of chancery

FIGURE 2. Instituting a language of state: the mausoleum of Isma'il Samani (r. 892–907), Bukhara. Photograph by Nile Green.

practice and court patronage under the Samanids, coinage remained resistant to Persian. Indeed, it was not until the Safavid period, specifically the time of Shah Tahmasp (r. 1524–76), that Persian as distinct from Arabic was regularly used on coins.[56] There was, then, in some sense a numismatic frontier that Persian would not cross for centuries, and in some regions not at all.

There were also significant inheritances from beyond Arabic, as seen in the case of the Middle Persian predecessors of the *Shah-nama* and the likely Sasanian prototypes of New Persian chancery documents. Even so, by the end of the Samanid period around 1000 CE, as a written language, the scope and functions of New Persian were still limited. Despite New Persian's expansion into prose under the Samanids, Arabic remained not only the dominant language of the sciences ('ulum) but also the preferred language for art objects such as ceramic ware. In terms of overall social impact, though, the Samanid chancery—and the provincial and local bureaucracy beyond it—was more important than court literature. It was only during the eleventh century, after the Samanids' fall, that New Persian's repertoire was expanded both in terms of literature and bureaucracy. The key patrons of this expansion were not ethnic Persians like the Samanids. They were Turks.

With the political ascent of Turkic former slave soldiers under the Ghaznavids (977–1186) and Great Saljuqs (1016–53), the role of the secretarial class became even more influential. For the secretaries served as administrative linchpins, political mentors, and propagandist encomiasts for the new Turkic dynasts. The contact between these different parties generated what Robert L. Canfield has called the "ecumenical mix" of "Turko-Persian Islamicate culture."[57] It is noteworthy that although Persographic Hindu secretaries would rise to prominence only centuries later, under the Mughal Empire, the Ghaznavids already employed Hindus in that capacity, among them the powerful Tilak (fl. ca. 1000–1040).[58] Although New Persian was to be the dominant written partner of Turkic, spoken social interactions gradually led to the absorption of numerous Turkic words into written Persian.[59] The incorporation of Turkish vocabulary into New Persian would never rival its earlier Arabization in scale, however, and neither did these linguistic interactions and lexical borrowings follow a simple linear pattern. The amount of Arabic vocabulary writers of New Persian adopted during the Ghaznavid and Saljuq ascendancy of the tenth and eleventh centuries did not expand chronologically so much as vary synchronically according to authors' locations, sources, audiences and genres. Thus, the *Kimiya-yi Sa'adat* (Alchemy of Happiness), composed in 1105 by the erstwhile Saljuq employee Abu Hamid al-Ghazali (d. 1111), contains few Arabic words compared to the densely Arabized *Kashf al-Mahjub* (Revelation of the Hidden) that 'Ali ibn 'Usman al-Hujwiri (d. ca. 1075) had composed under the Ghaznavids several decades earlier and considerably further east.[60]

Under the Turkic dynasties, written New Persian was increasingly endowed and empowered in both the court and chancery. The rapid expansion of both poetic and prose genres under the Ghaznavids created prestigious models of kingship and statecraft that would be imitated by many subsequent Turkic dynasties, a development that was arguably the most enduring cultural outcome of "Turko-Persian" contact.[61] Persian prose would no longer be a derivative medium for earlier works translated from Arabic. Instead, through the efforts of such prominent Ghaznavid secretaries as Abu al-Fazl Bayhaqi (d. 1077), original dynastic histories were composed in New Persian to present Turkic dynasts in the grandiloquent and increasingly normative terms of Persian kingship.[62] Even as a physical entity, the Ghaznavid court was Persianized through grand Persian inscriptions on palace walls.[63] Then under the Saljuqs, the language was adopted for formal manuals of statecraft in the "mirror for princes" genre, most famously with the *Siyasat-nama* (Book of Politics) of the influential secretary Nizam al-Mulk (d. 1092).

These new Turkic dynasties, whose founders had first emerged under Samanid tutelage, would bring about the most important shift to ever occur in the historical status and function of New Persian. In Fragner's terms, it was the shift from a "mother tongue" (*Muttersprache*) to a "second language" (*Zweitsprache*). Only from this point would New Persian start to serve as a written lingua franca. But to do so, it would also need to be introduced to new regions beyond those in which it was a spoken vernacular.

THE EXPANDING SPACES OF PERSIAN LEARNING
(CA. 1200–CA. 1500)

Enabling this geographic expansion of the frontiers of the Persianate world were two key institutions that helped not only to publicize works by established practitioners of written New Persian (henceforth simply Persian), but also to produce new works. In doing so, these institutions also incrementally transformed Persian into a learned second language rather than a written mother tongue. The Turkic ascendance of the eleventh and twelfth century was, in processual terms, more influential for its institutional than its bibliographical innovations. For by way of the madrasa and the *khanaqah*—the school and the convent—the Ghaznavids and particularly the Saljuqs patronized two new types of enduring institutions that not only enabled the production of more Persian texts but, more important, reared new generations of producers and readers of written Persian. Funded by property endowment (*waqf*), these new institutions for the overlapping parties of ʿulama and Sufis expanded through the new territories that were conquered by the Ghaznavids in India and the Saljuqs in Anatolia. Together with the royal court and the provincial courts and chanceries of local governors, the endowment of gradually increasing numbers of madrasas and *khanaqahs* spread the use of written Persian across new geographical frontiers. The later Ghaznavid capital of Lahore and the later Saljuq capital of Konya provide prime examples of Persian's new expanded geography by the twelfth century.[64] Then, from 1206, the establishment of the Delhi sultanate made Delhi a new regional hub of Persian learning. From there, within a century, a sequence of Persographic urban nodes irradiated as far as Gujarat, Bengal, and the Deccan.[65]

The pedagogic reproduction of the secretarial classes through the madrasa system and other forces of education was further enabled by formal manuals of ornate prose (*insha'*) and epistolography (*tarassul*) intended to train recruits for chancery work. The earliest surviving such manual was the *Dastur-i Dabari* written by the Saljuq secretary Muhammad al-Mayhani (d. 1129?).[66] Many other such manuals would follow, educating secretaries in Persianate numeracy (*siyaq*) as well as literacy, while also in some cases serving as guides on prosody for more literary forms of composition.[67] William L. Hanaway has argued that these writings served later generations as templates for imitative pedagogy and composition.[68] Based in their madrasas and *khanaqahs,* the overlapping circles of '*ulama* and Sufis who together with the secretaries and court poets formed the other major parties of text producers increasingly began to use Persian for religious works, both in poetry and prose. By around the mid-eleventh century, 'Ali ibn 'Usman al-Hujwiri (d. ca. 1075) had written his aforementioned pioneering handbook of the Sufi path, *Kashf al-Mahjub.*[69] By the early twelfth century, religious scholars from Samarqand such as Abu Hafs 'Umar Najm al-Din al-Nasafi (d. 1142) were crafting increasingly sophisticated Quran translations in Persian rhyming prose.[70] Although Arabic retained its hold over certain religious disciplines (notably law), especially at the higher level, Persian's religious ambit expanded enormously under the Turkic dynasties. The *Hadiqat al-Haqiqa* (Walled Garden of Truth) of Hakim Sana'i (d. 1131) showed the increasing literary sophistication of didactic poetry, and the *Tazkirat al-Awliya* (Lives of God's Friends) of Farid al-Din 'Attar (d. 1220) signaled the rise of a type of hagiography that would soon spread into Anatolia and India as part of the Persianate making of new Muslim sacred geographies.[71]

Across the expanding geography of their interconnected networks, the growing personnel of these madrasas and *khanaqahs* distributed, copied, and further contributed to this expanding corpus of Persian religious works.[72] Together, such manuals and curricula, whether of the secretarial or Sufi life, forged a relatively standardized version of Persian that spread southwards into India, westwards into the Balkans and eastwards into the Tarim Basin. Intelligible to readers across this wide Eurasian space, this was what John R. Perry has termed a "homoglossic" Persian.[73]

Undoubtedly, this dominant Arabic-script Persian—the last of the orthographically plural Persians of the post-Sasanian domains to emerge and be exported to the dar al-Islam—was a Muslim Persian promoted by powerful Muslim-ruled states and their administrative and religious establishments. Yet, however hegemonic, this Islamo-Persian never fully occluded other users of Persian, who survived (as with Judeo-Persian) or emerged (as with Hindu-Persian) through the social and political interactions of subsequent centuries. This point brings out the importance of the distinction between geographical and social frontiers. For the horizontal spatial expansion of Persian as part of the administrative and religious equipment of royal courts and Sufi lodges should not automatically be equated with the vertical social expansion of the language. The expanding new geographies of Persian were multilingual spaces in terms of both spoken and written language. The introduction of Persian added another layer to preexisting regional patterns of written multilingualism—whether in Sanskrit, Byzantine Greek, Armenian, or Georgian—that were the legacy of earlier religious and political institutions.

This becomes especially clear when we come to the interaction of Persian with Armenian and Georgian (Kartuli) literature of the twelfth century in the cultural and political frontier regions of the southern Caucasus. Here we are dealing with a different dimension and degree of the Persianate than in Hodgson's original model in which Persian generated new literary offspring in its imitative shadow. For both Armenian and Georgian were much older as written languages than New Persian, with Christian Armenian literature beginning around 405 with the invention of the Armenian alphabet by Mesrop Mashtots (362–440), and Georgian after the evolution of the Old Georgian (Asomtavruli) script, first attested in the Bolnisi Sioni church inscriptions of 494.[74] As a result of Iranian influences going back to the Achaemenian Empire, around 60 percent of the Classical Armenian lexicon consisted of borrowings from Old and Middle Persian (largely Parthian). However, from the fifth century on, Mashtots's Armenian alphabet acted as an enduring barrier against further lexical borrowing from Persian, forming a kind of orthographic frontier that constitutes an important contrast with the more familiar Persianate languages that adopted the Arabic script.

Over the centuries after their alphabetization, both Armenian and Georgian developed, initially for ecclesiastical purposes, as literary languages, which continued to evolve after the early Arab Muslim conquests of the seventh century. Nonetheless, literary production sharply increased after the reestablishment of Christian rule by the Bagratid kingdom of Armenia in 885 and the Georgian Bagrationi monarchs of Abkhazia and Georgia in 978 and 1008, respectively. Under their aegis, Armenian and Georgian literature expanded their formerly ecclesiastical remits into the realms of historiography and court poetry, with Georgian acquiring its subsequently standard Mkhedruli script. From the eleventh and especially twelfth century, as Persian entered its own ascendance in the lands to the immediate south, the Armenian and Georgian courts did adapt aspects of Persianate court and literary culture (albeit less than they borrowed from Byzantium in other spheres). An early instance of this was the impact of Firdawsi's *Shah-nama,* the composition of which coincided with Leonti Mroveli's Georgian *Kartlis Tskhovreba* (Life of Kings), composed around 1070.[75] Yet over the next few centuries, what developed was less the emergence of new Christian Persianate literatures under the dominant shadow of Persian than a pattern of highly selective adaptations, even appropriations, of Persian stories and motifs by a series of poets and chroniclers associated with the independent medieval Armenian and Georgian courts. Compared with the Persianate literatures in Indic and Turkic languages, there were far fewer Persian loanwords in Armenian and Georgian, into which motifs or entire stories were adapted without taking on Persian's script or lexicon. Thus, what Peter Cowe has written of the Persian and more broadly Islamic literary impact on Armenian can equally be said of Georgian, namely, that after the initial stage of contact, the verse type or literary motif first becomes indigenized in its new setting and then begins to be employed creatively so as to explore aspects of its expressive potential that were untapped in its culture of origin.[76] Yet it is important not to overstate the point for, unlike Armenian, Georgian also absorbed hundreds of literary loanwords from Persian, whether basic terms for "love" (Georgian: *mijnuroba,* from the name Majnun) and songbirds

(Georgian: *bulbul*) or the name of a particular poetic form (Georgian: *shairi* from Arabo-Persian *shi'r*).[77]

In this way, a series of major medieval Armenian and Georgian authors incorporated into their own works tales and motifs from Persian texts. The latter comprised not only the *Shah-nama* but more particularly the writings of Nizami Ganjawi (d. 1209) and the old romance cycle of *Vis u Ramin* (Vis and Ramin), via the eleventh-century version of Fakhr al-Din Gurgani (fl. 1040–54).[78] That Persian's impact on Georgian came via Nizami, who apparently spent his whole life in the city of Ganja in the southern Caucasus, is a further pointer to the multiple vectors centers and shifting centers of the Persianate world. In Georgian literature, the three most important such works are *Visramiani* (Vis and Ramin, ca. 1150), *Amiran-Darejaniani* (Tale of Amiran Son of Darejan) and Shota Rustaveli's *Vepkhistqaosani* (Knight in Panther's Skin, ca. 1189–1207).[79] The deliberate selectivity of these poets' appropriations from the Persian originals is perhaps most vividly seen in the way that *Visramiani* omits the long apology for Islam in its Persian source text by Gurgani.[80] Yet there is no doubting the self-consciousness with which the Georgian poets drew on Persian models. In the prologue to his *Vepkhistqaosani*, Rustaveli openly declared his 1,600-quatrain epic in the aforementioned *shairi* genre as a "Persian tale, translated into Georgian / Like an orphaned pearl, like a toy passed from hand to hand."[81] For, if not necessarily hegemonic, in the Georgian royal courts of King David (Davit) IV ("the Builder," r. 1089–1125) and Queen Tamar (r. 1184–1213), where such literary works flourished, the prestige of Persianate and more broadly Islamicate culture was widely recognized, most plainly in the use of both Arabic and Georgian scripts on their coinage.

To some extent, this was a pattern echoed in Armenian in such works as the romance of Farhad (an unsurprising choice given that Shirin was long identified in Persian versions of the story as an Armenian princess). Yet while entirely Persianate in onomastic, atmospheric, and geographic respects, the romance of Farhad, like other Armenian works, was far more impervious to lexical imports from Persian. While medieval Armenian poets adapted motifs from Persian works, the more Byzantine orientation of the Armenian courts (in Cilicia especially) meant that there were no lengthy Armenian renditions of Persian *masnawi* romances to compare with the Georgian *Vepkhistqaosani*. There were oral epics, though, such as *Rustam Zal*, which offers a partial parallel to the literate Georgian versions of Firdawsi. However, the greatest impact of Persian on Armenian literature came via the motifs of the lyrical *ghazal*. This is best seen in the poetry of Kostandin Erznkac'i (d. ca. 1330), where the Persian imagery of the rose and nightingale (the latter as *bulbul* in a rare example of a loanword into Armenian) was adapted for the purposes of Christian devotional poetry.[82] The later monks and abbots, such as Xač'atur (d. 1341), who subsequently followed Kostandin's model, further developed this Persianate imagery for their own distinctly Christian purposes in ways that, to quote Cowe again, found "expressive potential untapped in its culture of origin."[83] Persianate subtlety and refinement also characterized the poetry of Grigoris Aght'amarts'i (1485–1544), who is also notable for a series of Armeno-Persian macaronic verses.[84] Yet overall, having established its own alphabet, lexicon, norms, and concerns before the medieval ascent of Persian, Armenian literature made only selective adoptions of Persian motifs and loanwords, the latter being in any case mediated mainly through Turkish. (Conversely, what we might term "Georgianate" Turkish texts would later be written in the Georgian Mkhedruli script).[85] Indeed, it was probably in terms of book illustration rather than literary or linguistic content that Persianate models had their greatest impact on Armenian literary culture. Thus, one of the Persianate world's most testing frontiers lay in the Georgian royal courts and mountain-ringed Armenian monasteries that stretched from Tbilisi in the Caucasus to Sis in Cilicia.

This perspective is amplified when we turn from the southern to the northern Caucasus (particularly what is today Daghestan), where Arabic was much more widespread than Persian from the thirteenth century right through to the nineteenth, when Arabic served as the state language of Imam Shamil's imamate (1840–59).[86] Yet even in Daghestan, Persian served as a subsidiary language of Muslim learning. Medieval Persian classics by the likes of Firdawsi, Nizami, and Jami were read and inspired original works in Persian by Darghin poets such as Ibn Yusuf and Damadan of Mug in the sixteenth and seventeenth centuries, which also saw the composition of Muhammad Awabi's local history, the *Darband-nama* (Book of Derbent).[87] Many Persian inscriptions of this period are also extant from the northern Caucasus, as is Persian correspondence between local rulers and the Safavids, pointing to larger Persographic patterns of Persian as a written contact language. Persian thus embedded itself deeper in the Muslim than the Christian Caucasus.

Turning from the Caucasus to India, the medieval rise of Persian-using chanceries in Lahore, and then Delhi and beyond, coupled with the immigration of "Turko-Persian" Muslim settlers, generated new spoken vernaculars that would in time develop written forms that were more hegemonically Persianate. These notably included the various North Indian vernaculars generically referred to by medieval authors as Hindwi ("Hindi," that is, Indian). Compared to the older Christian written literary traditions of Armenian and Georgian, these languages and their literatures were much more clearly "Persianate" in the dominant partner sense that Hodgson intended. Amid these spaces of local linguistic pluralism and across the isoglossic language borders that separated them, written Persian served to connect literati in a common cultural framework. To what extent that interregional Persographic culture affected local life worlds, though, was a variable function of the Persianate as a process of literary and broadly cultural bricolage. As a dynamic process, the Persianate, then, was always contingent and contested.

We should therefore be cautious about assuming that Persian became the sole language of the various courts, chanceries, and Sufi lodges of the medieval period of Turko-Persian supremacy, particularly in frontier regions with their

own earlier traditions of literacy. Even under Muslim rule in the Delhi sultanate and its regional heirs in Gujarat, Bengal, and the Deccan, both bilingualism and biliteracy seem to have been practiced. This certainly happened at the
district (*pargana*) level, though there is every reason to see Persian as one linguistic (and especially written) stratum at the regionalizing courts.[88] This was a
practical outcome of the demography of literacy: in many regions preexisting
Hindu bureaucracies outnumbered immigrant Muslim secretaries. After Persian
emerged as a lingua franca between senior officials and their employees, between
the central chanceries and the districts, Persian did not stamp out other written languages but coexisted and ultimately interacted with them.[89] This was not
merely an Indian aberration on a distant Persianate frontier: the Jalayirid bureaucracy in Baghdad, at the heart of the "Middle East," issued documents in Arabic,
Persian, and Mongolian.[90]

In the expansion of these bureaucratic and in turn literary activities, we should
also recognize the material profile of Persographia based on increasing access to
the paper that had spread from China to Samarqand and then Khurasan by the
mid-eighth century, into Armenian and Georgian monastic usage in the Caucasus
by 981, then down into India by the thirteenth century.[91] When paper technology
reached Delhi, then Bengal and the Deccan, the Persian term *kaghaz* (a Soghdian
word that was possibly itself a borrowing from Chinese) was loaned and adapted
into many other languages of the subcontinent, from Bengali and Nepali to Marathi
and Telugu, as well as further west into such languages as Georgian, Kurdish, the
several varieties of Turkic, and Arabic (with early adoption into Arabic shaping the
spelling of the word in Persian).[92] Ottoman usage carried the word *kaghaz* even as
far west as the Balkans, where it generated the modern Serbian term for "documentation" (*ćage*), part of the larger Ottoman-borne Persian lexicon that survives to this
day in such other Balkan languages as Bulgarian and Romanian.[93]

After the multifarious spoken versions of Early New Persian, what by the fourteenth century had transformed the written language into the stable and standardized form of New Persian was therefore its adoption as a shared language among
various different groups of non-native users. That is to say, Arabic-script Persian
only gradually became a written lingua franca as a consequence of its expansion
by powerful Turkic (then Turko-Mongol) dynasties. This increasing orthographic
standardization is best seen in the contrast between Judeo-Persian and what we
might call Hindu-Persian. For as shown by the many surviving Jewish tombstone
inscriptions from Jam (Firuzkuh) during the Ghaznavid and Ghurid periods,
Persian-speaking Jewish communities were able to maintain their own Hebrew
script for centuries after the Muslim conquest of their homelands.[94] In the case of
Hindu adopters of Persian, however, being exposed to the language at a later stage of
its history meant that Persian was adopted together with the Arabic script through
Hindu exposure to the Islamo-Persian of the court, chancery, and *khanaqah*. The
key difference between these two situations was that Hebrew-script Judeo-Persian

was a community language intended for use within the Jewish community whereas Arabic-script Hindu-Persian was a contact language across community boundaries, albeit on terms set by Muslim orthographic norms. The synthesis of Turkish military power with Persian literary hegemony thus ensured that, from the twelfth century on, Persian did not adopt the writing systems of its new geographies but instead exported what would become a standard set of orthographic norms.

Together, the court secretaries, in their dual roles in the political-administrative and cultural-literary arenas, and the madrasa and *khanaqah* institutions, in their dual roles in pedagogy and text production, created a set of specific but connected spaces: court and chancery, school and shrine. In the latter case, we see the Islamic dimensions to the expansion of Persian as the language became associated with the education of *ulama* (albeit, in theory at least, in secondary status to Arabic at higher levels of study) and especially the transmission of Sufi doctrines. Here it is important to bear in mind that, from the twelfth century on, Sufi Islam became normative Islam rather than a mystical fringe. This was particularly the case insofar as the spread of Islam into new regions in this period meant that the Islam introduced as normative religion was Sufi Islam, and its introducers were more often than not members of the Sufi orders, whose syllabi were increasingly in Persian.[95] These highly mobile Sufis extended both the spatial and social frontiers of Persographia.

It was this combined expansion of both the Persian language and the Arabic script that enabled it to emerge as a written lingua franca that was transportable, imitable, and durable through the very fact of being written, and copied, on paper. What this in turn points to is the importance of shared and transferred writing practices, the acquired skill sets, and standard repertoires that distinguish written languages like Persian from the spoken languages like Hindwi, Turki, or demotic Greek with which Persian co-existed and interacted. Since the sociolinguistic landscapes that Persian traversed and connected were locally multilingual and multiscriptural, this returns us to the importance of keeping these other languages in view. As Marshall Hodgson emphasized in his original definition of the term "Persianate," it is this interlinguistic contact between Persian and its local subordinates that distinguishes the "Persianate" from the more narrowly "Persian." By the fourteenth and especially fifteenth century, such contact fertilized a rich field of linguistic and literary exchange between Persian and a ripening harvest of new regional literatures.[96] Attention to such multilingual environments, to languages in contact, therefore helps us understand how the "Persianate" actually worked.

In the thirteenth century, the geography of Persian was massively restructured by the conquests and then conversions of the Mongols. Initially, the Mongol obliteration of such key Khurasani cities as Balkh, Merv, and Nishapur destroyed the institutional basis of Persian's most important early region and dislocated its surviving personnel to places as distant as Delhi and Konya.[97] Yet inasmuch as the Mongols destroyed old geographies, they also created new political and cultural geographies that, however short-lived in their greatest extent, reached from Central Europe across the Iranian plateau to the Sea of Japan.[98] The impact was felt not only in the arts of the book—via marbled papers and brushwork clouds—but also in new textual visions of that wider Eurasian world, most famously in the Persian survey of world history, *Jami' al-Tawarikh* (Compendium of Histories), written by the Mongol vizier Rashid al-Din (1247–1318).[99] Its author, a convert from Judaism, was only one of many Persographic secretaries employed by the various Mongol states of the fourteenth century.[100] Through them, the Pax Mongolica afforded the expansion of Persian administrative practices further east across Eurasia as far as China and Mongolia. Despite claims to the contrary, Persian did probably not become one of the "official" languages of the Chinese Mongol (Yuan) bureaucracy.[101] Indeed, the importance of Mongolian as an administrative language saw dozens of Mongolian loanwords appear in the Persian poetry of the Ilkhanid and Timurid periods, most fully in the verse of the panegyrist of the Mongols, Pur-i Baha (d. ca. 1284?).[102]

Even so, the new diplomatic, commercial, and intellectual frontiers opened by the Mongols did see Persian carried further east than ever. Sufis expanded their activities across the Mongol domains, carrying Persian texts with them.[103] The Yuan (1271–1368)—and subsequent Ming (1368–1644) and Qing (1644–1912) dynasties—conducted part of their diplomatic and other political business in Persian. When the early Ming dynasty Muslim admiral Zheng He (1371–1433/35) led a trading mission across the Indian Ocean, Persian was one of the three languages—the others were Chinese and Tamil—selected for the stele he had erected in Galle on Ceylon (now Sri Lanka) in 1409.[104] Whether or not Zheng He was correct to consider written Persian a lingua franca of maritime trade, the Galle inscription is certainly testament to the importance with which the Chinese themselves had come to regard the language by the end of the Mongol era.[105] Another linguistic trace of the maritime interaction between Chinese and Persian is the adoption of the Mandarin word for an ocean storm, *dàfēng* (great wind), into Persian as *tufan* (and thence, probably via Portuguese, into English as *typhoon*).[106]

With the destruction of Khurasan, then the opening of China, the thirteenth and fourteenth centuries show the Persianate world to have comprised an unstable, evolving, and contingent set of frontiers. The early Mongol destruction of so many of the important early communities, institutions, and presumably libraries that had reared written Persian in Khurasan and the Iranian plateau witnessed in some sense a hollowing out of the Persianate world that saw its former fringes in Anatolia and northern India emerge as the self-conscious "canopies" (*qubba*) of Perso-Islamic culture. As the Central Asian Timurids and then the Thrace-based Ottomans began to build their own imperial cultures in the fourteenth and fifteenth centuries, the patronage of Persian poetical and historical works became a key part of their policies, particularly under Mehmet II (r. 1451–81) for whom Timurid Herat served as a model for his new imperial capital.[107] That Persian literary culture had a "natural" or "primordial" home in Iran is a fiction of latter-day nationalism. The geography of Persian was therefore a changing one, based less around dense town-and-country "homelands" than around a networked geography of dispersed and usually urban institutions by way of courts, chanceries, colleges, and khanaqahs.[108]

In the fourteenth and fifteenth centuries, this geography evolved again as new courts were established in places as distant as Edirne, Istanbul, Tabriz, Samarqand, Kazan, Tyumen, Pandua, and Bidar. Under mainly Turko-Mongolian rule—in claiming an ethnically Persian ancestry from the *Shah-nama*'s King Bahman, the Bahmanis of Bidar were unusual—these new capitals attracted Persographic poets, scribes, and mystics from as far as southeast Europe, Siberia, and southern India.[109] Aside from the paperwork of the chancery, the new texts composed in their courts and *khanaqahs* continued the characteristic genres established before the Mongol conquests. Chiefly they comprised epistolography, dynastic histories, hagiographies, mirrors of princes, and poetry in panegyric, epic, lyric, and narrative form. Though shared across wide regions, these conventional genres were adapted for local concerns and regional patriotisms.[110] Like literary watermarks visible in text rather than paper, conceptions of space were an indelible feature of the texts produced in these expanding and competing new capitals. Whether in royal histories or saintly hagiographies, genealogical geographies were articulated so as to map time (biological or inherited descent) onto space (areas of migration or conquest). In such ways, these textual tools of cultural transmission helped naturalize Persian (and its users) into its new geographies, many of which were themselves given Persian names through practices of urban and architectural onomastics.[111] Text and territory were in such ways perpetually in play as individual words, prose or poetic descriptions, and book illustrations were used to physically and semantically shape new built environments being created in radically different physical environments from the Mediterranean to Bengal and beyond. It was this mirroring, both mental and material, of both text and territory that rendered Persographia more than an eastern Utopia. Rather, as the medieval period's many migrant poets, mystics, and dynasts testify, its cities were intelligible to those who moved between them. Such cities could be far more navigable, linguistically, and thereby professionally, than the countryside around one's hometown. Because small towns and especially rural areas lay off the Persographic map.

It is worth pausing here to take stock of the geography of Persographia that had emerged from the different institutional spaces of Persian, by way of court, chancery, school, and shrine by the fifteenth century. It is in this respect that Richard Eaton has delineated a Perso-Islamic "cultural axis" connecting the cities of Khurasan and Central Asia to their urban interlocutors in Delhi, Bengal, and the Deccan.[112] Useful as this notion is, we require more specific geographical models based on the movement of actual texts and their producers.[113] In principle, these networked spaces could be mapped in a way that might mirror the "abstract models for a literary history" that Franco Moretti has developed in connection with English literature.[114] This would provide a much clearer cartography of written Persian than our current vague geographic notions of the Persianate world. Voluminous and diverse as the many textual products of these institutional spaces were, their connections should not blind us to the delineated geographies of their textual circulation. These Persian-producing institutions had very limited hinterlands in terms of the proximate reception and even comprehension of Persian texts. In many cases—notably the isolated semi-rural *khanaqahs* of India and the thinly populated Kazakh steppe—these institutions had no hinterlands at all. The reason for this is that the geography of written Persian was a networked geography. Rather than being dense and localized, the spaces of Persographia were sporadic and distant. This geographical formation shaped the profile of its linguistic medium. For Persian served as the shared written language of these courts, chanceries, madrasas, and *khanaqahs* precisely because of their spatial distance and distribution, which required a relatively stable, homoglossic, and transportable medium. These needs and functions are quite different from those of a locally dense spoken lingua franca, whether vernacular or not, suggesting again that Persographia is not identical with Persophonia.

This networked geography of written Persian contained its hubs as well as its nodes, that is, urban environments with larger numbers of Persian readers and writers as well as, in some regions, more or less dense or sporadic clusters of nodes around such a hub. These anchoring hubs were usually dynastic capitals (that is, sites of a court and chancery), where opportunities for education and employment combined with family- and kin-based forms of written language teaching to ensure relative density of Persian language use, or at least competence. Alternatively, hubs could be scholarly-cum-religious centers, such as Khuldabad in the Deccan, though as in the cases of Konya and Bukhara, such alternative hubs were often erstwhile dynastic capitals as well. The geography of Persian was then one of power, privilege, and authority, or at least proximity to them, taking us back to the hegemonic character of the "Persianate". Yet these hubs were also for this reason exceptional: a given region can only support so many capital cities with their expensive courts, schools, and salons. Except among the comparatively few such hubs with dense clusters—say, around Bukhara or the interfluvial North Indian *doab* region with its many small *qasba* towns—written Persian was therefore more typically a medium of distant rather than close communication. Its written character was essential to its function in connecting small groups of people—whether politically or culturally, administratively, or emotionally—in specific spaces along the distant nodes of this networked geography. In hubs and densely clustered nodes of Persian usage, the use of written and spoken Persian sometimes co-existed: though not identical, the geographies of Persophonia and Persographia most certainly overlapped, if to different degrees, in the streets of Shiraz, Delhi, and Samarqand. But by the same token, in each of its spaces—urban courtly hub or rural *khanaqah* node—Persian also competed with the usage of other spoken and sometimes written languages, whether Mongolian, Turkic, Indic, or Sinic. Across vast sections of Eurasia, Persian was often a literate island in a sea of spoken Turkic, a point that was no less true for large parts of post-Saljuq Iran.

Under the Saljuqs of Rum, and subsequently under the early Ottomans through the fourteenth century, the frontiers of Persian also expanded westwards across Anatolia and into the Balkans.[115] Given that Greek literary culture had dominated the region for more than a millennium, there was interchange with Greek as well as other Christian language groups in the region, via not only paper documents but also in few cases far more costly public inscriptions and Greek-inscribed coinage issued by Anatolia's Turkic dynasties.[116] This echoed the situation in India during this period, where the Gujarat sultans issued bilingual Sanskrit-Persian edicts on public monuments and steles.[117] Back in Anatolia, while Persian was the main language of the Saljuq chancery, the latter retained smaller Arabic, Greek, and possibly Armenian departments.[118] Even such influential Anatolian Persian literary figures as Jalal al-Din Rumi (d. 1273) and his son Sultan Walad (d. 1312) composed verses in Greek, albeit written in Arabic-script suggesting competence in vernacular spoken rather than written Greek.[119] These Anatolian interactions with Christian languages were sufficiently esteemed as to be imitated as far south as Aden, where, under the Turkic-origin Rasulid dynasty, Sultan al-Malik al-Afzal al-'Abbas ibn 'Ali (r. 1363–77) composed a dictionary of Arabic, Persian, Turkic, Mongolian, Greek, and Armenian.[120] After the brief bureaucratic replacement of Persian by Arabic in Mongol-ruled Saljuq Anatolia, the Ottoman chancery retained Persian as its chief chancery language, along with a smaller (and less linguistically competent) Arabic department. After a transitional period in the fifteenth century, during which many chancery documents were composed in a mixture of Persian and Turkish, it was only over the course of the sixteenth century that the Ottoman bureaucracy moved more fully to Turkish, along with Arabic for the empire's Arab provinces.

At this point, it is worth turning away from this continental Eurasian geography toward the Indian Ocean and the question of a maritime Persographic geography. This helps us understand the geographies of written Persian's expansion as distinct from the expansion of Islam per se. For between the twelfth and fifteenth centuries, Islam expanded across the Indian Ocean along both preexisting and expanding trade routes connecting coastal Iran, India, and crucially Arabia (notably Hadramawt) with the larger and smaller trading islands of the ocean. Yet, unlike some world-historical lingua francas, written Persian does not seem to have been significantly expanded by trade, except arguably where trade became linked to Persographic state diplomacy in the early modern period. There is some early evidence of the role of Persian-speaking traders from inland Fars and coastal Siraf in the spread of Islam through the western Indian Ocean. Twelfth-century Divehi-language *lomafanu* (copper-plate) inscriptions from the Maldives contain Persian rather than Arabic loanwords for their religious vocabulary.[121] But the written language here was Maldivian Divehi and not Persian. As written Divehi further evolved, it did adopt more Persian words, but these were part of a larger oceanic lexicon comprising borrowings from Sinhala, Sanskrit, Tamil, and Arabic.[122] Moreover, the earliest surviving history of the Maldives, *Tarikh Islam Diba Mahal* (Islamic History of the Maldive Islands) by Hasan Taj al-Din (fl. 1725), is in Arabic rather than Persian.[123] This does not rule out an earlier phase of "Persian" input, at least in terms of the spoken Persian of merchants and missionaries, but there is no evidence of Persian as a written contact language.

With regard to the expansion of Islam into Southeast Asia, there is a long academic debate about the importance of Persian vis-à-vis Arabic. It is true that when the North African Ibn Battuta (d. 1368) visited the court of Pasai on Sumatra, he found two Iranian experts in Islamic law in the sultan's employment.[124] But as legal experts, their expertise was presumably (like that of Ibn Battuta himself) in Arabic *fiqh* texts, placing Persian potentially on the spoken level attested in the Maldives. Although Iranian or more likely Indian Persian manuscripts may have circulated in Southeast Asia between the fourteenth and seventeenth centuries, leading to locally produced Malay translations, the lack of surviving early manuscripts in Persian from tropical Southeast Asia makes it extremely difficult to trace the details of Persian's reception in the region. While such limited evidence does not suggest a role for written Persian as an oceanic lingua franca, it does point to the importance of translation practices as the processual vector of the Persianate. The earliest significant case is a Malay translation of the *Tuti-nama* (Book of the Parrot) entitled *Hikayat Bayan Budiman* (Story of the Virtuous Parrot), which dates to 1371.[125] Through this and subsequent translations, the Persian *hikayat* (tale, narrative) laid the basis for what became the definitive classical Malay prose genre, pointing to a vector of "Persianate" influence according to Hodgson's formulation. In the *Hikayat Bayan Budiman* and other translated texts highly regarded in the fifteenth- and sixteenth-century Malacca court, Persian terms and idioms were passed over into the Malay versions in a manner that echoes the cases of other Persianate vernaculars then emerging in fourteenth- and fifteenth-century India and Central Asia. Beyond such narrative prose works, excerpts from major Persian poetic texts, such as the *Masnawi* of Rumi and the *Bustan* and *Gulistan* of Sa'di, were included in Malay anthologies in which interlinear translations were incorporated into the original Persian text.[126] There is, then, evidence of Fragner's *Sprachkontakt*, but not evidence of a sufficiently robust localization of Persian—comprising, say, the composition of Persian texts in Malacca—to suggest that the region had fully entered the domains of Persographia. There were also many cases in which Malay scholars accessed Persian literature via Arabic texts, as with the influential Malay work *Hikayat Iskandar Zulkarnain* (Story of the Two-Horned Alexander), which points to the larger and longer influence of Arabic rather than Persian texts in Southeast Asia.[127] Thus, while the current state of research allows us to point to the presence of short-lived corridors of Persian learning across the Indian Ocean, the evidence nonetheless seems to show the limits of the language's reach in the Malay zone. Persian crossed Eurasian land frontiers very effectively, not least through its adoption by state bureaucracies, but its expansion across maritime frontiers appears at present to have been more restricted.

Although the debate over the relative importance of Persian or Arabic in Southeast Asia is unsettled, certain things appear clear. Whatever the scale of early Persianate influence on the formation of Malay literature, written Persian was never an Indian Ocean lingua franca in the way that Arabic was, or even in the way written Malay subsequently became a "cosmopolitan vernacular" connecting peoples across peninsular and insular Southeast Asia. After all, the number of Persian loanwords in classical Malay stands at a little less than a hundred, compared to around a thousand Arabic words.[128] The maritime frontier of Persian in Southeast Asia, then, was not a uniquely (still less a hegemonically) Persianate space, but rather a space in which Arabic was a more important shared language of learning. In terms of the sheer number of surviving texts, there seems little doubt that, taken as a whole, the Indian Ocean appears more as an "Arabic cosmopolis" (in Ronit Ricci's formulation) than a Persian one.[129] Yet, as with regard to the Maldives, further research may find a more sequenced process of an early Persian-based influence on Malay court culture giving way to a greater expansion of Arabic usage that has bequeathed more surviving texts. The replacement of the generic notion of an "Indian Ocean world" by a more evidence-based and networked geography may reveal particular maritime corridors of Persian-usage that were distinct from those of Arabic. The Bengal-Burma and Iran-Gujarat axes across the Bay of Bengal and Arabian Sea seem to be two such smaller maritime spatial units in which Persian flourished in a way that is less apparent for the Arabia-Sumatra axis.[130]

Even so, for the most part, Arabic does appear to have been considerably more important in the Indian Ocean than Persian. The role of written Persian across the vast spaces of the Indian Ocean in no way parallels that of Persian across the comparable overland distances of Eurasia. Until European merchants in India created new Persian-based connections with Europe, from the thirteenth century on, the geography of Persographia reflected the reach of Turko-Mongolian power across Eurasia. Within that networked geography, courts, chanceries, madrasas, and *khanaqahs* functioned as the mechanisms and markers of Persian's expansion.

BETWEEN COSMOPOLITAN VERNACULARS AND PERSOGRAPHIC EMPIRES (CA. 1500–CA. 1800)

From the early sixteenth century on, the emergence of the Safavid, Mughal, and Shaybanid dynasties provided many new opportunities for Persian-writing secretaries, savants, and Sufis. Echoing wider "early modern" patterns, this was a period of increased interaction and mobility, which was in considerable part enabled by the shared usage of written Persian. Over the course of the sixteenth and seventeenth centuries, for example, between 20 and 30 percent of Mughal courtiers were émigrés from Safavid Iran, particularly its eastern provinces.[131] Even so, what can easily appear like the unassailable expansion of Persian between the late fifteenth and seventeenth centuries should not be overstated. In each of its hubs, Persian's users were necessarily in contact with the languages of their more proximate environments. While the "homoglossic" Persian texts described by John Perry may have neglected local languages because of the need to maintain a standardized lexicon that was intelligible "across the network," their writers were in varying degrees forced into familiarity with the spoken languages of their surroundings. Even that homoglossia was less apparent by the sixteenth and seventeenth centuries and was arguably undermined by deliberate literary policies arising from the increasing self-confidence of Persian-writing literati in India. Through his prose manual *Insha-yi Abu al-Fazl,* Akbar's chief secretary Abu al-Fazl 'Alami (1551–1602) promulgated a new secretarial style (*sabk-i munshiyana*) that promoted a distinctive "Indian usage" (*isti'mal-i Hind*).[132] A great influence on the Mughal literati, Abu al-Fazl's manual contributed to increasing lexical and stylistic differences between Persian in India, Central Asia, and Iran.[133]

This brings us back to one of the other core aims of this book: recognizing the multilingual environments from and between which Persian texts emerged. For long periods, these multilingual environments had been merely oral. But in the late fifteenth century and especially the sixteenth, Persian's local linguistic interlocutors began to be written down in a multitude of different regions, thus generating what Hodgson conceived as Persianate languages.[134] In Timurid Herat, this meant the Chaghatai Turkic promoted by court literati like Mir 'Ali Shir Nawa'i (1441–1501), which subsequently spread through much of Central and even South Asia, if very much as the junior partner to Persian.[135] For whatever the rhetorical claims of Nawa'i's *Muhakamat al-Lughatayn* (Contention of the Two Languages), the appearance of Chaghatai texts at the court of Sultan Husayn Bayqara (r. 1469–70, 1470–1506) never amounted to anything approaching a systematic Timurid program to promote Turkic at the expense of Persian: both the Timurid court and chancery remained wedded to Persian.[136] Indeed, the scope of Persographia expanded, since Persian began to be deployed as a language of jurisprudence (*fiqh*) under the late Timurids precisely after Bayqara's chief magistrate in Herat compiled *Mukhtar al-Ikhtiyar,* a legal textbook that remained in use till the twentieth century.[137]

Nonetheless, several written varieties of Turkic were emerging as new literary languages that qualify as Persianate in Hodgson's original terms of definition, that is as languages that "depended upon Persian wholly or in part for their prime literary inspiration."[138] A generation or two after Nawa'i, over a thousand miles west, the corpus of Old Anatolian, Azeri, and then Ottoman Turkic poetry, and in time prose, was expanded. As with multilingual poets such as the Azerbaijani Muhammad bin Sulayman, called Fuzuli (1494–1556), and his many successors, this occurred through court patronage (or in Fuzuli's case, an unsuccessful bid for

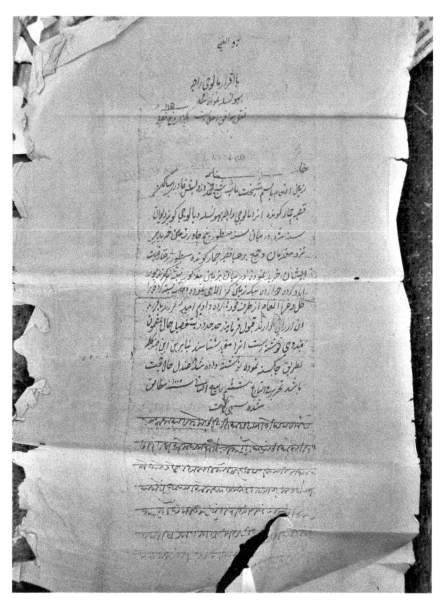

FIGURE 3. Mughal secretarial bilingualism: Persian-Marathi *In'am* document of Maloji Bhosle. Photograph courtesy of Dušan Deák and Riyaz Babasaheb Śekh.

patronage) in contexts in which, as in Timurid Herat, Persian literature remained a model of immense prestige.[139] These were not oral folk poets, then, still less nativist or proto-national figures. Indeed, it is worth pointing out that Fuzuli spent most of his life not in Anatolia but in Aq-Quyunlu Turkoman–ruled Iraq, where he learned Arabic and Persian in addition to his Azeri Turkic. It was only after the Ottoman sultan Sulayman I conquered Baghdad in 1534 that Fuzuli turned his poetic attentions to the Ottoman imperial literary economy.

Crucially, given the court-chancery nexus that long empowered Persian, these new language policies affected bureaucratic as well as literary texts, particularly in regions with large non-Muslim populations that had their own written languages. In the sultanates of southern India, the Bijapur ruler Ibrahim ʿAdil Shah I (r. 1535–58) had the language of judicial and revenue records changed from Persian to Marathi and Kannada, while in the neighboring Qutb Shah sultanate, public inscriptions were issued bilingually in Persian and Telugu, the latter including many loanwords in testament to a degree of Persian (if not hegemonically "Persianate") lexical influence.[140] In the Buddhist-ruled kingdom of Mrauk U in Arakan, on the borders of South and Southeast Asia, in 1495, the earliest extant bilingual inscription was engraved in Arakanese and Persian as the frontiers of Persographia began to expand into the numismatic, diplomatic, and mercantile spheres of Mrauk U court life only to subsequently witness the rise of literary Bengali.[141] For under the Bengal sultanate, and then in Mrauk U, a court literature in Middle Bengali was developed by such figures as Shah Muhammad Saghir and Alaʾol (fl. 1651–71), who translated poetic works from Persian into Bengali.[142] Meanwhile, in the North Indian cities under Afghan Lodi control, Arabic-script Hindwi works that recast Persian idioms in more vividly vernacular forms were patronized by Indian Sufis such as Mir Sayyid Manjhan (fl. 1545).[143] In each of these cases, we see Hodgson's definition of "Persianate" in varying degrees of action and with varying degrees of dominance. Here Persianate was an unsteady, variable process, a set of literary developments shaped by social dynamics, political changes, and patronage fashions in what were quite distinct environments.

Although all of these newly written vernaculars qualify to varying extents as being "Persianate" in Hodgson's terms through their adoption of words, genres, and subject matter from Persian, from the sixteenth century on, they were developing as rich (and sometimes richly patronized) literary fields in their own right. They were becoming "cosmopolitan vernaculars," in line with Sheldon Pollock's concept.[144] In addition to rival regional languages, the interregional hegemony of written Persian was also being threatened by literary Turki (whether what would eventually be termed "Chaghatai" or "Ottoman" Turkish), itself an increasingly interregional language, whose chefs-dʾoeuvre were read from the Tarim Basin to the Balkans.[145] Although Chaghatai was never nearly as widespread as Persian in Mughal India, it was arguably more socially and ethnically exclusive, being chiefly associated with elite families of *moghol* immigrants. Even so, a tradition of Chaghatai text production continued in the subcontinent during the entire Mughal era.[146] Moreover, even within empires, the politics of pluralism meant that Persian was not the only language being patronized, as Mughal support for Sanskrit treatises and Brajbhasha poetry shows.[147]

What is more striking—and less assimilable to Hodgson's model of assumed Persianate hegemony—is Persian's interaction with preexisting "classical" literary languages that had their own traditions, genres, and literary specialists. In differing degrees, such interactions occurred in each of the regions into which Persian expanded from the thirteenth century on, whether Anatolia, India, or China. In Anatolia, this was the case with Byzantine Greek. But while a few Greek texts were influenced by Persian, the prestige of Byzantine court culture also influenced the Rum Saljuqs and Ottomans in turn.[148] In India, this was the case with Sanskrit: by the sixteenth century, the Mughals supported both scholarship in Sanskrit and translations of Sanskrit works into Persian.[149] In China, this was the case with Chinese, for the bilingual inscriptions framed in Chinese decoration on the foundation steles of Ming-period mosques in no way suggest that Persian was the dominant partner.[150] Trade along the Silk Roads to China had led to the gradual emergence of a new community of "Persianate Chinese," who eventually became known as the Hui, but it was Chinese rather than Persian literary culture that emerged as dominant.[151] From the mid-seventeenth century on, Hui scholars began to create a new Muslim literature in Chinese based on translations from Persian texts. Known collectively as the *Han Kitab* (Chinese books), this new corpus was built on the foundations of four key Persian Sufi texts, *Mirsad al- 'Ibad* (Path of God's Servants) by Najm al-Din Razi (d. 1256); *Maqsad-i Aqsa* by 'Aziz al-Nasafi (d. 1263); and *Ashi'at al-Lama'at* (Commentary on the Divine Flashes[of Fakhr al-Din 'Iraqi]) and *Lawa'ih* (Gleams) by 'Abd al-Rahman Jami (d. 1492).[152] In each case, these translations had to adapt Persian Sufi vocabulary and concepts to the dominant Chinese literary and Confucian semantic order of the Ming imperial literati.

The linguistic traffic of the sixteenth and seventeenth centuries was not only one-way from Persian into other languages. In India, this is apparent from texts such as the *Qasida dar Lughat-i Hindi* (Panegyric on the Hindi Language), a versified vocabulary of Hindwi medical terms written by a physician who migrated to Delhi from Herat.[153] Sanskrit scholars also created their own dictionaries and teaching manuals of Persian, as well as absorbing Persian influences into their Sanskrit works.[154] As in many other regions of Eurasia, Jami was a key figure in this: in 1505, at the Kashmir court of Muhammad Shah (r. 1500–1526), Jami's *Yusuf wa Zulaykha* was rendered into the Sanskrit *Kathakautuka* (Curious Story) by the poet Śrivara.[155] Correspondingly, the Mughal elite sponsored large translation projects rendering Sanskrit works into Persian.[156] The desire of various other non-native speakers across the subcontinent to learn or master the Persian language—particularly its more recondite lexicons and technical jargons—led to the increasing production of pedagogic works. Having begun with the late thirteenth-century *Farhang-i Qawwas* (Dictionary of Qawwas), the production of such pedagogical and lexicographical works rapidly increased with the greater demand for mastery of Persian under the Mughals.[157] Many similar such works were written in Central Asia to enable Turki speakers to learn Persian, but also—reflecting the increasing status of Turkic languages—for Persian-speakers to learn to read Chaghatai.[158] Meanwhile, in China, Hui Muslims prepared similar glossaries of Chinese-Persian vocabulary.[159]

Whether in the Ottoman Empire or in post-Timurid Central Asia, literary Turkic expanded considerably in the sixteenth and seventeenth centuries. Over the course of the sixteenth century, the Ottoman imperial chancery steadily replaced Persian with Turkish for all forms of administration (except in the Arab provinces, where Arabic was retained).[160] Even so, the Ottomans did continue to issue documents in Persian—as, for example, when Selim I (r. 1512–20) issued a decree to the citizens of Bursa in Persian—and so it was likely not until the reign of Suleyman (r. 1520–66) that the Ottomans fully replaced chancery Persian with Turkish, except for diplomatic correspondence.[161] In Central Asia, however, although Muhammad Shaybani Khan (r. 1500–1510) and his successors sponsored an extensive program of translations from Persian into Chaghatai Turkish, Persian remained the paramount bureaucratic language under the Shaybanid dynasty. It also remained the chief literary and administrative language in the Safavid Empire, though Turkic literature was also written and patronized at the Safavid court, not least by its founder Shah Isma'il (r. 1501–24).[162] Even so, via the chanceries of the Safavids, Shaybanids, and Mughals, from the sixteenth century on, Persian was the preeminent language of state power across a vast region connecting Iran to Central Asia and India.

The Safavid conquest of the Georgian kingdoms of Kartli and Kakheti and the Armenian region of Erevan in the 1500s also deepened the reach of bureaucratic and in turn literary Persian in the Caucasus. Safavid mints issuing Persian coinage were established in Tblisi and Erevan (Yerevan), while for almost two centuries in Erevan and three centuries in Kartli and Kakheti decrees (farman) and other official documents were issued either in Persian or in a combination of Persian and either Armenian or Georgian.[163] Some such decrees concerned the patriarchal rights of the Armenian Catholicos and the landholding rights of Georgian monasteries. The state imperial status of Persian meant that various Georgian and Armenian poets continued either to adapt Persian motifs or to compose poetry in Persian alongside their mother tongues. For much of the sixteenth century, the main preoccupation of Georgian poets was to translate the first half of the Shah-nama into Georgian verse in the form known as Rostomiani (The Story of Rustam), as in the case of the monk of Khevi, Sogratisdze Sabashvili (fl. 1530), and Parsadan Gorgijanidze (fl. 1610) almost a century later.[164] Aside from Firdawsi and Nizami of Ganja, the other major Persian poetic model during these centuries was the Timurid literary colossus Jami. The most celebrated of Jami's transmitters into Georgian was King Teimuraz I (r. 1605–16, 1625–48) of Kartli and Kakheti, an erstwhile Safavid vassal turned rebel, who had been raised as a political hostage at the court of Shah 'Abbas.[165] In creating his own rival court culture, Teimuraz went on to adapt Jami's versions of the stories of Layli and Majnun (as Leilmajnuniani) and Yusuf and Zulaykha (as Iosebzilikhiani) before ending his days in a Safavid

FIGURES 4A and 4B. Safavid Christian borderlands: trilingual inscription in Persian, Georgian, and Armenian, Tarsa Church (1593–95), Gremi, Georgia. Photographs by Nile Green.

prison.[166] Yet, in the words of Donald Rayfield, Teimuraz had "made his enemies' tongue an integral part of his own."[167] Sharing Persianate tastes through such literary court cosmopolitanism was not, then, an automatic antidote to conflict.

King Vakhtang VI (r. 1716–24), Teimuraz's successor as ruler of Kartli and resister of the Safavids, continued to imbue his poetry with Persian metaphors and symbols, while his own successor Teimuraz II (r. 1732–44 in Kakheti, 1744–62 in Kartli) translated the tale of Sindbad (as *Timsariani*) from Persian.[168] Their coinage was also issued with both Georgian and Persian script. This too was the era of the celebrated court poet Harutyun Sayatyan, better known as Sayat Nova (Persian: *sayyad-i nawa,* 'Master of Song,' 1712–95), an Armenian by birth who composed verses in Armenian, Georgian, Azeri Turkish, and Persian and was put to death for refusing to apostatize by the invading Qajar shah of Iran, Agha Muhammad Khan.[169] But though even Sayat Nova's Georgian songs were filled with Persian words and phrases, after his death, with the Russian conquest of southern Caucasia looming on the horizon, Persian would soon give way to the new imperial literary and intellectual lingua franca of Russian. With the opening of the Tbilisi mint in 1804 after the Russian conquest of 1801, the use of Persian also disappeared from the region's coinage.

Armenian poets had also continued to incorporate Persianate elements into their literature during the Safavid era. In 1606, Shah 'Abbas had deported over 150,000 Armenians from the old town of Julfa in Nakhichavan to the suburb of New Julfa in his capital at Isfahan,[170] and between the late seventeenth century and the 1780s, Armenian bards composed oral poetry (particularly in the *du-bayti* and *dastan* genres) in both Persian and the New Julfan dialect of Armenian, itself replete with Persian vocabulary.[171] As in the case of Georgian, though, when writing in Armenian, there was only a selective incorporation of Persianate elements by adopting motifs and metaphors, rather than script. Even so, as late as the eighteenth century, Petros Lapʾancʾi (d. 1784) continued to use the imagery of the rose and nightingale.[172] However, in the Safavid period, the impact of Persian on Armenian literature as a whole was still less than on Georgian. The Ottoman conquest of eastern Anatolia (including much of the historically Armenian region of Vaspurakan) at Chaldiran in 1514 and of the western half of the Caucasus in 1639 rendered imperial Turkish (and subsequently European languages) an important counterweight to Persian in the lives of the Armenians who fell under Ottoman dominion.[173] When western Armenian writers did adopt Persian motifs, they were more likely to be channeled via Ottoman Turkish writers, pointing to the imperious rising power of the Persianate languages themselves.

It was in Mughal India, east of the Ottoman and Safavid imperial realms, that Persian made its greatest advances in the sixteenth and seventeenth centuries. The Mughals' Persianizing turn occurred especially after the return to Delhi in 1556 from his Safavid exile of the emperor Humayun (r. 1530–40, 1555–56), bringing to India a cohort of artists and writers from the Safavid court in Qazvin. More important for the broader impact of Persian beyond the Mughal imperial courts in Delhi, Lahore, and Agra, the social frontiers of Persian were expanded by the introduction to Persographic norms of many Hindu secretaries. It was not in the central Mughal chancery but through the regional bureaucracy that knowledge of Persian offered employment to the largest numbers of people. The chancery systems that the Mughals inherited from their Lodi Afghan and Deccani predecessors in India appear to have employed Hindu scribes using local languages such as Hindwi and Marathi at the level of local administration, sometimes transcribing Persian into Devanagari script.[174] However, despite the close affiliation of the early Mughal rulers and immigrant elite with Chaghatai Turkish, the imperial Dar al-Insha increasingly promoted the use of Persian. In 1582, the emperor Akbar (r. 1556–1605) declared Persian the official language of the Mughal bureaucracy, expanding its domain to even the local levels of administration previously conducted in the vernaculars.[175]

This increased state-driven demand for skills in Persian literacy, and particularly for mastery of epistolary forms, was the impetus for more and more Hindus to learn Persian in search of work in the imperial civil service. Echoing the importance of court secretaries in creating the earliest works of Persian prose during the Samanid period, six centuries later the larger Mughal Empire only increased the importance of bureaucracy as a vector of Persian literacy. The imperial elite in Safavid Iran had some Persian Jewish physicians, but they were far fewer than the numerous Hindus (mainly of the Kayastha and Khatri castes) who acquired literacy in Persian through the requirements of the Mughal bureaucracy. Although it was the rewards of regular employment that attracted Hindus to learn Persian, what actually enabled them to do so was the opening to them of madrasa education through another of Akbar's edicts.[176] By the reign of Jahangir (r. 1605–27), the number of Hindu scribes (*muharrir*) and secretaries (*munshis*) led Har Karan Das

Kambuh of Multan (d. 1625) to write his widely imitated epistolary manual *Insha-yi Harkaran.*[177] Within a generation, other Hindu munshis were writing Persian literary as well as administrative works. The most celebrated was Chandarbhan Brahman (d. 1662), the Lahore-born author of *Chahar Chaman* (Four Meadows) and several other works.[178] Far from disappearing with the retraction of Mughal rule, such Hindu Persian poets continued to flourish into the eighteenth and even nineteenth centuries, particularly in the successor state of Awadh.[179] Stefano Pellò has calculated that between 1760 and 1819, up to 30 percent of the poets writing in Persian in the Awadh capital of Lucknow were Hindus.[180] However, as seen in the partial translation of the *Bhagavata Purana* into Persian verse made during the 1730s in Delhi by the munshi Amanat Ra'i (d. after 1750), a Vaisnava follower of the metaphysical poet 'Abd al-Qadir Bidil (d. 1720), this was not a one-way "Persianate" street,[181] although the dominant direction was evidently what Pellò has termed "literary conversion to Islam [*conversion 'letteraria' all'islam*]."[182] For while we know of Hindu secretaries and poets who converted to Islam through their exposure to Muslim texts in Persian (such as the Punjabi Khatri Diwali Singh who became Hasan Qatil), we do not as yet know of Muslims apostatizing as result of reading Persian translations of Hindu scriptures.[183] In most Muslim-ruled contexts, there were of course legal and social limits to heterodoxy, apparent in the brutal murder by his brother Awrangzeb (r. 1658-1707) of the Mughal heir-apparent Dara Shikuh (d. 1659), who supported religious engagement with Hindu mystics.

As in the Caucasus, Persographia flourished in South Asia even in the midst of conflict between religious groups. Thus, whether motivated by political or religious concerns, the Mughal persecution of the Sikh gurus did not prevent the latter's followers from adopting the official language of Mughal Empire. As the Sikh religion gradually emerged through the teachings of the ten gurus under Afghan Lodi and Mughal rule, not only did Persian verses find their way into the Sikh holy book but a subsidiary Sikh religious literature was also composed in Persian.[184] The last Sikh Guru, Gobind Singh (1666–1708), composed his *Zafar-nama* (Letter of Victory) to the emperor Awrangzeb (whose successor had him assassinated) in the imperial lingua franca, while Persian was also the language of the *Rahit-nama* (Book of Conduct) and *Bandagi-nama* (Book of Discipleship) of Gobind Singh's favorite disciple, the Ghazni-born Bhai Nand Lal (1633–1713). To recognize conflict is not, then, wholly to reject Pellò's view of Persian as the Mughal Empire's "inter-ethnic/ecumenical language [*lingua sovranazionale/ecumenica*]" but to recognize that this did not automatically lead to wider sociopolitical ecumenism.[185]

The other important social frontier that Persian literacy increasingly crossed in the sixteenth and seventeenth centuries was that of gender, because increasing numbers of elite women learned to read Persian, and in some cases composed works in that language.[186] Here it was the court and the sub-imperial elite households, rather than the bureaucracy, that were important. Timurid cultural traditions of high female status and education found new expressions in India, most famously with the princesses Gulbadan (ca. 1523–1603) and Jahanara (1614– 81). The imperial courts of the Mughals and Safavids also increasingly exposed other groups to Persian, particularly leading representatives of the "tribal" peoples who occupied the mountainous borderlands over which the Mughal and Safavid states sought closer control than their predecessors. The examples of the Kurds and Afghans show how two peoples with their own languages—Kurmanju and Pashto—chose to adopt the language and genre of the Persian chronicles (*tarikh*) favored at the imperial court for writing their earliest histories. This occurred in the case of the *Sharaf-nama* of Sharaf al-Din Bitlisi (d. 1599), an erstwhile Kurdish protégé of both the Ottomans and Safavids, and the *Tarikh-i Khan Jahani* of Khan Jahan Lodi (d. 1631), an Afghan courtier and companion of the Mughal emperor Jahangir.[187] Even when Pashtun tribal elites did begin patronizing texts in Pashto, being unable to write themselves, they had to make use of non-Pashtun secretaries who were only literate in Persian, a collaboration that resulted in Persian shaping the evolution of written Pashto.[188]

Turning from the mountain to the maritime fringes of these empires, the "Parsi" Zoroastrians of Gujarat form another revealing case study of the Mughal social expansion of Persian. Having settled in India for many centuries, the descendants of Zoroastrian émigrés from the Iranian plateau had come to speak Gujarati and retained Middle (Pahlavi) Persian only as a liturgical language. However, in the wake of Akbar's conquest of Gujarat between 1572 to 1584, members of the literate Zoroastrian priesthood learned New Persian so as to engage with the conquering elite. Echoing such works as the *Sharaf-nama* and the *Tarikh-i Khan Jahani*, the *Qissa-yi Sanjan* (Tale of Sanjan), written in 1599 by Bahman Kaikubad, a priest from Navsari, used the norms of imperial literary culture to tell the story of his own community.[189] A subsequent Zoroastrian work, the 1655 *Dabistan-i Mazahib* (School of Religions), likely by Mir Zu al-Fiqar Ardistani, drew the Zoroastrians of the Mughal coastal periphery more closely into imperial norms through an ethnography of the empire's various religions that interpreted Zoroastrianism itself through the lenses of *ishraqi* (illuminationist) Sufi philosophy.[190]

Far from Mughal Gujarat, as mentioned earlier, Persian texts also had an impact on the emergence of a Muslim courtly and religious literature in the Malay language during the sixteenth and seventeenth centuries. This occurred through the roles of the itinerant religious teachers Hamza Fansuri (d. 1527 or 1590) and Nur al-Din Raniri (d. 1658). Born in Southeast Asia, Fansuri travelled west to Mecca, Baghdad, and even Palestine before returning to teach Sufi doctrines in his home region. This itinerary in itself suggests a more complex geographic movement than a simple center-to-periphery transfer of Persian ideas.[191] On his return to Southeast Asia, Fansuri's subsequent poetic and doctrinal writings in Malay saw him borrowing various key terms from the original Sufi lexicons of Arabic and Persian.[192] But though Fansuri adapted into several of his Malay works extracts from Persian works by such authors as Ghazali, 'Attar, and Sa'di, as well as from the *Lawa'ih* of 'Abd al-Rahman Jami (which we have already seen being rendered into Chinese), Fansuri was probably more practiced in Arabic than Persian poetical composition, since his translations were based on Arabic rules of prosody, and replete with Arabic vocabulary.[193] His competence in Persian remains uncertain. Between fifty and a hundred years after Fansuri's death, Nur al-Din Raniri migrated from the Gujarati port of Rander to the court at Aceh in Sumatra, where he attained the influential position of *shaykh al-islam* and, around 1638, composed his *Bustan al-Salatin* (Garden of Sultans), an encyclopaedic work in Malay that appears to have drawn even more than Fansuri's earlier writings on Arabic rather than Persian sources.[194] As Paul Wormser has succinctly phrased the matter, "when Persian culture and literature was at the height of its international fame, it was often accessed in the Malay world through an Arabic filter."[195] Even if Fansuri and Raniri did translate parts of Persian works into Malay, they did not produce Persian texts that genuinely linked Southeast Asia to Eurasian Persographia.

Turning to commercial rather than religious transfers across the Indian Ocean, while the poor survival of merchant records makes the picture unclear, it appears that non-Muslim merchant groups used their own languages, such as Gujarati and Julfan Armenian, rather than Persian, except presumably for their dealings with merchants who could only read Persian. Based on the small but significant set of surviving trade documents in Arabic and Persian, a case has been made for the existence of standardized mercantile "epistolary structures," though the argument here has been expressly for the importance of the Arabic script rather than of any particular language, whether Arabic or Persian.[196] A counterargument could be made that many such commercial documents were in varying degree Persianate: Armenian trade documents from New Julfa were replete with Persian vocabulary, which also crept into the Ondaatje Letters (1729–37), Tamil correspondence related to the Chettiyar merchant Nicolaas Ondaatje (Tamil: Ukantacci).[197] Yet while non-Muslim merchant communities shared technical vocabularies and loanwords with Persian users, their commercial transactions appear to have been written in their own scripts and languages. When Persian was important for Indian Ocean trade, it was mainly as a diplomatic language, not a merchant lingua franca, as evidenced by a handful of surviving Persian documents from Southeast Asia, comprising a letter to the king of Portugal produced in Malaka in 1519; two letters written in Aceh during the reign of Sultan 'Ala al-Din Ahmad Syah (r. 1725–35); and another diplomatic letter sent to Ottoman Istanbul in 1869 by the Burmese ruler, King Mindon (1853–78).[198] Only further research will allow us to speak with any certainty about these mercantile and maritime dimensions of Persographia but the discovery of such diplomatic documents does conceivably point to a greater knowledge of Persian in the chanceries of Southeast Asia than has previously been recognized.

The rise of the English East India Company (1600–1858), the Dutch Verenigde Oost Indische Compagnie (VOC; 1602–1799), the Danish Østindisk Kompagni

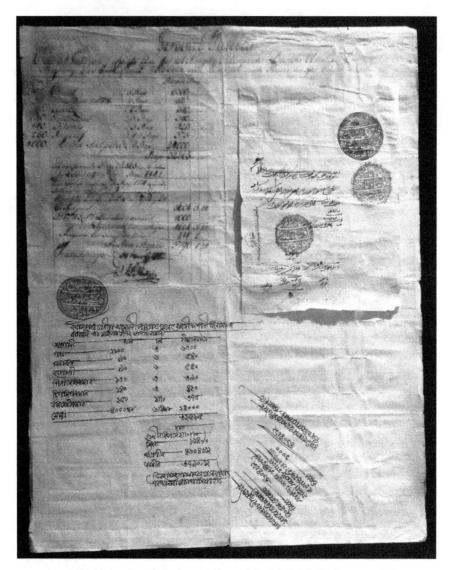

FIGURE 5. Mixed languages of merchants: trilingual Danish East India Company trade document in Persian, Bengali, and Danish. Photograph by Nile Green. Courtesy of the M/S Maritime Museum of Denmark, Elsinore.

(1616–50, 1670–1729), and the Compagnie française pour le commerce des Indes orientales (1664–1794) further expanded the geographical frontiers of Persian correspondence. In some such cases, a single document might feature Persian alongside Danish and Bengali. Thus, between the sixteenth and eighteenth centuries, trade and diplomacy with European states and their trading companies also led to an expansion of formal Persian correspondence east to the Burmese and Thai kingdoms of Pegu and Siam and west to Europe.[199]

Similarly, Iranian trade with Siam resulted in the settling of Iranian and Indian traders in Shahr-i Nav (City of Boats), as the Siamese capital Ayutthaya was called in Persian. The city, its peoples, and its goods were described in the *Safina-yi Sulayman* (*The Ship of Sulayman*), Muhammad Rabiʿ ibn Muhammad Ibrahim's official record of the embassy sent in 1685 by the Safavid Shah Sulayman (r. 1666–94) to the ruler of Siam Narai (r. 1656–88).[200] Increasing European engagement with the Safavids and then the Mughals produced an increasing amount of Persian-based diplomatic paperwork, beginning with the Republic of Venice and the Portuguese Empire and subsequently including France and England (while Russia developed its own diplomatic connections with the Central Asian khanates).[201] In its earlier phase, this involved the employment of various kinds of Persianate non-Muslim middlemen, particularly Armenians, who by the eighteenth century used Persian for communications between the English East India Company in Bengal and the Buddhist Konbaung dynasty in Burma.[202] But over the longer term the result was the production of new lexicographical works aimed at teaching Persian and its epistolary forms to Europeans, fostering a small cadre of Persian-trained European translators who were in some measure the latter-day heirs (and competitors) to the earlier Persographic munshis on the eastern half of Eurasia. A side-effect of this new intellectual axis was the creation, from around 1770 perhaps, of intellectual networks in which Persian-writing intellectuals in India and to some extent Iran translated and otherwise responded to recent developments in the "European sciences" (*ʿulum-i farangi*).[203] Even so, the case should not be overstated, insofar as the major power of concern to Europe—the Ottoman Empire—conducted its diplomatic correspondence with Europe in Turkish, which generated a cadre of European linguistic middlemen more "Ottomanate" than Persianate.[204]

Thus, even at the peak of Persian's usage, the fortunes of written Persian were marked by contingent conditions and regionally variable patterns of diplomatic practice, elite patronage and administrative policy. This became all the more visible from the mid-eighteenth century on, as the collapse of Mughal and Safavid power diverted court patronage and chancery practice toward a series of alternative languages. In different regions, this promoted the fashionable Urdu of the successor state of Awadh; the Pashto briefly promoted by the ethnically Afghan new elite of the Durrani Empire; and the Modi-script Marathi of the Peshwa Daftar, the Maratha chancery whose officials also created the Marathi historiographical genre of the *bakhar* (the name taken from the Persian *akhbar,* "news report").[205] In Central Asia, Chaghatai had by now similarly gained ground in both bureaucratic and literary contexts, though Persian works were still read, and sometimes written, in such regional hubs as Bukhara and Kashgar, the latter falling under Qing Chinese control by the 1760s. The age of the Safavid and Mughal empires that had so richly supported Persian was now over. The successor states and new empires that replaced them would develop their own policies regarding the Persian language and its by now expansive and increasingly diverse personnel.

THE RISE OF NEW IMPERIAL AND NATIONAL LANGUAGES (CA. 1800–CA. 1930)

Although the earlier expansion of Turkic bureaucracy under the Ottomans and the more limited patronage of Chaghatai literature under the Timurids and their successors in Central Asia had introduced Turkic into some of Persian's domains, the case for a vernacular ascendance in the eighteenth century observed by Bert Fragner and others should not be overstated. Even by the early nineteenth century, too many families, professional groups, and institutions were invested in Persian for its power to quickly crumble. In Iran, the founders of the new Qajar dynasty in the 1780s upheld Persian's status in spite of writing Turkic poetry themselves.

By this time, the southward push given by the Mughal Empire had also embedded the language deep in India, where it would continue to be important in such successor states as Hyderabad and Arcot.[206] Despite Ahmad Shah Durrani's flirtations with founding a Pashto-based bureaucracy, when the capital moved from Qandahar to Kabul in 1772, Durrani and post-Durrani Afghanistan retained Persian as its chancery and chief court language.[207] One key reason was the influence, and older skill set, of professional bureaucrats like Muhammad Taqi Khan (d. 1756) of Shiraz who were brought from Iran by Ahmad Shah Durrani to oversee his short-lived imperial administration.[208] Even as the erstwhile Durrani provinces of Punjab and Kashmir fell respectively under Sikh and Hindu rule in the early nineteenth century, Persian remained an important language for the scribes and literati of the Sikh and Doghra courts.[209] As late as 1849, when the East India Company conquered Punjab, the Lahore-based munshis who had served the Sikh Empire were only able to write in Persian and not in Gurmukhi-script Punjabi, which was the preserve of Sikh religious teachers.

Similarly, when the expanding Russian Empire annexed the Caucasus provinces from the Qajars during the Russo-Persian wars of the early nineteenth century, Persian was still an important bureaucratic language in a region with multiple spoken and written competitors.[210] Turning to Central Asia, in the khanate of Khiva, despite the fact that the overwhelming majority of the population spoke Turkic languages, Persian remained the chancery language until 1857, when the Qonghrat dynasty mandated its replacement by Chaghatai.[211] Meanwhile, in the khanate of Qoqand, although the broader culture of the khanate was bilingual, Persian dominated its chancery later still. New Persian literary works also continued to be patronized in nineteenth-century Qoqand.[212] And Persian remained the dominant bureaucratic language of the Manghit dynasty in Bukhara till the very end of the khanate in 1920. Beyond the realm of the state, even occult texts in Persian continued to be used right up to the Sovietization of Central Asia, pointing to Persian-based intellectual continuities during a period usually understood as dominated by the Russian-influenced modernist Jadids who wrote in Tatar Turkish.[213] Even in the Russian-ruled Volga-Ural region and Siberia, as well as Chinese-ruled East Turkistan, small numbers of Sufis and scholars continued to read if not necessarily write Persian works until the early twentieth century.[214] As old hubs such as Bukhara retained their connections to Persian learning, in some cases Persian found new intellectual connections, as with the late renaissance of Judeo-Persian in Russian-ruled Bukhara through the reinvigorating contact with other Jews of the tsarist empire.[215]

Even so, the new non-Muslim empires that were expanding through the old geographies of Persographia had little or no interest in Persian as a court, literary, or religious language. Their linguistic concerns were primarily practical and administrative. Except in India, whose post-Mughal states had upheld Persian bureaucracy, this was eventually—if less immediately and thoroughly than was once thought—to undermine the old lingua franca in favor of written vernaculars and new imperial languages, particularly English and Russian. Faced with this situation, the new Eurasian empires of the late eighteenth and nineteenth centuries—British, Russian, and Chinese—were forced in different degrees to adapt to the literate status quo. These were pragmatic policies. Except when it seemed politically expedient to engage with the culture of native elites, the new imperial ruling class would not be Persianized like the conquering Turks of an earlier era. They dealt with the language situation—particularly the availability of literate bureaucratic middlemen—as they found it. As a result, imperial Russia required its officials and intermediaries to deal far more with Turkic and Mongolian languages than with Persian.[216] After the Qing conquest of what they called the "New Territories" (Xinjiang) of Eastern Turkistan in the 1750s, Persian was used by Qing officials as diplomatic correspondence increased with China's new frontiers with Qoqand, the principalities of Badakhshan and the Pamirs, and Ladakh.[217] But in Chinese-ruled Xinjiang itself, by the time of the Qing conquests, written Turki had become far more important than Persian among the literate local population. Whether to their rulers in Beijing or their co-religionists in Bukhara and Kazan, by 1900, the Muslim inhabitants of Xinjiang were overwhelmingly writing in Turki (which, with some modifications, they renamed Uyghur).[218]

It was, then, only Britain's East India Company that made large investments in Persian, which remained the Company's official language of law and bureaucracy until the administrative reforms of 1832–37.[219] Until this time, the employment of Hindu and Muslim munshis remained a necessity not only for administering the Company's expanding empire, but also for training British officials competent in Persian paperwork.[220] Residing in India for decades, some of these British Company servants wrote poetry in Persian and adopted Persian noms-de-plume (*takhallus*), among them the Reverend Bartholomew "Sabr" Gardner, as did some of the Armenian merchants who had settled in Calcutta and other Indian cities.[221] In this respect, such members of the Company's administrative and commercial cadres were following the acculturating path taken by Hindu munshis over the previous centuries, whereby the acquisition of a practical skill set led to exposure to new aesthetic tastes. But the results of the Company's pragmatic policy of convenient continuity with Mughal administrative practices also charted new directions for Persian, with the establishment of the Calcutta Madrasa in 1781 and the Fort William College in 1800 as schools for British secretaries.[222] As a consequence of these educational policies, the geographical and social frontiers of Persian expanded as far as England through the teaching of Persian to hundreds of British students at the East India Colleges founded in England at Haileybury in 1806 and Addiscombe in 1809.[223] Demand from the East India Company's colleges, students, and scholars led in turn to the beginning of Persian printing in Calcutta and London, with the earliest publications including such bureaucratic works as the Mughal-era epistolary manual *Insha-yi Harkaran* by the Hindu munshi Har Karan Das, and several successors to Sir William Jones's 1771 *Grammar of the Persian Language*.[224] The beginning of Persian printing in Britain coincided with the minting of Persian coins there, and in 1786, the frontiers of Persian reached Birmingham, in the far west of Eurasia, when the pioneer of the steam engine Matthew Boulton (1728–1809) began using the new machinery at his Soho Foundry to produce Indian coinage with English obverse and Persian reverse inscriptions.[225] In purely quantitative terms, minting far outstripped printing: in just a few decades the Soho Foundry issued over 220 million Persian-script coins for the East India Company.[226]

In the longer term, though, the largest consequences for written Persian came from print rather than mint technology. The diffusion of print followed the new imperial frontiers of Russian and British power as they skirted across Central and South Asia to surround Iran and Afghanistan.[227] One direction of print diffusion followed a Russian imperial axis from Saint Petersburg to Kazan (where Turkic and some Arabic texts had been printed by Russian-ruled Tatars since 1797) and thence to Tbilisi and Tabriz, the latter a short distance beyond the new imperial Caucasian frontier with Qajar Iran.[228] The other direction comprised a British imperial axis from London to Calcutta to Lucknow (whence to North India more generally), as well as to Bombay (whence to south India and Iran). Between 1817 and 1819, print technology thus moved out of European hands as the first printing presses reached Lucknow and Tabriz from Calcutta and Saint Petersburg respectively. The first Persian text printed in Tabriz was the *Jihad-nama* (Book of Holy War), a collection of fatwas legitimizing war against Russia as jihad.[229] In Lucknow, the first printed text was the *Haft Qulzum* (Seven Oceans), a Persian dictionary and grammar. Even as more books followed from such Muslim-operated presses, for years to come the largest print runs for any Persian text remained those of the New Testament, issued by the British and Foreign Bible Society, which regularly ran to 5,000 copies.[230] Since the missionary societies needed literate local helpers for their work in their evangelizing frontier outposts around Bengal, the

Caucasus, and the ports of the Caspian, Christian missionaries were also respon-sible for transferring the skills of the printer to Persographia's former "men of the pen" (*ahl-i qalam*).[231]

This spread of printing was not a belated Persianate participation in the "Gutenberg Revolution," which had formerly been confined to Europe and a small number of its enclaves in the Americas and Asia. Instead, the spread of print-ing in the Persianate (and more generally, the Islamic) world was part of the truly global reach of the "Stanhope Revolution" based on the more portable, ro-bust, simplified, mass-produced, and thereby inexpensive iron hand presses that emerged as a consequence of industrialization in Europe.[232] The earliest machines used to print Persian were typographic presses, which in locations like Tabriz and Lucknow presented their Iranian and Indian owners with the difficulty and ex-pense of casting or purchasing imported Arabic-script type. With a few elegant exceptions, mainly works printed in London's typographic bazaar, Persian books printed in type looked unfamiliar to readers whose eyes were trained to pass over pages of flowing calligraphic *diwani, shikasta* or *nast'aliq.* Another by-product of the European industrial revolution, the invention of lithography by the German playwright Alois Senefelder in 1796, produced a method of printing that was able to overcome these problems.[233] Thus, within around fifteen years, the technique that Senefelder invented for printing scores of theatrical music was adapted for issuing texts in Persian calligraphy. Fixed to the new iron presses, slabs of im-ported Bavarian limestone could be written on by hand by traditionally trained calligraphers using wax crayons. This not only produced more familiarly read-able books, but it also solved the shortage of trained typesetters by employing former manuscript copyists to transfer their skills. After its initial introduction to Calcutta, then Bombay, where several Persian works were issued by Company scholars in the 1820s, lithography quickly reached Lucknow (from Calcutta) and Tabriz (from Russian-ruled Tbilisi).[234] From both cities, the technique, combining local skills with imported presses and stones, spread more widely, particularly in northern India, from whose commercial printers Persian books were exported to Afghanistan, and thence Bukhara, and to Kashmir, and thence Kashgar.

With lithography, the manuscripts of former centuries could now be printed. But faced with centuries of backlog, only a small proportion were, such that only a fraction of Persian's literary heritage was printed. The selection of what was print-ed—and hence more readily available to future generations—was based on the demands, ideologies, and tastes of mid-nineteenth-century state and commercial publishers. The uneven transition to printing brought a great caesura in the his-tory of Persographia and of the ideas Persian had carried through eight centuries of manuscripts.

Many of the major hubs of the precolonial geography of Persian did not partici-pate in this early nineteenth-century transfer from manuscript to printed text. In Central Asia, printing did not begin in the main former Persian hub of Bukhara but rather in Khiva, where the ruler, Muhammad Rahim Khan II (r. 1864–1910), employed a Russian-educated printer, Ata-djan Adbalov, in 1874. Khiva's first printed book—the first to be printed in Central Asia—was not issued till 1880.[235] Similarly in Afghanistan, printing did not begin until the ruler, Shir ʿAli Khan (r. 1863–66, 1868–79), established his government press in Kabul in 1873, and even then only a few dozen texts were issued until the press was reestablished in the 1910s (though many postage stamps were printed, albeit in Arabic not Persian).[236] Private printing and commercial publishing were slower to develop than printing by and for the state, be it tsarist or Qajar. Whether in Lucknow, Tabriz, Khiva, or Kabul, in all of these state-driven cases, printing was not equivalent to publishing: most of the books printed for Ghazi al-Din Haydar in Lucknow sat rotting in palace storerooms for lack of the distributive mechanisms of publishing; the Khiva printed texts were intended only for circulation and consumption at court; and Kabul printing was of legislation or propaganda intended to be distributed by state employees.

Moreover, as printing empowered older literary languages, ascendant imperial languages, and newer vernaculars, outside of Iran and Afghanistan, most of the printing being done was not in Persian. After King Vakhtang VI set up the first printing press in Tbilisi on the shifting frontiers of the Safavid Empire in 1708, its books were printed in Georgian, a practice revived under Russian patronage after the destruction of Vakhtang's press during the Qajar invasion of 1795.[237] Although in 1741–42 the final book issued by the pioneer Ottoman printer Ibrahim Müteferrika (1674–1745) had been the Persian-Turkish dictionary Lisan al-ʿAjam (Language of Persia) of Hasan Shuʿuri, with the revival of Ottoman printing in the early nineteenth century, his successors favored books in Ottoman Turkish, Arabic, or regional languages of the empire. If there was a dominant language, it was Turkish, as with the Greek-script Turkish works printed by the Karamanli Greeks of Anatolia.[238] Most of Central Asia relied on Turkic printed books imported from the vibrant private Tatar publishing houses of the Russian-controlled Volga-Ural region (chiefly in Kazan). Printing did not reach Eastern Turkistan until 1893, when the first press—for Turkic not Persian—was established in Yangihissar by a former tailor called Nur Muhammad Hajji, who had learned lithography on a journey through India en retour from the pilgrimage to Mecca.[239] After printing two popular Turkic classics by Sufi Allahyar and Mir ʿAli Shir Nawaʾi, Nur Muhammad was soon commissioned by the Qing government to print the Turkic translation of a morality text by the Qing Shunzhi emperor, followed by a translated military instruction manual. Whether in Tabriz or Lucknow, Yangihissar, or Kazan, non-Muslim empires played a part in each of the nodes of the new geography of printing. These empires' practical agendas saw them favoring more widely understood vernaculars than the old Persian lingua franca of the few. By the 1850s, only in Iran and eventually Afghanistan were there independent Muslim ruled-states that were committed to printing in Persian, and even then only for narrow statist purposes.

The new geography of print was therefore not at all the old geography of the former hubs and nodes through which Persian manuscripts had once circulated. Until the 1840s or 1850s, there were probably more Persian texts printed in London and Calcutta than anywhere else. By the end of the nineteenth century, even Jerusalem had become the chief center of Judeo-Persian printing through the efforts of the Bukharan émigré Shim'on Hakham (1843–1910). By the time print technology did spread to old hubs like Delhi and Shiraz in the mid-nineteenth century, the vernacularizing developments of the eighteenth and earlier nineteenth centuries meant that in most of the former sites of Persian literary culture, demand was primarily for books printed in various former vernaculars that had by now become literary, and in some cases bureaucratic, languages in their own right.

In the second half the nineteenth century, only in Iran (and later Afghanistan) was Persian the hegemonic language of printing. To some extent, this reflected state policy, as when the East India Company replaced Persian with Urdu (and Bengali) as its bureaucratic language in 1832–37, a policy extended to Punjab after its annexation in 1849, with formally independent Hyderabad State following suit in 1885.[240] In the tsarist and Qing territories, ever since their conquest, the more widely understood Turkic and Mongolian languages had been used for official purposes for similarly practical reasons (though various Iranian émigrés were able to print Persian works in tsarist Tbilisi).[241] Whether promoted by the colonial state, or by indigenous reformists exposed to colonial ideas, modern education increasingly came to mean education in literary vernaculars like Tatar and Urdu, or else in imperial languages like Russian and English. Even the literati and colonial munshis were now abandoning Persian for the written and now imperial vernaculars. Persian was able to hang on longer in the bureaucracies of some of India's princely states and as late as 1877, when Victoria was declared Empress of India (with the Persianate title Qaysar-i Hind), several princes sent as congratulatory gifts Persian local histories, such as Sultan Shah Jahan Begum's *Taj al-Iqbal* (Crown of Fortune, 1873) and Pandit Ra'i Narayan's *Siraj al-Tawarikh* (Torch of Histories, 1875). But in British India proper, Persian was by now disenfranchised by Urdu and other vernaculars, chiefly Bengali. The East India Company had established Delhi College back in 1823 to educate Indian bureaucrats, and by 1840 its syllabi were no longer Persian-based but instead consisted of Urdu textbooks translated from English.[242] This pattern was echoed by Muslim reformists, eager to seize on the wider social reach of the vernaculars for their own purposes. Thus, the Jadid and Aligarh movements, the main Muslim educational reformers in Russian Eurasia and British India, likewise favored what they saw as the more "modern" vernaculars of Tatar and Urdu over the "degenerate" medium of Persian.[243] Even a self-consciously traditionalist institution like the great Dar al-'Ulum madrasa at Deoband, founded in 1867, dropped Persian to teach mainly in Urdu (and to teach more Arabic, albeit via Urdu).[244] Its model was imitated by Deoband's countless ancillary schools across the subcontinent where Persian had once reigned supreme.

Yet such pervasive vernacularization of literacy, education, and thereby publishing was also a result of printing itself. Inherent economies of scale mean that, ceteris paribus, texts in languages without a sufficient number of likely readers are less likely to be printed. It is a striking echo of this general principle that a large proportion of the new Persian works composed in India in the second half of the nineteenth century were never printed and remained in manuscript.[245] For the logic of mass-production required commercial printers to issue books in the languages that would reach the maximum number of purchasing readers. Both government and missionary presses followed parallel tracks of maximal outreach. This was quite the contrary of the model of manuscript production, in which expensive individual texts had been produced for small numbers of readers. In this way, a general pattern can be observed with the rise of printing, whereby texts in geographically dense vernacular languages were increasingly favored over texts in the geographically dispersed former lingua franca of Persian. In India, commercial publishers thus issued increasing numbers of books in Urdu, Bengali, Hindi, and other vernaculars.[246] This was also the case across the vast sway of Central Eurasia controlled by the tsarist and Qing empires, where, from the Volga-Urals to Eastern Turkistan, the vast majority of printed books were in Turkic languages.[247] It was even the case in Iran, where Armenians and Azeri Turks read books imported from the larger print market of the neighboring Ottoman Empire, and the early introduction of printing to Armenian and Assyrian Christians by foreign missionaries led to increasing literacy in Armenian and Syriac.[248]

Printing, then, had a paradoxical effect on the fortunes of Persian. On the one hand, it enabled the reproduction of Persian texts in larger numbers than at any point in history, pushing mass-produced and thereby cheaper texts across various spatial and social frontiers. Persian books printed by some of the many commercial presses that had spread across India since the 1840s were exported to Central Asia. India also exported many Persian books to Iran, where commercial publishing remained poorly developed until the early twentieth century.[249] Whether as writers, readers, or simply listeners, women and broader groups of men gained increasing access to Persian texts. On the other hand, printing offered the same possibilities to vernacular languages, which had the vast comparative advantage of being more widely understood among Eurasia's masses. While the technological and political disruption of the printing revolution and Sino-European colonization combined to spread printing in Persian, these developments also spread printing in a far wider number of Persian's vernacular competitors.

By the turn of the twentieth century, these vernaculars—and arguably printing itself – became inseparable from the new ideology of nationalism, with its "modular" formulation of "one people, one language."[250] This powerful new ideology affected all of the languages of Eurasia. In the late tsarist era, Turkic languages were given new names like Tatar and Kazakh by local nationalists keen to create written successors to interregional Chaghatai that could be tied to local populations. In the 1920s, this policy of literary fragmentation was taken further by Soviet ideologues. In the process, these policies undermined the legitimacy of older contact languages, whether Persian, Chaghatai, or Arabic.[251] Even in important former hubs like Bukhara, Persian was undermined by the Soviet promotion of Uzbek as the national language, while in the one case where Persian received official status, in Soviet Tajikistan, it was cut off from Afghan and Iranian Persian by the adoption of the Cyrillic script and large numbers of Russian loanwords.[252] In nationalist China, self-styled Uyghur nationalists printed books and journals in their "own" Uyghur language, while Hui Muslims rejected what ties they still had to Persian in favor of either national Chinese or transnational Arabic, both of which were more easily available in print than Persian works.[253] In colonial India, competing nationalisms empowered a number of different languages—Hindi, Urdu, Bengali, Tamil, Marathi, Punjabi—but Persian was not one of them. In Afghanistan, influential nationalists like Mahmud Tarzi (1865–1933) even tried to break the hold of Persian in favor of Pashto in what had become its last stronghold as an interethnic lingua franca. Though the "Young Afghan" and then outright Pashtun nationalists failed to suppress Persian in Afghanistan, they did succeed in raising both the official status and literary infrastructure of Pashto, which from the 1920s on was taught and printed as never before.[254] Even in twentieth-century Iran, the one nation-state that unambiguously promoted Persian as its national language, new literary orthodoxies among the intelligentsia and language policies by the state separated readers from the textual and even lexical heritage of Persian's pre-national past.[255] The literary ideology of *bazgasht-i adabi* (literary return) demoted the "Indian style" (*sabk-i Hindi*) in favor of poets with closer (if, for Afghans and Tajiks, far from contested) connections to the national geography of Iran.[256] Echoing policies of linguistic purification in neighboring Turkey, in the 1930s, the Iranian Language Academy, or Farhangistan, promoted more than 1,600 "purely Persian" neologisms to replace words of Arabic or European origin in a deliberate policy of lexical divergence from pre-national Persian.[257] As mass education brought this nationalized lexicon and canon to millions of schoolchildren, even in Iran, Persian as language and literary culture was transformed and separated from what were now the other national Persians, dubbed "Dari" in Afghanistan and "Tajiki" in Tajikistan for which similarly nationalist dictionaries and literary histories were being composed.[258] Insofar as Persian ever had been "homoglossic," from the 1920s on, it was no more, especially at the written level that had sustained its former interregional literary culture.[259]

Unlike the thinly spread, networked geography of written Persian as lingua franca, its new national geographies were dense with vernacular readerships on the scale of the nation rather than diffused on the scale of the transregional network. Whether court or chancery, madrasa or *khanaqah,* the old institutional spaces of Persian whose hubs and nodes had been staffed by a mobile personnel of text producers had been replaced by new national and imperial institutions, in which Persian had little role outside Iran, Afghanistan, and Tajikistan. This reduced sphere of Perso-graphia also sat on the economic, political, and cultural periphery of the globalized world of the late nineteenth century. By the turn of the twentieth century, imperial politics, the introduction of printing, and the ideology of nationalism had com-bined to redraw the frontiers of the Persianate world. Though new enclaves of Per-sian-use—nodes if not quite hubs—would emerge through the globalizing oppor-tunities of the twentieth century (whether interwar Berlin or Southern California's "Tehrangeles"), there is no doubt that by 1900, the "Persianate world" had gone: Persian was no more a language to be imitated. On contrary, through borrowed words and genres, writers of Persian in Kabul, Dushanbe, and Tehran alike imitated and adapted European literature, especially via the *roman* (Farsi) or *naval* (Dari) as the novel was differently dubbed. Not only was Persian no longer an aesthetic role model, it was also no longer a contact language or lingua franca. Except for small diasporic enclaves, the geography of Persian now only existed at the level of the na-tion, in Iran, Afghanistan, and (separated by the Cyrillic alphabet) Tajikistan.

CHARTING FRONTIERS: TWELVE CASE STUDIES AND AN APERÇU

In focusing on the five centuries between around 1400 and 1900, the following case-study chapters trace the geographical, social, and linguistic frontiers that ex-isted during the period when the use of written Persian reached its greatest reach from Beijing to London and from Sri Lanka to Siberia. Collectively, what these chapters offer is therefore a critical as much as a celebratory approach to Persian drawn from the intersection of historical, sociolinguistic, and literary approaches. For the overall aim of this volume is to chart together both the reach and limits of Persographia, to assess not only its broadest extent but also its breaking points and fault lines. In this way, the book as a whole is intended as a problem-solving exercise focused on identifying the limits of Persian's usage and usefulness over the four centuries or so that marked the maximal extent and then retraction of Persographia. At the same time as it maps the furthest expansion of Persian, *The Persianiate World* therefore also serves as an exercise in tracing the constraints of the cosmopolitan. The implications of this networked geography of geographi-cally broad but socially shallow linguistic frontiers has rarely been factored into scholarly understandings of the texts that this geography produced. Yet as Franco Moretti has shown, aggregate "maps" of literary cultures deepen our understand-ing of their individual literary components. A text is inseparable from its territory: each is inscribed on the other.[260]

The first section of the book, "Pan-Eurasian Expansions, ca. 1400–1600," charts the widest reach that Persian usage achieved under the early modern empires and regional polities that followed the breakup of the Mongol and Timurid empires that had done so much to expand and promote the prestige of Persian. The first chapter, by Murat Inan, turns to the westerly frontiers of Persian in the Ottoman imperial territories of Anatolia and Rumelia (that is, the Balkans). Inan's chapter surveys the study and teaching of Persian in the Ottoman Empire, with a focus on the reception of the language in imperial and mystical contexts. With an emphasis on the period from 1450 to 1600, the first part of the chapter explores how Persian contributed to the making of an Ottoman imperial language and identity as Persian learning flourished in venues ranging from the royal court and elite households to Sufi lodges. The second part then investigates the practices involved in Persian learning under the Ottomans with reference to teacher-scholars whose works were intended for readers and students alike. In the second chapter, by Thibaut d'Hubert, we turn to the southeasterly reaches of Persian in Bengal. Unlike the Ottoman Empire, where Inan shows a new Ottoman Turkish or *zeban-ı Rum* ("language of Rum") emerging under the literary and orthographic shadow of Persian, this was a context in which Persian's chief linguistic interlocutor was a preexisting literary medium with its own distinct script. Pursuing Persian's various places—at the court as well as the village—the chapter addresses key questions about the history of Persian in Bengal that concern its links alternatively with the court culture of the Muslim sultanates and what are often presented as the antithetical lower, "vernacular" strata of society. After a general discussion of the study of Persian in Bengal, the first half of the chapter provides a historical interpretation of a celebrated poem by Hafiz of Shiraz that became emblematic of the assumed patronage of Persian poetry at the court of Bengal. This close inspection of the literary situation in Bengal shows that the region does not comply with predominant models of the patronage of Persian, pointing to the need to explore elsewhere in Bengal's cultural landscape. In response, the chapter's second half turns to the less well-known yet paradoxically better-documented spread of Persian literacy across the rural frontiers of Bengal as the era of the independent sultanate of Bengal gave way to that of the Mughal Empire.

The third chapter turns to Persian's northeastern frontiers in the capitals of the Ming Empire in China. Focusing on the *Siyiguan* imperial translation college founded in 1407 in the new Ming capital of Beijing, Graeme Ford examines the various records that describe the arrangements made for translating different kinds of documents between Persian and Chinese. Ranging from Sino-Persian exam papers from Beijing to a fifty-meter-long Buddhist scroll from Tibet and a trilingual stele from Ceylon, the documentary record of the Ming's use of Persian shows that the language was used for written communication not only within the empire itself, but with distant polities in Central, South, and Southeast Asia with which China sought diplomatic and commercial ties. Through a circuitous route via Beijing, the chapter shows how Persian reached the Malay royal ports of Sumatra as a language of Chinese diplomacy. With China's own rich literary heritage, the Ming made no attempt to adopt, still less imitate, Persian as a literary language. Rather, it served practical imperial purposes as a bureaucratic medium of governance, diplomacy, and trade. The final chapter in the first part of the volume turns to the vast interconnected spaces of central and northern Eurasia, where from the Volga-Ural region to Siberia, Persian was in constant interaction with the increasingly written Turkic languages of the region. Here Devin DeWeese charts the northerly frontiers of Persian from the fifteenth down to the nineteenth century. His chapter argues that, despite the overwhelmingly Turkic-speaking Muslim population, and despite the steady increase in the production of literary works in Turkic, Persian continued to serve as a language of learned communication right across central and northern Eurasia, albeit increasingly in the shadow of Turkic as these regions fell under Russian domination. After a series of general observations about the gradual shift from Persian to Turkic, and a consideration of the clearer patterns of Persian's persistence in Central Asia to the south, DeWeese turns to a detailed survey of manuscript catalogues to reveal the character of both Persian literary production and consumption from the Volga-Ural basin to the villages of Siberia.

The second section of the book, "The Constraints of Cosmopolitanism," focuses more specifically on the period between around 1600 and 1800. While the main focus of this section is on the uses of Persian in the new Eurasian empires of the Mughals, Qing, and Romanovs, the section's last chapter turns to the frontiers of Chinese and Turkic rule in Eastern Turkistan, renamed Xinjiang (New Territory) after the Qing imperial conquest of the late 1750s. The section's first chapter, by Purnima Dhavan, examines the expansion of Persian scholarly networks in the Mughal province of Punjab during the seventeenth century. Dhavan examines the careers of four Indian-born scholars who used Persian literary skills to achieve great professional success to reveal how self-fashioning, professional rivalries and self-promotion animated both the acquisition and perpetuation of Persian learning in the Mughal Empire. Treating a milieu in which Hindu bureaucrats also acquired and displayed their mastery of both bureaucratic and literary Persian, the chapter focuses on the crucial importance to professional success of access to specific social networks. Showing how social and political contexts shaped the contours of literary production, Dhavan shows how the competitive provincial networks of Punjab turned toward prose and pedagogical works, which in turn helped perpetuate and expand Persographia across the Mughal domains.

The next chapter turns from Mughal India, where Persian had been made the official language of state under the emperor Akbar, to the contemporaneous Qing Empire in China. Looking across the broad multilingual domains of the Qing, David Brophy reconsiders the hoary question of the "decline" of Persian's status as a Eurasian lingua franca. His chapter argues that far from showing a straightforward picture of decline, the centuries of Qing rule saw an ongoing if limited role for Persian in various spheres, even including brief periods of increased significance. The chapter takes two perspectives on the uses of Persian in Qing China. The first, building on Graeme Ford's chapter on the Ming period, is that of the imperial state and the translation infrastructure it inherited and adapted from the Ming in accordance with the evolving needs of communication with the Qing's expanding imperial frontiers in Xinjiang and Central Asia more generally. The second perspective is that of the status of Persian among the empire's own Chinese- and Turkic-speaking Muslim communities, which promoted efforts to vernacularize Persian texts into their own languages. Nonetheless, Brophy shows how Persian continued to enjoy considerable prestige in China's powerful Sufi milieus.

Turning to the west and north of the Qing territories, Alfrid Bustanov's chapter examines the circulation of Persian texts in imperial Russia. The chapter describes the multilingual and multiliterate contexts of imperial Russia, where the Persian language was often mixed in writing with other languages such as Chaghatai Turkish and Arabic. Bustanov covers the vast and varied territories of the Romanov Empire by means of three geographically distinct case studies. The first looks at the Volga-Ural region, where from the seventeenth century on, the Persian language became crucial to Quranic exegesis, Sufi writings, and jurisprudence. The second case brings to light the importance of Persian for the communities of "Bukharans" who settled around the Siberian city of Tobolsk in the early eighteenth century, while the third case study considers an exiled Sufi shaykh from the Caucasus who used Persian for his letters to fellow Sufis in the Russian-ruled towns of the Volga-Ural basin.

In the final chapter in this section, Alexandre Papas considers the evolution of Persian learning in Eastern Turkistan (Xinjiang), where spoken and written Turkic came to dominate from the eighteenth century. Yet rather than making the facile assertion that Persian declined into a dead language by the nineteenth century, Papas reveals a more complex scenario through an analysis of manuscript catalogues and a case study of several talismanic scrolls. By these means, the chapter moves from the early modern period, when Eastern Turkistan's elite mastered Persian, to the nineteenth century, when Persian texts were still sometimes written, but only in simplified forms. Through a close inspection of seven talismanic scrolls, Papas shows how the social prestige of Persian combined with the waning linguistic competence of its users to transform Persian from a lingua franca to a lingua magica, a magical language that was widely used but that was limited to specific and supernatural linguistic functions.

The third section of the book, "New Empires, New Nations," moves on to the rapidly changing period between around 1800 and 1920. In line with the preceding history given in this Introduction, rather than reiterate a conventionally simplistic model of Persian's collapse in the face of new imperialisms and nationalisms, the chapters in this section show how Persian continued to be read, and valued, throughout the nineteenth century, and indeed crossed new geographical frontiers to reach Britain through its connection to the East India Company's empire. In the first chapter of the section, Michael H. Fisher leads us through the long transition between the Mughal Empire and the British Empire. when the Persian language and Persianate culture continued to enjoy great prestige in India. But as the British East India Company replaced the Mughals, Persianate culture acquired conflicting meanings, at once valorized and denigrated. To trace this complex shift in status, Fisher's chapter considers the career of D. O. Dyce Sombre (1808–51). The doomed, mixed-race heir to a North Indian principality, Dyce Sombre struggled to maintain his identity in both the old Mughal imperial world as it fragmented and the rising British one as it expanded. Fisher reveals, through his private manuscript diary and correspondence, how, even during his decades living in London, Dyce Sombre clung to Persian, appraised others by Persianate standards, and was measured by the British by them as well.

The next chapter moves from the waning principalities of India to the khanates of Central Asia during their parallel transition to Russian imperial rule. Here Marc Toutant shows how both before and after the Russian conquest of Khiva in 1873, its court culture underwent a process of "de-Persification" by means of a translation program into more readily comprehendible Chaghatai Turkish. Toutant argues that, unlike in India, where the Company and then British Empire was instrumental in the vernacular replacement of Persian, Khiva's translation program was promoted less by the Russians than by cultural competition between the Qonghrat dynasty and its rival local khanates. After centuries in which Central Asia remained a key outpost of Persian—exporting and maintaining the language as far away as Siberia, as Bustanov's chapter shows—in the nineteenth century the situation rapidly changed. Toutant's chapter traces this monumental retraction of what was arguably Persian's core Eurasian territory by means of a case study of Khiva's extensive translation program from Persian into Chaghatai Turkish. In this way, the chapter examines the major cultural shift that brought to an end the era of Persian as Central Asia's main language of the arts and sciences.

Examining another of the longtime frontiers of Persian, the next chapter turns to the Caucasus. After outlining the earlier history of Caucasian Persian, Rebecca Gould focuses on the century after the region was conquered from Qajar Iran by imperial Russia. In this way, echoing Fisher's chapter, Gould explores, not so much the outright disappearance of a Persianate frontier, as its transformation into a new imperial and intellectual environment. The chapter follows the career of the Iranian reformer 'Abd al-Rahim Talibuf (1834–1911), who spent the last decades of his life in Daghestan after his initial migration from the Iranian city of Tabriz to the Russian-ruled Caucasian *carrefour* of Tbilisi. Despite the stronger traditional hold of Arabic in the region, Talibuf wrote eight books in his highland refuge in Daghestan that shaped the subsequent trajectory of intellectual history across the border in Iran. In this way, Gould traces the effects and circumstances of "dissidence from a distance," the process by which diasporic Iranian communities used Persian to influence political events in their homeland.

The final chapter in this section by Abbas Amanat continues this theme of border-crossing in the new imperial and national contexts of the late nineteenth century with a study of the migrant Indian poet Adib Pishawari. Having been born and raised in precolonial Peshawar, Adib was forced into exile as a result of his family's involvement in an anticolonial rebellion. After travelling, and studying, across independent Afghanistan, Adib settled in the Iranian cities of Mashhad and then Tehran, where this Indian émigré made his name as one of the last living repositories of the old literary culture that had formerly sustained Persian learning for centuries. With a new nationalist literary culture taking shape in Iran, however, Adib became an increasingly marginal figure, living out his last years in the Iran of Riza Shah as a survivor of, and transmitter from, the Persianate world of old. In this way, Amanat's chapter captures through a single life the travails of Persian's retraction from a Eurasian lingua franca to a national language that by the 1930s was preserved by just three modern nation-states.

By way of a concluding epilogue, the book's final chapter returns to the big picture of Persographia laid out earlier in this introduction. Here Brian Spooner takes a macrohistorical and structural approach to both the expansion and retraction of Persian across the *longue durée* of what he terms the "Persianate millennium." Moving from Old Persian's initial use as a language of administration in the sixth century BCE, Spooner follows the expansion of Persian through the cuneiform, Aramaic, and then Arabic scripts of its multiple incarnations as a *koine* used from China to the Balkans, before its retraction in the face of the official vernaculars of new nation-states. Focusing on the processes at work in the previous chapters, Spooner emphasizes Persian's standardization and stability as a written language that underlay its continued importance for a full millennium. In the final sections of the book, he brings us through developments in the twentieth century that saw an esteemed yet abandoned language become the forgotten Latin of a formerly Persianate world.

Before finally turning to the chapters that explore the various frontiers of Persian during its main centuries of expansion and retraction, it is worth taking stock of the scale of that literary eclipse by way of a bibliographical statistic from the library of a twentieth-century South Asian Muslim. Among the several thousand books collected by Jamal al-Din 'Abd al-Wahhab (1919–2012), 55 percent were in Urdu, 30 percent in Arabic, 10 percent in English, and a mere 5 percent in Persian.[261] Even for this religious scholar, educated in the great Farangi Mahal madrasa founded under Mughal patronage, Persian had been sidelined by other, national, religious, and imperial languages.

NOTES

1. I am most grateful to Domenico Ingenito and Andrew Peacock for advice on early New Persian and Ottoman Persian, as well as to Peter Cowe and Rebecca Gould for guiding my reading on Armenian and Georgian literature. I also thank my anonymous referees for their comments on this introductory essay as a whole. Needless to say, any errors and overstatements remain my own.

2. Marshall G. S. Hodgson, *The Venture of Islam,* 3 vols. (Chicago: University of Chicago Press, 1974), 2: 293.

3. Bruce B. Lawrence, "Islam in Afro-Eurasia: A Bridge Civilization," in *Civilizations in World Politics: Plural and Pluralist Perspectives,* ed. Peter J. Katzenstein (London: Routledge, 2009), 157–75.

4. Abbas Amanat, ed., *The Persianate World: Rethinking a Shared Sphere* (Leiden: Brill, forthcoming).

5. Bert G. Fragner, *Die "Persophonie": Regionalitat, Identitat und Sprachkontakt in der Geschichte Asiens* (Berlin: Das Arabische Buch, 1999), 33–36.

6. Ibid., 6–8, 16–21.

7. Ibid., 33.

8. Ibid., 100–104, with the quotation at 101.

9. Brian Spooner and William L. Hanaway, eds., *Literacy in the Persianate World: Writing and the Social Order* (Philadelphia: University of Pennsylvania Museum of Archaeology and Anthropology, 2012).

10. Brian Spooner and William L. Hanaway, "Preface," in Spooner and Hanaway, eds., *Literacy in the Persianate World,* xi.

11. Ibid., xiii.

12. Brian Spooner and William L. Hanaway, "Introduction: Persian as *Koine:* Written Persian in World-Historical Perspective," in Spooner and Hanaway, eds., *Literacy in the Persianate World,* 1–69.

13. Hamid Dabashi, *The World of Persian Literary Humanism* (Cambridge, MA: Harvard University Press, 2012), 42.

14. Ibid., ix and 2.

15. Ibid., viii.

16. Ironically, aside from a few pages on Ghalib, Iqbal, and the Tatar Jadids, Dabashi's emphasis on "cosmopolitan worldliness" ignores the past three centuries of contributions to Persian literature and culture by non-Iranians. See ibid., chaps. 7 and 8, with the quotation at 302.

17. Shahab Ahmed, *What Is Islam? The Importance of Being Islamic* (Princeton, NJ: Princeton University Press, 2015).

18. Ibid., 84.

19. Ibid., 84–85.

20. Ibid., 85. The italicized emphasis is Ahmed's own.

21. Stefano Pellò, *Ṭūṭiyān-i Hind: specchi identitari e proiezioni cosmopolite indo-persiane (1680–1856)* (Florence: Società editrice fiorentina, 2012).

22. Ibid., 33.

23. Ibid., 18, 169.

24. Ibid., 83.

25. I am grateful to Domenico Ingenito for this point. For a detailed study of Sudi's career, see Murat Umut Inan, "Writing a Grammatical Commentary on Hafiz of Shiraz: A Sixteenth-Century Ottoman Scholar on the Divan of Hafiz" (PhD diss., University of Washington, 2012).

26. This seems to have been particularly the case after the Safavid promotion of Shi'ism in the sixteenth century. This is not to say that Shi'ism created an unsurmountable "barrier of heterodoxy," for Shi'i Islam created its own networks between India and Iran, albeit often based on Arabic rather than Persian learning. See Juan R. I. Cole, *Roots of North Indian Shi'ism in Iran and Iraq: Religion and State in Awadh, 1722–1859* (Berkeley: University of California Press, 1988), and Robert D. McChesney, "'Barrier of Heterodoxy'?: Rethinking the Ties Between Iran and Central Asia in the Seventeenth Century," in *Safavid Persia: The History and Politics of an Islamic Society,* ed. Charles Melville (London: I. B. Tauris, 1996).

27. *Literacy in Traditional Societies,* ed. Jack Goody (Cambridge: Cambridge University Press, 1975).

28. For a standard, if somewhat dated, general survey, see Gilbert Lazard, "The Rise of the New Persian Language," in *The Cambridge History of Iran,* vol. 4, *The Period from the Arab Invasion to the Saljuqs,* ed. Richard N. Frye (Cambridge: Cambridge University Press, 1975), 595–632. More recently,

see John R. Perry, "The Origin and Development of Literary Persian," in , *A History of Persian Literature*, ed. J. T. P. de Bruijn, vol. 1, *A General Introduction to Persian Literature* (London: I. B. Tauris, 2009).

29. Mary Boyce, "The Parthian *Gōsān* and Iranian Minstrel Tradition," *Journal of the Royal Asiatic Society of Great Britain and Ireland* 89, nos. 1–2 (1957): 10–45, and Rahim Shayegan, "Old Iranian Motifs in *Vis o Ramin,*" in *Essays in Islamic Philology, History, and Philosophy,* ed. Alireza Korangy, Wheeler M. Thackston, Roy Mottahedeh, and William Granara (Berlin: De Gruyter, 2016).

30. William Hanaway, "Secretaries, Poets and the Literary Language," in Spooner and Hanaway, eds., *Literacy in the Persianate World,* 100–101.

31. Gilbert Lazard, *La langue des plus anciens monuments de la prose persane* (Paris: C. Klincksieck, 1963), 32.

32. Ludwig Paul, "Persian Language: i: Early New Persian," *Encyclopædia Iranica,* www.iranicaonline.org/articles/persian-language-1-early-new-persian.

33. Gilbert Lazard, *"Pahlavi, pârsi, dari:* Les langues de l'Iran d'après Ibn al-Muqaffa," in *Iran and Islam, in memory of the late Vladimir Minorsky,* ed. C. E. Bosworth (Edinburgh: Edinburgh University Press, 1971), 361–91. Ibn al-Muqaffa mentioned five languages in total, the other two being non-Iranian-group languages.

34. W. B. Henning, "The Inscriptions of Tang-i Azao," *Bulletin of the School of Oriental and African Studies* 20, 1–3 (1957): 335–42, and Bo Utas, "The Jewish-Persian Fragment from Dandān-Uiliq," *Orientalia Suecana* 17 (1968): 123–36.

35. N. Sims-Williams, "Early New Persian in Syriac Script: Two Texts from Turfan," *Bulletin of the School of Oriental and African Studies* 74, 3 (2011): 353–74, and W. Sundermann, "Ein manichäischer Lehrtext in neupersischer Sprache," in *Persian Origins: Early Judaeo-Persian and the Emergence of New Persian,* ed. Ludwig Paul (Wiesbaden: Harrassowitz, 2003), 243–74.

36. Hassan Rezai Baghbidi, "New Light on the Middle Persian-Chinese Bilingual Inscription from Xi'an," in *The Persian Language in History,* ed. M. Maggi and P. Orsatti (Wiesbaden: Harrassowitz, 2011), 105–14.

37. Ela Filippone, "The Language of the Qor' ān-e Qods and Its Sistanic Dialectal Background," in *The Persian Language in History,* ed. Maggi and Orsatti, 179–235, and Gilbert Lazard, "Lumières nouvelles sur la formation de la langue persan: Une traduction du Coran en persan dialectal et ses affinités avec le judéo-persan," in *Irano-Judaica* II, ed. S. Shaked and A. Netzer (Jerusalem: Ben Zvi Institute, 1990), 184–98. On conversion rates to Islam in Khurasan, see the classic study by Richard W. Bulliet, *The Patricians of Nishapur: A Study in Medieval Islamic Social History* (Cambridge, MA: Harvard University Press, 1972).

38. John R. Perry, "New Persian: Expansion, Standardization & Exclusivity," in Spooner and Hanaway, eds., *Literacy in the Persianate World,* 72.

39. Bo Utas, "A Multiethnic Origin of New Persian," in *Turkic-Iranian Contact Areas: Historical and Linguistic Aspects,* ed. Lars Johanson and Christiane Bulut (Wiesbaden: Harrassowitz, 2006), 241–51.

40. Sheldon Pollock, "The Cosmopolitan Vernacular," *Journal of Asian Studies* 57, 1 (1998): 6–37. By way of response, see Pnina Werbner, "Vernacular Cosmopolitanism," *Theory, Culture & Society* 23, 2–3 (2006): 496–98.

41. On the context for these developments, see Rocco Rante, "'Khorasan Proper' and 'Greater Khorasan' within a Politico-Cultural Framework," in *Greater Khorasan: History, Geography, Archaeology and Material Culture,* ed. Rante, Nathalie Gandolfo, Pascale Richardin, and Antoine Zink (Berlin: De Gruyter, 2015), and D. G. Tor, "Importance of Khurasan and Transoxiana in the Persianate Dynastic Period (850—1220)," in *Medieval Central Asia and the Persianate World: Iranian Tradition and Islamic Civilisation,* ed. A. C. S. Peacock and D. G. Tor (London: I. B. Tauris, 2015).

42. Perry, "New Persian," in Spooner and Hanaway, eds., *Literacy in the Persianate World,* 73.

43. Bosworth concluded that the Tahirids (r. 821–73) "were indeed highly Arabized in culture and outlook, and eager to be accepted in the Caliphal world where the cultivation of things Arabic gave social and cultural prestige. For this reason, the Tahirids could not play a part in the renaissance of New Persian language and literature." See C. E. Bosworth, "The Ṭāhirids and Persian Literature," *Iran*

7 (1969): 103–6, citation at 106. See also Richard N. Frye, "The Sāmānids," in *The Cambridge History of Iran*, ed. Frye, vol. 4, *From the Arab Invasion to the Saljuqs*, 136–61.

44. Gilbert Lazard, *Les premiers poètes persans (IXe–Xe siècles)*, 2 vols. (Paris: Librairie d'Amérique et d'Orient Adrien Maisonneuve, 1964), 1:10 et seq.

45. W. B. Henning, "Persian Poetical Manuscripts from the Time of Rudaki," in *A Locust's Leg: Studies in Honour of S. H. Taqizadeh*, ed. Henning and Ehsan Yarshater (London: Percy Lund, Humphries & Co., 1962), 89–104.

46. A. C. S. Peacock, *Mediaeval Islamic Historiography and Political Legitimacy: Bal'ami's Tarikh-namah* (London: Routledge, 2007), 36–37, and Lutz Richter-Bernberg, "Linguistic Shu'ubiya and Early Neo-Persian Prose," *Journal of the American Oriental Society* 94, 1 (1974): 55–64. My thanks to Andrew Peacock for these references.

47. The source for Muhammad ibn Wasif as a poet is the thirteenth century *Tarikh-i Sistan*, cited in William Hanaway, "Secretaries, Poets and the Literary Language," in Spooner and Hanaway, eds., *Literacy in the Persianate World*, 105.

48. Lazard, *La langue des plus anciens monuments*, 36–37, and Vladimir Minorsky, "The Older Preface to the Shāh-nāma," in *Studi Orientalistici in onore di Giorgio Levi Della Vida* (Rome: Istituto per l'Oriente, 1956), 2: 159–79.

49. Ludwig Paul, "The Language of the *Šahnama* in Historical and Dialectal Perspective," in *Languages of Iran: Past and Present. Iranian Studies in Memoriam David Neil MacKenzie*, ed. Dieter Weber (Wiesbaden: Harrassowitz, 2005).

50. Bert Fragner has also observed Persian's importance as an administrative language (*Verwaltungssprache*). See Fragner, "Persophonie," 76–78.

51. Julie Scott Meisami, "Why Write History in Persian? Historical Writing in the Samanid Period," in *Studies in Honour of Clifford Edmund Bosworth*, ed. Carole Hillenbrand (Leiden: Brill, 2000), 2: 348–71, and Peacock, *Mediaeval Islamic Historiography*, chaps. 3–4.

52. Travis Zadeh, *The Vernacular Qur'an: Translation and the Rise of Persian Exegesis* (Oxford: Oxford University Press, 2012), chap. 6.

53. Brian Spooner and William L. Hanaway, "*Siyaq*: Numerical Notation and Numeracy in the Persianate World," in *The Oxford Handbook of the History of Mathematics*, ed. Eleanor Robson and Jacqueline Stedall (Oxford: Oxford University Press, 2009), 429–47.

54. Ibid., 437.

55. Ibid., 438.

56. I am grateful to John E. Woods for this information.

57. Robert L. Canfield, "Introduction: The Turko-Persian Tradition," in *Turko-Persia in Historical Perspective*, ed. Robert L. Canfield (Cambridge: Cambridge University Press, 1991), 1.

58. S. Jabir Raza, "Hindus under the Ghaznavids," *Proceedings of the Indian History Congress* 71 (2010–11): 213–25.

59. Gerhard Doerfer, "The Influence of Persian Language and Literature among the Turks," in *The Persian Presence in the Islamic World*, ed. Richard G. Hovannisian and Georges Sabagh (Cambridge: Cambridge University Press, 1998), and John R. Perry, "The Historical Role of Turkish in Relation to Persian of Iran," *Iran & the Caucasus* 5, 1 (2001): 193–200.

60. My thanks to Domenico Ingenito for this point.

61. C. E. Bosworth, "The Development of Persian Culture under the Early Ghaznavids," *Iran* 6 (1968): 33–44.

62. C. E. Bosworth, "The Titulature of the Early Ghaznavids," *Oriens* 15 (1962): 210–33. and id., "An Oriental Samuel Pepys? Abu'l-Faḍl Bayhaqī's Memoirs of Court Life in Eastern Iran and Afghanistan, 1030–1041," *Journal of the Royal Asiatic Society*, 3rd ser., 14, 1 (2004): 13–25.

63. Alessio Bombaci, *The Kufic Inscription in Persian Verses in the Court of the Royal Palace of Mas'ud III at Ghazni* (Rome: Ismeo, 1966); Viola Allegranzi, "Royal Architecture Portrayed in Bayhaqī's *Tārīḫ-i Mas'ūdī* and Archaeological Evidence from Ghazni (Afghanistan, 10th–12th c.)," *Annali*

dell'Istituto orientale di Napoli 74 (2014): 95–120, and id., "The Use of Persian in Monumental Epigraphy from Ghazni (Eleventh-Twelfth Centuries)," *Eurasian Studies* 13 (2015): 23–41.

64. Saïd Amir Arjomand, "Evolution of the Persianate Polity and Its Transmission to India," *Journal of Persianate Studies* 2 (2009): 115–36, and A. C. S. Peacock and Sara Nur Yıldız, "Introduction: Literature, Language and History in Late Medieval Anatolia," in *Islamic Literature and Intellectual Life in Fourteenth- and Fifteenth-Century Anatolia,* ed. Peacock and Yıldız (Würzburg: Ergon, 2016).

65. Hasan Anusha, *Danishnama-yi Adab-i Farsi,* vol. 4 *Adab-i Farsi dar Shibh'qara (Hind, Pakistan, Bangladish)* (Tehran: Mu'assasa-yi Farhangi wa Intisharat-i Danishnama, Wizarat-i Farhang wa Irshad-i Islami, 1383/2005); Syeda Bilqis Fatema Husaini, *Critical Study of Indo-Persian Literature during Sayyid and Lodi period, 1414–1526 A.D.* (New Delhi: Syeda Bilqis Fatema Husaini, 1988); Nargis Jahan, *Tarikh-i Adabiyat-i Farsi-yi Hind dar Dawrah-'i Khaljiyan* (Dehli: Anjuman-i Farsi-yi Dihli, n.d. [199–?]), Muhammad Kalim Sahsarami, *Khidmatguzaran-i Farsi dar Bangladish* (Dhaka: Rayzani-yi Farhang-i Jumhuri-yi Islami-yi Iran, 1999); and M. H. Siddiqi, ed., *Growth of Indo-Persian Literature in Gujarat* (Baroda: Department of Persian, Arabic and Urdu, M.S. University of Baroda, 1985).

66. Hanaway, "Secretaries, Poets and the Literary Language," in Spooner and Hanaway, eds., *Literacy in the Persianate World,* 108.

67. Spooner and Hanaway, "*Siyaq,*" in *Oxford Handbook,* ed. Robson and Stedall, 444–47.

68. Hanaway, "Secretaries, Poets and the Literary Language," in Spooner and Hanaway, eds., Literacy in the Persianate World.

69. 'Ali ibn 'Uthman al-Hujwiri, *The Kashf al Maḥjúb: The Oldest Persian Treatise on Súfism,* trans. R. A. Nicholson (London: Luzac & Co., 1936). For context, see Hamid Dabashi, "Historical Conditions of Persian Sufism during the Seljuq Period," in *Classical Persian Sufism: From its Origins to Rumi,* ed. Leonard Lewisohn (London: Khanaqahi Nimatullahi Publications, 1993).

70. Zadeh, *Vernacular Qur'an,* 279.

71. Nile Green, *Making Space: Sufis and Settlers in Early Modern India* (New Delhi: Oxford University Press, 2012), and Jawid A. Mojaddedi, *The Biographical Tradition in Sufism: The "ṭabaqāt" Genre from al-Sulamī to Jāmī* (Richmond, Surrey: Curzon Press, 2001).

72. Feliz Çağman and Zeren Tanındı, "Manuscript Production at the Kazaruni Orders in Safavid Shiraz," in *Safavid Art and Architecture,* ed. Sheila R. Canby (London: British Museum Press, 2002), and Omid Safi, *The Politics of Knowledge in Premodern Islam: Negotiating Ideology and Religious Inquiry* (Chapel Hill: University of North Carolina Press, 2006).

73. John R. Perry, "Persian as a Homoglossic Language," *Cultures et sociétés contemporaines* 3 (2003): 11–28, and id., "New Persian: Expansion, Standardization & Exclusivity," in Spooner and Hanaway, eds., *Literacy in the Persianate World,* 70–94.

74. Stephen H. Rapp Jr., *The Sasanian World through Georgian Eyes: Caucasia and the Iranian Commonwealth in Late Antique Georgian Literature* (London: Routledge, 2017).

75. Donald Rayfield, *The Literature of Georgia: A History,* 3rd ed. (London: Garnett Press, 2010), 65–69.

76. Peter Cowe, "The Politics of Poetics: Islamic Influence on Armenian Verse," in *Redefining Christian Identity: Cultural Interaction in the Middle East since the Rise of Islam,* ed. J. J. van Ginkel, H. L. Murre-van den Berg, and Theo Maarten van Lint (Leuven: Peeters, 2005), 379–403.

77. Thanks to Rebecca Gould for this point.

78. Jost Gippert, "Towards an Automatical Analysis of a Translated Text and Its Original: The Persian Epic of *Vīs u Rāmīn* and the Georgian *Visramiani,*" *Studia Iranica, Mesopotamica et Anatolica* 1 (1994): 21–59. On the pre-Islamic origins of the story cycle, see Vladimir Minorsky, "Vis u Ramin: A Parthian Romance," *Bulletin of the School of Oriental and African Studies* 11 (1943–46): 741–63; 12 (1947–1948): 20–35; 16 (1954): 91–92.

79. D. M. Lang and G. M. Meredith-Owens, "*Amiran-Darejaniani*: A Georgian Romance and Its English Rendering," *Bulletin of the School of Oriental and African Studies* 22, 1–3 (1959): 454–90, and Rayfield, *Literature of Georgia,* 75–92.

80. Rayfield, *Literature of Georgia*, 81, 85.

81. Translated in ibid.,91. For a fuller linguistic analysis of the text, see Farshid Delshad, "Studien zu den iranischen und semitischen Lehnwörtern im georgischen Nationalepos 'Der Recke im Pantherfell'" (PhD diss., Friedrich-Schiller Universität, Jena, 2002).

82. James R. Russell, "Here Comes the Sun: A Poem of Kostandin Erznkats'i," *Journal of the Society for Armenian Studies* 3 (1987): 119–27. For translations and commentaries on Kostandin's works, see Theo Maarten van Lint, *Kostandin of Erznka: An Armenian Religious Poet of the XIIIth–XIVth Century. Armenian Text with Translation and Commentary* (Leiden: T. M. van Lint, 1996).

83. Cowe, "Politics of Poetics," in *Redefining Christian Identity*, ed. van Ginkel et al.

84. James R. Russell, "An Armeno-Persian Love Poem of Grigoris Aght'amarts'i," *Journal of the Society for Armenian Studies* 6 (1992–93): 99–105.

85. Joakim Enwall, "Turkish Texts in Georgian script: Sociolinguistic and Ethno-Linguistic Aspects," in *Turcology in Mainz*, ed. Hendrik Boeschoten and Julian Rentzsch (Wiesbaden: Harrassowitz, 2010).

86. Michael Kemper, "An Island of Classical Arabic in the Caucasus: Daghestan," in *Exploring the Caucasus in the 21st Century: Essays on Culture, History and Politics in a Dynamic Context*, ed. Françoise Companjen, László Marácz, and Lia Versteegh (Amsterdam: Amsterdam University Press, 2010), and Anna Zelkina, "The Arabic Linguistic and Cultural Tradition in Daghestan: An Historical. Overview," in *Arabic as a Minority Language*, ed. Jonathan Owens (Berlin: Mouton de Gruyter, 2000).

87. Gadzhi Gamzatovich Gamzatov, "Daghestan: Cultural Relations with Persia," *Encyclopædia Iranica*, 6, fasc. 6, 568–76, www.iranicaonline.org/articles/dagestan.

88. Francesca Orsini and Samira Sheikh, "Introduction," in *After Timur Left*, ed. Orsini and Sheikh (New Delhi: Oxford University Press, 2014), 17–18.

89. Stefano Pello, "Local Lexis? Provincializing Persian in Fifteenth-Century North India," in *After Timur Left*, ed. Orsini and Sheikh.

90. Anne F. Broadbridge, *Kingship and Ideology in the Islamic and Mongol Worlds* (Cambridge: Cambridge University Press, 2008),157.

91. Jonathan M. Bloom, *Paper before Print: The History and Impact of Paper in the Islamic World* (New Haven, CT: Yale University Press, 2001). Recent excavations at the erstwhile Soghdian town of Sanjar-Shah have found the earliest evidence (from between ca. 720 and 780) of the transmission of Chinese-made paper to Muslim usage. See Ofir Haim, Michael Shenkar, and Sharof Kurbanov, "The Earliest Arabic Documents Written on Paper: Three Letters from Sanjar-Shah (Tajikistan)," *Jerusalem Studies in Arabic and Islam* 43 (2016): 141–91.

92. For varied positions on the possible Chinese etymology of *kaghaz*, see *Encyclopaedia of Islam*, 2nd ed., vol. 4, ed. C. E. Bosworth, E. van Donzel, B. Lewis, and Ch. Pellat (Leiden: E. J. Brill, 1960–2005), s.v. "Kāghad," and Berthold Laufer, *Sino-Iranica: Chinese Contributions to the History of Civilization in Ancient Iran* (Chicago: Field Museum of Natural History, 1919), 557–58.

93. I am grateful to Bojan Petrovic for lexicographically confirming this etymology.

94. On the epigraphic evidence for the Jews of Jam (Firuzkuh), see Gherardo Gnoli, *Le inscrizioni giudeo-persiane del Gur (Afghanistan)*, Serie Orientale Roma, vol. 30 (Rome: Istituto Italiano per il Medio ed Estremo Oriente, 1964); Erica E. Hunter, "Hebrew-Script Tombstones from Jām, Afghanistan," *Journal of Jewish Studies* 61, 1 (2010): 72–87; and Eugen L. Rapp, *Die jüdisch-persisch-hebräischen Inschriften aus Afghanistan* (Munich: J. Kitzinger, 1965).

95. Nile Green, *Sufism: A Global History* (Oxford: Blackwell, 2012), chap. 2.

96. In *After Timur Left*, ed. Orsini and Sheikh, see Richard M. Eaton, "The Rise of Written Vernaculars: The Deccan, 1450–1650"; Dilorom Karomat, "Turki and Hindavi in the World of Persian: Fourteenth- and Fifteenth-Century Dictionaries"; Francesca Orsini, "Traces of a Multilingual World: Hindavi in Persian Texts"; and Ramya Sreenivasan, "Warrior-Tales at Hinterland Courts in North India, 1370–1550."

97. Early Khurasani customs such as the *'urs* death anniversary were exported by migrants to Anatolia and India alike. See Nile Green, "The Migration of a Muslim Ritual," in Green, *Making Space*.

98. Saïd Amir Arjomand, "Unity of the Persianate World under Turko-Mongolian Domination and Divergent Development of Imperial Autocracies in the Sixteenth Century," *Journal of Persianate Studies* 9, 1 (2016): 1–18.

99. Stefan T. Kamola, "Rashīd al-Dīn and the Making of History in Mongol Iran" (PhD diss., University of Washington, 2013), and *Rashīd al-Dīn: Agent and Mediator of Cultural Exchanges in Ilkhanid Iran*, ed. Anna Akasoy, Charles Burnett, and Ronit Yoeli-Tlalim (London: Warburg Institute, 2013). On the Il-Khanid cultural context, see Judith Pfeiffer, "From Baghdad to Maragha, Tabriz, and Beyond: Tabriz and the Multi-Cephalous Cultural, Religious, and Intellectual Landscape of the 13th to 15th Century Nile-to-Oxus Region," in *Politics, Patronage and the Transmission of Knowledge in 13th–15th Century Tabriz*, ed. Pfeiffer (Leiden: Brill, 2014).

100. George Lane, "Persian Notables and the Families Which Underpinned the Ilkhanate," in *Nomads as Agents of Cultural Change: The Mongols and Their Eurasian Predecessors*, ed. Reuven Amitai and Michal Biran (Honolulu: University of Hawai'i Press, 2015).

101. For the ongoing debate on the official status of Persian in Yuan China, see Stephen G. Haw, "The Persian Language in Yuan-Dynasty China: A Reappraisal," *East Asian History* 39 (2014): 5–32; David Morgan, "Persian as a Lingua Franca in the Mongol Empire," in *Literacy in the Persianate World*, ed. Spooner and Hanaway, 160–70; and Huang Shijian, "The Persian Language in China during the Yuan Dynasty," *Papers on Far Eastern History* 33–34 (1986): 83–95. The fullest study of Sino-Persian contact in this period is Mas'ud Tarumsari, 'Abd al-Rahman 'Alim, and Bahram Mustaqimi, *Chin: Siyasat-i Khariji wa Ravabit ba Iran (1328–57)* (Tehran: Daftar-i Mutala'at-i Siyasi wa Bayn al-Milali, 1986).

102. Vladimir Minorsky, "Pūr-i Bahā's Mongol Ode," *Bulletin of the School of Oriental and African Studies* 18, 2 (1956): 261–78.

103. Tommaso Previato, "Pre-modern Globalization and Islamic Networks under Mongol Rule: Some Preliminary Considerations on the Spreading of Sufi Knowledge in Gansu-Qinghai," *Journal of Muslim Minority Affairs* 36, 2 (2016): 235–66.

104. The Galle Trilingual Inscription has been surprisingly neglected by scholarship. See the inadequate Lorna Dewaraja, "Cheng Ho's Visits to Sri Lanka and the Galle Trilingual Inscription in the National Museum in Colombo," *Journal of the Royal Asiatic Society of Sri Lanka*, n.s., 52 (2006): 59–74, and S. Paranavitana, "The Tamil Inscription on the Galle Trilingual Slab," *Epigraphia Zeylanica, Being Lithic and Other Inscriptions of Ceylon* 3, 36 (1933): 331–41.

105. I am grateful to David Brophy for this astute observation.

106. Frederick Hirth, "The Word 'Typhoon': Its History and Origin," *Journal of the Royal Geographical Society* 50 (1880): 260–67.

107. Michel Balivet, "La conquête ottomane comme vecteur de l'expansion de la culture persane (XIV–XVI siècle)," in Balivet and Homa Lessan Pezechki, *Études turco-iraniennes: Anatolie-Iran du Moyen-Âge à l'époque moderne* (Istanbul: Isis Press, 2017); Murat Umut Inan, *Ottomans Reading Persian Classics: Literary Reception and Interpretation in the Early Modern Ottoman Empire* (forthcoming); and Sara Nur Yıldız, "Ottoman Historical Writings in Persian, 1400–1600," in *Persian Historiography*, ed. Charles Melville (London: I. B. Tauris, 2012), 436–502.

108. I am grateful to James Pickett for encouraging me to more carefully consider this "networked geography." See James R. Pickett, "The Persianate Sphere during the Age of Empires: Islamic Scholars and Networks of Exchange in Central Asia, 1747–1917" (PhD diss., Princeton University, 2015).

109. On Persian works from these regions, see O. F. Akimushkin, A. B. Khalidov and G. J. Roper, "Russian Federation," in *World Survey of Islamic Manuscripts*, ed. Geoffrey Roper, 4 vols. (London: Al-Furqan Islamic Heritage Foundation, 1992–94), 665–701; Hasan Anusha, *Danishnama-yi Adab-i Farsi*, vol. 6: *Adab-i Farsi dar Anatuli wa Balkan* (Tehran: Mu'assasa-yi Farhangi wa Intisharat-i Danishnama, Wizarat-i Farhang wa Irshad-i Islami, 1383/2005); and Alfrid Bustanov, *Knizhnaia Kul'tura Sibirskikh Musul'man* (The Book Culture of Siberian Muslims) (Moscow: Mardzhani, 2013).

110. Sanjay Subrahmanyam, "Early Modern Circulation and the Question of 'Patriotism' between Central Asia and India," in *Writing Travel in Central Asian History*, ed. Nile Green (Bloomington: Indian University Press, 2014).

111. Amid a vast historiography, see the more recent approaches of Ali Anooshahr, "Mughals, Mongols, and Mongrels: The Challenge of Aristocracy and the Rise of the Mughal State in the Tarikh-i Rashidi," *Journal of Early Modern History* 18 (2014): 559–77; Jonathan Brack, "Was Ede Bali a Wafāʾī Shaykh? Sufis, Sayyids and Genealogical Creativity in the Early Ottoman World," in *Islamic Literature and Intellectual Life*, ed. Peacock and Yıldız ; Mimi Hanaoka, "Visions of Muhammad in Bukhara and Tabaristan: Dreams and Their Uses in Persian Local Histories," *Iranian Studies* 47, 2 (2014): 289–303; Hanaoka, "Perspectives from the Peripheries Strategies for 'Centering' Persian Histories from the 'Peripheries,'" *Journal of Persianate Studies* 8, 1 (2015): 1–22; Agnieszka Kuczkiewicz-Fraś, "History Preserved in Names: Delhi Urban Toponyms of Perso-Arabic Origin," in *Islam on the Indian Subcontinent: Language, Literature, Culture and History*, ed. Kuczkiewicz-Fraś (Kraków: Kraków Księgarnia Akademicka, 2009); Sunil Sharma, "Amir Khusraw and the Genre of Historical Narratives in Verse," *Comparative Studies of South Asia, Africa and the Middle East* 22, 1–2 (2002): 112–18; and Sharma, "The City of Beauties in Indo-Persian Poetic Landscape," *Comparative Studies of South Asia, Africa and the Middle East* 24, 2 (2004): 73–81.

112. Richard M. Eaton, *Islamic History as Global History* (Washington, DC: American Historical Association, 1990).

113. *A Worldwide Jami*, ed. Thibaut d'Hubert and Alexandre Papas (Leiden: Brill, 2019), most substantially pioneers this approach.

114. Franco Moretti, *Graphs, Maps, Trees: Abstract Models for a Literary History* (London: Verso, 2005).

115. "The secondary literature often mentions that Turkish was made the official language by the Karamanid ruler of south-central Anatolia, Mehmed Beg, on his conquest of Konya in 1277. However, this derives from a statement by the Persian historian Ibn Bibi that was probably intended to discredit Mehmed Beg as a barbaric Turkmen. There is no other evidence that the Karamanids ever used Turkish for official purposes, or even much for literary ones." Andrew Peacock, personal communication, May 10, 2017.

116. There were, for example, several coins issued with Greek script by the twelfth-century Danshimendid dynasty, as well as a bilingual Greek-Arabic inscription dated to 1215 from Sinop. See Scott Redford, *Legends of Authority: The 1215 Seljuk Inscriptions of Sinop Citadel, Turkey* (Istanbul: Koç University Press, 2015), and Estelle Whelan, "A Contribution to Danishmendid History: The Figured Copper Coins," *American Numismatic Society Museum Notes* 25 (1980): 133–66. My thanks to Andrew Peacock for these references.

117. Samira Sheikh, "Languages of Public Piety: Bilingual Inscriptions from Sultanate Gujarat, c. 1390–1538," in *After Timur Left*, ed. Orsini and Sheikh. For epigraphic evidence from Southeast Asia, with which Gujarat was connected, see Claude Guillot and Ludvik Kalus, *Les monuments funéraires et l'histoire du sultanat de Pasai à Sumatra (XIIIe–XVIe siecles)* (Paris: Harmattan, 2008).

118. Andrew Peacock, "Islamisation in Medieval Anatolia," in *Islamisation: Comparative Perspectives from History* (Edinburgh: Edinburgh University Press, 2015), ed. Peacock: 141 and 144. I am very grateful to Andrew Peacock for his generous additional advice about the linguistic profiles of both the Saljuq and Ottoman chanceries.

119. On the Arabic-script Greek poems, see Paul Burguière and Robert Mantran, "Quelques vers grecs du XIIIe siècle en caractères arabes," *Byzantion* 22 (1952): 63–80.

120. Peter B. Golden, "The World of the Rasūlid Hexaglot," in *The King's Dictionary: The Rasūlid Hexaglot: Fourteenth Century Vocabularies in Arabic, Persian, Turkic, Greek, Armenian and Mongol*, trans. and ed. T. Halasi-Kun, P. B. Golden, L. Ligeti, and E. Schütz (Leiden: Brill, 2000).

121. Jost Gippert, "Early New Persian as a Medium of Spreading Islam," in *Persian Origins*, ed. Paul.

122. C. H. B. Reynolds, "Linguistic Strands in the Maldives," *Contributions to Asian Studies* 11 (1978): 155–66.

123. Hasan Taj al-Din, *The Islamic History of the Maldive Islands* [Arabic text], ed. Hikoichi Yajima, 2 vols. (Tokyo: Institute for the Study of Languages and Cultures of Asia and Africa, 1982).

124. Claude Guillot and Ludvig Kalus, "La stèle funéraire de Hamzah Fansuri," *Archipel* 60, 4 (2000): 3–24, at 18–19.

125. The following lines draw on Paul Wormser, "The Limits of Persian Influence in the 17th Century Malay World" paper presented at "The Frontiers of Persian Learning" conference II, UCLA, February 2016.

126. Alessandro Bausani, "Note su una antologia inedita di versi mistici persiani con versione interlineare malese," *Annali dell'Istituto universitario orientale di Napoli* 18 (1968): 39–66.

127. Wormser, "Limits of Persian Influence," 3.

128. Alessandro Bausani, "Note sui vocaboli persiani in malese-indonesiano," *Annali dell'Istituto universitario orientale di Napoli*, n.s., 14 (1964): 1–32. On this topic, see also Muhammad Abdul Jabbar Beg, *Arabic Loan-words in Malay: A Comparative Study*, rev. ed. (Kuala Lumpur: Universiti Kebangsaan Malaysia, 1979), and Muhammad Khush-Haykal Azad, *Wazhiha-yi Farsi-yi Dakhil dar Zaban-i Malayu* (Tehran: Wizarat-i Farhang wa Irshad-i Islami, 1378/1999).

129. Ronit Ricci, *Islam Translated: Literature, Conversion, and the Arabic Cosmopolis of South and Southeast Asia* (Chicago: University of Chicago Press, 2011).

130. Sanjay Subrahmanyam, "'Persianization' and 'Mercantilism' in Bay of Bengal History, 1400–1700," in Subrahmanyam, *Explorations in Connected History: From the Tagus* (New Delhi: Oxford University Press, 2005).

131. Ali Anooshahr, "Shirazi Scholars and the Political Culture of the Sixteenth-Century Indo-Persian World," *Indian Economic & Social History Review* 51, 3 (2014): 331–52; Abolghasem Dadvar, *Iranians in Mughal Politics and Society, 1606–1658* (New Delhi: Gyan Publishing House, 1999); Masashi Haneda, "Emigration of Iranian Elites to India during the 16th–18th Centuries," *Cahiers d'Asie centrale* 3–4 (1997): 129–43; and Riazul Islam, *Calendar of Documents on Indo-Persian Relations* (Tehran: Iranian Culture Foundation, 1979).

132. Momin Mohiuddin, *The Chancellery and Persian Epistolography under the Mughals, from Babur to Shahjahan, 1526–1658* (Calcutta: Iran Society, 1971), 157, 180–81.

133. Arthur Dudney, "Sabk-e Hendi and the Crisis of Authority in Eighteenth-Century Indo-Persian Poetics," *Journal of Persianate Studies* 9, 1 (2016): 60–82, and Rajeev Kinra, "Make it Fresh: Time, Tradition, and Indo-Persian Literary Modernity," in *Time, History, and the Religious Imaginary in South Asia*, ed. Anne C. Murphy (London: Routledge, 2011).

134. For fifteenth- and early sixteenth-century South Asian vernacularization, see the essays in *After Timur Left*, ed. Orsini and Sheikh (2014). For a larger world historical view on this process, see Benoît Grévin, "La lente révolution des cultures linguistiques," in *Histoire du monde au XVe siècle*, ed. Patrick Boucheron (Paris: Fayard, 2009), 651–67.

135. Marc Toutant, *Un empire de mots: Pouvoir, culture et soufisme à l'époque des derniers Timourides au miroir de la Khamsa de Mīr 'Alī Shīr Nawā'ī* (Leuven: Peeters, 2016), and id., "La Khamsa de Mīr 'Alī Shīr Nawā'ī (1441–1501) ou le triomphe de l'imitation créatrice," *La Timuride* 38 (2016): 17–25.

136. Colin Paul Mitchell, "To Preserve and Protect: Husayn Va'iz-i Kashifi and Perso-Islamic Chancellery Culture," *Iranian Studies* 36, 4 (2003): 485–507.

137. I am grateful to an anonymous reader for these details on the status of Persian versus Chaghatai under the Timurids.

138. Hodgson, *Venture of Islam*, 2: 293.

139. Hamide Demirel, *The Poet Fuzuli: His Work, Study of his Turkish, Persian and Arabic Divan* (Ankara: Ministry of Culture, 1991), and Halil Inalcık, "The Origins of Classical Ottoman Literature: Persian Tradition, Court Entertainments, and Court Poets," *Journal of Turkish Literature* 5 (2008): 5–75.

140. Richard M. Eaton and Phillip B. Wagoner, *Power, Memory, Architecture: Contested Sites on India's Deccan Plateau, 1300–1600* (New Delhi: Oxford University Press, 2014), 128, 210–11. See also Philip Wagoner, "The Multiple Worlds of Amin Khan: Crossing Persianate and Indic Cultural Boundaries in

the Quth Shahi Kingdom," in *Sultans of the South: Arts of India's Deccan Courts, 1323–1687*, ed. Navina Najat Haidar and Marika Sardar (New York: Metropolitan Museum of Art, 2011).

141. Thibaut d'Hubert, "The Lord of the Elephant: Interpreting the Islamicate Epigraphic, Numismatic, and Literary Material from the Mrauk U Period of Arakan (ca. 1430–1784)," *Journal of Burma Studies* 19, 2 (2015): 341–70, with the inscription as Appendix 1.

142. Syed Ali Ashraf, *Muslim Traditions in Bengali Literature* (Karachi: Bengali Literary Society, 1960), chap. 1; Thibaut d'Hubert, "Pirates, Poets, and Merchants: Bengali Language and Literature in Seventeenth-Century Mrauk-U," in *Culture and Circulation: Literature in Motion in Early Modern India*, ed. Thomas de Bruijn and Allison Busch (Leiden: Brill, 2014); and d'Hubert, "Compositional Patterns in the Seventeenth-Century Bengali Literature of Arakan," in *Tellings and Texts: Music, Literature and Performance Cultures in North India*, ed. Francesca Orsini and Katherine Brown (Cambridge: Open Books Publishers, 2015).

143. Adiya Behl and Simon Weightman, "Introduction," in *Madhumalati: An Indian Sufi Romance*, trans. Behl and Weightman (Oxford: Oxford University Press, 2000), and *Culture and Circulation*, ed. de Bruijn and Busch.

144. Sheldon Pollock, "Cosmopolitan and Vernacular in History," *Public Culture* 12, 3 (2000): 591–625.

145. Eleazar Birnbaum, "The Ottomans and Chagatay Literature," *Central Asiatic Journal* 20 (1976): 157–91, and Aftandil Erkinov, "Persian-Chaghatai Bilingualism in the Intellectual Circles of Central Asia During the 15th–18th Centuries: The Case of Poetical Anthologies (*bayāz*)," *International Journal of Central Asian Studies* 12 (2008): 57–82.

146. See Agnieszka Kuczkiewicz-Fraś, "Turkic in India and Its Elements in Hindi," *Studia Turcologica Cracoviensia* 8 (2001): 43–48; the literature on this subject is miniscule.

147. Allison Busch, "Hidden in Plain View: Brajbhasha Poets at the Mughal Court," *Modern Asian Studies* 44, 2 (2010): 267–309, and Busch, *Poetry of Kings: The Classical Hindi Literature of Mughal India* (New York: Oxford University Press, 2011), chaps. 4 and 5.

148. Burguière and Mantran, "Quelques vers grecs du XIIIe siècle en caractères arabes." On Turkic parallels, see Bernt Brendemoen, "Greek and Turkish Language Encounters in Anatolia," in *Language Encounters across Time and Space: Studies in Language Contact*, ed. Bernt Brendemoen, Elizabeth Lanza, and Else Ryen (Oslo: Novus, 1999).

149. Audrey Truschke, *Culture of Encounters: Sanskrit at the Mughal Court* (New York: Columbia University Press, 2016).

150. On inscriptions, see Chen Da-sheng et Ludvik Kalus, *Corpus d'inscriptions arabes et persanes en Chine* (Paris: P. Geuthner, 1991) and Clement Huart, *Inscriptions arabes et persanes des mosquées chinoises de K'ai-fong-fou et de Si-ngan-fou* (Leiden: Brill, 1905). On the mosques more generally, see Nancy Shatzman Steinhardt, *China's Early Mosques* (Edinburgh: Edinburgh University Press, 2015).

151. On Hui history, see Jonathan Lipman, *Familiar Strangers: A History of Muslims in Northwest China, Studies on Ethnic Groups in China* (Seattle: University of Washington Press, 1997).

152. On the Han Kitab and their milieu, see Françoise Aubin, "Islam en Chine et confucianisme," *Études orientales* 27–28 (2016); Zvi Ben-Dor Benite, *The Dao of Muhammad: A Cultural History of Chinese Muslims in Late Imperial China* (Cambridge MA: Harvard University Press, 2005); Anthony Garnaut, "Chinese Muslim Literature," in *Encyclopaedia of Islam*, 3rd ed., ed. Kate Fleet, Gudrun Krämer, Denis Matringe, John Nawas, and Everett Rowson, http://dx.doi.org/10.1163/1573-3912_ei3_COM_27604; and Kristian Petersen, *Interpreting Islam in China: Pilgrimage, Scripture, and Language in the Han Kitab* (New York: Oxford University Press, 2017).

153. Walter N. Hakala, "On Equal Terms: The Equivocal Origins of an Early Mughal Indo-Persian Vocabulary," *Journal of the Royal Asiatic Society* 25, 2 (2015): 209–27.

154. Sreeramula Rajeswara Sarma, "Sanskrit Manuals for Learning Persian," in *Adab Shenasi*, ed. Azarmi Dukht Safavi (Aligarh, India: Aligarh Muslim University, Department of Persian, 1996); Sarma, "From Yāvanī to Saṃskṛtam: Sanskrit Writings Inspired by Persian Works," *Studies in the History of*

Indian Thought 14 (2002): 71–88; and Audrey Truschke, "Defining the Other: An Intellectual History of Sanskrit Lexicons and Grammars of Persian," *Journal of Indian Philosophy* 40, 6 (2012): 635–68.

155. Rani Majumdar, "The Kathākautuka—A Persian Love Poem in Sanskrit Garb," *Journal of the Oriental Institute, Baroda,* 47, 3–4 (1998), 283–87, and Luther James Obrock, "Translation and History: The Development of a Kashmiri Textual Tradition from ca. 1000–1500" (PhD diss., University of California, Berkeley, 2015), chap. 7.

156. Supriya Gandhi, "Retelling the Rāma Story in Persian Verse: Masīḥ Pānīpatī's Maṣ navī-yi Rām va Sītā," in *No Tapping around Philology: A Festschrift in Honor of Wheeler McIntosh Thackston Jr.'s 70th Birthday,* ed. Alireza Korangy and Daniel J. Sheffield (Wiesbaden: Harrassowitz, 2014), and Truschke, *Culture of Encounters.*

157. Solomon I. Baevskiĭ, *Early Persian Lexicography: Farhangs of the Eleventh to the Fifteenth Centuries,* trans. John R. Perry (Folkestone, England: Global Oriental, 2007), esp. chap. 4, and Rajeev Kinra, "Cultures of Comparative Philology in the Early Modern Indo-Persian World," *Philological Encounters* 1, 1–4 (2016): 225–87.

158. Muhammad Mahdi Khan, *Sanglax: A Persian Guide to the Turkish Language by Muhammad Mahdī Xān,* facsimile text with introduction by Sir Gerard Clauson (London: Luzac, 1960).

159. Shinji Ido, "New Persian Vowels Transcribed in Ming China," in *Iranian Languages and Literatures of Central Asia: From the 18th Century to the Present,* ed. Matteo de Chiara and Evelin Grassi, *Cahiers de Studia Iranica* 57 (2015): 99–136.

160. My thanks to Andrew Peacock for advice on this matter.

161. On related matters, see Christopher Markiewicz, "The Crisis of Rule in Late Medieval Islam: A Study of Idrīs Bidlīsī (861–926/1457–1520) and Kingship at the Turn of the Sixteenth Century" (PhD diss., University of Chicago, 2015), 140–45.

162. Vladimir Minorsky, "The Poetry of Shah Isma'il I," *Bulletin of the School of Oriental and African Studies* 10, 4 (1942): 1006–53.

163. Helen Giunashvili and Tamar Abuladze, "Persian Historical Documents of Georgia (Sixteenth to Eighteenth Centuries): Aspects of Linguistic Analysis," *Journal of Persianate Studies* 5,1 (2012): 35–42.

164. Rayfield, *Literature of Georgia,* 108–9.

165. Rebecca Gould, "Sweetening the Heavy Georgian Tongue: Jāmī in the Georgian-Persianate Ecumene," in *A Worldwide Literature: Jāmī (1414–1492) in the Dār al-Islām and Beyond,* ed. Thibaut d'Hubert and Alexandre Papas (Leiden: Brill, 2019).

166. Rayfield, *Literature of Georgia,* 114–17.

167. Ibid., 118. On this literary response to the Safavids, see Z. Avalishvili, "Teimuraz I and His Poem 'The Martyrdom of Queen Ketevan,'" *Georgica* 1, nos. 4–5 (1937): 17–42.

168. Rayfield, *Literature of Georgia,* 125–26, 140.

169. Charles Dowsett, *Sayat'-Nova: An 18th-Century Troubadour: A Biographical and Literary Study* (Leuven: Peeters, 1997), and Xi Yang, "Sayat'-Nova: Within the Near Eastern Bardic Tradition and Posthumous" (PhD diss., University of California, Los Angeles, 2016).

170. Peter Cowe, "The Armenian Oikoumene in the 16th Century: Dark Age or Era of Transition?" in *Reflections of Armenian Identity in History and Historiography,* ed. Houri Berberian and Touraj Daryaee (Irvine, CA: UCI Jordan Center for Persian Studies, forthcoming).

171. Xi Yang, "Sayat Nova," 84.

172. Cowe, "Politics of Poetics" in *Redefining Christian Identity,* ed. van Ginkel et al.

173. However, on Ottoman influence in Georgia, see Güneş Işıksel, "L'emprise ottomane en Géorgie occidentale à l'époque de Süleymân Ier (r. 1520–1566)," in *Collectanea Islamica,* ed. Nicola Melis and Mauro Nobili (Rome: Aracne Editrice, 2012).

174. Mohiuddin, *Chancellery and Persian Epistolography,* 28.

175. Muzaffar Alam, "The Pursuit of Persian: Language in Mughal Politics," *Modern Asian Studies* 32, 2 (1998): 317–49. More generally, see Muhammad Abdul Ghani, *History of Persian Language and Literature at the Mughal Court,* 3 vols. (Allahabad: Indian Press, 1929).

176. Muzaffar Alam, and Sanjay Subrahmanyam, "The Making of a Munshi," *Comparative Studies of South Asia, Africa and the Middle East* 24, 2 (2004): 61–72.

177. Mohiuddin, *Chancellery and Persian Epistolography,* 215–20, with Har Karan's death date given as 1034–35 AH.

178. Rajeev Kinra, *Writing Self, Writing Empire: Chandar Bhan Brahman and the Cultural World of the Early Modern Indo-Persian State Secretary* (Berkeley: University of California Press, 2015).

179. Pellò, *Ṭūṭiyān-i Hind,* chap. 3.

180. Ibid.,139.

181. Stefano Pellò, "Black Curls in a Mirror: The Eighteenth-Century Persian Kṛṣṇa of Lāla Amānat Rāy's *Jilwa-yi ẕāt* and the Tongue of Bīdil," *International Journal of Hindu Studies* 22 (2018): 71–103.

182. Pellò, *Ṭūṭiyān-i Hind,* 18.

183. Ibid., 161–68, and Stefano Pellò, "A Linguistic Conversion: Mīrzā Muḥammad Ḥasan Qatīl and the Varieties of Persian (ca. 1790)," in *Borders: Itineraries on the Edges of Iran,* ed. Pellò (Venice: Edizione Ca' Foscari, 2016).

184. Purnima Dhavan, "Redemptive Pasts & Imperilled Futures: The Writing of a Sikh History," in *Time, History, and the Religious Imaginary,* ed Murphy; Louis E. Fenech, "Persian Sikh Scripture: The Ghazals of Bhā'ī Nand La'l Goyā," *International Journal of Punjab Studies* 1 (1994): 49–70; and Christopher Shackle, "Approaches to the Persian Loans in the *Ādi Granth*," *Bulletin of the School of Oriental and African Studies* 41, 1 (1978): 73–96.

185. Pellò, *Ṭūṭiyān-i Hind,* 135.

186. Ruby Lal, "Rethinking Mughal India: The Challenge of a Princess's Memoir," in *Challenges of History Writing in South Asia,* ed. Syed Jaffar Ahmed (Karachi: University of Karachi, 2013), 251–83, and Sunil Sharma, "From 'Äesha to Nur Jahān: The Shaping of a Classical Persian Poetic Canon of Women," *Journal of Persianate Studies* 2, 2 (2009): 148–64.

187. Nile Green, "Idiom, Genre and the Politics of Self-Description on the Peripheries of Persian," in *Religion, Language and Power,* ed. Nile Green and Mary Searle-Chatterjee (New York: Routledge, 2008); Green, "Tribe, Diaspora and Sainthood in Afghan History," *Journal of Asian Studies* 67, 1 (2008): 171–211; and Christoph Werner, "Taming the Tribal Native: Court Culture and Politics in Eighteenth Century Shiraz," in *Court Cultures in the Muslim World: Seventh to Nineteenth Centuries,* ed. Albrecht Fuess and Jan-Peter Hartung (New York: Routledge, 2011).

188. I am grateful to Mikhail Pelevin for this insight.

189. Alan Williams, *The Zoroastrian Myth of Migration from Iran and Settlement in the Indian Diaspora: Text, Translation and Analysis of the 16th Century Qeṣṣe-ye Sanjān, "The Story of Sanjan"* (Leiden: Brill, 2009).

190. Syed Hasan Askari, "Dabistān-i Madhāhib and Dīwān-i Mubad," in *Indo-Iranian Studies Presented for the Golden Jubilee of the Pahlavi Dynasty of Iran,* ed. Fathullah Mujtabai (New Delhi: Indo-Iran Society, 1977), 85–104. The authorship of the *Dabistan* is contested, but I have followed the attribution of Fathullah Mujtabai, "Dabestān-e Maḏāheb," in *Encyclopædia Iranica,* 6, fasc. 5, 532–34, www.iranicaonline.org/articles/dabestan-e-madaheb.

191. For variant evidence on Fansuri's biography and death date, see Vladimir I. Braginsky, "Towards the Biography of Hamzah Fansuri: When Did Hamzah Live? Data from his Poems and Early European Accounts," *Archipel* 57, 2 (1999): 135–75, and Guillot and Kalus, "La stèle funéraire de Hamzah Fansuri." On Fansuri's travels in their larger regional context, see Peter G. Riddell, *Islam and the Malay-Indonesian World: Transmission and Responses* (London: C. Hurst, 2001).

192. On Fansuri's language, see Syed Muhammad Naquib al-Attas, *The Mysticism of Ḥamzah Fanṣūrī* (Kuala Lumpur: University of Malaya Press, 1970), 142–75.

193. Wormser, "Limits of Persian Influence," 3.

194. G. W. J. Drewes, "Nūr al-Dīn al-Rānīrī's Charge of Heresy against Hamzah and Shamsuddin from an International Point of View," in *Cultural Contact and Textual Interpretation,* ed. C. D. Grijns and S. O. Robson (Leiden: KITLV, 1986), and Paul Wormser, *Le Bustan al-Salatin de Nuruddin ar-Raniri: Réflexions sur le rôle culturel d'un étranger dans le monde malais au XVIIe siécle* (Paris: MSH, 2012). On

this period's Indo-Malay connections, see also Vladimir I. Braginsky, "Structure, Date and Sources of Hikayat Aceh Revisited: The Problem of Mughal-Malay Literary Ties," *Bijdragen tot de Taal-, Land- en Volkenkunde* 162, 4 (2006): 441–67.

195. Wormser, "Limits of Persian Influence," 4.

196. Gagan D. S. Sood, "'Correspondence Is Equal to Half a Meeting': The Composition and Comprehension of Letters in Eighteenth-Century Islamic Eurasia," *Journal of the Economic and Social History of the Orient* 50, 2/3 (2007): 172–214. For discussion and comparison with the more abundant surviving Julfan Armenian correspondence, see Sebouh D. Aslanian, *From the Indian Ocean to the Mediterranean: The Global Trade Networks of Armenian Merchants from New Julfa* (Berkeley: University of California Press, 2011), 268–69, n20.

197. On the Julfan Armenian commercial documents and their many lexical borrowings from Persian, see Aslanian, *From the Indian Ocean,* chap. 5; Edmund Herzig, "Commercial Law of the New Julfa Armenians," in *Les Arméniens dans le commerce asiatique au début de l'ère modern,* ed. Sushil Chaudhury and Kéram Kévonian (Paris: Éditions de la Maison des sciences de l'homme, 2007), 73–74; and Herzig, "Borrowed Terminology and Shared Techniques in New Julfa Armenian Commercial Documents," in *Iran and the World in the Safavid Age,* ed. Herzig and Willem Floor (London: I. B. Tauris, 2015). On Persian as a language of correspondence more broadly, see Sood, "Correspondence." On the Ondaatje Letters, see *Between Colombo and Cape Town: Letters in Tamil, Dutch and Sinhala Sent to Nicolaas Ondaatje from Ceylon,* ed. and trans. Herman Tieken (Delhi: Manohar, 2015).

198. Jorge Dos Santos Alves and Nader Nasiri-Moghaddam, "Une lettre en persan de 1519 sur la situation à Melaka", *Archipel* 75 (2008): 145-166; Andrew Peacock, "Notes on Some Persian Documents from Early Modern Southeast Asia," *Sejarah* 27 (2018): 81-97; and Subrahmanyam, "'Persianization' and 'Mercantilism.'"

199. Michael H. Fisher, "Contested Political Representations: Early Indian Diplomatic Missions to Britain, 1764-1857," *Journal of Interdisciplinary Studies in History and Archaeology* 1, 1 (2004): 87–100; Giorgio Rota, "Diplomatic Relations between the Safavids and Siam in the 17th Century," in *Aspects of the Maritime Silk Road: From the Persian Gulf to the East China Sea,* ed. Ralph Kauz (Wiesbaden: Harrassowitz, 2010), 71–84; Rota, "Safavid Persia and Its Diplomatic Relations with Venice," in *Iran and the World,* ed. Herzig and Floor (2015).

200. Muhammad Ibrahim Rabi', *Safina-yi Sulaymani (Safarnama-yi Safir-i Iran bih Siyam),* ed. 'Abbas Faruqi (Tehran: Danishgah-yi Tihran, 1977), trans. John O'Kane as *The Ship of Sulaimān* (New York: Columbia University Press, 1972). See also Muhammad Ismail Marcinkowksi, *From Isfahan to Ayutthaya: Contacts between Iran and Siam in the 17th Century* (Kuala Lumpur: Pustaka Nasional, 2005); Christoph Marcinkowski, "The Safavid Presence in the Indian Ocean: A Reappraisal of the Ship of Solayman, a Seventeenth-Century Travel Account to Siam," in *Iran and the World,* ed. Herzig and Floor; and Subrahmanyam, "'Persianization' and 'Mercantilism.'"

201. Artyom Andreev, "Ashur Bek's Letters and Prince A. B. Cherkassky's Mission," *Manuscripta Orientalia* 22 (2016): 9–28; Andreev and M. Rezvan, "Khiwa and Bukhara Legation Missive Letters of the Late 17th–Early 18th Centuries," ibid., 50–55; Jean Calmard, "The French Presence in Safavid Persia: A Preliminary Study," in *Iran and the World,* ed. Herzig and Floor (2015), R. W. Ferrier, "The European Diplomacy of Shāh 'Abbās I and the First Persian Embassy to England," *Iran* 11 (1973), 75–92; *Asnad wa Rawabit-i Tarikhi-yi Iran wa Purtughal,* ed. Luis de Matos (Tehran: Markaz-i Asnad wa Khadamat-i Pazhuhish, 2003); Nader Nasiri-Moghaddam, "Les documents persans des Archives nationales du Portugal (Torre do Tombo) et leur importance pour l'histoire du golf Persique aux XVIe–XVIIe siècles," in *Revisiting Hormuz: Portuguese Interactions in the Persian Gulf Region in the Early Modern Period,* ed. Dejanirah Couto and Rui. Manuel Loureiro (Lisbon: Fundação Calouste Gulbenkian; Wiesbaden: Harrassowitz, 2008), *Asnad-i Farsi, 'Arabi wa Turki dar Arshiv-i Milli Purtughal dar bara-yi Hurmuz wa Khilij-i Fars,* ed. Jahangir Qai'mmaqami (Tehran: Sitad-i Buzurg-i Artishtaran, 1976); and Giorgio Rota, "Safavid Envoys in Venice," in *Diplomatisches Zeremoniell in Europa und im Mittleren Osten in der frühen Neuzeit,* ed. Ralph Kauz, Giorgio Rota, and Jan Paul Niederkorn (Vienna: Österreichische Akademie der Wissenschaften, 2009), 213–49.

202. Arash Khazeni, "Merchants to the Golden City: The Persian *Farmān* of King Chandrawizaya Rājā and the Elephant and Ivory Trade in the Indian Ocean: A View from 1728," *Iranian Studies* (forthcoming).

203. Simon Schaffer, "The Asiatic Enlightenments of British Astronomy" and Kapil Raj, "Mapping Knowledge: Go-Betweens in Calcutta, 1770–1820," in *The Brokered World: Go-Betweens and Global Intelligence, 1770–1820*, ed. Simon Schaffer, Lissa Roberts, Kapil Raj, and James Delbourgo (Sagamore Beach, MA: Science History Publications, 2009).

204. For an early example of such Ottoman Turkish diplomatic correspondence, see S. A Skilliter, "Three Letters from the Ottoman 'Sultana' Safiye to Queen Elizabeth," in *Documents from Islamic Chanceries*, ed. S. M. Stern (Oxford: Cassirer, 1965). More broadly, see Antoine Gautier with Marie de Testa, *Drogmans, diplomates et ressortissants européens auprès de la Porte Ottomane* (Istanbul: Isis Press, 2013).

205. Arthur Dudney, "Urdu as Persian: Some Eighteenth-Century Evidence on Vernacular Poetry as Language Planning," in *Texts and Traditions in Early Modern North India*, ed. Jack Hawley, Anshu Malhotra, and Tyler Williams (Delhi: Oxford University Press, 2017); Prachi Deshpande, *Creative Pasts: Historical Memory and Identity in Western India, 1700–1960* (New York: Columbia University Press, 2007), 19–39; and Sumit Guha, "Speaking Historically: The Changing Voices of Historical Narration in Western India, 1400–1900," *American Historical Review* 109, 4 (2004), 1084–1103. On the Mughal news system, see Michael H. Fisher, "The Office of Akhbar Nawis: The Transition from Mughal to British Forms," *Modern Asian Studies* 27, 1 (1993): 45–82.

206. Muhammad Yousuf Kokan, *Arabic and Persian in Carnatic, 1710–1960* (Madras: "Copies may be had from Hafiza House," 1974).

207. Vladimir Kushev, "Areal Lexical Contacts of the Afghan (Pashto) Language (Based on the Texts of the XVI–XVIII Centuries)," *Iran & the Caucasus* 1 (1997): 159–66.

208. Sajjad Nejatie, "Iranian Migrations in the Durrani Empire, 1747–93," *Comparative Studies of South Asia, Africa and the Middle East* 37, 3 (2017): 494–509, esp. 500.

209. On Persian in nineteenth-century India, see Alessandro Bausani, "The Position of Ghālib (1796–1869) in the History of Urdu and Indo-Persian Poetry," *Islam* 31 (1958): 99–127; Shamsur Rahman Faruqi, "Unprivileged Power: The Strange Case of Persian (and Urdu) in Nineteenth Century India," *Annual of Urdu Studies* 13 (1998): 3–30; *Early Nineteenth-Century Panjab*, trans. and ed. J. S. Grewal and Indu Banga (New Delhi: Routledge India, 2016); Sharif Husain Qasemi, "Persian Chronicles in the Nineteenth Century," in *The Making of Indo-Persian Culture: Indian and French Studies*, ed., Muzaffar Alam, Françoise Delvoye Nalini, and Marc Gaborieau (New Delhi: Manohar, 2000); and Chitralekha Zutshi, *Kashmir's Contested Pasts Narratives, Sacred Geographies, and the Historical Imagination* (New Delhi: Oxford University Press, 2014), chaps. 2 and 3.

210. Garnik Asatrian and Hayrapet Margarian, "The Muslim Community of Tiflis (8th–19th Centuries)," *Iran & the Caucasus* 8, 1 (2004): 29–52. On the codicological heritage of the region, see Hasan Anusha, *Danishnama-yi Adab-i Farsi*, vol. 5: *Adab-i Farsi dar Qafqaz (Azarbayjan, Armanistan, Gurjistan, wa Jumhuri-yi Khud'mukhtar-i Daghistan)* (Tehran: Mu'assasa-yi Farhangi wa Intisharat-i Danishnama, 1383/2005).

211. I am grateful to Marc Toutant for advice on Persian bureaucracy in Khiva, Qoqand, and Bukhara.

212. Susanna S. Nettleton, "Ruler, Patron, Poet: 'Umar Khan in the Blossoming of the Khanate of Qoqand, 1800–1820," *International Journal of Turkish Studies* 2, 2 (1981–82): 127–40.

213. James R. Pickett and Matthew Melvin-Koushki, "Mobilizing Magic: Occultism in Central Asia and the Continuity of High Persianate Culture under Russian Rule," *Studia Islamica* 111, 2 (2016): 231–84.

214. Alfrid K. Bustanov, *Knizhnaia kul'tura sibirskikh musul'man* (Moscow: Mardjani, 2013) and Allen J. Frank, *Bukhara and the Muslims of Russia: Sufism, Education, and the Paradox of Islamic Prestige* (Leiden: Brill, 2012).

215. Thomas Loy, "Rise and Fall: Bukharan Jewish Literature of the 1920s and 1930s," in *Iranian Languages and Literatures of Central Asia*, ed. Matteo Di Chiara and Evelin Grassi, *Cahier de Studia Iranica* 20 (2015): 307–36.

216. Michael Khodarkovsky, *Russia's Steppe Frontier: The Making of a Colonial Empire, 1500–1800* (Bloomington: Indiana University Press, 2002) and David Schimmelpenninck van der Oye, *Russian Orientalism: Asia in the Russian Mind from Peter the Great to the Emigration* (New Haven, CT: Yale University Press, 2010).

217. On the texts, see David Brophy, "High Asia and the High Qing: A Selection of Persian Letters from the Beijing Archives," in *No Tapping around Philology,* ed. Korangy and Sheffield . On the context, see Alexandre Papas, "Fonctionnaires des frontières dans l'Empire mandchou: Les *beg* musulmans du Turkestan oriental (1760–1860)," *Journal asiatique* 296, 1 (2008): 23–57.

218. David Brophy, "A Tatar Turkist in Chinese Turkistan: Nushirvan Yavshef's travels in Xinjiang, 1914–1917," *Studies in Travel Writing* 18, 4 (2014): 345–56, and Alexandre Papas, "Muslim Reformism in Xinjiang: Reading the Newspaper *Yengi Hayat* (1934–1937)," in *Kashgar Revisited: Uyghur Studies in Memory of Ambassador Gunnar Jarring,* ed. I. Bellér-Hann, B. N. Schlyter, and J. Sugawara (Leiden: Brill, 2016), 161–83.

219. Bernard S. Cohn, "The Command of Language and the Language of Command," in *Subaltern Studies IV: Writings on South Asian History and Society,* ed. Ranajit Guha (Delhi: Oxford University Press, 1985), and Tariq Rahman, "The Decline of Persian in British India," *South Asia* 22, 1 (1999): 63–77.

220. Hayden Bellenoit, "Between Qanungos and Clerks: The Cultural and Service Worlds of Hindustan's Pensmen, c.1750–1900," *Modern Asian Studies* 48, 4 (2014): 872–910, and Bellenoit, *The Formation of the Colonial State in India: Scribes, Paper and Taxes, 1760–1860* (London: Routledge, 2017).

221. Ram Babu Saksena, *European & Indo-European Poets of Urdu & Persian* (Lucknow: Newul Kishore Press, 1941), chaps. 7 and 8.

222. C. A. Storey, "The Beginning of Persian Printing in India," in *Oriental Studies in Honour of Cursetji Erachji Pavry,* ed. Jal Dastur Cursetji (London: Oxford University Press, 1933), 457–61.

223. Michael H. Fisher, "Persian Professor in Britain: Mirza Muhammed Ibrahim at the East India Company's College, 1826–44," *Comparative Studies in South Asia, Africa, and the Middle East* 21, 1–2 (2001): 24–32, and Fisher, "Teaching Persian as an Imperial Language in India and in England during the Late 18th and Early 19th Centuries," in *Literacy in the Persianate World,* ed. Spooner and Hanaway, 328–59.

224. Nile Green, "The Development of Arabic-Script Typography in Georgian Britain," *Printing History,* n.s., 5 (2009): 15–30, and Éva M. Jeremiás, "Matthew Lumsden's *Persian Grammar* (Calcutta, 1810)," *Iran* 50 (2012): 129–40 and 51 (2013): 197–206.

225. Sue Tungate, "Matthew Boulton and the Soho Mint: Copper to Customer" (PhD diss., Birmingham University, 2010), 236–40.

226. Ibid., 240. On subsequent unsuccessful attempts to introduce mechanized minting to Iran, see Rudi Matthee, "Changing the Mintmaster: The Introduction of Mechanized Minting in Qajar Iran," *Itinerario* 19, 3 (1995): 109–29.

227. On the wider development of early Islamic printing more generally, see *Das gedruckte Buch im Vorderen Orient,* ed. Ulrich Marzolph (Dortmund: Verlag für Orientkunde, 2002).

228. Nile Green, "Journeymen, Middlemen: Travel, Trans-Culture and Technology in the Origins of Muslim Printing," *International Journal of Middle East Studies* 41, 2 (2009): 203–24, and Michael Kemper, *Sufis und Gelehrte in Tatarien und Baschkirien: Der islamische Diskurs unter russischer Herrschaft* (Berlin: Klaus Schwarz, 1998), 43–50.

229. Ulrich Marzolph, "Persian Incunabula: A Definition and Assessment," *Gutenberg-Jahrbuch 2007,* 205–20. On the subsequent spread of printing in Iran, see Husayn Mirza'i Gulpayigani, *Tarikh-i Chap wa Chapkhana dar Iran* (Tehran: Intisharat Gulshan-i Raz, 1999), and Farid Qasimi, *Awwalinha-yi Matbu'at-i Iran* (Tehran: Nashr-i Abi, 2004).

230. For figures, see Green, "Development of Arabic-Script Typography."

231. Nile Green, "The Trans-Colonial Opportunities of Bible Translation: Iranian Language-Workers between the Russian and British Empires," in *Trans-Colonial Modernities in South Asia,* ed. Michael Dodson and Brian Hatcher (London: Routledge, 2012).

232. Nile Green, "Persian Print and the Stanhope Revolution: Industrialization, Evangelicalism and the Birth of Printing in Early Qajar Iran," *Comparative Studies of South Asia, Africa and the Middle East* 30, 3 (2010): 473–90.

233. Nile Green, "Stones from Bavaria: Iranian Lithography in Its Global Contexts," *Iranian Studies* 43, 3 (2010): 305–31.

234. Olimpiada P. Shcheglova, *Katalog litografirovannykh knig na persidskom yazyke v sobranii Leningradskogo otdeleniya Instituta vostokovedeniya AN SSSR*, 2 vols. (Moscow: Institute of Oriental Studies of the Academy of Sciences of the USSR, 1975), and Zahra Shah, "'Bringing Spring to Sahbai's Rose-Garden': Persian Printing in North India after 1857," in *The Global Histories of Books: New Directions in Book History*, ed. Elleke Boehmer, Rouven Kunstmann, Priyasha Mukhopadhyay, and Asha Rogers (New York: Palgrave Macmillan, 2017).

235. Seymour Becker, *Russia's Protectorates in Central Asia: Bukhara and Khiva, 1865–1924* (Cambridge, MA: Harvard University Press, 1968),206 and Adeeb Khalid, "Muslim Printers in Tsarist Central Asia: A Research Note," *Central Asian Survey* 11, 3 (1992): 113–18.

236. ʿAbd al-Rasul Rahin, "Aghaz-i Kitabnawisi wa Tabʿ-i Kitab dar Afghanistan," *Aryana-yi Birun Marzi* 5, 3 (Skärholmen, Sweden: Afghanistan Cultural Association, 2003): 3–16.

237. Tamaz Varvaridze, Sophia Kintsurashvili, and Nana Churghulia, *Georgische Schrift und Typographie / Georgian Script & Typography: Geschichte und Gegenwart / Past and Present* (Tbilisi: Graphic Design Association, 2016), 266–68, 278.

238. Evangelia Balta, *Beyond the Language Frontier: Studies on the Karamanlis and the Karamanlidika Printing* (Istanbul: Isis Press, 2010).

239. Rian Thum, *The Sacred Routes of Uyghur History* (Cambridge MA: Harvard University Press, 2014), 178–80.

240. On Punjab and its surroundings, see Jeffrey M. Diamond, "A 'Vernacular' for a 'New Generation'? Historical Perspectives about Urdu and Punjabi and the Formation of Language Policy in Colonial Northwest India," in *Language Policy and Language Conflict in Afghanistan and its Neighbors*, ed. Harold Schiffman and Brian Spooner (Leiden: Brill, 2012), and Farina Mir, *The Social Space of Language: Vernacular Culture in British Colonial Punjab* (Berkeley: University of California Press, 2010), chaps. 1 and 2. On Hyderabad, see Nile Green, "The Antipodes of Progress: A Journey to the End of Indo-Persian," in *The Persianate World*, ed. Assef Ashraf and Abbas Amanat (Leiden: Brill, 2018).

241. Marina Alexidze, "Persians in Georgia (1801–1921)," *Journal of Persianate Studies* 1 (2008): 254–60.

242. *The Delhi College: Traditional Elites, the Colonial State, and Education before 1857*, ed. Margrit Pernau (Delhi: Oxford University Press, 2006).

243. Adeeb Khalid, *The Politics of Muslim Cultural Reform: Jadidism in Central Asia* (Berkeley: University of California Press, 1998), and David Lelyveld, *Aligarh's First Generation: Muslim Solidarity in British India* (New Delhi: Oxford University Press, 1978).

244. Barbara Daly Metcalf, "The Madrasa at Deoband: A Model for Religious Education in Modern India," *Modern Asian Studies* 12, 1 (1978): 111–34, with the reference to Urdu replacing Persian on 119.

245. Thum, *Sacred Routes*, says the same of East Turkistan.

246. Anindita Ghosh, *Power in Print: Popular Publishing and the Politics of Language and Culture in a Colonial Society, 1778–1905* (New Delhi: Oxford University Press, 2006), and Ulrike Stark, "Hindi Publishing in the Heart of an Indo-Persian Cultural Metropolis: Lucknow's Newal Kishore Press (1858–1895)," in *India's Literary History: Essays on the Nineteenth Century*, ed. Stuart Blackburn and Vasudha Dalmia (Delhi: Permanent Black, 2004).

247. Alexandre Bennigsen and Chantal Lemercier-Quelquejay, *La presse et le mouvement national chez les Musulmans de Russie avant 1920* (Paris: Mouton, 1964), and Adeeb Khalid, "Printing, Publishing, and Reform in Tsarist Central Asia," *International Journal of Middle East Studies* 26, 2 (1994): 187–200.

248. Adam H. Becker, *Revival and Awakening: American Evangelical Missionaries in Iran and the Origins of Assyrian Nationalism* (Chicago: University of Chicago Press, 2015), chap. 3. On multilingual

late Ottoman printing, see Johann Strauss, "Kütüp ve Resail-i Mevkute: Printing and Publishing in a Multi-Ethnic Society," in *Late Ottoman Society: The Intellectual Legacy,* ed. Elizabeth Özdalga (London: Routledge, 2005).

249. On Indian book exports to Iran, see Nile Green, *Bombay Islam: The Religious Economy of the West Indian Ocean, 1840–1915* (New York: Cambridge University Press, 2011), chap. 4, and Afshin Marashi, "Parsi Textual Philanthropy: Print Commerce and the Revival of Zoroastrianism in Early 20th-Century Iran," in *India and Iran in the Longue Durée,* ed. Alka Patel and Touraj Daryaee (Irvine, CA: UCI Jordan Center for Persian Studies, 2017). On later developments, see Afshin Marashi, "Print-Culture and Its Publics: A Social History of Bookstores in Tehran, 1900–1950," *International Journal of Middle East Studies* 47, 1 (2015): 89–108.

250. The *locus classicus* for this argument remains Benedict Anderson, *Imagined Communities: Reflections on the Origin and Spread of Nationalism,* rev. ed. (London: Verso, 1991).

251. Alexandre Bennigsen and Chantal Quelquejay, *The Evolution of the Muslim Nationalities of the USSR and Their Linguistic Problems* (Oxford: Central Asian Research Centre, 1961), and Michael Bruchis, "The Effect of the USSR's Language Policy on the National Languages of Its Turkic Population," in *The USSR and the Muslim World: Issues in Domestic and Foreign Policy,* ed. Yaacov Ro'i (London: George Allen & Unwin, 1984).

252. John R. Perry, "Differential Assimilation of Some Arabic Loanwords in Tajik and Uzbek," *Folia Slavica* 7, 1–2 (1984): 268–82, and Perry, "Script and Scripture: The Three Alphabets of Tajik Persian, 1927–1997," *Journal of Central Asian Studies* 2, 1 (1997): 2–18.

253. On the Uyghurs, see David Brophy, *Uyghur Nation: Reform and Revolution on the Russia-China Frontier* (Cambridge MA: Harvard University Press, 2016). On the Hui, and the decline of Persian among them, see Masumi Matsumoto, "Secularization and Modernization of Islam in China: Educational Reform, Japanese Occupation, and the Disappearance of Persian Learning," in *Islamic Thought in China: Sino-Muslim Intellectual Evolution from the 17th to the 21st Century,* ed. Jonathan Lipman (Edinburgh: Edinburgh University Press, 2016). On Iranian contact with China in this period, and the place of Persian within it, see Nile Green, "From the Silk Road to the Railroad (and Back): The Means and Meanings of the Iranian Encounter with China," *Iranian Studies* 48, 2 (2015): 165–92.

254. Senzil Nawid, "Language Policy in Afghanistan: Linguistic Diversity and National Unity," in *Language Policy and Language Conflict,* ed. Schiffman and Spooner.

255. The evolution of Iranian nationalist thought is neatly contextualized in Firoozeh Kashani-Sabet, "Cultures of Iranianness: The Evolving Polemic of Iranian Nationalism," in *Iran and the Surrounding World: Interactions in Culture and Cultural Politics,* ed. Nikki Keddie and Rudi Matthee (Seattle: University of Washington Press, 2002).

256. Matthew C. Smith, "Literary Connections: Bahār's *Sabkshenāsi* and the *Bāzgasht-e Adabi,*" *Journal of Persianate Studies* 2, 2 (2009): 194–209. For a longer and more complex interrogation of this concept, see Kevin Schwartz, "Bâzgasht-i Adabî (Literary Return) and Persianate Literary Culture in Eighteenth and Nineteenth Century Iran, India, and Afghanistan" (PhD diss., University of California, Berkeley, 2014).

257. Ludwig Paul, "Iranian Language Reform in the Twentieth Century: Did the First Farhangestān (1935–40) Succeed?" *Journal of Persianate Studies* 3 (2010): 78–103.

258. Nile Green, "Introduction," in *Afghanistan in Ink: Literature between Diaspora and Nation,* ed. Green and Nushin Arbabzadah (New York: Columbia University Press, 2012) and Brian Spooner, "Persian, Farsi, Dari, Tajiki: Language Names and Language Policies," in *Language Policy and Language Conflict,* ed. Schiffman and Spooner.

259. How to conceptualize this "post-Persianate" era is briefly theorized in Mana Kia and Afshin Marashi, "Introduction: After the Persianate," *Comparative Studies of South Asia, Africa and the Middle East* 36, 3 (2016): 373–83.

260. See Green, *Making Space.*

261. Francis Robinson. *Jamal Mian: The Life of Maulana Jamaluddin Abdul Wahab of Farangi Mahall, 1919–2012* (Karachi: Oxford University Press, 2017), 336.

PART ONE

Pan-Eurasian Expansions, ca. 1400–1600

Imperial Ambitions, Mystical Aspirations

Persian Learning in the Ottoman World

Murat Umut Inan

The preface to the 1504 commentary on the introduction to the *Gulistan* (Rose Garden) of Sa'di (d. 1292) of the Ottoman scholar Lami'i Çelebi (d. 1532), a Naqshbandi Sufi translator of the Timurid-era Sufi poet 'Abd al-Rahman Jami (d. 1492), begins:

It should be known that Persian is a language built upon beauty and elegance. Dari is another name of Persian. Lexicographers explain the reason [why Persian is also called Dari] as follows: Bahram Gur forbade the people in his palace to speak in Persian and to write the letters and edicts in Persian. Because at that time the language became associated with his palace, people called it Dari. . . . Since this language is founded on elegance, its alphabet does not include many letters [that are found in the Arabic alphabet]. First, it does not have the letter "s" [ث]. Second, it does not have the letter "h" [ح]. The words that are pronounced in this language with "h" [ح] are either of Arabic origin or borrowed from another language or have been corrupted by common use. The word "hiz" [حیز], which is a common word in Persian, means catamite. This word was originally spelled with "h" [ه], but people have corrupted the word, pronounced it harshly and spelled it with "h" [ح]. As a matter of fact, if one looks at Asadi Tusi's [d. 1072–73] *Mustashhadat* [Evidences], Hindushah Nakhichawani's [d. ca. 1375] *Sihah al-Furs* [Correct Meanings of Persian Words], or at the works of Qatran Urumawi [d. ca. 1072] and Shams Fakhri [d. unknown], may God have mercy on them, one can see that these scholars note that the original word is "hiz" [هیز].[1]

Designed as a textbook for Ottoman students, Lami'i's text is an early example of a growing corpus of commentaries produced for the teaching and study of Persian language and belles lettres in the Ottoman Empire. The passage above reflects Lami'i's erudite engagement with Persian language: his references to the oldest dictionaries of Persian are eye-catching in terms of showing the way an Ottoman scholar of Persian language and literature connects his work to the scholarship produced in Central Asia and Iran. Based in Bursa, the first Ottoman capital, which was the final destination of the trade caravans coming from Tabriz, a city in the northwest of Iran, Lami'i Çelebi enjoyed and was influenced by the Persian atmosphere in the city, which gave him access to many Persian artifacts and books, including fine copies of Persian literary classics. As such, Lami'i Çelebi's life and work present a telling example of the close literary, cultural, and scholarly ties the Ottomans had with the broader geographies of "Persographia," a world interconnected by Persian literacy.[2]

The wide presence and influence of the Persian language in the Ottoman Empire is well known and has been repetitively pointed out in scholarship, from Orientalist philology to modern studies.[3] Some basic, yet critical, questions have remained largely unexplored, however. For example, what interested a scholar like Lami'i Çelebi, or the Ottomans in general, in Persian? How and for what purposes did they study or teach the language? And on a larger scale, how and why was Persian gradually incorporated into Ottoman language, literature, scholarship, and culture? This chapter explores these questions by mapping out the reception of Persian in the Ottoman world between 1400 and 1800, an overarching period during which Persian learning gradually gained momentum in various circles in the Ottoman capital and beyond. In charting a history of Ottoman engagements with the language, the chapter focuses on the work of major Ottoman Persianists, namely those scholars who devoted most of their time to the study and teaching of Persian and produced a range of learning materials for Ottoman students and readers, and particularly seeks to shed light on the contexts of Persian learning and to understand the motivations of the teachers and students of Persian.

The following pages argue that the Ottoman interest in Persian went beyond a fascination with the richness and beauty of the language but was rather informed predominantly by imperial intentions and mystical aspirations. For the flowering of Persian learning in the Ottoman world coincides with the launching of literary, artistic, and intellectual projects in the fifteenth century by Murad II (r. 1421–51) and his son Mehmed II (r. 1451–81) who, along with the imperial elite, not only showed particular interest in Persian but also encouraged and sponsored the study and appropriation of the language and its culture by scholars and literati. Pursued by the Ottoman dynasty for generations, these projects arguably contributed, among other things, to creating and cultivating an imperial language, identity, and culture for an empire both modeled on and in competition with the Arabic and Persian worlds, and particularly with the latter. Alongside this imperial reception, there developed a mystical interest in Persian, which is perhaps the second major phenomenon that paved the way for the efflorescence of Persian learning in the Ottoman world. On the one hand, Ottoman mystical orders took the Persian tradition as a model and established close relations with Persian schools of mysticism, which gave rise to an exchange of texts and scholars between the Ottoman lands, Iran, and Central Asia. This vibrant mystical network contributed to, and kept alive, a broader Ottoman interest in the language as well as in Persian mystical literature and culture. On the other hand, within the Ottoman mystical canon itself, the Mawlawi and Naqshbandi orders, in particular, took the lead in promoting the study of the language through instruction in the classics of Persian mysticism.

The next section begins by discussing the imperial aspects of the appropriation of Persian in the Ottoman world with examples from the mid-fifteenth to the late sixteenth century, a period during which the Ottoman state became an empire. On the one hand, the discussion draws attention to the way in which Persian, along with Arabic, was increasingly integrated into Turkish in the making of an imperial language. On the other hand, the discussion highlights how mastery of Persian reading and writing became an indispensable component of Ottoman imperial identity. Finally, the chapter turns to the careers and works of a sample selection of Ottoman Persianists, placing an emphasis on their connections with imperial and mystical circles of Persian learning.

A NEW LANGUAGE AND IDENTITY
FOR A NEW EMPIRE

The rise of Persian in the *diyar-ı Rum* (Land of Rome), which is to say Ottoman Anatolia and Rumelia (i.e., the Balkans), begins in the second half of the fifteenth century, when Sultan Mehmed II, following in the footsteps of his father, Murad II, encouraged the crafting of an Ottoman imperial identity, designated as *Rumi* (literally, "the one from Rum") and *Rumiyan* (plural of *Rumi*, "people of Rum").[4] This identity-making process involved a language inspired by the literary and bureaucratic vernacular of Persia. Determined to foster the creation of a new language and literary-artistic culture for his blossoming court in Istanbul, Mehmed II urged those under his patronage to engage with the models offered by Persian cultural capitals such as Shiraz and Tabriz, and particularly by the Timurid court of Husayn Bayqara (r. 1469–1506) in Herat in what is today northwestern Afghanistan. The writings of two famous Timurid figures associated with Bayqara's court held sway on the Ottoman court and high culture as well as on Istanbul's mystical scene: the language and style of the bureaucrat, scholar, and poet ʿAli Shir Nawaʾi (1441–1501) were perused and emulated by court literati, and those of the Naqshbandi scholar and poet ʿAbd al-Rahman Jami, who was invited to Istanbul by Mehmed II, were widely embraced in Sufi circles.[5]

Called alternatively *lisan-ı Türki, zeban-ı Türki* (both meaning "Turkish language"), *lisan-ı Rum,* or *zeban-ı Rum* (both meaning "the language of Rum"), the new language of the Ottomans was infused with extensive borrowings from Arabic and especially from Persian. It functioned as an imperial language in the sense that it served for centuries as the language particularly of the Ottoman court, bureaucracy, diplomacy, and literature.[6] Beginning in the mid-fifteenth century, the language was gradually developed in the hands of Ottoman bureaucrats, historians, and literati, who turned to Persian models to create and enrich a literary and chancery language through lexical appropriations, syntactic adaptations, and stylistic reworkings. The outcome was an amalgam of Turkish, Arabic, and Persian that was celebrated as a language fit for an empire that laid claim to the heritage of the Arabo-Persian world. "The language of Rum is the most beautiful, ornate, sparkling, and elegant of all languages," the Ottoman court historian Ta'likizade (d. 1606?) states in the preface to his *Şehname-i Hümayun* (Imperial Book of Kings). This, he implies, is thanks to its reception and blending of the rhetorical and artistic resources of Arabic and Persian. Drawing a parallel between the language and its users, Ta'likizade adds that the "Rumiyan" (meaning learned Ottomans) are "adorned" with the intellectual heritage of the "Arabs" and "Persians" because they are "in between." The Ottoman world is thus tied to and draws upon the Arabic and Persian worlds. Ta'likizade goes on to say that Murad III (r. 1574–95) had particularly asked him to write, not in Persian, but in the "pleasing language of Rum," which suggests that by the late sixteenth century, Ottoman Turkish, the language of Rum, was prestigious enough to compete with Persian.[7]

Ottoman Turkish is similarly portrayed in the writings of Ta'likizade's contemporaries. In biographies of Ottoman poets in his *Künhü'l-Ahbar* (Essence of Histories), for instance, the bureaucrat, historian, and litterateur Mustafa 'Ali (d. 1600) frequently touches on the significance of the hybrid language of Rum, of which he clearly saw Persian as a key component. One of the poets 'Ali discusses at length is Mehmed II's favorite vizier, poet, and adviser Ahmed Pasha (d. 1496), who, to quote the Ottoman literary critic Latifi (d. 1582), "studied books and *diwans* [poetry collections] in the Persian language carefully and extensively" in honing his poetic style and constructing a literary language furnished with "Rumi words."[8] A poet himself, 'Ali introduces Ahmed Pasha as the "forerunner of [Ottoman] poets and rhetoricians" and agrees with his contemporaries that he pioneered in adapting Persian language and poetry into the vernacular. 'Ali celebrates Ahmed as a skilled panegyrist, but nonetheless finds him insufficiently eloquent, arguing that he fails to articulate a language in which Turkish, Persian, and Arabic are harmoniously intertwined with each other. Since "the Turkish language is harsh by nature and is in every respect hardly eloquent, it should always be blended with the honey-sweet words of the Persian language and should sometimes be intermingled with the sugary expressions of the Arabic language," 'Ali says.[9] The language of Ahmed Pasha, a poet of the previous century, seemed unrefined to late sixteenth-century imperial elites, who frequently sprinkled their writings with Persian words and phrases.

By the sixteenth century, Persian increasingly permeated Ottoman Turkish, and the consensus among learned Ottomans was that the less Persianized Turkish of the preceding eras had been uncourtly and unsophisticated. Reviewing the works of the early fifteenth-century poet Şeyhi (d. after 1429) in his *Tezkiretü'ş-Şu'ara*

(Biography of Poets), for example, Latifi writes that Şeyhi's *Hüsrev ü Şirin* (Khusraw and Shirin), a romance modeled on Nizami's (1141–1209) famous romance of the same title, features some "Oghuzid [Turkic] and nomadic" words and expressions, which he finds "strange" and even "barbaric." Şeyhi should be excused for this, Latifi adds, since "at that time the Turkish language was not as elegant as it is now, and the style of the poets of the era was hardly eloquent."[10]

As Turkish was elaborated with Persian and Arabic and began to establish itself as an imperial language, there emerged a growing need to teach this language to budding scribes, secretaries, and bureaucrats of the empire. Beginning especially in the mid-fifteenth century, a series of chancery manuals appeared, featuring refined samples of letter writing in Persian as well as in the language of Rum. Highlighting the style and conventions of chancery prose, these manuals were composed by Ottoman scholars proficient in Arabic, Turkish, and especially Persian. One famous example is the *Gülşen-i İnşa* (Rose Garden of Prose Writing) by Mahmud ibn Edhem (d.?), an Ottoman Naqshbandi scholar of Arabic and Persian, written in 1496 and presented to Sultan Bayezid II (r. 1481–1512). In the preface to his manual, Mahmud ibn Edhem remarks that he studied all the "major books" and "famous letters" by the masters of chancery writing in preparing his work, an indication that he was inspired by Persian and Arabic chancery models.[11] Unsurprisingly, those who became famous for their skills in bureaucratic and diplomatic language were often promoted. One important example is the case of Karamani Mehmed Pasha (d. 1481), one of Mehmed II's favorite bureaucrats, who later became his grand vizier. For many years, Mehmed Pasha worked closely with the sultan, and advised him on the making of laws and on structuring the empire's bureaucracy, playing a key role in the early stages of the making of a bureaucratic language and culture for the emerging empire. Also a trilingual poet with lineage ties to Jalal al-Din Rumi, Mehmed Pasha patronized literary composition, which spurred the poets in his entourage to hone a poetic language interwoven with Persian. Mehmed Pasha was noted by his contemporaries for his dexterity with the language of Rum and for his mastery of prose writing. In particular, the style and language of a diplomatic letter he composed in Turkish and sent on behalf of Mehmed II in response to a Persian letter from the Aqqoyunlu ruler Uzun Hasan (r. 1453–78) was greatly admired by courtiers and bureaucrats, so much so that he was promoted to the grand vizierate.[12] Mehmed Pasha's enviable command of the language had a long-standing impact on later generations of Ottoman bureaucrats. A century later, for instance, the Ottoman bureaucrat and historian Feridun Ahmed (d. 1583) included a copy of Mehmed Pasha's ornate letter in bureaucratic Turkish in his *Münşeatü's-Selatin* (Correspondence of Sultans), a collection of writings presented as exemplars of high-style Turkish and Persian prose, including diplomatic letters, imperial edicts, and warrants. Even a fastidious figure like Mustafa ʿAli welcomed Mehmed Pasha's rich, flowing language and applauded his letter as an "eloquent" piece of writing, embellished with "artistic words."[13]

Not only was Persian mined to make Turkish an imperial language, but Ottoman royalty and the elite developed a growing interest in both reading and writing it. Starting especially with the fifteenth century, Persian learning became one of the integral components of imperial training. As candidates for running a fast-growing empire with ties and networks with the Persianate and Arabic worlds, Ottoman princes were schooled in Arabic and particularly in Persian. During his princely education, Murad II regularly studied Persian with his tutor Ahmed-i Da'i (d. after 1421). Early schooling in Persian spurred Ottoman sultans to internalize the language, which they incorporated as part of their imperial identity. 'Abdülhamid-i Sivasi's *Şahname* (Book of Kings), a Persian grammar and glossary he prepared for Murad II, says that the sultan was "very enthusiastic about using Persian words in his writings and correspondence as well as in his daily speech."[14] Indeed, Ottoman sultans' interaction with the language went beyond memorizing vocabulary and learning grammar rules. Most of them developed a keen interest in Persian poetry and experimented with the works of the master poets of Persia, leading them sometimes to compose Persian verses, sometimes to incorporate Persian into their Turkish poetry, and sometimes to do both. Some Ottoman sultans, like Selim I (r. 1512–20) and his son Süleyman I (r. 1520–66), went further: they adopted pen names, regularly composed poetry, and compiled *diwan*s of their poems. Fashioning themselves as poets skilled in Persian, they frequently compared their poetry to that of Persian masters. Persian literary language and culture defined their poetic identity, which was also one of the key constituents of their imperial identity.

With the accession of Mehmed II, royal interest in Persian increased dramatically. Mehmed's reign was a time when "Persians were sought after and deeply respected," Latifi writes. The new sultan invited Persian men of letters and scholars to his court, and "on hearing this, many well-educated people from Persia came to the land of Rum."[15] As Istanbul attracted more and more Persian speakers, knowledge of the language gradually spread into all venues of the city, from the imperial palace to elite households and gradually to the wider society. One particularly significant venue of Persian learning was the palace school established by Mehmed II, the *Enderun*, where a select body of students was trained for high-rank bureaucratic, administrative, and military service. As the seventeenth-century British diplomat and historian Paul Rycaut (1628–1700) informs us, Ottoman students read Farid al-Din 'Attar's (1145–1221) *Pand-nama* (Book of Advice), Sa'di's *Gulistan* (Rose Garden) and *Bustan* (Orchard), and the *Diwan* of Hafiz of Shiraz, which were the most popular texts in the royal curriculum.[16]

Mehmed's successors followed the imperial tradition of Persian learning. Selim I and his son Süleyman were particularly ambitious to read and write in Persian. Selim was bilingual to the extent that he composed a Persian *diwan*. He was also "very fond of speaking Persian," Latifi tells us.[17] Inspired by his father, Süleyman was an avid reader of Persian literary classics and composed poetry in both

Turkish and Persian. According to Mustafa ʿAli, the sultan tried his hand in Persian poetry to acquire "a refined disposition," both as a poet and as a member of Ottoman royalty, which implies that in the eyes of a member of the Rumi elite like ʿAli, Persian learning was seen as essential for courtliness.[18] The extensive military campaigns in Persia launched by Selim and Süleyman opened the door to a significant number of Persian-speaking scholars, artists, and literati, who relocated to the Ottoman capital particularly from Tabriz and its environs. As more and more Persian speakers moved in, Istanbul became a full-fledged imperial metropolis, where Persian enjoyed wide usage and prestige.[19] In the case of both sultans, the interest in Persia and Persian was driven by, among other things, an imperial ambition to create a Rumi language, literature, and arts that were meant to supersede the Persian models. Sultan Selim's intention to make Istanbul a center of Persian learning and of craftsmanship inspired by the Persianate world is shown in an anecdote recorded by the sixteenth-century Ottoman poet and biographer ʿAşık Çelebi. Visiting the sultan after his return from the Tabriz campaign, Hayali Çelebi, one of Selim's close companions, found him downhearted and asked him why he was low-spirited. "We arrived in the land of the Persians and forced the talented ones to emigrate to the land of Rum," the sultan replied angrily. "My goal was that the talented men of Rum would surpass the Persians and achieve high rank in arts and crafts. But I hear that people still consult Persian masters, and that they feel ashamed to consult the Rumis. . . . It seems there is no one [among the learned Rumis] who can beat the Persians as I beat the [Safavid] king." Upon hearing these words, Hayali cited many examples to prove that Ottomans had produced works that would rival and even outshine those of the Persians, saying: "Oh my sultan, under the shadow of your felicity, Istanbul is now like Tabriz."[20] With Istanbul turning into a Persian city like Tabriz, knowledge of Persian became almost a necessity, and a cadre of scholars specializing in Persian grammar, literature, and rhetoric emerged, who produced a spectrum of texts tailored to diverse needs and interests.

OTTOMAN PERSIANISTS: CANONIZATION AND DIVERSIFICATION

Ahmed-i Daʿi (d. after 1421), a gifted writer of both Persian and Turkish poetry, joined the Ottoman court at Edirne (formerly Adrianople) in eastern Thrace during the reign of Mehmed I (r. 1413–21). The first major Ottoman scholar of Persian, Daʿi was responsible for the education of Mehmed' son, the future Murad II, and inspired the latter's deep interest in Persian language and literature.[21] Daʿi's *Müfredat* (Basics), one of the earliest Ottoman Persian manuals, was intended as an elementary textbook. It consists of two main parts, which are preceded by a preface, in which Daʿi observes that "in the cities of Rum" knowledge of Persian grammar is poor, both lexically and semantically. A common complaint of the learned men of the time is that few people care about the correct use of Persian, he adds, and his friends and colleagues had therefore encouraged him to write this textbook illustrating correct Persian grammar and including a glossary of words frequently used in the works of Persian men of letters, which he hopes "beginners" (*mübtediyan*) will find helpful.[22] The first part of the manual features two Persian-Turkish glossaries, a thematic glossary followed by a glossary of the most common Persian verbs, while the second part is devoted to the rudiments of Persian grammar. Da'i concludes: "This much is enough for beginners. If they would like to acquire more information, they should study the works of men of eloquence and the *diwan*s of poets, so that they can advance [their Persian]."[23] Textbooks and glossaries are for novices, he observes; Persian poetry and rhetoric are for advanced students.

In the mid-to-late fifteenth century, men sponsored by Mehmed II and his son Bayezid II come to prominence in Ottoman scholarship. Lütfullah Halimi (d. shortly after 1497), who in his youth traveled to Iran to receive his scholarly training in Islamic jurisprudence and mysticism and to improve his Persian and acquire familiarity with Persian scholarship, was perhaps the most celebrated Persianist of the time. Upon his return, Halimi began working on his *Bahrü'l-Garayib* (Ocean of Subtleties), a three-part compendium of the Persian language, which he completed in 1446. The first part is a dictionary in verse where 2,930 Persian words are followed by their Turkish equivalents. The second part is a concise handbook that covers a variety of topics, ranging from the Persian calendar and astrology to literary genres and figures of speech. The last part features a manual of Persian prosody, to which is appended an elementary grammar of the language. As such, *Bahrü'l-Garayib* is a multifaceted text and the first of its kind in the Ottoman world, aiming to provide a basic yet thorough guide to the language for students of Persian, whom Halimi calls "nightingales in school gardens." Besides the dictionary he included in his *Bahrü'l-Garayib,* Halimi compiled the first comprehensive Persian-Turkish dictionary in alphabetical order, *Lügat-i Halimi* (Halimi's Dictionary), listing 6,060 Persian words with Turkish glosses. His works, particularly his *Lügat,* quickly enjoyed popularity and wide circulation, and Halimi attracted the attention of court circles, whereupon Mehmed II appointed him to tutor his son Bayezid (1447–1512), then the governor of Amasya, a city in northern Turkey. In 1467, Halimi prepared an abridged version of his *Lügat* for Bayezid. As the abundance of the manuscript copies suggests, the reception of Halimi's *Lügat* went well beyond his own time. It became not only a major scholarly text, frequently referenced by later generations of Ottoman Persianists, but also a canonical textbook that would be used by teachers and students of Persian for centuries.[24]

In the first half of the sixteenth century, Persian learning spread well beyond the courtly and princely setting and thrived mainly in three sociocultural spaces. The first was the Naqshbandi community based in the city of Bursa. This vibrant community of Persian learning formed around the Naqshbandi poet, translator and scholar Lami'i Çelebi (d. 1532), who was inspired by the writings of 'Abd al-Rahman Jami. For readers who lacked knowledge of Persian, Lami'i translated a series of Persian literary and mystical classics including Jami's hagiographical compilation *Nafahat al-Uns* (Breezes of Intimacy), and his allegorical romance *Salaman and Absal*. The text Lami'i used for Persian instruction was the introductory portion of Sa'di's *Gulistan,* on which he wrote a commentary designed specifically to assist his students working with Sa'di's text and, more generally, to cater to those studying Persian grammar and vocabulary. For elementary classroom instruction, Lami'i compiled a Persian-Turkish glossary in verse form to help schoolboys memorize basic Persian vocabulary, *Lügat-i Manzume* (Glossary in Verse).[25]

The community gathered around the Mawlawi Sufi master and scholar Şahidi İbrahim Dede (1470–1550) was the second major Ottoman focus of Persian learning. In a range of Mawlawi circles, from Muğla, his native town located in the southwest of Turkey, to Konya, the hub of the Mawlawi order in central Anatolia, Şahidi regularly taught Rumi's *Masnawi* (Spiritual Verses) and interpreted the text for audiences eager for spiritual growth. In 1515, Şahidi prepared a Persian-Turkish glossary in verse for schoolboys and beginning students receiving a Mawlawi education, *Tuhfe-i Şahidi* (Gift of Şahidi), which contains a significant number of words from *Masnawi*. After the glossary, as a guide for advanced students and readers of Persian wanting to get into Rumi's text, Şahidi started working on *Gülşen-i Tevhid* (Rose Garden of Unity), a commentary in verse on selected parts of *Masnawi,* which he composed in Persian and completed in 1530. For the same students and readers, Şahidi authored another Persian commentary, this time on *Gulistan,* in which he glossed and annotated Sa'di's text in Persian. Among his works, it was *Tuhfe* that brought Şahidi recognition in the Ottoman world of Persian learning and had an influence far beyond his own time: it remained a popular work that attracted commentaries from instructors and scholars and was eventually printed in the nineteenth century.[26]

Madrasa-based circles formed the third strand of Persian learning in the early sixteenth-century Ottoman world, a strand in which the works of the polymath Kemalpaşazade (1469–1534) loomed large.[27] A preeminent scholar and madrasa professor, Kemalpaşazade was born into a distinguished family with Iranian roots on his mother's side. He began learning Persian at an early age in Amasya, where he was taught by notable scholars and studied *Gulistan* and presumably Halimi's *Bahrü'l-Garayib,* which was already circulating in the city at that time. Given that one of his Persian works, *Nigaristan* (Garden of Images), draws the inspiration for its title and content from *Gulistan,* Sa'di's text seems to have had an enduring influence on Kemalpaşazade's immersion in Persian learning. As we can also tell from the preface to his *Risale-i Yaiyye,* a treatise on the Persian letter ى (the long *i*), the Persian language remained an integral aspect of Kemalpaşazade's scholarly life: he not only engaged in discussions with his colleagues about grammatical issues, but devoted part of his oeuvre to Persian linguistics. His most famous work in this regard is *Dakayıku'l-Hakayık* (Subtleties of Truth), a handbook of Persian homonyms, synonyms, and antonyms, where each entry is amply glossed in Ottoman Turkish, with examples from Persian poetry. Halimi's *Bahrü'l-Garayib* was one of the main sources Kemalpaşazade relied on in preparing his handbook, though we frequently find him criticizing his predecessor's semantic glosses. One particular feature of *Dakayık* is that, while explaining the phonetic, semantic, and morphological aspects of the Persian words, Kemalpaşazade employs Arabic grammatical terms freely and frequently. Presented to Süleyman I's grand vizier Ibrahim Pasha (ca. 1493–1536), the handbook remained in high demand not only by courtly audiences but by madrasa scholars and students of Persian, such that in 1550 a new edition was prepared by a scholar from Skopje in Macedonia, who now organized Kemalpaşazade's text alphabetically for easy reference. The second text Kemalpaşazade compiled for Persian instruction was a manual entitled *Kava'idü'l-Fürs* (Rules of Persian), which is the first Persian grammar written in the Ottoman world not in Turkish but in Arabic. Besides these two texts, Kemalpaşazade also wrote two treatises on Persian, *Risale-i Yaiyye* (Treatise on the Letter *Y*) and *Maziyyat al-Lisan al-Farisi 'ala Sair al-Alsinat ma Khala al-'Arabiyyat* (Virtues of Persian over Other Languages except Arabic). The former, written in Ottoman Turkish and replete with Arabic terms, is an in-depth study of the diverse and often puzzling grammatical functions of the Persian adjective suffix –*i*, while the latter, penned in Arabic, presents an overview of the history, culture, and languages of Persia and argues with examples that the world's most important and richest lingua franca after Arabic is Persian. Obviously, Kemalpaşazade's Ottoman Turkish titles presumed an audience familiar with Arabic grammatical terminology, and presumably his Turkish-speaking madrasa students were acquainted with Arabic. His Arabic titles, on the other hand, seem to be introductory works intended for madrasa students and scholars from the Arab lands now claimed by the empire, who were new to Persian but eager to study the language out of personal interest or for intellectual reasons.[28]

In the second half of the sixteenth century, the Ottoman interest in Persian continued to flourish, but now with an unprecedented momentum, particularly thanks to three teachers of Persian specializing in commentary writing, Muslihüddin Süruri (1491–1562), Şem'ullah Şem'i (d. ca. 1603), and Ahmed Sudi (d. ca. 1600), who resided in Istanbul, authored commentaries devoted to the analysis and translation of Persian classics, and became canonical voices in circles of Persian reading and learning across the empire. A madrasa professor with a Naqshbandi Sufi affiliation, Süruri focused on a set of four classics, Sa'di's *Bustan* and *Gulistan*, Hafiz's *Diwan*, and Rumi's *Masnawi*. In all of his commentaries, Süruri concerned himself less with Persian instruction and more with mystical education. Şem'i, a reputed Mawlawi who enjoyed close relations with the Ottoman court, not only shared the same concerns as Süruri and revisited the texts he expounded, but also expanded his predecessor's repertoire by writing mystical commentaries on new texts including Jami's *Baharistan* (Garden of Spring), 'Attar's *Mantiq al-Tayr* (Conference of the Birds) and *Pand-nama,* and Nizami's *Makhzan al-Asrar* (Treasury of Secrets). Unlike Süruri and Şem'i, Sudi did not come from a mystical milieu and was exclusively trained in Arabic and Persian philology. Born in Bosnia and educated in Istanbul, Sudi traversed the empire from Anatolia to the Arab lands to study further Arabic and Persian literary and philological works under the guidance of established scholars such as the Persian historian and philologist Muslih al-Din al-Lari (ca. 1510–72), who was then based in Amid (Diyarbakır) in southeastern Turkey. Returning to Istanbul, Sudi worked on Sa'di and Hafiz only and approached their texts from a purely grammatical perspective, immersing his readers in a thorough analysis of the phonetic, morphological, semantic, and syntactic features of *Bustan, Gulistan,* and *Diwan* while criticizing his predecessors' interpretations. Once a Persian tutor at the Ibrahim Pasha Palace School in Istanbul, one of the leading imperial institutions where outstanding slave boys recruited into the Ottoman service were educated, Sudi constructed his commentaries in such a way that learners of Persian as a second language could acquire a good grasp of grammar through reading the works of classical authors. He was acclaimed, contemporaneously and posthumously, as one of the authoritative scholars of Persian, inasmuch as his texts proved accessible and appealing to a wide audience, whether beginning or advanced, mystical or not. Perhaps one of the most noteworthy things about Sudi's commentaries is that they provide a framework with which to map the diverse contours of Persian learning in the Ottoman world up to the 1600s, since his texts include references to and citations from predecessor scholars, including not only Süruri and Şem'i but also almost all the other Persianists traced here so far.[29] What is also noteworthy about his commentaries is that they were well received particularly in the Balkans, which constituted one of the vibrant frontiers of the Ottoman world of Persian learning. Before moving on to the post-1600s, it is therefore worth pausing here to take a brief look at the spread and influence of Persian in the Ottoman Balkans, which the Ottomans called Rumili (Rumelia).

Though Persian learning was widespread across the Balkans, certain cities were distinguished by their long-standing traditions in the study of the Persian language and classics. One of these cities was Sudi's hometown, Saraybosna (Sarajevo), where he first encountered the Persian language as a young boy while attending a local school, as revealed by an anecdote found in his commentary on *Gulistan.*[30] Sudi's case was far from being unique: a significant number of Ottoman Persianists who made their careers in Istanbul received their early Persian training in Saraybosna.[31] Located to the southwest of Sarajevo, the town of Mostar was the second major locus of Persian learning, which owed its status mainly to the patronage of Derviş Paşa (d. 1603), one of Sudi's students from Mostar who graduated from the Ibrahim Pasha Palace school and became an imperial bureaucrat under Murad III. In particular, the *waqf* (pious endowment) complex established by Derviş Paşa in the heart of Mostar attracted students and scholars of Persian from across Rumelia: the madrasa attached to the *waqf* offered Persian classes, and its library was famous for its rich collection of Persian classics and learning materials, including Sudi's commentaries.[32] On the other hand, the Mawlawi lodge in the same complex offered instruction in Persian grammar and mystical literature. One notable teacher who created a legacy that lasted for generations was Shaykh Fevzi of Mostar (d. 1747), who completed his Sufi training in Istanbul before returning to elucidate and translate the *Masnawi* for the Mawlawi community in his home town. Vardar Yenicesi (or Yenice-i Vardar, now Giannitsa, in northern Greece), on the other hand, was a city where Persian was not only taught and studied but was also widely spoken.[33] The Persian spoken in the town and across Rumelia differed from formal Persian in accent and vocabulary, to such an extent that the Ottomans called it *Rumili Farsisi* (Rumelian Persian).[34] Since Vardar Yenicesi was frequented by students, scholars, and literati, a rich Persianate linguistic and literary culture quickly sprang up there. 'Aşık Çelebi (1520–72), an Ottoman poet and literary scholar from Prizren in what is today Kosovo, was very impressed by the Persian-speaking and -writing communities of the city, which he called a "hotbed of Persian."[35]

The post-1600 era saw no decline in the Ottoman interest in Persian. New scholars appeared and new materials were produced for contemporary learners and readers, gradually creating a new canon. Representatives of the pre-1600 tradition nevertheless continued to have an influence, providing models for new teachers of Persian, who not only studied and taught their works but drew on them in writing their own books. Audiences, too, remained under the spell of some, if not all, texts of the pre-1600 era. As we learn from the preface of an eighteenth-century manuscript, for instance, Sudi's commentary on Hafiz remained unmatched as late as 1794, when it was considered "the best commentary" providing a full discussion of all aspects of the Persian language.[36]

The post-1600 era opens with the writings of the Mawlawi scholar Isma'il Ankaravi (d. 1631) who was famed for his commentary on *Masnawi*, which played a central part in his teaching and scholarship. Ankaravi first experienced Rumi's text through Şahidi's *Tuhfe*, a *Masnawi* glossary he studied at an early age. Later he read and lectured on *Masnawi* to audiences attending Mawlawi gatherings in Ankara, his hometown, and Konya. During his twenty-one-year career as the chief shaykh of the famous Mawlawi convent in the Galata district of Istanbul, he regularly taught and discussed *Masnawi* in his classes, wrote treatises focusing on selections from it, and finally embarked on an extensive commentary on the whole text. Completed in 1627, the commentary quickly became a canonical text in the literature on *Masnawi*, not only remaining in vogue among Mawlawi readers and reciters across the empire but also engaging the interest of the courtly community and finally of Sultan Murad IV (r. 1623–40) who requested a fine copy of the text in 1629. Ankaravi's commentatorial approach is along the same lines as that of

Süruri and Şem'i, the two former commentators of Rumi whose writings formed a backdrop to Ankaravi's text. Interested in unearthing the esoteric meanings and divine messages layered in *Masnawi,* Ankaravi, too, concentrated his and his readers' attention not so much on the grammar of the text but rather on its translation and mystical interpretation.

Neşati Ahmed (d. 1674) followed Ankaravi as the second major Mawlawi scholar of the century. Neşati taught Persian language and poetry for many years in the Mawlawi convent in Edirne, where he compiled a concise reference grammar for his students. A poet himself, he was particularly accomplished in Persian poetry and influenced by 'Urfi of Shiraz (1555–91), whose poetry suited the taste of most seventeenth-century Ottoman poets and triggered nearly a hundred commentaries. Neşati was no exception: he compiled a commentary to translate and interpret a selection from 'Urfi's nuanced poems for Ottoman readers and students of Persian poetry who were now interested in the works of poets like 'Urfi writing in the so-called Indian style, as noted by Mirak Muhammad Naqshbandi, a Persianist from Tashkent (d. after 1613), who visited Istanbul at the turn of the seventeenth century.[37]

As the eighteenth century unfolded, a number of commentators appeared on the scholarly stage, where Isma'il Hakkı Bursevi (1653–1725) and Ebubekir Nusret (d. 1793) distinguished themselves. A Sufi exegete steeped in Islamic sciences, Bursevi came to the fore with his detailed commentary on 'Attar's guidebook of morality, *Pand-nama.* Unlike Şem'i, the former commentator of 'Attar, Bursevi paid special attention to the grammatical texture of *Pand-nama,* translated the text, and elaborated on the mystical teachings interspersed in it. Perhaps this is why Şem'i's commentary was overshadowed and gradually replaced by Bursevi's work, which became a popular classroom commentary among students and teachers of mysticism who looked for a thematic and grammatical analysis of a mystical classic like 'Attar's text. The mystical scholar and poet Ebubekir Nusret established himself as a sought-after teacher of Persian language and literature in Istanbul after 1750. Like Neşati, Nusret made an effort to move scholarship in a new direction: he focused, not on the works of poets that had been heavily studied, but on poets like Saib of Tabriz (d. 1676), whose poetry was gaining a readership in Istanbul's poetic circles, but was still left largely unexplored. Perhaps more significantly, what motivated Nusret to devote his scholarly energy to the study of Saib's poetry is better explained by the fact that Saib served as a source of inspiration for Nusret's poetic creativity and deeply shaped the language and style of his poems. As with Neşati's approach to 'Urfi, Nusret's emphasis was predominantly on the mystical meanings and imagery in Saib's poems, which he translated and explicated for the growing number of students coming to his classes, in his three commentaries on selections from the poet's *Diwan.*[38]

While almost all Persianists of the post-1600 era preferred commentary writing and were concerned less to teach their readers Persian vocabulary and grammar than to furnish them with—mostly mystical—tools of reading and interpretation, a small number of scholars adopted a different approach to Persian learning and compiled reference works with a broader audience in mind. Notable among these scholars were Hasan Şu'uri (d. 1694), Sünbülzade Vehbi (d. 1809), and Ahmed 'Asım (1755–1819), whose works on Persian-Turkish lexicography filled a long-existing lacuna in the tradition of dictionary writing, which had dwindled away since Halimi's *Lügat* and Şahidi's *Tuhfe,* the two representative lexicographical works of the pre-1600 period.

Şu'uri's comprehensive Persian-Turkish lexicon *Lisanü'l-'Acem* (Persian Language), better known as *Ferheng-i Şu'uri* (Şu'uri's Dictionary), was compiled between 1662 and 1681, drawing on a range of dictionaries from Anatolia, Iran, Central Asia, and India. One of the largest compilations in the history of Persian-Turkish lexicography, *Ferheng-i Şu'uri* was also the first Persian-Turkish dictionary to be printed in the Ottoman Empire, appearing in two volumes in Istanbul in 1742. As part of the short-lived but pioneering venture of Ibrahim Müteferrika (1674–1745), it was also one of the earliest Muslim-printed books anywhere.

Vehbi's Persian-Turkish verse glossary, *Tuhfe-i Vehbi* (Gift of Vehbi), compiled in 1783, a much smaller-scale work, reminiscent of Şahidi's 1515 glossary, reflects Vehbi's experiences and work in Isfahan and Shiraz, the two cities he visited as the Ottoman ambassador to Iran. It became immensely popular shortly after it was printed in 1798. Reprinted more than fifty times until 1909, the glossary brought Vehbi a reputation that eclipsed that of Şahidi.

Completed in 1797 and presented to Sultan Selim III (r. 1789–1808), 'Asım's translation of *Burhan-i Qati'* (Definitive Proof), a famous Persian dictionary compiled in the southern Indian city of Hyderabad in 1652 by Muhammad Husayn of Tabriz (d. unknown), made its debut in print in 1799. 'Asım's work is hardly a word-for-translation: he expanded on Muhammad Husayn's dictionary by adding new entries selected from a pile of dictionaries on his desk, including Şu'uri's *Ferheng* and Halimi's *Lügat*. With 'Asım's translation, one of the landmarks of Persian lexicography now became a text available to a broader community of learners rather than one used only by scholars. Printed four more times by 1885, the lexicographer's work captivated the Ottoman world of Persian learning for almost a century.[39]

CONCLUSIONS

The history of Persian in the Ottoman lands is intertwined with multiple histories of the empire: the language left its imprint on the linguistic, literary, and cultural histories of the Ottomans who, torn between admiration and envy, looked to Persia in the making of an empire, particularly after the conquest of Constantinople in 1453. As the Ottoman Turks learned Persian, the language and the culture it carried seeped not only into their court and imperial institutions but also into their vernacular language and culture. The appropriation of Persian, both as a second language and as a language to be steeped together with Turkish, was encouraged notably by the sultans, the ruling class, and leading members of the mystical communities. Persian learning sometimes had much to do with personal curiosity, but it was mostly interwoven with imperial ambitions and mystical aspirations. The imperial and mystical underpinnings of the Ottoman world of Persian learning were far from excluding each other. Rather, the two spaces often appeared as intersecting and interrelated, each influencing and influenced by the other. In this regard, Ottoman commentarial circles present us with a venue where the imperial and mystical spaces of Persian learning more visibly converged and intertwined: major Ottoman commentators on Persian belles-lettres, like Şemʿi, were mostly steeped in mystical tradition or had mystical affiliations, but they were also closely involved with court circles. Accordingly, works of these commentators appealed to a diverse range of audiences, including members of the imperial elite and Sufi orders.

Looking back at my survey of teachers and learners of Persian, some general conclusions can be drawn regarding different aspects of Persian teaching and learning in the Ottoman world. First, teachers of Persian came from a miscellany of backgrounds ranging from royal tutors and madrasa professors to Sufi masters, and they specialized mostly in commentary writing and translation. Secondly, learners of Persian, too, formed a diverse community, which included members of the dynasty, the imperial elite, students studying at various institutions, from palace schools and madrasas to Sufi lodges, and, last but not least, interested readers and listeners particularly inclined toward mysticism. Thirdly, Persian learning materials spanned a variety of texts, each reflecting different concerns, needs, and teaching methodologies. Grammars, glossaries, and commentaries were the most popular texts for learning and teaching Persian. Often treated as supplementary materials, these texts were devised to help students who studied or were taught Persian classics, among which the *Gulistan, Bustan, Masnawi, Pand-nama,* and Hafiz's *Diwan* formed the core of the Ottoman curriculum. Fourthly, the contexts of Persian teaching and learning present us, again, with a spectrum of practices and goals. Sometimes, as in the cases of Ahmed-i Daʿi, Kemalpaşazade, and Sudi, the context was a classroom setting, where the main purpose was to teach Persian grammar and vocabulary. Sometimes Persian learning came to mean mystical learning, as in the case, for instance, of Şemʿi or Ankaravi, who sought to edify their students, readers, or listeners morally by introducing them to the seminal texts of Persian mysticism. And sometimes these two purposes overlapped, as in the case of Bursevi. Though in most cases, students of Persian learned the language through texts and textbooks, in some cases, like those of Şahidi and Ankaravi, learning was mainly an oral activity, in which the audience was exposed to the recitation, performance, or discussion of a text in a less formal and more interactive setting.

Historically speaking, there seems to be no clear-cut difference or contrast between the pre- and post-1600 periods in the Ottoman Empire, particularly considering that there is a continuity of texts and transmission of pedagogical practices between the two periods. Nevertheless, perhaps one can make a general, if not definitive, distinction by saying that while the former period can be characterized as an age of Persian grammatical learning, the latter period presents itself more as an age of Persian mystical learning, an age brimming more with mystical readings and interpretations than with grammars and glossaries. This distinction can be explained by arguing, first, that in the post-1600s there was mostly no need for new grammars and glossaries, since those produced between 1400 and 1600 continued to be relevant and popular with students and readers, and, second, that the interests and concerns of the audiences shifted from the grammatical to the mystical, inasmuch as mysticism was in higher demand and a dominant discourse in Ottoman centers of Persian learning after 1600.

Finally, it is worth highlighting the place of the Ottoman world of Persian literacy in the broader Persographic world. On the one hand, standing at the intersection of Eastern and Western geographies of Persographia, the Ottoman world, and particularly Istanbul, seems to have functioned as a diverse hub in which students, poets, and scholars from Persia, Anatolia, and the Balkans crossed paths and influenced one another. On the other hand, the same hub also seems to have provided a network through which a range of texts, ideas, and practices circulated and were exchanged among readers, authors, and scholars of Persian. Ottoman scholarship, too, seems to be nourished and framed by this diversity, especially by the influx of philological traditions from Persia and the Arab lands. As Ottoman Persianists benefited from Arabic and Persian philological models, they introduced new works and approaches, which, in turn, traveled across the interconnected terrains of the Persianate world. This brought recognition and prestige, not only to some Ottoman scholars, like Sudi from Sarajevo, but also to the cities where they were based, among which Istanbul, unsurprisingly, ranked first. The imperial capital of the Ottomans gradually established itself as a Persographic center that exported learning and teaching materials to the wider Persianate world, as exemplified by the wide reception and influence of Ottoman scholarship in the Balkans.

NOTES

1. Lamiʿi, *Şerh-i Dibace-i Gülistan* (MS Hacı Selim Ağa 956, Hacı Selim Ağa Manuscript Library, Istanbul), folios 4a–b. Unless noted otherwise, all translations from Ottoman Turkish are mine.

2. On the term "Persographia," see Nile Green's Introduction to this volume.

3. For the ways in which the Persian influence in the Ottoman world is treated in Orientalist scholarship, see Murat Umut Inan, "Rethinking the Ottoman Imitation of Persian Poetry," *Iranian Studies* 50, 5 (2017): 671–89. For modern scholarship, see, among others, Muhammad Amin Riyahi, *Zaban wa Adab-i Farsi dar Qalamraw-i ʿUsmani* (Tehran: Pazhang, 1990), 225–37, and Ilhama Miftah and Wahhab

Wali, *Nigahi ba Rawand-i Nufuz wa Gustarish-i Zaban wa Adab-i Farsi dar Turkiya* (Tehran: Shura-yi Gustarish-i Zaban u Adabiyat-i Farsi, 1995), 161–216.

4. For the terms "Rum" and "Rumi," see Cemal Kafadar, "A Rome of One's Own: Reflections on Cultural Geography and Identity in the Lands of Rum," *Muqarnas* 24 (2007): 7–25.

5. For the influence of Timurid literary culture in the Ottoman world, see Michele Bernardini, "Ottoman Timuridism: Lami'i Çelebi and His *Şehrengiz* of Bursa," in *Irano-Turkic Cultural Contacts in the 11th–17th Centuries*, ed. Éva M. Jeremiás (Piliscsaba, Hungary: Avicenna Institute of Middle Eastern Studies, 2003),1–16. For the ways in which the works of 'Ali Shir Nawai were appropriated by Otto-man literati, see Yusuf Çetindağ, *Ali Şir Nevai'nin Osmanlı Şiirine Etkisi* (Ankara: Kültür ve Turizm Bakanlığı, 2006). On the Ottoman reception of Jami, see Hamid Algar, *Jami* (New Delhi: Oxford University Press, 2013), chap. 7. For the intellectual connections between the Ottomans and the Timurids, see İlker Evrim Binbaş, *Intellectual Networks in Timurid Iran: Sharaf al-Din 'Ali Yazdi and the Islamicate Republic of Letters* (Cambridge: Cambridge University Press, 2016), chap. 4. On the development of a Persianate court culture in the reign of Mehmed II, see Franz Babinger, *Mehmed the Conqueror and His Time*, trans. Ralph Manheim and ed. William C. Hickman (Princeton, NJ: Princeton University Press, 1978), 467–77.

6. For a history of the Turkish language under the Ottomans, see Linda Darling, "Ottoman Turkish: Written Language and Scribal Practice, 13th to 20th Centuries," in *Literacy in the Persianate World: Writing and the Social Order*, ed. Brian Spooner and William L. Hanaway (Philadelphia: University of Pennsylvania Museum, 2012), 171–95.

7. Christine Woodhead, *Ta'liki-zade's Şehname-i Hümayun: A History of the Ottoman Campaign into Hungary, 1593–94* (Berlin: Klaus Schwarz, 1983), 134.

8. Latifi: *Tezkiretü'ş-Şu'ara ve Tabsıratü'n-Nuzama*, ed. Rıdvan Canım (Ankara: Atatürk Kültür Merkezi Başkanlığı, 2000), 155–56.

9. *Künhü'l-Ahbar'ın Tezkire Kısmı*, ed. Mustafa İsen (Ankara: Atatürk Kültür Merkezi, 1994), 131.

10. *Latifi*, ed. Canım, 339–40.

11. Mahmud bin Edhem, *Gülşen-i İnşa* (MS A2276, National Library, Ankara), folio 3a.

12. *Latifi*, ed. Canım, 528–29.

13. *Künhü'l-Ahbar'ın Tezkire Kısmı*, ed. İsen, 146.

14. Yusuf Öz, *Tarih Boyunca Farsça-Türkçe Sözlükler* (Ankara: Türk Dil Kurumu, 2010), 91.

15. *Latifi*, ed. Canım, 474.

16. Paul Rycaut, *The Present State of the Ottoman Empire*, 3rd ed. (London: John Starkey and Henry Brome, 1670), 31.

17. *Latifi*, ed. Canım, 150.

18. *Künhü'l-Ahbar'ın Tezkire Kısmı*, ed. İsen, 187. For Süleyman's interest in Persian poetry, see Inan, "Rethinking the Ottoman Imitation of Persian Poetry," 674–84.

19. Ahmet Kartal, *Şiraz'dan İstanbul'a: Türk-Fars Kültür Coğrafyası Üzerine Araştırmalar* (Istanbul: Kurtuba, 2011), 447–48. For a detailed study of the cultural networks between the Ottomans and the Safavids, see Sinem Arcak, "Gifts in Motion: Ottoman–Safavid Cultural Exchange, 1501–1618" (PhD diss., University of Minnesota, 2012). The Mughal capital Lahore presents a case similar to that of Ottoman Istanbul. For comparison, see Purnima Dhavan's chapter 5 in this volume.

20. '*Aşık Çelebi: Meşa'irü'ş-Şu'ara*, ed. Filiz Kılıç, 3 vols. (Istanbul: Istanbul Araştırmaları Enstitüsü, 2010), 3: 1538–40.

21. On Da'i and his works, see İsmail Hikmet Ertaylan, *Ahmed-i Da'i: Hayatı ve Eserleri* (Istanbul: Üçler Basımevi, 1952).

22. Abdülbaki Çetin, "Ahmed-i Da'i'nin Farsça Öğretmek Amacıyla Yazdığı Bir Eser: *Müfredat*," *Selçuk Üniversitesi Türkiyat Araştırmaları Dergisi* 20 (2006): 119.

23. Ibid., 123.

24. On Halimi's works, see Öz, *Tarih Boyunca*, 94–100 and 103–9. Halimi's *Lügat* is one of the early examples of Ottoman lexicography modeled on the Persian lexicographical tradition. For a history

of Persian lexicography, see Solomon I. Baevskii, *Early Persian Lexicography: Farhangs of the Eleventh to the Fifteenth Centuries*, trans. N. Killian and ed. John R. Perry (Folkestone, England: Global Oriental, 2007).

25. On Lami'i Çelebi's life and works, see Günay Kut Alpay, "Lami'i Chelebi and His Works," *Journal of Near Eastern Studies* 35, 2 (1976): 73–93.

26. On Şahidi and his works, see Öz, *Tarih Boyunca*, 138–43. For commentaries on Şahidi's glossary, see Yusuf Öz, *Tuhfe-i Şahidi Şerhleri* (Konya: Selçuk Üniversitesi Fen-Edebiyat Fakültesi, 1999).

27. Though Persian, unlike Arabic, was not included in the typical curriculum of an Ottoman madrasa, the language was offered as an elective course or recommended for study in some madrasas. For those Ottoman madrasa curricula featuring Persian, see Cevat İzgi, *Osmanlı Medreselerinde İlim*, 2 vols. (İstanbul: İz, 1997),1: 167–69.

28. For the *Dakayıku'l-Hakayık*, see MS Amcazade Hüseyin Paşa 372, Süleymaniye Manuscript Library, Istanbul. On the *Kava'idü'l-Fürs*, see Éva M. Jeremiás, "Kamalpašazada as Linguist," in *Irano-Turkic Cultural Contacts*, ed. id., 79–110. For the Turkish and Arabic treatises, see, respectively, MS Izmir 704 and MS Murad Molla 1831, folios 352b–54b, Süleymaniye Manuscript Library.

29. On the life and works of Süruri and Şem'i, see İsmail Güleç, "Gelibolulu Musluhiddin Süruri: Hayatı, Kişiliği, Eserleri ve *Bahrü'l-Ma'arif* İsimli Eseri," *Osmanlı Araştırmaları* 21 (2001): 211–36, and Şeyda Öztürk, *Şem'i Efendi ve Mesnevi Şerhi* (Istanbul: İslam Araştırmaları Merkezi, 2011). On Sudi, see Murat Umut Inan, "Crossing Interpretive Boundaries in Sixteenth-Century Istanbul: Ahmed Sudi on the *Divan* of Hafiz of Shiraz," *Philological Encounters* 3, 3 (2018): 275-309.

30. Nazif M. Hoca, *Sudi: Hayatı, Eserleri ve İki Risalesi'nin Metni* (İstanbul: İstanbul Üniversitesi Edebiyat Fakültesi, 1980), 12.

31. On the lives and works of the Ottoman scholars from Sarajevo, see Sabaheta Gačanin, "Persian Language as Vehicle of Islamic Cultural Memory in Ottoman Bosnia," *Tarih İncelemeleri Dergisi* 31, 1 (2016): 165–75. For a survey of the reception of Persian language and literature in Bosnia, see *Danishnama-yi Adab-i Farsi: Adab-i Farsi dar Anatuli wa Balkan*, ed. Hasan Anusha, vol. 6 (Tehran: Wizarat-i Farhang wa Irshad-i Islami, 2005), s.v. "Busni wa Hirziguwin."

32. Gačanin, "Persian Language," 167.

33. On Fevzi's life and scholarship, see Hamid Algar, "Persian Literature in Bosnia-Herzegovina," *Journal of Islamic Studies* 5, 2 (1994): 260–61.

34. For references to the Persian spoken in Rumelia, see *Latifi*, ed. Canım, 541–42; *'Aşık Çelebi*, ed. Kılıç, 1: 205.

35. *'Aşık Çelebi*, ed. Kılıç, 2: 904. For a history of the city of Vardar Yenicesi, see Heath W. Lowry and İsmail E. Erünsal, *Yenice-i Vardar'lı Evrenos Hanedanı: Notlar ve Belgeler* (Istanbul: Bahçeşehir Üniversitesi Yayınları, 2010).

36. *Muhtasar-ı Şerhü's-Sudi* (MS 577, National Library, Ankara), folio 1b.

37. On the life and works of Ankaravi, see *The Oxford Encyclopedia of Philosophy, Science, and Technology in Islam*, s.v. "Anqarawi, Isma'il." For Neşati, see Bayram Ali Kaya, *Neşati* (Istanbul: Şule, 1998). For Mirak Muhammad's observations, see *Mirek Muhammed-i Taşkendi: Şehri ve Güli, Bir Şehir Bir Gül*, ed. Bahattin Kahraman and Yusuf Öz (Ankara: Akçağ, 2012), 216–17.

38. For Bursevi's commentary, see Kezban Paksoy, "Bursevi İsmail Hakkı: *Şerh-i Pend-i Attar* (İnceleme-Metin-Sözlük)" (PhD diss., Erciyes University, 2012). For Nusret's, see Osman Ünlü, "Ebubekir Nusret'in Saib-i Tebrizi Şerhleri," *Turkish Studies* 4, 6 (2009): 442–55.

39. For the works of the three lexicographers, see Öz, *Tarih Boyunca*, 204–9, 245–49, and 251–53.

2

Persian at the Court or in the Village?

The Elusive Presence of Persian in Bengal

Thibaut d'Hubert

Persian[,] which was closely connected with the life of the court, does not seem to have had any direct impact on the ordinary people, nor could it produce literature of any importance in our period.
MOMTAZUR RAHMAN TARAFDAR, HUSAIN SHAHI BENGAL, 1494–1538

When listening to Persian from someone else's mouth, one cannot understand properly and be content.
ʿABD AL-HAKIM, NUR-NAMA (BOOK OF LIGHT, CA. 1660)

The available historiography of Persian in Bengal tells the story of travelling saints, men of letters, and political elites, with occasional signs of indigenization; or else it tells of its opposite: a fierce resistance to identifying the Bengali environment with the Persianate cultural ethos.[1] Then, we have the influential historiographical notion of the influence of Persian on Bengali language and culture, which appears as the natural outcome of the cultural hegemony of Persianate elites in the region.[2] In such narratives, Persian belongs to the cosmopolitan elite. Correspondingly, the Bengali expression of whatever is Persian is primarily seen as a matter of translation, usually performed by some intermediary figures located between the elite and the lower, vernacular strata of Bengal's society.[3] This schema foregrounds narratives of successive colonizations and the attempts by vernacular agents to negotiate with hegemonic cultures so as to survive and elevate their status. Part of this historiographical narrative can indeed be verified in the primary sources that have come down to us. But as one might expect, a closer look at the economy of Persian in Bengal reveals a more complex situation, which points to many unanswered questions. This chapter provides a critical survey of the primary evidence available for the scope and character of Persian use in Bengal, particularly during the fifteenth and sixteenth centuries prior to the Mughal conquest of the region during the 1570s.

In addition to providing a synthetic overview of the available sources for the study of Persian in Bengal, the following pages revisit the historical narrative of the presence of Perso-Arabic learning in the Bengal frontier of the Persianate world.[4] The chapter dwells on two cases that are representative of the issues surrounding the history of Persian in the region. The first case study invites us to reconsider how the sultanate of Bengal was integrated into the geography of the Persian-using world, while the second case study looks at the presence of Persian outside the court, in the remote rural areas of eastern Bengal in Noakhali, Chittagong, and Sylhet.

It is sometimes instructive to tread the paths of previous scholarly traditions, and in the present case to have a fresh look at *the* quote that located Bengal on the map of Bert Fragner's *Persophonie* in the fourteenth century. No piece of scholarship dealing with Persian in the Indian subcontinent generally or in Bengal specifically would omit to quote the following verse by Hafiz of Shiraz:

> *Shakkar-shikan shawand hama tutiyan-i hind/z'in qand-i parsi ki ba bangala mi-rawad*

All the parrots of India started crushing sugar/this Persian candy that goes to Bengal.

This verse became emblematic of the Persianization of South Asia's Muslim courts. Already in premodern times, commentators strove to locate the poet's ghazal within a specific historical context. This contextualization of Hafiz's poem would later become a landmark in the historiography of Persian in the Bengal sultanate (1205–1574) and the ultimate proof of the patronage of Persian literature at that regional court. The problem is that this prestigious poetic anecdote is a rather isolated clue. As we shall see below in further detail, this one poem and the commentaries that surround its reception tell us more about the perception of the expanding geography of poetic patronage than about the actual cultivation of Persian in Bengal.

The subsequent section of the chapter then turns to a later period of Bengal's history and to the eastern margins of the province. It studies a body of texts that contrast with the previous example to show how deeply the Persian language had penetrated into rural areas by the seventeenth century. After a brief overview of the use of Persian in didactic religious literature, the analysis focuses on the anonymous Persian *Nur-nama* and its several Bengali versions. The chapter argues that both the Persian and the Bengali texts testify to the formation of a regional Islamic idiom in Bengal. We shall also see that the topic of cultural and linguistic hegemony, although present in the discourse of the Bengali translators, offers a wide range of possible attitudes to Persian. What *Nur-nama* clearly shows is the availability of a little-known corpus of "popular" Persian texts that were instrumental in the religious instruction and ritual life of Bengali Muslims.

THE ELUSIVE PRESENCE OF PERSIAN IN BENGAL

Historians have highlighted the fact that, until the late Mughal or the early British period—that is the mid-eighteenth century—we lack a consistent and substantive body of Persian sources on the basis of which one could write the political and cultural history of Persianate Bengal.[5] This observation could also apply to belles-lettres: judging from the available texts from that period and from the *tazkira* (anthology) literature, no noteworthy Persian poet seems to have received the patronage of Bengali sultans.[6] Only one manuscript of Nizami's *Sharaf-nama* testifies to the cultivation of calligraphy and miniature paintings based on classics of Persian poetry in Bengal's royal ateliers.[7] On the other hand, religious literature is fairly well represented in the corpus of Persian texts from Bengal.[8] Among the oft-mentioned sources from that period are the letters and treatises of the Chishti saint of Pandua, Nur Qutb-i 'Alam (d. 1415).[9] The works of this Chishti Sufi are extremely valuable sources about the cultivation of Persian in urban elite milieus in the Bengali sultanate. They have been mostly used by historians for the information they contain about the conflicts surrounding the accession to the throne of Raja Ganesh after the death of the Ilyas Shahi ruler, and Nur Qutb-i 'Alam's role as the spiritual master of Bengali sultans.[10] Stone inscriptions also provide further pieces of the puzzle, but it is worth noting that until the Mughal period these were mainly in Arabic and therefore provide little positive information about the status of Persian under the Bengali sultans.[11]

What can be gathered from the sultanate period shows that Persian was mainly used in urban centers—that is in Gaur, Pandua (near Malda in today's Indian state of West Bengal), and Sonargaon further east (near Dhaka in today's Bangladesh). There is no doubt about the fact that Persian was used at the court as a language of communication, as well as in the chancery's administration, if perhaps not to the same extent that it was used in the neighboring kingdom of Jawnpur and in later, Mughal times.[12] Chinese travelers noted the use of Persian at the Bengal court and identify it as the second language of the kingdom after Bengali. The court protocol, titles, and architecture of the sultanate also indicate the role of Persian models in the political idiom of the period.[13] But despite all these clues, the actual language of official statements composed for both inside and outside the kingdom was predominantly Arabic.[14]

The majority of stone inscriptions from the sultanate period were written in Arabic. Most of them were formulaic, containing quotes from the Quran and Hadith. Some titles evince the desire of Bengali Sultans to claim recognition in both the 'Arab and 'Ajam domains of the Muslim world.[15] But the most visible attempts at gaining supraregional fame are linked to traditional Arabic learning, jurisprudence (*fiqh*) in particular. The establishment of educational institutions in the sultanate is well attested by numerous inscriptions, as well as by later records that point to the supraregional significance achieved by some centers of learning.[16]

Sonargaon was one such center of learning that seems to have attracted scholars from abroad.[17] Accounts of the contribution of Bengal to Islamic learning point to Sharaf al-Din Abu al-Tawwama, the teacher of Sharaf al-Din Yahya Maneri (1263–1381). Very little is actually known about him, though, and almost none of his works have come down to us. The only exception is a versified treatise on jurisprudence entitled *Nam-i Haqq* (Name of the Truthful God), but the evidence for attributing this popular work to either him or one of his direct disciples is extremely thin to say the least.[18] The other instance of supraregional scale in the fostering of Arabic traditional learning was the foundation in 1410 of al-Madrasa al-Bangaliyya, the Bengali madrasa founded in Mecca by Ghiyas al-Din A'zam Shah (r. 1389–1410). This case differs in the sense that we have much information regarding the foundation of this educational institution from a variety of Arabic and Persian sources.[19] Here again jurisprudence played a central role, because this was the first madrasa in Mecca in which the four legal schools (*mazahib*) were all taught: twenty students would each study Shafi'i and Hanafi *fiqh,* and ten each Maliki and Hanbali *fiqh.*[20] As we shall see, this instance of long-distance patronage of an institution fostering Arabic learning probably contributed to the inclusion of Bengal in the geography of *'Ajam.*

HAFIZ AND THE INDIAN PARROTS

If Amir Khusraw was the first Indian poet to gain fame throughout the Persian-using world and self-consciously to include Hind in the imaginary of Fragner's *Persophonie,* the following ghazal by Hafiz is perceived as an acknowledgement of the role of India in the economy of patronage of Persian poetry:

> *Saqi hadis-i sarw-u-gul-u-lala mi-rawad . . .*
> Cup-bearer, so goes the story of the cypress, the rose, and the tulip,
>   and this conversation goes with three purifying cups of wine.
> Serve wine because the bride of speech is fully adorned; now, what's
>   to be done is done through the intermediary's craft.
> All the parrots of India began crushing sugar; this Persian candy
>   that goes to Bengal.
> See the crossing in space and time of the poem's journey: This child
>   born yesterday sets off for a year-long trip.
> See this bewitching eye that tricks the pious man; the caravan of
>   enchantment follows his trail.
> Lest you depart from the path for the sake of worldly pleasures;
>   it is an old woman who sits there, deceitful, and acts like
>   a procuress.
> Warmed up, he wanders, and on the cheeks of jasmine, ashamed by
>   his face, sweat drips like dew.

The spring wind blows from the king's garden and morning dew
   flows like wine in the tulip's cup.
Hafiz, do not silence your eagerness to join Sultan Ghiyas-i Din's
   gathering because your work is only done by ways of laments
   and requests.[21]

The interpretation of this ghazal has a long and complicated history. Modern
scholars have seen in it clear evidence of Hafiz's relations with Indian sultans, but
premodern commentators equally strove to uncover the context, which may help
explain its otherwise obscure images.[22] Before scrutinizing the various accounts
found in the commentarial literature and the speculations of historians as to the
identity of the Sultan Ghiyas-i Din mentioned in the last verse of the poem, let us
first see what a decontextualized reading of the poem can reveal.

The first couplet brings the reader right in the middle of a banquet that takes
place in a pleasure garden. The poet reflexively comments on the completion of a
poem ("the bride of speech is fully adorned") and the role of the messenger who
will deliver the poem to its addressee. The destination of the poem is given in the
third couplet in which Hafiz says that Indian parrots began crushing the candy of
Persian poetry, which reaches even the far end of the world that is Bengal. Pushing further his reflection on the commissioning of a poem by a sultan living in a
faraway land, the poet identifies the work that he composed the day before with
a newborn baby who must set off on a year-long journey. With this line, Hafiz
manifests a clear awareness of the economy of poetic patronage in the Persianate
world and subtly conveys the amazement—and perhaps the anxiety—of a poet
who sends the product of his labor to a region of the world that he can barely
comprehend. Here the poetic images are not so much conceived as hyperbolic
statements about a familiar environment than as default ways to depict a world
beyond the reach of experience. Couplets five to seven are particularly difficult to
include in a unified interpretation of the poem. Most commentators chose to identify the figure of the beloved with the patron: the bewitching eye, the path, and face
covered with sweat might all refer to the sultan.[23] Yet this interpretation is problematic: the various orders in which the verses have been arranged by premodern
commentators and modern editors show that they struggled to make them fit in
the poem's general schema.[24] If the poet was talking about the patron, then why
focus on the journey, the caravan, and the sweating caused by the journey? It almost seems as though Hafiz was addressing the messenger and warning him about
the temptations of the world that could cause a delay in the delivery of the poem
to the sultan. Indeed, verse eight comes as the goal of the messenger's journey,
with the refreshing "spring wind" and the wine served in the perpetual banquet
in the king's garden—his mission is over and we are back to the scene that opened
the poem. The final couplet is also very self-reflexive in the sense that, after some
observations about the economy of patronage in the geographical space of the

Persianate world, the poet comments on the transgression of courtly etiquette that he is forced to make when manifesting his desires and lamenting on his inability to join Ghiyas-i Din's banquet.

Attempts to identify the sultan mentioned in the signature line started early in the commentarial tradition. The Ottoman commentator Sudi Busnawi (d. 1600) is vague about the identity of the addressee and simply says that Bengal is the capital (!) of the rulers of India.[25] Around the same time in Mughal India, we find two historical interpretations of this ghazal: one is a brief mention of the poem in the *'Ain-i Akbari* of Abu al-Fazl (1551–1602), reviewing the rulers of Bengal, and the other is from the entry on the term *thalatha ghassala* in *Madar al-Afazil*, the dictionary of Allahdad Fayzi Sirhindi (d. 1595). In the latter work, the source of the story is said to be the *tazkira* (anthology) devoted to the poetry of sultans in the Muslim world compiled by Sultan Muhammad ibn Muhammad Harawi "Fakhri" (fl. 1551–55), the *Rawzat al-Salatin* (Garden of Sultans). The critical edition of this text by Sayyid Husam al-Din Rashidi gives the story in the chapter on the poet-sultans of Hind. The editor placed this account in the notes because it was only found in one manuscript kept in Istanbul, which was copied in 1628. The account given in both the *Rawzat al-Salatin* and the *Madar al-Afazil* goes as follows:

> Sultan Ghiyas al-Din of Bengal was a protector of the arts and patron of many poets at his court. One of his ministers had three sons named Sarw, Gul, and Lala. The sultan was fond of the three young men. As they grew in beauty and intelligence, the sultan one day composed the line: "Cup-bearer, so goes the story of Sarw, Gul, and Lala." He liked it a lot, and he decided to send one of his ministers to Shiraz with gifts for Hafiz to get him to complete the ghazal. The emissary went by sea, but was caught in a storm that made the ship drift "below the wind." After a year's travel, he eventually reached Shiraz, gave Hafiz Ghiyas al-Din's presents, and submitted his request. The next morning, Hafiz handed the completed ghazal to him, and the messenger went back to Bengal.

After this, the text of the Istanbul manuscript adds a piece of information that is absent from the *Madar al-Afazil*, namely, that one Mawlana Muhammad Bihbahani, who was a respected figure in Shiraz and who was old by then, had heard the story from his father and testified to its accuracy by saying: "This account is correct" (*in waqi'a sahih ast*). In order to close his demonstration, the author then took the poem as evidence of the accuracy of this story and invited the reader to verify his account by reading Hafiz's poem.

This first account of the circumstances of the writing of this poem by Hafiz shows the need to provide a narrative context for this ghazal in order to make sense of its images. The conventional scene of a springtime banquet in a garden with the recitation of poetry on the tropes of the cypress, the rose, and the tulip turns into an actual story. The tropes become characters at the court of Ghiyas al-Din of Bengal. In this version of the story, the episode of the storm is hardly relevant to the unfolding of events. Of course, the fact that the messenger eventually takes a year to reach Shiraz is reminiscent of the "year-long trip" of the fourth verse. But it is also reminiscent of another story involving Hafiz and India that was recorded in Firishta's chronicle and later repeated by various anthologists.[26]

The story is also related in the commentary on Hafiz's *Diwan* attributed to Khatmi Lahawri (fl. 1615)—supposedly one of the earliest complete commentaries written in the subcontinent.[27] The author mentions as his sources both the *Rawzat al-Salatin* and the *Madar al-Afazil*.[28] But Khatmi provided a second account drawn from another commentary that he simply calls *Sharh-i Diwan:*[29]

> When sultan Ghiyas al-Din, the ruler of Hind, conquered Bengal, he fell ill. Three servants took care of him and, thinking that he was about to die, they gave him his last bath. The servants' names were Sarw, Gul, and Lala. The sultan was eventually cured, and the three servants became his favorites. The other courtiers became jealous and started making fun of the untimely bathing of the sultan. One day the sultan heard about the mockeries and wrote this line: "Cup-bearer, so goes the story of Sarw, Gul, and Lala." Then the poets of the court tried to complete it, but they failed, and the ghazal was sent to Hafiz [to complete].

In this version, it is the Arabic term *thalatha ghassala* (literally, "the three that wash," that is the three cups of wine drunk in the morning to clear the body and mind) that triggers the contextual account of the poem's composition. The term is lexicalized and it is found in several premodern dictionaries, including the *Madar al-Afazil*, which first gives its proper definition and then turns to the story.[30] It is this story that later authors kept retelling, whether in the commentarial tradition on Hafiz's *Diwan* or in the Persian historiography of Bengal. For instance, this version of the story opens the section devoted to Ghiyas al-Din in the 1792 *Riyaz al-Salatin* (Garden of Sultans) of Ghulam Husayn Zaydpuri (d. 1817), the first Persian chronicle entirely devoted to the history of Bengal.[31]

The second story, as related in Khatmi Lahawri's commentary and some other later commentaries from South Asia, does not make explicit the identification of Ghiyas-i Din with A'zam Shah of Bengal. The mention of the conquest of Bengal seems to indicate that the author had in mind the sultan of Delhi. As a matter of fact, none of the rulers of the time seems to match exactly with the possible time of the composition of the poem by Hafiz (ca.1315–90). The first Ghiyas al-Din ibn Tughlaq ruled too early (between 1320 and 1325), and the second Ghiyas al-Din Tughlaq (r. 1388–89) and A'zam Shah of Bengal (r. 1389–1410) both succeeded to the throne at the very end of Hafiz's lifetime. The absence of the name Ghiyas-i Din in the final verse and in verses 3, 4, and 8 in one of the earliest manuscripts of the *Diwan* dated November 1415 (Rabi' I 818) that was edited by Nazir Ahmad makes it very probable that the references to Bengal and India were added after the death of the poet.[32]

But the identification of Ghiyas al-Din is not what should monopolize our attention here. What is more relevant is the expression of an awareness of the "new" frontiers of the Persianate world and the making of a wider geocultural domain in which Persian poetry circulates. Regarding the historiography of Bengal, this poem and the commentarial tradition that surrounds it thus show how the region was integrated into an imaginary of the Persianate world.

One reason that may have led to the association of Hafiz's ghazal with Ghiyas al-Din is a well-attested instance of long-distance patronage: the aforementioned foundation of al-Madrasa al-Bangaliyya in Mecca in 1410. This provided Ghiyas al-Din with an unprecedented aura in the wider Muslim world for a Bengali sultan. As a matter of fact, Ghulam 'Ali Azad Bilgrami (1704–84), who always drew a wealth of information from Persian and Arabic historiography in addition to mining previous biographical dictionaries, made the connection between sultan Ghiyas al-Din A'zam Shah's correspondence with Hafiz and the founder of the madrasa in Mecca. In Bilgrami's entry on Hafiz in his biographical dictionary *Khazana-yi 'Amira*, after quoting verse 3 ("All the parrots of India . . ."), Bilgrami identifies Ghiyas al-Din with the Bengali sultan and provides a Persian translation of a passage drawn from the Arabic *Tarikh Makka* (History of Mecca) about the foundation of al-Madrasa al-Bangaliyya.[33]

Rather than the accuracy of the historical reading of this poem, what is significant is the role that it played in the inclusion of Bengal in a wider imaginary of the Persianate world. The late fourteenth and early fifteenth centuries constituted a key period for the formation of Bengal as a political and cultural entity. As a matter of fact, Hafiz's use of the term *bangala* to designate the region is contemporaneous with the term's adoption in Persian chronicles.[34] It was during the Ilyas Shahi and Husayn Shahi periods that the Bengali sultanate reached its maximum territorial expression. Yet in the decades that followed Ghiyas al-Din's rule, no major developments seem to have occurred regarding the patronage of Persian poetry at the court. We find some sporadic evidence of the cultivation of Persian classics through the compilation of the *Sharaf-nama-yi Maneri/Farhang-i Ibrahimi* under Rukn al-Din Barbak Shah (r. 1459–74) and the production of illustrated manuscripts in the ateliers of the Husayn Shahi rulers. Whereas the practice of long-distance patronage of Arabic learning via madrasas in Arabia continued with Jalal al-Din (r. 1415–32), Raja Ganesh's son who had converted to Islam at the hands of the Chishti saint Nur Qutb-i 'Alam, nothing seems to indicate that the Bengali sultans tried to turn their court into a proper center of Persian learning.

PERSIAN IN PREACHING AND RITUAL CONTEXTS

The Bengali literature of the restored Ilyas Shahi (1433–86) and Husayn Shahi (1493–1538) periods does, however, provide evidence for the diffusion of Persian literacy in Bengal. The principal domains of cultivation of Persian were administration, religious education, and public performances involving narratives in preaching and ritual contexts—which would have involved a certain level of bilingualism absent from the context of court poetry.[35] Among the Persian texts that are attributed to authors who lived in Bengal during the sultanate, we find the famous Persian rendering of the earlier Sanskrit *Amritakunda* ('Pool of Nectar'), the *Hawd ma al-Hayat* (1210); a versified text on Sufi theory (*tasawwuf*) by Shaykh Sufi 'Abd al-Rahman Fathabadi entitled *Ganj-i Raz* (ca.1433–59); and *Nam-i Haqq,* another versified treatise, on elementary principles of religious obedience (*'ibadat*), attributed to the scholar of Sonargaon, Abu Tawwama (d. 1300).[36] Bilingualism appears in the collected letters (*maktubat*) of Nur Qutb-i 'Alam, a Sufi who composed multilingual verses using eastern Indic words.[37] Texts written during this period in Bengali, which was then emerging as a written literary idiom, already contained several Persian loanwords. Elements of the narrative poems composed around this time outside of courtly contexts also show that at least some elements of Persianate culture had reached Bengal's rural areas and non-Muslim populations.[38]

It is in the seventeenth century that we find the first texts that testify to the presence of Persian learning among Bengali Muslims in the rural areas of Bengal's eastern frontiers. In the kingdom of Arakan, starting from the late sixteenth and early seventeenth century, Muslim authors began to compose texts using the Bengali literary idiom.[39] Although no Persian works from this early period have come down to us, the Bengali texts often acknowledge their reliance on earlier Persian and Arabic sources. The Bengali Muslim population of Arakan, and of other small kingdoms in eastern Bengal such as Bhulua (in today's Noakhali district of Bangladesh), was at least partly constituted of descendants of soldiers and officers formerly in the Bengali sultanate's employ,[40] and we can assume that their literary and religious culture reflected that of the sultanate. It seems, too, that in addition to narrative literature, it was ritualistic literature and treatises on religious obedience (*'ibadat*) conveyed through a regional religious idiom—but not courtly poetry—that constituted the main field of the spread of Persian literacy.

A unique manuscript excerpting texts dealing with Islamic jurisprudence, devotional practices, and mysticism (*tasawwuf*), copied in the late seventeenth century by a shaykh and his son in Sylhet, and kept at the Dhaka University, sheds a great deal of light on the uses of Persian literacy in rural areas and the integration of local elements into religious practice.[41] This is therefore a unique source through which to study the texts that were part of the curriculum of the provincial imams and shaykhs in eastern Bengal. For instance, we find the Persian versified treatise of Yusuf Gada entitled *Tuhfa-yi Nasa'ih* (A Gift of Guidance; 1393) translated entirely by the poet Alaol in Arakan in 1663, and also partly by 'Abd al-Hakim in Bhulua around the same time.[42] The excerpts given in this compendium are drawn from classical Persian literature, Indo-Persian Sufi texts (such as the treatises attributed to Shah Madar or the *Tuhfa-yi Nasa'ih*), and anonymous handbooks on how to perform remembrance of God (*zikr*) or bio-cosmological knowledge known as *nuzul-i tawhid* (the descent of Unicity). In the margins of folios 26b to 30a, we find an abridged version of an anonymous ritual text about the creation of the world entitled *Nur-nama* (Book of Light), which was very popular in northern South Asia at the time. This is a perfect example of both the rooting of Islam in the subcontinent and the role of Persian in the daily religious practices of Bengali Muslims.

THE "NUR-NAMA" AND YOGIC SUFI LITERATURE IN BENGAL

Among the traces of the diffusion of Persian literature outside urban centers and institutionalized religious movements (the Sufi orders particularly), we find the fascinating corpus of eastern Bengali treatises on Islamic mysticism (*tasawwuf*) and bio-cosmological practices.[43] Historically speaking, these texts remain in a void: we have a fairly coherent corpus that can be dated from the late sixteenth to the eighteenth century, but very little is known about their authors, social status, and readership, or about the precise textual and doctrinal background of their teachings on *'ibadat, tasawwuf,* and bodily/yogic practices.

These Bengali Muslim treatises on yoga were composed in the regions of Chittagong, Comilla, and Mymensingh. The earliest author of this tradition is believed to be Sayyid Sultan (fl. 1630–45). Ali Raja is considered one of the latest and most accomplished. Other authors such as Mir Muhammad Shaphi may have been relatives and/or disciples of Sayyid Sultan.[44] The anonymous *Yoga-Kalandar* is one of the most popular texts of this corpus.[45] The manuscripts were consistently found in eastern Bengal. Besides the Bengali alphabet, some manuscripts have been copied in fully vocalized Arabic *naskh* script. To this we may add the Sylhet Nagari texts that deal with cosmogony and Sufi practices, though they belong to a somehow different and later tradition in which the place of yogic knowledge remains to be assessed.[46]

The structure of these treatises is stable, and if all the usual topics are not treated, they appear in the same order. After the *hamd* and *nat* (in Persian spelling, *na't*), that is, the praises of God and the Prophet, the author gives an account of the creation, from the formless God through his beloved consciousness that is the Light of Muhammad (*Nur Muhammad*). Then we find the exposition of the *manjil-tattva*, or science of the stages of spiritual realization. The author then proceeds with teachings about various aspects of the *deha-tattva*; that is, bio-cosmological knowledge per se. The last part of the treatise is typically dedicated to the development of the fetus in the womb and the interpretation of omens.

If we look at the doctrinal content of Bengali treatises on bio-cosmology, the transmission from classical Sufi and Nath traditions may be obvious, but the exact nature of the textual transmission is not.[47] The texts themselves do mention precise Persian sources, but, as far as is known, no Sanskrit or Bengali Tantric texts are explicitly cited. Very few references are given to the field of Persian literature. But at least one of these texts is known to be a Bengali rendering of a Persian work, namely, the *Nur-nama*. This text is a cosmogony dealing with the creation of the universe by the Light of Muhammad.[48] The researcher Raziya Sultana provides a preliminary survey of the six Bengali versions of this text.[49] Several manuscripts bearing this title are preserved in various libraries around the world.[50] A manuscript in the Bibliothèque nationale de France contains a complete version of the *Nur-nama* in prose.[51] Its content largely matches that of the Bengali texts consulted in researching this chapter, namely, 'Abd al-Hakim and Muhammad Shaphi's *Nur-nama*s. The Bibliothèque nationale manuscript was copied in Central Asia in the mid-nineteenth century.[52] The creation story just takes a few folios at the beginning of the manuscript, then we find indications about the merits gained from reading, copying, or reading the *Nur-nama* aloud. Then there follows a story about al-Ghazali (d. 1111), who sent a manuscript of the *Nur-nama* to Mahmud of Ghazna. The Sultan read it and redeemed himself of all his sins. The manuscript ends with a prayer in Arabic relating how the body of the Prophet was created from the qualities of various elements of God's creation. The text emphasizes the importance of the daily recitation of the *Nur-nama*. If one cannot copy it, one should have it copied; if one cannot read it, one should have it read; and if one cannot have it read aloud, one should keep a copy at home.[53]

The abridged version of the Dhaka manuscript differs slightly from that of the Bibilothèque nationale de France; and as one might expect, its version is closer to the Bengali versions of the *Nur-nama*—especially that of 'Abd al-Hakim. The manuscript provides an exposition of bio-cosmological correspondences in Persian that agrees with the Bengali texts on the topic. It also contains Hindwi terminology.[54] The *Nur-nama* is thus an Islamic creation story in Persian and Arabic with characteristically Indic features.[55]

It goes without saying that even if the Persian *Nur-nama* is claimed to be the direct source of the Bengali versions, this does not imply that the original text came from outside South Asia.[56] For instance, its creation story shows the influence of Nath Yogi cosmogonies. Nur Muhammad is not only the medium of God's epiphanies and it is through the exudation of drops from his own "body" that the elements of the universe are created. In Muhammad Shaphi's version, the reformulation of the account by means of a local religious idiom makes the likeness with Nath cosmologies even more striking.[57]

Following Simon Digby, Carl Ernst, and Aditya Behl's works on 'Abd al-Quddus Ganguhi, the *Amritakunda,* and Shattari literature respectively, the example of the transmission of the *Nur-nama* illustrates the inclusion of Indic bio-cosmological knowledge in South Asian Persian literary culture.[58] The presence of Indic elements is not a new phenomenon of doctrinal synthesis engendered by the vernacular rendering of the Persian text: by the time Bengali versions were composed, the Persian *Nur-nama* was itself conveying elements of a South Asian religious idiom.

The *Nur-nama* was thus a ritual Persian text that was part of the daily environment of the Bengali Muslims from at least the seventeenth century on. 'Abd al-Hakim's Bengali version is particularly instructive regarding the transmission of this text and the attention given not only to its ritual reading, but also to its meaning. The prologue of 'Abd al-Hakim's *Nur-nama* is often quoted for its elaborate apology for treating religious matters in a written work in Bengali. As a matter of fact, in some milieus, using the regional language (*deshi-bhasha*) rather than Arabic or Persian to discuss Islamic topics deserved some kind of disclaimer.[59] But in 'Abd al-Hakim's case, things are more complicated than a mere dichotomy between the classical languages of Islam, of which most Bengali Muslims were supposedly ignorant, and the easily accessible regional idiom. Here is a prose translation of the famous passage in which the author presented his arguments against meaningless rituals and in favor of the use of the vernacular to access Arabic and Persian texts:

> All those accounts about religions are remarkable and everything is related in [Perso-Arabic] books [*kitaba*]. Those friends who are not trained to read [Perso-Arabic] books came to me and affectionately submitted their complaint. Therefore, I strove to satisfy everyone by rendering the poem about the creation of light into the language of Banga, and by composing it I fulfilled everyone's wish. When listening to Persian from someone else's mouth, one cannot understand properly and be content. This is why I address you in a Bengali composition and satisfy everyone with my work. Treatises in Arabic convey no emotion, but one is deeply moved when he understands a work in the regional idiom. It makes no difference if God writes about the Prophet's qualities in Arabic, Persian, or in the language of Hind. Whether in Arabic, Persian, or Hinduyani, God wrote the Prophet's story in treatises. In the Arab country, the Lord provided Muhammad with a Quran [*musapha phorkana*] in Arabic language. In the country of the Uryan, he sent the Torah to the prophet Musa in Uryani. In Greece, he sent the Psalms [*jabbura*] to David in Greek. In the country of Syria, it is in the Syriac language that he sent the Gospel to Jesus. In all countries, whatever the language people speak, the Lord understands all of them, be it Hinduyani, the language of the country of Banga, or any other idiom. Whoever worships the Lord in his own tongue, he will address him accordingly. The lord does not ignore any language; whatever the kingdom, he knows its language. Allah, Khuda, Gosai, all these are his names; Niranjan is the receptacle of all qualities. The savant wrote with Indic letters a Muslim speech and understood its explanation. Letters never had any importance; it is the teaching of the treatises one ought to know. If one does not follow the conduct prescribed by treatises, it is useless for him to read Arabic and Persian texts. Whether in a *pustaka* or a *kitaba*, letters manifest a hidden message. *Alif*, or *anji*, are God's creations; there is no other creator besides God. Whether in Arabic, Persian or Bengali, God wrote the Prophet's teachings in treatises. He ordered meritorious deeds and forbade sin.[60]

This passage is typically quoted to illustrate the tensions between those in favor of Bengali and traditional Islamic scholarship associated with Arabic and Persian.[61] 'Abd al-Hakim put his defense of the use of the regional language in the clearest terms possible. But this side of his discourse should not lead us to miss the testimony regarding the cultivation of Arabic and Persian in rural areas that this text, as well as the rest of his oeuvre, illustrates. For his *Nur-nama* constitutes a very elaborate commentary on the Persian source text, and somehow brings back the focus to its semantic content, which may seem counterintuitive considering the text's own invitation to talismanic use.[62] Among 'Abd al-Hakim's other works, we find a poem that may be described as a "popular" Persian text that was circulating between Central Asia and Bengal, *Durr al-Majalis* (Pearl of Gatherings). This is not a ritual work; it is rather a prose compendium of stories about the prophets that also contains didactic sections in which 'Abd al-Hakim inserted renderings of other didactic works such as *Tuhfa-yi Nasa'ih* mentioned earlier. 'Abd al-Hakim was a very self-aware mediator who was himself multiliterate and was addressing an audience with various degrees of familiarity with Perso-Arabic literacy. He does not describe a blunt opposition between a knowledgeable elite and an ignorant popular mass. People were variously exposed to Perso-Arabic literacy through their education and religious life—a fact he clearly expresses in the trope of the friends' request and in his mention of the difficulties one might encounter when "listening to Persian from someone else's mouth."

Another domain in which some nuance is needed is the form that "Musul-mani"—that is, regionally Islamic—literacy might take. At some point 'Abd al-Hakim turns to the alphabet and what we should understand as a codicological definition of the book's religious identity. A text could be defined by its language, its alphabet, or the shape of the manuscript itself. The Bengali alphabet is designated as *hinduyani akshara* (Indic letters), and the Indic "book" is called a *pustaka*, in contrast to the Perso-Arabic-derived term *kitaba*. He also draws a contrast between the first letter of the Arabic alphabet, *alif*, and *anji*, the auspicious sign inscribed at the beginning of both Hindu and Muslim Bengali manuscripts right up to the late nineteenth century. Indeed, the *anji* sign had a crucial function in the sanctification of Islamic texts written in the Bengali/*hinduyani* alphabet.[63] We have other evidence during this period of emerging debates about the Islamization of literacy and of the book as a physical artifact. It is very probable that the practice of writing Bengali in vocalized Arabic *naskh* script and of arranging the pages of books (even ones written in the Bengali alphabet) from right to left began sometime in the seventeenth century.[64] But the vast majority of the manuscripts displaying such features were apparently produced in the nineteenth century.[65]

In order to gather the various threads of this chapter, let us turn to a final example of the impact of Perso-Arabic literacy in rural Bengal by way of an undated manuscript of Muhammad Shaphi's version of the *Nur-nama*. The copy bears no date, but judging from the quality of the paper, it may be from the late eighteenth or early nineteenth century, that is to say, approximately a century after the author's roughly seventeenth-century lifetime. The copy was produced by Muhammad 'Abd al-Hamid for Shaykh Asalat Khan, son of Musa Khan, of the village of 'Ashah (?) in the *chakla* of Pata in the district of Islamabad, also known as Chatgam (corresponding to Chittagong in today's Bangladesh). The manuscript is kept at the

Bangla Academy in Dhaka. The text was edited a few decades ago, but only on the basis of manuscripts written in the Bengali script.[66] The Bangla Academy manuscript is complete, but it has been copied from a model whose first one or two pages were missing. At the end, we find magic formulas in Persian, Arabic, and Indic languages, as well as diagrams that highlight the ritual use of the text.

The Bengali text of the manuscript is meticulously pointed and vocalized. We find a few marginal notes in Persian indicating that the scribe of the model from which the copy was prepared made errors (e.g., *dar inja katib ghalat karda ast*: "here the scribe made a mistake"). We also find other orthoepic signs to guide the recitation and indicate the sections of the text (such as *la la* for *la waqf; ta* for *faqat,* used when the end of a verse coincides with the end of a line, or to indicate the end of a section). The annotations and orthoepic apparatus indicate the dual function of the text, which conveyed meaningful teachings and was meant to be used in ritual contexts.

The copy has two scribal colophons in Persian conveying almost the exact same information. Its first part, written in Persian *naskh* script, informs us about the copy's patron and contains conventional statements forbidding other claims of ownership. The second part identifies the scribe (*katib*) and is written in a cursive Persian *nasta'liq* script. A marginal note provides further information on the copyist and is in *nasta'liq* with elements of *shikasta* script for the verb *ast* in both lines. The second colophon is entirely written in *nasta'liq,* though the text is almost exactly the same, with the addition of minor conventional expressions. The copyist signed the second colophon with an elaborate calligraphic monogram (*tughra*). A marginal note indicates the names of the copyist and his father, as well as his place of residence.

The conventional expressions, belonging to the formal register of legal discourse, indicate that we are dealing with a professional *munshi* (secretary). In the two lines that he adds in the margin of each colophon, the scribe tells us:

> *[Agar] kase pursid ki in katib chi nam ast bi-nawisam muhammad hamidullah bi-dani 'arabi ast* If someone asks what is the name of the scribe I shall write that it is Muhammad Hamidullah, know that it is Arabic

The reference to the Arabic origin of his name suggests that besides the ritual and practical dimensions of this scribal tradition, some ethnic claim may have motivated the adoption of this Arabicized system of transcription. In another text, similarly composed in the eighteenth century in the same region of Chittagong, we find the family history of a local landlord who claims to be the descendant of a saint who came from Baghdad. The text itself is said to be a translation from an Arabic original.[67] This manuscript from Chittagong shows how Perso-Arabic literacy shaped the vernacular tradition, or perhaps more accurately that Perso-Arabic literacy was instrumental in shaping Islamic modes of transmission of local forms of religiosity.

CONCLUSION

Writing the history of Persian in Bengal requires us to distinguish between the representation of the region in the geocultural space of the Persophone world and the actual uses of Persian in Bengal. We have seen that Hafiz's famous poem recognizes Bengal as a distinct region associated with the far end of Hind, but tells us very little about the patronage of Persian poetry by Bengali sultans. On the other hand, Hafiz's poem does testify to an awareness of the broadening of the landscape of literary patronage, in which Bengal stands as a landmark for the far frontier of Persian learning. Arguably, Bengal would find its place as a center of Persian literary production only in the Mughal period among the circles of governors and princes who were posted to the region.[68] The study of the formation of the stories linking Ghiyas al-Din A'zam Shah with Hafiz also testifies to the influence of the reputation of a ruler in the *'Arab* world on the making of his fame in *'Ajam*. These two domains—*'Arab* and *'Ajam*—converged again in Azad Bilgrami's eighteenth-century account of Ghiyas al-Din in his biographical notice on Hafiz. The ghazal of the poet from Shiraz thus comes across as a *poème de circonstance* that required some kind of historical context in order to be understood. In fact, it actually ended up creating history.

When we turn to the linguistic economy of the Bengali sultanate, we see that whatever can be retrieved of its courtly culture does not fit with already established models of Persianate courts observable in Delhi, Jawnpur, or the Bahmanid sultanate in the Deccan. In these three polities, sultans had full-fledged Persian chancelleries, regularly used Persian in inscriptions, and patronized Persian poets. Nothing seems to indicate that the Bengali sultans followed this pattern, and the exact nature of their courtly culture demands further study on the basis of the relatively little evidence at our disposal. The spread of Perso-Arabic literacy in the rural regions of Bengal took place through preaching and a variety of religious practices centered on Arabic and Persian texts. For the earlier periods of the Bengal sultanate, we have a set of texts that suggests the efforts made to reach a broader audience by including regional linguistic and cosmological features in treatises. The recourse to verse forms to compose treatises on the basics of jurisprudence and religious observances is yet another sign of a deliberate attempt to popularize Islamic learning through Persian.

The formation of Bengali Muslim literature sheds light on a body of texts that we may term "popular" Persian literature. Yusuf Gada's *Tuhfa-yi Nasa'ih*, the *Nur-nama*, the *Durr al-Majalis*, and the *Iblis-nama*—which would become an important source for later Bengali Muslim literature—are all representative of this popular Persian literature.[69] These texts were not classics, nor were they associated with courtly culture or prestigious figures of Islamic scholarship. But they were instrumental in the making of Bengali Muslim religiosity. It is also remarkable to see the very limited amount of scholarship devoted to such texts—ironically, Hafiz is virtually absent from the intertext of Middle Bengali literature, but these popular Persian texts that are virtually unknown to modern scholarship are omnipresent. Overall, the case studies presented in this chapter point to the need to revisit the dichotomy between Persianate urban centers versus vernacular rural areas. The situation is much more complex, and many pieces of the puzzle are missing. But we can still distinguish important trajectories of Perso-Arabic learning in Bengal, one of which led to the Bengali manuscripts in Arabic script that were produced in southeastern Bengal.

NOTES

1. Chapter epigraphs: Momtazur Rahman Tarafdar, *Husain Shahi Bengal, 1494–1538 A.D.: A Socio-Political Study,* 2nd rev. ed. (Dhaka: University of Dhaka, 1999), 253; *Nur-nama* in 'Abd al-Hakim Racanavali, ed. Raziya Sultana (Dhaka: University of Dhaka , 1989), 471. On Bengali resistance to the Persianate cultural ethos, see Richard M. Eaton, *The Rise of Islam and the Bengal Frontier, 1204–1760* (Berkeley: University of California Press, 1993),159–93.

2. Richard M. Eaton, N. H. Ansari, and S. H. Qasemi, "Bengal," *Encyclopædia Iranica* (1989), 4, fasc. 2, 137–43, www.iranicaonline.org/articles/bengal; *Danishnama-yi Adab-i Farsi: Adab-i Farsi dar Shibh-i Qarra-yi Hind (Hind, Pakistan, Bangladish),* ed. Hasan Anushe, vol. 4 (Tehran: Wizarat-i Farhang wa Irshad-i Islami, 1996), s.v. "Bangâlî"; and Abu Musa Mohammad Arif Billah, "Persian," in *Banglapedia,* ed. Sirajul Islam et al. (Dhaka: Asiatic Society of Bangladesh, 2006).

3. Asim Roy, *The Islamic Syncretistic Tradition in Bengal* (Princeton, NJ: Princeton University Press, 1983).

4. This chapter uses the term "Perso-Arabic" alongside "Persian" and "Persianate." Persian literacy cannot be dissociated from the Arabic episteme. The transmission of Persian literacy invariably required a certain degree of familiarity with Arabic language and literary culture. Moreover, the cases studied in this chapter clearly show a close connection between Persian, Arabic, and Bengali in the making of Muslim literary idioms in Bengal from the arrival of Islam in the region up to the nineteenth century.

5. Simon Digby, "Review of Husain Shahi Bengal, 1494–1538 A.D.: A Socio-Political Study by Momtazur Rahman Tarafdar," *Bulletin of the School of Oriental and African Studies, University of London* 30, 3 (1967): 713–15.

6. Muhammad Kalim Sahsarami, *Khidmatguzaran-i Farsi dar Bangladish* (Dhaka: Rayzani-i Farhang-i Jumhuri-i Islami-i Iran, 1999), 11–38.

7. For references to this manuscript, see Eloïse Brac de La Perrière, *L'art du livre dans l'Inde des sultanats* (Paris: Presse de l'Université Paris-Sorbonne, 2008), 73, n. 54.

8. For a comprehensive survey of the Persian sources on Sufism in the Bengali Sultanate, see Abdul Latif, *The Muslim Mystic Movement in Bengal, 1301–1550* (Calcutta: K. P. Bagchi, 1993).

9. Nur Qutb-i 'Alam Pandawi, *Anis al-Ghuraba,* ed. Ghulam Sarwar (New Delhi: Markaz-i Tahqiqat-i Farsi, 2010). See also Zuhur al-Din Ahmad, *Pakistan men Farsi Adab,* vol. 1 (Lahore: Yunivarsati Buk Aijansi, 1965), 608–38; Sahsarami, *Khidmatguzaran-i Farsi dar Bangladish,* 16–31.

10. Eaton, *Rise of Islam,* 89–91.

11. Abdul Karim, *Corpus of the Arabic and Persian Inscriptions of Bengal* (Dhaka: Asiatic Society of Bangladesh, 1992); Muhammad Yusuf Siddiq, *Rihla ma'a al-Nuqush al-Kitabiyya al-Islamiyya fi Bilad al-Banghal: Dirasa Tarikhiyya Hadariyya* (Damascus: Dar al-Fikr, 2004); and Mohammad Yusuf Siddiq, *Epigraphy and Islamic Culture: Inscriptions of the Early Muslim Rulers of Bengal (1205–1494)* (New York: Routledge, 2016).

12. Qeyamuddin Ahmad, *Corpus of Arabic & Persian Inscriptions of Bihar (A.H. 640–1200)* (Patna: K. P. Jayaswal Research Institute, 1973). On Persian and Arabic learning in Jaunpur, see Mian

Muhammad Saeed, *The Sharqi of Jaunpur: A Political & Cultural History* (Karachi: University of Karachi, 1972), 169–210.

13. Eaton, *Rise of Islam*, 40–50; Syed Ejaz Hussain, *The Bengal Sultanate: Politics, Economy and Coins, A.D. 1205–1576* (New Delhi: Manohar, 2003), 219–40.

14. Regarding the predominance of Arabic in the inscriptions and the absence of actual patronage of Persian literature in the Husayn Shahi period of Bengal, see Tarafdar, *Husain Shahi Bengal*, 278–80.

15. Siddiq, *Rihla ma'a al-Nuqush al-Kitabiyya al-Islamiyya fi Bilad al-Banghal*, 62.

16. A. K. M. Yaqub Ali, "Education for Muslims under the Bengal Sultanate," *Islamic Studies* 24, 4 (1985): 421–43. See also Siddiq, *Epigraphy and Islamic Culture*, 48–52.

17. M. Saghir Hasan al-Masumi, "Sunargaon's Contribution to Islamic Learning," *Islamic Culture*, no. 105 (January 1, 1953): 8–17; Mohammad Yusuf Siddiq, "Sonārgā' on," *Encyclopaedia of Islam*, 2nd ed., ed. C. Edmund Bosworth et al., http://dx.doi.org/10.1163/1573-3912_islam_SIM_7095.

18. Abdul Karim, *Social History of the Muslims in Bengal, Down to A.D. 1538*, 2nd rev. ed. (Chittagong: Baitush Sharaf Islamic Research Institute, 1985), 96–102.

19. Z. - A. Desai, "Some New Data Regarding the Pre-Mughal Muslim Rulers of Bengal," *Islamic Culture* 32 (1958): 195–207; Richard T. Mortel, "Madrasas in Mecca during the Medieval Period: A Descriptive Study Based on Literary Sources," *Bulletin of the School of Oriental and African Studies, University of London* 60, 2 (January 1, 1997): 236–52.

20. Mortel, "Madrasas in Mecca during the Medieval Period," 244.

21. Hafiz, *Diwan-i Khwaja Shams al-Din Muhammad Hafiz-i Shirazi*, ed. Muhammad Qazwini, Qasim Ghani, and Rahim Zu al-Nur (Tehran: Intisharat-i Zawwar, 1374/1995), 345–346, *ghazal* no. 225. Verse no. 6 is given in the notes.

22. Ghulam 'Ali Azad Bilgrami already quoted verse no. 3 of this *ghazal* to illustrate the category of poets who praised an Indian ruler but did not travel to India. These considerations are included in his biographical notice on Fayzi (1547–95). Ghulam 'Ali Azad Bilgrami, *Tazkira-yi Sarw-i Azad (Tahrir-i Nahayi)*, ed. Mir Hashim Muhaddis (Tehran: Safir-i Ardihal, 2014), 55.

23. See, e.g., Fouchécour's comments: "Les beyts 5 à 7 sont à l'éloge du prince, décrit comme un bien-aimé, avec son œil ensorceleur (beyt 5), sa fière démarche et la beauté de sa sueur qui rend honteux, par comparaison, le jasmin, pourtant si beau par sa 'sueur', la rosée sur sa 'joue' (beyt 7)." Hafiz *Le divân: Oeuvre lyrique d'un spirituel en Perse au XIVe siècle*, ed. Charles-Henri de Fouchécour (Lagrasse: Verdier, 2006), 597–98.

24. Fouchécour refers to Neysari's edition in which verses 5 and 7 are paired and 6 comes after—we find the same order in Sudi Busnawi. Khatmi Lahuri moves *bayt* 6 before *bayt* 4.

25. Sudi Busnawi, *Sharh-i Sudi bar Hafiz*, trans. 'Ismat Sattarzada (Tehran: Nawbahar, 1390/ 2011), 1289. On Sudi and Persian philology in the Ottoman Empire, see Murat Inan's chapter 1 in this volume.

26. Aqa Husayn Quli Khan 'Azimabadi and Kamal Hajj Sayyid Jawadi, *Tazkira-yi Nishtar-i 'Ishq* (Tehran: Markaz-i Pizhuhishi-i Miras-i Maktub, 1391), 430–31.

27. Abu al-Hasan 'Abd al-Rahman "Khatmi" Lahuri, *Sharh-i 'Irfani-i Ghazal-ha-yi Hafiz*, ed. Baha al-Din Khurramshahi, Kurush Mansuri, and Husayn Amin, 4 vols. (Tehran: Nashr-i Qatra, 1378). See also Anushe, *Danishnama-yi Adab-i Farsi*, s.v. "Hafiz dar Shibh-i Qarra."

28. The absence of Muhammad Bihbahani's testimony seems to indicate that Khatmi only consulted the *Madar al-Afazil*.

29. At this point, I cannot identify which commentary he was referring to.

30. See also the many parallels in Arabic and Persian poetry given in Hafiz, *Diwan-i Hafiz: Lisan al-Ghayb: Nuskha-yi Faridun Mirza-yi Taymuri*, ed. Ahmad Mujahid (Tehran: Mu'assasa-yi Intisharat wa Chap-i Danishgah-i Tihran, 2001), 334, 894, *ghazal* no. 284.

31. Ghulam Husayn Zaydpuri, *Riyaz al-Salatin: Tarikh-i Bangala*, ed. al-Haqq 'Abid, Bibliotheca Indica, n.s., vol. 129 (Calcutta: Matba'-i Biptist Mishin, 1890), 105–9; *The Riyaẓu-s-Salāṭīn: A History of Bengal*, trans. Maulavi Abdus Salam (Calcutta: Asiatic Society, 1902), 108–9.

32. Hafiz, *Diwan-i Hafiz: bar Asas-i Nuskha-yi Muwarrakh-i 818 Hijri*, ed. Nazir Ahmad (New Delhi: Markaz-i Tahqiqat-i Farsi-i Rayzani-i Farhangi-i Sifarat-i Jumhuri-i Islami-i Iran, 1988), *kaf*, 61n3, *ghazal* no. 108.

33. Ghulam 'Ali Azad Bilgrami, *Khazana-yi 'Amira*, ed. Human Yusufdihi (Tehran: Kitabkhana-yi Muza wa Markaz-i Asnad-i Majlis-i Shura-yi Islami, 2014), 275–80.

34. One of the first instances of the use of *bangala* to designate the region of Bengal in Persian historiography is found in Diya al-Din Barani's *Tarikh-i Firuz Shahi* (1357). In Dihkhuda's *Lughat-nama*, the first example of the use of the term in Persian poetry is Hafiz's poem. A. H. Dani, "Bangala," *Encyclopaedia of Islam*, 2nd ed., ed. P. Bearman et al.,http://dx.doi.org/10.1163/1573–3912_islam_SIM_1182; 'Ali Akbar Dihkhuda, "Bangala," *Lughatnama-yi Dihkhuda* (Tehran: Intisharat-i Danishgah-i Tihran, 2002).

35. We assume that Persian was used in the administration but we have very little evidence regarding the existence of a Persian chancellery in the Bengali sultanate. It is very probable that the administration was still very much "Indic." The presence of Hindu kayastha, vaidya, and brahman ministers at the court and the cultivation of Sanskrit and increasingly vernacular literacy and literature suggest the rather limited impact of Persian on courtly culture. See, e.g., the table of Hindu officers in Hussain, *Bengal Sultanate*, 237–38. See also the discussion on the rise of Raja Ganesh and the warnings of Sufis regarding the presence non-Muslims in the sultan's entourage in Eaton, *Rise of Islam*, 50–56.

36. Carl W. Ernst, "The Islamization of Yoga in the 'Amrtakunda' Translations," *Journal of the Royal Asiatic Society*, 3rd ser., 13, . 2 (2003): 199–226; Sahsarami, *Khidmatguzaran-i Farsi dar Bangladish*, 33–36. The dating of *Ganj-i raz* is very tentative.

37. Nur Qutb-i 'Alam Pandawi, *Anis al-Ghuraba*, ed. Ghulam Sarwar (New Delhi: Markaz-i Tahqiqat-i Farsi, 2010), 41.

38. E.g., the episode of the war against the characters called Hasan/Husen in various versions of the *Manasa-magala*. Other often quoted examples are the complaints by Vaishnava authors about bearded brahmans reading the *Masnawi* (or *masnawis?*) and the description of Muslim city-dwellers in Mukundaram's *Candi-mangala*. Momtazur Rahman Tarafdar, "Husain Shah in Bengali Literature," *Indian Historical Quarterly* 32, 1 (1956): 56–80; and Eaton, *Rise of Islam*, 100–102.

39. For a refutation of Md. Enamul Haq's early dating of various Muslim authors who were believed to have written Bengali texts in the sultanate period, see Karim, *Social History of the Muslims in Bengal*, 9–12. Regarding Bengali literature in Arakan, see Thibaut d'Hubert, "Pirates, Poets, and Merchants: Bengali Language and Literature in Seventeenth-Century Mrauk-U," in *Culture and Circulation: Literature in Motion in Early Modern India*, ed. Thomas de Bruijn and Allison Busch (Leiden: Brill, 2014); and d'Hubert, "Arakan aur Janub-i Mashriqi Bangala-desh men Musulamanon ki Tahzib aur Zabanen," trans. Timsal Masud, *Ma'arif* 194 (2014): 265–88.

40. Mawlawi Hamidullah Khan Bahadur, *Ahadith al-Khawanin, Ya'ni Tarikh-i Islamabad Chatgam ki Ham Musamma ba-Tarikh-i Hamid Ast* (Calcutta: Mazhar al-'Aja'ib, 1871), 54; Sha'barid Khan, *Sha'barid Khaner Granthavali*, ed. Ahmed Sharif (Dhaka: Bangla Academy, 1966), cha-tha.

41. A. B. M Habibullah and Md. Siddiq Khan, *Descriptive Catalogue of the Persian, Urdu & Arabic Manuscripts in the Dacca University Library*, Dacca University Library Publication (Dacca: University Library, 1966), 338–45, MS no. 336; call no. HR/11–21.

42. Simon Digby, "The Tuḥfa i Naṣā'iḥ of Yūsuf Gadā: An Ethical Treatise in Verse from the Late-Fourteenth-Century Dehlī Sultanate," in *Moral Conduct and Authority: The Place of Adab in South Asian Islam*, ed. Barbara Daly Metcalf (Berkeley: University of California Press, 1984), 91–123; Alaol and Muhammad Yusuf Gada, *Tohpha*, ed. Ghulam Samdani Quraishy (Dhaka: Bangla Academy, 1975); 'Abd al-Hakim Racanavali (cited n. 1 above), 446–51.

43. Ahmed Sharif, *Bamlar Suphi Sahitya*, 2nd ed. (Dhaka: Samaya Prakashan, 2003); Tony K. Stewart, "In Search of Equivalence: Conceiving Muslim-Hindu Encounter through Translation Theory," *History of Religions* 40, 3 (2001): 260–87; France Bhattacharya, "Un texte du Bengale médiéval: *Le yoga*

du kalandar (*Yoga-kalandar*)," *Bulletin de l'Ecole française d'Extrême Orient* 90, 1 (2003): 69–99; Shaman Hatley, "Mapping the Esoteric Body in the Islamic Yoga of Bengal," *History of Religions* 46, 4 (2007): 351–68; Ali Raja, *The Ocean of Love: Ali Raja's Agama/Jnana Sagara*, trans. David G. Cashin (Dhaka: Bangla Academy, 1993); David Cashin, *The Ocean of Love: Middle Bengali Sufi Literature and the Fakirs of Bengal* (Stockholm: Föreningen för Orientaliska Studier, 1995); Carol Salomon, "Review of *The Ocean of Love: Middle Bengali Sufi Literature and the Fakirs of Bengal* by David Cashin," *Journal of the American Oriental Society* 118, 4 (1998): 554–58.

44. 'Ali Raja, *The Ocean of Love; Sharif, Bamlar Suphi Sahitya*. The latest and most comprehensive study of Saiyad Sultan's life and works is Ayesha A. Irani's "Sacred Biography, Translation, and Conversion: The 'Nabivamsa' of Saiyad Sultan and the Making of Bengali Islam, 1600–Present" (PhD diss., University of Pennsylvania, 2011).

45. Bhattacharya, "Un texte du Bengale médiéval."

46. Shah Arman Ali, *Nura Paricae*, ed. Muhammad Abdul Mannan (Dhaka: Utsa Prakashan, 2011).

47. David Cashin argues for a *sahajiya vaishnava* influence, but this theory raises historical problems regarding the demography of such movements in eastern Bengal in the sixteenth and seventeenth centuries. See Cashin, *Ocean of Love*.

48. U. Rubin, "Nur Muhammadi," *Encyclopaedia of Islam*, 2nd ed., ed. P. Bearman et al., http://dx.doi.org/10.1163/1573-3912_islam_SIM_5985.

49. Raziya Sultana, '*Abd al-Hakim, Kavi o Kavya* (Dhaka: Bangla Academy, 1987); Thibaut d'Hubert, "'Abd al-Hakīm," in *Encyclopaedia of Islam*, 3rd ed., ed. Denis Matringe, Everett Rowson, and Gudrun Krämer, http://referenceworks.brillonline.com.proxy.uchicago.edu/entries/encyclopaedia-of-islam-3/abd-al-hakim-COM_27231. See also the edition, translation, and commentary on various Middle Bengali creation texts, including Shekh Paran's *Nur-nama*, in Cashin, *Ocean of Love*, 59–115.

50. See the entry "*Nur-nama*" in the index of Ahmad Munzawi, *Fihrist-i Nuskha-ha-yi Khatti-i Farsi*, vol. 5 (Tehran: Mu'assasa-yi Farhangi-i Mintaqa'i, 1348/1969-), 341. The *Nur-nama* is often found in compendia such as the MS from Sylhet kept at the library of the Dhaka University. See, for instances, Wilhelm Pertsch, *Die Handschriften-Verzeichnisse der königlichen Bibliothek zu Berlin. Vierter Band. Verzeichniss der persischen Handschriften der königlichen Bibliothek zu Berlin* (Berlin: A. Asher, 1888), 126, no. 62.7, MS orient. 8. 102. See the versified version in Vladimir Ivanow, *Concise Descriptive Catalogue of the Persian Manuscripts in the Collections of the Asiatic Society of Bengal First Supplement*, Bibliotheca Indica (Calcutta: Asiatic Society, 1927), 379, MS no. 832.

51. Anonymous, "Nur-nama, Shama'il-nama, Wasiyat-nama" (Transoxiana, ca. nineteenth century), Supplément Persan 1679, Bnf. Manuscrits orientaux.

52. E. Blochet, *Catalogue des manuscrits persans*, vol. 4 (Paris: Imprimerie nationale, 1934), 179–80, MS no. 2219.

53. Anonymous, "Nur-Nama, Shama'il-Nama, Wasiyat-Nama," fol. 12–16b.

54. Compare with the table in Bhattacharya, "Un texte du Bengale médiéval," 97.

55. The *Nur-nama* was present in Central Asia in the nineteenth century. There are also several versions in northwestern Indic vernacular languages (Gujarati, Sindhi, Kashmiri) and in Urdu. The chronology of the diffusion of the text and whether or not it was originally composed in Bengal remains to be clarified. For the western versions of the *Nur-nama*, see Wafi Ahmed Momin, "The Formation of the Satpanth Ismaili Tradition in South Asia" (PhD diss., University of Chicago, 2016).

56. The success of Yusuf Gada's *Tuhfa-yi Nasa'ih* (1393) is also proof to the fact that an Islamic literature in Persian produced in South Asia was already used as the basis for the formulation of vernacular Islamic idioms at the regional level. Simon Digby pointed out that "an independent reason for the popularity of the *Tuhfa i Nasa'ih* is that it provided for South Asian Muslims with a lower level of education, and especially for the children of such Muslims, a comprehensible guide to the good life in an easy mnemonic verse form. It can be classified with numerous other short verse treatises, mostly of later date and often bilingual vocabularies, under the heading *niṣab aṣ-ṣibyān* (the capital stock of

children)." See Digby, "Tuḥfa i Naṣā'iḥ," 98. Versified treatises such as *Nam-i Haqq* or *Ganj-i Raz* were also "popular" didactic texts meant for a wide readership.

57. For instance, the "drops" (*qatra*) of the Persian text become "drops of sweat" (*gharma*) in the Bengali version. The sweat is reminiscent of accounts of primordial act of love making between the Adi Purusha and the Shakti.

58. Ernst, "Islamization of Yoga"; Simon Digby, "'Abd al-Quddus Gangohi (1456–1537 A.D.): The Personality and Attitudes of a Medieval Indian Sufi," *Medieval India: A Miscellany* 3 (1975): 1–66; Aditya Behl, *Love's Subtle Magic: An Indian Islamic Literary Tradition, 1379–1545,* ed. Wendy Doniger (New York: Oxford University Press, 2012).

59. Ahmed Sharif, *Madhyayuger Sahitye Samaj o Samskritir rup* (Dhaka: Samay Prakashan, 2000), 63–65.

60. *Nur-nama* in *'Abd al-Hakim Racanavali* (cited n. 1 above), 471–72.

61. Perween Hasan et al., *Essays in Memory of Momtazur Rahman Tarafdar* (Dhaka: Centre for Advanced Research in the Humanities, Dhaka University, 1999), 442–45.

62. On the talismanic usage of Persian in the context of Eastern Turkistan, see Alexandre Papas's chapter 8 in this volume.

63. Mohammad Abdul Qayyum, *Pandulipi Patha o Patha-samalocana* (Dhaka: Gatidhara, 2000), 25–26.

64. Another seventeenth-century author from southeastern Bengal mentioned the issue of the use of the Bengali alphabet in Islamic texts. See e.g., Hajji Muhammad, "Suratnama," in *Bamlar Suphi Sahitya,* ed. Ahmed Sharif, 2nd ed. (Dhaka: Samay Prakâshan, 2003), 117–18, 134.

65. Thibaut d'Hubert, "La diffusion et l'usage des manuscrits bengalis dans l'est du Bengale, XVIIe–XXe siècles," ed. Maria Szuppe and Nalini Balbir, *Eurasian Studies, Special Issue: Lecteurs et copistes dans les traditions manuscrites iraniennes, indiennes et centrasiatiques; Scribes and Readers in Iranian, Indian and Central Asian Manuscript Traditions* 12 (2014): 335–45.

66. Ahmed Sharif, "Nurnama," in *Banlar Suphi Sahitya,* 2nd ed. (Dhaka: Samay Prakashan, 2003),151–61.

67. Muhammad Ujir 'Ali, "Nasle Osman Islamabad va Shahnama" (MS no. 253), 'Abd al-Karim "Sahityavisharad," Dhaka University Library.

68. Eaton, *Rise of Islam*, 167–74; Sahsarami, *Khidmatguzaran-i Farsi dar Bangladish*, 40–70.

69. See Habibullah and Khan, *Descriptive Catalogue* , 345, for a dialogue between Iblis and the Prophet Muhammad to be found in the seventeenth-century MS from Sylhet in the Dacca University Library alluded to in nn. 41 and 50 above.

3

The Uses of Persian in Imperial China

The Translation Practices of the Great Ming

Graeme Ford

The reach of Persographia extended to the imperial court of the Great Ming Empire (1368–1644), where language specialists were employed for the important task of translating the emperor's written edicts to tributary countries from Chinese into Persian, and letters and petitions in Persian addressed to the emperor into Chinese. As was appropriate to the task of translating the emperor's words, the translators were highly educated officers of the Hanlin Academy (*hanlinyuan*). They worked alongside translators of Mongolian, Uyghur, Tibetan, and other languages. This chapter presents an overview of the surviving documents that demonstrate how Persian was used in the Great Ming Empire. These extant relics of Ming court translations attracted the attention of bibliophiles in the Qing dynasty. Later, European orientalists took an interest in Persian translating: the French Sinologist Paul Pelliot published a detailed study of the Siyiguan translating college as early as 1948.[1] More recently, scholars in China, notably Liu Yingsheng of Nanjing University, have published articles on this subject.[2] This chapter revisits this question of the scale and kind of Persian-usage under the Ming emperors by surveying the various surviving primary documents from the period.

The practice of using Persian in imperial documents at the Ming court was inherited from the previous Mongol dynasty of the Yuan Empire (r. 1271–1368). Historians such as David Morgan and Stephen Haw have recently debated whether Marco Polo spoke Persian as a lingua franca when he was employed at the Mongolian court, and whether Persian was or was not an official language of the Yuan government in China.[3] Records state that an Imperial Muslim College (*huihui guozixue*) was established alongside the Chinese and Mongolian Colleges, and young men of the official class were selected to be trained in languages written in *istifi* (Arabic script) to work as translators.[4] Under the Yuan, official documents of all kinds—including edicts, patents, letters, and orders—must have been created in several languages, including Persian. However, none of these documents have survived, and only a few "safe-passes" (*paizi*) bearing Persian words attest to the use of Persian under the Yuan rulers of China.[5]

The situation is different for the Great Ming Empire, at least for its first century. As this chapter discusses in detail, several records describe the arrangements made at the Ming court for translating different kinds of documents into and out of Persian. These surviving texts show that Persian was used in communications within the empire; with countries along the Silk Road to the west; with Tibet to the south; and with countries along the sea routes to Calicut in India and Hormuz in Iran. This was expressly not Persian as a literary language. For the Ming, Persian served the practical imperial purpose of proclaiming the emperor's power abroad. Yet no special status can be claimed for it: it was a practical, bureaucratic medium of imperial governance, trade, and diplomacy.

The Persian College was one of ten colleges established within the Hanlin Academy. All ten languages were primarily used in the tributary process and in the emperor's communications with foreign lands. Persian never appears alone in a document: all surviving Persian translations appear alongside translations in one or more other languages. In some texts Persian precedes the other languages, while in others it comes last. Persian translators probably had a greater volume of work to do than the others, especially during the Yongle era from 1402 to 1424, when embassies arrived from many Central Asian countries and countries along the sea route to Hormuz.

While no original Persian tributary documents survive, several edicts and letters from Ming emperors to Tibetan leaders have been preserved and are held in Tibetan archives.[6] They are on large scrolls, some of plain white linen paper, some of yellow linen paper patterned with dragon-and-cloud design, and some of silk brocade in broad stripes of different colours.[7] A letter from 1453 in Chinese and Mongolian enumerating imperial gifts of silk, held in the Topkapi Museum in Istanbul, is also on dragon-and-cloud-patterned yellow paper.[8] Of hundreds of fine scrolls in Chinese and other languages carried to tributary countries, only these few have survived.

The Ming History (Ming shi) and the Ming Veritable Records (Ming shilu), compiled from daily court records, provide a meticulous account of envoys and tribute missions, from which the amount of translation at the court can be gauged.[9] The Great Ming Statutes (Da Ming huidian) contain information about the translation of documents and tribute activity.[10] These records show that tribute missions took place regularly for most of the first Ming emperor's reign, called Hongwu (1368–98), but increased in frequency during the Yongle era (1402–24), when thousands of ambassadors and sometimes rulers themselves arrived with large retinues.

The first Persian translators at the Ming court were semuren, the administrative class of non-Mongolian peoples from the lands to the northwest, from Central Asia, and elsewhere. These included the Huihuiren, that is, Muslims who spoke Turkish and wrote Persian, and who served the Yuan administration, often in positions that Chinese people could not take.[11] When Zhu Yuanzhang's forces rode into Khanbalik in 1368, an amnesty was proclaimed, and officers of the former

FIGURE 6. Ming imperial Muslims: Niujie (Ox Street) Mosque, Beijing, rebuilt 1443. Photograph by Nile Green.

regime were employed in the new Ming administration at Nanjing.[12] Linguists from the old Imperial Muslim College probably translated the letters of accession that were sent overland to Samarqand and by sea to Calicut.[13]

THE SIYIGUAN TRANSLATION COLLEGE

In 1407 a translation college, known as Siyiguan was established within the Hanlin Academy in Beijing. This occurred when the Yongle Emperor began large-scale missions by sea to the Indian port of Calicut and by land to the Timurid cities of Samarqand and Herat. The resulting flood of tribute-bearers to the Ming court made it necessary to begin training translators and give them substantive posts.[14] The overall Siyiguan translation college contained separate sub-colleges for Mongolian, Nüzhen, Tibetan, Xitian (Indian), Huihui (Persian),, Gaochang (Uyghur), Miandian (Burmese), and Baiyi (Tay).[15] A Babai (Chiangmai) College was added in 1511, followed by a Xianluo (Thai) College in 1578.[16]

In order to pass their regular examinations, candidates who aimed to become officers of the Hanlin Academy had to master, not only language translating skills, but also neo-Confucian dogma, historical and administrative knowledge, and composition and calligraphy skills in Chinese. A treatise on statecraft presented to the throne in 1487 states that translators were selected from candidates of *juren* status, that is, those who had passed the provincial examinations. They had not only to write the demanding series of essays in Chinese on the prescribed neo-Confucian curriculum, but also to translate one or more of the essays they had written into the other language, a task requiring a high level of ability.[17]

The regulations of the Translating College (*Siyiguan ze*) that were compiled between 1543 and 1688 contain edicts, regulations, precedents, and name lists relating to teachers, students, courses, and examinations, as well as rules for seconding to other departments.[18] The organization the regulations describe is not a translating bureau, where documents would be received, translated, and checked, but rather a translation training college that was staffed by teachers, and where translators could be trained, tested, and assigned official rank, and seconded for translation, calligraphic, or editing work within the overall Ming secretariat (*neige*). The Great Ming Statutes inform us that translating documents was part of the duties of the Patents Office (*gaochifang*).[19] The Veritable Records also list translating officers as compilers.[20] They worked on the detailed records of tribute missions, recording the correct Chinese forms of country names, and names of sovereigns and ambassadors. However, it was not until 1494, during the *Hongzhi* reign (1487–1505), that supervisors (*tidu*) were appointed to oversee the translating colleges.[21] Records of personnel and procedures were kept after that time, but the compilers of *Siyiguan ze* could not locate any materials for the period before 1490. Hence, we cannot see what the organization was like at its busiest during the *Yongle* era. Nonetheless, the surviving evidence does allow us to detail a range of different imperial functions for Persian.

MING COMMUNICATION WITH THE TIMURID EMPIRE

The Timurid and Ming empires both emerged from the breakup of the Mongol Empire of Chinggis Khan. The Hongwu Emperor soon sought to establish tribute relations with Timur (r. 1370–1405), but a series of tribute missions recorded in the Veritable Records did not begin until 1387, the twentieth year of the reign.[22] In the sixth mission in 1394, Timur's ambassador arrived with tribute of two hundred horses and a letter. The original letter no longer exists. A letter from Timur to Charles VI of France written eight years later in 1402, preserved in the French archives, is in Persian, on a plain sheet of paper 47 × 20 cm, written in black ink, with the salutation and the title of the recipient in gold ink.[23] Timur probably also sent a Persian letter to the Hongwu Emperor (r. 1368–98), which was translated at the Chinese court. The translated letter so pleased the emperor that it was copied into the daily record and later into the Ming history.[24] It is the only surviving example of Persian tributary correspondence from the Hongwu period, and the only example of a translation from Persian into Chinese for the whole of the early Ming period. It is in polished literary style, using bureaucratic terminology, and shows that the standard of Persian-Chinese translating was high. The obsequious tone of the letter has led to claims of it being a forgery, inasmuch as some consider it impossible that the proud Timur would have written such a letter.[25] But it is equally unlikely a merchant would have risked the ire of Timur, crossed the desert with a large tribute of 200 horses, and impersonated an ambassador at the Ming court, where five genuine embassies had arrived in the past six years. Others argue the letter is genuine; its elaborate language expresses the nature of the tributary relationship that existed at that time and confirms Timur's important wish to keep the roads open for commerce.[26]

Timur inexplicably detained subsequent envoys, and tribute relations were discontinued for the rest of the first Ming emperor's long reign. When the emperor's fourth son, Zhu Di, usurped the throne and proclaimed *Yongle* in 1403, a series of major tribute missions soon began with Timur's successors Khalil and Shah Rukh. The Persian translations of two letters from the Yongle Emperor to Shah Rukh at his capital at Herat, together with two of Shah Rukh's letters in reply, are preserved in a Persian historical work *Zubdat al-Tawarikh* (Cream of Histories). This was compiled by Hafiz-i Abru (d. 1430), a historian at the court of Shah Rukh (r. 1405–47), who must have sorted through the original scrolls in the Timurid chancery archives at Herat and copied several of them into his history.[27] He gives a valuable description of the letters, including the useful information that all of the letters from the Chinese emperor were written in three languages: Chinese, Persian, and Turkish in Uyghur script.[28] These three languages were also used for communications with the Silk Road oasis town of Hami.[29]

The Yongle Emperor's two letters to Shah Rukh are the best examples of court translation that have come down to us. Each is a long, continuous text, dealing with a variety of subjects. The first is the Yongle Emperor's first letter to Shah Rukh, which reached Herat in 1412.[30] A shorter Chinese version of the same letter is preserved in the Ming Veritable Records.[31] A deeper comparison reveals that the Chinese text is the first draft, perhaps made in the presence of the emperor and copied into the daily record, thus finding its way into the Veritable Records. This draft was enlarged before being translated into Persian and Uyghur and copied onto scrolls. The Persian translation of the longer final Chinese version was preserved by Hafiz-i Abru. The imperious tone of the Chinese draft is softened and made friendlier-sounding in the longer translated version, while an injunction concerning Shah Rukh's relationship with his nephew Khalil is moderated and considerably shortened. Details of previous tributary activity, names of envoys, and lists of gifts are added, as well as the assurance that roads will be open for commerce. The translation is plain and grammatically correct, apparently by a native speaker of Persian who was accustomed to producing high-quality translations routinely.[32]

The Chinese embassy that carried this letter to distant Herat, in what is today western Afghanistan, was the first of a series that continued to the end of the Yongle Emperor's reign. His fourth embassy, which reached Herat in 1419, carried the second of the letters preserved by Hafiz-i Abru.[33] The plain, accurate Persian translation, with literal phraseology, is similar in style to the letter of 1412, and might have been done by the same translator. It expresses gratitude for presents of a lion, horses, a leopard, and falcons, and like the other letter, expresses the wish that envoys and merchants should continue to come and go. It differs from the letter of 1412 in that terms of equal address are used throughout. The relationship between the two rulers is described as friendship in the closest terms: "Our friendship is heart to heart, reflecting like a mirror, although there be such a distance between us."[34]

The subsequent return mission to China is recorded in the Persian diary of Ghiyas al-Din, a member of a large group of tribute-bearers from several Central Asian princes who arrived together at the new capital at Beijing in 1420. He provides vivid pictures of the magnificent tribute ceremonies, including the presentation of tribute letters.[35] His account is preserved in several Persian histories, and has been translated into European languages, including English, since the eighteenth century.[36]

No other Persian translations survive from the regular missions that went back and forth annually, until the Yongle Emperor's death in 1424, and thereafter continued to do so at longer and longer intervals. Tribute missions came from Herat until 1463. Shah Rukh's successors continued to send missions from Samarqand. The last tribute missions from Samarqand recorded in the court history were from Uzbek rulers in 1508 and 1514. A mission from Babur, who briefly recaptured Samarqand, is also recorded in 1512.[37]

THE TSURPHU SCROLL IN TIBET

The Tsurphu scroll, currently displayed at the Tibet Museum in Lhasa, is a large scroll some 49.68 meters long and 66 centimeters wide. It depicts the miraculous phenomena observed when the Tibetan Fifth Karmapa carried out a Buddhist ceremony for the salvation of the souls of the dead on behalf of Emperor Zhu Di's late parents at the Linggusi monastery in Nanjing in 1407. In Chinese, the scroll is called *Gamaba wei Ming Taizu jianfu tu* (Pictures of the Karmapa Performing a Ceremony for Ming Emperor Taizu). Such lavish patronage of Tibetan Buddhism by the imperial family was a court practice adopted from the Mongolian rulers.[38] The ceremony and the scroll supported the Yongle Emperor's claim to legitimacy. Although he was the first Ming emperor's fourth son by a concubine, he ordered a ceremony for his parents, the emperor and empress, thereby asserting that his mother was the empress, and that his own reign was legitimate.[39]

Twenty-one sections of text on the scroll describe the mystical phenomena in Chinese, with accompanying translations in Persian, Tibetan, Mongolian, and Tay (Shan).[40] The sections of text are interspersed with forty-nine fine paintings depicting the miraculous phenomena of colored clouds, rays of light, cranes, bodhisattvas, and flowers. The scroll resided at the Tsurphu Monastery, at some distance from Lhasa, where Hugh Richardson photographed it in 1949, and Luo Wenhua and Patricia Berger have commented on it more recently.[41] The publication in 2000 of high-quality photographs of the entire scroll now allow its text and images to be studied in detail.[42] Luo Aili and Liu Yingsheng, who have published a study of the Persian language in the scroll, point out that the overall text, its choices of vocabulary, grammar, and sentence structure, as well as its practiced, fluent calligraphy, indicate that the translator's first language was Persian, or at least that he knew Persian very well indeed.[43]

Mirza Haydar Dughlat (d. 1551), who served the first Mughal emperor, Babur (r. 1526–30), his cousin, as governor of Kashmir, records in his *Tarikh-i Rashidi* (Rashidi History) of Mughulistan that in 1553, at a place called Zunka in Tibet, he saw a stone inscribed in Chinese, Tibetan, and Persian relating to repairs to a temple. The vertical Chinese inscription took up the right side, with Tibetan above and Persian below on the left. Prince Haydar thought the inscription was about a hundred years old.[44] Although the identity and location of Zunka are unknown, the stele evidently stood in a temple, where it had possibly been since the *Yongle* era, which is to say for more than a hundred and twenty years. It would presumably have been carved in Nanjing or Beijing before being transported to its location. It is unlikely that the emperor would have repaired a temple further away than southern Tibet, and transporting a stele to northern Tibet would have been difficult. So Haydar possibly saw the stele at a temple close to Lhasa, perhaps at the Tsurphu Monastery, where it might have been erected in the years immediately following the Karmapa's visit. Tibetan records state the Karmapa returned to Tsurphu and rebuilt many shrines and stupas and completely renovated all the living accommodations there.[45]

Another surviving document is the Yongle Edict (*Yongle chiyu*), an edict of the Yongle Emperor in 1407 granting security to one Mir Hajji, a Muslim living in China. It is the only surviving example of an imperial edict from the Ming period. The text is in Chinese, with Persian and Mongolian translations. The Yongle Edict shows that Persian was used not only for communications with other countries, but also for administrative matters within the borders of the empire. The document is now held at Puhading Garden (*Puhading yuan*), a mosque complex in Yangzhou. Unfortunately, only an unclear black and white photograph has been published, in which the Persian and Mongolian texts are not clear enough to read.[46] The Tsurphu scroll was probably produced soon after the departure of the Karmapa from Nanjing on a pilgrimage to Wutaishan on the thirteenth day of the third month in 1407. The Yongle Edict was issued just eight weeks later on the eleventh day of the fifth month. It is therefore possible that the same translators and calligraphers worked on both of these texts.

COMMUNICATIONS ALONG THE SEA ROUTE
TO HORMUZ

Wang Zongzai, the supervisor of the Translating College in 1578–79, compiled a series of documents stored in the ten colleges into a work that he entitled Translating College Examinations (*Siyiguan kao*).[47] It was evidently intended as a preparation book for the Translating College examinations (*kao*). The compilation provides tribute histories as well as information about geography, local products, and customs for each of the countries dealt with by each of the colleges. In an interesting pointer to the maritime trade routes in which Ming China was taking such interest, the *Siyiguan kao*n states that Islam was practiced in Champa, Cambodia, Java, and Malacca; and that Persian was used to communicate with these regions.[48]

An entry in the Veritable Records of 1487 concerning communications with Thailand tells us that tribute letters were presented in Thai and Persian together at first, but that later Persian alone was used.[49] Liang Chu, chief minister in charge of the Patents Office (*Gaochifang*), the agency in charge of preparing these translations, stated in a submission to the Zhengde Emperor (r. 1505–21) that when tribute documents from maritime countries like Champa, Xianluo, and elsewhere, were encountered in local languages and scripts, the Persian College translated them with the help of the interpreters. He also stated that Persian only was used in reply in the case of all the imperial orders and letters accompanying the gifts.[50]

The first three voyages of the Chinese Muslim admiral Zheng He (1371–1433 or 35), all reaching as far as Calicut in India, set out at two-year intervals in 1405, 1407, and 1409. The next three, setting out in 1413, 1417, and 1421, at four-year intervals, went to Hormuz in southern Iran and to other countries beyond. The final voyage, ordered by the Xuande Emperor, set out in 1431, also going as far as Hormuz.[51] Tribute missions from many lands beyond the Sumatran port of Semudera (including the island of Ceylon, and the ports of Calicut, Hormuz, and Aden), arrived with Zheng He's returning fleets, usually going back with the next fleet. No tribute missions are known to have arrived from these countries independently of Zheng He's fleets.

Several geographical works were created following the voyages. Chief among them is *Yingya shenglan* by Ma Huan, a Persian translator who took part in Zheng He's fourth, sixth, and seventh voyages.[52] Ma Huan took care to note the presence of Muslims in each place, along with their status in local society; he also occasionally provided information about their writing systems.[53] Some of Ma Huan's material was novelized in 1597 by Luo Maodeng in *The Well-Known Romance of the Grand Eunuch Sanbao's Record of the Western Ocean* (*Sanbao taijian xiyang ji tongsu yanyi*), which was supplemented by personnel lists, letters, and tribute lists that are not authentic documents but bravura inventions of the author.[54] These scarcely add to the historical record.

THE GALLE STONE IN CEYLON

The only surviving Persian document relating to Zheng He's voyages is the so-called Galle Stone, a stele erected in Ceylon (*Xilan,* modern Sri Lanka) by Zheng He in 1411, which records the emperor's donations to various temples. The text is in Chinese, with Tamil and Persian translations. The text, translations, and calligraphy were completed in 1409 at the Ming court in Nanjing, where the stele was carved and then carried to Ceylon by Zheng He.[55] Galle was the major trading port in southwestern Ceylon, and there seems no doubt that Zheng He's fleets stopped there. Devundara, the "city of gods," a vast temple precinct and busy port on Ceylon's southernmost promontory, was nearby, and its great gilt roof was a landmark for mariners.[56] This was a fitting location for an imperial monument, and the stele must have stood there for 178 years, before the temple precinct was looted and destroyed by Portuguese forces in 1588.[57] An account by a Portuguese missionary written between 1671 and 1686 records that the stone still stood among the ruins in the seventeenth century.[58] This suggests that it was not located within any of the temples, which were destroyed, but instead stood in a public place.

When the stele was rediscovered in a culvert in Galle in 1911, British colonial scholars were rapidly mobilized. Rubbings were made, followed by transcriptions and translations of the Chinese text by Edmund Backhouse, of the Tamil text by S. Paranavitana, and of the Persian text by Khwaja Muhammad Ahmad.[59] Less than half of the Persian text is legible, but it is clearly a translation of the Chinese inscription. All three texts variously indicate that gifts were offered to Buddha, Vishnu, and Muhammad. The stone now stands in the Colombo Museum, but no rubbing or image of the Persian text has been published, and only the transcription by Khwaja Muhammad Ahmad is available for study. The 600th anniversary of the Zheng He voyages prompted publications on every aspect of Zheng He.[60] Among them, the contribution of Liu Yingsheng, the leading contemporary Chinese scholar of Persian, demonstrated the importance of the Galle stone as evidence of the use of Persian as a language of international communication for the Ming maritime expeditions.[61]

In 1431, seven years after the end of the Yongle era, the Xuande Emperor commissioned Zheng He's final voyage and also sent a large-scale mission to Herat, Samarqand, and several smaller kingdoms in 1432, which produced a final round of tribute-bearers, but no tribute missions came from beyond Southeast Asia after them. When Malacca fell to the Portuguese in 1511, bearers of tribute and even of letters from countries in the Southern (Indian) Ocean decreased to a trickle. Tribute relations with the Timurid rulers in Herat were also discontinued. However, missions from Samarqand, Turfan, and elsewhere in Central Asia, accompanied by large numbers of merchants seeking to trade, continued to arrive at Jiayuguan, where the Silk Road passes through the Great Wall, for the rest of the fifteenth century. Many such merchants sojourned within the wall at Ganzhou and Suzhou, where border officials dealt with them and issued them entry permits.[62]

THE PERSIAN EXEMPLARY BILINGUAL LETTERS

Chinese translations of four tribute letters, together with five petitions from Hami and other places within Ming jurisdiction, all from the last three decades of the fifteenth century, which were translated from Persian into Chinese at the court, have survived by their inclusion as "exemplary bilingual letters" (*laiwen*), in the Persian section of the word-List collections (*huayiyiyu*). They are the only surviving examples of the work of Persian translators after the Yongle period.

The first bilingual language learning material was produced at the court of the first Ming Emperor, before the Translating College was established. Huo Yuanjie and Mashaykh were ordered to write up this bilingual material in 1382, and it was published in 1389. Entitled *Huayiyiyu* (Chinese and Foreign Word List), it consists of a bilingual Chinese and Mongolian word list with 844 entries under seventeen topic headings.[63] It also has an appended section containing twelve Mongolian "exemplary letters" (*laiwen*), of which seven are authentic Mongolian letters to the court and five are Chinese imperial letters translated into Mongolian. It was not until the Siyiguan translation college was established in 1407 that the work of compiling the complete set of such word lists in the languages of each college was begun.[64] They consisted at first only of bilingual lists called *zazi* (collected words), forming a series that were called *huayiyiyu* like the Mongolian word list compiled in the Hongwu period.[65] The second element of the *huayiyuyu* model, the *laiwen*, examples of letters, was not added until much later. Some collections contain word lists and *laiwen* for the Thai College, which was not established until 1578, the sixth year of the Wanli era, so the date of compilation could be even later than that.[66] Supplementary vocabulary lists (*zengxu zazi*) derived from the exemplary letters, were added at the same time.

Several manuscripts and old printed editions of *Huayi yiyu* contain Persian word lists and exemplary letters under the title *Huihuiguan yiyu*.[67] They include *zazi*, *laiwen*, and a *zengxu zazi* (additional word list). Correspondences of dialect forms and place-names show that the additional word list was compiled partly from the exemplary letters. Liu Yingsheng has published an annotated edition of the Persian word lists, and Honda Minobu has published a transcription of the word lists and the exemplary letters, which is the only published text of Persian *laiwen*.[68] Liu Yingsheng collated twenty-six *laiwen* from four manuscripts.[69] The most interesting of these manuscripts as far as the *laiwen* are concerned is a Ming manuscript in the Tōyō Bunko in Tokyo, called B, or the Toyo Bunko text. Its fine calligraphy in all languages indicates that it was written by officers of the translating colleges. It contains the original *Huihuiguan zazi* vocabulary, but without the additional *zengxu zazi* vocabulary, and thirty *laiwen*.

The Persian *laiwen* texts have baffled scholars, who have thought them examples of ungrammatical Persian. However, they are neither original Persian letters nor even Persian translations. Rather, they are deliberate word-for-word Persian glosses of the Chinese translations of original Persian letters, and of Chinese tribute lists, which were created to test students at the Persian College during regular seasonal tests called *jike* (季課). The tests are described in the regulations of the Siyiguan.[70] They were carried out in each language and, according to the results, students were recruited to work in the Gaochiguan translating office, or the history department, or to do copying work.[71] In his library catalogue the Qing bibliophile Qu Zhongrong describes a finely bound collection of seasonal tests of a candidate in the Tibetan College. It consisted of forty-five texts of the exemplary letter (*laiwen*) genre, with corrections by college tutors, which were made for each of the five seasons from winter 1575 to winter 1576.[72]

Collections of *ke* examination texts in the different languages of the translation colleges were made using the Chinese texts stored in each language college. This was not done grammatically in accordance with the rules of the different languages being examined, but rather by closely following the word order of the Chinese source text. The uniformity of the glossing, with identical glosses used for the same words in all the texts, indicates that the texts were all glossed at one time. This evidently occurred when a decision was made to create uniform testing materials for all of the language colleges. This might have been soon after the appointment of supervisors to oversee the language colleges in 1494.[73] Several of the Persian exemplary letters (*laiwen*) can indeed be dated between 1472 and 1494. Another possible date is the supervisorship of Yang Zishan and Zhang Jisheng, who instituted the keeping of records and personnel lists between 1516 and 1519.[74] Their zeal may have given rise to the testing procedures. These supervisors evidently saw a need to establish uniform testing for all languages, and the glossed texts were a somewhat clumsy bureaucratic answer to that need. One collection of tests survives, titled *Gaochangguan ke* (高昌館課; Tests of the Uyghur College).[75] It contains eighty-seven Chinese texts of the *laiwen* type, including translations of letters referring to rulers in Turfan and Hami, as well as tribute lists, all glossed uniformly and systematically word for word in Uyghur. The letters are from the same period as the Persian *laiwen*.

Another Qing bibliophile, Qian Zeng, in a catalogue of his family's rare books made between 1669 and 1674, described a collection entitled *Huihuiguan ke* (Tests of the Persian College), which also contains texts of the *laiwen* type.[76] Elsewhere Qu Zhongrong describes slips of paper, inserted into an old book, bearing the titles *Huihuiguan ke* (Persian College Tests), *Miandianguan ke* (Burmese College Tests), and *Baiyiguan ke* (Baiyi [Tay] College Tests).[77] Collections of *ke* tests later provided the texts for the *laiwen* exemplary letters that were appended to vocabulary lists in the *huayiyiyu* collections some time after 1579.

The Chinese versions of the *laiwen* are the only examples of Persian court translation after the Yongle era ended in 1424. They are plain and correct, showing that the translators had a good knowledge of both Persian and Chinese. The chapters in the *Ming shi* (Ming History) on Hami and Turfan give a detailed account of Great Ming's loss of control over the oasis kingdom of Hami and the subsequent breakdown of relations with the Mughul rulers of Turfan in eastern Turkistan. These events form the historical background to several of the letters preserved in the exemplary letters. The earliest dateable letter is an appeal from Hami for help following its invasion by Sultan ʿAli of Turfan in 1473.[78] Another letter refers to the return of detained Turfan ambassadors in 1499.[79] A tribute letter from Egypt is probably from al-Malik al-Ashraf Sayf al-Din Qaytbay (r. 1468–96), the eighteenth Burji Mamluk sultan of Egypt. The letter was most likely sent during the years when his reign prospered before 1481.[80]

The French Sinologist Paul Pelliot scrutinized Ming records in his classic *Le Ḫōja et le Sayyid Ḥusain de l'histoire des Ming* to solve the problem of the identity of the prince of Hami who became a favorite of the Zhengde (正德) Emperor (r. 1505–21), and whose name appears in one or more of the Persian *laiwen*.[81] A petition from a military commander (*dudu*) named Sayyid Husayn asks that official status be given to a mosque. Since he was granted *dudu* status only in 1494, the letter can be no earlier than that.[82] In another letter, Mawla Hasan, a prince of Hami enfeoffed as a military commander there, petitions the Ming court seeking confirmation of his status. The Ming History records a mission by Military Commander Mawla Hasan to Turfan in 1511, so the letter is from before that time.[83] A surviving request from a Muslim holy man for a travel permit, and tribute letters from Turfan, Balkh, and Basra, unfortunately cannot be dated. In future, an overall study of the exemplary letters from all ten colleges may come up with more secure dating.

Only nine of the twenty-six *laiwen* are Chinese translations of Persian tributary letters or petitions. Seventeen of them are not actual letters, but rather tribute lists (*fangwuzhuang*), which were declaimed at audiences and listed goods brought and gifts bestowed. (The "Edicts of Hongwu" describe how the lists were declaimed.)[84] These documents list tribute from Mecca, Samarqand, Turfan, and Hami. Such tribute lists were an indispensable element of the tribute audience ritual, though the public declaiming of a tribute letter could be waived. The tribute lists are all inserted within the same few formulas, using the same wording each time. They were not translations from Persian, like the other *laiwen* letters, but are instead lists composed in Chinese by officers of the Board of Rites. They lay alongside the Chinese translations of letters in the college, and when the order was given to create collections of glossed examination texts, they were also taken up and used for this purpose.

CONCLUSIONS

Beyond the materials discussed here, no other Persian documents exist from the era of the Great Ming, so we cannot know what work translators did in the last

150 years of the dynasty. However, the lists in *Siyiguan ze* show that small numbers of officers continued to be appointed in each college.[85] Five were appointed to the Persian College in 1490, when records begin; six in 1509; one in 1537; four in 1566; one in 1578; six in 1605; and one in 1627. Collectively, these appointments show that the college remained active until the end of the Ming dynasty. The Tibetan seasonal tests recorded by Qu Zhongrong also show that testing was still being done in 1576, while Wang Zongzai states that he compiled *Siyiguan kao* in moments of leisure while supervising *ke* examinations in 1579. It is reasonable to tentatively conclude that language testing, including in Persian, possibly continued until the end of the dynasty.[86]

The ten translating colleges were maintained to ensure that the Ming emperors could address tributary states in their own languages and understand the messages they sent. Alongside other languages, Persian was used exclusively for the emperor's purposes. Although the writing of Persian was practiced by a small number of translators, it did not serve as a lingua franca in China. Rather, it was used for a specific purpose, namely, the emperor's communications with countries in Central Asia, along the sea route to Hormuz in Iran, and, perhaps more surprisingly, with Tibet. As in other regions of Eurasia, the use of Persian was underwritten by an imperial state bureaucracy.

NOTES

1. Paul Pelliot, *Le Ḫōǰa et le Sayyid Ḥusain de l'histoire des Ming* (Leiden: Brill, 1948) (*T'oung Pao* 38), app 3: *Le Sseu-yi-kouan et le Houei-t'ong-kouan*, 207–92.

2. See Liu Yingsheng, *Hailu yu Lulu, Zhongguo gu shidai dong xi jiaoliu yanjiu* (Maritime and Continental Routes between East and West) (Beijing: Beijing daxue chubanshe, 2011).

3. David Morgan has summarized the arguments for this proposition. See David Morgan, "Persian as a Lingua Franca in the Mongol Empire," in *Literacy in the Persianate World: Writing and the Social Order,* ed. Brian Spooner and William L. Hanaway (Philadelphia: University of Pennsylvania Museum of Archaeology and Anthropology, 2012), 160–70. However, Stephen Haw has refuted all the arguments; Marco Polo's supposed use of Persian terms, the use of the term *huihui* in a Persian context, and Persian inscriptions on a small number of *paizi* safe-passes, arguing that in the Great Mongolian Empire, Turkic, not Persian, was the lingua franca of the *semuren* ("persons with special status," i.e., confederates of the Mongols such as Turks or Middle Eastern Muslims), and the language that Marco Polo spoke. Stephen G. Haw, "The Persian Language in Yuan-Dynasty China: A Reappraisal," *East Asian History* 39 (2014): 5–32.

4. Thomas T. Allsen, "The Rasūlid Hexaglot in Its Eurasian Cultural Context," in *The King's Dictionary: The Rasūlid Hexaglot,* ed. Peter B. Golden (Leiden: Brill, 2000), 37, traces the references to the Persian College in *Yuan shi;* Stephen Haw defines the term *istifi* in "The Persian Language in Yuan-Dynasty China," 28.

5. Igor de Rachewiltz, "Two Recently Published *P'ai-tzu* Discovered in China," *Acta Orientalia Academiae Scientiarum Hungaricae* 36 (1982): 414–17.

6. *Xizang lishi dangan huicui* (A Collection of Historical Archives of Tibet), compiled by the Archives of the Tibet Autonomous Region (Shekou: Cultural Relics Publishing House, 1995), nos. 23–30.

7. Su Bai, "Lasa Budalagong zhuyao diantang he kuzang de bufen Mingdai wenshu," *Wenwu* 8 (1993): 40–48.

8. Francis Woodman Cleaves, "The Sino-Mongolian Edict of 1453 in the Topkapi Sarayi Müzesi," *Harvard Journal of Asiatic Studies* 13 (1950): 431–36.

9. Zhang Tingyu et al., eds., *Ming shi*, 1736; repr. 28 vols. (Beijing: Zhonghua shuju, 1974); *Ming shilu*, 1418–mid-seventeenth century. Facsimile repr. of Guoli Beiping tushuguan cang hongge chaoben, 133 vols. (Taibei: Zhongyang yanjiuyuan lishi yuyan yanjiusuo, 1961–66).

10. *Da Ming huidian* (Collected Statutes of the Ming Dynasty), comp. Li Dongyang et al. (Taibei: Zhongwen shuju, 1963).

11. See a full discussion of this term in *Menggu shi cidian* (A Dictionary of Mongolian History), ed. Bao Yinhu (Huhehot: Nei Menggu daxue chubanshe, 2010), 203.

12. *Taizu shilu* (Ming Annals), 34: 9v. Cf. Henry Serruys, *The Mongols in China during the Hung-wu Period , 1368–1398* (Brussels: Institut belge des hautes études chinoises, 1980), 57.

13. *Taizu shilu*, 38: 7v–8r (0338–9); 53: 9r. (1049).

14. *Ming shi* (Ming History) 74: 1797. Cf. Pelliot, *Ḫōǰa*, 226–27.

15. The language of Baiyi, identified as Mäng² Maaw², land of the Dai, present-day southwestern Yunnan. See Christian Daniels, "Script without Buddhism: Burmese Influence on the Tay (Shan) Script of Mäng² Maaw² as Seen in a Chinese Scroll Painting of 1407," *International Journal of Asian Studies* 9, 2 (2012): 147–76.

16. *Siyiguan ze*, 2: 3r; *Siyigu an kao* (1924 Oriental Society imprint), comp. Wang Zongzai (Taibei: Shangwu yinshuguan, 1972), pt. 2, 21v–22r.

17. Qiu Jun,*Daxue yanyi bu* (Taibei: Shijie shuju, 1988), *juan* 145, 14–15.

18. *Siyiguan ze*, ed. Lü Weiqi (Taibei: Wenhai chuban she, 1985).

19. *Da Ming huidian*, 221: 6v–7r (pp. 2939–40).

20. Wolfgang Franke, "The Veritable Records of the Ming Dynasty (1368–1644)," in *Histories of China and Japan*, ed. W.G. Beasley and E.G. Pulleyblank (London: Oxford University Press, 1961), 742–43.

21. *Siyiguan ze* 2: 3r (p. 45). Cf. Norman Wild, "Materials for the Study of the Ssǔ i Kuan," *Bulletin of the School of Oriental and African Studies* 11, 3 (October 1945): 617–40, at 625, https://doi.org/10.1017/S0041977X00072311.

22. These records are listed in Liu Yingsheng's chapter "Baiaerxintai ji qi chushi," in *Hailu yu lulu*, 316–17.

23. Silvestre De Sacy, "Observations on a Correspondence between Tamerlane the Great and Charles the Sixth, King of France," *Monthly Magazine, or British Register* 38, 2 (1814): 15–16.

24. The Chinese text of this letter is in *Ming shilu*, 8: 3420, and also in the chapter on Samarqand in *Ming shi*, 332: 8598. English translation in Emil Bretschneider, *Mediaeval Researches from Eastern Asiatic Sources: Fragments towards the Knowledge of the Geography and History of Central and Western Asia from the 13th to the 17th Century* (London: Kegan Paul, 1910), 2: 258.

25. Morris Rossabi, *China and Inner Asia* (London: Thames & Hudson, 1975), 27. "The letter . . . was undoubtedly forged by a Central Asian merchant. It is inconceivable that Tamerlaine, who aspired to world conquest, could have written such a fawning, self-deprecatory missive." Also Rossabi, "The Ming and Inner Asia," in *The Cambridge History of China: The Ming Dynasty (1368–1644), Part 2*, ed. Denis C. Twitchett and Frederick W. Mote, vol. 8 (Cambridge: Cambridge University Press, 1998), 247, "the Hong-wu emperor had faith in these forged missives &c."

26. Zhang Wende, "Lun Ming yu Zhongya Tiemuer wangchao de guanxi," *Lishi dangan* 1 (2007): 58.

27. Hafiz Abru, *Zubdat al-Tawarikh*, ed. Sayyid Jawadi (Tehran, 1993), 3: 460ff. Also Kamal al-Din 'Abd al-Razzaq Samarqandi, *Matla'-i Sa'dayn wa Majma'-i Bahrayn*, ed. Muhammad Shafi (Lahore, 1946–49), 2, pt. 1: 130ff.

28. Hafiz Abru, *Zubdat al-Tawarikh*, 3: 467.

29. *Siyiguan kao*, 2: 1v.

30. Hafiz Abru, *Zubdat al-Tawarikh*, 3: 460.

31. *Taizu shilu*, 101: 3v (1316), and in Herat chapter in *Ming shi*, 332: 8610.

32. Liu Yingsheng, "Baiaerxintai ji qi chushi," in *Hailu yu lulu*, 325.

33. Hafiz Abru, *Zubdat al-Tawarikh*, 4: 697. Translation by Joseph F. Fletcher, "China and Central Asia, 1368–1884," in *The Chinese World Order: Traditional China's Foreign Relations*, ed. John. K. Fairbank (Cambridge MA: Harvard University Press, 1968), 212–14.

34. Fletcher, "China and Central Asia, 1368–1884," 213.

35. *A Persian Embassy to China, Being an Extract from Zubdatut Tawarikh of Hafiz Abru*, trans. K. M. Maitra, intro. L. Carrington Goodrich (New York: Paragon Book Reprint, 1970).

36. Étienne Quatremère published his French translation of this text in 1843 and lists earlier translations into Turkish, French, and Dutch, including one by Antoine Galland in 1696. Quatremère, "Notice de l'ouvrage persan qui a pour titre: *Matla-assaadeïn ou-madja-albahreïn* et qui contient l'histoire des deux sultans Schah-Rokh et Abou-Saïd," *Notices et extraits des manuscrits de la Bibiliothèque du Roi et autres bibliothèques* 14, 1 (1843): 10.

37. Ralph Kauz, *Politik und Handel zwischen Ming und Timuriden: China, Iran und Zentralasien im Spätmittelalter* (Wiesbaden: Reichert, 2005), 244.

38. David M Robinson, "The Ming Court and the Legacy of the Yuan Mongols," in *Culture, Courtiers and Competition: The Ming Court (1368–1644)*, ed. Robinson (Cambridge, MA: Harvard University Asia Center; distributed by Harvard University Press, 2008), 371.

39. Patricia Berger, "Miracles in Nanjing: An Imperial Record of the Fifth Karmapa's Visit to the Chinese Capital," in *Cultural Intersections in Later Chinese Buddhism*, ed. Marsha Weidner (Honolulu: University of Hawai'i Press, 2001), 149–50.

40. On the Tay (Shan) language, see n. 15 above.

41. Hugh Edward Richardson, "The Karma-pa Sect, A Historical Note," in *High Peaks, Pure Earth: Collected Writings on Tibetan History and Culture* (London: Serindia Publications, 1998), 335–78; Berger, "Miracles in Nanjing," 145–69; and Luo Wenhua, "Ming Dabao Fawang jian pudu dazhai changjuan," *Zhongguo Zangxue* 1 (1995): 89–97.

42. "Gamaba wei Ming Taizu jianfu tu changjuan," in *Baozang: Zhongguo Xizang lishi wenwu*, vol. 3: *Yuanchao shiqi, Mingchao shiqi* (Beijing: Zhaohua chubanshe, 2000), 96–115.

43. Luo Aili and Liu Yingsheng, "Gamaba wei Ming Taizu jianfu tu Huihuiwen chutan" (A Preliminary Survey of the Persian Text in the Tsurphu Scroll), *Xibei minzu yanjiu* 48, 1 (2006): 55.

44. *Mirza Haydar Dughlat's Tarikh-i-Rashidi: A History of the Khans of Moghulistan*, trans. and ed. W. M. Thackston (Cambridge, MA: Harvard University, Department of Near Eastern Languages and Civilizations, 1996), 182. See also *A History of the Moghuls of Central Asia: Being the Tarikh-i-Rashidi of Mirza Muhammad Haidar, Dughlát*, trans. Sir E. Denison Ross, ed. Ney Elias (London: Sampson Low, & Marston, 1898), 416. Dr. Anya King of the University of Southern Indiana made me aware of this record.

45. Nik Douglas and Meryl White, *Karmapa: The Black Hat Lama of Tibet* (London: Luzac, 1976), 64.

46. *Quanzhou Yisilanjiao shike* (Islamic Inscriptions at Quanzhou), ed. Chen Dasheng, (Ningxia: Ningxia renmin chubanshe, 1984), 7–8.

47. Zhang Wende, "Wang Zongzai ji qi 'Siyiguan kao'" (Wang Tsung-Tsai and His "Ssu I-Kuan K'ao"), *Zhongguo bianjiang shidi yanjiu* 10, 3 (2000): 1.

48. *Siyiguan kao*, 1: 10v.

49. *Xiaozong shilu*, 2: 14v.

50. Liang Chu, *Yuzhou yi gao* (Manuscripts Bequeathed by Yuzhou) (Taibei: Shangwu yinshuguan, 1973), 1: 10rv.

51. Jan J. L. Duyvendak, "The True Dates of the Chinese Maritime Expeditions in the Early 15th Century," *T'oung Pao* 34 (1939): 341–412.

52. Ma Huan, *Yingyai shenglan jiaozhu* (Overall Survey of the Ocean's Shores Annotated), ed. Feng Chengjun (Taibei: Shangwu yinshuguan, 1962).

53. All sources summarized in Ma Huan, *Ying-Yai Sheng-lan, "The Overall Survey of the Ocean's Shores" [1433],* trans. and ed. J. V. G. Mills (Cambridge: Cambridge University Press, 1970).

54. Luo Maodeng, *Sanbao taijian xiyang ji tongsu yanyi* (Shanghai: Shanghai guji chubanshe, 1985).

55. Liu Yingsheng, "Mingchu Zhongguo yu Yazhou zhongxibu diqu jiaowang de waiwen yuyan wenti" (On the Diplomatic Language in the Communication between China and Midwestern Asia in Ming Dynasty), in *Chuancheng wenming, zou xiang shijie, heping fazhan, jinian Zheng He xia Xiyang liubai zhounian guoji xueshu luntan lunwenji* (Carry on Civilization, Open to the World, for Peace and Development; Proceedings of the International Forum in Memory of the 600th Anniversary of Zheng He's Expeditions) (Beijing: Social Sciences Academic Press, 2005), 107.

56. W. I. Siriweera, *A Study of the Economic History of Pre-Modern Sri Lanka* (New Delhi: Vikas, 1994), 142–43.

57. P. E. Pieris, *Ceylon and the Portuguese 1505–1658* (Tellippalai, Ceylon: American Ceylon Mission Press, 1920), 108–9.

58. Fernão de Queyroz, *The Temporal and Spiritual Conquest of Ceylon,* trans. S. G. Perera (Colombo: A. C. Richards, 1930), 35.

59. Edward W. Perera, "The Galle Trilingual Stone," *Spolia Zeylanica* (Colombo Museum) 8 (1913): 122–32; Tamil and Persian texts in S. Paranavitana, "The Tamil Inscription on the Galle Trilingual Slab," *Epigraphia Zeylanica* (London: Frowde, 1912–33), 3: 331–41.

60. This was the International Forum in Memory of the 600th Anniversary of Zheng He's Expeditions (*Jinian Zheng He xia xiyang 600 zhounian guoji xueshu luntan*).

61. Liu Yingsheng, "Mingchu Zhongguo yu Yazhou zhongxibu diqu jiaowang de waiwen yuyan wenti," 113.

62. Enoki Kazuo, "Su-chou in Late Ming," in *Studia Asiatica: The Collected Papers of the Late Dr. Kazuo Enuki* (Tokyo, Kyuko-Shoin, 1998), 538.

63. Antoine Mostaert, *Le matériel mongol du Houa i i iu, Huayi yiyu, de Houng-ou, 1389,* ed. Igor de Rachewiltz, Mélanges chinois et bouddhiques, 18 (Brussels: Institut belge des hautes études chinoises, 1977).

64. Liu Yingsheng, *Huihuiguan Zazi yu Huihuiguan Yiyu yanjiu* (Beijing: Renmin chubanshe, 2008) 13.

65. Ibid.

66. Wang Zongzai, *Siyiguan kao,* pt 2: 21v–22r.

67. Liu Yingsheng, *Huihuiguan Zazi yu Huihuiguan Yiyu yanjiu,* 15–17.

68. Ibid. and Honda Minobu本田實信, 回回館譯語に就いて/*On the Hui-hui-kuan I-yü (Chinese-Persian Vocabulary)* (Sapporo, Japan: Hokkaido University, 1963).

69. The manuscripts are described in detail in Liu Yingsheng, *Huihuiguan Zazi yu Huihuiguan Yiyu yanjiu,* 14–22.

70. *Siyiguan ze,* introduction: 2v (p.16).

71. Ibid.

72. Qu Zhongrong, *Guquanshanguan tiba* (Prefaces and Postscripts from Ancient Spring Mountain Hostel), in *Song Yuan ban shumu tiba jikan,* ed. Jia Guirong and Wang Guan, vol. 1 (Beijing: Beijing tushuguan chubanshe, 2003), 326–28. Cf. Pelliot, *Ḥōja,* 279.

73. *Siyiguan ze,* 2: 3r (p. 45). Cf. Wild, "Materials for the Study of the Ssŭ i Kuan," 625.

74. *Siyiguan ze,* 18: 3rv.

75. Hu Zhenhua and Huang Runhua, *Mingdai wenxian "Gaochangguan ke": Ladingwen zimu yizhu* (The Gaochangguan ke Documents Transcribed in Latin Letters) (Wulumuqi: Xinjiang renmin chubanshe, 1981).

76. *Du shu min qiu ji,* ed. Qian Zeng and Ding Yu (Beijing: Shumu wenxian chubanshe, 1983), 189ff.

77. Qu Zhongrong, *Guquanshanguan tiba,* 329.

78. *Ming shi,* 329: 8516. Rossabi, *China and Inner Asia,* 35–36, identifies Sultan 'Ali as Yunus Khan of Moghulistan.

79. *Ming shi,* 329: 8532.

80. C. F. Petry, *Twilight of Majesty: The Reigns of the Mamlūk Sultans al-Ashrāf Qāytbāy and Qānṣūh al-Ghawrī in Egypt* (Seattle: University of Washington Press, 1993), 73–88.

81. Pelliot, *Ḫōǰa,* 81–206.

82. *Dictionary of Ming Biography, 1368–1644,* ed. Chaoying Fang and L. Carrington Goodrich (New York: Columbia University Press, 1976), 1152.

83. *Ming shi,* 329: 8521.

84. *Da Ming huidian,* 58: 10v.

85. *Siyiguan ze,* 7: 1rff.

86. Wang Zongzai, *Siyiguan kao,* 2: 21v–22r.

4

Persian and Turkic from Kazan to Tobolsk

Literary Frontiers in Muslim Inner Asia

Devin DeWeese

Our understanding of the widespread use of Persian in literary culture from the sixteenth to the nineteenth centuries has been shaped largely by attention to what we might call the southern route of Persian linguistic penetration, from Iran proper through Central Asia to India and Southeast Asia; less often considered are the remarkably long-lasting legacies of Persian literacy and Persian literary production along a more northerly trajectory, in which the northern and eastern frontiers of Persian literary culture largely correspond with the northern and northeastern frontiers of Islam in Eurasia. This trajectory mostly reflected Central Asian roots—though also patterns of transmission from Azerbaijan through the Caucasus or via Astrakhan—and led to the widespread production, use, and transmission of works in Persian in the Volga and Ural valleys, in western Siberia, and in "Eastern Turkistan" (i.e., Altïshahr, the Tarim basin).

It is the first two of these regions that will be the focus of this chapter. In the next part of this book, Eastern Turkistan (or Xinjiang) is treated in David Brophy's chapter 6, which is complemented by Alexandre Papas's discussion in chapter 8 of a particular niche of Persian "literary" production there. Although the regions discussed in this chapter are also covered in chapter 7 by Alfrid Bustanov—upon whose work part of the present survey depends—the overview offered here reflects a somewhat different approach, and a different perspective, rooted to the south, in Central Asia, where the trajectory of Persian usage helps frame the basic pattern that might be expected to the north, from the Volga valley to western Siberia. Indeed, the extent and longevity of Persian's domination of literary expression in Central Asia is not always recognized. It is therefore helpful to outline the contours of the late use of Persian in much of Central Asia, which may explain, and certainly parallels, its longevity further north.

First, however, some general observations of relevance for all the frontier regions considered here are in order. To begin with, the players and the general direction taken in the game are fairly clear: the contest was between Persian and various written forms of Turkic, with regional differences in the latter largely subsumed within the literary language now usually referred to as Chaghatai. The latter term can cover all literary forms of "Eastern Middle Turkic," from the thirteenth century to the early twentieth, and represents the "other" sphere of Turkic literary culture, beyond the Ottoman. Ironically, the term "Chaghatai" was in fact used more often in Ottoman, Indian, and, to a lesser extent, Iranian contexts than in the geographical range in which "Chaghatai" was actually deployed. There it was more often referred to simply as "Türki." Despite regional differences in orthography and, to a lesser extent, in grammar and morphology, the written Chaghatai language served as a common literary medium throughout Central Asia, including Eastern Turkistan, and throughout western Siberia and the Volga valley as well (though in the latter region, elements of Ottoman orthography combined with local linguistic particularities to distance "Türki" from "standard" Chaghatai, creating a third distinct Turkic literary sphere by the end of the eighteenth century). That common literary medium largely masked local differences, and was used by communities whose languages would devolve into the host of "national" languages in the twentieth century, from Noghay and Tatar and Bashkir to Qazaq and Uyghur and Türkmen.

As for the general direction of the contest, Persian eventually lost out, and the major languages used across western "Inner Asia" today, though filled with Persian elements, are Turkic. If we can speak more broadly of the "retraction" of Persian language and literary culture into Iran alone by the nineteenth century, the case of Persian's fate in Central Asia is in some ways even more dramatic: it retreated into the small country of Tajikistan and parts of Afghanistan. The dramatic contraction of the Persian sphere—of written Persographia, that is, more readily measurable than the sphere of spoken Persophonia—came quite late, however, as noted below.

A second general point to note is the enormous impact of Persian language and literary culture on the varieties of Turkic spoken, and later written, throughout northern and northeastern Eurasia. It is no exaggeration to say that Islamic Turkic literature is practically entirely modeled on and inspired by Persian genres and styles. Moreover, Persian was the chief "mediating" language for entire swaths of cultural assimilation. Direct influence from Arabic certainly occurred, but Persian had a much greater direct impact. If we consider linguistic influence, Persian's impact on Turkic languages throughout northern Eurasia was immense. That influence extends even beyond the frontiers of Islam. The religious vocabulary of various "pagan" peoples of the north of Russia, including parts of Siberia, includes numerous Persian borrowings, such as *khuda* (Persian: God) and *karamat* (Persian: miracle). Whether these came directly from Persian, or through contacts with Turks who had already borrowed the Persian terminology, is less clear. But the latter is more likely, and in fact the likelihood that Turks were transmitting an originally non-Turkic cultural vocabulary says even more about the *linguistic* (as opposed to simply human) impact of Persian.

Third, throughout the regions considered here, Persian tended to dominate in particular fields. In his studies of Siberian Muslim literature, Alfrid Bustanov has referred to Persian as the language of poetry and Sufism. Although there were clearly other fields in which Persian retained its importance, there is certainly some truth in this. However, it is not so much Turkic that Persian competed with in particular fields of learning in these regions, but Arabic. Turkic did compete with Persian in historiography, and in that field came to replace Persian in the more northerly regions (and in Eastern Turkistan as well, though only by the middle of the eighteenth century). But Arabic remained the dominant language of the Quranic sciences and jurisprudence (*fiqh*), and continued to compete with Persian in the natural sciences—above all medicine and astronomy.

Fourth, and finally, there are in principle various means for gauging the late and gradual transition from Persian to Turkic, or, put another way, the lingering prominence of Persian. One way might be to focus on the sponsorship of translations from Persian into Turkic. As discussed below, this approach turns out to be not of much help. Another way is to focus on the creation of original works in Persian, representing composition in Persian by local inhabitants, or immigrants, based in these distant outposts of "Persianate Islam." Such original works are of particular interest in terms of the use of Persian to frame local and regional history and religious consciousness, or to memorialize locally or regionally prominent individuals or dynasties. Adopting this approach, however, would lead us to date the demise of Persian quite a bit earlier than is suggested by other evidence.

That other evidence may be drawn from data on the continued copying of Persian manuscripts in regions where we would expect to find Turkic literary production dominating. In some cases, that expectation can be confirmed, but must be balanced by recognition that there was ongoing manuscript production in Persian, reflecting the copying of Persian works for a local and regional readership. There was, that is, a market for Persian manuscripts, and, presumably, an educated readership for material in Persian alongside Turkic, well after the time in which writers in these regions had ceased to use Persian for the creation of original literature or works of learning. The extent, and longevity, of this phenomenon are just now becoming clear through the cataloguing and description of Islamic manuscript collections in the Volga-Ural region, and in western Siberia. Although such cataloguing and description is now under way, coverage is still quite incomplete, and as a result we can apply this promising strategy only unevenly.

A PERSIAN/TURKIC LITERARY CURVE: THE CASE OF CENTRAL ASIA

For western Central Asia (the portion that came under Russian and then Soviet rule), the general pattern of the late shift from the literary domination of Persian is reasonably clear. However, the issue is now fraught with nationalistic claims and

counterclaims, rooted in the Soviet-era relegation of Tajikistan to a relatively marginal status vis-à-vis the more numerous, and more populous, republics dominated by Turkic speakers. That is, Turkic literary production remained a small part of
literary culture in most of Central Asia until the nineteenth century, with Persian
remaining by far the major medium of learned expression in all parts of the region
down to the nineteenth century, and only slowly giving way to Turkic—and then
not in all parts of Central Asia—in the course of the nineteenth century.[1] It may
be helpful to sketch this development, as a sort of benchmark for considering the
status of Persian in more northerly regions.

Turkic literary production had hardly begun before the Mongol conquest. The
fourteenth and fifteenth centuries still saw only a handful of Turkic-language
works produced—with many surviving only in copies made in the sixteenth century. However, the Timurid era of the fifteenth century did see an increase in the
body of Turkic literature produced in Central Asia—in part through the individual efforts of Mir 'Ali Shir Nawa'i toward the end of the Timurid century—but it
was still dwarfed by the Persian literary production patronized by the Timurid
elite. After all, this was the era of the small explosion of historiography reflected
in the works of Nizam al-Din Shami, Hafiz-i Abru, Sharaf al-Din 'Ali Yazdi, Kamal
al-Din 'Abd al-Razzaq Samarqandi, Mirkhwand, and Khwandamir, to name only
the most notable authors. All of them wrote in Persian, defining and framing the
legacy of a dynasty rightly regarded as reflecting Central Asia's growing Turkification following the Mongol conquest. The fifteenth century also saw the beginnings
of a dramatic rise in hagiographical production in Central Asia that would reach
its peak in the sixteenth century; it is virtually all in Persian, and hagiographical
production remained an almost entirely Persian undertaking in the region until
the genre began to wither in the latter part of the nineteenth century.

Ironically, then, just as the Mongol conquest, and the new waves of Turkic-
speaking communities it brought into Central Asia and Iran, had yielded a flowering of Persian historiography under the Il-Khans, the Timurid era likewise
saw the proliferation of historical works in Persian in Iran and Central Asia, and
extensive patronage of Persian literature in general. Two Turkic histories were
evidently written in Timur's own day, before the flowering of Timurid historiography in Persian, but no Turkic historical work has survived from the Timurid
era—unless we include 'Ali Shir Nawa'i's prose contributions, which are focused
not on the Timurid dynasty, but on the pre-Islamic prophets and the ancient kings
of Iran. The case of Nawa'i is particularly instructive, insofar as he himself wrote
in Persian too and used Persian classics as the models for his Chaghatai Turkic
literary production. Though Nawa'i is now typically regarded as a sort of patron
saint of Turkic literature, especially in Uzbekistan, despite his praise for the greater
versatility of Turkic over Persian and Arabic (he devoted one work to this claim),
he may be regarded as the major "Persifier" of Turkic language and literature in
the Timurid era.[2]

Although Turkic historiography got under way in the early sixteenth century, through the patronage of the Shïbanid, or Abu al-Khayrid, clan that ousted the Timurids and restored Chinggisid rule, its products were relatively few. The career of Muhammad Shïbani Khan inspired one Chaghatai Turkic historical work in verse (Muhammad Salih Bilgüt's *Shïbani-nama*), and the khan himself sponsored another (the *Tawarikh-i Guzida-yi Nusrat-nama*). Yet his career also inspired at least two substantial Persian histories (the works of Bina'i and Shadi), thus balancing the use of Turkic. More striking, in some regards, is the extensive program of translations from Persian sponsored by Muhammad Shïbani Khan and his successors in the various appanage centers of Mawarannahr ("the Land beyond the River," viz. Transoxiana), yielding six known Chaghatai translations of important Persian works dating from the first three decades of the sixteenth century.[3] In addition, a major universal history, known as the *Zubdat al-Asar,* was compiled in Turkic in this era, which may be regarded as a translation of sorts, since its author relied almost entirely upon earlier Persian historiography, and there appears to be little original in it.[4] Here, too, Abu al-Khayrid patronage is balanced between Persian and Turkic. Soon after the *Zubdat al-Asar* was completed, another Khurasani in Mawarannahr produced yet another universal history that culminates in the career of the dynasty's founding figure. The *Tarikh-i Abu al-Khayr-khani,* as this work is called, was thus sponsored by, and celebrated, the Turkic-speaking Chinggisid dynastic clan that came to power and prominence in the steppes of the northern Dasht-i Qïpchaq and depended on the nomadic Uzbek tribal groups for its military power; but it is written in Persian.[5]

Despite this balance of Persian and Turkic historiography in terms of original works, the translation program of the early Abu al-Khayrid polity suggests that the early sixteenth century might have become a tipping point in a transition toward Turkic literary dominance; but this was not the case. In other contexts, that is, patronage of translations might be understood as marking, in effect, the passing of one language's dominance and the emergence of a new learned language—one "made learned," indeed, by the sponsored translations. Such patronage may be understood as preparing the way for a new literary, and historical, idiom, and as clearing away a past linguistic and literary legacy—in this case, Persian—by rendering it in the new soon-to-be dominant language and thus making the works in the old language disposable.

Yet this did not happen in sixteenth-century Central Asia. Despite the translation program, and the patronage of Turkic literature,[6] which seems to have reached its peak in the 1520s, the brief experiment in promoting or sponsoring Turkic literature seems to have come to an end by the second half of the sixteenth century.[7] The substantial body of historical—and hagiographical—literature prompted by the centralization of rule in Central Asia under 'Abdullah Khan ibn Iskandar (d. 1598) was again all in Persian. If we consider the *central* Central Asian region of Mawarannahr during the seventeenth and eighteenth centuries, Turkic literary production practically ceases, outside occasional Turkic verse (recorded, moreover, not in substantial *diwan*s or even anthologies, but mostly in the ad hoc form of the *bayaz*). The one notable exception to this overwhelmingly Persian literary scene is a medical work in Chaghatai Turkic ascribed to Subhan-Quli Khan (r. 1681–1702) of the Ashtarkhanid dynasty, based in Bukhara.[8] Otherwise there is practically no evidence of the use of Turkic as a literary language, much less a language of learning, in Mawarannahr from the second half of the sixteenth century down to the nineteenth. Indeed, a sign of a reversion from Turkic to Persian may be found already in the early Ashtarkhanid era in the translation into Persian of ʿAli Shir Nawaʾiʾs *Tarikh-i Anbiya wa Hukama wa Muluk-i ʿAjam,* done in 1640–41 at the request of an official at the court of Imam-Quli Khan.[9]

It was only in Khwarazm that Turkic literature had a greater presence than Persian, though in this case literary production was in general much more limited. Aside from two translations from Persian into Turkic sponsored by the Khwarazmian Uzbek dynasty during the second half of the sixteenth century—of Rashid al-Din, again, and of a Persian Quran commentary (*tafsir*)—three Turkic historical works (one from the 1550s and two from the middle of the seventeenth century) dominate the Khwarazmian literary scene during the sixteenth and seventeenth centuries. This meager production is noteworthy primarily because Persian literary production during this period was even less substantial, making Khwarazm the only part of Central Asia for which we can claim some sort of parity between Persian and Turkic before the nineteenth century.

Persian continued to dominate in the rest of Central Asia during the eighteenth century, and it was not until the emergence of dynastic states dominated by the Uzbek tribal elites in the nineteenth century that the situation began to change. That change was again most pronounced in Khwarazm, where the Qonghrat dynasty sponsored historiographical production in Chaghatai Turkic, as well as an extensive program of translations into Turkic from Persian (and in some cases from Arabic), as discussed by Marc Toutant in chapter 10 of this volume. The Khivan khanate's patronage of Chaghatai letters during the nineteenth century yielded by far the largest body of literary material in Central Asian Turkic, and this patronage continued into the early twentieth century. In this case, the 'tipping point' was reached very quickly. Yet even as Chaghatai Turkic literature dramatically overtook production in Persian, and as Turkic came to be used overwhelmingly (and indeed exclusively, from the late 1850s on) in official documents, a preference for Persian was maintained in some spheres well into the nineteenth century. Endowment deeds (*waqf-nama*s) and other documents produced by *qazi*s were often written in Persian until the second half of the nineteenth century; deeds of sale (*wasiqa*s) preserved in the Khivan archives are overwhelmingly in Persian until 1857, when they abruptly begin to be written exclusively in Chaghatai, suggesting a deliberate bureaucratic decision to switch.[10]

Another feature of the shift from Persian to Turkic in Khwarazm is worth noting. The ornate Chaghatai literary language used in the historical works of the early nineteenth century, above all the *Firdaws al-Iqbal* of Mu'nis (d. 1829) and his nephew Agahi (d. 1874), is filled, not simply with Persian terminology, but with extensive Persian syntactic units fitted into a broader Turkic structure that sometimes all but disappears for line after line. Indeed, reading some of the introductory sections of the *Firdaws al-Iqbal,* one can find Persian phrasings continuing for pages, with just a few Turkic suffixes occasionally interspersed to remind the reader that this is a Chaghatai work. The prevalence of this high style, with Turkic infused with (and sometimes crowded out by) Persian, prompted a new, if smaller, wave of literary production in Khwarazm at the end of the nineteenth century and the beginning of the twentieth. At that time, several writers were commissioned to produce *simplified* Chaghatai Turkic versions of the earlier histories produced by Mu'nis and Agahi, with the florid Persian material reduced substantially or omitted altogether. It is thus not until the early twentieth century that we can rightly speak of the replacement of Persian by a more substantially de-Persified Turkic, even in the most thoroughly Turkified region of Central Asia.

Elsewhere in the region, Chaghatai literary production increased substantially in the khanate of Khoqand, especially through the activity of poets writing in Turkic, but never displaced Persian as in Khwarazm, at least not before the liquidation of the khanate in 1876. The historiography of the Ming dynasty of Khoqand is again almost entirely in Persian, and bureaucratic practice, while including some document production in Turkic, continued the overwhelming dominance of Persian. Under the Manghït dynasty in Bukhara, finally, Persian continued to dominate literary and bureaucratic culture, down to the end of the khanate in 1920. With the inclusion of much of Mawarannahr, including the major cities of Samarqand and Bukhara, into the Uzbek Soviet Socialist Republic during the mid-1920s, the question of the relationship of Persian and Turkic literary cultures entered the realm of Soviet language and nationalities policy.

A final phenomenon worthy of note in the interplay of Persian and Turkic in the western part of Central Asia is the creation of what might be considered hybrid texts, in which Persian and Turkic syntax and vocabulary were integrated to a degree not encountered in earlier times. The adoption of Persian lexical elements—not just words, but *izafat* constructions and other compounds—into Turkic was under way before the Mongol era, and was a standard feature of Chaghatai, leaving a substantial Persian element still today in most Central Asian Turkic languages. Borrowing went in the other direction as well, especially after the increasing prominence of Turks in the wake of the Mongol conquest. Timurid Persian historiography is filled with Turkic and Mongolian terminology, above all dealing with military and administrative matters. But in the second half of the nineteenth century, we find works such as the *Tarikh-i Jadida-yi Tashkand,* an enormous compilation by one Muhammad Salih, completed already after the Russian conquest of Tashkent in 1865. Tashkent was another heavily Turkified part of Central Asia, with a large Uzbek and even Qazaq population base, but the basic framework of this work is Persian. Nevertheless, we find entire Turkic phrases inserted into the Persian structures, and vice versa, on a far greater scale than before; a particular saint is identified, for instance, as the *sarwar-i toqsan-toquz ming masha'ikh* (leader of 99,000 shaykhs), combining Arabic, Persian, and Turkic words in an essentially Persian construction. This sort of hybridization goes well beyond the incorporation of Persian words and syntactically significant phrases into Turkic languages, or the imitation of Persian style in Chaghatai literature.

BEYOND CENTRAL ASIA: PERSIAN LITERATURE IN NORTHERN EURASIA

A similar pattern, and a similar timetable, might be expected in areas closely linked with Central Asia, such as western Siberia and the Volga-Ural region. In fact, the situation appears to be different in each of these regions, reflecting both the different kinds of information available to us about these connected, but distinct, regions and doubtless genuinely different patterns.

To a large extent Persian literary production in these regions has fallen through the cracks of scholarly interest, at least until recently; attention has tended to focus on Turkic literary production in the regions, as the precursor of modern literary cultures. Indeed, the prominence of Persian in all these regions—including even the western part of Central Asia—has been obscured by twentieth-century historical constructions framed by and for politically dominant Turkic constituencies—especially in the Volga-Ural region, Eastern Turkistan, and four of the five former Soviet republics of Central Asia—determined to project a Turkic literary heritage deep into the past. With access to manuscript collections assembled from throughout the Russian Empire and the USSR, Soviet-era specialists based in Leningrad were well equipped to comment on the literary legacies of the Volga-Ural region and western Siberia, but for the most part they paid scant attention to Persian writings there.[11]

The Volga-Ural Region

In the Volga-Ural region, despite the overwhelmingly Turkic-speaking Muslim population, there was a remarkable continuation of Persian literary culture through the nineteenth century.[12] Persian language and literature appeared relatively early in this region, as evidenced by the extensive Persian *masnawi* produced in Crimea during the reigns of Özbek and Jani-bek, khans of the Jochid *ulus* (the khanate of Chinggis Khan's eldest son, Jochi, or Golden Horde), in the first half of the fourteenth century.[13] This clearly reflects the transplantation of Persian speakers and writers from Anatolia, but Muslim jurists and scholars from Khwarazm were also influential in the Golden Horde, ensuring access to Persian literary production from Central Asia as well. During the fourteenth century, moreover, the central lands of the Golden Horde yielded a Turkic rendering of the story of Khusraw and Shirin, clearly based on a Persian model, by a poet named Qutb from Saray.[14] Here we can only infer the circulation of Persian literature, based on the influence of Persian models on Turkic literature produced in the Golden Horde and on evidence of Persian speakers from Iran and Central Asia dwelling for a time in the Volga valley.

It becomes increasingly difficult to trace Persian literary production—or Turkic, or Arabic, for that matter—in the central lands of the Golden Horde during the latter part of the fourteenth century and through the fifteenth century, a time of major political disorders. The bureaucratic language reflected in the few surviving documents from the late fourteenth and early fifteenth centuries is Turkic, usually in the Uyghur script. But the fifteenth century saw still more Central Asian scholars moving through the lands of the Golden Horde (by then largely defunct), and there is no reason to assume that Persian (or Arabic) letters disappeared at this point. Scattered references to the education of the Chinggisid elites of the Dasht-i Qïpchaq, and to the presence of both schools (*maktabs*) and learned tutors for princes of the blood, suggest that some knowledge of both Persian and Arabic, and hence at least a limited market for literary production in multiple languages, were sustained through the fifteenth century. In his early sixteenth-century anthology (*tazkira*) of royal poets, *Rawzat al-Salatin,* Fakhri Harawi devotes an entry to Muhammad Amin Khan, "ruler of the province of Qazan," characterizing him as an intelligent, good-natured ruler with the heart of a dervish, and affirming that he wrote poetry in Persian.[15] Muhammad Amin was a great-grandson of Ulugh Muhammad Khan (who was a grandson of Toqtamïsh), and ruled what was left of the Golden Horde in the late fifteenth and early sixteenth centuries as khan in 1484–85, 1487–95, and 1502–18. We unfortunately know next to nothing of Persian literary training or production in this region during that period. Things worsen from the time of the Russian conquest of the region in the middle of the sixteenth century, as we mostly lose sight of any literary activity or continuity. It is not until the eighteenth century that we can trace substantial literary production again, with Persian well represented alongside Turkic ("Tatar") and Arabic.

Here again, seeking a translation-based "tipping point" is of no avail.[16] The only prominent translation from Persian into Turkic from this region was an adaptation of portions of Rashid al-Din's *Jami' al-Tawarikh* (Compendium of Chronicles), with additional information about the Golden Horde during the fourteenth, fifteenth, and sixteenth centuries, compiled by Qadir-'Ali Bek Jalayiri at the beginning of the seventeenth century. This was produced in the khanate of Kasimov, a Chinggisid principality under Moscow's rule, in 1602, and bears a dedication to the tsar, Boris Godunov.[17] It is of interest chiefly for the additional material on the later Chinggisid lineages active in the territory of the former Golden Horde, but for present purposes its production attests to the continued circulation there of Rashid al-Din's Persian original at the end of the sixteenth century.

As regards original works in Persian in the Volga-Ural region, we have little
to go on; but there is one remarkable work worthy of note, with a relatively late
date, from this thoroughly Turkified frontier of Persian literary culture. The
chief manuscript collection at the Institute of Oriental Manuscripts in Saint Petersburg preserves a short text, written in Persian by an anonymous author,
probably in the last quarter of the eighteenth century, and copied in the Volga
valley during the first half of the nineteenth century on Russian paper water-
marked 1820. It was acquired for the collection in Soviet times, in Astrakhan;
the manuscript catalogue assigns it the title *Hikayat* (Tales) and it also bears
the heading *Jaza-yi Jang*,[18] but neither title is very illuminating. Its contents, described in the manuscript catalogue, were explored more extensively by M. A.
Salakhetdinova over half a century ago.[19] The manuscript comprises "legends
and narratives relating to the history of the Kazan Tatars and Bashkirs," and is
divided into two sections. The first occupies just two folios (37b–38b) and presents a legendary account of Timur's campaign against the city of Vladimir,
and of his conquest of Bulghar, as well as an account of the founding of Kazan, a list
of the khans of Kazan, and an account of the conquest of Kazan by the Russians in
1552; the material on Timur echoes some of the narratives known from the Turkic
Tawarikh-i Bulghariyya.[20] The second part (38b–45b) contains various accounts
dealing with the history of the Bashkirs, covering the period from the second half
of the sixteenth century to the first half of the eighteenth. This section appears
to have been based on accounts of oral informants, and includes an account of a
Bashkir uprising that lasted from 1735 to 1741.

A "Tatar" version of this work was known to exist, but only a Russian translation of that Turkic version survives. A comparison undertaken by Salakhetdinova revealed that the Persian version was often more complete and more detailed
(judging by the Russian translation). Whether this indicates that the Persian version was original is less clear. But in any case, the use of Persian to render such
material on the history of the Volga River Basin's Muslim communities in the late
eighteenth century is certainly worthy of note, as is the copying of this text in the
first half of the nineteenth century.

Unlike the situation with western Siberia (or Eastern Turkistan), there is more
abundant, and above all more accessible, evidence on the production, and importation, of such copies of Persian manuscripts in the Volga-Urals. That evidence
comes from manuscript catalogues, which are by no means uniform in their descriptive practices or quality, but nevertheless allow a picture of the Persian manuscript market to emerge. The evidence such catalogues provide, of both local
manuscript production and importation, suggests a substantial, and lively, readership for Persian material in the Volga-Urals through most of the eighteenth and
nineteenth centuries.

In the mid-1960s, Yuri Bregel published an article on the historical manuscripts preserved in Kazan (chiefly in the collection of Kazan University).[21] Most

of the works he discussed were in Persian, reflecting his interests in Central Asian historiography. The collection was significantly enlarged through the efforts of Mirkasym Usmanov, Marsel' Akhmetzianov, and Al'bert Fatkhiev in the 1970s and 1980s, but little was done in terms of actually utilizing this rich manuscript heritage, whether in Turkic or Persian, until after the collapse of the Soviet Union. In the late 1990s, Allen Frank and Michael Kemper published important studies that began to make the manuscript culture of the Volga-Urals more widely known, if still not widely used in historical study of the region.[22]

In the latter connection, it is worth noting the clear impact of Muslim educational institutions in the maintenance of Persian literacy. The studies of Kemper, Frank, and of others have explored the topography of Muslim learning in the Volga-Urals and western Siberia, and the major madrasa centers under the jurisdiction of the Orenburg Muslim Spiritual Assembly (*Dukhovnoe sobranie*), established in 1788. Such studies highlight the vibrant intellectual activity in Orenburg itself, but especially in Omsk and Semipalatinsk, as well as in Ufa and Kazan, alongside other regional centers such as Sterlitamak. Persian works were studied in these madrasas down to the early Soviet era. Although it is difficult to link this activity directly with the region's Persian manuscript legacy, it is clearly part of the story of Persian's persistence there.

As for that manuscript legacy, it is still not possible to give a thorough accounting of the Persian manuscripts preserved in Kazan (much less Ufa), as a marker of local production or consumption of Persian materials. But partial catalogues of three important collections with significant holdings of manuscripts obtained in the Volga-Urals are now available, and allow some preliminary observations about the contours of Persian literary production in the region.

To begin with, the most important, and largest, collection of Persian manuscripts in Russia is that of the Saint Petersburg Institute of Oriental Manuscripts, noted above. To date, nine volumes of a descriptive catalogue of the institute's Persian manuscripts have been published, beginning in the mid-1950s. However, a far larger number of works is covered in a two-volume handlist published in 1964, giving minimal information (author, copy date, foliation), but including each manuscript's provenance.[23] The catalogue reveals Persian manuscript production and use in the Volga-Ural region throughout the eighteenth and nineteenth centuries, and throughout the region, from the major cities to small villages. The sample of material produced and/or obtained in the Volga-Ural region is relatively small overall, but the profile it yields for the circulation of works in Persian corresponds reasonably well with what is suggested by the larger samples made available more recently.

More specifically, regarding the chronological range represented by the manuscripts from this collection, the dates of copying in the region are all in the eighteenth and nineteenth centuries. The earliest dates to 1738–39 and the latest to 1884. Of the twenty-eight separate manuscripts (rather than works) clearly from the Volga-Ural region, six are undated, nine belong to the eighteenth century, and thirteen date from the nineteenth century. The eighteenth-century distribution is of particular interest, insofar as Persian manuscripts were being copied extensively both before and after the administrative, and intellectual, impact of the Orenburg Muslim Spiritual Assembly's establishment in 1788 (as is borne out by data from the other collections as well).

As noted, in geographical terms the Persian manuscripts were produced throughout the Volga-Ural region. There was a heavy concentration (twelve) from present-day Tatarstan, with half of these copied in or near Kazan,[24] and half from elsewhere in Tatarstan.[25] One was produced as far west as the Chuvash republic;[26] and no fewer than six came from Bashqortostan—and not just from the prominent towns of Ufa and Sterlitamak (one each), but from small towns and villages throughout the Bashkir territory.[27] The small sample of works copied in Bashqortostan represents the major genres in which Persian was most important (two Sufi works, a copy of Sa'di's *Gulistan,* one work on Arabic grammar, one *tafsir,* and one Persian translation of a collection of hadiths). Several more were evidently produced southward along the Volga valley.[28] Three came from much further south and east, with two from Astrakhan and one from Ural'sk (along the middle course of the Ural River, not far west of Orenburg).[29] The manuscripts from Bashqortostan skew somewhat earlier than the rest, with two from the eighteenth century, and the latest from 1837. This pattern might be held to signal the longer persistence of Persian literacy closer to the "learned" center of Kazan, but the nineteenth-century manuscripts from as far away as Astrakhan and Ural'sk seem not to confirm this, and of course the sample is quite small in the first place.

The most extensive catalogues so far available for any manuscript collection in the Volga-Ural region—two volumes compiled by Alsu Arslanova—are devoted to Persian manuscripts in the collection of Kazan University.[30] Unfortunately, the descriptions rarely include information on *where* the manuscripts described were copied.[31] It is sometimes possible to infer a general location from the *nisbas* (onomastic place attributions) of the copyists. Even the copyists' *nisbas* are of limited value, however, given the extensive contacts between the Volga-Ural region and Central Asia, for instance, both before and after the Russian conquest, and the pattern of "Tatar" students travelling to study in the madrasas of Bukhara (where their studies might also include the copying of manuscripts), as explored recently by Allen Frank.[32]

At the same time, those same contacts and patterns may help us to contextualize the current state of the collection in Kazan. In other words, given both the particular status of the Volga-Ural region within the Russian empire prior to the second half of the eighteenth century, and the relative isolation of the region in Soviet times—through most of the twentieth century, that is—it stands to reason that both the importation and local copying of Persian manuscripts would have peaked between the latter eighteenth century and the early twentieth century. The peak may have been pushed toward the earlier part of that range—say, the second quarter of the nineteenth century—by the broader pattern of increasing Turkifica-tion, or "Tatarification."

Arslanova's catalogue confirms the presence in the Kazan collection of many manuscripts copied in Central Asia—above all, Bukhara, less often, Samarqand, and occasionally Kabul—that were brought to the Volga-Ural region in the nine-teenth century (the approximate dates of their arrival in the region are often in-dicated through owners' marks). Together with a few manuscripts copied in In-dia and presumably transported through Central Asia, we can see the tangible evidence of the market or readership for Persian manuscripts in the Volga-Ural region during the nineteenth century. Some of these manuscripts were clearly cop-ied in the eighteenth and nineteenth centuries. This suggests again that travelers and students from Kazan and elsewhere were obtaining manuscripts in Central Asia, or copying them themselves. But quite a few old manuscripts held in Kazan most likely reflect this avenue for the acquisition of Persian manuscripts as well, and thus likewise confirm a readership for—or, more properly, a constituency that valued the ownership of—Persian manuscripts in the Volga-Ural region. There are some manuscripts, to be sure, produced in Iran or in the Caucasus, and more (mostly in Turkic) from Istanbul. But it seems clear that collections in the Volga-Ural region were substantially enriched, not only by ongoing local production, but by the importation of Persian literature from and through Central Asia.

For instance, an old manuscript of 'Abd al-Rahman Jami's *Shawahid al-Nubuw-wa* (on the life of the Prophet), copied in 1489, had made its way to the Volga-Urals by 1847.[33] A sixteenth-century copy of Mirkhwand's *Rawzat al-Safa,* completed in 1595, was evidently brought to the region in the late eighteenth or early nine-teenth century.[34] And the same is most likely true of the sixteenth-century copy of Dawlatshah's *Tazkirat al-Shu'ara,* dated 1580.[35] The collection also holds much older Persian material, and although it is not impossible that it was brought to the Volga-Ural region in earlier centuries, the shifts in the Russian administration of the Muslim communities in the region point to the second half of the eighteenth century, at the earliest, as the time in which private collections were being assem-bled, even when a particular work's acquisition in the late eighteenth or nineteenth century is not explicitly confirmed. This era in turn points, again, to Central Asia as the immediate source.[36]

On the other hand, not just classical or old and rare works, but later works as well evidently held appeal for the Volga-Ural community and were in all likelihood sought by travelers and students who spent time in Central Asia. For instance, the collection holds a copy of the *Matlab al-Talibin,* a hagiography of the Juybari *khwaja*s of Bukhara compiled in the second half of the seventeenth century, which was copied in Central Asia in the early nineteenth century.[37] It also holds two copies of Muhammad Yusuf Munshi's *Tazkira-yi Muqim-Khani,* from the early eighteenth century—a work of much more local Central Asian interest than the universal history of Mirkhwand—both produced in Bukhara in the nineteenth

FIGURE 7. Sufi Protector of the Steppe: the shrine of Ahmad Yasawi, Turkistan, Kazakhstan.
Photograph by Nile Green.

century.[38] And it holds single copies of two other works likewise of local Central Asian focus: Muhammad Vafa Karminagi's *Tuhfat al-Khani*, from later in the eighteenth century, on the emergence of the Manghït dynasty in Bukhara, copied in 1844, and the *Tarikh-i Shahrukhi* of Muhammad Niyaz Khuqandi, a history of the khanate of Khoqand completed in 1871–72.[39] Also of interest, from roughly the same era, is a nineteenth-century copy of *Fawa'id-i Khaqaniyya,* a relatively uncommon work in the "Mirror for Princes" genre, written in the second half of the seventeenth century by the Yasawi shaykh Muhammad Sharif Bukhari (who dedicated the work to Nazr Muhammad Khan, of the Ashtarkhanid dynasty).[40] Two other copies are known in Tashkent, and two in Saint Petersburg. This copy was made by Sarïghay ibn Yana-si [*sic*] Qazani, but it is not clear whether he produced it during a stay in Bukhara—where he or some intermediary must have come into contact with this relatively obscure work—or in his native town.

The Kazan University collection thus holds a number of manuscripts from the fifteenth and sixteenth centuries, as well as works from the eighteenth century, that seem to suggest an interest in, or close connection with, Central Asia. More broadly, Arslanova's catalogue offers an idea of what local readers of Persian were having copied, and there seem to be clear patterns in the kinds of literature in which Persian continued to be important.

First of all, the catalogue reveals a particularly strong representation of Persian-language grammars of Arabic, certainly in the eighteenth century but still in the nineteenth century as well; this is evident in the materials from Saint Petersburg outlined above, but Arslanova's catalogue is of particular interest for reflecting additional examples of locally collected manuscripts.[41] What this pattern suggests about when and where Persian might have been used as a medium for studying or teaching Arabic remains uncertain, but Arabic grammar was clearly a subject that prompted considerable copying, and original production, of works in Persian. Of interest in this connection is a lexical work, intended for teaching children, entitled *Sharh Nisab al-Sibyan*, using Persian to teach Arabic, which was composed in the second half of the sixteenth century by Muhammad ibn Fasih ibn Muhammad al-Dasht-bayazi and was copied in 1755 by Salim-Jan ibn Dust-Muhammad Bulghari.[42] An exception to this rule, however, reflecting direct interest in Persian itself (rather than its apparent use in mediating knowledge of Arabic), is an eighteenth-century copy—evidently done in the Volga-Ural region, to judge from the description of its target language as "Tatar"—of the *Lughat-i Ni'matullah,* a sixteenth-century Persian-Ottoman lexicon, evidently adapted to the local Turkic language when copied in 1731.[43]

Persian was also notable in the field of medicine. Three Persian medical works, including the famous *Jami' al-Fawa'id* of Yusuf al-Harawi, were copied by 'Abd al-Jabbar ibn 'Abd al-Mannan al-Bulghari in Kazan in 1842.[44]

As expected, there is a heavy preponderance of Sufi works among the Persian manuscripts held at Kazan University. These include some important old copies of both well-known and obscure works, noted above, but the later copies produced in the Volga-Ural region are instructive about particular currents of Sufism and their impact in the region. Not surprisingly, Naqshbandi works are well represented, and aside from some works produced in Central Asian Naqshbandi circles in the fifteenth, sixteenth, and seventeenth centuries, works reflecting the northward spread of the Mujaddidiyya, through Central Asia but often through the Ottoman realm, in the form of the Khalidiyya, are more common.[45] Two biographies of Shaykh Ahmad Sirhindi (d. 1624), the *mujaddid* (Renewer) himself, copied together in Istanbul, in 1828, by Muhammad Rajab Badakhshani, may reflect this more complex transmissional and personal history.[46] However, one of these works, and yet another hagiography focused on Sirhindi, are represented in the collection in much older copies.[47] The collection also holds six copies of Sirhindi's *Maktubat.*[48] The oldest of these, copied in 1721, may not have been produced locally, but at least three of the others were clearly copied in the Volga-Ural region, on paper produced in Russian factories (including one copied in the late nineteenth century by Mulla Hasan ibn Mulla Ja'far al-Naratbashi). Similarly, the five copies of the *Maktubat* of Sirhindi's son, Muhammad Ma'sum, include one from 1772 that is not clearly a local product, but also two clearly produced in the region, likewise copied on Russian factory-produced paper.[49] One was copied as early as the late 1780s or 1790s, and another was copied in 1811 by 'Ubaydullah ibn Kalimullah al-Aldirmishi, who later, in 1840, copied treatises of Makhdum-i A'zam, as noted above.

The Kazan University collection holds two copies, including one produced in the Volga-Urals in 1830, of a Persian work by the Central Asian Mujaddidi, Musa Dahbidi (d. 1776).[50] Not surprisingly, it also holds numerous locally produced copies of Persian works by the famous Sufi Allahyar (d. ca. 1720), a Naqshbandi Mujaddidi shaykh whose works—some in Persian, some in Turkic—became quite popular throughout the Volga-Ural region.[51] His *Maslak al-Muttaqin* is represented in twenty-eight copies in this collection,[52] and his *Murad al-'Arifin* is preserved there in nine copies.[53] But perhaps more telling with regard to the extent of the use of Persian in Sufi intellectualism are the two manuscripts of the Persian commentary on Sufi Allahyar's *Murad al-'Arifin,* entitled *Tuhfat al-Talibin,* written by the prominent "Tatar" litterateur 'Abd al-Rahim ibn 'Uthman ibn Sarmaqi Utïz-Imani al-Bulghari (d. 1834).[54] A Mujaddidi teaching certificate (*ijaza*) preserved in the collection reflects Central Asian links,[55] but the origins of particular works included in a collection of Mujaddidi treatises suggest more diverse connections, including links to the North Caucasus.[56]

The Kazan catalogue thus confirms an ongoing presence of Persian-language Sufi works well into the nineteenth century. However, it is also worth noting the extent and range of religious literature in Persian outside the sphere of Sufi literature, and in fields normally dominated by Arabic, represented in the Kazan University collection. This includes numerous locally copied Persian works on Hanafi jurisprudence (*fiqh*) from the eighteenth and nineteenth centuries.[57] Among them are copies of a Persian discussion of Hanafi inheritance law, evidently compiled by a local scholar, Yunus ibn Mulla Ivanay, active in the second half of the seventeenth century.[58] The collection also includes a dozen locally produced copies—mostly from the eighteenth century—of several old Persian Quran commentaries (*tafsir*).[59] Of particular interest are the three manuscripts in the Kazan University collection—two from the late eighteenth century and evidently locally copied—preserving a late-sixteenth-century Persian work on Quran recitation (presenting and explaining particular verses to be recited in various situations), entitled *Riyaz al-Abrar,* by Muhammad Sadiq ibn 'Abd al-Baqi ibn 'Izz al-Din al-Farghani, completed in 1591; one manuscript copy was finished in 1784, by a copyist whose *nisba* of al-Bulghari suggests its production in the Volga-Ural region, while the other was copied in Kazan a year later, in 1785.[60]

A final sample of Persian manuscripts from the Volga-Ural region is presented by a recent catalogue published by a Tatar scholar, S. M. Giliazutdinov, describing Persian manuscripts from a substantial collection in Kazan, that of the Institute of Language, Literature, and Art.[61] The first volume covers 332 manuscript works. This material substantially confirms the impression conveyed by the smaller Saint Petersburg sample and by Arslanova's catalogue, with regard to both the kinds of Persian material produced or held in the Volga-Ural region, and the wide distribution of Persian manuscript copying—again, not only in urban areas, but in the countryside as well. For example, let us take the case of the sixteen copies of the Persian commentary on the Arabic grammatical work commonly referred to as *al-Mu'izzi* (ascribed to 'Izz al-Din Zanjani, d. 1257) included in the first volume of Giliazutdinov's catalogue.[62] Of these, only three give both the date and place of copying, and all were done in rural villages.[63] An additional ten indicate the date of copying, or provide evidence for a range of dates (one was copied before 1772, another in 1781, five in the first half of the nineteenth century—1812, 1813, 1822, 1837, and 1844—and three in the mid-1880s—1883, 1884, and ca. 1886). Another work represented by a substantial number of copies in Giliazutdinov's catalogue is a very short Persian poem recounting an episode from the Prophet's life.[64] Of the twenty-one copies, seven, ranging in date from 1756 to 1867, indicate where they were copied, and of these only one was produced near Kazan[65] (seven of those that do not indicate the place of copying give a date or provide evidence for arguing a range: 1717–18, between 1742 and 1769, ca. 1787, 1823, 1865, 1879, and 1915).

Western Siberia

Unlike western Central Asia and Eastern Turkistan, Siberia is not, to say the least, a region immediately associated with Persian literary culture, or with a strong, or deep, literary culture of any sort; nevertheless, we are just beginning to appreciate the wealth of Islamic manuscripts preserved there, and indeed the long presence there of Persian literacy. A gravestone discovered in 1991 in the nature preserve known as Saadak-Terek, on the right bank of the Khemchik River in the Tuvan Republic (now officially Tyva), bore an inscription, in Arabic and Persian, dated to 1194, identifying the deceased as a *sayyid*, or descendant of Muhammad, Shaykh Rashid al-Din 'Umar ibn Muhammad ibn 'Ali al-Balkhi.[66]

Still further east, in the Mongol steppe, an inscription in Persian celebrating the establishment of a Sufi *khanaqah* in the Mongol capital of Qaraqorum, dated 1341-42, was discovered and published in 1999 by a team of Japanese scholars. Among the figures identified as responsible for the *khanaqah*'s establishment are several bearing Central Asian names and *nisbas*. These include as Khwaja Sa'd al-Din Balasaghuni, Hamid al-Din Almalighi (identified as a donor), and two figures to whose name the honorific *'azizan* is attached, namely. Khwaja Taj al-Din Andukani (i.e., a native of the town later known as Andijan), and 'Imad al-Din Bulghari.[67]

These inscriptional relics clearly reflect the migration of individuals or small groups into these northerly and northeasterly regions, above all from Central Asia. The inscriptions can hardly stand as evidence of a significant implantation of Persian literary culture among the local population. Yet it was precisely this sort of movement that eventually led to the Islamization of Western Siberia, beginning from the sixteenth century and continuing into the twentieth. The Central Asians involved in that movement, who brought Islam and came and settled in towns and villages of the region, chiefly for commercial reasons (usually becoming known locally as Bukharans), also brought Persian literature to Siberia.

There is, to be sure, little evidence so far available to confirm the endurance or continuity of any sort of Persian literary culture in the West Siberian region. We cannot point to major works produced locally in Persian and neither have any local Turkic works been identified as clear translations from Persian. Much less do we have any evidence of a local translation program of the sort encountered elsewhere. The region was, after all, in Russian hands nearly by the time such translations from Persian to Turkic were being sponsored in Mawarannahr, and prior to those done in eastern Turkistan.

We likewise find little help from manuscript cataloguing with regard to western Siberia. Local collections have scarcely begun to be inventoried and described. As a result, what we know of literary production in the region must come from the relatively few specialists who have utilized local historiographical and literary production in sketching the history of the region both before and after the establishment of Russian rule in the latter sixteenth century. Among the pioneers in this regard have been specialists based in Kazan, such as Mirkasym Usmanov and Marsel' Akhmetzianov, or in Ufa (R. G. Kuzeev). Usmanov in particular has expanded the reach of the archaeographical expeditions he conducted in Tatarstan and Bashkortostan further east, into the Baraba steppe.[68] Most of the material explored so far has been in Turkic, and is now typically classified as "Tatar."

Special mention must be made, however, of the remarkable researches of Alfrid Bustanov. Almost single-handedly, over the past several years Bustanov has delved into the manuscript culture of his native Siberian region, yielding above all an important monograph on the book culture of Siberian Muslims.[69] It is chiefly because of his work that we can begin to piece together something of the role of Persian literary culture in this region, and to understand how long Persian remained part of the cultural arsenal of Siberian Muslims.

Bustanov's focus in his recent study is on private collections, in which it seems clear that works in Turkic (Tatar) and Arabic predominated. This suggests that Persian material might have been squeezed out into public collections. In other words, Persian manuscripts were given up by recent owners who by contrast kept their Turkic and Arabic materials (Turkic for comprehension, Arabic for sacrality). Such a pattern is suggested by one manuscript Bustanov discusses, produced in Tara in the 1860s, containing copies of Persian and Arabic religious works. The Persian texts alone have been supplied with Tatar translations under each line. Other manuscripts, however, provide Turkic equivalents for Arabic texts as well.[70]

Another work of particular interest is a section of a nineteenth-century manuscript Bustanov discusses, containing an account, by Rahmatullah ibn Mulla Yusuf al-Tarawi, of the status of Muslims in Siberia. The author—who also uses the *nisba* al-Sibiri (the Siberian) wrote in 1858–59, and although the basic text is in Tatar, he freely includes Persian verse and passages in Arabic as well.[71] This work thus cannot be said to represent the use of Persian to recount local history and religious issues. But it does attest to a degree of literacy in Persian, and Arabic—as would be expected, after all—among those with an interest in local history and local religious culture.

Bustanov also devotes substantial attention to the Biktimerov collection. This is a private collection of eighteenth- and nineteenth-century manuscripts from Siberia (mostly from the region of Tiumen'), comprising 182 works in all.[72] The majority by far are in Turkic or Arabic, but a few Persian works are named. Finally, in his description of numerous other manuscripts from private collections, Bustanov suggests the same pattern as found in the case of the Volga-Urals: Persian was used for Sufi works—whether *ijazat* and *silsilas*,[73] defenses of the vocal *zikr*,[74] the letters of Ahmad Sirhindi,[75] or Sufi Allahyar's *Murad al-'Arifin*[76]—and for works on Arabic grammar.[77]

CONCLUSIONS

Overall, it seems safe to conclude that literacy in Persian, and the reading of Persian literature, continued on a much wider scale, and considerably later, than might have been assumed on the basis of the contemporary linguistic situation, or of the remoteness of the regions explored here from other historic homes of Persian literature, Iran and Central Asia. Educated Muslims from Kazan to Tobolsk appear to have read Persian and to have sought out materials in Persian, keeping Persian manuscript culture alive until well toward the end of the nineteenth century. To be sure, by that time, Persian literary production was dwarfed by that in various Turkic vernaculars. Its persistence is worth noting, but it was no longer in serious competition with Turkic. Nor did Persian, in certain spheres, offer competition with Russian, the imperial language in most of the regions considered here. It should also be kept in mind that the educated reader in these regions expected to read Persian above all when dealing with certain distinct spheres. As we have seen, Persian was still routinely important in Sufi literature, and Persian-language interpretations of the Quran remained popular, as did Persian poetry. The high representation, in manuscript collections, of grammars of Arabic written in Persian suggests that Persian may have served as a medium for studying Arabic, or may have been studied in conjunction with Arabic. It is also, finally, worth stating the obvious: literacy *exclusively*, or even primarily, in Persian is not what we observe here. This, perhaps, may be the lesson of those earlier periods marked by extensive translations from Persian into Turkic, inasmuch as Turkic was *made* into a literary language, able to compete with Persian, on the model of Persian.

NOTES

1. The linguistic shift in literary production happened somewhat earlier in Eastern Turkistan, where Persian was dominant into the early eighteenth century; by the second half of that century, however, Turkic literary production had largely replaced that in Persian, and the nineteenth century brought a dramatic expansion of the corpus of Chaghatai literature produced in the region.

2. Mir 'Ali Shir [Nawa'i], *Muhakamat al-Lughatain*, trans. R. Devereux (Leiden: Brill, 1966), praises Turkic as more versatile than Persian and Arabic .

3. Four of these translations, evidently done at the Köchkünjid court in Samarqand, are discussed in Devin DeWeese, "Chaghatay Literature in the Early Sixteenth Century: Notes on Turkic Translations from the Uzbek Courts of Mawarannahr," in *Turkish Language, Literature, and History: Travelers' Tales, Sultans, and Scholars since the Eighth Century (A Volume of Studies in Honor of Robert Dankoff)*, ed. Bill Hickman and Gary Leiser (London: Routledge, 2016), 99–117. Two others (translations of al-Ghazali's *Nasihat al-Muluk* and of Najib Hamadani's *'Aja'ib al-Makhluqat*) were done at the court of Muhammad Shïbani Khan himself.

4. See Devin DeWeese, "A Note on Manuscripts of the *Zubdat al-āthār*, a Chaghatay Turkic History from Sixteenth-Century Mawarannahr," *Manuscripts of the Middle East*, 6 (1992), 96–100, with further references.

5. On the *Tarikh-i Abu al-Khayr-khani*, see Ch. A. Stori, *Persidskaia literatura: Bio-bibliograficheskii obzor*, trans. Iu. È. Bregel', 3 vols. (Moscow: Nauka, 1972), 1: 397–99.

6. On another product of this patronage, from Bukhara, see Devin DeWeese, "Telling Women's Stories in 16th-Century Central Asia: A Book of Guidance in Chaghatay Turkic for a Royal Lady of the Bukharan Court," *Oriens* 43, 1–2 (2015), 154–222.

7. The translation gauge is somewhat more helpful for Eastern Turkistan (see David Brophy's discussion of translations from Persian in his chapter 6 in the present volume). Undoubtedly, more evidence of Turkic translations from Persian will come to light as manuscript collections are better described, but nearly all of the Turkic translations from Persian known from catalogued collections were produced in two periods: the first half of the eighteenth century—a time that indeed seems to correspond to the transition from Persian to Turkic in literary production—and the first half of the nineteenth century (especially the second quarter)—ironically, before the major expansion of literary production associated with the rule and patronage of Ya'qub Beg, but reflecting the patronage of local elites that administered regions in Eastern Turkistan on behalf of the Qing emperor.

8. See *A Turkic Medical Treatise from Islamic Central Asia: A Critical Edition of a Seventeenth-Century Chagatay Work by Subḥān Qulï Khan*, ed. and trans. László Károly, Brill's Inner Asian Library, 32 (Leiden: Brill, 2015).

9. Manuscripts of this translation by one Salihi are preserved in Saint Petersburg and Kazan.

10. The shift is noted, and its possible implications suggested, in Iu. È. Bregel', "Arkhiv khivinskikh khanov (Predvaritel'nyi obzor novykh dokumentov)," *Narody Azii i Afriki*, 1966, no. 1: 67–76 (p. 72). Bregel' estimated that one-sixth of the documents he surveyed from the Khivan archives were in Persian. Of 1,700 Khivan documents (dating from the second half of the eighteenth century down to the 1920s) described in *Katalog khivinskikh kaziiskikh dokumentov XIX–nachala XX vv.*, ed. A. Urunbaev, T. Khorikava, T. Faiziev, G. Dzhuraeva, and K. Isogai (Tashkent/Kyoto: Institut Vostokovedeniia im. Abu Raikhana Beruni Akademii nauk Respubliki Uzbekistan / Kyoto University of Foreign Studies, 2001), 199 (just under 12 percent) are in Persian, all of them dated before 1860.

11. See the survey of Persian manuscript production by the noted Iranist O. F. Akimushkin, "Persidskaia rukopisnaia kniga," *Rukopisnaia kniga v kul'ture narodov Vostoka: Ocherki*, Kniga pervaia (Moscow: Nauka, GRVL, 1987), 330–406. In the same volume, L. V. Dmitrieva, "Tiurkoiazychnaia arabopis'mennaia rukopisnaia kniga po ee arealam," 407–77, discusses the Volga-Ural region (437–42) and Eastern Turkistan (417–23), along with Central Asia, Azerbaijan, and Asia Minor, as distinctive regions of manuscript culture, but only in terms of Turkic literary production.

12. This designation, though by now conventional, is somewhat misleading, being derived from the regions in which the Muslim population of European Russia has historically been concentrated; this population—now mostly counted as "Tatars," but including the Bashkirs as well, and historically linked with the legacy of Islam in the Mongol successor state of the Golden Horde—in fact extends from the Volga-Kama confluence, near Kazan, down the Volga to Astrakhan, west and south to the Crimea, and east to the Ural mountains and the valley of the Ural/Yayïq River. Before the late tsarist

and Soviet eras, many in this Muslim community seem to have preferred to identify themselves with the Muslim legacy of Bulghar rather than with the ethnonym "Tatar," but the latter term—long used by Russians, somewhat indiscriminately, to refer to the indigenous inhabitants, of diverse linguistic and "ethnic" affiliations, of the region through which Russian control spread during the sixteenth and seventeenth centuries, especially in the Volga valley and Western Siberia—gained wide acceptance during the twentieth century.

13. See Devin DeWeese, "A Persian Sufi Work from the Golden Horde: The *Qalandar-nāma* of Abū Bakr Rūmī," in *Mongols, Tatars and Turks in the Persianate World*, ed. Benedek Péri and Ferenc Csirkes (Leiden: Brill, forthcoming). See also Devin DeWeese, "*Khāns* and *Amīrs* in the *Qalandar-nāma* of Abū Bakr Rūmī: Praise of the Islamizing Jochid Elite in a Persian Sufi Work from Fourteenth-Century Crimea," *Archivum Eurasiae Medii Aevi* 21 (2014–15 = *Festschrift for Thomas T. Allsen in Celebration of His 75th Birthday*, ed. P. B. Golden, R. K. Kovalev, A. P. Martinez, J. Skaff, and A. Zimonyi [Wiesbaden: Harrassowitz, 2015]), 53–66.

14. Ananiasz Zajączkowski, *Najstarsza wersja turecka Ḫusräv u Šīrīn Quṭba*, 3 vols. (Warsaw: Państwowe Wydawnictwo Naukowe, 1958-61), 1 (*Tekst*), 2 (*Fac-similé*), 3 (*Słownik*).

15. Sultan Muhammad ibn Muhammad Harawi Fakhri, *Tazkira-yi Rawzat al-Salatin*, ed. 'Abd al-Rasul Khayyampur (Tabriz: Intisharat-i Mu'assasa-yi Tarikh wa Farhang-i Iran, 1345/1966), 26.

16. Dmitrieva comments that in the Volga-Ural region, translations into "Tatar" were not uncommon from Arabic, but were less often done from Persian. See Dmitrieva, "Tiurkoiazychnaia arabopis'mennaia rukopisnaia kniga," 441.

17. On Jalayiri's work, see H. F. Hofman, *Turkish Literature: A Biobibliographical Survey; Section III, Moslim Central Asian Turkish Literature*, 6 vols. in 2 (Utrecht: University of Utrecht, 1969), 5: 114–15, and M. A. Usmanov, *Tatarskie istoricheskie istochniki XVII–XVIII vv.* (Kazan: Izdatel'stvo Kazanskogo Universiteta, 1972), 33–96. Kasimov is in the district of Ryazan, 160 km east-southeast of Moscow.

18. MS B4070, fols. 37b–45b; described in N. D. Miklukho-Maklai, *Opisanie persidskikh i tadzhikskikh rukopisei Instituta vostokovedeniia*, no. 3: *Istoricheskie sochineniia* (Moscow: Nauka, GRVL, 1975), 400–401, no. 509.

19. M. A. Salakhetdinova, "Ob odnom neizvestnom persidskom sochinenii po istorii narodov Povolzh'ia," *Strany i narody Vostoka*, no. 4 (Moscow, 1965), 147–54.

20. On this work, most likely compiled in the early nineteenth century, see especially Allen J. Frank, *Islamic Historiography and "Bulghar" Identity among the Tatars and Bashkirs of Russia* (Leiden: Brill, 1998), esp. 47–91, and Michael Kemper, *Sufis und Gelehrte in Tatarien und Baschkirien, 1789–1889: Der islamische Diskurs unter russischer Herrschaft* (Berlin: Klaus Schwarz, 1998), 324–54, with further references.

21. Iurii Bregel', "Vostochnye rukopisi v Kazani," *Pis'mennye pamiatniki Vostoka, Ezhegodnik 1969* (Moscow, 1972), 355–73.

22. Frank, *Islamic Historiography*; Kemper, *Sufis und Gelehrte*; Allen J. Frank, *Muslim Religious Institutions in Imperial Russia: The Islamic World of Novouzensk District and the Kazakh Inner Horde, 1780–1910* (Leiden: Brill, 2001).

23. *Persidskie i tadzhikskie rukopisi Instituta narodov Azii AN SSSR (Kratkii alfavitnyi katalog)*, ed. O. F. Akimushkin, V. V. Kushev, N. D. Miklukho-Maklai, A. M. Muginov, and M. A. Salakhetdinova (Moscow: Nauka, 1964), hereafter *Kratkii alfavitnyi katalog*. Works are listed by title, with each copy of distinct works numbered consecutively (nos. 1–4680, with an additional 110 items in a supplement, nos. 1*-110*).

24. *Kratkii alfavitnyi katalog*, no. 340, B2717 (128ff.), a copy of Sa'di's *Bustan* done in Kazan in 1182/1768–69; no. 2467, A1090 (fols., 1b–28a), a copy of the *Sharh-i Sarf-i Mir*, a commentary on the beginning section of al-Jurjani's (d. 1413–14) grammar of Arabic, here called the *Sharh-i Da'ud* (the commentary is by Da'ud ibn 'Abd al-Baqi ibn 'Isa ibn Baba Turkistani), done in Kazan, n.d.; no. 2748, B2531 (2b–20b), a copy of the *Sarf-i Mir* itself, by Jurjani, a Persian grammar of Arabic, done in Kazan in 1881; no. 2758, B2856 (1b–14b), another copy of the *Sarf-i Mir*, done in Kazan, n.d.; no. 829, B2592

(91ff.), a copy of Ya'qub Charkhi's Persian *tafsir* done in the village of Tashkichu, northeast of Kazan, n.d.; no. 48* [suppl.], B4401 (68b–94a), a defective copy of the *Siraj al-Qulub*, a Persian work by Abu Nasr Sa'id ibn al-Qasim al-Ghaznawi, likewise done in Tashkichu, near Kazan, in 1738–39 (1151).

25. Manuscripts from elsewhere in present-day Tatarstan: *Kratkii alfavitnyi katalog,* no. 3573, B3315 (126ff.), a copy of Sa'di's *Gulistan* done in the village of Kishit in 1775–76 (1189); no. 344, B2941 (25b–156b), a copy of Sa'di's *Bustan* done in the village of Urnash in 1813 (1228); no. 4374, B3300 (52b–64a), a copy of the Persian poetic work known as *Nan-u-Halwa* by Baha al-Din Muhammad ibn Husayn al-'Amili done in 1849 in the village of Bikbak; no. 1588, B4104 (27b–36b), a copy of the poetic *Diwan* of Farishta done in Kargaly, in Chistopol' district, in 1806; no. 1287, A1416 (106ff.), a copy of Nawbahari's Sufi work, *Durr al-Majalis,* done in the village of Baraskai in 1748–49 (1162); no. 2339, B2729 (11b–60b), a copy of a Persian commentary on part of an Arabic grammatical work known as *al-Mu'izzi,* ascribed to 'Izz al-Din Zanjani (d. 1257), done in the village of Darvish in 1771–72 (1185).

26. *Kratkii alfavitnyi katalog,* no. 2345, B2856 (18a–65b), a copy of the Persian commentary on *al-Mu'izzi* done in 1782–83 (1197) in the village of Alman, in the present-day Chuvash republic.

27. Manuscripts from present-day Bashqortostan: *Kratkii alfavitnyi katalog,* 1: no. 2366, MS B3676 (1b–75a), a copy of a Persian commentary on the Arabic grammar known as *al-Mu'izzi* done in Ufa, n.d.; no. 3570, B2574 (104ff.), a copy of Sa'di's *Gulistan* done in 1778–79 (1192) in the village of 'Abdul-lah; no. 831, B4008 (1b–202a), a copy of Ya'qub Charkhi's Persian *tafsir* done in the village of Babalar in 1781–82 (1196); no. 1296, B2975 (107ff.), a copy of Nawbahari's *Durr al-Majalis* done in 1812 in the village of Qïzïl Chapchak; no. 4061, B3984, 200ff., a copy of Sufi Allahyar's *Maslak al-Muttaqin,* a famous Sufi work, copied in 1837 in the town of Tuymaza; no. 2651, B3695 (12b–86a), a copy of the *Shifa al-Qulub* by Muhammad ibn Muhammad al-Jami al-Almasi, presenting Persian translations of forty *hadith*s, with commentary (the original collection was compiled in 1445–46 [849]), done in Sterlitamak in 1829–30 (1245).

28. *Kratkii alfavitnyi katalog,* no. 3556, B168 (98ff.), a copy of Sa'di's *Gulistan* done in 1775 in the village of Salman; no. 2392, C2080 (19b–91b), a copy of a Persian commentary on the Arabic grammar *al-Mu'izzi* done in Yangi-Kulatka in 1879; no. 2365, B3636 (42b–99b), another copy of a Persian commentary on *al-Mu'izzi,* done in 1870 in the village of Iski Yarmak; o. 2780, B3753 (89b–103b), a copy of the Persian *Sarf-i Mir,* by Sayyid Sharif al-Din 'Ali Jurjani, done in Kulatka, n.d.; no. 3703, B2681 (39b–72b), a copy of the Persian Sufi work by Muhammad Siddiq al-Badakhshi al-Kishmi, called *al-Mabda' wa'l-Mu'ad,* done in Kulatka, n.d.; No. 16, B3333 (ff. 1a–5b), a collection of *hadith*s, with verse Persian translations, compiled by Muhammad Yar ibn 'Ala al-Din, in the village of Yanga Tazlar in 1884; no. 103*, B4401 (3a–60a), a defective copy of the *Mawahib-i 'Aliyya* of Husayn ibn 'Ali al-Wa'iz al-Kashifi done in the village of Kazaklar in 1738–39 (1151).

29. *Kratkii alfavitnyi katalog,* no. 2779, B3725 (3b–25b), a copy of the Persian *Sarf-i Mir* by Sayyid Sharif al-Din 'Ali Jurjani done in "Qal'a-yi Jayiq," evidently Ural'sk, in 1865; no. 3506, C297 (2b–368a), a copy of the lexicographical work *Kanz al-Lughat* by Muhammad ibn 'Abd al-Khaliq ibn Ma'ruf done in Astrakhan in 1827–28 (1243); no. 4233, B4441 (101ff.), a full copy of the second volume of the *Maktubat* of Ahmad Sirhindi as compiled by Yar-Muhammad al-Jadid al-Badakhshi al-Taliqani, evidently done in Astrakhan in 1865–66 (1282).

30. A.A. Arslanova, *Opisanie rukopisei na persidskom iazyke Nauchnoi biblioteki im. N.I. Lobachevskogo Kazanskogo gosudarstvennogo universiteta,* no. 1 (Moscow/Kazan: Kazanskii gosudarst-vennyi universitet/Institut istorii im. Sh. Mardzhani Akademii nauk Respubliki Tatarstan/Institut vostokovedeniia Rossiiskoi Akademii nauk, 2005); A.A. Arslanova, *Opisanie rukopisei na persidskom iazyke Nauchnoi biblioteki im. N.I. Lobachevskogo Kazanskogo (Privolzhskogo) federal'nogo universiteta,* no. II (Kazan: Kazanskii federal'nyi universitet/GBU "Institut istorii im. Sh. Mardzhani" Akademii nauk Respubliki Tatarstan/Institut vostokovedeniia Rossiiskoi Akademii nauk, 2015).

31. The principle seems to have been to avoid mentioning the place of copying unless it was explic-itly mentioned, but in some cases this information is shown in excerpts from colophons but still not

included in the general description (and not indexed). Manuscripts from the Volga-Ural region often display distinctive handwriting, and can at least be generally assigned to that region to distinguish them from manuscripts copied in Central Asia, for instance; but this information and the editor's judgments about the provenance of the manuscripts have not been included.

32. Allen J. Frank, *Bukhara and the Muslims of Russia: Sufism, Education, and the Paradox of Islamic Prestige* (Leiden: Brill, 2012).

33. Arslanova, *Opisanie*, 1: 37–39, no. 4.

34. Ibid., 1: 117–19, no. 54.

35. Ibid., 1: 43–46, no. 7.

36. For example, the Kazan collection holds a fourteenth-century copy of Najm al-Din Razi's famous Sufi work the *Mirsad al-ʿIbad*, copied in 1360 (762) by a native of Shiraz (Arslanova, *Opisanie*, 1: 209–11, no. 112), and an early fifteenth-century excerpt from the much rarer Sufi work by a grandson of Sayf al-Din Bakharzi, the *Fusus al-Adab*, copied in 1412 (815) (Arslanova, *Opisanie*, 1: 302, no. 172), as well as an astrological work (*Lataʾif al-Kiram*, by "Sayyid Munajjim") copied in 1434 (838) (Arslanova, *Opisanie*, 1: 51–52, no. 10) and a copy of Kashani's Persian translation of the popular Sufi compendium of Shihab al-Din ʿUmar Suhravardi, the *ʿAwarif al-Maʿarif*, completed in 1491 (897) (Arslanova, *Opisanie*, 1: 249–50, no. 137); these no doubt travelled to Kazan via Central Asia, a path even more likely in the case of an old copy of Khwaja Muhammad Parsa's *Fasl al-Khitab*, completed in 1495 (901), and the sixteenth-century copies of Sufi treatises by Mawlana Yaʿqub Charkhi, including one completed in 1558–59 (966), evidently by a native of Merv (Arslanova, *Opisanie*, 1: 298–302, nos. 166–71).

37. Arslanova, *Opisanie*, 2: 18–20, no. 391.

38. Ibid., 1: 122–25, nos. 56–57.

39. Ibid., 2: 183–84, no. 491, and 186–88, no. 493, respectively.

40. Ibid., 1: 363–64, no. 244. Cf. 2: 414–16, nos. 626–27, identified as the same work but assigned the title *al-Kitab al-Khaqaniyya fi Bayan al-Jihad*.

41. For instance, the Kazan University collection holds at least a dozen copies of a Persian-language manual of Arabic grammar, assigned its "title" from its first word, *ba-dan* ("Know . . . ") and in some versions ascribed to Baha al-Din al-ʿAmili (Arslanova, *Opisanie*, 1: 86–93, nos. 33, 36–39; 2: 32–40, nos. 401–8); all were evidently produced in the Volga-Ural region, in the eighteenth and (mostly) nineteenth centuries. Likewise registered are at least a dozen copies, produced from the late eighteenth century through the nineteenth, of a locally produced Persian commentary ascribed to a certain ʿAbdullah ibn Aq-Muhammad (see n. 62 below) on *al-Muʿizzi* (Arslanova, *Opisanie*, 1: 94–99, nos. 40–43, 2: 23–31, nos. 393–400; additional copies or fragments are mentioned among the *majmuʿa*s described by Arslanova), including one (no. 43) copied in Kazan in 1800 (1215) by ʿUbaydullah ibn Kalimullah al-Bulghari (who also copied Sufi works noted below); original Persian works on Arabic grammar evidently written by this copyist are registered in Arslanova, *Opisanie*, 2: 43–44, no. 411, and 51–52, no. 419. For a copy of the Persian grammatical work known as the *Sarf-i Zanjani*, done in the Volga-Urals in 1742 (1155), see Arslanova, *Opisanie*, 1: 100–101, no. 45; cf. 2: 40–43, nos. 409–10. In the second volume of Arslanova's catalogue, the section on grammatical works (in which the overwhelming majority are Persian works dealing with Arabic grammar) is the second-largest (II, 23–173, nos. 393–484), surpassed only by the catch-all section on belles lettres (pp. 476–714, nos. 667–820), comprising chiefly works of poetry.

42. Arslanova, *Opisanie*, 1: 143–44, no. 66.

43. Ibid., 1: 132–34, no. 61.

44. Ibid., 1: 165–66, nos. 86–88; cf. the mostly anonymous Persian medical treatises described in 2: 214–28, nos. 511–16.

45. The collection includes, e.g., a Persian treatise of Khwaja Muhammad Parsa copied in Kazan in 1871 (1288) by Mulla Khwaja ibn Mulla Muzaffar al-Bulghari (Arslanova, *Opisanie*, 1: 277–78, no. 154); five copies of the famous hagiography *Rashahat-i ʿAyn al-Hayat*, most ascribed to the eighteenth century and probably "local" (Arslanova, *Opisanie*, 1: 266–72, nos. 147–50, 2: 323–24, no. 584); two

apparently partial sets of the treatises of the sixteenth-century shaykh known as Makhdum-i A'zam, one of which was copied in Bukhara in 1840 (1256), but by "'Ubaydullah ibn Kalimullah al-Bulghari al-Ghazani al-Aldirmishi" (Arslanova, *Opisanie*, 1: 312–25, nos. 180–205 [misidentified], and 338–40, nos. 223–25); and copies of treatises, otherwise unknown from Central Asian collections, ascribed to the rather obscure sixteenth-century Naqshbandi shaykh Khwajagi Darwish Imkanagi (Arslanova, *Opisanie*, 1: 344–45, nos. 230–31).

46. Arslanova, *Opisanie*, 1: 284–85, no. 158.

47. Arslanova, *Opisanie*, 2: 281–82, no. 554 (the *Zubdat al-Maqamat* of Muhammad Hashim Kishmi, copied in 1670 (1081)), and 291–92, no. 561 (the *Hazarat al-Quds* of Badr al-Din Ibrahim Sirhindi, copied in 1648 (1058) by Miftah al-Din ibn Sabit al-Jamaqi al-Bulghari). It is not clear whether these older copies reflect an earlier Mujaddidi presence in the Volga-Urals, or the later importation of these manuscripts into a region with a strong Mujaddidi presence.

48. Ibid., 225–29, nos. 123–25; 2: 279–81, no. 553, 283–85, nos. 555–56.

49. Ibid., 1: 229–33, nos. 126–28; 2: 285–88, nos. 557–58.

50. Ibid., 243–44, no. 134, and 2: 321, no. 582 (the *Zubdat al-Haqa'iq*).

51. On Sufi Allahyar, see Hofman, *Turkish Literature*, 2: 71–81.

52. Arslanova, *Opisanie*, 1: 214–22, nos. 114–20; 2: 240–68, nos. 523–43.

53. Arslanova, *Opisanie*, 2: 293–303, nos. 562–70 (with an anonymous commentary on the work, 303–3034, no. 571).

54. Arslanova, *Opisanie*, 1: 287–89, no. 160, 2: 317–18, no. 580. On Utïz-Imani, see Kemper, *Sufis und Gelehrte*, 174–212, and Frank, *Islamic Historiography*, 37.

55. Arslanova, *Opisanie*, 2: 322–23, no. 583.

56. Arslanova, *Opisanie*, 2: 348–51, no. 593.

57. Arslanova, *Opisanie*, 1: 366–91, nos. 246–64, among which one (no. 254) deals with Shafi'i *fiqh*; 2: 438–74, nos. 641–65.

58. Arslanova, Opisanie, 2: 455–60, nos. 653–56; on the author, see Kemper, *Sufis und Gelehrte*, 217.

59. Arslanova, *Opisanie*, 1: 346–55, nos. 233–38, including copies of works by Ya'qub Charkhi, Muhammad Parsa, and Husayn Wa'iz Kashifi, as well as still older works from twelfth- and thirteenth-century Mawarannahr; cf. 2: 371–73, nos. 601–2 (one "local" and one much older "imported" copy of Charkhi's *tafsir*), and 374–80, 383–86, nos. 603–7, 610–11 (copies of Kashifi's works).

60. Arslanova, *Opisanie*, 1: 194–97, nos. 103–4; 2: 236–37, no. 521 (dated 1857 [1274], of less certain provenance).

61. S. M. Giliazutdinov, *Opisanie rukopisei na persidskom iazyke iz khranilishcha Instituta iazyka, literatury i iskusstva* [Akademii nauk Respubliki Tatarstan] (Kazan: Fiker, 2002); the second and third volumes appeared in 2006 and 2007, respectively, but have not been available to me. See also S. M. Giliazutdinov, *Persidsko-tatarskie literaturnye sviazi (X–nachalo XX v.)* (Kazan: Akademiia nauk Respubliki Tatarstan, Institut iazyka, literatury i iskusstva im. G. Ibragimova, 2011); the author surveys the development and holdings of manuscript collections in Kazan, elsewhere in Tatarstan, and Saint Petersburg (but not Bashqortostan), with attention to the dates and places of copying (pp. 19–59), with the bulk of the work devoted to the presumed impact of various classics of Persian literature on "Tatar" literature, and literary figures, of the eighteenth and nineteenth centuries.

62. Giliazutdinov, *Opisanie*, 100–107, nos. 156–71. Here the popular commentary is ascribed to 'Abdullah ibn Aq-Muhammad, of whom nothing is known; but the work is said to have been popular already in the late seventeenth and early eighteenth centuries as the chief "textbook" on Arabic in use in "Tatar" madrasas.

63. Giliazutdinov, *Opisanie*, no. 156, copied in Khan-Kirman, Kasimov, in 1811 (1226); no. 159, copied in the village of 'Abdullah in 1870 (1287); no. 162, copied in Nurkaevo in 1888.

64. Giliazutdinov, *Opisanie*, 80–87, nos. 112–32.

65. Giliazutdinov, *Opisanie*, no. 117, copied in the village of Torna in 1756; no. 112, copied in the village of Ayman in 1847; no. 130, copied in Tegermen in 1855; no. 114, copied in the village of Bikbau, in

Ufa *guberniia,* in 1858; no. 128, copied in Tashkichu (northeast of Kazan) in 1864; no. 119, copied in the village of Taulyk in 1867; no. 132, copied in village of Salaush (Agryz *raion*), n.d.

66. A. M. Mukhtarov, "Dvuiazychnaia nadpis' XII v. iz Novosibirsk," *Istoriia, filologiia i filosofiia,* no. 1 (Novosibirsk, 1991), 68–70.

67. N. Uno, H. Muraoka, and K. Matsuda, "Gencho kouki karakorumujyoushi hankaa kensetsuki-nen perushagohibun-no kenkyu" (Persian Inscription in Memory of the Establishment of a Khanqah at Qara-qorum) (in Japanese, with Persian text and English translation of the inscription), in *Studies on the Inner Asian Languages,* 14 (1999): 1–64 + plates I–V.

68. M. G. Gosmanov, *Kauriy kaläm ezennän: Arkheograf yazmalarï* (Kazan, 1994), 35–36.

69. Al'frid Bustanov, *Knizhnaia kul'tura sibirskikh musul'man* (Moscow: Izdatel'skii dom Mardzhani, 2013).

70. Ibid., 27.

71. Ibid., 31, and facsimiles of 14b–19a as *Faksimile* 2 at the end.

72. Ibid., 45–52.

73. Ibid., 88–91.

74. Ibid., 95, 97, 99.

75. Ibid., 171.

76. Ibid., 159, 165.

77. Ibid., 103–5.

PART TWO

The Constraints of Cosmopolitanism, ca. 1600–1800

5

Persian Scholarly Networks in Mughal Punjab

Purnima Dhavan

Soon after Emperor Jalal al-Din Muhammad Akbar adopted Persian as the language of state in 1581, both the Mughal Empire and the cultural sphere of Persian expanded together in South Asia. Persian had a long history in South Asia before the Mughals, which would continue in South Asia even as the Mughal Empire slowly retrenched, but the stories of the language and the state that advanced it in India are intrinsically linked. Its official role in state administration and also as the language of the cultural elite encouraged numerous young men from the diverse communities of Mughal India to study the language and also embrace the cultural habits associated with Persianate traditions. The extent to which Persian soaked into the cultural fabric of South Asia, however, remains a matter of debate.[1] Was it mostly a language of the empire's elite, propelled by administrative needs and imperial patronage? What role did Persian play in the multilingual literary circles of the time, and to what extent did it shape ideas of self and community? This chapter engages these questions by focusing on a cluster of Persian scholars from the northwestern Mughal province of Lahore who were active under Shah Jahan (r. 1626–58).

Lahore during Shah Jahan's reign was a bustling mercantile center and a major of hub of Persian learning and scholarship. The repeated journeys of the Mughal courts under the emperors Akbar, Jahangir, and, later, Shah Jahan had elevated the *suba* (province) of Lahore and also the city, as one of seasonal capitals of the empire, where the court frequently spent time on its way to its summer retreat in Kashmir. With the start of the cooling monsoons, the court returned to the plains of Hindustan, passing through Lahore again. Offensive and defensive military campaigns on the empire's northwestern borders with the Safavids of Persia and the Uzbeks were also launched from Lahore.[2] Unsurprisingly, too, as an important economic, political, and literary imperial hub, Lahore was a desirable destination for Persian-speaking scholars hoping to forge careers in Mughal India. By the time Shah Jahan had secured his hold on the Mughal throne, the role of Lahore as a meeting ground of home-grown and émigré talent in Persian circles was so entrenched that there is perhaps no better place to explore their interactions.[3]

By the opening years of Shah Jahan's reign in the late 1620s, Persian literary circles occupied a particularly thick set of interlinking circles centered in Lahore. The interaction of these clusters of poets, scholars, bureaucrats, and administrators reveals much about the immense reach of Persian as a cosmopolitan language of empire, as well as the limits to its connections with other literary communities in Punjab. Tracking the flows of patronage, mentorship, and social connections that fueled the trajectory of Persian-knowing bureaucrats and scholars in these circles also lays bare the competitive and aspirational motivations in the use of Persian in North India, particularly in its form as an instrument of self-fashioning. One such cluster of scholars in Lahore was that of Munir Lahawri, Chandarbhan Brahman, and the two Kanbu brothers, Muhammad Salih and 'Inayatullah.[4] These men, like many of their Indian peers, had connections with provincial literary elites, who were usually the second or third generation of their families to be employed in Mughal service. They shared the distinction of having long family connections to both the province and the imperial officers of the Mughal court. They were also known to interact frequently with many of the Persian-speaking scholars who had relocated to Mughal India from other regions or had visited Mughal India during the reigns of Jahangir and Shah Jahan. An awareness and celebration of these interlinked cosmopolitan literary circuits saturates their work, but their writing also reveals a deep ambivalence about their place in this literary network. A close reading of the works of this Lahori quartet suggests that their attempts to craft literary personas that commanded the respect of their peers and were attractive to patrons had far-reaching effects on the genres of literary Persian they favored. The cultivation of their image as scholars, teachers, and literary models through the dissemination of their cohort's works burnished their reputations in their own time and also influenced their perceived pedagogical worth among later scholars of Persian in Mughal India. In the works of these four men, we see Persian used as a tool for competitive self-crafting, and also as the very site of that competition, since they evaluated the literary merit of other scholars as well. At the peak of their careers, they chose to focus on prose, rather than poetry, as the medium of literary self-presentation. At a time when performance at the majlis, or poetic salon, and the ability to compose elegant poetry ex tempore were greatly valued, these four Punjabi scholars forged a divergent path, focusing in particular on literary criticism, epistolography, and writing introductions to one another's collected works. Munir and Chandrabhan Brahmin were also successful poets, but the most important part of their literary self-fashioning and legacy was their ornate prose.

PARROTS OF HIND OR BROTHERHOOD OF THE PEN?

Abu al-Barakat Munir Lahawri (1610–44), the son of 'Abd al-Majid Multani, an established scholar during Akbar's reign, was among the literati who benefitted from the frequent presence of the imperial court at Lahore during the reign of Shah Jahan,[5] as were his childhood friends Muhammad Salih Kanbu and 'Inayatullah Kanbu, the sons of a man who enjoyed high status in the atelier of Prince Salim (the later Emperor Jahangir), the well-known calligrapher 'Abdullah Muskhin Qalam, whose sobriquet was "musky-scented [*mushkin*] pen" (a perhaps ambiguous play on words, since *mushkin* also means "black").[6] Chandarbhan Brahman, the son of a former provincial Mughal bureaucrat, Dharamdas of Lahore *suba*, was another of the eminent young men at Shah Jahan's court.[7] The correspondence among these four men testifies to their long professional and personal intimacy. Indeed, favorable notices about one another's talents in the realm of Persian literary mastery inserted into their literary offerings burnished this cluster's reputations, not only for their peers, but also for later generations of Persian scholars.[8] Lahore was also visited by a stream of Persian émigré scholars and poets, some of whom remained in North India.

What makes this cluster particularly compelling to any scholar of Persian literature in Mughal India is their self-reflective meditation in their works about mastery of Persian and the significant role this skill had played in their achievement of literary success, emotional development, and spiritual discipline. Rajeev Kinra has recently discussed the investment that bureaucrat scholars such as Chandrabhan had in preserving a Mughal cultural sphere defined by cosmopolitan inclusivity as practiced by its most famous Persian poets and scholars.[9] As Muzaffar Alam and Sanjay Subrahmanyam have argued, this specifically Mughal literary and political tradition created a context in which Persian literary practices molded the shared imaginative and philosophical outlook of its practitioners.[10] A close look at the Lahori quartet on which this chapter focuses also suggests, however, that their relationship with Persian was not always celebratory: it was also tinged with an awareness of competitive and sometimes brutal competition with their peers. Their works also offer glimpses of their group as inhabiting a literary frontier, and of themselves as bridge builders and skilled interpreters in this world. Finally, it should be noted that the cultivation of Persian literary art and multilingual dexterity of these Punjabi scholars was to a large degree the result of a very privileged place in a network of imperial patronage. Barely visible in their works are their connections with and status in regional and subregional Persian, Hindawi, and Punjabi literary networks.

For the sake of brevity, I will use Munir Lahawri as an entrée into this cluster, particularly since recent studies of his work *Kar-nama* have been central to way in which scholarship has conceived of the fault lines of Persian literary culture in Mughal India. Munir Lahawri famously criticized the hyperbolic admirers of four Persian poets associated with the *tazagui* "fresh-speaking" aesthetics of his own time, 'Urfi Shirazi, Talib Amuli, Zulali, and Zuhuri.[11] Munir's critique of this blind admiration of the contemporary style over the master poets of the classical past was also an attempt to assert the superior literary merits of the two classical poets that Munir most admired, Amir Khusraw and Salman Mas'ud Sa'd Salman. In particular, the excessively convoluted metaphorical imagery of his own time is contrasted in Munir's reading of these four émigré poets with the restrained classicism of the masters of the past. *Kar-nama*'s goals, while much discussed in recent studies, remain opaque in the larger context of his oeuvre and literary network. Even if Munir's literary critiques of émigré and Mughal poets are clear in their intent in individual pieces, his target shifts and changes over time. Some recent studies have linked *Kar-nama* with the rivalries of the professionalizing Indian and Iranian intellectuals of the period as a "plea for cosmopolitan egalitarianism over parochial favoritism" and meditation on the problems of poetic communication in a diverse poetic milieu that serves as an opening salvo to the great Persian literary debates of the following century.[12] All of these positions have some validity, since Munir's own point of attack and imagined goals in *Kar-nama* shift considerably. Yet they are also framed, and each of these studies acknowledges this, by the masterful analysis of Munir's critique by Siraj al-Din Khan-i Arzu (1687–1756), a formidable scholar of Indo-Persian.[13] A somewhat different picture of Munir and his famous essay emerges if it is inserted back into its own historical context.

Munir's self-presentation in *Kar-nama* is central to how this piece has been interpreted by later readers. The narrative framework presents a young, modest, but deeply erudite Munir as the quiet spectator in a majlis gathering of poets. Incensed with what he considers the ridiculous fawning of his colleagues at this gathering for the poetry of the four *tazagui* poets, he feels compelled to offer a fairer and, in his own opinion, more balanced view of the relative merits of these four poets as compared to the old masters of Hind, such as Amir Khusraw. Yet he hesitates to voice them as he sits quietly in a corner, held back by his belief that the validity of his defense will be ignored by an audience with a partiality for older men, men of wealth, Iranian origins, and a disputatious nature, all of which he lacks. He thus presents his *Kar-nama* to discerning readers in Hind and Iran as a restrained and judicious defense of the masters they all cherish.

Notably, contrary to his self-presentation in this work, Munir did not compose *Kar-nama* as a youth in Lahore, although certainly some of the references to the literary biases of his time were shaped in that environment. We know from Munir's correspondence that it was actually a work of his mature years, likely written in his early thirties, shortly before his death. Significantly, the work was composed while Munir accompanied his patron Sayf Khan to the imperial court at Agra and later to the *suba* of Bengal, where Sayf Khan would die in 1639. The prominent broadcasting of Munir's Lahori identity in *Kar-nama*, distracts from the actual place of its writing.[14] The self-presentation of the tentative young scholar within the imagined majlis of its setting also cloaks the fact that this work was crafted at a time of great professional success, something Munir gestures to at the end of the essay. The mask of the talented, but bashful narrator slips at the end of the essay when Munir describes himself as the writer of "one hundred thousand couplets, of which every verse is like an exalted house for that star of [poetic] meaning [*sad hazar bayt kih har yik bayt al-sharaf-i kaukaba-yi ma'ani ast*]."[15]

In spite of these accomplishments, Munir had reached an uncertain period in his life by 1640, the year in which the *Kar-nama* was written. For much of that period, his letters and works, both prose and poems, are full of homesickness for Lahore, its gardens, and its literary spaces. With the sudden death of his patron, this was also a time in which Munir, writing to his friends, was desperate to find a new patron, and in one of these letters, he declares his intent to dedicate *Kar-nama* to Prince Dara Shikuh, the heir apparent.[16] In these circumstances, writing the introduction to *Kar-nama* was a struggle, and Munir describes his labors to finish the work in a letter to Nawwab Sa'dullah Khan.[17] In another letter from this time to his friend Muhammad Sadiq, a frequent correspondent, this period of professional turmoil ends with an offer of a post with I'tiqad Khan.[18] There is some irony in the fact that both Sa'dullah Khan and I'tiqad Khan were prominent members of the extended family of Persian émigrés to which Nur Jahan and Asaf Khan, Chandrabhan's mentor, also belonged. Thus, despite the angst Munir expressed about his Hindustani roots being a barrier to his career, it would seem that access to such men among the prominent Irani émigré community was also key to Munir's later success, and these patrons received him warmly. This suggests that these two men likely did not view the work as an exercise in regional chauvinism. But what did they make of Munir's harsher comments?

Let us briefly look at the possible roots of Munir's resentment of young Indian poets being held in little regard by his peers, keeping in mind that he feels that wealth and an argumentative nature attract undeserved notice and patronage. Munir never became as wealthy as some of his famous peers, but he was not entirely free of an argumentative streak. That a flood of poets from the Persian Safavid court and Central Asia came to India is a well-established fact, and the peculiar circumstances may well have made Munir's circle—longtime residents of Lahore—especially aware of this stream. For much of the youth and maturity of these scholars, the extended family of I'timad al-Dawla, Empress Nur Jahan's father, had held the governorship of the important border provinces of Lahore, Kashmir, Kabul, and Multan. Well educated, erudite, and powerful, this family lavishly patronized poets and scholars, many of whom were their own kin.[19] Several generations of this family, other than the well-known branch that married into the royal family, were also poets who found patronage in India, beginning with Shapur Tehrani early in Akbar's reign, followed by I'timad al-Dawla's older brother Wasli, and later the poet Hijri. Some sense of this family's pride in these poetic connections can be taken from the extremely ornate and costly commemorative *diwan*s (poetic collections) of his relatives that Ja'far Khan, the grandson of Wasli, commissioned in 1670 to mark the four generations of poets in this remarkable family.[20] Thus both the bureaucratic heights of the provincial administration and the cultural space of its court were dominated by numerous offshoots of the same family and its associates, cemented by the marital ties of this clan to the imperial family. Not surprisingly scholars and poets who shared *nisbat* (genealogical) and *watan* (homeland) ties with this clan flourished, as the commemorative divans of Ja'far Khan suggest.

Yet before we assume that Munir's complaint is valid, let us remind ourselves of his place in the equally well-documented quartet of scholars whose mutual support of one another thrust their Punjabi brotherhood of the pen into the spotlight in Shah Jahan's court. Their mutual promotion not only elevated their status among their peers but also helped them become master scholars whose works were foundational for later generations of Persian munshis (secretaries) and other bureaucrats in the Mughal Empire. Munir himself wrote much admired flattering introductions to the collected volumes of *insha'* of both Kanbu brothers, Muhammad Salih's *Bahar-i Sukhan* (The Springtime of Eloquence) and 'Inayatullah's *Gulshan-i 'Inayat* (Garden of Commitment, 1651).[21] At the time when Munir wrote the introduction to 'Inayatullah's work, it was still incomplete. Muhammad Salih would edit and organize his brother's letters into the final version of the *Gulshan-i 'Inayat* in 1661.[22] That each of these works helped promote the scholarly image of their network is quite clear, and particularly in the case of Munir, whose early death appears to have fostered a desire to memorialize him. The burnishing of his memory is very apparent in some cases. Muhammad Salih, for example, insists in his notice of his departed friend in his *'Amal-i Salih* that Munir was the unsurpassed master of both prose and poetry of his age, and was the first to reach this height since the death of Fayzi (the much admired court poet of Akbar's reign). Furthermore his chief contribution, according to his friend, was that Munir had renewed and made the *tazagui* style fresh again (*rasm-i tazagui-ra taza sakhta*).[23]

The idea that this quartet of Lahori scholars were engaged in reviving Persian literary mastery in India is also found in other works of their circle. Muhammad Salih, who had originally compiled *Bahar-i Sukhan* in 1655 and later revised it in 1663–64, notes that the encouragement to compile a volume of the letters he had penned during his long career in service to some of the leading men of the empire had come from Munir himself. He recalls Munir saying, "If they could see this sweet new nightingale in the garden of meaning, the parrots of Hind could once again fill their hearts with the nectar of beauty and the ornamentation of inspiration [*ilham*]." However, his busy professional life kept Muhammad Salih from perfecting this work.[24] What is remarkable about its long gestation is that Munir wrote the *dibacha* (preface) to his friend's volume before it was completed, since we know he died in 1644, long before the first draft of *Bahar-i Sukhan* was compiled in 1655. The ideas expressed by both Munir and Muhammad Salih were not unique to just this work, however, but broadly shared within their circle.

Munir's preface to *Baharistan-i Sukhan* closely traces the path that he would take in his introduction to his own collections of letters, elevating prose works to the same level of literary sophistication as poetry. Comparing the writing of such elegant prose to the creation of a beautiful bride, paradise, or a bounteous garden in his preface to Muhammad Salih's work not merely repeated what now seem like clichéd reworkings of its title (The Springtime of Eloquence). These analogies served to underline Munir's emphasis on elegant writing as full of the light of gnosis (*nur-i ma'rifat*) and the pathway to the gardens of paradise, where the reader can dwell in the company of holy martyrs.[25] This closely parallels the benefits of self-improvement and self-fashioning he argued would follow those who studied prose writing in the introduction to his own letter collections. The first collection was a work of *insha'* that compiled his correspondence along with some of his prose writings, but a year later, in November 1641, he was encouraged to bring together another collection, *Nawbada* (New Wine), which is specifically dedicated to his Hindu pupil Nik Rai, whom Munir affectionately describes as his adopted son (*farzand-i banda Munir ast*).[26] Nik Rai had urged him to put together letters that had not been compiled into the earlier work, which Munir protests were as dissimilar from each other as "the patched robes of dervishes."[27] This seemingly modest dismissal of this eclectic letter collection appears to point, not to the poverty displayed by the patched robes of dervishes, however, but rather to the variety of their ethical insights.

Indeed, Munir picks up this theme of self-improvement repeatedly in the introduction to this work. He instructs his reader that letters are a source of civility (*adab*) and a suitable inheritance to men of the pen (*ahl-i qalam*); reading such works is akin to sitting in a majlis of learned men.[28] The reader is also introduced by such works to ethical thought (*akhlaq*). Furthermore, Munir hints that the act of writing is almost spiritual, as some other spirit rather than the author moves the pen: "When the pen begins to speak, it makes itself the master of eloquence [*sahib-i sukhan*] and I become the silent transmitter . . . in this state, the pen is not in my hand, but I in the grasp of the pen."[29] Indeed, much of this later collection for his pupil is full of more intimate letters to those close to Munir, including former patrons, close friends, and companions. It also includes their responses to him, reflecting a more intimate network of correspondents than the earlier, more formal collection of letters for his patron Sayf Khan. In a letter to Chandarbhan Brahman, Munir mentions reading the works of a mutual friend, but also encloses his own poetry with the letter for *istilah,* or correction.[30] In another, Munir confesses that having read many divans, he now thinks of himself as resident of the city of literature (*shahristan-i sukhan),* and he goes on to claim a relationship with his fellow scholars as brothers of the same lineage, a sentiment that is in strong contrast to the more defensive and nativist view of his fellow poets in his *Kar-nama.*[31] But we also get a sense of other ambitions when Munir concludes this work by citing the influence of the emperor Akbar's famous scholar-bureaucrat Abu al-Fazl as his inspiration. Munir claims the reflected glory of this comparison, not for himself alone, but also for his friends and companions, without whose help he would have been unable to complete the work and who are as integral to his world as "the four

humors," "the four elements," "the four corners of the world," and the four corners of his house.[32] Repeatedly in these letters addressed to a large cross-section of
Mughal India's literati, Munir asserts his fellowship with them, as when he affirms
that despite his love of Lahore, his true *watan* (homeland) is that of the *farsi-guyan*
(Persian speakers).[33]

Stepping back from this discussion of the intimate collaborations of Munir
and his circle, and even that of his presumed rivals, we can see the parallels between these seemingly dissimilar groups. If some of the poets of Iranian origin
are criticized in *Kar-nama,* in other works they are reclaimed as brothers, even
given the shared identity of the *ahl-i qalam.* Munir appears to recognize that the
diverse network he drew on was crucial to his later success. He did not reach
the heights of power and wealth that Nur Jahan's relatives achieved in the seventeenth century, but the efforts of the Lahori cluster to which Munir, the Kanbu
brothers, and Chandarbhan belonged certainly launched them into an elevated
place in Indo-Persian culture. It is also appropriate to note that each member of
this Punjabi circle benefitted from the patronage of Irani nobles as well. Thus, neither the circles of patronage nor the networks of professional promotion in Mughal
India were dominated by those from the same *watan,* or homeland. But we should
also not dismiss the anxieties and insecurities we find expressed by Munir and
his circle. Their perception of being judged less able, perhaps even provincial, although not dominant modes of self-presentation in their wider work, suggest that
such perceived differences did occasionally spark strong heartfelt criticism of the
different spheres of power held by this cluster of scholarly friends and those they
perceived as rivals. This imagined frontier was real enough to motivate Munir to
write works like *Kar-nama* and police the boundaries of the imagined *shahristan-i
sukhan,* and for his colleagues in the quartet frequently to compare themselves to
the acknowledged masters of Persian of the recent past. Likewise, this seems
to be related to their perception that it was necessary to "revive" the flagging literary arts of the Mughal Empire in their own generation, and their hope that their
own works might serve as models for aspiring students.

FROM MAJLIS TO *MAKTAB* (SCHOOLS): THE PLACES
AND PRACTICES OF ACQUIRING PERSIAN

Strong identification with their *watan* is found in many of the quartet's works.
However, they occupied very privileged spaces in the Mughal imperial structure.
After his first patron, Sayf Khan, died, Munir apparently found himself another
one—I'tiqad Khan, a wealthy, powerful Irani. both the Kanbu brothers held lifetime positions in the court's central bureaucracy, which enabled the three, still
alive in 1658, to survive the transition to the reign of Aurangzeb. Chandrabhan
became the caretaker of the Taj Mahal, and the Kanbu brothers were able to build
themselves a substantial tomb, which was still a landmark in colonial-era Lahore.[34]

But as the quartet's own works remind us, their positions were only available to those who had spent years mastering the demanding curriculum, etiquette, and practices of the Mughal imperial bureaucracy, and, what is more, also had some access to the network of influential men who commanded the ability to make (or break) careers. So what about those who did not have such access?

We know little of the training of the quartet, but the hints they drop in their work reveal different pathways to literacy in areas within and outside imperial cities. Both Kanbu brothers and Munir, as sons of families with already close linkages with the imperial court and the eminent scholars, poets, and teachers clustered around it, likely did not lack for instruction and mentoring either in the intricacies of court etiquette as it related to bureaucrats, or the use of Persian in the court. Chandrabhan, born into a family of Punjabi bureaucrats, was a decidedly different case. His father appears to have had only mid-level provincial postings. As Rajeev Kinra has noted, in his letters to family members Chandrabhan mentions learning to write the fiendishly difficult *khatt-i shikasta* from the "shudra" scholar Jatmal, one of many low-caste scribes skilled in calligraphy.[35] It is tempting to see this as a reference for the little-studied Jat author Jatmal Nahar, now known chiefly known for his *Gora Badal ki Katha,* a reworking of the Padmavat Sufi narrative in a *masnawi* of 1628 written for his Afghan patrons in Punjab, but who is also known to have written two other works, *Lahore Ghazal* and *Zingar Ghazal.*[36] Lahore in the early part of the seventeenth century, at the center of a growing engagement not only with Persian and Indic literary languages such as Sanskrit and Braj but with vernaculars like Punjabi, Sindhi, and the Haryanwi dialects, was flooded with Jains, Kayasths, Khatris, Brahmins, and Jats employed in various literary and scholarly capacities.[37] Many of the scholars engaged in these multilingual, cross-cultural literary exercises were associated with new forms of religiosity such as the Adhyatmi Jains and the increasingly diversifying forms of Sikhism. New status groups appear to have used the opportunities presented by the expanding cultural literacy of the time to scale social ranks as well. For example, we learn from the family chronicles of the Ahulwalia Sikhs who would eventually establish a small Sikh state in the eighteenth century, that the ancestors of this family, originally distillers of the Kalal caste, had moved into two very different professions during the seventeenth and early eighteenth century: some, claiming a mixed Jat and Rajput status in the countryside, became zamindars (rural revenue collectors), and others found bureaucratic jobs in Lahore, where a quarter was named for this clan.[38]

How did such families achieve this dramatic leap in both rural and urban mobility? This is a difficult question to answer since our sources for the day-to-day life of rural Punjab are limited. However, British Agency records for east Punjab in the early 1800s and a mid-nineteenth-century land survey offer some tentative answers. Most relevant to our discussion of the frontiers of Persian are the numerous charitable grants for which colonial officers were asked to survey and confirm deeds—these included a large number of Sufi *khanaqah*s, as well as non-Muslim religious institutions including Hindu *maths* and *thakurdwaras* and Sikh *gurud-waras*.³⁹ Some had titles going back to the time of the early Mughal emperors, but the larger spikes are from the seventeenth century, and then again later in the period of the Sikh *misals*. The multifunctional role of these spaces in rural Punjab is particularly interesting for our discussion of languages, literature, and community. One of their primary functions for many of these spaces, particularly of *khanaqa-hs*, was to serve as hubs of social and cultural life for these rural communities. Most had a weekly market, or *hat*, and they also served as rest houses for travelers, merchants, and wedding parties. The annual *'urs* (death anniversary) festivals attracted poets and musicians from around the region, but most significantly, they also had schools. Like the market, rest house, and *'urs* festivals, these schools were open to all in the community, not just Muslims.⁴⁰ For these reasons, even in the eighteenth century, after political control of Punjab moved from the Mughals and later the Afghans to the Sikh chiefs, the latter confirmed most of these grants and often initiated new grants for Muslim teachers who ran schools.⁴¹

Very little survives of the instructional aids from the period. Walter Hakala's work on bilingual dictionaries and commentaries on Persian literary works, for example, has unearthed the substantial work of 'Abd al-Wasi' Hansiwi, who hailed from Hansi, a town and *khanaqah* complex situated on the imperial highway from Kabul to Delhi in the eastern part of the Punjab region now associated with Haryana. Among these works were a bilingual dictionary intended to help with the composition of verse, a grammar of Persian, and commentaries on Sa'di's *Bustan* and Jami's *Yusuf wa Zulaykha*. Their inclusion in the traditional madrasa curriculum would lead to a dismissive view of such works by later scholars of Persian in India, which only recently has begun to reverse with Hakala's groundbreaking study.⁴² The ostensibly "rustic" register of the vernacular received more criticism than the scholarly work on the challenging aspects of Persian acquisition in earlier studies.

This supposedly "rustic" vernacular served an important pedagogical purpose, however, helping Punjabi speakers learn and read Persian from difficult literary texts and creating a formal system of script, pronunciation, and standardized grammar for them, which until then had not been formulated in any systematic way. The Punjabi case closely follows the forms of multilingual literacy described by Thibaut d'Hubert and Paul Wormser with respect to the crucial bridging role of Persian in both language and spiritual instruction in the Bengali and Malay contexts. This form of early instruction of Punjabi Muslims in Arabic script, which includes works such as the *Baran Anwa* of Mawlawi 'Abdullah, known by his pen-name (*takhallus*) 'Abdi, now lies mostly neglected in archives. Such treatises instructed Punjabi Muslims in the vernacular, but the title headings and scholarly apparatus were in Persian.⁴³ These works should command our attention because, although not written in literary Persian, they mark the edges of the Persophone world in the *khanaqah*s, small *qasba* (towns), and villages of rural India. Their intentions were not that different from the intentions of Munir, Chandarbhan, and the Kanbu brothers in trying to expand the knowledge of Indian Persian learners beyond basic literacy—enabling them to use the shared language of the Mughal empire fluently—to some grasp of the literature of Persian. It was the scale of these educational initiatives that was different. In small towns and settlements, they were geared to teaching functional command of a script that was not fully suited to the more copious sounds of Punjabi or Braj, but could be adapted to allow children to achieve a basic literacy in two languages at the same time. An important side effect was that Punjabi, which was not taught formally even within Punjab, but remained a mostly spoken vernacular, was now beginning to achieve the shape and form of a literary culture, both in the Arabic script taught alongside Persian, and also the Gurmukhi script taught and passed down in the Sikh community. As the archival material from Punjab inevitably reminds us, those who achieved literacy were often bilingual, if not multilingual in Persian, Punjabi, or Braj, often working in tandem and combinations with each other. Unlike in the later colonial period, when speakers increasingly began to see each language as the province of a particular religious or regional community, neither in the rural spaces of Punjab's *khanaqah*s and *dharamsala*s, nor in the urban spaces of the literary majlis was the community of scholars and poets monolingual or exclusively from one religious group. Much like Allison Busch's Braj poets at the Mughal courts, the numerous Jats—or, as she puts it, Shudra scribes and scholars—that Chandrabhan remembers with both affection and respect were "hiding in plain view," as were the mid-to-low status Arains, Aroras, and others who would grasp literacy as a pathway to social mobility later in the eighteenth century.[44]

Adjusting our perspective in this way then, we begin to see how the linguistic and scholarly leavening of engaged scholarship in these small towns fed the hungry demands of the Mughal Empire's great need for trained, multilingual officials necessary for the day-to-day working of the empire. Although we tend to focus on the specific demands of the more rarified environs of the imperial secretariat, every bureaucrat to some degree, but particularly those in the mid-to-lower rungs of the administration, had to be bilingual by necessity. The oral orders given to messengers, servants, soldiers, village account keepers, most likely in vernaculars, did not make it into the epistolography (*insha'*) collections, but in their written forms, these were organized, analyzed, and rendered into Persian. Much as imperial buildings were both functional and exquisitely crafted, so too were these bureaucratic building blocks, written in beautiful scripts on decorated papers, or bound into elegant volumes. Even in the unadorned paper of everyday use, these were made beautiful by the conscientious use of exquisite civility, polished imagery, and pleasing themes. In this guise, they cloak the sheer labor and painstakingly acquired skills of their many anonymous crafters, both native speakers, and those who acquired Persian knowledge later in *maktab*s, madrasas, or in their family circles.

If we turn back then to the early generations of Indian-born bureaucrats who first came into imperial service like our Lahori quartet, we begin to see how and why both imagined barriers and carefully cultivated connections with the wider cosmopolitan world of Persian literature dominate their works. While not trail-blazers, they appear to have been conscious of the need to create works, particularly in the prose forms suitable for training bureaucrats, works that would allow other young men to achieve the hard-won mastery of these complex texts. It is notable that the while each of the individuals in this Punjabi quartet of scholars wrote poetry, the vast majority of their work was in the prose valued by Mughal bureaucrats—letters, short debates, and charmingly rendered prose vignettes that are collectively found in their *insha'* works, as well as the histories such as *'Amal-i Salih* (Work of Salih) and the *Padshah-nama* (Book of the Emperor). The prose works of the Kanbu brothers such as *Bahar-i Danish* (Springtime of Learning) and *Bahar-i Sukhan* (Springtime of Speech), both of which contain letters as well as short prose extracts, and certainly the works of both Munir and Chandarbhan would actually become part of the standard curriculum for Persian learners in India, surviving into the period of printed texts in early lithographed versions.[45] This was not by accident. As mentioned earlier, Munir crafted his letter collections with a pedagogical purpose in mind. 'Inayatullah, too, expresses this purpose in his own *Bahar-i Sukhan.* Nor were the efforts of this group unique. Owing in part to agrarian expansion that made generous endowments possible, there were similar, if more modest, efforts throughout Punjab's small towns and villages.

CONCLUSIONS

Much has been said about the "cosmopolitan" nature of Persian in Mughal India, but while there is ample evidence of the inclusivity of the literary circles in the empire, we must be careful not to overextend this view when studying how Persian became rooted in imperial cultures, or the extent to which it engaged with regional cultures. Particularly in the seventeenth century, when the reforms of Akbar were finally beginning to get an impetus from agrarian expansion, on the one hand, and the expanding need for literate men, on the other, the contexts in which Persian was acquired, mastered, or used were quite varied. In Punjab, the contexts of Persian and Punjabi literary acquisition often closely related, and while the full tide of Persian mastery acquired in the smaller towns of the province does not become evident until the late seventeenth and early eighteenth century, the roots of this expansion can be traced to the network of schools, mentors, and early patrons active the period of Shah Jahan. Later, famous figures from these smaller towns would include the *tazkira* writer Sarkhush and his childhood friend Nasir 'Ali Sirhindi from the Naqshbandi complex in Sirhind; Sialkoti Mal "Warista" from Punjab's prime paper-producing center, Sialkot; and the veritable tide of *khatris* from towns like Batala, Thanesar, and Qasur who flooded into many parts of the empire starting under Aurangzeb (r. 1658–1707). Equally important here was the bilingual production in Punjabi and Persian in a variety of Sufi *khanaqah*s that grew steadily over the course of the seventeenth century. In these contexts, Persian was equally a frontier, a bridge, and a path.

Most Persian learners or users in the early decades of the seventeenth century functioned, not in the rarified inner circle of the imperial court, but in much more eclectic settings all over the province and in the cities of the empire. The urban majlis however, operated in a more competitive milieu. Dominated by affective ties of kinship, regional origins, and patronage, each literary circle had its own sense of collective belonging to a wider literary world, but also of the fissures perceived within it. This is true of the four men discussed in this paper—Munir Lahawri, the Kanbu brothers, and Munshi Chandarbhan. Even as they pushed Persian to become an even more expansive, inclusive, and triumphant medium of their collective sense of success, we find discordant notes of competitive regionalism, status anxiety, and a failure to imagine the very cosmopolitanism they ardently desired. Not all frontiers are concretely rendered in geographical or political solidity, and one may argue that even such frontiers require feats of collective imagination. The imagined topography of Persian as presented in the works of these masters of the language in Punjab is simultaneously expansive and restrictive, its borders patrolled by gatekeepers who were often self-appointed. Farsi was itself both the territory they fought over and the weapon they wielded.

NOTES

1. See Muzaffar Alam, "The Culture and Politics of Persian in Pre-colonial Hindustan," in *Literary Cultures in History: Reconstructions from South Asia*, ed. Sheldon Pollock (Berkeley: University of California Press, 2003), 131–98, and Abdul Ghani, *A History of Persian Language and Literature at the Mughal Court in Three Parts* (Allahabad: Indian Press, 1929). On claims of a one-way influence of Safavid culture on the Mughals, see Ehsan Yarshater, "The Indian or Safavid Style: Progress or Decline?" in *Persian Literature*, ed. Ehsan Yarshater (New York: Bibliotheca Persica, 1988). Paul E. Losensky, *Welcoming Fighānī: Imitation and Poetic Individuality in the Safavid-Mughal Ghazal* (Costa Mesa, CA: Mazda, 1998), offers a nuanced counterargument for cross-regional influence.

2. These journeys to and from Lahore are mentioned at length in key primary sources such as the emperor Jahangir's *Tuzuk-i Jahangiri*, ed. Henry Beveridge (1909; repr. New Delhi: Low Price Publications, 1999), 67–77, 239–46, and Muhammad Salih Kanbo, *'Amal-i Salih, Shahjahan-nama*, ed. Ghulam Yazdani (Lahore: Majlis-i Taraqqi-yi Adab, 1972), passim.

3. A large number of such scholars and learned men are cited in Salih Kanbo, *'Amal-i Salih*, 264–346.

4. For their works and collaborations, see D. N. Marshall, *Mughals in India: A Bibliographic Survey of Manuscripts* (London: Mansell, 1985) 120–21, 203–4, 338–39, and 353–55.

5. Abu al-Barkat Munir Lahawri, *Kar-nama wa Siraj-i Munir*, ed. Dr. Sayyid Muhammad Akram Ikram (Rawalpindi: Iran Pakistan Institute of Persian Studies, 1977).

6. A portrait of the Kanbo brothers' father appears in the illustrated manuscript of the *Diwan-i Hasan Dihlawi* in the Walters Art Museum, fol. 187a. See "Walters Ms. W.650, Collection of Poems (Divan)," www.thedigitalwalters.org/Data/WaltersManuscripts/html/W650/description.html

7. Rajeev Kinra, "Master and Munshi: A Brahman Secretary's Guide to Mughal Governance," *Indian Economic and Social History Review* 47, 4 (2010): 536.

8. Ibid., 534–37.

9. Rajeev Kinra, "Making It Fresh: Time, Tradition, and Indo-Persian Literary Modernity," in *Time, History and the Religious Imaginary in South Asia*, ed. Anne Murphy (London: Routledge, 2011), 12–39.

10. Muzaffar Alam and Sanjay Subrahmanyam, "The Making of a Munshi," *Comparative Studies of South Asia, Africa, and the Middle East* 24, 2 (2004): 61–72.

11. For a more detailed discussion of this, see Kinra, "Making It Fresh," 28–30; Alam, "Culture and Politics of Persian," 182–84.

12. Mohamad Tavakoli-Targhi, *Refashioning Iran: Orientalism, Occidentalism, and Historiography* (New York: Palgrave, 2001), 26–28; Kinra, "Making It Fresh," 30; Alam, "Culture and Politics of Persian," 182–84.

13. Kinra, "Making It Fresh," 30; Alam, "Culture and Politics of Persian," 183.

14. Munir, *Nawbada wa Ruq'at Mulla Munir*, Salar Jang Museum and Library, Acc. no. 3428, Adab Nasr 333, fol. 511b, Also see D. N. Marshall's discussion of dated works, *Mughals in India*, cited in n. 4 above.

15. 'Abu al-Barkat Munir Lahawri, *Kar-nama wa Siraj-i Munir*, ed. Dr. Sayyid Muhammad Akram 'Ikram' (Rawalpindi: Iran Pakistan Institute of Persian Studies, 1977), 27. I am grateful to Daniel Sheffield for pointing out the astrological significance of *bayt al-Sharaf* as the "exalted house."

16. Munir, *Nawbada*, fol. 511b.

17. Ibid., fol. 67a.

18. Ibid., fols. 64b–65a.

19. No major study of this family's literary activities has been attempted; only glimpses of it occur in some of the works on Indo-Persian discussed above, although the archival legacy of this clan is immense. The only major monograph on the prominent noblemen in this family remains Anil Kumar's *Asaf Khan and His Times* (Patna: Kashi Prasad Jayaswal Research Institute, 1986).

20. These commemorative volumes are now in the Salar Jang collection, each is lavishly decorated with gold and blue floral margins. The autograph of Muhammad Ja'far Khan appears on the flyleaf. Salar Jang Museum and Library, *Diwan-i Wasli*, Cat. no. 1824, Adab Nazm 1093/2. In the same bound volume fol. 29a starts the section by Shapur. The volume was rebound in 1983. The section between Wasli and Shapur's poetry, which contained Ja'far Khan's own poetry and that of Hijri, another relative, is now a separate manuscript shelved as Adab Nazm 1155. Yet another section is Adab Nazm 1156 with the *Diwan-i Wasli*.

21. Muhammad Salih Kanbo, *Bahar-i Sukhan*, British Library, Oriental MS 178. Munir's introduction is on fols. 2a–4a of this work.

22. See Marshall, *Mughals in India*, 203–4, 354.

23. Muhammad Salih Kanbo, *'Amal-i Salih*, 342–42.

24. Muhammad Salih Kanbo, *Bahar-i Sukhan*, 9b.

25. Munir in introduction to Muhammad Salih Kanbo's, *Bahar-i Sukhan*, fols. 2a–4a.

26. Munir, *Nawbada*, fol. 57a.

27. Ibid., fol. 57a.

28. Ibid., fol. 581b.

29. Ibid., 59b.

30. Ibid., fols. 70b–71b.

31. Ibid., fol. 99b.

32. Ibid., fols. 106b–109b. The comparison of groups of four intimately connected objects goes on at length to stress this point.

33. Ibid., fol. 34b.

34. Rajeev Kinra, *Writing Self, Writing Empire: Chandar Bhan Brahman and the Cultural World of the Indo-Persian State Secretary* (Oakland: University of California Press, 2015), 56; Muhammad Salih Kanbo, *'Amal-i Salih*, intro.

35. Kinra, *Master and Munshi*, 536–58.

36. Marshall, *Mughals in India*, 230–31. Ramya Sreenivasan identifies him as an Osval Jain working for the Pathan chief 'Ali Khan Niazi Khan in Simbala Village near Lahore. However, as she herself makes clear, the question of his identification either as a Jat or an Osval Jain is not clear. Ramya Sreenivasan, *The Many Lives of a Rajput Queen: Heroic Pasts in India, c. 1500–1900* (Seattle: University of Washington Press, 2007), 77, 113n57. It is important to note that these are not mutually exclusive. Since the Nahar *gotra* caste are included in Jain, Jat, and even Afghan genealogies in Modern India today, this may reflect a longer history of caste mobility and transformation.

37. For Jains, particularly the Adhyatmis, see Mukund Lath, *Ardhakathanak, Half a Tale—A Study in the Interrelationship between Autobiography and History* (Allahabad: Rupa, 1981), 46. The interface between Punjabi and Braj, particularly in the life of the noted seventeenth-century Sikh poet and intellectual Bhai Gurdas, is also relevant here; see discussion in Rahuldeep Singh Gill, "Growing the Banyan Tree: Early Sikh Tradition in the Works of Bhai Gurdas Bhalla," (PhD diss., University of California, Santa Barbara, 2009), 72–79.

38. Ram Sukh Rao, *Jassa Singh Binod*, M/772, Punjab State Archives, Patiala, fols. 57a–58b.

39. These records are currently available, organized by date and district, in the National Archives in New Delhi under "Foreign and Political Proceedings."

40. See, e.g., the cluster of grants to Muslim shrines in the village of Nimaneewal near Sialkot, mostly beginning in the Mughal period and later confirmed by subsequent Sikh rulers. Foreign and Political Proceedings, January 9, 1857, Nimaneewal, Jila Sialkote, Lahore Division, no. 221, 1–12. I have retained the original spelling of the colonial officials who compiled this file.

41. See, e.g., Foreign and Political Proceedings, National Archives of India, January 9, 1857, no. 233, entries 27 and 28. The first grant cited here was by Jahan Khan, a Mughal-era *lambardar* (revenue collector), for a school on the premises of a mosque in Chaudhriwalla; the second was a Sikh-era grant for a mosque with a school.

42. See, e.g., discussion of the "Haryanvi" diction in Walter Nils Hakala, "Diction, and Dictionaries, Language, Literature and Learning in Persianate South Asia," (PhD diss., University of Pennsylvania, 2010), 381–420.

43. For a full description of these works in English, see Christopher Shackle, *Catalogue of the Sindhi and Punjabi Manuscripts in the India Office Library* (London: British Library Publishing Division, 1977), 39–40.

44. Allison Busch, "Hidden in Plain View: Brajbhasha Poets at the Mughal Court," *Modern Asian Studies* 44, no. 2 (2010): 267–309.

45. For details of this, see Marshall, *Mughals in India*, cited in n. 4 above.

6
———

A Lingua Franca in Decline?

The Place of Persian in Qing China

David Brophy

The Qing dynasty (1636–1912) inherited a large community of Chinese-speaking Muslims from the Ming, and in the eighteenth century incorporated a new population of Turkic-speaking Muslims, the inhabitants of Xinjiang (or Eastern Turkistan), into its territory. The conquering Manchus also took possession of an existing Chinese infrastructure of translation, which had served the Ming court in its dealings with Persophone neighbors. Across this imperial expanse, the question of the place of Persian can therefore be considered on two levels: the institutional level and the level of Muslim society. These two lines of inquiry provide the structure for this chapter, which looks at the place of Persian in the Qing, both in terms of the language's position within the empire's bureaucracy, and the production and consumption of Persian texts among Chinese-speaking and Turkic-speaking Qing Muslims.

Given that the scholarly literature tends to depict the use of Persian as declining through this period, it is worth beginning this discussion with a look back at earlier periods of Chinese history. In the case of the Mongol Yuan dynasty (1271–1368), strong claims have been made for the role of Persian in China, where it is said to have been both a "lingua franca" and an "official" language.[1] Viewed in such a light, the situation during the Qing would indeed represent a decline in the language's status. Recently, though, Stephen Haw has subjected these claims to extensive criticism, arguing that both the place of Muslims among the foreigners who served in the Yuan bureaucracy and that of Persian-speakers among these Muslims have been exaggerated. While there undoubtedly were Persian-speakers in the service of the khans, far more "Semu ren" (as the Yuan classified them) can be confidently identified as speakers of Turkic: among them the Uyghurs, who held a prominent position in the Yuan bureaucracy, but also various Qarluq, Qangli, Öngüt, and Qipchaq migrants to China. Contrary to the received wisdom on Marco Polo, the Venetian's travelogue does not in fact offer conclusive evidence for the preeminence of Persian. Here, and elsewhere in sources on the Yuan, Turkic toponyms and terminology crop up just as frequently as Persian, including, for example, the name (*khanbalïq*) by which the Yuan capital was known among foreigners, or the name for the dynasty's Mongol-Muslim trading enterprises (the *ortoq*). From his wide-ranging discussion, Haw draws the conclusion that Turkic, not Persian, was "the predominant language of the Semu ren" in the Yuan.[2]

Haw's contribution highlights a methodological issue that is equally important for the following period. Chinese authors frequently confuse the distinction between script and language, but strictly speaking, references to "Muslim writing" (*Huihuizi, Huizi, Huiwen*, etc.) refer only to the Arabic script, and tell us nothing about the language of the text in question. Only when we have further evidence at hand can we identify the language intended. Surviving records show, for example, that during the Ming, staff of the "Muslim" office of the College of Translators studied Persian. It would be wrong, though, to infer from this that all Ming references to "Muslim writing" or "Muslim language" (*Huiyu*) should be interpreted to mean Persian. All this really tells us is that during the early Ming, Persian was a language of diplomacy between China and its Muslim neighbors. Equally, it seems excessive to infer from the fact that its bureaucracy had some facility with Persian that the language had any kind of "official" status under the Ming dynasty. Leaving aside the question of whether the concept of an "official" language is applicable to an empire such as the Ming, it was in any case standard diplomatic practice to permit tributaries to present letters in their own language, and the Ming invested in translation expertise accordingly. If Persian was an "official" language of the Ming, then the dynasty had many such languages.

In the case of Xinjiang, too, there is reason to be wary of a simplistic narrative of decline. The fall of the ruling Chaghataiid dynasty at the end of the seventeenth century is commonly associated with the end of a Persianate courtly culture, the isolation of the Tarim Basin from the rest of the Islamic world, and a decline in standards of Persian learning. There is some evidence that the Chaghataiids were participants in a common post-Mongol Turco-Persian cultural synthesis in the sixteenth and seventeenth centuries. The Chaghataiid khans and princes kept up correspondence in Persian with their neighbors in Western Turkistan, India, and occasionally China.[3] The dynasty's founder Sa'id Khan (1487–1514) spoke Persian, and could versify in the language, as could his son, 'Abd al-Rashid Khan (1508–60).[4] Yet on the whole the Chaghataiids were no great patrons of Persian letters. There was never a sizable community of native Persian-speakers in the Tarim Basin, and the language never occupied the position in Yarkand that it did in neighboring Khoqand or Bukhara. Naturally, allowance must be made for the vagaries of manuscript survival, but to this date little evidence has come to light for court sponsorship of poetry or prose in Persian. Nor was Persian the language of administration: the textual record shows that the Chaghataiid chancellery made exclusive use of Turkic.[5]

These facts would seem to rule out the idea that Persian ever had "official" status across the territory that became the Qing Empire, or that it served as a lingua franca (whether that term is intended to mean a common spoken language or a medium of written communication). From this more modest, but realistic, starting point, we are in a better position to appraise the role of Persian in the Qing. The language was not incorporated into multilingual expressions of Qing imperial universality, in which the empire's Muslim constituency was addressed exclusively in Turkic. Persian did, though, play a limited role in imperial diplomacy, and for a brief period connected the Qing to parts of the Islamic world. Persian was not a language of daily use among any of the empire's Muslims, and very few original works were written in the language, but a canon of Persian texts continued to be studied in madrasa networks across China. In examining the state of Persian literacy and learning among the empire's Muslims, this chapter treats the Chinese-speaking Hui and the Turkic-speaking Muslims of Xinjiang (today's Uyghurs) side by side. While there are significant differences between the intellectual histories of these two communities, there are also enough commonalities to justify this approach. Particularly striking is the simultaneous emergence in these communities around 1700 of traditions of translation into Chinese and Turkic.

THE INSTITUTIONAL USE OF PERSIAN IN THE QING

As Graeme Ford describes in chapter 3 of this volume, the Ming dynasty (1368–1644) established the College of Translators (Siyiguan) within the prestigious Hanlin Academy as the dynasty's main institution for the training of translators. *Siyiguan* literally means the "Bureau of the Four Barbarians," where "four" refers to the four cardinal points (i.e., "all directions"). However, the Siyiguan usually had at least eight subdivisions. Of these, two dealt with the languages of peoples and polities that were part of, or were becoming part of, the Islamic world during the Ming: the Gaochang Office, whose name reflects the proximity to Ming China of the Turkic-speaking people of Gaochang, the Chinese name for Turfan; and the Muslim Office, which received envoys from the Timurid realm and beyond. These designations give the impression that geographic or cultural divisions determined each office's jurisdiction, but the division of labor was based on the scripts that they dealt with. In the Gaochang Office, translators studied the Sogdian-derived Uyghur script; in the Muslim Office, translators learned Persian in the Arabic script.[6]

The divisions of the Siyiguan reflected the state of the world outside China at the time of the Yuan-Ming transition in the mid-fourteenth century. This picture was constantly changing, though, and political and cultural shifts in the international environment increasingly brought these bureaucratic forms into conflict with reality. The spread of Islamic rule in Turkistan at the expense of the remaining Buddhist principalities is a case in point. Following the eastward expansion of the Muslim Chaghataiids in the fifteenth and sixteenth centuries, Arabic script displaced Uyghur for written communication in the Tarim Basin, as well as in the principalities of Turfan and Hami. In his *Siyiguan kao* (1580), a late-Ming description of the Siyiguan, Wang Zongzai points out that in his day, tribute missions from Gaochang were led by Muslims, who wrote, not in the Uyghur script that was still studied in the Gaochang Office, but in Arabic script. "Although Gaochang originally fell within the Gaochang Office for translation," he writes, "recently there have been a lot of Muslims among them. When they bring tribute they use the Muslim script, so they too come within the purview of the Muslim Office." Ming officials referred to these Turkic letters in Arabic script as the "Gaochang language in the Muslim script" (*Gaochanghua Huihuizi*).[7]

Despite these growing incongruities, the Siyiguan survived the end of the Ming era. The Qing initially maintained the bureau's divisions intact, and there is some evidence that the Muslim Office kept up the study of Persian into the early Qing.[8] As time went by, though, the bureau atrophied, dwindling to a skeleton staff, with infrequent recruitment of new pupils. In 1748, the Qianlong emperor issued a decree significantly downsizing these institutions of translation, merging the Siyiguan into the Bureau of Interpreters, and reducing its eight subdivisions to two: one for the Western Regions (*Xiyu guan*), and one for the Hundred Barbarians (referring to peoples to China's southwest). The restructuring led to the dismissal of the entire staff of the Gaochang Office, with only a small group retained from the Muslim Office.

The main reason for the Qing court's neglect of this inheritance from the Ming was that it had alternative organs for the conduct of foreign affairs. In 1636, at the proclamation of the new dynasty, Hong Taiji created the Mongolian Office (*Monggo yamun*) as his regime's main institution for handling relations with its Mongol allies. In 1638 he enlarged the Mongolian Office into the Court of Colonial Affairs (*Lifanyuan*). Although this ostensibly widened its remit, the primary task of the new Court of Colonial Affairs was still to manage relations with the Mongols. At the same time, the Grand Secretariat's Mongolian Copying Office (*Menggufang* or *Menggutang*) also played an important role in translating incoming correspondence and preparing outgoing letters and decrees. Insofar as these institutions reflected a view of the Muslim world, it was one quite different from that of the Ming. The first foreign Muslims with whom the Qing court had contact were members of Junghar Mongol trading missions, men who were bilingual in Turkic and Mongolian, drawn from that group of Turkistani Muslims who were in the service of the Junghars. For this reason the Qing court saw no need to add Muslim staff to either the Court of Colonial Affairs or the Mongolian Copying Office. Archival evidence indicates that when the Mongolian Copying Office encountered texts in "Muslim script," it relied on ad hoc intermediaries to translate via Mongolian into Manchu.[9]

As the Qing extended their sway from Jungharia into the Tarim Basin in the 1750s, they encountered a complex linguistic situation, and officials became aware of the linguistic diversity of the Islamic lands. Yet for the most part, this diversity was treated in terms of discrete geographic spheres, with little recognition given to the idea that the local learned tradition was itself multilingual, with texts circulating in Arabic, Persian, and Turkic. The first officially published gazetteer of Xinjiang, the *Qinding huangyu xiyu tuzhi* (commissioned in 1755), situated each of these three Islamic languages in distinct territories: "There are a total of three languages in the Muslim territory. From Hami and Pichan as far west as Kashgar, Yarkand, and Khotan, the language is basically the same, and they call it Turki. Among foreign tributaries such as Badakhshan, Bolor, etc., the language they use is called Parsi. There is also the language of the Quran [*He-er-ang*], which is only spoken in the Muslim homeland of Mecca and Medina, and differs from Turki and Parsi."[10]

In this account, typical of Qing reports on Xinjiang, we see that linguistic identity aligns not only with geography, but with political status: the language of Muslims incorporated into the Qing empire is Turkic; Persian belongs to the empire's immediate tributary rim, while Arabic is a language of the far-flung western regions with which the Qing had no direct contact. Qing scholars and officials writing on Xinjiang would occasionally note that local toponyms, or individual items of vocabulary derived from Persian, but the prevailing view of Persian was thus strictly as a language of diplomacy, and limited to a sector of its frontier stretching from the khanate of Kokand to the kingdom of Ladakh.

As is the case for the Ming, so too in the Qing, we cannot confidently identify the language intended in every reference to "Muslim script" (i.e., Arabic letters). By the middle of the eighteenth century, though, the default meaning of "Muslim language" had settled decisively on Turkic. It was in a form of literary Turkic that the corpus of official "Muslim language" texts commissioned during the Qing was written, including the inscription of the mosque that the Qianlong emperor had built in Beijing in 1764 (with Turkic alongside Manchu, Mongolian, and Chinese), along with the "Muslim" sections of Qing dictionaries and linguistic handbooks.[11] In the Tarim Basin itself, a distinctive idiom of Turkic "translationese" emerged within the Qing bureaucracy. Here too, officials customarily referred to Turkic simply as the "Muslim language," while Persian texts were specified as Persian (Manchu *parsi*).

Persophone interactions between Qing China and its neighbors to the south and west of Yarkand built on the Chaghataiid court's earlier exchange of letters with this region. The great majority of Persian letters in the Qing archive belong to the first fifteen years following the conquest of Xinjiang (1760–75), when the Qing actively intervened in diplomacy across the Pamirs and Himalayas, and local elites saw an opportunity to exercise regional hegemony with Qing support. An initial count of surviving Persian letters in the Manchu section of Beijing's First Historical Archive has yielded more than a hundred such documents.[12] Badakhshan, as well as the surrounding Pamiri principalities of Ghund, Shughnan, and Shakhdara, were the source of much of this correspondence. The Wakhan Corridor, being the

Qing court's gateway to Afghanistan, was an important supplier of intelligence. Further east, Ladakh and Kashmir also wrote to the Qing in Persian in the 1760s. Following this initial flurry of contact, though, the flow of communication all but ceased, and from the 1780s on we have only the highly formulaic letters that representatives of Hunza (or Kanjut, as it was known to the Qing) brought with them on their semi-annual tribute missions to Yarkand. Local sources from Hunza add to the evidence for this ongoing communication: Qudratullah Beg's history of Hunza, for example, contains the text of Persian letters to the Qing.[13]

Before they reached Beijing, letters from regions bordering Xinjiang were usually rendered into Manchu by local translators, known as *tongchi* (from Chinese *tongshi*). This system worked well for Turkic, but not, it seems, for Persian. The corps of *tongchi* largely consisted of Muslims from Hami and Turfan, the oases most closely involved in the long-running Qing-Junghar conflict, and scribes from this part of Xinjiang were more likely to know Mongolian than they were to know Persian. As a consequence, translating incoming and outgoing correspondence from Persian-speaking neighbors tested the capabilities of the fledgling Qing bureaucracy in the Tarim Basin. We know this from a report sent by an official in Yarkand in 1763, describing a complicated three-step translation process:

> The letters that places such as Afghanistan, Badakhshan, Bolor, Wakhan, Tibet, or Kashmir submit to the emperor or to the *amban*s (Manchu high officials) are all written in Persian, but among the mullahs and *akhund*s (a synonym for mullah), there are very few here who know this language. Since only the Akhund Shah 'Abd al-Qadir knows Persian, whenever the *beg*s [local governors] and heads of these various countries send a Persian letter, it is entrusted to him. He translates it into Muslim [*hoise gisun*, i.e., Turkic], and transmits this to a mullah who knows how to write in Muslim. The Muslims in the Seals Office then translate it into Mongolian and give it to the *amban*s, who translate it into Manchu.[14]

Following this lengthy procedure, and having digested the letter's contents and replied, Qing officials filed a report on the emissary's arrival to the court, attaching to it the original letters with translations. There is little evidence for the nature of outgoing correspondence, though it seems likely that the reverse procedure applied: official missives would be issued exclusively in Turkic, with local officials commissioning translations into Persian (if they were translated at all) before sending them on. Although multilingual imperial decrees in Manchu, Mongolian, and Turkic have survived, nothing of comparable significance was ever written in Persian. Not surprisingly, therefore, it seems that neighboring polities equipped to communicate in Turkic came to realize that this was the best medium for dealing with Kashgar and Yarkand. While the Khoqand court did occasionally dispatch letters to Xinjiang in Persian, it tended to write to Qing officials in Turkic.[15] Bukhara, as far as we can tell from limited records, also wrote to the Qing in Turkic.[16]

A rare, possibly even unique, exception to this rule is an inscription that was erected in the western Pamirs in 1768, the only instance of the quasi-official use of Persian that I have encountered in my research. This text was set in stone to delineate the domains of the *amir* (emir) of Ghund from the district of Suchan, subordinate to the *amir* of Shughnan, in an effort to mediate a dispute between the two. The text is a quatrain, which reads: "By decree of the emperor of China, with worldly and spiritual support, this is his pronouncement on the boundary between Ghund and Suchan [*bi-farman-i haqan-i Chin / bi-'umda-i dunya-u-din / dar miyana-i Ghund-u-Suchan / in ast ada-yi suhan*]."[17] The poetic form seems to conform to a distinctly Pamiri style of proclamation, in which such quatrains were inscribed onto the naked rock of the steep mountain valleys.[18] The production of the inscription was indeed an entirely Pamiri affair, with the authority of the Qianlong Emperor delegated to the *ishikagha beg* (deputy governor) of Sarikol (the valley through which the Chinese-built highway between Kashgar and Pakistan now runs), a man by the name of Abu al-Hasan. It was presumably Abu al-Hasan who was responsible for the choice of language and the wording of the inscription.

Unfortunately for Qing officials in Xinjiang, this intervention did not achieve its intended goal of ending raids between the mountainous Pamir principalities to the south of Yarkand. Ongoing feuding in this region was among the reasons that the court gradually withdrew from an active role in the Pamirs in the 1770s, and in so doing, withdrew from the world of Persophone diplomacy. As the authority of the *khaqan-i Chin* receded, local memory transposed this inscription to a more remote past. In 1885, the British explorer Ney Elias approached the western Pamirs through Badakhshan, entering territory that was now at the center of the Great Game between Britain and Russia. Along the route he heard of the inscription in the Ghund Valley. Locals told him it was some six hundred years old, and Elias wondered what purpose it might have served: "It is difficult to see what concern the Chinese Emperor can have had in the boundary disputes of villagers." When Sayyid Haydar Shah wrote the first narrative history of Shughnan in the early years of the twentieth century, he told a similar story: the Qing inscription was a relic of unknown antiquity, from a time when Shughnan had been part of the Chinese emperor's realm, before the Chinese were succeeded by pagan fire-worshippers, and in turn, by the arrival of Shughnan's first Muslims. To Shughnanis such as Sayyid Haydar Shah, the time when China spoke Persian was well and truly ancient history.[19]

PERSIAN AMONG THE QING EMPIRE'S MUSLIMS

Kashgar and Yarkand have never been thought of as great centers of Islamic learning. Still, it is surprising to think that it was hard for Qing officials to find *anyone* capable of translating letters written in Persian in the middle of the eighteenth century. As I have suggested, this difficulty may reflect the fact that the cohort of translators that the Qing invasion brought with it had likely served as go-betweens in earlier Muslim-Mongol liaisons and may not have had any kind of madrasa education. In the case of Western Turkistan, it has been argued that the employment of Tatars as translators in the Russian administration contributed to the declining status of Persian in the nineteenth century, and something similar may have occurred in Xinjiang in the eighteenth century.[20] It is also probable that knowledge of Persian survived best among sections of Tarim Basin society that were less likely to collaborate with the Qing at this point, for example, among Sufi networks, whose activities involved the communal reading of Persian texts.

It is tempting to think of the use of Persian as in decline in this period, coinciding with the demise of the Chaghataiid court, but the available evidence does not map easily onto that narrative. Surviving Persian compositions from the Tarim Basin only begin at the very end of the Chaghataiid period. In the late seventeenth and early eighteenth centuries, Mahmud Churas penned two works, the hagiographic *Anis al-Talibin,* and a continuation of *Tarikh-i Rashidi,* known to scholarship simply as the "chronicle" of Mahmud Churas.[21] Following Churas, the eighteenth century saw a series of hagiographies in the Naqshbandiyya-Afaqiyya tradition, leaving little doubt that the language was best kept up in Sufi circles: Mir Khal al-Din Yarkandi's *Hidayat-nama,* Shams al-Din Ibn ʿAli's *Siyar al-Mukhlisin,* Kafshin Khoja's *Jamiʿ al-Asrar* and *ʿIqd al-Gawhar,* and anonymous works such as *Tazkirat al-Hidayat.*[22] Although best known for their Turkic compositions, eighteenth-century authors Zalili and Khoja Jahan ʿArshi also wrote mystical poetry in Persian.[23] There were certainly more such texts in the eighteenth century than in the seventeenth, permitting the hypothesis that the dominance of the Naqshbandiyya following the fall of the Chaghataiids gave the Persian language a temporary boost in the Tarim Basin. Following this, there was no local writing in Persian for around a century, until the anti-Qing uprising of the 1860s. Among the flurry of historical writing that these events inspired were two *masnawi* poems in Persian describing the rebellion in Kucha and praising its leader Khwaja Rashid al-Din.[24]

The Sinophone Hui community presents a similar picture, with only a handful of original compositions in Persian. The earliest Persian work written in China seems to have been *Minhaj al-Talab,* a description of Persian grammar from the early seventeenth century, which has been tentatively attributed to a Bukharan migrant to China, Chang Zhimei (or Yunhua).[25] This book seems to have circulated widely, with copies being found as far afield as Qarghiliq (Yecheng) in the south of Xinjiang.[26] The late nineteenth century saw the publication of a second work on Persian grammar by a Sinophone Muslim, Ma Lianyuan's *Kimiya al-Farsiyya.*[27] Apart from these grammatical studies, as in Xinjiang, it seems to have been Sufi networks that kept alive a tradition of Persian composition. In his recent study of Sinophone Muslim intellectual history, Nakanishi Tatsuya has edited and translated a doctrinal work called *Khulasat al-Maʿrifa,* a Qadiriyya text kept in the library of a shrine in Linxia, a religious center in the south of Gansu Province.[28] Nakanishi also brings to our attention *Nuzhat al-Qulub,* a hagiographic text belonging to the Beizhuang brotherhood (*menhuan*), which describes a chain of transmission connecting the Beizhuang lineage to the Naqshbandiyya-Mujaddidiyya of Afghanistan.[29]

FIGURE 8. Xinjiang's Sufi bastion of Persian: the gateway to the shrine of Afaq Khwaja (d. 1694) near Kashgar in China's far west. Photograph by Nile Green.

In both the Chinese and Turkic traditions, the transition to Qing rule coincided with an increase in translation from Persian into the dominant literary language, be it Chinese or Turkic. Among Chinese-speaking Muslims, the mid-seventeenth century saw the emergence of a body of Sinophone Islamic texts that eventually became known as the "Han Kitab."[30] Incorporating both translations and original compositions, these Chinese works represent a body of Islamic texts in a distinctly neo-Confucian idiom. Hui studies scholars have done much to identify the original Arabic and Persian works behind these translations and adaptations, showing that the most popular texts derive from a Timurid-period canon in which Sufi doctrinal and hagiographic works in Persian predominated.[31]

Meanwhile, from the late seventeenth century on, there was also an increased output of translations from Persian into Turkic in Xinjiang. Beginning with Sufi and *beg* patrons in the 1680s, this wave of translation continued through the Qing period, encouraged by the rise of a new local aristocracy in collaboration with the Manchus (primarily the hereditary *wang* dynasties, but including lesser *beg* families). Today's manuscript collections hold some thirty such Turkic translations of Persian works. Some of these translations belong to the same corpus of Sufi works as those translated by Chinese Islamic scholars, but the *beg* patrons were interested in a wider range of genres than this. As in the case of the Khiva school of translation, described in chapter 10 of this volume by Marc Toutant, some texts were translated more than once, and the period also saw revisions of Chaghatai classics into more colloquial form.

Translation testifies to an ongoing interest in the translated text, but it may also reflect the declining utility of the text in its original form. Not surprisingly, the turn to translation is often treated as a measure of the declining knowledge of Persian (see Devin DeWeese's discussion in chapter 4 of this volume of a potential "tipping point" into Turkic literary dominance in the Russian Empire). Certainly, evidence can be found that standards of Persian were not high at this time. A ditty from a Sinophone Islamic schoolroom included in *Jingxue xichuan pu* (Register of Lineage and Transmission of Classical Learning) describes Persian texts as "a hundred times harder than the Confucian classics" (*jiao rushu baibei nan*), an indication of how difficult the language was seen in such settings.[32] As Nakanishi points out, in the preface to his *Minhaj al-Talab*, the seventeenth-century Sinophone Muslim scholar Chang Zhimei mourns the fact that scholars in his day preferred the study of Arabic grammar to that of Persian. Nakanishi credits Chang's work with reviving the study of Persian to some extent, at least in northeast China. The accounts of early twentieth-century Hui intellectuals would seem to support this view. These identified the madrasas of Shandong, Beijing-Tianjin, and Manchuria as giving equal emphasis to Persian and Arabic texts, while the so-called Shaanxi school taught a curriculum that was almost exclusively Arabic.[33]

Among Turkic translations of Persian in Xinjiang, the difficulty of the Persian text is typically given as the primary reason for the translation. This, for example, is from the preface to a Turkic translation of a hagiography of the Sufi saint of Samarqand, Makhdum-i A'zam: "Since some Turk devotees were worried that they couldn't grasp its meaning, they requested from me that I translate this important treatise into Turkic, so that it would be easy to understand, and that readers and listeners would obtain the full benefit of its blessings."[34] By this time, though, such introductions were highly formulaic: the patron requests that a text to be translated into Turkic, the translator wrestles with his conscience for a while and then commits to the task. A nineteenth-century translation of *Tazkira-i Bughrakhan* begins in this way:

> One day there was a private party in which many learned men were honored. Stories were told from all sides—not just stories but traditions. Finally, *Tazkira-i Bughrakhan* was read, and we were greatly enlivened by it. But because it was composed in Persian, many could not comprehend its meaning. I served as translator for the gathering, or indeed as reciter. As I explained the meaning, I clarified it for those who had not understood. Then the *amir* declared to me: "You should translate this and gain merit! It was written in Persian, you should get to work on a Turkic version. [The book] has been very beneficial for Persian speakers, let the Turkic speakers enjoy it too!" With the *amir* making such a request, there was no way that I could refuse.[35]

Here the translator's depiction of the communal consumption of the *tazkira* has a realistic feel, and no doubt Xinjiang's Turkic-speakers would have found a Persian text like this difficult. Yet his picture of the linguistic situation in Qing Xinjiang may be misleading, and his reference to distinct Persian-speaking (*farsi eli*) and Turkic-speaking (*turki eli*) communities is a trope of the genre, deriving from earlier translations in communities that really were divided between native speakers of Persian and Turkic, in Mawarannahr.[36] Clichéd stories such as this do not tell us very much about the actual state of knowledge of Persian in Xinjiang.

Literacy in Persian must have been a relatively rare accomplishment in the Qing, but it is difficult to show that the state of Persian learning in the eighteenth century was significantly different from the situation in the sixteenth: it was weak, that is to say, but still appreciated and cultivated in certain spheres. It seems that most translations had only limited distribution, and whether or not a translation of a text existed, the ideal was still to read it in the original Arabic or Persian. Take, for example, Najm al-Din Razi's *Mirsad al-ʿIbad*, a popular thirteenth-century Persian instructional work on Sufism, which was rendered into both Chinese and Turkic versions during the Qing. In 1651, Wu Zunqi (or Zixian) translated it into Chinese as *Guizhen yaodao* (The Essentials of Returning to the Truth), but forbade its printing, and his translation did not circulate widely until the end of the Qing.[37] In Xinjiang, one Muhammad Rahim Kashghari translated the text into Turkic in Aqsu in the 1760s, known from a lone copy in Ürümchi. Meanwhile, multiple manuscripts of the Persian original have been found in China.[38] Matsumoto Akiro makes a similar point regarding the Chinese translation of Jami's *Ashiʿat al-Lamaʿat*, arguing that "the Persian version . . . might have exerted greater influence on Sino-Muslims than its Chinese translation did."[39]

Descriptions of madrasa curricula are unfortunately lacking for much of the Qing period, yet late nineteenth- and early twentieth-century accounts show that

Persian was still accessible to Muslims in China, if not widely taught. Within the so-called "scripture-hall education" (*jingtang jiaoyu*), as Islamic schooling among Sinophone Muslims became known, Persian texts were studied up until the middle of the twentieth century. The "thirteen books" that Sinophone Muslims read in the madrasa always included some Persian works—such as Razi's *Mirsad*—though the emphasis was on Arabic. In Xinjiang, primary schools would provide a limited introduction to Persian classics such as Sa'di's *Gulistan,* while reading ability in Persian could be obtained in a madrasa, though possibly only in a few locations in the province. In the 1890s, a Tatar visitor to the town of Astana in the Turfan oasis found a teacher (*mudarris*) who had great expertise in Persian. Chief among the texts that he imparted to his pupils was *Maktubat* by the great Naqshbandi Sufi 'renewer' Ahmad Sirhindi (1564–1624), no doubt among the most widely read and recited Persian texts in late Qing Xinjiang.[40] Apart from this, a madrasa education might have included Persian literary and hagiographic works such as Rumi's *Masnawi,* the *diwan* of Hafiz, and Jami's *Nafahat al-Uns.* Martin Hartmann offers an interesting observation from his visit to Kashgar in 1902, that Persian literature and poetry was studied in the hot summer months, while the more difficult fields of jurisprudence and grammar were tackled during the winter, primarily on the basis of Arabic texts.[41]

These twin traditions of translation sprang up alongside the ongoing study of Arabic and Persian, therefore, not as a substitute for it. In the case of the Sino-Islamic school of translation, scholars such as Jonathan Lipman and Zvi Ben-Dor Benite have highlighted a series of social and cultural factors at work among Chinese-speaking Muslims in the early Qing era: the growth of a new Islamic schooling network; the influence of Chinese literati, and Chinese moral discourse, on learned Muslims; along with a desire to reconcile the foundational narrative of Islam with Chinese tradition. Such studies also point to the turbulence of the Ming-Qing transition, and the fact that these works could serve to demonstrate Islam's compatibility with Confucian orthodoxy, at a time in which the loyalties of China's Muslims were being questioned. The complexity of this interpretative question reflects the fact that translation from Persian (and Arabic) into Chinese was a double motion: to do so was to render the text both into the native language of its intended audience, and into the prestigious intellectual language of the environment. It was also an innovation—these were the first such translations to be carried out.[42]

Xinjiang represents a more straightforward case of vernacularization, and one that drew on well-established precedents of translation from Persian to Turkic. At the same time, the cultural history of Qing Xinjiang has not been as well studied as the Sinophone Islamic tradition. Scholars of various parts of the globe associate the choice to patronize the vernacular in the early modern period with a range of factors, including rising literacy, and the increasing wealth of nontraditional elite groups. Some emphasize the importance of the new cultural forms to the cultivation of loyalty, and political mobilization, in a period that saw increasing competition between elite actors.[43] Political instability from the late seventeenth century to the period of the Qing conquest may well have provided a pressure such as this. If it is the case, as I suggested above, that Persian was most closely identified with Xinjiang's Sufi milieu, this may have also been a reason for the *wangs* and *begs* to eschew it. For this stratum at least, the fact that Turkic had become the default "Muslim language" of the Qing would equally have enhanced its suitability as a literary medium. Patronage of translation, then, represented an effort to maintain a semblance of courtly culture in Qing Xinjiang, while mediating between Qing officialdom and local society. This involved drawing on texts such as those narrating local royal traditions (the Bughra Khan cycle), the mirror of princes genre (e.g., *Qabus-nama*), as well as more accessible historical and hagiographic vignettes from the Islamic tradition (such as Nawbahari's *Durr al-Majalis*, Kashifi's *Rawzat al-Shuhada*, and *Qisas al-Ghara'ib*, a compendium of translations).[44]

This literary activity during the Qing breathed new life into works that seem to have been poorly known in Xinjiang by the eighteenth century. To give one example, while hardly any Persian copies of Mirza Haydar's *Tarikh-i Rashidi* have come to light in Xinjiang, several Turkic translations received wide circulation. While serving as *hakim beg* of Yarkand in 1805–11, Yunus ibn Iskandar commissioned Muhammad Sadiq Kashghari to produce one such translation. Kashghari's preface depicts Yunus as conscious of the significance of *Tarikh-i Rashidi* as a repository of local traditions of royal authority. Outlining his instructions to the translator, he says:

> The rise of Chinggis Khan, the end of the 'Abbasid caliphs, Sultan Muhammad Khwarazmshah's martyrdom, and his conquest of the world—all of these events are recorded in detail in *Zafar-nama* and *Timur-nama,* which were incorporated into *Tarikh-i Rashidi.* The events beginning with Tughluq Temür Khan down to 'Abd al-Rashid Khan are recounted in *Tarikh-i Rashidi,* along with an account of what rights these Moghul khans had in this region, which khan exercised justice and was praised for it and came to a good end, and which acted cruelly and fell into ruin and destruction. But this book was composed in Persian, with delicate expressions and subtle wording, and much obscure vocabulary. It relies on allusions and similes, and is full of rhyming prose. Because of this, the historical narratives in this book were hidden from the people of Mughulistan like a veiled virgin. Thus it is necessary for you to render this into the Turkic speech that is current in Kashgar, so that the common people can understand it and gain insight into its secrets.[45]

In associating himself with *Tarikh-i Rashidi,* Yunus was not simply advertising his interest in models of good governance. The translation can be read as part of a deliberate policy to link his Turfani family (of obscure origins) to the Chaghataiid heritage of Yarkand. During his tenure there, Yunus also funded the restoration of one of 'Abd al-Rashid Khan's constructions—the shrine of Muhammad Sharif, a Sufi shaykh prominent at the court in the sixteenth century. The long Persian inscription in the rebuilt shrine's interior, a text linking Yunus to Muhammad Sharif's deputy Mir Wali Sufi, is a rare exception to the preference for Turkic among the *begs*.[46]

CONCLUSIONS

This chapter has touched on a variety of ways in which Persian was encountered and utilized in China in the period 1600–1900 (if not all such ways, as seen in Alexandre Papas's chapter 8 in this volume on the ritual and magical applications of Persian in Xinjiang). The evidence is incomplete, and still leaves room for speculation; both in the Chinese interior and in Xinjiang, there is important work yet to be done in cataloguing Islamic manuscript collections. Nonetheless, the picture that emerges is of a limited role for Persian in a series of disconnected spheres. From the viewpoint of the court, the "Muslim language" of the empire was Turkic, not Persian or Arabic. From the second half of the eighteenth century onward, Turkic served as Xinjiang's interface with the cosmopolitan linguistic culture of the high Qing. For Qing officials, Persian was the language of a set of relatively insignificant tributary polities to the west of Xinjiang. Although the Manchus inherited translation capacity in Persian from the Ming, it was never utilized, and Persian correspondence was filtered at the frontier. The court had little to no knowledge of Iran as a distinct political actor, nor did it have direct diplomatic contact with Mughal India, and it therefore saw no need to enhance its ability to communicate with the outside world in Persian.

Among the empire's Muslims, Persian texts were collected, read, and valued, although the language never became a popular vehicle for original literary or scholarly expression. The trajectories in this period of Persian in Qing China and further west in Central Eurasia, for example—particularly in a place like Khiva, where there was little or no native Persian-speaking population, in contrast to Khoqand and Bukhara—had much in common. While Sufi circles and madrasas kept up the tradition of reading Persian texts, considerable intellectual energy was expended during the Qing on translation from Persian into Chinese and Turkic. Of these two traditions, it is the Chinese Islamic scholars, who rendered Sufi discourse into the scholarly lexicon of Confucianism that not unsurprisingly attracts the most interest today. Hui studies specialists continue the painstaking task of identifying the originals of these texts and analyzing the translation techniques of China's Muslim literati. These translations made some of the Persian tradition's most significant religious and historical texts available to a wider readership, though in both the Chinese and Turkic traditions, the question of how these texts were received calls for further study.

In the People's Republic of China today, Persian survives in restricted ritual form among Chinese-speaking Muslims, with only a few Islamic schools providing instruction in the language. Outside the religious sphere, Peking University teaches Persian language and literature, and acts as a focal point for a small circle of scholars of Persian studies in China. A few dedicated language institutes also offer instruction in Persian, producing Persian-speaking graduates to service the nation's needs in trade and diplomacy. In Xinjiang, there have been various efforts to revive the study of Persian, which is an important accompaniment to the study of the Chaghatai Turkic tradition, but even at Xinjiang University it has never become an established part of the curriculum. This may in part be due to the political sensitivities that surround Islamic studies in Xinjiang, though it can equally be seen as a product of the modernist and nationalist critiques of Persian that Turkic-speaking intellectuals participated in from the late nineteenth-century on. Will this picture change in the age of Xi Jinping's "One Belt, One Road"? Certainly, the policy seems to signal a new level of economic and diplomatic investment in the Eurasian continent. Time will tell whether or not this will be accompanied by a revival of China's interest in the history and culture of its Persophone neighbors.

NOTES

This research was carried out with the support of an ARC Discovery Early Career Researcher Award (DE170100330), funded by the Australian Government.

1. The most commonly cited source for this view is Huang Shijian, "The Persian Language in China during the Yuan Dynasty," *Papers on Far Eastern History* 34 (1986): 83–95.

2. Stephen G. Haw, "The Persian Language in Yuan-Dynasty China: A Reappraisal," *East Asian History* 39 (2014): 5–32, primarily a response to David Morgan, "Persian as a Lingua Franca in the Mongol Empire," in *Literacy in the Persianate World: Writing and the Social Order,* ed. Brian Spooner and William L. Hanaway (Philadelphia: University of Pennsylvania Museum of Archaeology and Anthropology, 2012), 160–70.

3. E.g., a set of Persian letters from the Chaghataiids to eminent Bukharan shaykhs were copied into Badr al-Din Kashmiri's *Rawzat al-Rizwan wa Hadiqat al-Ghilman* (1589), IV RUz 2094.

4. Mirza Haydar, *Mirza Haydar Dughlat's Tarikh-i Rashidi: A History of the Khans of Moghulistan,* trans. W. M. Thackston (Cambridge, MA: Harvard University, Department of Near Eastern Languages and Civilizations, 1996), 76; Shah Mahmud Churas, *Khronika: Kriticheskii tekst, perevod, kommentarii, issledovanie i ukazateli O. F. Akimushkin* (Moscow: Nauka, 1976), 11–2 (Persian text).

5. At the very least, all surviving decrees are in Turkic. See Hodong Kim, "Eastern Turki Royal Decrees of the 17th Century in the Jarring Collection," in *Studies on Xinjiang Historical Sources in 17–20th Centuries,* ed. James A. Millward et al. (Tokyo: Toyo Bunko, 2010), 59–119.

6. Parts of this discussion draw on David Brophy, "The Junghar Mongol Legacy and the Language of Loyalty in Qing Xinjiang," *Harvard Journal of Asiatic Studies* 73, 2 (2013): 231–58.

7. See, e.g., Xia Yan, *Nangong zougao* (Taibei: Taiwan shangwu yinshuguan, 1973), *juan* 4, 15b.

8. *Neige daku dang'an* (Grand Secretariat Archive), Academia Sinica, Taibei, doc. 186729–001.

9. E.g. *Dayičing gürün-ü dotuyadu yamun-u Mongyol bičig-ün ger-ün dangse,* ed. Zhongguo di-yi lishi dang'anguan and Nei Menggu daxue Mengguxue xueyuan (Hohhot: Nei Menggu renmin chubanshe, 2005), 15: 491, 512.

10. *Qinding huangyu Xiyu tuzhi, Zhongguo difangzhi jicheng,* comp. Fu-heng, vol. 1 of *Shengzhi ji: Xinjiang, Qinghai, Xizang* (Nanjing: Fenghuang chubanshe, 2012), 820.

11. Most notably, the five-language Manchu dictionary, *Wuti Qinwenjian* (published 1794). For linguistic handbooks, see E. Haenisch, "Ein dreifacher Sprachführer Mandschu-Mongolisch-Turki in

kurzer Auswahl von 110 Beispielen," in *Silver Jubilee Volume of the Zinbun-kagaku Kenkyusyo* (Kyoto: Kyoto University, 1954), 184–91, and Chen Zongzhen, "'Han Hui hebi' yanjiu," *Minzu yuwen* 5 (1989): 49–72.

12. For transcription and translation of a selection of these letters, see David Brophy, "High Asia and the High Qing: Persian Letters in the Beijing Archives," in *No Tapping around Philology: A Festschrift for Wheeler McIntosh Thackston Jr.'s 70th Birthday*, ed. Alireza Korangy and Daniel J. Sheffield (Wiesbaden: Harrassowitz, 2014), 325–67.

13. Qudratullah Beg, *Tarikh-i 'Ahd-i 'Atiq-i Riyasat-i Hunza* (Rawalpindi: Hafiz Shafiq al-Rahman, 1980), 150–51.

14. *Qingdai Xinjiang Manwen dang'an huibian*, ed. Zhongguo di-yi lishi dang'anguan and Zhongguo bianjiang shidi yanjiu zhongxin (Guilin: Guangxi shifan daxue chubanshe, 2012), 65: 314–5.

15. See, e.g., Onuma Takahiro et al., "An Encounter between the Qing Dynasty and Khoqand in 1759–1760: Central Asia in the Mid-Eighteenth Century," *Frontiers of History in China* 9, 3 (2014): 384–408.

16. An early nineteenth-century Bukharan *insha* compilation, which is otherwise entirely in Persian, contains a letter to Kashgar written in Turkic. *Maktubat wa Manshurat*, IVR RAN A212, fols. 115b–116b.

17. Sayyid Haydar Shah, "Istoriia Shugnana," *Protokoly zasedanii Turkestanskogo kruzhka liubitelei arkheologii* 21 (1917): 1. A Manchu memorial describing the carving of this inscription can be found in *Qingdai Xinjiang Manwen dang'an huibian*, 88: 372–73.

18. For other examples of such inscriptions, see A. Z. Rozenfel'd and A. I. Kolesnikov, "Materialy po epigrafike Pamira," *Epigrafika Vostoka* 19 (1969): 92–102.

19. Ney Elias, *Report on a Mission to Chinese Turkestan and Badakhshan in 1885–86* (Calcutta, 1886), 23 (repr., London: Routledge, 2008), and Sayyid Haydar Shah, "Istoriia Shugnana."

20. Alexander Morrison, *Russian Rule in Samarkand, 1868–1910: A Comparison with British India* (Oxford: Oxford University Press, 2008), 43.

21. Churas, *Khronika* and *Anis al-Talibin*, Bodleian Library Ind. Inst. Pers. 45.

22. For descriptions, see N. D. Miklukho-Maklai, *Opisanie tadzhikskikh i persidskikh rukopisei Instituta narodov Azii, vypusk 2: Biograficheskie sochineniia* (Moscow: Izdatel'stvo vostochnoi literatury, 1961), nos. 196, 197, and 202. On the *Siyar al-Mukhlisin*, see Rian Thum, "Beyond Resistance and Nationalism: Local History and the Case of Afaq Khoja," *Central Asian Survey* 31, 3 (2012): 307n16. Earlier Persian hagiographies in the Naqshbandi tradition touch on saintly activities in the Tarim Basin, e.g., the *Jalis-i Mushtaqin* and *Ziya al-Qulub* (Miklukho-Maklai, *Opisanie*, nos. 181 and 184), and were read and copied there, but the texts themselves give no indication as to the place of composition.

23. Unfortunately, Zalili's Persian works were not included in his published *diwan*, but they are mentioned by its editor. See *Zälili Divani*, ed. Imin Tursun (Beijing: Millätlär näshriyati, 1985), 22. Some of 'Arshi's Persian poetry is cited in Muhammad Sadiq Kashghari's *Tazkira-i 'Azizan*.

24. *Persidskie i tadzhikskie rukopisi Instituta narodov Azii AN SSSR (Kratkii alfavitnyi katalog)*, ed. N. D. Miklukho-Maklai (Moscow: Nauka, 1964), nos. 1709 and 3712.

25. Muhammad ibn al-Hakim al-Zinimi, *Minhaj al-Talab* (Isfahan: 1360/1981–82). On Chang Zhimei, see Ralph Kauz, "Chang Zhimei und der Islam in Shandong im 17. Jahrhundert: Akkulturation oder Abgrenzung? Zur Geschichte einer persischen Grammatik," *Saeculum* 60, 1 (2010): 91–114.

26. Mozafar Bakhtyar, "China," in *World Survey of Islamic Manuscripts*, ed. Geoffrey Roper, 4 vols. (London: Al-Furqan Islamic Heritage Foundation, 1994), 4: 113.

27. Iraj Afshar, "Jung-i Chini ya safina-i Ilani (Pu si) 2," *Ayanda* 8 (1361/1982): 485.

28. Nakanishi Tatsuya, *Chuka to taiwa suru isurāmu: Junana jukyu seiki chugoku musurimu no shisoteki eii* (Kyoto: Kyoto daigaku gakujutsu shuppankai, 2013), 203–88.

29. Ibid., 36, 353.

30. The term "Han Kitab" was first used only in the late nineteenth century, according to Barbara

Stöcker-Parnian, *Jingtang Jiaoyu: Die Bücherhallen Erziehung. Entstehung und Entwicklung der islamischen Erziehung in den chinesischen Hui-Gemeinden vom 17.–19. Jahrhundert* (Frankfurt a./M.: Lang, 2003), 60n47.

31. Donald Daniel Leslie and Mohamed Wassel, "Arabic and Persian Sources Used by Liu Chih," *Central Asiatic Journal* 26, 1–2 (1982): 78–104.

32. Zhao Can, *Jingxue xichuan pu* (Xining: Qinghai renmin chubanshe, 1989), 117–18.

33. E.g., Fu Tongxian, *Zhongguo Huijiao shi* (Taibei: Taiwan shangwu yinshuguan, 1959), 205.

34. *Majmuʻat al-Muhaqqiqin,* India Office Library Turki 7, fol. 2b.

35. Jarring Collection (Lund University Library), Prov. 155, fols. 4a–5b.

36. Some examples are given in Devin DeWeese, "Chaghatai Literature in the Early Sixteenth Century: Notes on Turkic Translations from the Uzbek Courts of Mawarannahr," in *Turkish Language, Literature, and History: Travelers' Tales, Sultans, and Scholars since the Eighth Century,* ed. Bill Hickman and Gary Leiser (London: Routledge, 2016), 99–117.

37. Min Chunfang and Ding Taoyuan, "'Guizhen yaodao' banben kaoshu," *Beifang minzu daxue xuebao* 2 (2015): 86.

38. Yusupbek Mukhlisov, *Uyghur klassik ädäbiyati qolyazmilirining katalogi* (Ürümchi: Shinjang yärlik muziyigha täyyarliq körüsh bashqarmisi, 1957), 34–35.

39. Matsumoto Akiro, "The Sufi Intellectual Tradition Among Sino-Muslims," in *Sufism: Critical Concepts in Islamic Studies,* ed. Lloyd Ridgeon, 4 vols. (London: Routledge, 2008), 2: 107.

40. Qurban ʻAli Khalidi, *Kitab-i Tarikh-i Jarida-i Jadida* (Kazan: Qazan universitetïnïng tabʻ-khanäsendä, 1889), 17. A public reading of the *Maktubat* in Khotan is mentioned in Näüshirvan Yaushef, "Törkestan-i Chinidä mäshräblär," *Waqït,* June 21, 1916, 3.

41. Martin Hartmann, *Chinesisch-Turkestan: Geschichte, Verwaltung, Geistesleben und Wirtschaft* (Halle a./S.: Schwetschke, 1908), 48.

42. Jonathan N. Lipman, *Familiar Strangers: A History of Muslims in Northwest China* (Seattle: University of Washington Press, 1997); Zvi Ben-Dor Benite, *The Dao of Muhammad: A Cultural History of Muslims in Late Imperial China* (Cambridge, MA: Harvard University Asia Center, 2005).

43. See, e.g., Victor B. Lieberman, "Transcending East-West Dichotomies: State and Culture Formation in Six Ostensibly Different Areas," *Modern Asian Studies* 31 (1997): 481–96.

44. Rian Thum, "Untangling the Bughrā-Khān Manuscripts," in *Mazar: Studies on Islamic Sacred Sites in Central Eurasia,* ed. Jun Sugawara and Rahile Dawut (Tokyo: Tokyo Foreign Studies University Press), 281–94; L. V. Dmitrieva, *Katalog tiurkskikh rukopisei Instituta vostokovedeniia Rossiiskoi akadamii nauk* (Moscow: Vostochnaia literatura, 2002), no. 373; Mukhlisov, *Uyghur klassik ädäbiyati,* nos. 56 and 65; and T. I. Sultanov, "Medieval Historiography in Manuscripts from East Turkestan," *Manuscripta Orientalia* 2, 1 (1996): 25–30.

45. Muhammad Sadiq Kashghari, *Tarjama-i Tarikh-i Rashidi,* IVR RAN C569, fols. 8–9.

46. David Brophy and Rian Thum, "The Shrine of Muhammad Sharīf and Its Qing-era Patrons," in *The Life of Muhammad Sharif,* ed. Jeff Eden (Vienna: Österreichischen Akademie der Wissenschaften, 2015), 55–75.

7

Speaking "Bukharan"

The Circulation of Persian Texts in Imperial Russia

Alfrid Bustanov

Unlike in Central Asia or Daghestan, Muslims in Russia historically often wrote a curious mixture of Arabic, Persian, and Turkic, with either Ottoman or Chaghatai Turkish influences, so that the study of Muslim texts there requires proficiency in at least three languages of Islam besides Russian.[1] This is not only true of collected volumes (*majmu'at*) that comprise several works, but also of individual narratives where switching between these languages was a widespread practice in the seventeenth and nineteenth centuries. As far as one can judge from the manuscripts still held privately across the Russian Federation, this linguistic feature mirrored the cultural orientations and fashions that evolved over a period of centuries across that vast region.[2] The Persianate literary tastes and preferences of the Muslim citizens of imperial Russia originated from the cultural and religious prestige of Bukhara as a major intellectual center. For as Allen Frank's ground-breaking research has demonstrated, since the late eighteenth and throughout the nineteenth centuries, the Muslims of imperial Russia used to go primarily to Bukhara to study Islamic subjects.[3] There were usually no native speakers of Persian in the remote Tatar villages of imperial Russia, and because almost nothing is known about the use of Persian as a spoken language among Russia's Muslims, the concept of Persographia, developed by Nile Green in his Introduction to this volume, is crucial in this chapter. The classics of Persian ethical literature, such as Sa'di, were widely copied in local madrasas across the Russian Empire, and in the nineteenth century, some Russian Tatars even tried to compose their own literary works in Persian, among them Ahmadjan Tobuli (1825–189?)[4] and his brother-in-law 'Abd al-Rahim al-Bulghari (1754–1834).[5]

The prestige of Bukhara is not a self-explanatory reason for the popularity of Persian in the northern Eurasian regions of the Russian Empire. There were many intellectual trends and schools of thought in Bukhara and other Central Asian centers of learning. Moreover, madrasas in a "geography of *'ajam*" that extended from Nizhnii Novgorod beyond Russian imperial territories to Kabul all used

Persian, and this language choice for scribes and authors meant a contribution to a Persianate sphere.[6] This is reflected in the thousands of Persian manuscripts that madrasa students in imperial Russia either produced locally themselves or imported from Central Asia, where they bought the originals or copied them. Catalogues of Persian manuscripts published by Alsu Arslanova and Salim Giliazutdinov in Kazan have made this landscape of literary production accessible.[7] Through their tremendous efforts to catalogue hundreds of previously unknown texts, these two scholars have identified numerous works from prerevolutionary private collections that are now preserved in state archives. The ill-conceived approach of describing manuscripts according to their language is part of the Soviet academic legacy that emphasized the study of the "Foreign Orient," that is Turkey, Iran, and Arab lands, rather than the USSR's "own Orient," leaving the latter to specialists in Soviet national republics who were rarely versed in Islamicate literary culture.[8] The same holds true for the current research on Persian manuscripts in Russia: the study of classics is rarely associated with the living tradition of Persian literacy in the Russian Empire. For Russian scholarship, the Persianate world is conceived of as lying outside of Russia's borders, particularly in the modern republics of Iran and Tajikistan. Despite the fact that Persian manuscripts in Inner Russia are the best catalogued and well described (better than Arabic and even Turkic-language texts), current research contains very little reflection on how Islamic literature functioned in the cultural realm of imperial Russia.[9] This is especially true of research on classical literature in Iranian studies. Regrettably, the transmission of knowledge and circulation of texts in Persian among the Muslims of Russia thus largely remains outside current scholarly interests in Russia.

As a counterweight to this tendency, this chapter shares some findings and tentative hypotheses on how the role of Persian learning evolved over the past three centuries among the Muslim communities of Russia. To do so, it maps some of the genres and individual works available in the manuscript libraries of Russia. Still, it would be a grave mistake to cut off and isolate the development of Persian texts from the rest of the literature that was in circulation in imperial Russia, including in the Russian language as the dominant vehicle of imperial information. This chapter is merely a modest attempt to highlight those places where Persian is in the forefront, often accompanied by other languages, in the literary history of Russia's Muslims. The role of Persian literacy in imperial Russia should in no way be overestimated on the basis of sources cited below. It is beyond any doubt that the various Turkic dialects, usually referred to under the rubric of Tatar literary language formed in the Golden Horde, played the central role in articulation of everyday matters, but also in historiography, poetry, and official documentation, while Arabic was reserved for the countless books on religious subjects. However, there were historical periods and cultural zones in which the use of Persian was deemed crucial by local actors who made their linguistic choices on the basis of societal expectations and their personal abilities and educational backgrounds. A more nuanced picture of the linguistic land-scape of Muslim culture in the Russian Empire might perhaps be achieved by digitally linking information from surviving manuscripts with the geography of their production and circulation, as well as with the evolution of linguistic choices over time and space.[10] However, such a map is not likely to appear soon, given the deplorable situation of cataloguing the Arabic-script manuscripts in Kazan, Ufa and elsewhere.

The present chapter looks at three geographically selected case studies. The first focuses on Yunus al-Qazani, a scholar from the Volga region who travelled to Bukhara and Eastern Turkistan in the seventeenth century and used Persian in Quranic exegesis, Sufi writings in the Naqshbandi tradition, and legal exposi-tion. The second highlights the role of the Persian language for the communities of Siberian Bukharans settled around the city of Tobolsk in the early eighteenth century, among whom Sufi texts were dominated by this language and references to literature produced in Central Asia. The third case concerns a Daghestani Sufi authority living in exile who used some Persian in the letters he addressed to his fellows in Tatarstan. This final section of the chapter demonstrates that migrant literati from the predominantly Arabic-using region of Daghestan in the Caucasus still had to satisfy the triple language mosaic of Islamic literature in Russia that was so heavily influenced by the canon of earlier reference works composed in the Persianate cities of Central Asia.

TATAR STUDENTS IN BUKHARA

Judging from available documentation, in the seventeenth and eighteenth cen-turies Persian was not just the language of pious didactic poetry that instructed Muslims youths on how to behave.[11] In the first centuries of Russian dominance over the former lands of the Golden Horde, Persian was also regularly used for legal purposes, Sufi doctrines, and even for teaching Arabic grammar. Most of this writing was a product of cultural influence stemming from the regular trips of Tatar students to Bukhara and other educational centers in Central Asia, where Persian was a language of instruction. The first author who left us a consider-able amount of written Persian is Akhund Yunus ibn Akhund Iwanay al-Qazani (d. 1689/90). When he was eighteen, Yunus al-Qazani copied the Quran and add-ed some interlinear translations in Persian.[12] He mainly studied in Transoxiana and was remembered by subsequent scholars as one of the first Muslims of Russia who went to study in Bukhara.[13] Some decades after his death, another scholar and Sufi shaykh called Taj al-Din al-Bulghari (1768–1838) discovered an Arabic poem by Yunus al-Qazani that lacked a commentary (*sharh*) in the Chaghatai Turkic language. To make these untitled verses available to his co-religionists, Taj al-Din al-Bulghari commented on them and added the following biography of Yunus al-Qazani:

This poet died in the land of Bulghar, in Kicha village near Kazan. He was a learned and pious person. Al-Qazani authored commentaries on *Fara'iz al-Sajawandi, al-Fiqh al-Kaidani,* and other works. Besides that, he possessed the ability to perform miracles [*al-karamat wa al-kashufat*] and belonged to the Naqshbandi Sufi path. He studied with Idris Afandi in Yarkand in the Kashgar region and became his successor. Idris Afandi was also originally from Kazan region, from Chally village, also previously known as Tarberdi. In 1110 [1698],[14] Idris Afandi granted him a Sufi diploma, which he received from his master Hidayatullah al-Yarqandi.[15]

This Russian link to the Eastern Turkistan (or Xinjiang) region discussed in Alexandre Papas's chapter 8 in this volume is notable, since religious figures with the attribution name (*nisba*) al-Yarqandi feature in Siberian legends of Islamization dating from the late eighteenth century.[16] Being able to consult and produce Persian texts was certainly part of this link, since in addition to his Arabic poetry, Yunus al-Qazani wrote an extensive commentary on an Arabic legal text on the subject of inheritance, *al-Fara'id al-Sirajiyya* by the twelfth-century scholar Siraj al-Din al-Sajawandi, which was subsequently known as *Sharh-i Yunus* (Yunus's Commentary) in Tatar madrasas and later circulated between Kazan and Tashkent, where at least six copies of it have been preserved.[17] Yunus cites his teacher Safar al-Turki, a mullah in Tobolsk, in this work. Its intended audience remains an open question,[18] but the choice of language tells us something about the readers envisaged, who would have had to know enough Persian to understand the legal details translated from the Arabic original and Yunus's comments.

Yunus al-Qazani also had something to say about the status of Muslim lands conquered by the Russians. In a bilingual Arabic-Persian work (*taqrirat*), he vaguely advised his co-religionists to accept the new situation of "infidel domination" as unthreatening to the basics of their beliefs.[19] The following question posed to him by 'Abd al-Karim al-Shirdani exemplifies the rhetoric and terminology used in this debate:

> Question: What is the reasoning in regard to a land that is currently in the hands of infidels, where the victory of Muslims was short-lived and the rules of infidels were installed? Are Kazan, Astrakhan, Kasimov, and other such places closed to merchants and traders? Do they belong to the land of war [*dar al-harb*] or to the land of Islam [*dar al-Islam*]? Is it strictly prescribed for each Muslim to leave [*hijrat kardan*] such places, or not?[20]

Irrespective of Yunus's opinion, it seems that the question of jihad and other forms of resistance against the non-Muslim government remained quite a popular issue among the Volga Tatars for a long period of time.[21] Tatar students copied the *Kitab al-Khaqaniya* composed by Muhammad Sharif Bukhari (d. 1697) in 1643, which contained a section on jihad. There are at least four copies of the work in the archives of Kazan, two of them produced in the seventeenth century.[22] Even throughout the nineteenth century, Muslims of the Volga region continued to

question the legal status of Russia as a "land of Islam," justifying their pious migrations to Central Asia or the Ottoman Empire.[23]

In 1726, another Bukharan student, Mansur ibn 'Abd al-Rahman ibn Anas
al-Burunduqi (also known as 'Ubaydullah al-Bulghari), compiled a work on Arabic
grammar in Persian entitled *Sharh al-'Awamil al-Mi'a,*[24] which subsequently became very popular in the madrasas of Inner Russia.[25] A similar Persian grammar
of Arabic of Central Asian origin, *Sharh 'Abdullah,* was widely copied in Tatar
madrasas throughout the nineteenth century.[26] It seems that, beyond the abundant
copies of grammatical or Sufi treatises brought from Central Asia or copied locally,
the legal discourse of Inner Russia's Muslims was also partly conducted in Persian
in the first half of the nineteenth century. This observation is supported by the fatwas of Mufti Muhammadjan ibn Husayn (1789–1824), dated from 1819, and of his
successor 'Abd al-Salam ibn 'Abd al-Rahim (1774–1840), dated from 1833, with regard to the Islamic calendar and against the drinking of alcohol and celebrating a
popular spring festival called *Sabantuy.*[27] Unlike many of his contemporaries, 'Abd
al-Salam never studied in Bukhara, but received his religious education in Kazan and Qarghala, an important trading and cultural center near Orenburg in the
Volga-Ural region.[28] Even a poem in praise of 'Abd al-Salam by 'Umar al-Qarghali
was written almost entirely in Persian.[29] The same preference for Persian writing
is evident in a collection of legal documents copied or authored by Fathullah al-
Uriwi (1765–1843), a famous legal scholar of the era, who nonetheless preferred to
write his longer legal treatises in Arabic, or sometimes in Tatar.[30]

Although the Arabic and Tatar languages undoubtedly dominated in the writings of Russia's Muslims in the nineteenth century, there were thus authors who
regularly produced original Persian texts, including a poem in praise of the Tatar
theologian and historian Shihab al-Din al-Mardjani (1818–89) and commentaries
on Sufi works.[31] 'Abd al-Rahim al-Bulghari was among the most prolific of these
authors, famous for his commentaries on the ethical works *Thabat al-'ajizin* and
Murad al-'arifin of Sufi Allahyar (1616–1713). Both commentaries enjoyed great
popularity and are known in numerous copies in state and private libraries across
the country.[32] While residing in Bukhara between 1788 and 1803, 'Abd al-Rahim
al-Bulghari penned an impressive number of works, partially in Persian. Among
the latter are his lexicological commentaries on Shams al-Din al-Kuhistani's *Jami'
al-rumuz ,* Ahmad Sirhindi's *Maktubat,* and al-Ghazali's *Ihya 'ulum al-din.*[33] His
key work on Sufi ethics, called *al-Sayf al-sarim,* was written half in Persian and half
in Arabic and aimed to provide a picture of the ideal Muslim.[34]

In short, among the Muslims of the Volga-Urals in and after the seventeenth
century, Persian literacy was greatly associated with scholarly credentials acquired
in Central Asia. But during the nineteenth century, active production of Persian
texts with no obvious links to Bukhara commenced in Tatar territory. Moreover,
as early fatwas from the imperial muftiate testify, Persian also served at times as a
language of legal debate.

PERSIAN IN WESTERN SIBERIA

Among learned Central Asian migrants in western Siberia during the late seventeenth century, Persian literacy was certainly a norm.[35] Most of the texts produced in this migrant milieu around this period were in Persian. For example, recently at the Institute of Oriental Manuscripts in Saint Petersburg, the present author came across a short manuscript work by Dawlat Shah ibn 'Abd al-Wahhab al-Ispijafi, a migrant Yasawi Sufi shaykh who had travelled between the Central Asian city of Sayram, the Siberian town of Tobolsk, and the cities of India. He is remembered in local Siberian hagiographies as a discoverer of the sacred tombs of those who supposedly first spread Islam in western Siberia. According to these legends of Islamization, composed chiefly in the seventeenth and eighteenth centuries, Dawlat Shah first occupied himself preaching among the Qalmyqs on the banks of Syr Darya river and then moved north in order to identify eighteen saintly graves, which then became veneration sites. Hagiographical sources also add that he collected saintly genealogies and became surrounded by local disciples (as documentary evidence attests).[36]

Dawlat Shah was a teacher of at least two local Siberian religious figures of the late seventeenth and early eighteenth centuries, namely, Khwajam Shukur[37] and Ibni Khwaja. Persian texts of their Sufi diplomas have been preserved by their families and are known from early twentieth-century copies.[38] In these documents, Dawlat Shah licensed his students to spread a Sufi "path" (tariqa), albeit without any specification as to which one. Due to the lack of sources, details of particular religious practices, and of the social context in which Dawlat Shah operated, remain a mystery. Drawing on Central Asian hagiographical sources, Devin DeWeese has identified Dawlat Shah as a Yasawi Sufi shaykh.[39] But it remains unclear what this Yasawi link meant for his Siberian disciples in an area where the Indian-derived Naqshbandi-Mujaddidi order soon became the dominant Sufi tradition.

Turning to comparable figures, it is striking that whereas Khwajam Shukur had previously received his "license" (ijazat-nama) in the Siberian city of Tobolsk, Ibni Khwaja had studied with his master in Bukhara and had been "licensed" there in around the 1680s, the latest possible date that we can calculate from a note in the copy of Ibni Khwaja's ijazat-nama produced in 1920. The note in question runs as follows: "This is a license brought from Bukhara by the ancestors of the Qomarow village mullah, 'Abd al-Jabbar Yankhujin, two hundred and thirty-three years ago."[40]

Dawlat Shah al-Ispijafi authored at least two Sufi works that have survived to the present day, one of them presumably in an autograph manuscript. The first of these works is devoted to the condition of soul before its unification with the human body, and to the legitimization of listening to music (sama') as a mystical practice. It has survived in a late nineteenth-century copy from Tatarstan.[41]

FIGURE 9. From Sayram to Siberia: Dawlat Shah al-Ispijafi's *Burhan al-Zakirin*. Courtesy of Kazan University Library. MS 747 F, fols. 2b–3a.

Fortunately, this copy bears the exact date and place of its composition, namely, Tobolsk in the year 1692.

In fact, this is one of the earliest examples of an original work on Sufi rituals to have been composed in the Muscovite state. Given the rarity of such texts, it is worth briefly outlining its contents. The treatise, which might have been part of a larger work, is organized as an answer to a tempting question by one of the author's fellow Muslims (*baradaran*): did the soul exist before its unification with the body; and if so, is the memory of that preexistence passed on? Dawlat Shah answered positively: the human soul continues to carry the experience it acquired before its unification with the body, but under the evil influence of worldly life, all the perfect sounds and forms that the soul had encountered in the eternal realms come to completely disappear from its memory. Citing verses from Jalal al-Din Rumi's *Masnawi*, Dawlat Shah claimed that "cleansing" the memory of the human soul went hand in hand with the sins of this world. The only way to remember the idyllic experience of paradise is to perform the ritual of *sama*, that is, to play musical instruments and sing beautiful songs that resemble the sounds of paradise. At this point the author made a reservation that *sama*'can be of two kinds: godly (*rahmani*) and demonic (*shaytani*). The difference lies in the participants' attitudes to the details of Shari'a, for only the strict following of even the smallest prescriptions of the religious law can guarantee the legitimacy of *sama*' as a ritual practice. Any music performed by impious persons must therefore be condemned and forbidden.

A second, somewhat larger, text by Dawlat Shah bears the title *Burhan al-Za-kirin*. It has come down to us as a manuscript in his own handwriting, bearing the date Rabiʻ al-Awwal 1117 (that is, July 1705).[42] The text, written in Persian and Chaghatai Turkish, consists of four chapters: on the preeminence of vocal *zikr* (remembrance of God); on Quranic verses and prophetic traditions that explain the ways of *zikr*; on the spiritual lineages of shaykhs who practiced vocal and silent forms of *zikr*; and on the ethical prescriptions of the Sufis (*baʻz-i adab-i silsila*). It is clear that the external, vocal form of ritual practice was central to Dawlat Shah's writings, and he had to defend his position against the proponents of the silent remembrance of God.

Regardless of the universality of arguments involved in this discussion, we can conclude that musical performance and a form of *zikr* spoken aloud were part of the teaching that Dawlat Shah al-Ispijafi spread among the Muslims of Siberia. Sufi ritual practice was also a highly disputed matter in other localities of the Russian Empire. This was why Dawlat Shah's short account had been copied somewhere in the Volga-Ural region in 1893. Other Persian texts that supported the vocal forms of *zikr* were also composed in what is today the Permʼ region of Siberia around the turn of the seventeenth century and were similarly associated with the Yasawi Sufi tradition.[43] Even as late as the 1860s, Sufi groups near Tobolsk continued to practice vocal *zikr* and public recitation of religious poems despite the warnings of their colleagues from Samarqand who contended that this did not bring due spiritual reward.[44]

Even so, it is doubtful that anyone actually spoke Persian in Tobolsk or its surrounding villages by the mid-nineteenth century. Written Persian was a different matter, though, and even in the 1840s, the Naqshbandi Sufis of the area who had received their education in Bukhara still used Persian to correspond with their peers back in Bukhara. An example is a letter written by ʻAbd al-Rahman ibn Damulla Sayfullah al-Bukhari to his friend Damulla Khwajam Wirdi Khalifa from the village of Sausqan near Tobolsk.[45] We know from biographical sources that Khwajam Wirdi had studied in Bukhara with Kalan Ishan Sahibzada and had many students in Siberia before he died in his native village in 1855.[46]

Thus, in Siberia probably more than in the Volga-Urals, literacy in Persian remained strong until the late nineteenth century as a result of the constant migration in both directions between Transoxiana (especially Bukhara) and the mid–Irtysh Valley. The Russian imperial bureaucracy called these migrants "Siberian Bukharans" in order to designate both their place of origin and of settlement.[47] In fact, from quite early on, western Siberia's religious communities were strongly bound to their peers in Central Asian centers of learning, which ensured the exchange of goods and ideas between the two regions. With its traditions of Islamic learning and Sufism, based on Persian-based literacy, Bukhara often meant more to Siberians than the great Tatar intellectual center of Kazan or any of the other Islamic centers of the Volga-Urals, not to mention Iran.

A DAGHESTANI SHAYKH SPEAKS "BUKHARAN"

Another case of linguistic polyphony evident in our sources comes from Daghestan, a land of mountains and, in Michael Kemper's words, an "island of classical Arabic literature" in the Caucasus.[48] For the second half of the nineteenth century and the first decade of the twentieth century, we know of a Naqshbandi-Khalidi Sufi network that united Daghestan and the Volga region via an important nodal point in Astrakhan.[49] A case study of this network is the Daghestani shaykh Mahmud al-Almali (1810–77), who was sent into exile by Russian officials and eventually settled in Astrakhan around the 1860s.[50] Not only was al-Almali able to create a large following in the city, he also integrated himself into the world of Tatar Sufis, merchants, and Muslim scholars ('ulama). From Astrakhan, he travelled widely in the heartlands of the Russian Empire, paid a visit to the sacred graves in the city of Bulghar near Kazan, and even married a Tatar woman, the daughter of a local saintly figure, Ibrahim Diwana. Moreover, in Tatarstan, he invited local Muslim authorities to join his Sufi lineage (silsila). Muhammad Zakir al-Chistawi (1815–93) was al-Almali's foremost admirer and closest friend. We know of many details of their personal contacts between 1862 and 1876 from a collection of letters that al-Almali sent to al-Chistawi. which survives in two manuscripts, one from a village in Tatarstan and another from Astrakhan.[51] These numerous letters discuss the phenomenon of the "double supervision" of Sufi initiates by al-Almali and al-Chistawi. Indeed, it was their joint students who preserved the letters, for the students of these two Sufi masters in turn travelled back and forth between Astrakhan and Chistopol', learning from both al-Almali and al-Chistawi.

What is striking about al-Almali's letters is that they follow the linguistic polyphony of the Islamic literature of Inner Russia. The letters start in Arabic, then move on to colloquial Turki, which is in turn broken up by al-Almali's custom of regularly quoting books in Persian. This linguistic practice was certainly not common in Daghestani writings of the period, when Arabic dominated the intellectual scene.[52] So al-Almali's usage of Persian is of particular interest in clearly demonstrating his deep integration into intellectual traditions and norms based on the use of written Persian, which were more accepted among the Tatar 'ulama at the time than by their Daghestani counterparts. Not only does al-Almali's language use point to this integration, so does the list of Persian bibliographical references in his texts. For these Persian citations link the author with literary canons established in Bukharan madrasas and familiar to the Tatar students who generation after generation were sent to study in Bukhara's "abode of knowledge."

Al-Almali was born in Shirwan and subsequently studied there. This is probably why he knew Persian so well and was able to make translations into both Persian and Chaghatai Turkish. In his letters he cited such authors as Ya'qub Charkhi (d.1447), 'Abd al-Rahman Jami (d.1492), and Ahmad Sirhindi (d. 1624), particularly his Maktubat (Letters), pointing to a core collection of Sufi classics that were copied en masse by the Muslims of Russia. Such references made Mahmud al-Almali's views on Sufi practices understandable by and popular among the predominantly Tatar audience he addressed. Thus, knowledge of Persian and familiarity with the Turkic language became key factors for al-Almali's smooth integration into Inner Russia's world of scholars, Sufis, and merchants. This audience was accustomed to the trilingual literature of the Persian Sufi treatises imported from Central Asia and recopied in Tatar rural madrasas. It is not surprising, therefore, that al-Almali's letters survived mainly in the Tatar milieu, where they had been disseminated by his followers.

This Daghestani case shows the power of the Persianate cultural sphere, which required scholars from a predominantly Arabic linguistic area to orient themselves toward and adopt the references of the Persian canon of Sufi literature established in Central Asia and shared by Muslims of the Russian Empire.

CONCLUSIONS

As this chapter's fragmentary overview has shown, the main source of inspiration for the Persianate culture that spread across the Muslim regions of imperial Russia was Bukhara. Under Russian governance, the empire's Turkic-speaking literati not only actively used and nativized classics of Persian poetry or Sufi manuals imported from Bukhara. They also contributed to maintaining a common cultural sphere across which Persian acted for centuries as a written lingua franca. In some cases, the Muslims of Russia played a significant role of intermediaries between the Arabic and Persian linguistic spheres. Suffice it to mention that the only Arabic translation of the Persian *maktubat* of Ahmad Sirhindi was made by the Tatar Naqshbandi shaykh Muhammad Murad al-Ramzi (1855–1935), who knew both Arabic and Persian very well and resided in Mecca for the last decade or so of his life.[53]

Among the learned Tatar Muslim subjects of imperial Russia, literacy in Persian defined the list of books and authors to be regularly cited and brought into circulation. This is why we have several thousand Persian manuscripts copied by Tatar students in Central Asia or produced in Inner Russia. But things had changed by the early twentieth century, when most Tatar students preferred to go to study in the Ottoman Empire or Egypt and thus found themselves immersed in different languages and literatures. From this point on, Persian began to be marginalized in writing, such that by the early Soviet period we encounter notes of readers that helplessly confess, "I do not understand Farsi."[54] During the subsequent Soviet era, students at the Mir-i 'Arab madrasa, the sole Muslim school permitted to remain open in Bukhara, received only elementary instruction in Persian and so did not engage in writing or reading Persian texts to any notable extent. Rather, in accordance with the usage of Russian academic dictionaries and the works of Soviet Orientalists, their efforts were aimed entirely at the practical ability to read Arabic texts on hadith and jurisprudence.[55] Today, Moscow has replaced "Bukhara the Noble" (Bukhara-yi Sharif) in attracting thousands of Central Asian migrants (who often barely speak Russian), and written Persian has become almost nonexistent in the Muslim culture of the Russian Federation.

NOTES

1. This chapter was written in the frame of "The Russian Language of Islam," project no. 360-70-490 of the Nederlandse Organisatie voor Wetenschappelijk Onderzoek (NWO; Netherlands Organisation for Scientific Research), and of project no. 17-81-01042 a(ts) of the Russian Foundation for Basic Research (RFBR). I am grateful to its anonymous reviewers for their criticisms and fruitful suggestions. All remaining mistakes are mine.

2. For an overview of my early expedition work in western Siberia, see Alfrid Bustanov, *Knizhnaia kul'tura sibirskikh musul'man* (Moscow: Mardjani Foundation, 2013).

3. Allen J. Frank, *Bukhara and the Muslims of Russia: Sufism, Education, and the Paradox of Islamic Prestige* (Leiden: Brill, 2012).

4. Institute of Language, Literature and Arts (Kazan), MS 6058, fols. 106b–107a. On the author, see Alsu Khasavnekh, *Akhmetzian Tubyli: zhizn' i tvorchestvo tatarskogo poeta-sufiia XIX veka* (Kazan, 2017).

5. So far the only comprehensive overview of Persian literature in Russia is Salim Giliazutdinov, *Persidsko-tatarskie literaturnye sviazi (X–nachalo XX vv.)* (Kazan, 2011).

6. Rebecca Gould, "The Geographies of 'Ajam: The Circulation of Persian Poetry from South Asia to the Caucasus," *Medieval History Journal* 18, 1 (2015): 87–119.

7. Alsu Arslanova, *Opisanie rukopisei na persidskom iazyke Nauchnoi biblioteki im. N. I. Lobachevskogo Kazanskogo gosudarstvennogo universiteta*, 2 vols. (Kazan, 2005, 2015); Salim Giliazutdinov, *Opisanie rukopisei na persidskom iazyke iz khranilishcha Instituta iazyka, literatury i iskusstva*, 3 vols. (Kazan, 2002, 2006, 2007). Another catalogue of Persian manuscripts collected at the Institute of Oriental Manuscripts (the former Saint Petersburg Branch of the Institute of Oriental Studies of the Russian Academy of Sciences) includes roughly 492 manuscripts, with about 298 titles copied in the Volga-Urals and western Siberia. See *Persidskie i tadzhikskie rukopisi Instituta narodov Azii AN SSSR*, ed. Nikolai D. Miklukho-Maklai, 2 vols. (Moscow, 1964). For an overview of the genres and popular works, see Devin DeWeese's chapter 4 in this volume.

8. See *The Heritage of Soviet Oriental Studies*, ed. Michael Kemper and Stephan Conermann (London: Routledge, 2015).

9. For a recent overview of cataloguing efforts in Russia, see Il'ya Zaitsev, "Izuchenie i katalogizatsiia sobranii arabskikh, persidskikh i tiurkskikh rukopisei v Rossiiskoi Federatsii za istekshie 25 let (1991–2016)," http://manuscriptaislamica.ru/storage/app/media/uploaded-files/Arabic_Persian_and_Turkish_Mss_Catalogue.pdf.

10. The late historian Mirkasym Usmanov authored a small, but informative, account on the fate of two manuscripts (one of them in Persian) that travelled between Kazan and Eastern Turkistan. See Mirkasym Usmanov, "Knigi-puteshestvennitsy," in *Dagestan i musul'manskii Vostok. Sbornik statei*, ed. Alikber Alikberov and Vladimir Bobrovnikov (Moscow: Mardjani Foundation, 2010), 273–79.

11. For an overview of the political importance of pious poetry in Russia, see Alfrid Bustanov, "Against Leviathan: On the Ethics of Islamic Poetry in Soviet Russia," in *The Piety of Learning: Islamic Studies in Honor of Stefan Reichmuth*, ed. Michael Kemper and Ralf Elger (Leiden: Brill, 2017), 199–224.

12. Kazan University Library MS 189T.

13. Shihab al-Din al-Marjani, *Mustafad al-Akhbar fi Ahwal Qazan wa Bulghar* (Kazan, 1900), 187.

14. This date must be wrong given the lifetime of Yunus al-Qazani, which is not surprising given Taj al-Din's notorious fame as a mystifier. See Allen J. Frank, *Islamic Historiography and 'Bulghar' Identity among the Tatars and Bashkirs of Russia* (Leiden: Brill, 1998), 94.

15. Kazan University Library MS 5882 Ar., 99b–100a (a late copy by Fathullah ibn Rahmatullah produced at the madrasa of Mulla 'Abd al-'Alim ibn Yahuda al-Bikbawi in 1845). Both Idris Afandi and

his teacher Hidayatullah figure prominently in local "Bulgharist" hagiographies. See Frank, *Bukhara and the Muslims of Russia,* 79.

16. Alfrid Bustanov, "'Rukopis' v kontekste sibirskogo islama," in *Kul't sviatykh v sibirskom islame: spetsifika universal'nogo,* ed. Aleksandr Seleznev et al. (Moscow: Izdatel'skii dom Mardjani, 2009), 181. For the study of local production of Sufi texts in Eastern Turkistan see Alexander Papas's chapter 8 in this volume.

17. Kazan University Library MS 440 F, 451 F, 473 F (copied by 'Abd al-Khaliq ibn Mulla Ahmar al-Mamdali), 506 F (autograph?). See the descriptions in Arslanova, *Opisanie rukopisei,* 2: 455–60. Michael Kemper mentions two copies of the book in Tashkent: Kemper, *Sufis und Gelehrte in Tatarien und Baschkirien, 1789–1889: Der islamische Diskurs unter russischer Herrschaft* (Berlin: Klaus Schwarz, 1998), 217n22.

18. Shihab al-Din al-Mardjani, *Mustafad al-Akhbar fi Ahwal Qazan wa Bulghar* (Kazan, 1900), 188. The proper spelling of al-Turki's attributive name is unknown.

19. Kazan University Library MS 5875 Ar., fols. 82b–88b; MS 399 Ar., fols. 168b–173a. MS 399 Ar. provides a date of composure as Ramadan 15, 1014/ January 24, 1606, which must be a mistake given the dates of al-Qazani's life. This small treatise (*mukhtasar*) is written in Arabic and Persian and contains questions posed by 'Abd al-Karim Shirdani with answers by Yunus ibn Iwanay al-Qazani.

20. Kazan University Library MS 399 Ar., fol. 168b.

21. Especially in the mid-eighteenth century, calls for jihad appear regularly in the written form. See, e.g., a proclamation by Zayn al-'Abidin al-Qarghali: *Rusiya müsilmannarïnï ikhtilälä dägvät idän khitabnamä* (1773), Institute of Oriental Manuscripts, Saint Petersburg, MS D566, fol. 1a.

22. Arslanova, *Opisanie rukopisei,* 1: 363–64; 2: 414–16. A manuscript kept at the Museum of National Culture (MS KP-14016) is peculiar, because the copyist, Bikash ibn Ish Muhammad al-Qazani, claims that he finished his work in 1015/1606 (fol. 77a), which is impossible given the date of tract's composition.

23. Kazan University Library MS 740 F, fols. 92b–97a; Murtaza ibn Husayn al-Burali, *Risala fi bayan dar al-kharb,* Kazan University Library MS 2400 Ar., fols. 63a–68b. For more details on the issue of *dar al-harb* in Russia, see Alfrid Bustanov, "The Bulghar Region as a 'Land of Ignorance': Anti-Colonial Discourse in Khorezmian Connectivity," *Journal of Persianate Studies* 9 (2016): 183–204, and Michael Kemper, "Imperial Russia as Dar al-Islam? Nineteenth-Century Debates on Ijtihad and Taqlid among the Volga Tatars," in *Islamic Law and Society: A Global Perspective,* ed. Sabrina Joseph, *Encounters: An International Journal for the Study of Culture and Society* 6 (2015): 95–124.

24. Fakhretdin Rizaetdin, *Asar. 1 tom* (Kazan: Rukhiiat, 2006), 36, provides a short biography of this author.

25. There are at least fourteen copies of the work: Arslanova, *Opisanie rukopisei na,* 2: 43–44, 51–52; Alfrid Bustanov, *Knizhnaia kul'tura sibirskikh musul'man,* 117–19; Giliazutdinov, *Opisanie rukopisei,* 1: 187–88, 2: 146–47, 3: 136–37.

26. E.g., Institute of Oriental Manuscripts, Saint Petersburg, MS B3477, an 1819 copy on Russian-manufactured paper by Sangatullah b. mulla Lutfullah al-Äjam. Other copies: Kazan University Library MSS 145 F, 180 F, 221 F, 261 F, 263 F, 277 F, 286 F.

27. Institute of Oriental Manuscripts, Saint Petersburg, MS B 3086, fols. 26ab; ibid., MS B 4375, fols. 163b–166a, copied by Imam 'Abd al-Hadi b. 'Abd al-Jabbar. Rizaetdin Fakhretdinov cites only his Turkic-language writings full of Russian loanwords. See Rida al-Din ibn Fakhr al-Din, *Athar,* vol. 1, fasc. 7 (Orenburg, 1904), 352–410.

28. Robert Crews, *For Prophet and Tsar: Islam and Empire in Russia and Central Asia* (Cambridge, MA: Harvard University Press, 2009), 67–71, 77–78; Kemper, *Sufis und Gelehrte,* 66–77.

29. 'Umar b. Muhammad al-Qarghalï, *Tadhkira janab 'ali shaykh al-islam wa mufti 'Abd al-Salam b. 'Abd al-Rahim Orenburghi Ufi,* Institute of Oriental Manuscripts, Saint Petersburg, MS B4089.

30. Institute of Oriental Manuscripts, Saint Petersburg, MS B3476, 96ff. This very important collection of legal documents was brought to Leningrad by members of the manuscript expedition, Vali

Zabirov and Sayid Vakhidi, from the scholar's home village Ura in 1934. The collection was never cata-logued or mentioned in the literature. On the author and his writings, see Nathan Spannaus, "The Decline of the Akhund and the Transformation of Islamic Law under the Russian Empire," *Islamic Law and Society* 20, 3 (2013): 372–74.

31. Institute of Oriental Manuscripts, Saint Petersburg, MS B2580, fols. 48b–50b. The author of this poem is *damullah* 'Ubaydullah b. Rahmatullah al-Qarlawi.

32. Giliazutdinov, *Persidsko-tatarskie literaturnye*, 113–19. Private collections in the Volga-Urals and western Siberia that conserve late-nineteenth-century copies include that of Kalam al-Din Shanga-reev, a Soviet-era imam in Rostov-on-Don and Perm, and the library of Rafis Shaikhadarov, a present-day imam in the village Iske Baltach in northern Bashkiria.

33. Giliazutdinov, *Persidsko-tatarskie literaturnye*, 119–22.

34. Kazan University Library MS 1204–1206 Ar.; Institute of Language, Literature, and Arts (Kazan), MS 44. For a Russian translation of the work, see Utyz-Imiani Gabdrakhim, *Izbrannoe*, ed. Ramil' Adygamov (Kazan: Tatarskoe knizhnoe izdatel'stvo, 2007), 184–236.

35. Historiography on Central Asian migrants in Siberia is abundant. To cite just a few studies: *En islam siberien*, ed. Stephane A. Dudoignon, *Cahiers du monde russe* 41, 2–3 (2000); Aleksandr Seleznev, Irina Selezneva and Igor' Belich, *Kul't sviatykh v sibirskom islame: spetsifika universal'nogo* (Moscow: Mardjani Foundation, 2009); Igor' Belich, "Vsemirnaia skazka v fol'klore sibirskikh tatar (opyt istor-iko-etnograficheskogo analiza)," *Etnografo-arkheologicheskie kompleksy: Problemy kul'tury i sotsiuma* 8, ed. Nikolai Tomilov (Omsk: Nauka, 2004), 63–96.

36. For more details, see Alfrid Bustanov, "Notes on the Yasaviya and Naqshbandiya in Western Siberia," in *Islam, Society and States across the Qazaq Steppe (18th–Early 20th Centuries)*, ed. Niccolo Pianciola and Paolo Sartori (Vienna: Österreichischen Akademie der Wissenschaften, 2013), 80–81.

37. On this person and the role of his family in the history of Islam in Siberia, see Igor' Belich, "Pis'mennye istochiki 80-kh godov XVIII—pervoi chetverti XIX veka o pravovykh traditsiiakh sibirskikh tatar," *Etnografo-arkheologicheskie kompleksy: problemy kul'tury i sotsiuma*, vol. 10, ed. Nikolai Tomilov (Omsk: Nauka, 2009), 170–94; Alfrid Bustanov, "Sviashchennye rodoslovnye i mezhregional'nye sviazi musul'man Severnoi Evrazii: Istoriia sem'i Shikhovykh v XVII–XX vv.," in *Sufizm i musul'manskaia dukhovnaia traditsiia: teksty, instituty, idei i interpretatsii*, ed. Aleksandr Knysh, Denis Brilev, and Oleg Yarosh (Saint Petersburg: Peterburgskoe vostokovedenie, 2015), 106–25; Zaituna Tychynskikh, *Sluzhilye tatary i ikh rol' v formirovanii etnicheskoi obshchnosti sibirskikh tatar (XVII–XIX vv.)* (Kazan: Fan, 2010); *Zakon, obychai, shariat: materialy po pravovoi kul'ture sibirskikh tatar (XVIII–nachalo XX v.)*, ed. Gul'sifa Bakieva (Tiumen, 2013), 13–80 (prepared by Igor' Belich and Alfrid Bustanov).

38. A resident of Tumen, Hasan khwaja b. Mir 'Ali khwaja of Bukharan origin, possessed a Persian "genealogy" listing the locations of Shi'i shrines in Central Asia and Iran. This manuscript was copied for the historian Gerhard Miller in 1154/ 1741 and thus survived in the Archive of Ancient Acts in Moscow: see Bustanov, *Knizhnaia kul'tura sibirskikh musul'man,*84.

39. Devin DeWeese, "The Yasawi Presence in the Dasht-i Qïpchaq from the 16th to 18th Century," in *Islam, Society and States across the Qazaq Steppe*, ed. Pianciola and Sartori, 59.

40. Kazan University Library MS 1575 T, fol. 26a. This copy of Ibni Khwaja's diploma is nearly un-intelligible: the copyist did not know Arabic and Persian and thus only mechanically reproduced what he saw in the original, which may have been the very document issued by Dawlat Shah in Bukhara.

41. Institute of Oriental Manuscripts, Saint Petersburg, A 1539, fols. 81a–85b. This manuscript was copied by 'Abd al-Wahid ibn Ahmadi ibn Baymat ibn 'Abdullah in 1893. In the catalogue, the location of the copy was mistakenly read as Kabul instead of Tabul (i.e., Tobolsk). See *Persidskie i tadzhikskie rukopisi Instituta narodov Azii AN SSSR*, ed. Miklukho-Maklai, 1: 508.

42. Kazan University Library MS 429 F, fols. 1a–34a. First description of the manuscript: Arsla-nova, *Opisanie rukopisei*, 2: 731–32.

43. Kazan University Library MS 747 F, fols. 27b–35a. Cf. Devin DeWeese, foreword to *Sobranie fetv po obosnovaniiu zikra dzhakhr i sama',* ed. Bakhtiyar Babadzhanov and S. Mukhammadaminov (Almaty: Daik-Press, 2008), 10–11.

44. Bustanov, *Knizhnaia kul'tura sibirskikh musul'man,* 97–100.

45. This letter, dated from Zu al-Qa'da 1256/December 1840–January 1841, is preserved in the private library of 'Abbas Bibarsov in the Penza region.

46. Alfrid Bustanov, "'Abd al-Rashid Ibrahim's Biographical Dictionary on Siberian Islamic Scholars," *Kazan Islamic Review* 1 (2015): 28–29, 67.

47. Erika Monahan, *The Merchants of Siberia: Trade in Early Modern Eurasia* (Ithaca, NY: Cornell University Press, 2016).

48. Michael Kemper, "An Island of Classical Arabic in the Caucasus: Daghestan," in *Exploring the Caucasus in the 21st Century: Essays on Culture, History and Politics in a Dynamic Context,* ed. Françoise Companjen, László Marácz, and Lia Versteegh (Amsterdam: Amsterdam University Press, 2010), 63–90.

49. See esp. Shamil' Shikhaliev and Michael Kemper, "Sayfullah-Qadi Bashlarov: Sufi Networks between the North Caucasus and the Volga-Urals," in *The Piety of Learning: Islamic Studies in Honor of Stefan Reichmuth,* ed. Michael Kemper and Ralf Elger (Leiden: Brill, 2017): 166–98.

50. Michael Kemper, "al-Almālī, Mahmūd," in *Encyclopaedia of Islam,* 3rd ed., ed. G. Krämer, D. Matringe, J. Nawas, and E. Rowson (Leiden: Brill, 2011), 29–31.

51. Kazan University Library MS 1TGF, fols. 55b–130a (copied by Ahmad al-Utiamishi in 1886); Institute of Oriental Manuscripts, Saint Petersburg, MS B3575, 32b–33a, 41b–42a, 57a, 78a, 79a, 80a–84b, and 90b–91a (copied by 'Abd al-Wahhab al-Hajji-Tarkhani). For an overview of these letters, see Alfrid Bustanov, "Sufizm bez granits: pis'ma Daghestanskogo shaikha Makhmuda al-Almali v Chistopol'," in *Istoricheskie sud'by narodov Povolzh'ia i Priural'ia,* ed. Il'dus Zagidullin, vol. 5 (Kazan, 2015), 51–66.

52. Amri R. Shikhsaidov, "Sammlungen arabischer Handschriften in Daghestan," in *Muslim Culture in Russia and Central Asia from the 18th to the Early 20th Centuries,* ed. Michael Kemper, Anke von Kuegelgen, and Dmitriy Yermakov (Berlin: Klaus Schwarz, 1996), 297–315.

53. Abdulsait Aykut, "The Intellectual Struggle of Murad Ramzi (1855–1935): An Early 20th Century Eurasian Muslim Author" (PhD diss., University of Wisconsin, 2015).

54. National Library of the Republic of Tatarstan, Kazan, MS 757T (copied in 1845), fol. 39b.

55. Eren Tasar, "The Official Madrasas of Soviet Uzbekistan," *Journal of the Economic and Social History of the Orient* 59, 1–2 (2016): 265–302.

8

Lingua Franca or Lingua Magica?

Talismanic Scrolls from Eastern Turkistan

Alexandre Papas

During the summer of 2010, I undertook fieldwork in Gansu and Qinghai among various Muslim minorities: Turkic-speaking Salar; Mongolian-speaking Dongxiang; Kargang Tibetans; and Chinese-speaking Hui. Accompanied by a Salar colleague, the ethnologist Ma Wei, I visited several holy places (called *gong-bei* in Chinese, from the Persian *gumbad,* "dome"). At the shrine of the Sufi saint Ma Taibaba (d. ca. 1680–90) in Linxia, we met Hui villagers from eastern Xinjiang who were performing a collective pilgrimage.[1] At a certain point of the ritual, which included Quran reading, prayers, incense burning, and cash distribution, I was asked to read aloud a Persian manuscript eulogy of the Prophet Muhammad, probably copied in the late nineteenth century. None of them could now read it, I was told, because it was written in Persian.[2]

This unusual experience raises a question on the status of Persian in western China: what happened to this language, which was no longer understandable but still so highly regarded that villagers carried with them a book written in it and wished to hear it read as a part of the ritual? My hypothesis is that Persian, at the height of its prestige, was read, spoken, and even sometimes written among the literate population, but then progressively became a "scriptural" language—that is, based exclusively on a limited number of written idioms—whose prestige verged on magic or devotions used by a large part of society. To flesh out this hypothesis and explain the paradox, this chapter limits its focus to Eastern Turkistan (designated Xinjiang since 1884), and explores two sources of information: manuscript catalogues of Eastern Turkistani collections and a corpus of talismanic scrolls, written either in Persian or in Chaghatai Turkish. Manuscript handlists and the fieldwork notes taken by their authors provide a rough but clear picture of the quantity and quality of Persian manuscripts that circulated throughout the Tarim Basin. A basic chronology can also be established. Less studied but more telling than the books, the scrolls allow an unusual insight into the everyday usages of Persian writing among not only the literate classes but also the lower strata of society. The following sections introduce seven original scrolls several meters' long, produced at different times, and then analyze them in the light of both art history and linguistics.

PERSIAN MANUSCRIPTS IN EASTERN TURKISTAN: THE SOCIAL PRESTIGE OF A LINGUA FRANCA

Like Devin DeWeese's chapter 4 in this volume, this chapter's case study brings together specific manuscripts with manuscript catalogues so as to reach more general conclusions. Three catalogues of Eastern Turkistani manuscripts are of particular interest in providing a consistent survey of books used in the oases of Xinjiang over a period of two centuries, whatever the language in which they were composed. Abdulladzhan Muginov's classic *Opisanie uigurskikh rukopisei Instituta Narodov Azii* (Description of the Uyghur Manuscripts of the Institute of the Peoples of Asia), published in Moscow in 1962, does not help us much in this comparative endeavor, being focused only on Turkic material.[3] Chronologically, the first of the three catalogues under scrutiny here is the manuscript collection of Jules-Léon Dutreuil de Rhins and Fernand Grenard, which remains understudied, because its documents are scattered in different places in Paris and its catalogue— or rather the notes written during the expedition—is unpublished and not always accurate. Although the explorer and the orientalist were clearly more interested in Turkic books, they also collected a few Persian items during their tribulations in southern Xinjiang, which started in 1891 and ended brutally in June 1894 with the murder of Dutreuil de Rhins by Tibetan highwaymen in Qinghai. Among the fifty manuscripts they sent from China to France, there are only two in Persian (a *diwan* by Hafiz, copied in 1731, and, translated from the Arabic, Qazwini's medieval cosmography, *'Aja'ib al-Makhluqat*, dated 1861), and two Chaghatai translations from Persian (a Sufi treatise of the late eighteenth century and a book on ethics copied in the first half of the nineteenth century). Persian manuscripts thus make up only 10 percent of the total, a figure that we will encounter again, although this is too small a selection to be representative. This collection of manuscripts will be discussed more closely in the second part of the chapter, devoted to scrolls.

The second catalogue under scrutiny is that based on the expedition of the German orientalist Martin Hartmann, who visited Eastern Turkistan in 1902–3 and came back with 133 manuscripts, all of which are now preserved in Berlin's Staatsbibliothek. In his catalogue, Hartmann did not provide dates, nor did he consistently identify the language of the books.[4] Yet it is possible to make a general evaluation based on the titles. For instance, we can safely assume that all professional manuals (simply called *risala*) (numbers 2, 5, 7, 8, 9, 10, 25, 26, 27, 84, 87, 90, 91, 92, 93, 94); Mir 'Ali Shir Nawa'i's *masnawi*s (numbers 15, 16, 68); Kharabati's *masnawi* (numbers 22, 29); and even the recent hagiographies (*tazkiras*) (numbers 6, 14, 66, 122) are all composed in Chaghatai. Hartmann lists only eight documents as being in Persian or including substantial Persian text (numbers 8, 28, 74, 75, 97, 102, 111, 131), but other books in the collection are certainly written in that language, such as 'Abdullah Ansari's works (numbers 28, 32) and Fayzullah's *Rahat al-Qulub* (numbers 55, 62, 73). This means that there are at least thirteen Persian manuscripts in the Hartmann collection, again 10 percent of the total. Like Dutreuil de Rhins and Grenard, Hartmann discovered that Persian manuscripts mainly if not exclusively comprised classics of literature and Sufism, both being prestigious genres in Xinjiang.

Far richer, the third collection is that of the Swedish ambassador and Turkologist Gunnar Jarring, which is preserved in the University Library of Lund, Sweden. The collection was first established by Swedish missionaries, such as Gustaf Raquette, who stayed in the Kashgar region from 1896 to 1921, and then expanded by Jarring himself during the 1930s. It now contains about 575 manuscripts, of which only a small proportion do not originate in Xinjiang.[5] With sixty-nine texts either fully in Persian or including significant Persian parts, we have again 10 percent of the total. This contrasts, on the one hand, with the linguistic distribution of literary production on the western side of the Tian Shan; and, on the other hand, with the Persianate culture of seventeenth- and eighteenth-century Eastern Turkistan. But Jarring's detailed cataloguing helps us to go beyond this basic evaluation.[6] Based on a commonly accepted periodization of the history of Eastern Turkistan, we may distinguish between three phases of manuscript copying. These were, firstly, the sixteenth to eighteenth century, which corresponds to the Chaghataiid and Khwaja regimes; secondly, the early nineteenth century to the 1870s, which covers the *begs* administration under Qing imperial suzerainty and the emirate of Ya'qub Beg (r. 1864–77); and thirdly, the 1880s to the early twentieth century, that is, the era of effective Qing domination. Generally speaking, we see a constant increase in the number of copies over time. This is of course due to the conditions of preservation of documents, which favor the most recent ones, as well as to the mass production and wide circulation of manuscripts in the modern times. Still, this upward curve shows that Persian did not end its career in the region as a dead language.

In the first period, from the sixteenth to eighteenth century, there are either practical documents, such as a marriage formula (Prov. 264) and a commentary on jurisprudence (*fiqh*) (Prov. 40), or quite sophisticated works such as the monumental philosophical poem of Nizami, *Makhzan al-Asrar* (Prov. 308), Jamal Husayni's *Rawzat al-Ahbab* (Prov. 244, a Timurid biography of the Prophet, the People of the House, and the Companions), and Abu Nasr Farahi's *Nisab al-Sibyan* (Prov. 350, a metrical Arabic-Persian glossary of the thirteenth century). As for the second historical period, from the early nineteenth century to the 1870s, while there are Sufi hagiographical dictionaries such as Lari's *Takmil-i Nafahat al-Uns* (Prov. 168, a commentary on Jami's famous fifteenth-century *Nafahat al-Uns*) and Badr al-Din Ishaq's *Asrar al-Awliya* (Prov. 66, an Indian compendium), we also find many didactic treatises on religious duties and ethics, among which the most worthy of mention are Sufi Allahyar's *Maslak al-Muttaqin* (Prov. 231 and Prov. 419, a classic on religious duties written in the spirit of Sufi beliefs), *Rahat al-Qulub* (Prov. 267), and a few other more obscure works (Prov. 192, Prov. 291).[7] Prov. 512 contains Arabic-Persian lexicons, and at least four manuscripts copied in Persian, but often including Arabic and Chaghatai segments, deal with devotion and magic (Prov. 75, Prov. 401 and Prov. 503 on prayers and amulets, and Prov. 193 on geomancy).

The third time period, from the 1880s to the early twentieth century, confirms this tendency toward less complexity and more ritualism. Linguistic material now includes Chaghatai and is reduced to short vade mecum (Prov. 306, Prov. 360, and Prov. 377). Sufi writings meanwhile are now limited to a few brief hagiographies (*tazkiras*) (Prov. 73, Prov. 307). Most of the manuscripts are devotional literature: books about or of prayers, mixing Arabic, Persian, and Chaghatai (Prov. 70, Prov. 71, Prov. 416, Prov. 157 and Prov. 505, both being Muhammad ibn Ahmad Zahid's *Targhib al-Salat*); prayers with amulets (Prov. 393); prayers with magic (Prov. 425); and a talismanic scroll (Prov. 452).

In sum, during the early modern period, the elite of Eastern Turkistan mastered Persian. This is confirmed by the fact that the sixteenth, seventeenth, and eighteenth centuries saw also a relatively important movement promoting Persian writings in the joint intellectual fields of historiography and hagiography, respectively patronized by the region's Chaghataiid sultans and Khwaja Sufi rulers. This is not the place to revisit a literary history that has partly been written, so it is sufficient to mention the following major works: Mirza Haydar Dughlat's *Tarikh-i Rashidi* (composed outside the Tarim Basin but by a Kashgari ruler of Kashmir); Mahmud Churas's *Tarikh* (a follow-up to Dughlat's historical work); the *Anis al-Talibin* by the same author; Mir Khal al-Din al-Yarkandi's *Hidayat-nama*; the anonymous hagiographical *Tazkira-yi Afaq Khwaja* (also known as *Tazkirat al-Hidayat*); and the Sufi oral commentaries on Rumi's *Masnawi-yi Ma'nawi* undertaken by experts known as *masnawi-khwan* (*masnawi*-reciters).[8] We may finally speculate that excerpts of Persian texts were quoted orally in sermons and preaching, as a recent if erratic survey of manuscript collections in Xinjiang suggests. Mozafar Bakhtyar found no fewer than three intriguing items comprising sermons in Persian: in Bishkiram, in the collection of the imam's Friday mosque, a text called *Firdaws al-Wa'izin*; in Yengisar's Friday mosque, a *Majmu'a-yi Khutbaha-yi Farsi Dawazdamahi*, and in Poskam, the *Khutba-nama-yi Dawazdamahi*.[9]

Evidently, Persian certainly did not disappear in nineteenth- and early twentieth-century Xinjiang. But the mastery of this prestigious language does seem to have vanished with the regional ruling elite: the Chaghataiid court was dismantled by the Khwaja dynasty of Sufis with the help of the Junggar Mongols in the 1680s, then the Khwajas themselves and their followers were partly forced into exile in Ferghana after the Qing conquest in 1759. Yet Persian learning maintained its prestige and even expanded in terms of book production, albeit at the price of a kind of leveling down. It was no coincidence that the high administration of Eastern Turkistan, led by *begs* (local governors) appointed by the Qing imperial authorities, commissioned translations of Persian classics into Chaghatai from the late eighteenth century on.[10] We find a comparable patronage of translations at the Khiva court in the nineteenth century, as seen in Marc Toutant's chapter 10 in this volume. In Xinjiang, there was for instance the case of an official named Khush Kipek Beg (d. 1781) who funded translations of Jami's *Nafahat al-Uns* and 'Attar's *Tazkirat al-Awliya*.[11] In the foreword of the former, the translator explained that "because of the use of Persian, profiting from this book has been easy for some people, possible for others, despite the difficulties, and completely impossible for most people ['*umum-i khala'iq*]. . . . This is why the knowledgeable and powerful Khwaja (Khush) Kifek Bek . . . asked me, the miserable one, to translate this work into Turki and continually to simplify [*asan*] its meaning for general readership [*khass-u-'am*]." Further examples are discussed in David Brophy's chapter 6 on the institutional use of Persian in Qing imperial China.

This translation process seems to have lasted until the mid-nineteenth century, as attested by the Jarring collection. Thus Prov. 334, copied in the late eighteenth century, is the Chaghatai version of *Shahr-i Gulshan*, a didactic religious treatise, which could correspond to Lahiji's *Sharh-i Gulshan-i Raz*, composed in the fifteenth century. Prov. 261, copied in 1841–42, is the Chaghatai version of the anonymous *Tazkirat al-Anbiya*. Prov. 341, copied around 1856–57, is a Chaghatai version of Fayzullah's *Rahat al-Qulub*. These are in addition to the two translations mentioned in the catalogue of the Dutreuil de Rhins and Grenard collection. Apparently, this translation process ceased abruptly with the emirate of Ya'qub Beg between 1864 and 1877, although these books still circulated in Khotan after 1863, according to Fernand Grenard.[12]

Whereas in the period stretching from the early nineteenth century to the 1870s, very few people seem to have been able to *write* Persian in Xinjiang, in the second period from the 1880s to early twentieth century, *reading* knowledge of Persian seriously declined. Hartmann and Jarring do not provide much detail about language learning among their local informants, but Grenard makes interesting observations about the language skills of his book suppliers and other literate people. According to him, there were schools (*maktabs*) attached to each mosque, but boys only attended classes episodically and merely learned Quran excerpts by heart. Very few people, even among officials, were able to read and write, except those whom Grenard calls "clergymen."[13] Given the general illiteracy in Xinjiang, the lower-class mullahs who constituted the majority of these "clergymen" not only served as public writers and gave public lectures, but also treated the sick, cast spells, and divined the future.[14] Among upper-class religious authorities—composed of muezzins, imams, qadis (Muslim judges), muftis, and the '*ulama*—only the latter could be considered highly educated.[15] In most serious madrasas, students learned the Quran by heart, studied some jurisprudence (*fiqh*) and listened to commentaries on the Persian classics such as Sa'di's *Gulistan*. In more precise linguistic terms, Chinese learning was very uncommon, and qadis and muftis did not master Arabic and Persian. In fact for most of them, Chaghatai (known as Turki) was so much in use in the region that it was called the "Muslim tongue" (*musulman tili*).[16]

The manuscript collectors' notes are often written in a condescending tone that does not do justice to the intellectual history of Xinjiang. Nevertheless, they are based on field experience and tell us a lot about the lower layers of Xinjiang society. What is important here, and should be discussed in connection with the popularity of devotional and magical books, is the overlapping of mullahs' language practices. On the fertile ground of popular beliefs and recourse to the supernatural (which, for instance, led the local constabulary to wear epaulettes with amulets to guard them against bullets), mullahs used their linguistic skills to cultivate an everyday life in which words and sentences were not only for technical or pragmatic use but equally for curing, assisting, and enchanting bodies and minds.[17] Grenard wrote that "they sell all kinds of amulets, i.e., coins, pieces of jade, consecrated strips of paper full of scriptures (*tumar*), fruit, and consecrated pieces of bread, which have the power to captivate the indifferent (*isitma*) or conversely to calm overenthusiastic lovers (*suutma*). The various offices of witchcraft [*sic*] are held by irregular mullahs, incomplete as people say (*chala*), who always wear a turban, affect scrupulous orthodoxy, and are no less exposed to the suspicion and contempt of the clergy."[18] In this way, armed with its early modern prestige, Persian continued to survive, almost better than ever, albeit now only as a *lingua franca cum mundo spirituum*, to pastiche Swedenborg. Or more simply as a *lingua magica*.

TALISMANIC SCROLLS: THE ADVENT OF A *LINGUA MAGICA*

Vertical scrolls have existed in Eastern Turkistan since the medieval period. But it seems that their economic and juridical usages have been abandoned in modern times, though the format was still very much in use in western Turkistan until the early twentieth century, especially for endowment deeds (*waqf-nama*), genealogical charts (*shajara*), or other secular and religious decrees and acts, such as *yarliq* (royal commands), *wasiqa* (endowments), fatwas, and so on.[19]

Three documents suggest that in Xinjiang, genealogy was also a major subject of scrolls, often covering a strong devotional aspect. The first of these is a calligraphic genealogical scroll of the Khwaja Sufi dynasty, which ruled over the Tarim Basin from 1680 till the Qing imperial conquest of 1759.[20] Comparable in size to other genealogical trees found in Central Asia, the scroll measures 424 × 27.5 centimeters. Attached one to the other, the ten sheets of paper that compose it are pasted onto canvas. With the exception of the title, the calligraphy is in fine *naskh* script, usually in black ink, except on the occasion of the second rendering of

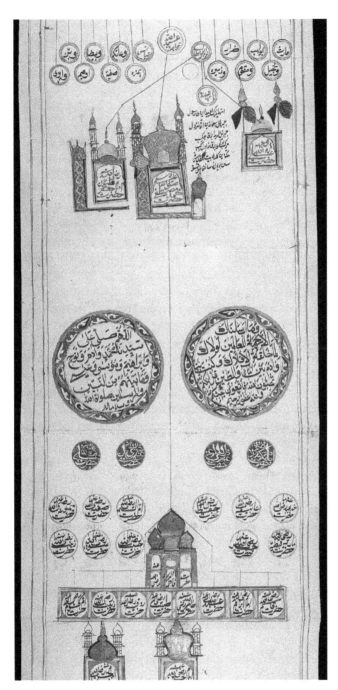

FIGURE 10. Sainthood inscribed: genealogical scroll of the Khwajas. Lund University Library, Lund, Sweden. MS Jarring prov. 561.

the Prophet Muhammad's name, which is instead given in white lettering. Verses 31–34 of the third *sura*, Ali 'Imran, along with the well-known *hadith qudsi* "Were it not for your sake, We would not have created the universe," close the section of the scroll devoted to the genealogies of the prophets who preceded Muhammad. The rest of the text is in Persian and is largely given over to short biographical notes of some of the people mentioned, including dates of death. The last section of the scroll repeats the prayers to Muhammad and quotes Quran 33:56, to wit "God and His angels bless his Prophet. O believers, do you also bless him, and pray him peace." Before concluding with a few last *salawat* (praises), the ending lines reveal the name of the scribe (*katib al-huruf*) as al-Hajji Isma'il Bukhari, a personage who has not yet been identified. The document is likely to have been produced at some point during the lifetime of the three last generations of Afaqi Khwajas, that is to say, between 1751 and 1826.

As for the work's geographical provenance, we have several clues. Together, the use of the Persian language, the quality of the calligraphy, the calligrapher's *nisba* (referring to his place of origin in Bukhara) and the fact that the Afaqi Khwaja Hasan left behind descendants after his exile and death in Transoxiana, suggest that the document may have come from that region. However, we know that Persian was still reasonably well known among members of a Xinjiang elite in the eighteenth and nineteenth centuries; that the *nisba* refers to an individual's birthplace or lineage, not to the place of a work's composition; and that, according to oral investigations, several families who claimed to be Khwaja Afaq's relatives long maintained themselves in eastern Central Asia, including southern Kazakhstan and the region around Kashgar. Therefore, a provenance from Xinjiang is also very possible.

Within the milieu of the Sufi order, meanwhile the production and exhibition of such a genealogical tree (*shajara*) may have served a number of more specific purposes. This is certainly the case in Eastern Turkistan, as I discovered during research in western China in July 2008 and August 2010. In both environments, I observed how *shajara* documents might serve in various ways to foster the workings of a particular Sufi order. Often, for instance, saintly genealogies perform a function in the initiation of new disciplines, their recitation from memory serving as a kind of initiatory devotional discipline. As consensually authoritative accounts of the past, genealogical documents also serve as a point of reference in the adjudication of controversies and conflicts within the order, particularly when relating to problems of succession. And as rich demonstrations of calligraphic skill, these documents are often presented to members as monuments of a Sufi order's aesthetic as well as spiritual achievements. We cannot be certain, of course, but the Khwaja Sufi scroll may very well have exercised a similarly diverse set of religious functions. Produced within a forum of competition with other aristocratic households, prestigious Sufi lineages in particular, the scroll served to highlight both the high-status Sharif origin of the family and the hereditary succession of its spiritual leaders. At the same time, the manuscript's remarkable aesthetic qualities served to impress upon those who saw in it the numinous force of the Khwajas' supernatural authority.

The devotional and magical nature of the Khwaja Sufi *shajara* is visible in a second document produced by the same calligrapher. Put on sale in Paris in March 2014, the scroll presents the same contents as the first scroll, including the Quran and hadith quotations. The design and the size, however, are different (being 608 × 29 centimeters), and here and there we find some variations. Hajji Isma'il Bukhari signed as *li-mu'allifih wa katibih* (by the author and scribe), and there are more biographical explanations in Persian, as for example in the case of Afrasyab, the mythical king of Firdawsi's *Shah-nama,* about whom we read in Persian on the scroll that "he was king of Turkistan beyond Transoxiana and the lands of China [*maliki-yi Turkistan az hadd-i Mawarannahr wa Diyar-i Chin bud*]." What is striking about this manuscript is the repetitive use of large circles, symbolizing halos of blessing power (*baraka*) for the names *Muhammad Rasulullah* and *Hazrat-i Fatima,* along with the multiplication of blessings (*salla allahu 'alayhi wa sallam*). These are all graphic signs that manifest, and call for, devotion. If Arabic of course remains the language of Islamic sacredness on this second scroll, Persian appears as the language of Sufi devoutness.

A third document confirms this impression that genealogies of the Khwaja Sufis can be understood as magical scrolls. This is not in the technical sense of *simiya* (occult science) or *sihr* (magic), but in the broader meaning of enchantment and intercession, of rendering the paper document a written intermediary between its readers and God. In this regard, the paper document acted in a similar way to the architecture of a shrine. Previously preserved in the collections of the Mission Covenant Church of Sweden and offered to the Lund University Library in 2008, the third *shajara* scroll is mostly composed in late Chaghatai Turkish with some Arabic and Persian.[21] Probably produced in the early twentieth century—a time of declining knowledge of Persian in the Sufi circles of Xinjiang—the document once again displays the detailed Afaqi family line of the Khwaja Sufis. The interesting point here is not the language but the particular iconic signs surrounding holy names. The anonymous artist drew little cupolas, minarets, and columns on the names of the prophets and saints in order literally to enshrine the holy figures listed in the document. This was particularly the case with the names of Muhammad and Fatima, both objects of great veneration. This colorful iconography, with its circles, strips, and scriptural use of language, recalls that of other magical objects in Central Asia, such as the Sufi talismanic shirts called *libas al-taqwa,* an expression from Quran 7:26.[22]

The four other documents under discussion here are talismans *stricto sensu.*[23] Unlike the preceding items, they were composed by mullahs who probably came from the lower classes. Thanks to the ethnographical study of Islamic clerics in Turfan region undertaken by Jianxin Wang in the 1990s, we know precisely how these talismanic scrolls were produced:

Ismayil Qarahaji practices two kinds of amulet (*retname tomari*). The amulet is used for preventing illnesses and misfortunes, and curing light ailments and vexations. It has a large range of applications such as healing unknown ailments or repelling the incantations cast by evil-willed sorcerers. It is made of a long narrow piece of white paper, about ten centimeters wide and 500 centimeters long, rolling up in the size of a cigar. It is written fully with fixed spells and selected Quranic verses. It consists of an introduction paragraph, twenty main paragraphs, and a conclusion paragraph. The introduction explains its purpose and merits, each of twenty main paragraphs contains two parts to introduce troubles and desired results in Uyghur and some Quranic verses showing expelling power in Arabic, and the conclusion is composed of some hymns written in Arabic. An amulet can be effective only as long as the owner keeps it at hand. For maintaining its effectiveness after getting the desired result, amulets must be recited, preferably once every month, but at least once in a year. A simple rite will be held when giving amulet to a client. Since the religious importance of this ceremony lies in its recitation by the maker or an Islamic leader, neither observers nor any complicated procedure involved. As Ismayil Qarahaji introduced to me what he did in the past, he usually puts a teacup full of water on a table, and takes out a prepared amulet, unfolds it and writes down the client's name at the end of the text. After that, he starts the presentation rite. He recites all content of amulet. Then after his concluding prayer, he blows his breath onto the water of the teacup (a symbolic action of soaking the sacred power of Quranic verses into the water), and let the client drink the water and hands over that amulet.[24]

Grenard and Dutreuil de Rhins also collected two comparable scrolls in the course of their expedition. Called *asnad-i du'a* (or *asna-du'a*), which means "prayer document," they both measure 170 × 9 centimeters and are written in Chaghatai with Arabic prayers and some Persian specific vocabulary. They both date from the late nineteenth century. The first talisman targets the demon Ibn Sabyan and stipulates that anyone who keeps the paper talisman with him will be under God's protection against djinns, evil spirits (*diw*), male demon (*albasti*), and other evils. Women especially must keep the talisman with them every day. This is explained by the following story. During a battle, King Solomon encountered a giant and asked him who he was. The giant said his name was Ibn Sabyan and explained that he penetrated the bodies of pregnant women to kill their fetuses. On hearing this, Solomon composed a prayer so as to struggle against Ibn Sabyan's devilry. We can therefore understand that the talisman was made to protect women during pregnancy. Concerning its language precisely, beside the reference to Solomon, famously known in the Persian tradition as the one who masters the secret 'language of birds' (*mantiq al-tayr*, taken from Quran 27:15), we find a series of terms holding negative, even nihilistic, values, which were quite unusual in Chaghatai and here served an apotropaic function. These terms were *ziyandash* (noxious), *zakhm* (trauma), *gunahkar* (sinner), and *nabud* (annihilated). In the same way that amulets represent wild beasts, or parents give children apotropaic names (the name of a physical or moral defect, for example), in explicitly naming calamities the talisman resorted to Persian words to ward off evil powers.

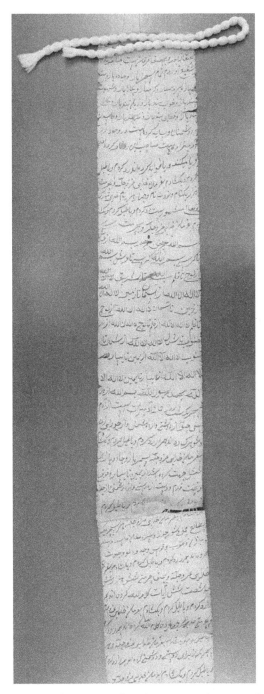

FIGURE 11. *Lingua magica:* talismanic scroll used as a countercharm. Lund University Library, Lund, Sweden. MS Jarring prov. 452.

The second talismanic scroll is dedicated to Kithmir, the dog of the Companions of the Cave (*ashab al-kahf*, from Quran 18:7–26). The text does not provide any explanation about this attribution. Like the first talisman, it is said that anyone who keeps the document with him will be under God's protection against evil forces. The bearer will likewise be cherished in both worlds, and protected against afflictions, the devil's oppression, the wrath of kings, false accusations, and all manner of other calamities. The second half of the scroll is more precise and focuses on love affairs. If someone was in love with someone else, the scribe would read this amulet and blow on either an apple, candy, or anything sweet and edible, and then the lover would give it to the beloved, rendering the latter madly in love with him or her. If a husband did not behave correctly with his wife, the scribe would write this amulet, and she would then keep it with her: the couple would live thereafter in happy tenderness. If a woman wants to bind (*öru bol*) someone, she would blow three times to the left of the beloved and he would become mad with love for her. For a man, the procedure would be that he blows three times to her right. As regards the uses of Persian what is interesting in this second section, and in the invocation at the end of the scroll, is the rich lexis of love and pain (quite common in Chaghatai), which comes from Persian elegiac poetry. It includes syntagmas like *dard-i firaq* (pain of separation), *diwana-yi shayda* (love madness), *khun-i jigar* (deep affliction), *'ashiq-i biqarar* (passionate lover), *khar khar* (anxious desire) and so on. Clearly, the language of love is Persian, which here serves the purpose of reification. Inspired by the technique of elegiac poetry, objectifying its heroes, the talisman makes a diverse and comprehensive use of the poetic vocabulary of passion to arouse that same passion and make it a reality rather than a literary fiction.

The third item in this talismanic corpus deals also with love stories, using the same idioms in a different way. Preserved in the Jarring collection in Lund (Prov. 14), the scroll measures 110 × 12 centimeters and can probably be dated to the early twentieth century. The text is in Arabic and late Chaghatai/early Uyghur, mixed with Persian.[25] Explicitly called a talisman (*tumar*), the scroll is made for both men and women and should be kept on one's person in order to be effective. Its aim is to awaken love and unite couples, either by drawing a lover to their beloved or by maintaining long-term relationships. In the latter case, it is stipulated that the lover must carry the talisman on a Thursday and whisper to the right of the beloved three times, "By order of God." Other magical techniques are also described. Then, in the final invocation (which mentions God, Adam and Eve, the archangels, Muhammad and Fatima), reference is made to the legendary literary couples Layla and Majnun and Yusuf and Zulaykha, who thus appear less as inaccessible mystical allegories than as embodiments of the vicissitudes of ordinary emotional life. Here again, the talisman maker had recourse to the Persian elegiac tradition. At the linguistic level, the text on the talisman mainly repeated the expression "passionate lover" (*'ashiq-i biqarar*), used in lines 9, 11, 17, 35, and 50, which characterizes the overall usage of Persian in that scroll. By recurrence and anaphora rather than by the literary synonymization of the preceding case, this locution assumes a performative function similar to the more usual ritualistic iterations of Islamic talismanic scrolls. It is this repetition of specific phrases, whether Quranic or not, that empowers the efficacy of the written talisman.[26]

To focus more squarely on their shared linguistic features, all of these documents were written in Chaghatai Turkish with Persian usages. This does not mean that Xinjiang did not issue talismans in Persian. In fact, the Jarring collection features a very long scroll of approximately five meters in length that was composed in Persian and Arabic sometime between the late nineteenth and early twentieth centuries. This is more precisely a counter-charm (*radd-nama*) against all kinds of magic, which ends with a series of invocations in Arabic. Against each of the magical actions listed extensively in the text, using astrology, horoscope, divination, spells, the Quran, hadith, and the names of God, the prophets, the martyrs and the saints, the scribe wrote the same formula: "all of them, I rejected I dissolved I subdued by God's order the Mighty and Majestic [*hama-ra radd kardam wa batil kardam wa bikushadam bifarman-i khuda-yi 'azza wa jalla*]."[27] The Persian sentence is repeated over and over in order to draw on divine power and to activate the counter-charm in a way that is comparable with other crucial phrases used in Islamic talismans to activate the text by means of verbal incantations in the first-person singular (e.g., the Arabic *as'aluk*, "I ask you," and *a'udhubik* "I take refuge in you").[28]

CONCLUSIONS

Overall, we have seen four talismanic scrolls that manifest not only the survival of Persian until the early twentieth century, but also its transformation into a *lingua magica* in Xinjiang. This *lingua magica* functioned through a rhetorically limited but socially widespread set of linguistic functions that the scrolls performed by way of apotropaic reification, performativity by recurrence, and verb activation.

In contrast with a top-down historiography of Persian that tends to focus on high literary production to observe the social realities of a language and the culture it carries, this chapter has taken another methodological path by looking at both the quantity of that production in the pre-print age and its most popular, albeit overlooked, documents, namely, talismans.[29] As Thibaut d'Hubert shows in his chapter 2 in this volume, on eastern Bengal, recognizing the ritual usage of Persian refines our understanding of the literary economy of this lingua franca as it operated at the level of masses across the frontiers of Eurasia. On the basis of a brief survey of what Persian texts were actually copied, written, and understood in Xinjiang from the eighteenth century to the early 1900s, it appears that Persian learning experienced a paradoxical fate in the region. As if the prestige of Persian had given birth to a lingua franca and then killed it because of its confinement to a small elite, that prestige also generated a linguistic aura that transformed poetic vocabulary into magic tricks.

The social profile of Xinjiang's Persian-speakers, or rather Persian-users, remains difficult to identify with precision. Yet for the majority of them, an ideal-type can still be recognized. Far from being a cosmopolitan *homme de lettres* and citizen of a republic of letters, the Persian-user in Xinjiang was generally a mullah or an *akhund* (cleric) who had been trained in a local *maktab* school, sometimes in a more senior madrasa, and who had been appointed to a mosque or shrine in a village or urban neighborhood. His circle of acquaintances was composed of Muslim men and women from various backgrounds. But it was limited to a local scale, obeying rules of spoken sociability that were expressed exclusively in the Chaghatai Turkic language.

NOTES

1. Ma Taibaba was one of the three representatives (*khalifas*) of the Naqshbandi Sufi master Hidayatullah/Afaq Khwaja (d. 1694) in northwestern China (excluding Eastern Turkistan at this period). The famous Abu al-Futuh al-Sini/Ma Laichi (d. 1753) was among Ma Taibaba's successors. See Alexandre Papas and Ma Wei, "Sufi Lineages among the Salar: An Overview," in *Muslims in Amdo Tibetan Society: Multidisciplinary Approaches,* ed. Marie-Paule Hille, Bianca Horlemann, and Paul Nietupski (Lanham, MD: Lexington Books, 2015), 109–34.

2. For a recent discussion on the disappearance of Persian learning in China proper, see Masumi Masumoto, "Secularization and Modernization of Islam in China: Educational Reform, Japanese Occupation and the Disappearance of Persian Learning," in *Islamic Thought in China: Sino-Muslim Intellectual Evolution from the 17th to the 21st Century,* ed. Jonathan Lipman (Edinburgh: Edinburgh University Press, 2016), 171–96, which shows that Persian, perceived as the Sufi idiom par excellence, came to be considered a barrier to modern reform and eventually disappeared in Reformist curricula in favor of Chinese and Arabic. Persian learning was nonetheless preserved in a few villages of northern China until the Cultural Revolution.

3. Neither *Uyghur, özbek, tatar qädimki äsärlär tizimliki* (Kashgar: Qäshqär Uyghur Näshriyati, 1989) nor Amina Abdurahman and Jin Yu-Ping, "Une vue d'ensemble des manuscrits tchagatay du Xinjiang," *Cahiers d'Asie centrale* 8 (2000): 35–62, help much here either. The *Sobranie vostochnykh rukopisei Akademii Nauk Uzbekskoi SSR* (Catalogue of Oriental Manuscripts of the Academy of Sciences of the Uzbek Soviet Republic), edited by Aleksandr A. Semenov et al. between 1952 and 1987, and cited below as *SVR,* is not representative, but it includes little-known Persian references from Eastern Turkistan such as Nasir 'Ali Sirhindi's *Takhmis-i Diwan-i Hafiz* copied by Rahim Baqi Yarkandi in 1712 (1124) (*SVR,* 2: 149, MS 176); a collection of Sufi texts copied in Tashmaliq (outside Kashgar) by Mulla Genje-yi Kashghari in 1844 (1260) (*SVR,* 3: 270, 288 and 4: 39, MS 586); and *Nawadir al-Ma'arif* by Muhammad Dahbidi al-Naqshbandi (d. 1776), copied by Mulla Muhammad Nazar Qaraqashi in 1846 (1262) (*SVR,* 8: 439–40, MS 8590/1). See also the composite volume of Sufi poetry and prose copied by Ibrahimjan ibn Mulla Fayzi Ishan in Kashgar in 1858 (1275) described in *Katalog sufiiskikh proizvedenii XVIII–XX vv. iz sobranii Instituta Vostokovedeniia im. Abu Raikhana al-Biruni Akademii Nauk Respubliki Uzbekistan* (Stuttgart: Franz Steiner, 2002), 54, MS 9884/2.

4. Martin Hartmann, "Die osttürkischen Handschriften der Sammlung Hartmann," *Mitteilungen des Seminars für Orientalische Sprachen zu Berlin* 7, 2 (1904): 1–21.

5. Officially 560 but recent discoveries increased the amount.

6. Lund University Library: Jarring Collection, http://laurentius.ub.lu.se/jarring/browse/idno/1. html. Call numbers start with "Prov." (provisional no.). A current project aims at updating the

catalogue, electronically digitizing, annotating, and editing a part of the collection; see "Chaghatai 2.0," https://uyghur.ittc.ku.edu. Both catalogue and manuscripts themselves provide, from time to time, names or titles of ownership (mainly *akhund*s in fact), but it remains extremely difficult to trace the itinerary of books. E.g., Prov .73 gives Qadir Akhund (fol. 1a), Sabit Akhund (fol. 93b, misspelled Sa'it by Jarring) and, in Chinese (cover), "This book is the property of Han Ziyuan of Yarkand East Gate trading [*Shache Dongguan shangye Han Ziyuan shu*])." Thanks to Arienne Dwyer and Akbar Amat for these last data. The name Niyaz Agha Khan also appears on the cover, apparently as an agent (*katim*, miswritten *katam?*).

7. Jarring did not correctly identify these two hagiographical dictionaries; on the impact of Sufi Allahyar (d. 1723) on madrasa education in Eastern Turkistan, see Abudurehemu Wubuli, "Doğu Türkistan medreselerinde islam düşüncesi: Sûfî Allahyar'ın Sebatü'l-âcizin adlı eseri ekseninde inceleme" (PhD diss., Ankara Üniversitesi, 2015).

8. See esp. Oleg Akimushkin, introduction to *Sha-Mahmud Churas khronika* (Moscow: Nauka, 1976); Minoru Sawada, "Three Groups of *Tadhkira-i khwājagān*," in *Studies on Xinjiang Historical Sources in 17–20th Centuries*, ed. James Millward, Shinmen Yasushi, and Sugawara Jun (Tokyo: Toyo Bunko, 2010), 9–30; Alexandre Papas, introduction to *Soufisme et politique entre Chine, Tibet et Turkestan* (Paris: Jean Maisonneuve, 2005).

9. Mozafar Bakhtyar, "China," in *World Survey of Islamic Manuscripts*, ed. Geoffrey Roper, vol. 4 (supplements) (London: Al-Furqan Islamic Heritage Foundation, 1994), 88, 113–15.

10. Less significant but worthy of note, there is also the commission of rewritings of Chaghatai classics into late Eastern Chaghatai, as when the poet 'Abd al-Rahim Nizari (d. ca. 1850), with the support of Kashgar's district governor (*hakim beg*) Zuhur al-Din, himself a versifier, recomposed parts of 'Ali Shir Nawa'i's pentalogue (*khamsa*). See *Nizari Dastanliri*, ed. Ghulam Ghopuri (Urumqi: Millätlär Näshriyati, 1985), 2–3, 123, and 382; *Nizari Lirikliri*, ed. Muhämmättursun Bahawidin (Urumqi: Shinjang Khälq Näshriyati, 1995); *Diwani Zuhuri*, ed. Qurban Barat (Urumqi: Shinjang Khälq Näshriyati, 1995) with a facsimile of the *diwan*.

11. For more details, see Alexandre Papas, "Individual Sanctity and Islamization in the *Ṭabaqāt* Books of Jāmī, Navā'ī, Lāmi'ī, and Some Others," in *Jami and the Intellectual History of the Muslim World*, ed. Thibaut D'Hubert and Alexandre Papas (Leiden: Brill, 2019), 378–423.

12. Jules-Léon Dutreuil de Rhins, *Mission scientifique dans la Haute Asie, 1890–1895, troisième partie par F. Grenard* (Paris: Ernest Leroux, 1898), 2, 86.

13. Ibid., 132.

14. Ibid., 161.

15. Ibid., 232.

16. Ibid., 273, 235, 168, 188, and 10.

17. Ibid., 121.

18. Ibid., 257.

19. Bakhtiyar Babajanov, "About a Scroll of Documents Justifying Yasawi Rituals," in *Persian Documents: Social History of Iran and Turan in the Fifteenth to the Nineteenth Centuries*, ed. Nobuaki Kondo (London: Routledge, 2003), 53–72; *Mazar Documents from Xinjiang and Ferghana*, ed. Jun Sugawara and Yayoi Kawahara, vol. 1 (Tokyo: Tokyo University of Foreign Studies, 2006); *Mazar Documents from Xinjiang and Ferghana*, ed. Ashirbek Muminov, Nodirbek Abdulahatov, and Yayoi Kawahara (Tokyo: Tokyo University of Foreign Studies, 2007); and El'ior Karimov, *Kubraviskii vakf XVII–XIX vv.: Pis'mennye istochniki po istorii sufiiskogo bratstva Kubraviia v Srednei Azii* (Tashkent: Fan-Institut français d'étude sur l'Asie centrale, 2008).

20. Here I summarize the results of Alexandre Papas, "Joining the Dots between the Ḫwājas of East Turkestan: A *Šağara* Scroll Preserved at the Louvre Museum," *Der Islam* 88 (2012): 352–65.

21. I was able to consult this scroll briefly in June 2015 in Lund. A full study will be available on the website of the "Chaghatai 2.0," project mentioned in n. 6 above.

22. *Heaven on Earth: Art from Islamic Lands: Works from the State Hermitage Museum and the Khalili Collection*, ed. Mikhail B. Piotrovsky and J. Michael Rogers (Munich: Prestel, 2004), 98–99;

Elena Tsareva, "Talismanic Shirts of Central Asia," *Manuscripta Orientalia* 17, 2 (2011): 54–58. Cf. Alain Epelboin, Constant Hamès, and Anne Raggi, "Cinq tuniques talismaniques récentes en provenance de Dakar (Sénégal)," in *Coran et talismans: Textes et pratiques magiques en milieu musulman,* ed. Constant Hamès (Paris: Karthala, 2007), 147–74.

23. Yasmine Alsaleh, "'Licit Magic': The Touch and Sight of Islamic Talismanic Scrolls" (PhD diss., Harvard University, 2014), 3, 12–13, and 81–83, shows, however, that talismans are tools of devotion.

24. Jianxin Wang, *Uyghur Education and Social Order: The Role of Islamic Leadership in the Turpan Basin* (Tokyo: Research Institute for Languages and Cultures of Asia and Africa, Tokyo University of Foreign Studies, 2004), 213–14 (the entire description). See also Abdurähim Häbibullah, *Uyghur Etnografisi* (Urumqi: Shinjiang Khälq Näshriyati, 1993; rev. ed., 2000), 249–50, 393–98.

25. More details, including pictures, on that document in Alexandre Papas, "Un rouleau talismanique du Xinjiang musulman," *Eurasian Studies* 12 (2014): 555–59, xxiv–xxvi.

26. Alsaleh, *"Licit Magic,"* 56, 59, 64, 124, 128, and 139–40.

27. This formula is repeated on lines 9–10, 12, 26–27, 34–35, 36–37, 40–41, 43–44, 47–48, 53–54, 81–82, 83–84, 88–89, 91–92, 93–94, 96–97, 101–2, 103, 105, 108, 110, 113–14, 124–25, 130–31, 134–35, 156–57, 158–59.

28. Alsaleh, *"Licit Magic,"* 202.

29. Lithographs from Tashkent and India had circulated in Xinjiang since the late nineteenth century by the time printing started there in the 1910s.

PART THREE

New Empires, New Nations, ca. 1800–1920

9

Conflicting Meanings
of Persianate Culture

An Intimate Example from Colonial India and Britain

Michael H. Fisher

During the long period of transition from Mughal to British imperial rule over India, the Persian language and Indo-Persianate culture conveyed conflicting meanings to various individuals and classes of Indian and British people in India and in Britain. These powerful meanings shifted over time and were context-sensitive. In India, the frontier of Persian and its associated culture had advanced from the sixteenth century on, especially with the expanding rule of the Mughal imperial family. Much of the power of the Mughal Empire came from its capacity to incorporate a range of Indian people and Indic elements into its Persianate imperial culture.[1] Indeed, this cultural force meant that the Mughal imperial dynasty and court lasted for a century and a half after the military power and effective rule of these emperors had largely fragmented (conventionally dated from the death of the emperor Aurangzeb in 1707).

Until the official end of the Mughal Empire in 1858, many Indian princely states and the English East India Company both continued nominally to respect Mughal sovereignty and to emulate parts of its imperial Indo-Persianate culture, albeit to different degrees and in inconsistent and often conflicting ways. Many of the fading Indian rulers and traditional service elites continued to value and to identify themselves strongly with that Indo-Persianate culture. However, in the context of expanding British political, cultural, military, and economic assertions in Asia, the Persian language was no more than a useful tool. Simultaneously, there were also debates in Britain, however, over the meanings of Persian and Indo-Persianate culture, which involved both "Orientals" in the abstract and some Asians in person, and concepts of biological racial difference increasingly inflected them in the nineteenth century. This chapter complements a substantial existing body of insightful scholarship on the lives of Persophone Asians who visited or settled in Britain in that era.[2]

In order to explore these conflicts and transitions as the Persian and Persianate frontiers advanced, retreated, and persisted at various social strata in India and Britain, this chapter contextualizes and analyzes the early nineteenth century case of a hybrid heir to the doomed north Indian principality of Sardhana: D. O. Dyce Sombre (1808–51). For him, Persian was the most intimate and status-giving of languages. While his tendentious life in both India and in Europe was eccentric, it provides especially rich primary source material about what Persian meant to him personally—from his private diary and letters as well as from the extensive evidence about his words and actions from his contemporaries. When placed in the larger historical context of whole classes of Indians and Britons in India and in Britain, this case suggests the conflicting effective and affective meanings of Persian and Indo-Persianate culture in various times and places during this crucial period, as power and prestige were more broadly shifting to English and Anglicized culture globally.

HISTORICAL CONTEXTS IN INDIA AND IN BRITAIN FOR PERSIAN AND INDO-PERSIANATE CULTURE, SIXTEENTH TO EARLY NINETEENTH CENTURIES

Especially as strengthened by the innovations of the Mughal emperor Akbar (r. 1556–1605), Persian language and culture diffused into key parts of society in India's cities, towns, and even villages.[3] After the Mughal dynasty entered India (starting in 1526) and sporadically expanded its power there, it adapted Iranian (especially Safavid imperial) culture and also built on and synthesized existing Deccani and Delhi sultanate Persianate and also Indic cultures into its distinctively Mughal Indo-Persian model. Increasingly, the Mughal court attracted into imperial service a range of Indians (both Indian Muslims and non-Muslims, including Rajput and other Hindus, as well as Jains and members of other Indian religious communities). Additionally, the flow of Persophone service elites from Iran (and Central Asia) into the Mughal Empire continued for two centuries.

Over time, the Mughal imperial court became the model for many subordinated but also independent Indian regional courts. Various elite and scribal communities also studied and adapted to its Indo-Persianate culture. Hence, in north, central, and even parts of south India, many official histories, high literature, and documents, including landholding and revenue records, were in the Persian language and script. Wide sectors of society used Persian terms and concepts in daily and official activities, appreciated and contributed to its literature, and displayed the associated Indo-Persianate etiquette and deportment.[4] Thus, as shown by Purnima Dhavan's chapter 5 in this volume, "Persianate clusters" developed within and around the Mughal Empire, where competitive expertise in Persian language and literature brought prestige and attracted people of various sociocultural origins.

Even after the Mughal Empire fragmented over the eighteenth and early nineteenth centuries, many regional successor states sought to perpetuate and/or revive various forms of its imperial and cultural Indo-Persian traditions. Rulers and scholar-officials in these states in various degrees valued Persian as their court, administrative, and high-cultural language, even if they also wrote and domestically spoke in "Hindustani" (Urdu, Deccani, Hindawi, or Hindi) or another regional language (within either the Indo-European or the Dravidian language families). Sharif Husain Qasemi argues that the early nineteenth century saw an unprecedented volume of Persian literary production, as the surviving Mughal successor courts sought to establish their cultural and political credentials through lavish (if anxious) patronage of Persian-language arts, especially the writing of histories about their dynasties and states, that referenced their connections with historic Mughal glory.[5] Further, these rulers, courtiers, and scholar-officials in part strongly supported these arts so as to resist British Anglicizing assertions.

Hence, even as many Indian rulers perforce submitted politically, and traditional service elites accepted employment under the British from the late eighteenth century on, many of these men still sought to instruct Britons in the established Indo-Persian modes of high-cultural etiquette and its related administrative techniques and technologies of rule. Inherent in their efforts was their conviction that Britons who became their students and who accepted Indo-Persianate high culture would better understand, appreciate, and govern Indians, including themselves. Some individual Britons also personally adopted key aspects of Indo-Persianate culture, including various British political residents at Indian courts, for example, Lt. Colonel David Ochterlony, the East India Company's political resident agent at the Mughal imperial court from 1803 to 1806 and 1818 to 1822.[6]

In contrast, many Britons in Britain and in India had long believed that gaining access to Persian instrumentally empowered them to master and control Indian peoples and polities, without necessarily accepting the inherent Indo-Persian culture. As Bernard Cohn puts it: "The British realized that in seventeenth-century India, Persian was the crucial language for them to learn. They approached Persian as a kind of functional language, a pragmatic vehicle of communication with Indian officials and rulers through which, in a denotative fashion, they could express their requests, queries, and thoughts, and through which they could get things done. To use Persian well required highly specialized forms of knowledge."[7] By the late eighteenth century, the East India Company largely recognized the value of Persian as the "language of command," although many British officials and officers simultaneously rejected the Indo-Persianate manners and morality of the old regime they were displacing.[8]

To advance the implementation of its policies, the new British colonial regime established state-supported institutions where Indians taught Persian (among other subjects) to arriving British officials. The Calcutta Madrasa (established in 1781) perpetuated many established traditions of Persian-based education. However,

FIGURE 12. Machine-minted Persian: East India Company coinage from the Soho Foundry, Birmingham, England, 1803. Photograph by Jon Augier. Museums Victoria, Melbourne, Australia.

reflecting growing British cultural assertions, at Fort William College (established in Calcutta in 1800), British professors took charge, with Indian teachers in subordinate roles as assistants (munshis) and tutors to incoming British officials. But these young British students customarily treated their Indian instructors as hirelings. Thus, "the teacher-taught relation with which the Indian teachers were familiar did not exist in the College of Fort William. It was a new relationship, that of *Sahibs* and *Munshis,* that of European officers and their servants."[9] Such policies at Fort William degraded Indian scholars, but they at least preserved Persian as a major subject, albeit under British curricular and pedagogic control. These "Orientalist" policies, however, themselves gradually gave way to even more powerful British cultural assertions of Anglicization (peaking with the Governor-General's Council's 1835 Minute on Education). Nevertheless, many Indian courtiers and scholar-officials who embodied Indo-Persianate culture continued to resist such Anglicizing pressures. A few traveled to England to create positions for themselves as expert Persian-language teachers. There, they found different conditions from colonial India, including the pedagogy they had to use, the meaning of Persian and Indo-Persian culture, and their own social lives.

From the early seventeenth century on, many Persian-speaking male visitors, travelers, and members of royal diplomatic and commercial missions from Persia and India, together with their servants, lived for considerable periods in London.[10] By the mid-nineteenth century, as many as forty thousand Indians alone had reached Britain.[11] Many of these men married or formed liaisons with British women, the Persophones among them presumably informally teaching Persian domestically or for profit. Their Indo-Persianate culture (in public most visibly expressed in their clothing) during this period carried an attractive oriental

exoticism for many (albeit not all) Britons, as many of these Indian visitors themselves noted, and occasionally used to their own advantage.

With the growth of British commercial and political assertions in India over
these centuries, increasing numbers of Britons demanded Persian-language training, sometimes from a personal or an abstract academic interest but more often to
empower themselves in India over Indians. However, interest in Persian remained
limited at universities such as Oxford until much later.[12] Consequently, some Britons
turned to private instruction in Persian under the direction of Asian teachers who
had traveled to Britain as part of their own larger effort to educate Britons in the
superior moral and literary values inherent in Persian and Persianate culture. For
instance, Mirza Sayyid I'tisam al-Din of Bengal went to Britain in 1766–68 as a
diplomat representing the Mughal emperor; while there he also taught Persian
privately.[13] Various other Indian teachers of Persian published advertisements in
London newspapers for British pupils to whom they could teach, for a fee, "the
true Court Persian Tongue, as also the Arabic and Hindostannee Languages, as
Pronounced in the Country," skills they believed a cultured Briton going to India
should desire.[14] By stressing their accurate pronunciation, unattainable by a native
English speaker, these Indians thus highlighted their own superiority. Most, but
not all, of such scholars going to England were Muslim. A Bengali Hindu by birth,
Goneshamdass, traveled to England and testified in English before Parliament in
1773 as an expert on Indian legal practices customary under the Mughal emperors
and other Muslim rulers.[15]

Most famously, Mirza Abu Talib Khan Isfahani (1752–1806) ventured from
Calcutta to England in 1799 and remained there for three years, famous in British
society as "the Persian Prince."[16] He was already prominent in north India for his
Persian-language books of history, poetry, and other literary forms. In Britain, he
taught Persian privately, intending that the study Persian would spread through
the country "as one candle lights a hundred."[17] Abu Talib recalled how he had saved
at least one eager pupil from ill-informed rival British "false teachers" who were
outrageously charging a guinea and a half for each useless ninety-minute lesson in
inaccurate Persian:

> an amiable young man, Mr. [George] Swinton . . . agreed that . . . he would attend me
> at *eight* o'clock in the morning. . . . Thanks be to God, that my efforts were crowned
> with success! and that he having escaped the instructions of *self-taught* masters, has
> acquired such a knowledge of the principles of the [Persian] language, as so cor-
> rect an idea of its idiom and pronunciation, that I have no doubt, after a few years'
> residence in India, he will attain to such a degree of excellence as has not yet been
> acquired by any other Englishman![18]

Thus, in Abu Talib's judgment (as expressed in Persian for his peers back in India),
Europeans who presumed inappropriately to claim expertise in Persian needed
to be humbled and his own expertise in Persian recognized. Abu Talib particularly singled out the prominent Persian grammar written by the famous (and

recently deceased) Sir William Jones (1746–94): "Whenever I was applied to by any [British] person for instruction in the Persian language who had previously studied [Jones's] grammar, I found it much more difficult to correct the bad pronunciation he had acquired, and the errors he had adopted, than it was to instruct a person who had never before seen the Persian alphabet. Such books are now so numerous in London, that, in a short time, it will be difficult to discriminate or separate them from works of real value."[19] Abu Talib graciously excused Jones for his immature efforts: "Far be it from me to depreciate the transcendent abilities and angelic character of Sir William Jones; but his Persian Grammar, having been written when he was a young man, and previous to his having acquired any experience in Hindoostan, is, in many places, very defective; and it is much to be regretted that his public avocations, and other studies, did not permit him to revise it, after he had been some years in India."[20]

While in England, Abu Talib himself wrote a Persian-language book and an English-language article about his experiences and his moral judgments of Britain.[21] Earlier, three other Indian teachers in Britain had also composed books in Persian about Britain for the edification of other Indians.[22] In all these books, the authors generally expressed their own Persianate-Islamic cultural superiority, criticizing Britain for its religious practices and the overly free treatment and behavior of British women. Visiting English libraries, these Asians were impressed by the vast, and growing, collections of books and manuscripts in them, especially those in Persian and Arabic, showing British respect for those languages. Abu Talib was astonished, as well as proud, that Oxford held some "ten thousand" books about Islamic sciences.[23]

One of Abu Talib's main reasons for venturing to Britain was to establish a government-sponsored Persian-language training institute (a madrasa, as he saw it) under his own direction in London or Oxford. It would have created a firm foundation in England for the knowledge of Persian, as well as for his own fame. Despite Abu Talib's reasoned advocacy, his plan met delay (partly due to the ongoing Napoleonic wars). To temporize, Lord Pelham, British secretary of state for the Foreign Department, requested that Abu Talib extend his stay in London for an additional sixteen months to give the government more time to consider his proposal. Finally, just before Abu Talib finally left England in June 1802, the government belatedly authorized him to create and direct such an institute, with a handsome annual salary (£600 plus expenses).[24] However, his letter of appointment letter did not reach his home in India until shortly after his death.

Overall, many Indian visitors to Britain used knowledge of Persian language and Indo-Persian culture to prove British moral inferiority. Yet, growing British military, political and technological assertions clearly threatened their self-confidence. In India, British cultural assertions and Indian resistance even more powerfully created conflicting understandings of Persian and Indo-Persian culture for whole classes of Indians.

THE INTIMATE MEANINGS OF PERSIAN FOR A NORTH INDIAN COURT AND PRINCE

In order to explore what the Persian language and Indo-Persian culture meant in personal terms, we can consider the admittedly unusual case of Col. David Ochterlony Dyce Sombre, MP, heir to the north Indian regional principality of Sardhana and an immigrant to Britain.[25] It is striking to find such an extensive, first-hand written record of the intimate feelings of someone from this period in India. In the last decade of Dyce Sombre's life, British courts convicted him of lunacy six times, and he died facing the seventh trial, but as with individuals studied in other chapters of this volume, his case nonetheless provides insight into larger cultural patterns among Britons and Asians in India and in Britain during this transitional period.

Asian-born but of mixed Indian and European cultural and biological ancestry, "Davey" (as David was known by his extended family) was raised by the notorious Farzana, Begum Sombre, also known as Begum Somru (ca. 1750–1836), at the court of the small (250-square-mile) princely state of Sardhana, located about thirty miles from the Mughal imperial capital of Shahjahanabad. This principality emerged in 1777, when Emperor Shah 'Alam II (r. 1759–1806) awarded it to a German-speaking Catholic mercenary, Walter Reinhardt (ca. 1720–78), whose nom de guerre was (for disputed reasons) Sombre, but whose Mughal imperial Persian titles were Zafaryab Khan, Muzaffar al-Dawla. Setting aside Reinhardt's legal wife and son, his slave mistress Farzana succeeded him in 1778 as Begum Sombre, independent ruler of Sardhana. During her fifty-eight-year rule, she created a multilingual, multicultural princely court, in which Persian was, however, the most prestigious of the many languages used by her courtiers, and Indo-Persian etiquette largely prevailed. Farzana had evidently been born Muslim, but she openly converted to Roman Catholicism after she took the throne of Sardhana. Hence, her identification with Persian and Indo-Persian culture were not religious, but these remained culturally powerful for her throughout her long reign.

Hence, Begum Sombre constantly nurtured and highly valued her relations with the Mughal imperial family, showing much deference and also providing much funding for them. She appreciated (and perhaps could read) Persian poetry, keeping a copy of the famous thirteenth-century Iranian poet Sa'di's works always by her bedside. Her diverse courtiers composed poetry in Persian, as well as Urdu and English, as did David himself. Her chief secretary, Munshi Lalla Gokul Chand, penned an extensive, eulogistic Persian-language poetic history of the Begum, entitled *Zib al-Tawarikh*.[26] This was not just the consumption of Persian literature, it was also the creation of new works in that tradition.

At the same time, she recognized the military and political dominance of the invading British. She pragmatically submitted her army, her state, and herself to them in 1803—at the time of their capture of nearby Shahjahanabad (that is, Delhi) and the incumbent Mughal emperor. Her principality was located in the shadow of

Meerut, which gradually became the major British military base in upper Gangetic north India. Hence, for most of her long career as ruler of Sardhana, she made persistent efforts to create and sustain a valued place in both Mughal Persianate and British Anglicized worlds.

Soon after the birth of her owner-lover's biological great-grandson in 1808, she took him as her heir, having no biological children of her own. His full name, David Ochterlony Dyce Sombre, reflected his hybrid biological and cultural identity: his foster-mother named him after her "brother," Delhi Resident David Ochterlony; his half-Indian, half-Scots biological father's surname was Dyce; and Sombre was the adopted name of both the Begum and his biological maternal great-grandfather. In one system of Western biological cultural terms, he was half Indian in "blood"; in another Western cultural system, he was "Anglo-Indian," "Indo-Briton," and/or "Eurasian"; in yet another, more binary Western system, he was "black."

While David spoke Hindustani, and had a limited Anglophone education with Protestant and Catholic clergymen in Sardhana (learning Latin from the latter), Persian was clearly the language he most highly and intimately valued. His strong affective relationship with Persian is clear from his private diary (which he kept for most of his life) and also from how he used Persian in his most personal relationships with various men and women, both in India and then in Britain. In some contexts—for example, when attending an Indian nautch (*nach*) dance performance—David wore Indo-Persian dress, but in others wore British clothing.

In many aspects of his life, he struggled (often in vain) to ingratiate himself with the domineering British, first in India and later in Britain. In his youth, he learned to gain access to the British officers in nearby Meerut by losing heavily in gambling. But he also led Britons into the world of Indo-Persianate nautch performances, strongly associated with cultured courtesans, where he was the expert connoisseur and his British guests the often awkward neophytes. Indeed, many of David's most sympathetic companions were other young elite men with similarly mixed Indian-European biological and cultural heritage.

David transgressed boundaries of genre and language in his diary. Many volumes of it were destroyed during his later legal struggles, but parts have survived: the earliest set starting with his twenty-fifth birthday (December 18, 1833) and ending with his arrival in London (June 7, 1838), plus one later twelve-month period (1847–48).[27] For the last of these, for example, he used a printed, bound English-language and style daybook, with a lined half-page for each day. But he began in August, proceeding to the end of that calendar year, and then continued from the front of the book, even though this made his notations a calendar year behind the printed date, and uncoordinated with the days of the week, on that page. Furthermore, he often wrote across, rather than within, the printed blank spaces.

David wrote most of his diary in English, but he reverted to Persian for his most intimate thoughts and record of his deeds and thoughts, usually of a poetic or erotic nature. He evidently associated Persian with both elegance and sexuality, and he apparently also intended these remarks to be unintelligible to English readers. On occasion, in an otherwise English paragraph, he transcribed the names of British men or women into Persian characters, especially when he thought of them in sexual terms. He also seems to have thought in Persian about Indians, and his transliterations of many Muslim names omit unmarked vowels as Persian script does (e.g., writing "Mhmd" for "Muhammad").

He also used mastery of Persian language and culture to assess the status of various elite Indians and Europeans, relative to himself. Repeatedly, David demonstrated, at least to himself, his superiority over them based on their lesser expertise in Persian. Given his ambivalent and hybrid background and social and political status, his psychological need for self-esteem is understandable.[28] Nonetheless, his use of expertise in Persian as the measure of a person's true worth is significant, and characteristic of an entire class of his contemporary Indian elites in India and then in Britain.

A few brief examples from India in David's private diary illustrate the role of Persian language and culture as a key element in his personal relations. The Sardhana court's relationship to the Mughal imperial family was complex. Begum Sombre was far wealthier than many of the Mughal imperial princes. But she (and they) believed that the imperial family stood far higher than her in protocol and social standing. Thus, unsurprisingly, David tried to convince himself that he was actually superior to the Mughal princes he encountered. He privately ridiculed the imperial prince Mirza Muhammad Shah as "very foolish," for example, because Mirza lacked an education beyond the Quran and Sa'di's *Gulistan* and did not read the *Jam-i Jahan Numa,* a Persian weekly newspaper from Calcutta, as David regularly did.[29]

Persian was also David's standard for assessment of both Europeans and Indians. For a time, he considered marrying one of the half-Indian daughters of the French Catholic mercenary General Jean-François Allard (1785–1839), a cavalry officer under Napoleon who, after Waterloo, served for many lucrative years under Maharaja Ranjit Singh (1780–1839), ruler of the Punjab. In 1834, on Allard's way back to France, he stayed at the Begum's court, France's King Louis-Philippe having delegated the Begum to invest Allard with the Légion d'honneur on his behalf (the French and Sardhana monarchs earlier having exchanged correspondence and portraits of themselves).[30] David felt a special affinity for Allard, noting, "Monsr Allard . . . talks Persian pretty well for a foreigner."[31] But he did not end up marrying either of Allard's daughters.

As Begum Sombre aged, she sought an heir for her vast fortune of some five million rupees (approximately £500,000 then; between £3 and £54 million today, depending on the basis of calculation).[32] On December 16, 1831, just two days before David's twenty-third birthday, the Begum signed her final will (*hibbanama,* with Persian and English versions), bequeathing him almost everything she owned, including her treasury and her properties in Sardhana and elsewhere. She also made him colonel-commander of her small army and had Pope Gregory XVI knight him in the Pontifical Order of Christ.

Immediately upon her death in 1836, however, the British annexed Sardhana, making David homeless. Various legal cases, including ones by his own biological father, were brought against David, seeking possession of various parts of his inheritance. Indeed, the final lawsuit over this estate was not settled until more than two decades after his death.

On his part, David refused to live in his lost Sardhana, instead traveling across north India, with thoughts of emigrating to Britain. Unrealistically, he considered marrying the young Queen Victoria (1819–1901). As a departing warning, a neighboring British-Indian ruler, Colonel James Skinner (1778–1841), paternalistically composed a poem in Persian to persuade David not to venture to England, correctly warning that he was unprepared for what he would encounter there.[33]

As David traveled down the Ganges River, he met other culturally Indo-Persianate rulers, in various stages of suppression or exile at British hands. In Lucknow, he observed the self-proclaimed Padshah (emperor) Nasir al-Din Haydar (r. 1827–37), who still ruled the large Indian state of Awadh. David noted that Nasir also wore both European (sometimes European women's) clothing and elaborate Indo-Persianate garments. David judged Sardhana's Indo-Persianate (and Anglicized) architecture and court culture superior to Lucknow's. Early in January 1837, David visited the newly completed Palladian-style palace of Humayun Jah, Mubarak 'Ali Khan Bahadur (r. 1824–38), the pensioned Nawab of Bengal, in Murshidabad. There, David met and conversed comfortably in Persian with the Nawab's chief eunuch and his chief astrologer, again judging that language the most appropriate and congenial medium. Here, too, David in his diary lauded Sardhana's cultural superiority.

Later that month, he entered Calcutta, the British imperial capital of India. There, he met both with Europeans (some of whom made him aware for the first time that he was a "black") and also Indians of a range of social classes, from sex workers through members of the Bengal Renaissance. One of his supporters among the British establishment was Henry Thoby Prinsep (1792–1878), longtime Persian secretary to the government (in charge of the Company's political relations with Indian states that used Persian as the language of diplomacy), a published historian, and also an acting member of the Governor-General's Council. They had met briefly in Shahjahanabad six years earlier. Prinsep invited David to his office (not his home). But in this case, Prinsep's interest in Persian was mostly professional; his household was Anglo-Indian in style, and they evidently conversed in English.

David's attitudes toward Calcutta's elite Indians were complex; they treated one another with both reserve and sympathy. Governor-General Sir George Eden's unmarried sisters Emily and Fanny (Frances) invited David, other Indian royalty and elite men, and high-status European men and women, to their parties. David considered his own mastery of sophisticated Persian as the criterion for rating elite Indians. He noted, in the Eden sisters' drawing room. "a Baboo, who pretends to be, I am told, a very clever man. I introduced myself to him, and talked to him in Persian, wh [sic] he talks pretty fair."³⁴

Wherever he travelled, David always carried his library of Persian and Urdu books. He endeared himself to Dr. L. Burlini, librarian of the Asiatic Society of Bengal, by donating Begum Sombre's copy of Saʿdi's poetic *diwan*, "always kept by H. H.'s [her highness's] bedside," and a rare early manuscript of that poet's *Gulistan*.³⁵

After a traumatic stay in the British imperial capital of Calcutta (1837–38, interrupted by a short trip to China), David ventured to Britain. Amid the confined passenger community aboard ship, David experienced social and cultural alienation. He salaciously detailed in his diary a rich social and sexual world he believed was rampant among the other paying passengers (all Europeans), using Persian character transcriptions of the names of the parties involved. He also devoted himself to reading Persian poetry, as well as solving European mathematical puzzles. When he disembarked in Britain, he faced complex social conflicts, many of them centering around the ambivalent meanings there of Persian and Indo-Persianate culture, and his personal identification by others and by himself with these.

BEING PERSOPHONE IN EARLY NINETEENTH-
CENTURY BRITAIN

While in Britain, David continued to demonstrate his affinity with Persian and Indo-Persian culture, using it both to reassure himself of his own often challenged social status and self-worth and also in his personal relationships with others. He frequently directed his Sardhana correspondents to write him in Persian—to which he remained committed, in so doing both evoking his earlier life in India and concealing the contents of these letters from his Anglophone associates and quarrelsome relatives.³⁶ He proposed in 1839 bringing to Europe, as his scribe and private tutor, a scholar of Persian, Kullender Buksh "Meanjee," whom he had known in India: "If he has no better employment, perhaps he would not mind coming to this country. I would allow him 15 rupees a month for his trouble, & 5 shillings a day, & finding a lodging for him here. I want his assistance in some work I am doing for my amusement. . . . Of course, I would pay for his passage out and back again, unless he took employment in England, in case I do want him to remain beyond a year . . . & then he need not be afraid of losing his caste."³⁷ This plan never worked out.

While Persian conveyed intimate parts of David's identity, it also occasionally erupted antisocially into the public sphere. He had known an Italian general, Jean César Baptiste, Comte Ventura de Mandy (1794–1858), in Sardhana, and they met again socially in Europe. But they eventually quarreled bitterly. In one altercation in Paris, David verbally assaulted Ventura in the presence of his daughter using (according to Ventura) "every abusive term that the English, French, Persian, or Hindustanee language can furnish; in fact he ransacked the vocabularies of the four languages for filthy and disgraceful epithets."[38]

David also socialized with many of the thousands of Asians then living in Britain, including with other Indian princes, or would-be princes. These included Nawwab Iqbal al-Dawla Bahadur, a claimant to the throne of Awadh, recently made vacant by the death of his cousin, Nawwab Nasir al-Din Haydar. This prince, exactly Dyce Sombre's own age, had entered British high society just before him, in 1837, remaining in Britain for nearly two years. At Iqbal al-Dawla's lavish apartments near Regent's Park, he and Dyce Sombre repeatedly dined together.[39] Their conversations were presumably in Persian, as would be appropriate for the etiquette their respective courts. In addition to savoring all that London offered, Iqbal al-Dawla futilely lobbied the British government and East India Company for his enthronement.

David also met socially with Mirza Ibrahim, an Iranian who was currently professor of Persian at the East India Company's college for civilian officials at Haileybury (near Hertford, established 1806).[40] Mirza Ibrahim was the fifth in a series of Indian and Iranian teachers between 1806–44 holding full-time, permanent, and well-paid appointments in the faculty at Haileybury and the East India Company's military seminary at Addiscombe (in Croydon, south of London, established 1809). Experts in Persian and Hindustani languages and literatures, they provided formative language training to thousands of young Britons bound for colonial rule over India for nearly four decades. They also profitably wrote and translated texts on "Oriental" subjects, generating British-style grammars and other teaching aids. Four took European wives or longtime mistresses (generally of lower social status than themselves), and several had children there, thus demonstrating how their male gender and professional class standing overcame their difference by "race" in English metropolitan society at the time. The staffing of the Oriental language departments of these two colleges in England was contested from the outset, since British scholars and veterans of the East India Company's service in India argued that they had the moral right to be handsomely employed to teach these languages. Yet even they recognized that only Asians could provide "that idiomatical accuracy (which never can be attained by any foreigner) so essential to such works."[41]

For their part, these Asian faculty members regarded themselves as doing their British students a service by teaching them the Persian language and modelling Persian culture for them. They generally enjoyed far superior salaries to what they would have received teaching languages in Asia, took positions of authority over their British students, and also held the status of scholar, professional, and gentleman in English society. Nonetheless, they taught in institutions designed and run by Britons, using British codifications and pedagogy, to British students who were preparing to administer and militarily expand a colonial state ruling large parts of India. Nor was Persian-language instruction very much valued by the colleges, most British faculty, or most British students. Like that of these professional teachers of Persian at the Company's Colleges, Dyce Sombre's Indo-Persianate identity proved to be both one of his most attractive features to some Britons, but also a source of his ultimate alienation from European society.

SANE IF ORIENTAL, LUNATIC IF EUROPEAN

In Europe during the last thirteen years of his life, David faced conflicting racial, gendered, and other cultural forces. Many Britons and other Europeans highlighted his putative biological race, which they increasingly associated with all "Orientals." He was publicly tagged by diverse European and American newspapers, journals, and other publications as "Black," "a half-washed Blackamoor," "Copper-coloured," "Dark," "Indian," "mixed breed," "Negro," "Orientalist," "Othello," "sable," "Sambo," and a "tawny alien." French newspapers identified him as "excessivement brun" and "le prince noir."[42]

David's vast wealth and oriental exoticism inevitably attracted many, including some British aristocrats, and within two months of his arrival in London, he had become engaged to Mary Anne Jervis (1812–93), the twenty-seven-year-old youngest daughter of the second viscount St. Vincent. Said to be a highly accomplished composer and singer who had performed at Covent Garden (as a gracious amateur, of course, not as a professional), she was also widely rumored to be the mistress of the duke of Wellington (1769–1852). To woo Mary Anne, David taught her loving phrases in Persian, his language of intimacy, and recited what he said was an "Indian Love Song." Despite her Low Church Anglican family and his Roman Catholicism, they married after a tumultuous, two-year-long engagement. David hoped to gain stature and legitimacy with British society generally from her family and by getting himself elected in 1841 to the House of Commons (from Sudbury in Suffolk)—the first-ever Asian and second nonwhite British MP. After he became estranged from his wife, she futilely tried to win him back by writing him notes including what she recalled as the Persian poetry he had taught her, saying: "You see, tho' I am obliged to write it in an English way, that I have not quite forgot what taught me, Boht hub, Persian hub; you must say Wah, Wah."[43]

In fact, he proved unable to sustain most of his relationships with British society. Nearly two years after Dyce Sombre's election, Parliament expelled him for the blatant corruption of his electors. Then his wife's family had him arrested, confined, and convicted of lunacy. Over the next decade until his death, he faced six retrials for lunacy which largely revolved around his Indo-Persianate cultural and racial identity. On one side, his defenders tried to excuse his obsessions as natural in a "black man" raised in Oriental culture, who could never really become morally British or European. Since a major charge against him was his demanding that his wife not go out in public, this defense asserted that all Asians are obsessed with their womenfolk observing purdah, making him sane if he was Asian. However, Dyce Sombre himself consistently and heatedly rejected this public identification of him as non-European, even though it might have led to his legal reclassification as sane. Yet privately he clearly continued to value and identify with Persianate culture. For their part, his British accusers highlighted his Anglophone education in court, saying no man of European culture would act as he had done toward British women, thus making him a lunatic.

In these multiple, highly contested retrials of Dyce Sombre, his identity was so complex that most of the presiding judges could not come to a definitive judgment. Hence, his initial conviction as a lunatic was never overturned. We should not, however, overlook the unspoken dimensions of these prolonged and repeated court cases, where a rich but isolated nonwhite man faced his powerful, aristocratic English in-laws during a period when the Victorian bourgeois values of the husband's responsibility for protecting his wife and family fortune were rising and elite male autonomy (even for white British men) being questioned. Significantly, when Dyce Sombre fled confinement, escaping to continental Europe, the courts and the general public judged his behavior sane and well within the sociocultural bounds for an elite male, especially an Oriental one.

Over the decades that followed his early death in 1851 (as his seventh trial for lunacy commenced), his widow continued to draw upon the prestige of Indo-Persian culture (supported by much of his vast wealth, which she had won after protracted legal battles). She occasionally dressed in high society in the Indo-Persianate garments he had given her and was known in her elite social circles as "the Begum." Hence, for some elite Britons at least, Indo-Persianate culture (when performed by an aristocratic white woman) appeared safely and exotically attractive.

CONCLUSIONS

Through the particular (and perhaps peculiar) case of David Ochterlony Dyce Sombre, this chapter has explored some of the conflicting meanings of the Persian language and Indo-Persian culture in India and Britain during a period of increasing Anglophone dominance globally. Especially under the Mughal dynasty, the frontier of Persian and the development of imperial Indo-Persian culture had expanded across most of India. But even during the fragmentation of the Mughal Empire, the cultural power of this language and culture persisted, even strengthened, in the face of British imperialism and Anglicization. Many (but not all) Britons in India and in Britain regarded Persian as having effective utility, usually without identifying themselves with Indo-Persian culture. But for many Indians, Persian language and culture carried retained their affective power. Both in India and in Britain, some Indians attempted to convey this culture to Britons for their edification and moral improvement.

Culturally and ethnically mixed, David Dyce Sombre identified deeply with Persian during this crucial transitional period, using Persian language and Persianate culture as a measure of his own worth and that of others both in India and in Britain. But it was his very identification with Indo-Persian culture—by himself and by Britons—that led to his trials for lunacy, incarceration, and the confiscation of his vast wealth, sadly illuminating some of contested aspects of Persian learning and its social frontiers that this volume as a whole explores.

NOTES

1. Indigenous Indian linguistic and other cultural elements were also present and respected even at the Mughal imperial court and, though dominant, Indo-Persianate values were not hegemonic. See Audrey Truschke, *Culture of Encounters: Sanskrit at the Mughal Court* (New York: Columbia University Press, 2016). Brian Spooner's Epilogue to this volume explores what the literary tradition of classical Persian in particular has meant personally to native and non-native speakers in today's world.

2. Scholarship on these issues in the broadest sense for India and Britain is too voluminous to be cited here. However, studies of Indians and other Asians in eighteenth- and early nineteenth-century Europe include Antoinette Burton, *At the Heart of the Empire: Indians and the Colonial Encounter in Late-Victorian Britain* (Berkeley: University of California Press, 1998); Gulfishan Khan, *Indian Muslim Perceptions of the West during the Eighteenth Century* (Karachi: Oxford University Press, 1998); Shompa Lahiri, *Indians in Britain: Anglo-Indian Encounters, Race and Identity,1880–1930* (London: Frank Cass, 2000), Satadru Sen, *Migrant Races: Empire, Identity, and K. S. Ranjitsinhji* (Manchester: Manchester University Press, 2004); Rozina Visram, *Asians in Britain: 400 Years of History* (London: Pluto, 2002); and *Ayahs, Lascars and Princes: Indians in Britain, 1700–1947* (London: Pluto, 1984), plus the works cited below.

3. In addition to Thibault d'Hubert's chapter 2 and Purnima Dhavan's chapter 5 in this volume, see Muzaffar Alam, *The Languages of Political Islam: India, 1200–1800* (Chicago: University of Chicago Press, 2004). For the "curve" of the roles and genres of Persian during other transitions in Asia, which was similar and also differed in fascinating ways in each region, see Devin DeWeese's chapter 4 and Marc Toutant's chapter 10 in this volume.

4. N. S. Gorekar, "Persian Impact on Indian life," *Journal of the Asiatic Society of Bombay* 70 (1995):59–70. See also Michael H. Fisher, *A Short History of the Mughal Empire* (London: I. B. Tauris, 2015).

5. Sharif Husain Qasemi, "Persian Chronicles in the Nineteenth Century," in *The Making of Indo-Persian Culture: Indian and French Studies,* ed. Muzaffar Alam, Françoise Nalini Delvoye, and Marc Gaborieau (New Delhi: Manohar, 2000), 407–16.

6. Although born in Massachusetts, Lt. Colonel Ochterlony (1758–1825) served in India from age nineteen on.

7. Bernard S. Cohn, *Colonialism and Its Forms of Knowledge* (Princeton, NJ: Princeton University Press, 1996), p. 18.

8. For comparative examples of imperial states using Persian instrumentally, see Murat Umut Inan's chapter 1, Graeme Ford's chapter 3, and David Brophy's chapter 6 in this volume.

9. Sisir Kumar Das, *Sahibs and Munshis* (Calcutta: Orion, 1978), 108. Emphasis in original.

10. See Nile Green, *Terrains of Exchange: Religious Economies of Global Islam* (New York: Oxford University Press, 2015), and Mohamad Tavakoli-Targhi, *Refashioning Iran: Orientalism, Occidentalism and Historiography* (New York: Palgrave Macmillan, 2001, 2014).

11. See Michael H. Fisher, *Counterflows to Colonialism: Indian Travellers and Settlers in Britain, 1600–1857* (Delhi: Permanent Black, 2004).

12. Green, *Terrains*.

13. See Nile Green, *The Love of Strangers: What Six Muslim Students Learned in Jane Austen's London* (Princeton, NJ: Princeton University Press, 2015), 87–88, 140, and *Shigarf-nama-i Wilayat: Safarnama-i Mirza I'tisam al-Din ba Wilayat Englis, 1765-1766*, critical edition, ed. Mohamad Tavakoli-Targhi (Toronto: Iran Nameh Books, 2016).

14. E.g., *Public Advertiser*, November 5, 1777; *European Magazine* 39 (January–June 1801): 7–8; Home Political Consultation, May 15, 1797, no. 50, Home Miscellaneous Series, vol. 559, fols. 297–301, 405, National Archives of India.

15. *House of Commons Sessional Papers of the Eighteenth Century*, ed. Sheila Lambert, 147 vols. (Wilmington, DE: Scholarly Resources, 1975), 135: 546–49, 138: 124; *Memoirs of Sir Elijah Impey* (London, 1846), 237.

16. See Michael H. Fisher, "Representing 'His' Women: Mirza Abu Talib Khan's 1801 'Vindication of the Liberties of Asiatic Women,'" in *Indian Economic and Social History Review* 37, 2 (2000): 215–37.

17. Mirza Abu Talib Khan, *Masir Talibi fi Bilad Afranji*, Persian reprint of British Library, Add 8145–7 [my pagination hereinafter is from the Persian reprint edited and published by Husayn Khadiv-Jam, Tehran, 1983], 107–8, 175.

18. Mirza Abu Taleb Khan, *Travels of Mirza Abu Taleb Khan in Asia, Africa, and Europe during the Years 1799, 1800, 1801, 1802, and 1803*, trans. Charles Stewart, 3 vols., 2nd ed. (n.p.: Longmans, 1814), 101; see also 92. Emphasis in original.

19. Ibid., 173–74; *Morning Chronicle*, March 29, 1800, 4a; *European Magazine and London Review*, 43 (January–June 1803): 3;

20. Khan, *Travels*, 173–74.

21. Mir Muhammad Husain, Risala-yi Ahwal-i Mulk-i Farang, MS R.IV-51, K.R. Cama Oriental Research Library, Bombay, and Maulana Azad Library, Aligarh; Munshi Isma'il, Tarikh-i Jadid, in Simon Digby's private collection, discussed by him in "An Eighteenth Century Narrative of a Journey from Bengal to England: Munshi Ismail's New History," in *Urdu and Muslim South Asia: Studies in Honour of Ralph Russell*, ed. Christopher Shackle (London: School of Oriental and African Studies, University of London, 1989), 49–65; Mirza I'tisam al-Din, *Shigarf Nama-i Walayat*, translated into English and Urdu and published by James Edward Alexander and Munshi Shamsher Khan (London: Parbury, Allen, 1827). See also Tavakoli-Targhi, *Refashioning*, and Fisher, "Representing."

22. See Fisher, *Counterflows*.

23. Mirza Abu Talib Kahn, *Masir Talibi fi Bilad Afranji*, 116.

24. Minutes of the Court of Directors, February 10, 1801, fol. 1015, British Library [hereinafter BL]; Abu Talib to Pelham, Persian letter with translation, August 28, 1803, Add 33112, Pelham Papers, fols. 138–39, BL.

25. For a full biography, see Michael H. Fisher, *The Inordinately Strange Life of Dyce Sombre* (New York: Oxford University Press, 2013).

26. "Zeb al-Tawarikh," ADD 25,830, BL; *History of Zeb-ul-Nissa: The Begum Samru of Sardhana*, ed. Nicholas Shreeve (Crossbush, West Sussex, England: Bookwright, 1994).

27. These survived only due to his virtually all-encompassing legal entanglements later in life. *The Times* (London), March 7, 1857, 11. PROB 37/1700, National Archives of the United Kingdom [hereinafter PRO] and L/L/63–65, BL [hereinafter Dyce Sombre, Diary].

28. There is a large literature about "hyphenisation" and "hybridity" that seeks to analyze ambivalent identities like Dyce Sombre's. See, e.g., Pawan Dhingra, *Managing Multicultural Lives: Asian American Professionals and the Challenge of Multiple Identities* (Stanford, CA: Stanford University Press, 2001), and Homi Bhabha, *The Location of Culture* (New York: Routledge, 1994). A full psychological or somatic analysis of Dyce Sombre is beyond the scope of this paper. See Ronald Pies, Michael H. Fisher, and C.V. Haldipur "The Mysterious Illness of Dyce Sombre," *Innovations in Clinical Neuroscience* 9, 3 (March 2012): 16–8.

29. Dyce Sombre, Diary , December 24–31, 1833. He had a similar view of other Mughal princes:

ibid., February 17, November 25–28, and December 23–27, 1834; March 17, 1835.

30. Louis Philippe, Emperor of the French to Most Illustrious, Most Excellent and Most Magnificent Simrou Begum, Princess of Sardana, October 27, 1835, L/L/64 (438); PROB 37/1700, PRO.

31. Dyce Sombre, Diary, September 39, 1834.

32. "Measuring Worth," www.measuringworth.com/ppoweruk.

33. H. G. Keene, "Sardhana: The Seat of the Sombres," *Calcutta Review* 70 (1880): 458; V. C. P. Hodson, *List of the Officers of the Bengal Army,* 4 vols. (London: Constable, 1927–47), 4: 579.

34. Dyce Sombre, Diary, February 7, 1837.

35. Ibid., February 13 and March 6, 1837.

36. Dyce Sombre to Peter Solaroli, December 27, 1841, in *Mary Anne Dyce Sombre, Dyce Sombre against Troup, Solaroli (Intervening) and Prinsep and the Hon. East India Company (also Intervening) in the Goods of David Ochterlony Dyce Sombre, Esq., Deceased, in the Prerogative Court of Canterbury,* 2 vols. (London: Seyfand 1852) [hereinafter *DSAT*], 1: 868–69.

37. Dyce Sombre to Peter Solaroli, June 2, 1839, and May 1, 1841, *DSAT,*1: 867–68; Dyce Sombre to Antonio Reghellini, May 1, 1841, and December 30, 1842, PROB 37/1700, PRO.

38. Comte Ventura deposition, October 22, 1853, *DSAT,* 2: 472–79; John Warwick, affidavit, November 18, 1846, in David Ochterlony Dyce Sombre, *In Lunacy: In the Matter of David Ochterlony Dyce Sombre, a Person Found to Be of Unsound Mind* (London: Hansard, 1851), 93–98.

39. George Sigmond, depositions, July 28, 1851, April 6, 1852, *DSAT,* 1: 68–72, 686. See also Fisher, *Counterflows,* chaps. 7–10.

40. Dyce Sombre to Peter Solaroli, June 2, 1839, *DSAT,* 1: 867. For a study of all five of these faculty members, see Michael H. Fisher, "Teaching Persian as an Imperial Language in India and in England during the Late 18th and Early 19th Centuries," in *Literacy in the Persianate World: Writing and the Social Order,* ed. Brian Spooner and William L. Hanaway (Philadelphia: University of Pennsylvania Museum of Archaeology and Anthropology, 2012), 328–58.

41. Jonathan Scott, *Observations on the Oriental Department of the Hon. Company's East India College, at Hertford* (Hertford: The Author, 1806), 10.

42. E.g., G. Bobson, "Letter to T. Smith," *Blackwood's Edinburgh Magazine* 59, 367 (May 1846): 534–42; *Agra Ukhbar,* August 14, 1841, reproduced in *Friend of India,* September 2, 1841; *Satirist* (England) , March 10, 1849; *Saturday Evening Post* (U.S.), September 29, 1860; *The Diary of Philipp von Neumann, 1819 to 1850,* 2 vols., ed. and trans. E. Beresford Chancellor (Boston: Houghton Mifflin, 1928), 2: 164–65; *Le Siècle: Journal politique, littéraire et d'économie sociale* (France), March 21, 1844.

43. Mrs Dyce Sombre to David Dyce Sombre, September 28, November 3, and October 16, 21, and 24, 1843; January 8, 1844, *DSAT,* 2: 276, 281–85.

10

De-Persifying Court Culture

The Khanate of Khiva's Translation Program

Marc Toutant

Despite the expansion of Turkish-speaking populations and the efforts of several Turko-Mongol dynasties to promote the use of Chaghatai Turkish after the thir-teenth-century era of the Mongol Empire, Persian remained a favored language all over Central Asia in chanceries and belles-lettres till as late as the nineteenth century.[1] Only a small proportion of the literature created in Central Asia was in Chaghatai Turkish (hereafter simply called Turkish), and Persian was the ma-jor medium of learned expression in all parts of the region, as Devin DeWeese's chapter 4 in this volume reminds us. And as Alfrid Bustanov's chapter 7 shows, even in distant Tatar villages of the Russian Empire, where there were no native speakers of Persian, the classics of Persian ethical literature were widely copied in local madrasas, where some students even tried to compose their own literary works in Persian.

Nevertheless, the status of Persian as lingua franca did not remain unchal-lenged in Central Asia. Over the course of the fifteenth century, cultural patronage under the Timurid rulers brought about the composition of numerous Turkish texts in diverse fields of learning. At the court of the last great Timurid ruler, Husayn Bayqara (r. 1469–70, 1470–1506), one of the most important corpora of Central Asian Turkish literature was written by Mir 'Ali Shir Nawa'i (1441–1501). Albeit largely based on Persian models, the works of Nawa'i can be regarded as an attempt to forge a culture that was specific to his Turkophone audience. It was also the most significant endeavor to challenge the supremacy of Persian in Central Asia.[2] Yet after the collapse of the Timurids, Persian recovered and indeed con-siderably strengthened its position in the literary field. Being of recent nomadic origin, successive new rulers attached importance to their public image; that is, to their complete conformity with the existing artistic and cultural canon, which expressed itself in Persianate models.

It was therefore not until the nineteenth century that the situation began to change. The three new Uzbek dynasties that emerged in the eighteenth century—

namely, the Qongrats (1717–1920) in Khiva, the Manghits (1753–1920) in Bukhara, and the Mings (1710–1876) in Khoqand—displayed a new interest in the Turkish language. That interest was most pronounced in Khwarazm, a large oasis region on the Amu Darya River delta in western Central Asia where an extensive translation program was sponsored by the Qongrat dynasty, a Turkified branch of a Mongolian tribe. Consequently, the Khiva khanate's patronage of Turkish letters during the nineteenth century produced one of the largest bodies of literary materials in Central Asian Turkish.

Their translation program has been the subject of prior research, albeit mostly by Russian and Uzbek scholars.[3] Among the latter, Najmiddin Komilov investigated the way Turkish translations were crafted from a stylistic point of view.[4] Then, more recently, subsequent studies tried to contextualize the translations by placing them in their broader cultural environment and historical context.[5] Building on these important contributions to understanding this turning point in the history of the Persianate world, this chapter, for its part, focuses on the significance of a policy that led to the replacement of a cosmopolitan language on a political and cultural level by a vernacular language. In other words, taking into consideration the new political and intellectual demands of the eighteenth and nineteenth centuries in what was one of the most Turkified of Persographic regions, the main contribution of this chapter lies in reconsidering the meaning of the major shift that brought to an end Persian as Central Asia's main language of the arts and sciences.

PERSOGRAPHIA IN THE KHANATE OF KHIVA DURING THE NINETEENTH CENTURY

It is still difficult to give an accurate picture of Persographia, or the use of written Persian, in the khanate of Khiva during the nineteenth century. The relationship between Persian and Turkish was more balanced in Khiva than in Bukhara and Kokand. Of the three precolonial Central Asian states, Khiva was the most Turkic. Khwarazm underwent the process of Turkification earlier than the other agricultural regions of Central Asia, presumably between the eleventh and thirteenth centuries. A few centuries later, while the khanate was ruled by Turkish-speaking Uzbeks who were former members of the Qypchaq tribal federation, Abu al-Ghazi Bahadur Khan (r. 1603–63) supported the use of Turkish by himself writing two historical works in this language, the *Shajara-yi Tarakima* (Genealogy of the Turkmens) and the *Shajara-yi Turk wa Mughul* (Genealogy of the Turks and Mongols).[6] Khiva was actually the only one of the three khanates where the use of Turkish had been increasing since the sixteenth century.

Whereas the Qongrats were descended from these Uzbek nomadic tribes, there was another population, known as Sarts, that belonged to older settled groups. In Khiva in the nineteenth century, like everywhere in Central Asia, the term "Sart" in Khiva was used to denote urbanized merchant-elites of various pedigrees. They even held important positions in the khanate's civil administration, for we know that a Sart vizier (*mehter*) was executed in 1857.[7] Yet, it is still hard to identify all the characteristics that distinguished Sarts from Uzbeks. According to the Anglo-Hungarian explorer Ármin Vámbéry (1832–1913), who travelled across the region between 1862 and 1864, the idiom spoken by Sarts at that time was a variety of Turkish that differed from the Uzbek spoken by the Qongrats.[8] A century later, the scholar Yuri Bregel identified the Sarts as Turkicized descendants of the older indigenous Iranian population, suggesting that they would have had an interest in the preservation of Persian at a time when Turkish became the main administrative language in the late 1850s. Until this date, for instance, numerous deeds of sale for real estate in the southern districts inhabited by Sarts were written in Persian. When they began to write such deeds only in Turkish, Bregel noticed that numerous annotations were still made in Persian by the secretaries (*diwan*s) who kept the record books. Bregel accordingly concluded that these secretaries were probably of Sart origin, and that, even though the Sarts were not native speakers of an Iranian language, Persian remained a convenient written language for them.[9] Unfortunately, we do not know whether Sarts perceived themselves as heirs of a population of Iranian origin, for we lack conclusive evidence that could support such claim.[10] Given the current state of knowledge it is therefore difficult to suggest that Sarts were in some way as the last defenders of Persographia, especially against Uzbeks who favored the adoption of Turkish. What we do know is that until Turkish became the main administrative language, Persian was still used by jurists to produce legal documents. A document kept in one of the present-day manuscript libraries of the region reveals, for example, that in 1799–1800, an endowment document (*waqfiya*) issued by a member of the dynasty was written in Persian.[11] Persian was therefore used for notarial output related to Shari'a, as well as for correspondence with pastoral nomads such as the Turkmens.[12]

As far as belletristic literature is concerned, sources of various types show that Persian remained a major medium of cultural expression among the Turkish-speaking Uzbek elite. Some of the khans seem to have been well versed in Persian poetry. For example, the famous poet and historiographer Muhammad Riza Agahi (1809–74) wrote of Muhammad Rahim Quli (r. 1842–46) that "he knew all the difficult rules of writing poetry, knew by heart the dates and stories of all the men of past generations from the beginning of the world till our time, and in royal assemblies could easily interpret any difficult verse that puzzled the men of learning."[13] Moreover, at the beginning of the twentieth century, the library of Sayyid Isfandiyar Khan (r. 1910–18) boasted no fewer than eighteen manuscripts of the works of the Persian poet Jami (d. 1492) as well as three of the Indo-Persian poet Bidil (d. 1720).[14] Several copies of the quatrains (*ruba'iyat*) of 'Umar Khayyam (d. 1131) were also produced in Khiva during the nineteenth century.[15] At the royal court, even such members of the Turkish-speaking literati as Munis (1778–1829), his nephew Agahi, Kamil Khwarazmi (1825–99), and the renowned vizier and poet Ahmad Tabibi (1868–1910), wrote some of their works in Persian.[16] Anthologies of poems (*bayaz*) that were composed for the khan or high officials also included pieces written either in Persian or Turkish. Among one hundred and forty-six *bayaz* from Khiva kept at the Al-Beruni Institute for Oriental Studies in Tashkent, seventy-four are mostly in Persian, or are at least bilingual.[17]

The numerous notices left by the readers of the manuscripts that are conserved today at the regional museum of Nukus also show that in the nineteenth century, Persian was still largely used among provincial scholars of Khwarazm. The explanations and translations they wrote in the margins or between the lines of the Arabic texts are for the most part in Persian. Besides, the copyists' formulas that were added at the end of the texts were also mostly Persian, if also sometimes in Arabic and, very rarely, in Turkish. The holdings of manuscript libraries in Nukus thus confirm that Persian maintained its role among Khivan scholars.[18]

The translation program into Central Asian Turkish that was conducted throughout the nineteenth century serves as additional evidence of the importance and prestige that Persian literature long enjoyed in this early Turkified region. For among the many works that were translated into Turkish, some 85 percent were originally composed in Persian, the remainder having been written in Arabic or Ottoman Turkish.[19]

TRANSLATING FOR "THE COMMON PEOPLE" OF KHWARAZM?

The cultural efflorescence in Khwarazm that began in the reign of Muhammad Rahim Khan (r. 1806–25) and continued under his successors was reflected in the development of a more intense literary life. Translation played an especially important role in this. Indeed, a large proportion of Turkish classical literature consists of translations from Persian. But what was new here was the quantity of translations being made. For instance, during the reign of Muhammad Rahim Khan II from 1864 to 1910, which marked the peak of this cultural revival, more than a hundred works were translated, mostly from Persian into Chaghatai Turkish.[20] From the beginning of the nineteenth century till the demise of the khanate in 1917, we can identify at least eighty-two different translators at the court of Khiva.[21] Unfortunately, we have little information about these translators.[22] Aftandil Erkinov and Shadman Vohidov published an article about the *Fihrist-i Kitabkhana* (Library Catalogue), a handwritten record of all of the Arabic, Persian, and Turkish works to be found in the library of Muhammad Rahim Khan II. It mentions the names of forty-seven copyists and thirty-one translators, as well as art commissioners, most of them members of the khan's family.[23] According to the *tazkira* ('anthology') of Hasan Murad Laffasi, "There were always thirty-forty poets and worshippers of literature in the service of Muhammad Rahim Khan II, some of them dealing with books and translations."[24]

FIGURE 13. The last khanate: Kalta Minaret, Khiva, left uncompleted in 1855. Photograph by Nile Green.

The case of Muhammad Riza Agahi, one of the most prominent figures of this period, is illustrative. In the preface to his *diwan,* he gave the total number of his translations as nineteen (including one from Ottoman Turkish). Among them there are such prominent classical Persian works as Sa 'di's *Gulistan*; Jami's *Yusuf wa Zulaykha, Salaman wa Absal,* and *Baharistan;* Hilali's *Shah wa Gada;* Nizami's *Haft Paykar;* Muhammad Waris's *Zubdat al-Hikayat;* Kaykawus's *Qabus-nama;* Husayn Kashifi's *Akhlaq-i Muhsini;* Mahmud Ghijduwani's *Miftah al-Talibin;* Amir Khusraw's *Hasht Bihisht;* and Wasifi's *Bada'i' al-Waqa'i'.* Six translations of historical works also appear in this list: Mirkhwand's *Rawzat al-Safa,* of which Agahi translated the second part of the second volume and the whole of the third volume; Riza Quli Khan's *Rawzat al-Safa-yi Nasiri,* of which he translated only the third volume; Mahdi Khan Astarabadi's *Tarikh-i Jahangusha-yi Nadiri;* Sharaf al-Din Yazdi's *Zafar-nama; Tabaqat-i Akbarshahi;* and *Tazkira-yi Muqimkhani.*[25]

This impressive list gives an idea of the variety of works that were translated in Khiva. When looking at the *Fihrist-i Kitabkhana* catalogue, we notice that not only literary and historical works were translated, but also texts pertaining to medicine (such as *al-Aghraz al-Tibbiya*), pharmacology (such as *Tuhfat al-Muminin*), jurisprudence (such as *Mukhtasar al-Wiqaya*), hadith (such as *Sharh-i Dala'il al-Khayrat*), and Sufism (such as Jami's famous *Nafahat al-Uns*). Agahi's example also reveals that one work could be translated by several different people. This was the case with the translation of the historiographical works *Rawzat al-Safa* and *Tarikh-i Kamil,* the latter's twelve volumes being translated by a team composed of no fewer than eleven people. The translation of one text could thus turn into a collective endeavor that had to be continued from a reign to another. For example, while the first volume (*daftar*) of *Rawzat al-Safa* was translated by Munis at the behest of Muhammad Rahim Khan I, the other volumes were translated by Agahi, Muhammad Yusuf Raji, Muhammad Nazar, and Kamil Khwarazmi during the reigns of Allah Quli Khan (r. 1825–42), Rahim Quli Khan (r. 1842–45), Muhammad Amin Khan (r. 1845–55), Sayyid 'Abdullah Khan (r. 1855), and Muhammad Rahim Khan II (r. 1864–1910).

Another feature of Khiva's translation program is that the same work could be translated several times over. There are at least five Turkish translations of *Mahfilara,* and three translations of Wasifi's famous memoirs of Timurid Herat, *Bada'i' al-Waqa'i'.*[26] This reminds us of the fact that there were several different ways to translate any given work: the word *tarjuma* covers a much wider idea of transferring a text, or elements of it, into another language than is suggested by the modern English term "translation."[27] Thus, if we compare several translations of the same text, we find that none of them recreated the integral character of the original Persian work. Indeed, over the long term there seems to have been a clear trend toward simplification.[28] By way of illustration, the researcher Najmiddin Komilov compared three translations of *Bada'i' al-Waqa'i'.* The first was made in 1826 by Dilawar Khwaja; the second in 1860 by Agahi; and the third in 1917 by Muhammad Amin Töra. Komilov found that the 1826 translation was the closest to the original. The 1860 translation by Agahi shows that the latter took an interest in unusual words and refined expressions but nonetheless shortened a significant part of the book. And the 1917 translation went even further in representing a very simplified version of the Persian original.[29] Over the years, the need for linguistic accessibility evidently became more and more important. The first translations produced Turkish texts that looked very close to the Persian originals both from a grammatical and a lexical point of view, whereas after the second half of the nineteenth century, translators tried to "de-Persify" their translations as much as they could. When Muhammad Yusuf Bayani (1858–1923) crafted a new Turkish translation of *Tarikh-i Tabari*, for example, he replaced Persian and Arabic words with their Turkish equivalents, or at least included only Arabic and Persian words that were widely understandable to his readers at the time.[30]

Along with these practices of simplification and Turkification, the need to produce commentaries and explanations also emerged. A case in point is Mulla Babajan Sana'i's translation of *Haft Kishwar*, a treatise on ethics written by Fakhri Harawi at the beginning of the sixteenth century, made in 1859 during the reign of Sayyid Muhammad Khan (r. 1856–64). A comparison of the original and its translation reveals a notable difference in volume between original Persian passages and their Turkish versions.[31] What is particularly interesting are the instances where Sana'i added words and sentences because he felt the need to further explain the meaning to his readers. For example, a sample Persian segment of the text can be translated as:

> In ancient times [*dar zamani*], there was a wise sultan named 'Adil Shah. He was the king of all the earth and the master of the seven climes. In the land of Mashriq, he erected a city and succeeded in building it in a short amount of time, thanks to his many efforts. Since the grace of both worlds was found in the city, it was called Kawnayn.[32]

Sana'i's rather more prolix translation reads as follows:

> In the days of yore [*zaman-i madi*], that is to say, in bygone days [*ya'ni ötgän ayyamda*], there was such a just king, such a munificent king of the kings, that people gave him the name and title the wise sultan 'Adil Shah. . . . One day, this king imagined beholding his kingdom and showing one particle of the sun of his greatness and his majesty to the people of the world. In the land of Mashriq, he built such a city that the grace of the two worlds and the marvel of the two worlds became resplendent and apparent in it. Since in this auspicious time and propitious day, wise and learned men—whose wisdom, piety and eloquence were above all—were very numerous, and because in this blessed age, thanks to their instructions and indications, the buildings of the aforementioned city were shaped and fortified, for all of these reasons they named the city Kawnayn.

Obviously, such translation practices aimed at giving much more than a mere translation. Translators wanted to make their texts fully accessible to their readers. And they used various methods in order to provide readers with this kind of easy accessibility. They would translate verse passages into prose, for example, add synonyms and comments, or even change the structure of a passage.[33]

In the prefaces to their translations, Khiva's translators often stated this purpose explicitly: they wanted to produce a text that could be read by everyone. This was in fact an express demand of their patrons. When Khan Muhammad Amin Inaq and the high official Niyazbek entrusted Muhammad Qasim with the translations of *Abu Muslim* and the *Shah-nama* respectively, Muhammad Qasim was required to work with "the common people" (*khass u 'awam*) in mind.[34] Similarly, the ruler Muhammad Rahim Khan II asked Agahi to translate many passages of Nizami's famous poem *Haft Paykar* into Turkish prose for the same reason. This desire to produce texts that could be not only technically readable but also broadly intelligible was not new in the history of Central Asian Turkish literature. In one of the epilogues of the five narrative poems (*masnawi*) he composed between 1483 and 1485, Mir 'Ali Shir Nawa'i told his readers that he had begun to rewrite in Turkish Nizami's famous medieval Persian poem *Khamsa* because he wanted the "Turkic people" (*Türk eli*) to benefit from it, "for nowadays in the world many Turks have a good nature and a clear mind."[35] Almost two centuries later in Khiva, the ruler Abu al-Ghazi Bahadur similarly stated in the first pages of his *Shajara-yi Turk wa Mughul* that he had "tried to use a Turkish that is easily understandable even by a five-year-old child."[36] And as shown by Alexandre Papas's chapter 8 in this volume, when the high administration of Eastern Turkistan commissioned translations of Persian classics into Chaghatai Turkish from the late eighteenth century on, translators were also asked to continuously simplify the meaning of the text for a "general readership" (*khass u 'awam*).

At the end of the nineteenth century in Khiva, not only translators but also historians had to produce simplified versions of earlier Persian works. When in 1863 Hasan Murad Qushbegi instructed Sana'i to write a history of the khanate of Khiva, Sana'i was required to produce a text that could be intelligible even by the "common people" (*'awam ahli*). Even though the history of the Qongrat rulers had already been written by previous poets and scholars, these earlier chronicles had been written in such a refined style that they were barely understandable by their readers. While dominant, this was not an entirely uniform policy. Simplification was evidently less required under Allah Quli Khan (r. 1825–42), and translators had sometimes to keep the style of the original works. Nevertheless, during the subsequent reign of Muhammad Rahim Khan II, the demand for simplified translations regained momentum.[37] Talib Khwaja, who was asked by Muhammad Rahim Khan II to translate *Hikayat al-Salihin* from Persian to Turkish, wrote in his preface that its translation would be profitable for "all the people" (*jami'-i khala'iq*).[38] In fact, most forewords to translations mention the importance of providing access to culture to the "Turkic people of Khwarazm."[39]

We know that such literary translations could be appreciated by the khans of Khiva and high officials who belonged to the educated part of the Khiva society and were often engaged themselves in literary activity. But what about "the common people" of Khwarazm? To judge from the very small number of existing copies, the historical works translated by Munis, Agahi, and others did not enjoy wide circulation. It seems that they were read mostly at court, so that expressions like "the common people" should not be understood too literally. We might therefore wonder what really lies behind this claim of public outreach. That is, who did patrons, translators, and historiographers have in mind when they talked about "the common people" of Khwarazm?

NEW FRONTIERS OF CULTURAL LEGITIMACY

Even though ethnically all three of Central Asia's khanates remained highly heterogeneous, Khiva was the most Turkic in terms of population compared to the khanates of Khoqand and Bukhara. In Khiva, Uzbeks constituted a majority of almost 65 percent, with the similarly Turkic Turkmens forming a large minority of about 25 percent (roughly the size of the Tajik minority in Bukhara). Khiva thus had the greatest proportion of Turkish-speakers anywhere in the region, whereas Bukhara had the greatest percentage of Persian-speaking Tajiks. But were these Turkish-speaking people, who in demographic terms certainly did mostly constitute the "people of Khwarazm," the true target of this cultural policy, which eventually led to the replacement of Persian by Turkish? Given the fact that only 5 percent of the population lived in towns, there is no doubt that the number of those in the Khiva khanate who could read even translated works was very limited. The translators' claim that they worked for the common people who did not know Persian may be therefore considered as a topos and, as such, should not be taken at face value.

Further evidence confirms that the call for popular access to literary culture was more a motto than a true policy objective. In 1874, Muhammad Rahim Khan II, an ardent admirer of the West, established a court printing office in Khiva with a lithographic press, but beyond the court, its impact on intellectual life in Khiva was minimal. Its publications were available neither for sale nor for general distribution, but were solely for the use of the court. The principal subject matter was poetry, much of it written by the khan himself. The Russian orientalist A. N. Samoilovich observed during his visit to Khiva in 1908, "The press does not have a permanent home; it does not accept outside [i.e., commercial] orders, and works irregularly. . . . Its publications do not go on sale, but are given out as gifts by the Khan."[40] At the time of Samoilovich's visit, the press was housed in a pavilion in a royal garden. Two years later, after Muhammad Rahim Khan's death in 1910, the printing office was closed. This shows that rather than being a tool for popular enlightenment, Khiva's pioneering printing press was merely, in Adeeb Khalid's words, "an instrument of royal pleasure." As Khalid further explains, the press was used solely "to present the elegant courtly culture in a new form."[41]

The translation program reached its peak between 1864 and 1910 during the reign of Muhammad Rahim Khan II, who wrote poetry himself under the pen name Firuz and patronized poets and historians, promoting a vibrant literary life at court, in which more than thirty poets participated.[42] Restricted politically, especially in foreign policy, Muhammad Rahim Khan focused on regal court culture as the only means he had to voice his protest against the Russian protectorate. The Uzbek scholar Aftandil Erkinov has argued that the Russian invasion of 1873 was responsible for this cultural effervescence favoring Turkic culture, and that Muhammad Rahim Khan cultivated his court library as a means of resistance to the Russian Empire.[43]

Yet whatever impact Russian colonization may have had on the cultural life of the Khiva khanate, the translation program had certainly begun long before the coming of the Russians, as shown for instance by the translation of *Rawzat al-Safa* under way since the reign of Muhammad Rahim Khan I. We should thus not overstate the impact of the Russian invasion on the evolution of the khanate's culture. Russian occupation may have been the accelerator, but the turn of Khiva's court life toward Turkification, in which the translation program played a major role, was probably rooted in the new political situation that emerged in Central Asia during the eighteenth century with the disintegration of the traditional polities that had existed since the Uzbeks originally took over the region in the early 1500s. New tribal forces challenged central authority and ceased to recognize the charisma of the Chinggisid dynasts. Although none of them belonged to the house of Chinggis Khan, for the first time in Central Asian history, the rulers of the three new Uzbek dynasties that emerged in the eighteenth century adopted the title of "khan."[44] The "tectonic shift" of the eighteenth century ended the Chingissid period and launched that of the Uzbek khanates' "introversion," as Paolo Sartori has put it.[45]

After Muhammad Amin Inaq, the leader of the Qongrats, defeated and banished the Yomut Turkmen in 1770, he continued to enthrone puppet khans from the Kazakh Chinggisids, while ruling himself only as the *inaq* ("intimate") of the sovereign. It was his grandson, Eltüzer Inaq who was the first to discard these Chinggisid figurehead khans and have himself proclaimed khan in 1804 so as to rule in his own name, thus founding the new dynasty of the Qongrats. Like the two other khan dynasties established by the end of the eighteenth century in Bukhara and Khoqand, the khanate of Khiva enjoyed a certain degree of stability. This in turn led to internal centralization and administrative robustness as compared with the previous two hundred years.

However, since these Uzbek dynasties were theoretically deprived of ruling privileges—the old Chinggisid imperial legacy in Central Asia prescribed that only descendants of Chinggis Khan had the right to the throne—in order to facilitate their rule they had to sanction certain modes of legitimation. We might imagine that the Qongrats' cultural policy played a part in these efforts, promoting a specific culture that would help legitimize their power. In the beginning of the nineteenth century, the changes that affected politics in Central Asia also affected the cultural sphere. With the Qongrat dynasty asserting its own values, Persian no longer had the legitimacy it had once had.

The fact that the Qongrats fostered the Turkification of courtly life to a significantly greater degree than their counterparts in Khoqand and Bukhara could be explained by the particularities of Khwarazm. Since, as noted earlier, this region was one of the most Turkified, the Turkic component of its identity had always played an important role. Vámbéry remarks that "the Khivite has a legitimate pride in the purity of his ancient Özbeg nationality, as contrasted with that of Bukhara and Kashgar."[46] Furthermore, Khiva's connections with other Turkish-speaking regions of the Russian Empire inhabited by Muslim communities, such as Tatars, at least since the late eighteenth century, were another manifestation of the khanate's "Turkicness."[47] By contrast, the relative remoteness of the region, which is separated from Transoxiana and Iran by deserts and steppes, helped preserve the Turkic cultural specificity of the Khiva oasis as compared to more Persianized regions.[48] Turkish was still dominated by Persian in the khanates of Bukhara and Khoqand at the end of the nineteenth century, and the Qongrats khans of Khiva therefore used Turkish as a visible sign of their power and distinction. This sense of their distinctiveness was so pronounced that the Uzbeks of Khwarazm looked upon the khanate of Bukhara as "Tajik country." They would even refer haughtily to the troops of Bukhara, which were actually composed mainly of Uzbek soldiers, as "the Tajik army."[49] Several decades earlier, Vámbéry had already noticed that Khiva and Khoqand were regarded "as the constant enemies of Bukhara."[50] According to what Mary Holdsworth has called these "old patterns of internal rivalries," the external political relations of the three khanates should be considered first in relation to each other, and only secondly to Russia.[51] "The enduring rivalries" among the Central Asian khanates had prevented the formation of a united front against the Russian invader and created a cultural competition in which the translation program may have played its part. Tellingly, the animosity between Khiva and Bukhara was exacerbated in the literary sphere, especially in chronicles.[52] These rivalries may have "cultivated local feelings of belongings [sic], perhaps a kind of early 'patriotism,'"James Pickett observes.[53] The "de-Persification" process that occurred on a courtly level was another means for the Qongrats khans to distinguish their own court from those of their rivals in Bukhara and Khoqand. By promoting Turkish as the main cultural language at the expense of Persian, the dynasty gave a distinguishing significance to its royal imagery within the context of "a Central Asian vernacular century."[54] Well before the coming of the Russians, the numerous translations carried out throughout the nineteenth century show that the Qongrats wished to take over all the official signs of power in their khanate, including the language through which this power could be culturally articulated.

CONCLUSIONS

From the beginning of the nineteenth century on, the Qongrats khans of Khiva decided to implement a cultural policy that aimed to make Central Asia's literary legacy accessible to Turkish-speakers. Nevertheless, contrary to what the prefaces of many of Khiva's translations would suggest, the translations probably responded less to the demands of a Turkish-speaking readership than they contributed to forging a virtual reading community. The policy of translation from Persian to Turkish, along with the desire to compose new works in Turkish, was undertaken with the aim of establishing a vernacular literary culture. In Khwarazm, as well as elsewhere, the primary stimulus for vernacularization was provided by the royal courts; it was a "top-down" policy rather than a "bottom-up" process.[55] This cultural policy served a broader political project. For by reshaping the boundaries of their cultural universe, the Qongrat rulers contributed to the forging of a new political community: that of the Turkic people of Khwarazm. The new linguistic boundaries, within which a vernacular (Turkish) was called on to supersede a lingua franca (Persian), reflected a new way of ordering the political universe.

The role of these new cultural frontiers was therefore to offer a new vision of vernacular political space. The local Qongrat dynasty distinguished itself from its regional Manghit and Ming rivals by cultivating its own type of cultural legitimacy, in which Persian no longer had its former role or prestige. Khiva's translation program thus became "one of the means by which a new nation 'proves' itself, shows that its language is capable of rendering what is rendered in more prestigious languages." In the case of Khiva, as in others, the many translations amounted to a real "seizure of power."[56] In this way, the Qongrats' translation program illustrates the fact that the delimitation of frontiers, be they linguistic or cultural, remains a political act par excellence. It was a choice of the prince, or, in this case, of the khan, and his court. Not surprisingly, the delimitation of linguistic frontiers became a major issue several decades later with the Soviet policy on nationalities, leading to the definitive contraction of Persian throughout Central Asia.

NOTES

1. "Turkish" in this chapter refers to the Turkic language as spoken and written in Central Asia from the thirteenth century to the early twentieth, also known as "Eastern Middle Turkic" or "Chaghatai Turkish."

2. Marc Toutant, *Un empire de mots: La culture des derniers Timourides au miroir de la Khamsa de Mīr ʿAlī Shīr Nawāʾī (1441–1501)* (Leuven: Peeters, 2016).

3. Apropos of Uzbek studies here, we should acknowledge the work of Yuri Bregel, one of the most important heirs of the Russian Oriental School regarding Central Asian history and culture and the author of several articles about major historiographers at the Khivan courts, who were also known for their translation activities. See Bregel, "The *Tawārīkh-i Khōrazmshāhiya* by Thanāʾī: The Historiography of Khiva and the Uzbek Literary Language," in *Aspects of Altaic Civilization II: Proceedings of the XVIII PIAC, Bloomington, June 29–July 5, 1975,* ed. L. V. Clark and P. A. Draghi (Bloomington, IN:

Asian Studies Research Institute, 1978), 17 32; "Tribal Tradition and Dynastic History: The Early Rulers of the Qongrats according to Munis," *Asian and African Studies* 16, 3 (1982): 392–97. Bregel is also the editor and translator of the *Firdaws al-Iqbal*, a critical source for the history of Khwarazm; see Shir Muhammad Mirab Munis and Muhammad Riza Mirab Agahi, *Firdaws al-Iqbal: History of Khwarazm*, ed. Yuri Bregel (Leiden: Brill, 1988), and *Firdaws al-Iqbal: History of Khwarazm by Shir Muhammad Mirab Munis and Muhammad Riza Mirab Agahi*, translated from Chaghatai and annotated by Yuri Bregel (Leiden: Brill, 1999).

4. Najmiddin Komilov, "Khorezmskaja shkola perevoda (problemy tipologii i sopostavitel'noe issledovanie istorii perevoda)" (PhD diss., University of Tashkent, 1987); id., *Bu qadimiy san'at: Risola* (Tashkent: G'afur G'ulom nomidagi Adabiyot va san'at nashriyoti, 1988).

5. Aftandil Erkinov and Shadman Vahidov, "Une source méconnue pour l'étude de la production de livres à la cour de Muḥammad Raḥīm Khân II (Khiva, fin XIXe s.)," *Cahiers d'Asie centrale* 7 (1999): 175–93; Aftandil Erkinov, "A. N. Samojlovich's Visit to the Khanate of Khiva in 1908 and His Assessment of the Literary Environment," *International Journal of Central Asian Studies* 14 (2010): 109–46; id., "How Muḥammad Raḥīm Khân II of Khiva (1864–1910) Cultivated His Court Library as a Means of Resistance against the Russian Empire," *Journal of Islamic Manuscripts* 2 (2011): 36–49.

6. The Qypchaq confederation had begun to migrate to Transoxiana under Shibanid leadership since the early 1500s.

7. The *mehter* was "a sort of officer who has the charge of the internal affairs of the court and country" who "must always be from the Sart ancient Persian population of Khiva," according to Ármin Vámbéry, *Travels in Central Asia; Being the Account of a Journey from Teheran across the Turkoman Desert on the Eastern Shore of the Caspian to Khiva, Bokhara, and Samarcand Performed in the Year 1863* (New York: Harper & Brothers, 1865), 385. See also Yuri Bregel, "The Sarts in the Khanate of Khiva," *Journal of Asian History* 12, 2 (1978): 127–38.

8. The Sarts "are called Tadjik in Bokhara and Khokand, and are the ancient Persian population of Kharezm. Their number here is small. They have, by degrees, exchanged their Persian language for the Turkish. The Sart is distinguishable, not less than the Tadjik, by his crafty, subtle manners. He is no great favorite with the Özbeg, and in spite of the Sart and Özbeg having lived five centuries together, very few mixed marriages have taken place between them" (Vámbéry, *Travels*, 400).

9. Bregel, "Sarts in the Khanate of Khiva," 149–50.

10. About Sarts and the way Soviet historiography approached this issue, see Sergey Abashin, *Nacionalizmy v Srednej Azii: v poiskakh identichnosti* (Saint Petersburg: Aletejja), 101–76.

11. Ashirbek Muminov, Maria Szuppe, and Abdusalim Idrisov, *Manuscrits en écriture arabe du Musée régional de Nukus* (Rome: Istituto per l'Oriente C. A. Nallino, 2007), 37.

12. For a discussion of Bregel's hypothesis for this change of administrative language at the end of the 1850s, see Paolo Sartori, "Introduction: On Khvārazmian Connectivity: Two or Three Things That I Know about It," *Journal of Persianate Studies* 9 (2016), 148–49.

13. See Bregel's translation of the *Firdaws al-Iqbal*, 407.

14. Aftandil Erkinov, "Manuscripts of the Works by Classical Persian Authors (Hafiz, Jami, Bidil): Quantitative Analysis of the 17th–19th c. Central Asian Copies," in *Iran: Questions et connaissance*, vol. 2: *Périodes médiévale et modern*, ed. Maria Szuppe (Paris: Association pour l'avancement des études iraniennes, 2002), 216.

15. These copies are now kept at the Al-Beruni Institute for Oriental Studies in Tashkent.

16. Munis and Agahi devoted sections in their *diwan*s to poems in Persian; see H. F. Hofman, *Turkish Literature: A Bio-bibliographical Survey*, § 3, pt. 1, vol. 4 (Utrecht: Library of the University of Utrecht, 1969), 199–205. Ahmad Tabibi wrote five *diwan*s, two of them in Persian; see F. G'anixo'jaev, *Tabibiy (hayoti va ijodi)* (Tashkent: FAN, 1978).

17. There are no fewer than 134 Persian *ghazal* poems in the *Majmuat al-Shu'ara-i Mumtaz* (Al-Beruni Institute for Oriental Studies, Tashkent, MS no. 7081).

18. Muminov, Szuppe, and Idrisov, *Manuscrits en écriture arabe*, 37.

19. Komilov, *Bu qadimiy sanat,* 25.

20. Komilov, "Khorezmskaja shkola perevoda," 75.

21. A. Nosirov, *Xorazmga oid materiallar: Qo'lyozma,* quoted by Komilov, "Khorezmskaja shkola perevoda," 112.

22. One of our major sources remains the *tazkira* composed by Hasan Murad Qari Laffasi (1880–1945) in 1920, "Khiwa shâ'ir wa adabiyâtchilarining tarjima-i hâllari," MS, Fond. IV AN O'zSSR, no. 9494. See also P. Babajanov's edition: Laffasiy, *Tazkiratush Shuaro* (Urganch, Uzbekistan, 1992).

23. The manuscript is kept at the Uzbek Academy of Science. See Erkinov and Vahidov, "Une source méconnue," 178.

24. Quoted by Komilov, *Bu qadimiy sanat,* 15.

25. Muhammad Rizâ Âgahi, *Ta'wiz al-'Ashiqin,* ed. Rahmat Majidiy (Tashkent: O'zSSR Fanlar akademiyasi nashriyoti, 1960), 38–39.

26 *Mahfilârâ,* a work composed by Barkhurdâr Turkmen Mumtâz, is also known by its other title, *Mahbub al-qulub.*

27. See esp. Mona Baker, "The History of Translation: Recurring Patterns & Research Issues," in *Translations: (Re)Shaping of Literature and Culture,* ed. Saliha Paker (Istanbul: Boğaziçi University Press, 2002), 5–14.

28. Komilov, "Khorezmskaja shkola perevoda," 131–44.

29. Ibid., 145–61.

30. Komilov, *Bu qadimiy sanat,* 70.

31. The original Persian text and the Turkish translation are both given in Komilov, "Khorezmskaja shkola perevoda," 214–16.

32. "Kawnay" means "the two worlds." All translations are mine.

33. A good illustration is the way Muhammadniyaz translated Kashifi's *Anwar-i Suhayli.* See Komilov, *Bu qadmiy sanat,* 75–76.

34. Quoted by Komilov, *Bu qadmiy sanat,* 60.

35. This verse is taken from the prologue of *Layli-u-Majnun.* See the manuscript kept at the University of Michigan (Ann Arbor, Special Collections Library, Isl., no. 450), 345.

36. Abu al-Ghazi Bahadur, *Histoire des Mongols et des Tatares par Aboul-Ghâzi Béhâdour Khân,* ed. and trans. Petr I. Demaison (Amsterdam: Amsterdam Philo Press, 1970), 36.

37. Komilov, *Bu qadimiy sanat,* 58–59.

38. Quoted by Komilov, ibid., 68.

39. Ibid., 19–20.

40. Quoted by Adeeb Khalid, "Muslim Printers in Tsarist Central Asia: A Research Note," *Central Asian Survey* 11, 3 (1992): 114.

41. Ibid.

42. Several poetic anthologies were printed for the court. See Aftandil Erkinov, "Timurid Mannerism in the Literary Context of Khiva under Muhammad Rahim-Khan II (Based on the Anthology Majmu'a-yi Shu'ara-yi Firuz-Shahi)," *Bulletin of International Institute for Central Asian Studies* 8 (2008): 58–65.

43. See esp. Erkinov, "How Muḥammad Raḥīm Khān II . . . Cultivated His Court Library."

44. "The first [principle of the Uzbek state] was that only an agnatic descendant of Chinggis Khan was eligible to rule. The second was [that] the right to govern the state resided in the entire Chinggisid ruling clan (among the males who had reached the 'age of discretion') and not in an individual" (Robert D. McChesney, "Waqf at Balkh: A Study of the Endowments at the Shrine of 'Alī ibn Abī Tālib" [PhD diss., Princeton University, 1973], ix).

45. Sartori, "Introduction," 140.

46. Vámbéry, *Travels,* 396–97.

47. See Sartori, "Introduction," 150–51.

48. Certain narratives tended to exaggerate this isolation; see Sartori, "Introduction," 138.

49. Yuri Bregel, "Central Asia vii. In the 18th–19th Centuries," *Encyclopædia Iranica*, vol. 5, fasc. 2, 193–205.

50. Vámbéry, *Travels*, 481.

51. Mary Holdsworth, *Turkestan in the Nineteenth Century: A Brief History of the Khanates of Bukhara, Kokand and Khiva* (Los Angeles: Central Asian Research Centre in association with St. Antony's College (Oxford) Soviet Affairs Study Group, 1959), 3.

52. Seymour Becker, *Russia's Protectorates in Central Asia. Bukhara and Khiva 1865–1924* (New York: Routledge, 2004), 4, and James Pickett, "Enemies beyond the Red Sands: The Bukhara-Khiva Dynamic as Mediated by Textual Genre," *Journal of Persianate Studies* 9 (2016): 168.

53. Pickett, "Enemies," 159.

54. Sartori, "Introduction," 148.

55. Sheldon Pollock, "Cosmopolitan and Vernacular in History," in *Cosmopolitanism*, ed. Carol A. Breckenridge, Sheldon Pollock, Homi K. Bhabha, and Dipesh Chakrabarty (Durham, NC: Duke University Press, 2002), 15–53.

56. *Translation, History and Culture*, ed. Susan Bassnett and André Lefevere (New York: Pinter, 1990), 8.

11

Dissidence from a Distance

Iranian Politics as Viewed from Colonial Daghestan

Rebecca Ruth Gould

Unlike many modern nation-states and the regions they comprise, the Caucasus is defined neither by a single language nor by its affiliation to a single ethnicity or religion, but rather by its multiplicity. As a marginalized crossroads at the intersection of several imperial formations, the Caucasus is distinguished by the multilingual and multiconfessional identities that have developed within its ambit, as well as by its resistance to the kind of homogeneous narrative that characterizes the logic of nation-states. From the Sasanians to the 'Abbasids to the Mongols, to the Ottomans, Safavids, and Qajars, each empire that annexed or occupied this region shaped local literary production, in Persian, Arabic, and several Turkic languages, including Azeri, Qumyq, and Nogai. One of the distinctive features of the Caucasus is that, without ever being dominated by a single tradition, the many genres and texts that were authored on its terrain shaped multiple transnational literary traditions, including Persian, Arabic, and various Turkic literatures. This heterogeneous genealogy of influence applies above all to Persian, which generated a milieu, termed Persographic by Nile Green in the introduction to this volume, that transcended imperial borders. Indeed, it might be argued that the Caucasus, like much of South Asia, illustrates the broad divergence between the Persophone (Persian as a spoken language) and the Persographic (Persian as a written language), which this volume is uniquely suited to reveal.

For most of history, the Caucasus was not formally part of any Persian or Persianate dynasty (the Shirvanshahs, vassals of the Saljuqs, are one exception). Nonetheless, it has frequently been considered the northernmost periphery of the Persographic world. Yet, in the Caucasus, geographic peripherality has often coexisted with cultural centrality. Home to several centers of Persian literary production, including Shirvan, Ganja, and Derbent, the Caucasus has played a unique role in shaping Persian literary history. Nizami (d. 1209), whose cycle of literary romances (*masnawis*) were to become among the most frequently imitated works across the Persianate world, produced these works from his home in Ganja, not far from the Georgian border. In his prodigious confrontational verses, Khaqani of Shirvan (d. 1191) similarly depicted a sensibility that could only have been articulated by a poet who had come of age along imperial borderlands, and whose understanding of Islam was profoundly shaped by his contact with Christian culture. Entire genres, such as the prison poem, which Khaqani pioneered, were the product of a subaltern identity formed on the margins of empires and at a crossroads of cultures.[1]

The unique status of Persian as a language of writing in the Caucasus meant that the process whereby colonial modernity replaced what in chapter 12 of this volume Abbas Amanat calls the "once thriving sociocultural sphere that stretched from Khotan to Sarajevo and from Tbilisi to Mysore" did not follow the same trajectory as its gradual demise elsewhere. Although never wholly hegemonic, Persian continued to shape literary culture across the Caucasus even after much of the region was incorporated into the Russian Empire. Persian in the Caucasus was fragmented from the very beginning; it never encompassed the entirety of literary culture. Yet the fragmented, graphic status of this literary language in a geography wherein it was rarely spoken may have helped to keep its ethos alive in the Caucasus amid the rise of national identities. Far from representing a tradition that was being erased, Persian inflected all of the major literatures of the Caucasus, from Georgian to Armenian to Azeri. Even when Persian was overtaken in early modernity by Turkic and indigenous languages as the primary medium of literary culture, its historical role in creating a cohesive literary culture, woven together by common themes, tropes, genres, and narratives, persisted up to and after the Russian revolution.

Standard histories of Persian literature concentrate on the Caucasus during the twelfth and thirteenth centuries, but the influence of the Caucasus on the Persian literary imagination did not end with Nizami and Khaqani or the literary genres these poets pioneered (the *masnawi* and the *qasida*, respectively). As a result of Safavid deportations to regions around Isfahan of Georgian and Armenian communities, begun by Shah ʿAbbas I (r. 1588–1629), Iranian culture continued to be shaped by literary production in the Caucasus, and in new ways.[2] Whereas Saljuq-era experiments in Persian poetics primarily involved textual transmission from the periphery to the center, Safavid-era literary production in Persian travelled in the opposite direction. Georgian kings such as Teimuraz I of Kakheti (r. 1605–16, 1625–48), who came of age in Isfahan and was buried in Astarabad, used their training in Persian poetics to develop a new Persianate canon for Georgian literature.[3]

One consequence of the Safavid practice of having Georgians regularly serve as slaves (*ghulam*) of the shah was to enable extensive intermingling between Iranian rulers and non-Iranian subjects.[4] As Said Amir Arjomand has pointed out, "the mothers of all the Safavid shahs from Shah Safi I (r. 1629–42) onward were Georgians."[5] Equally salient is the fact that "the longest-serving grand vizier under

Sultan Husayn, Fath-'Ali Khan Daghistani (in office 1715–20), was a self-pro-claimed Sunni who hailed from the tribal, fervently Sunni region of Daghestan."[6] As a result of the extensive presence of Georgians at the Safavid court, Georgian intermingled with Persian in the harems of Isfahan, and Safavid shahs grew up hearing this language. For the first time in the literary history of the Caucasus, under Safavid rule, Georgian poets passed much of their life within the borders of Iran. Iran went from being an imaginary geography in Caucasus literary his-tory to being an ever-present, oppressive political reality. Safavid Iran could not be idealized, but, as a matter of political exigency, it had to be engaged. The Safavid court continued the tradition of exchange between the literary culture of Iran and the Caucasus from prior eras, but these new, early modern contacts could not be extracted from the broader coercive dynamics of Safavid rule.

Intermingling did not take place to this degree in earlier eras, not least because Tbilisi and Shirvan were centers of power in their own right, and Georgian rulers had no reason to reside in Iranian capitals such as Isfahan and Shiraz. With the weakening of Georgian sovereignty in the early modern era and the collapse of centralized rule in the Caucasus, the center-periphery relation changed. Rather than expanding outward, as Saljuq and Ghaznavid sultans had done, the Safavid shahs evinced a "relative lack of expansionist zeal . . . [and] never sought to extend their dominion far beyond the plateau."[7] Safavid rulers preferred to focus on sta-bilizing their immediate domains rather than engaging in wars of conquest and expansion. This meant cultivating literary culture closer to home, and pursuing a relatively insular approach to literary patronage. Yet Safavid rulers' lack of expan-sionist zeal did not mean that they were not guided by an imperial design. Rather, their imperial agenda prioritized securing the borders of the Safavid Empire rather than extending them. In order to achieve this goal, millions of Georgians and Ar-menians were deported to the environs of Isfahan. In making Iran their new home, the deportees often applied the names of the villages they had been forced to aban-don to their new abodes. Hence the paucity of conquests of the Caucasus during the Safavid period was compensated for by mass deportations, the emptying out of the Caucasus, and the incorporation of deported Georgians and Armenians into Safavid Iran. In the early modern Persianate world, the expansionist Saljuq state was replaced by the Safavids' aggressive assimilation.

By the late nineteenth century, in the late stages of Qajar rule (1785–1925), ag-gressive assimilation had given way to a different dynamic. Now that the geopo-litical center of gravity had shifted dramatically westward, official policy focused on the imitation of, and rivalry with, an ascendant Europe, as well as with the Ottoman Empire. Reform, revolution, liberty, equality, and constitutionalism were the keywords of this age. Literary culture reflected this shift. Poetry gave way to prose, and the imaginative stories about times past that had structured Nizami's medieval romances were replaced by political polemics, including castigations of the Qajar regime and calls for limiting the power of the sovereign and introducing new political forms through which the will of the people could be realized. For Qajar-era writers, being political meant engaging with the classical categories of European liberalism, and seeking to reform Islam along these lines, rather than praising the ruling regime.

MIGRATORY IDENTITIES IN THE CAUCASUS

Even when nineteenth-century Persian literary production in the Caucasus shifted away from poetry to engage with other genres, many of them in prose, Persian never ceased to figure heavily in the literatures of the Caucasus . The annexation of much of Georgia and Azerbaijan by the Russian Empire in the early nineteenth century, especially following the Treaty of Gulistan (1813), introduced a new orientation to print culture. These decades witnessed a proliferation of serial publications that circulated across the Ottoman, Mughal, and Russian empires, such as *Habl al-Matin* (The Strong Cord, 1893 to 1930), published in Calcutta, and the even more influential *Mulla Nasr al-Din* (1906–31), published first in Tbilisi, subsequently in Tabriz, and finally in Baku, as censors successively sought to bring its existence to a halt.[8] Eventually banned in Iran, *Mulla Nasr al-Din* reached Iranian readers by being smuggled in along with cloth and other merchandise.[9] In shaping what Nile Green has called the Persianate world's "paper modernity," this serial print culture, much of which originated in the Caucasus and Central Asia, greatly contributed to the spread of the ideas that inspired the Iranian Constitutional Revolution.[10]

The new print culture that these publications inspired and sustained was largely the creation of a merchant class that was increasingly detached from the 'ulama. Across Central Asia and the Caucasus, the publishers and contributors to these publications participated in an intellectual movement that sought to carve out a new sphere for public debate through the reform of the education system and the development of print culture.[11] Throughout the Russian empire, these reformers led the way in creating a new class of intellectuals, many of whom had religious educations but who chose to write for the general public rather than the 'ulama. Until recently, the general consensus in Central Asian history has been that "jadidism as a reformist project would have been inconceivable without the printing press, for the printed word allowed the Jadids to challenge the moral authority of the established rural elite, the *ulema*."[12] More recent years have witnessed a critical approach to this narrative, with Devin DeWeese, Paolo Sartori, and others challenging the binary opposition between the Jadid reformers and the 'ulama.[13]

Much like the Russian intelligentsia, individuals from the emergent social class that fostered the development of Persian print culture often had merchant backgrounds and worked in multiple languages. They were cosmopolitan in temperament, vocation, and biography. In some respects they resembled their predecessors from earlier centuries, except that these new figures choose prose, rather than poetry, as their medium of choice. Their writing engaged with the debates of the time, and drew heavily on the European Enlightenment, as mediated by Russian sources, and with substantive admixtures of Indian and Ottoman learning.[14] The reading publics they cultivated extended across the Caucasus and in many cases deep into Central Asia, all the way to South Asia. Often migrants to the Caucasus, these intellectuals, who were variously Iranian, Turkic, and mixtures of other ethnicities, made their home in the Caucasus, a region known for its ethnic and confessional diversity. The work these intellectuals produced reflects their intersecting migratory identities.

The impact of the Jadids of the Russian empire, in particular the Caucasus, on political developments within Iran harkens back to a pre-Safavid dialectic of center/periphery relations, whereby intellectual developments on the edges of the Persianate world came to be seen as the standard toward which Iranian intellectuals should aspire. Although the differences are so incommensurable as to preclude most reasonable comparison, Muslim reformers of this era in the Caucasus and the Saljuq-era poets had in common the fact that their learning was in many respects more cosmopolitan than that of their counterparts within Iran. Like the twelfth-century poets, Muslim reformers of the nineteenth-century Caucasus were luminaries of their age. Also like the earlier poets in and around the Saljuq court and their vassals, the Shirvanshahs, they were attentive to developments in Iran. There was also a demographic dimension to this connection, given that Iranians were the largest diasporic group in the Russian empire and most members of this diaspora resided in the Caucasus.

Coming to terms with Persian literature in the Caucasus after the Russian annexation means engaging with the particular kind of modernity that these political shifts and technological transformations fostered. Writers' global affiliations shifted during these years, with the introduction of rapid forms of communication such as the telegraph and the transregional networks that traversed new political boundaries. Moscow, Tbilisi, Baku, Tehran, Tabriz, Yerevan, and Tashkent became linked in hitherto unforeseen ways. In some instances, new alliances brought about linguistic shifts, including an increased use of Russian as a language of communication. In other instances, global realignments instead offered new frameworks for engaging with local traditions that were articulated in forms that were predominantly Persographic (including Persian as well as Persian-influenced forms). As had been the case for centuries, Persian functioned temporally as well as spatially to create mobile communities of readers who collectively engaged with the future of Islam, educational reform, and the challenges of modernity.

Thanks in part to exchanges between Russian, Iranian, Georgian, and Azeri writers, the Caucasus was a center for many cultural flows during the nineteenth century. Writers such as 'Abbas Quli Agha Bakikhanuf (1794–1847) and Mirza Fath 'Ali Akhundzada (1812–1878) each passed some of their lives in Tbilisi, the cultural capital of the Caucasus and a meeting place for writers, intellectuals, publishers, and merchants from Iran, Azerbaijan, and Armenia. When writers gathered in Tbilisi, their native ties to Iran, Azerbaijan, and Armenia intermingled, linguistically and politically, with new cosmopolitan identities. Through such assimilative processes, nineteenth-century Persian literature in the Caucasus became heterogeneous and resistant to attempts from Tehran to make Persian isomorphic with the Qajar state. Immersed as it was in advancing social transformation, the Persian literature of the nineteenth-century Caucasus—of Bakikhanuf and Akhundzada—was commensurately global in its imagination. Instead of the cities that had been centers of Persianate culture under the Ghaznavids and Saljuqs (namely, Ghazna, Lahore, Shirvan, and Ganja), the nineteenth-century centers of Persographic culture outside Iranian borders were Tbilisi, Baku, and Istanbul. Although Persian was not the official language in any of these cities, each of them nurtured a culture that was broadly Persianate. In each city, too, newspapers and journals banned in Iran were published and distributed. Hence, without being formally part of Iran, each of these cities has a central place in the history of Persian literature.

The remainder of this chapter focuses on an intellectual whose work and life epitomize the cultural and political flows that characterize the periphery/center relation instituted by Qajar rule. It brings together a perspective on the long history of Persian literature across the centuries with specific attention to the shaping of this imagination by currents in Russian political life and intellectual history. In many cases, these currents were mediated to Iran from Europe via Russia. It therefore responds, albeit schematically, to Ali Ansari's recent query, addressed to those who wish to reconstruct the intellectual history of the Iranian Constitutional Revolution: "If . . . as we know, a rich flow of intellectual traffic came via Russia, to what extent did Russian intellectualism affect the interpretation and transmission of those texts?"[15] In the writings of Mirza 'Abd al-Rahim Talibuf (1834–1911) we can better perceive both the trajectory of the Iranian enlightenment and the shaping influence on Iranian modernity of Russian ideas and the environment of the Caucasus.

'ABD AL-RAHIM TALIBUF: A BRIEF BIOGRAPHY

Born in the Iranian city of Tabriz, Talibuf was part of the wave of Iranian migrants who travelled north in search of greater economic opportunity as well as new intellectual horizons. As Hassan Hakimian has demonstrated, migration from Iran to the Russian empire, primarily to the Caucasus between 1880 and 1914, was unprecedented in scope and scale.[16] Indeed, existing data suggests that Iranians may have been "the largest group of foreign subjects in the Russian Empire."[17] Talibuf's trajectory fits into the demographic captured in the Russian Imperial Census of 1897, which recorded 73,920 Persian-speaking migrants throughout Russia, 60,405 of whom resided in the Caucasus. Roughly 17,000 of these Persian-speakers resided in Baku; 6,000 in Tbilisi; and just over 1,000 in Daghestan, where Talibuf

FIGURE 14. Across imperial frontiers: 'Abd al-Rahim Talibuf. Undated photograph by an unknown photographer in Talibuf, *Azadi u Siyasat,* ed. Iraj Afshar (Tehran, 1978), unnumbered plate.

was living when the census was completed.[18] Unlike Bakikhanuf and Akhundzada, Talibuf was not native to the Caucasus; like the migrants studied by Hakimian, he travelled to Tbilisi from Tabriz in search of a new life. He did well for him-self in Tbilisi and stayed behind, eventually relocating to Daghestan, where he blended into the local community, dedicated himself to writing, and quickly be-came a successor to the Persianate reformist tradition pioneered by Bakikhanuf and Akhundzada.

Within Iran, the Caucasus, and globally, the second half of the nineteenth cen-tury was an era of monumental changes. The fragmenting Russian and Qajar em-pires were both giving rise to new political formations, especially in the Caucasus. Geographically and temporally, Jadids of the Russian empire were both influenced by and influential on the revolutions that took place both to the north and to the south. From Tabriz to Tbilisi to Temir Khan Shura (at that time the capital of Daghestan, then a province of the Russian Empire), Persophone intellectuals were at the forefront of efforts to rethink the meanings of liberty, freedom, and political legitimacy in terms that could have traction within Muslim society. Bakikhanuf presided over the first generation of these intellectuals, who were ethnically Turkic but wrote primarily in Persian.[19] Akhundzada, another Azeri writer and thinker whose works attained notoriety in Iran, presided over the second generation. Al-though he migrated to the Caucasus late in life, in light of his prodigious output and significant influence on local intellectual life, Talibuf was among the most prominent figures in the third generation of Persianate thinkers that shaped intel-lectual life both within Iranian borders and throughout the Caucasus.

Talibuf's biography differs from those of his predecessors Bakikhanuf and Akhundzada, whose direct contact with Iran ranged from minimal to nonexistent. Born in Iran, he interacted directly with leading Iranian intellectuals during his lifetime. During the decades in which he resided in Temir Khan Shura, Iranian in-tellectuals undertook pilgrimages to see him. The poet Yahya Dawlatabadi, whose memoirs exhibit a broad fascination with the Caucasus, travelled to Daghestan to visit him.[20] Talibuf corresponded with the lexicographer, poet, and social critic 'Ali Akbar Dihkhuda (1879–1956) and other influential supporters of the Iranian Constitutional Revolution of 1905. He met the Iranian diplomat Hasan Taqizada (1878–1970) in person when the latter came to see him in Baku.[21]

In perhaps the strongest sign of his influence on the Iranian revolution, Talibuf was selected as a deputy to the first Iranian parliament (1906–8). To the surprise of his many readers, after having acquired such respect from his countrymen, Talibuf refused to travel to Tehran, even when invited to do so. He preferred to observe the revolution that he had inspired from afar. Whether out of principle or simply through historical happenstance, Talibuf practiced dissidence from a distance. Various reasons have been suggested for Talibuf's refusal to travel to Iran to take up a position in the parliament, but the most persuasive one has been given by the literary historian Yahya Aryanpur: having been declared persona non grata by the ʿulama, and indeed labeled an infidel (kafir) within Iran, Talibuf was not eager to return to a country where his books had been condemned.[22] Furthermore, his critical orientation may have benefitted from the distance he maintained between himself and the political turbulence of the era. Iraj Parsinijad for one has argued that Talibuf regarded literary criticism as a means of engaging with the social and political tribulations of his time.[23]

Bakikhanuf and Akhundzada were both born in what was to become during their lifetimes Russian (rather than Iranian) Azerbaijan. By contrast, Talibuf was born in Iranian Azerbaijan, in Tabriz, to a family of carpenters (hence his full name Mirza ʿAbd al-Rahim Talibi Najjar Tabrizi). At the age of sixteen, he left Tabriz for Tbilisi, where he worked for the Iranian merchant Muhammad ʿAli Khan, who made a fortune from obtaining concessions for the construction of roads and bridges across the Caucasus.[24] In Tbilisi, Talibuf also continued his studies. His education surely included Russian, a language that made many new European thinkers accessible to him, as it did for Akhundzada. An undated photograph reproduced in his own book Azadi u Siyasat (Freedom and Politics) shows Talibuf wearing the traditional Caucasian cloak (chokha) and having fully assimilated to local fashion.

A HOME AWAY FROM HOME: TEMIR KHAN SHURA

Talibuf's choice of permanent home was even more perplexing than his sudden departure from Tabriz to Tbilisi. Unlike the majority of Iranian migrants, Talibuf did not settle in cosmopolitan Baku, Tbilisi, Shirvan, or even Ganja, where he would have been surrounded by Persophone intellectuals who shared his reformist proclivities. Rather, he settled in the provincial capital of Daghestan, Temir Khan Shura (renamed Buynaksk in 1922), located on the other side of the Caucasus mountains, where he joined a community of only three and a half thousand speakers of Persian. Postcards of the time reveal Temir Khan Shura as a city that combined traditional ways of life with gestures towards urban planning along European lines. Another series of images collected by the American explorer and diplomat George Kennan (1904–2005) reveal urban boulevards intersecting with Oriental bazaars creating the impression of a city on the brink of a major transformation.[25]

While residing in Temir Khan Shura, Talibuf married a Daghestani woman with whom he had a daughter. He lived in Daghestan with his family until the end of his life, writing books and amassing what was probably Daghestan's most significant library of Persian writings, which became a resource well known to local intellectuals. During these years Talibuf also founded Temir Khan Shura's first girl's gymnasium, where, in true reformist fashion, a combination of secular intellectuals, ʿulama, and reformist Muslims taught. As a philanthropist who contributed intensively to the welfare of his community, Talibuf's grave in Temir Khan Shura is replete with elaborate Quranic inscriptions to this day.

Although, like all of Daghestan, Temir Khan Shura is recognized for its formative role in the intellectual history of Russian Islam, its relevance to Iranian
history and Persian culture is less known.[26] For Daghestani intellectuals, however,
the city, which was named after the Turco-Mongol conqueror Timur (Tamerlane)
who stayed there in 1396, was an important center for Muslim reform movements during and after Talibuf's lifetime. One of the most important of this city's
legacies is the Islamic publishing house founded by another influential reformer,
Muhammad Mirza Mavraev (Mawrayuf) (1878–1964) in 1903, during the height
of Talibuf's literary activities, two years before the beginning of the Iranian Constitutional Revolution, and three years before the first issue of the journal *Mulla
Nasr al-Din*.

Mavraev's was among the first publishing house in the Caucasus to specialize
in publishing in Arabic-script languages, including those of Daghestan. The publishing house of Mavraev (transliterated into Arabic script as Mawrayuf) released
many hundreds of books in Arabic. These comprised classical Islamic texts as well
as many works by Daghestani scholars in local Turkic and indigenous Arabic-
script languages.[27] Hundreds of volumes were also published in other languages,
including Qumyq, Avar, Dargin, Chechen, Azeri, Karachai, Kabardin, and Osse-
tian, all in Arabic and Persian scripts. Although he initially printed his books in
the simplified and less curvaceous *naskh* script in order to approximate modern
print, these books sold badly, and their publication brought Mavraev to the verge
of bankruptcy. Only when Mavraev turned to lithographs, a form of facsimile reproduction that most closely approximated manuscripts, was he able to make a
profit.[28] This same pattern of readerly reception, and preference for lithographs
over books printed according to the latest technology, has been recognized across
Islamic lands, including in Central Asia, where the curvaceous *nast'aliq* script "allowed script to continue under the guise of print," and hence to preserve a semblance of continuity with the manuscript age while also attaining commercial
success.[29] That Talibuf (and Mavraev initially) preferred the simpler *naskh* script
reflect their modernizing tendencies.

Although he was evidently inspired by the intellectual ferment that centered
around Mavraev's activities, Talibuf chose to work with publishers outside Daghestan who could guarantee his works a wider reception than Mavraev could have
done. He therefore published his books in Tbilisi, Grozny, Tehran, Istanbul, and
Cairo, in editions printed in the *naskh* script. But the intellectual activity that was
stimulated by this first Daghestani publishing house, which enabled local writers
to see their works printed for the first time, and acquainted Muslim readers with
the classics of Islamic learning in accessible format, left a mark on this transplanted Iranian reformer.

More direct evidence regarding the wide recognition Talibuf attained within Daghestan is offered by an Arabophone Daghestani intellectual, who was fluent in Persian although he wrote mostly in Arabic and Azeri. Almost his exact contemporary,

Hasan al-Alqadari (1834–1910) was born the same year as Talibuf and passed away only months before his death. They shared much more in common than their biographical chronology. Like Talibuf, al-Alqadari was multilingual, and fluent in Arabic, Azeri, and Persian. In contrast to Talibuf, al-Alqadari wrote primarily in Arabic, which was not his native tongue. The parallels between these two Daghestanis, one native-born and the other transplanted from Iran, suggest how Arabic and Persian productively interacted in this multilingual linguistic geography.

Arguably the most important Daghestani jurist, poet, and historian of the twentieth century, and regarded by many as a forerunner of the Jadid movement that would soon transform intellectual life across Muslim Russia and the Ottoman Empire, al-Alqadari dedicated to Talibuf two odes (*qasidas*) in his autobiographical Arabic-language collection of poetry and prose, *Diwan al-Mamnun*. Although this work was published by Mavraev/Mawrayuf in 1913, after al-Alqadari's death, it was composed in the 1890s, during which decade it circulated in manuscript form. Although the text is entirely in Arabic, at many points al-Alqadari deploys tools from the Persian literary repertoire, such as his pen name (*takhallus*), which means "thankful one [*mamnun*]." Al-Alqadari references Talibuf in two places to thank him for his assistance in securing much-needed books for him.[30] In the expression of gratitude preceding the first of these *qasidas,* al-Alqadari refers to Talibuf as his spiritual grandfather (*al-jad al-ruhani*).[31] Even though he was his exact contemporary, al-Alqadari felt compelled to defer to Talibuf when addressing him.

Another major Daghestani reformer who was fluent in Persian, Abu Sufiyan Akaev (1872–1931), from a somewhat younger generation, recollected passing many hours in Talibuf's library in Temir Khan Shura during his childhood, where he read Firdawsi's *Shah-nama* and other Persian classics.[32] After returning from an extended sojourn in Egypt, where he impressed Rashid Rida (1865–1935) so much with his learning and ideas that the latter went on to write an article entitled "The Daghestani Awakening," Akaev founded Daghestan's first school based on "new method" (*jadid*) principles.[33] This school may have been partly inspired by the gymnasium that Talibuf founded to support the instruction of girls. While none of these Daghestani thinkers, who circulated primarily within Arabic, Turkic, and Russian worlds, were directly involved with the Iranian Constitutional Revolution, their proximity to Talibuf brought them into indirect contact with the latest ideas coming from Iran. Although Persian, along with Turkish, was accessible to most of Talibuf's Azeri readers to the south, Daghestani readers in his immediate environment were more likely to read works in Arabic and various Turkic dialects. And yet, as the 1897 census showed, thousands of Persian speakers resided in Daghestan. Still, we might ask, why did Talibuf elect to pass his life, and elaborate his plea for Iranian Enlightenment, among Daghestanis who were unlikely to read his work? In light of these linguistic differences, the close connections Talibuf cultivated with Daghestani reformists who were more likely to write for Turkic, Arabic, and Russian audiences is all the more striking.

IDEAS AND TEXTS

In his recent study of Talibuf's theory of liberty, Mehran Mazinani notes that the most influential and progressive Iranian thinkers passed the majority of their adult lives outside the borders of Iran.[34] During these same years, the Iranian diplomat Mirza Malkum Khan (1833–1908), whose writings similarly influenced the trajectory of the Constitutional Revolution, was observing events within Iran from afar, first in London and subsequently as Iran's ambassador to Italy.[35] Akhundzada remained safely within the borders of Russian Azerbaijan while he penned his biting satires of Persian and Muslim culture. Only twice in his life did he travel to Iran.[36] Talibuf's biography conforms to this pattern of dissidence from a distance that features frequently in Iranian intellectual history, and indeed in the intellectual history of many empires with politically influential diasporas. By situating themselves on the margins of imperial formations, writers gain a unique vantage point on their own societies, and acquire a capacity for critique that eludes those who operate closer to the centers of power. Hence, the emergence of the concept of critique in nineteenth-century Persian literature is coeval with the tendency of writers critical of sovereign power to settle in a physical space far away from the regime.[37] This may help to explain why certain forms of Persian literary criticism flourished in the Caucasus even more than within the borders of Iran. The polemical writings of Akhundzada strikingly exemplify this trend.

Particularly in the decades leading up to the Constitutional Revolution, Persophone intellectuals who were most forthrightly critical of the state were most productive while residing outside the borders of Qajar Iran. In further evidence of this pattern, Talibuf's own framing of his life suggests that remaining far from Tabriz, where he was born, and Tehran, the center of Iranian power, was a deliberate choice. Reflecting on the benefits of exile, Talibuf wrote in 1908, just after the dissolution of the first Iranian parliament, "although there are critics and satirists more talented than I, located as I am, distant from my homeland, I do not fear to write the truth."[38] In his own eyes, Talibuf's physical location in the Caucasus was central to his claim to originality. A few years earlier, contrasting his position to that of his more politically ambitious contemporaries, Talibuf had declared on the opening pages of his *Masalik al-Muhsinin* (Ways of the Righteous, 1905), a fictional travelogue interspersed with philosophical and literary-critical digressions: "I am not an Iranian tycoon [and I] . . . strongly oppose injustice; I seek neither power nor titles."[39] Informed by his merchant background, Talibuf reconfigured this relation to capital as a tool for the critique and moderation of sovereign rule. His words testify to an emergent bourgeois consciousness among the Iranian intellectual elite. For Talibuf, as for so many of his contemporaries, distance from Iran was a precondition for effective social critique. Exile from Iran enabled Talibuf to articulate his vision of a just social order within Iran.

Having made most of his income while working as a merchant in Tbilisi, Talibuf did not begin publishing books until he reached the age of fifty-eight. His first book, *Nukhba-i Sipihri* (Best of the Spheres, 1892), was a biography of the Prophet Muhammad, which he first published in Istanbul and, a decade later, in Grozny in his own translation into Russian.[40] An autodidact whose knowledge was acquired in the politically peripheral locations of Tabriz and Tbilisi rather than Tehran, Istanbul, and Cairo, Talibuf published eight books during the last two decades of his life. These were eclectic and aphoristic reflections, written in an accessible style, on the major political and philosophical issues of his day, ranging from child-rearing, to educational reform, to political sovereignty and the distribution of power.

Alongside his original writings, which constitute the bulk of his oeuvre, Talibuf translated three books. Each of the translations was done from Russian, even when the original texts were in Greek and French, which returns us to Ansari's query concerning the extent to which "Russian intellectualism affect[ed] the interpretation and transmission" of European texts. One such example is his *Hayat-i Jadid* (New Astronomy, 1894), which was largely a translation of a treatise on astronomy by the French writer Camille Flammarion (1842–1925).[41] Another is Marcus Aurelius's *Meditations,* which Talibuf Persianized by situating it within the classical genre of advice literature (*pand-nama*).[42] Talibuf also composed poetry with a strongly political orientation that was praised by the firebrand Iranian critic Ahmad Kasrawi (1890–1946).[43]

In the preface to his Russian translation of *Nukhba-yi Sipihri,* Talibuf explained that he wanted to make available to Muslim students within the Russian empire his "short history of the life of the Prophet and his teachings, and to provide Muslims, without regard to sectarian differences, instruction to which no Muslim scholar or European orientalist could object."[44] At the same time, Talibuf hoped with this translation of his life of the Prophet to give the Russian reader "a brief source for becoming acquainted with the history of Islam." Hence Talibuf's reformist agenda was directed to the many different constituencies to which his works circulated: to readers of Persian residing throughout the Persianate world, including of course Iran, who were interested in the latest advances in European thought, to Russophone Muslims of the Russian Empire of all sectarian, cultural, and linguistic backgrounds, and to Russians, for whom Islam was a foreign religion in their midst, concerning which they wished to know more.

STYLE AND FORM

Having examined the context and reception of Talibuf's writing, this chapter concludes by briefly considering its style and form, which also sets him apart from his contemporaries within and outside Iran. In stylistic terms, one feature that sets Talibuf's writing apart from his predecessors such as Akhundzada and Bakikhanuf is the simplicity of his language. It was due to this simplicity that the Russian Persianist E. Bertel's classed Talibuf's *Kitab-i Ahmad* (Book of Ahmad, 1893) as written within the rubric of children's literature in imitation of Jean-Jacques

Rousseau's *Émile* (1762). Talibuf's simple style conceals a complex literary strategy, as well as unmatched clarity of thought. As he explained in the preface to *Masalik al-Muhsinin*, Talibuf preferred simplicity of prose and had little use for excessive flourishes in language.[45]

Much like Akhundzada and to a lesser extent Bakikhanuf, Talibuf took a particular interest in foreign, particularly European, sources. With both thinkers, however, their engagement with European writers was multifarious and never directed exclusively at Europe. Akhundzada combined an interest in European enlightenment thinkers with an idealized account of pre-Islamic Persia and of Zoroastrianism before Islam.[46] Instead of celebrating the ancient past, Talibuf directed his attention to political transformations under way elsewhere in the world during his lifetime. *Masa'il al-Hayat* (Questions of Life, 1906), Talibuf's most detailed meditation on the different forms of government and the types of sovereignty appropriate to them, concluded with an extended translation from Japan's Meiji Constitution of 1868.[47] As a country that had emerged triumphant over a major European empire during the Russo-Japanese War (1904–5), and which had also creatively appropriated the most recent advances in European civilization, Japan for Talibuf and many like-minded Iranian thinkers represented a model for Iran to follow, of a non-European country that adopted the best practices of European empires without becoming subservient to them. The epic poem *Mikadu-nama* (Book of the Mikado, 1907) by Mirza Husayn-'Ali Tajir Shirazi, written to congratulate the "Emperor of the Sun and the Japanese people in the aftermath of Japan's victory," over Russia and discussed in Abbas Amanat's chapter, belongs to this same tradition.[48] Neither Talibuf nor Shirazi criticizes the Meiji Constitution's close relationship to the Prussian model.[49] They therefore miss the link between nationalist revivals and authoritarian governance. Focusing instead on the Meiji Restoration as a political process to emulate, Talibuf promoted the Meiji Constitution in his translation and in the commentary that accompanied it as a means of inspiring his readers to learn from modern methods of governance, and to advocate for a political system based on constitutional rights.

Like many of his predecessors, and particularly Akhundzada, Talibuf relies on pastiche as a literary method. He associates Voltaire with the claim that "complete sovereignty is contrary to nature."[50] Numerous passages from Sa'di's *Gulistan* also populate his work, including the first page of his collected teachings, *Siyasat-i Talibi* (Talibuf's Politics), where quotations from Sa'di frame a photograph of himself. These citations elide distinctions in culture and chronology as they amalgamate the world's learning into a universal repository. Finally, Talibuf resembles Akhundzada in his strategic deployment of techniques derived from fictional literary narrative throughout his nonfiction. Among Akhundzada's most famous works is *Maktubat* (Letters), an epistolary exchange between a fictional Mughal prince and an equally fictional Qajar ruler. Talibuf's nonfiction similarly deploys fictional devices, such as a father addressing his son in his *Kitab-i Ahmad* or his fictional travelogue *Masalik al-Muhsinin*.

Like Akhundzada, whose *Maktubat* was published with a special lexicon of foreign words for progressive ideas, and his fellow exile Mirza Malkum Khan, Talibuf's Persian overflows with a borrowed European lexicon, even in contexts where Persian words could have been used.[51] Terms like *qanun, impiratur,* and *diplumasi* suffuse Talibuf's prose, as if the repeated invocation of European keywords could facilitate the reception of European ideas within Islamic and Iranian thought.[52]

CONCLUSIONS

Talibuf's legacy is important for, among other reasons, the pressure it puts on us to rethink the circulation of knowledge between Russia and Iran during the early twentieth century. As Moritz Deutschmann has argued, "Although the Russo-Iranian border in the early twentieth century was not a serious obstacle to contacts between Iran and the South Caucasus . . . the border did start to have an impact on the field of politics in the region" during the second half of the nineteenth century.[53] The Constitutional Revolution was a turning point in this progressive transformation of border identities. The outcome of the revolution that Talibuf observed from afar is well known, but the vision that motivated it has broader implications for the study of Islamic modernism and the role of diasporic constituencies in shaping intellectual history. Across the Russian empire, the decades leading up to the 1905 revolution were a period of tremendous intellectual ferment. The same questions that were being asked in Iran during those years by Persian writers such as Talibuf were also asked by Daghestani reformers in Arabic, Azeri, and other languages of the Russian empire. The groundwork for posing many of these questions had been laid by Bakikhanuf and Akhundzada in prior decades.

To varying degrees, each reformer within this Persianate world reconceptualized the place of Islam in modernity along lines inaugurated by thinkers like Jamal al-Din al-Afghani (1838–97), although they had their disagreements, of course, with this pioneer of modern Islamic thought. While their Iranian counterparts worked to develop parliamentary forms of governance that incorporated classical liberal principles of the division of powers, Muslims of the Russian Empire turned to the Islamic past to develop a Muslim-majority society grounded in the rule of law and promising equality for all. Just as developments within Iran resonated with the reform movements that were transforming the Russian Empire during these years, the efforts of the Muslims of the Russian empire to create a new society should be considered with reference to the political transformations taking place in Iran during these same years, most notably the Constitutional Revolution.

In his efforts to introduce European learning as mediated by Russia to his Persian readers, Talibuf reveals a dimension of Russian-Iranian exchange that was too frequently submerged by the tense geopolitics that motivated Russia's generally obstructionist policies with respect to domestic politics in Iran. This extended to the bombardment of the first Iranian parliament (*majlis*), and to backing the shah against the Constitutionalists, even to the point of inflicting violence and hanging revolutionaries.[54] Even as these state-perpetrated actions expressed geopolitical might and power, new forms of cross-border affiliation were developing among intellectuals on both sides of the Iranian-Russian border. Talibuf's oeuvre is one of the most significant instances of these cross-border activities.

Talibuf's incorporation of the European Enlightenment in its Russian iteration into the Persian canon bears the mark of interpretive traditions that developed within the Russian empire, many of which resonated with key insights of Jadidism. The heterogeneity of the Iranian Constitutional revolution itself, which was, as Iago Gocheleishvili notes, "multi-national and multi-ideological" has been vastly underestimated.[55] At the same time, the role of revolutionaries from the Caucasus, in particular Georgians, in shaping the events in Iran, was fraught with ambiguities. As Deutschmann has shown, non-Muslim revolutionaries from the Caucasus, particularly Georgians, imposed their own sense of civilizational superiority on the very Iranians whose constitutional rights they sought to defend.[56] Meanwhile, writers such as Talibuf remained by and large above the fray and rejected such hierarchies, even while they refrained from directly commenting on the events of the day. Amid the false dichotomies propagated by revolutionaries and reactionaries past and present, Talibuf's work, which evolved according to a time scale different from that of many of his contemporaries, clarifies that neither democracy nor constitutionalism can legitimately be claimed as the exclusive possession of any specific culture.

NOTES

This research has been supported by the European Union's Horizon 2020 Research and Innovation Programme under ERC-2017-STG [grant agreement no. 759346].

1. For the genre of the prison poem, see Rebecca Ruth Gould, "Wearing the Belt of Oppression: Khāqānī's Christian Qaṣīda and the Prison Poetry of Medieval Shirvān," *Journal of Persianate Studies* 9, 1 (2016): 19–44, and for the specific spatial coordinates of this genre, Gould, "The Geographies of 'Ajam: The Circulation of Persian Poetry from South Asia to the Caucasus," *Medieval History Journal* 18, 1 (2015): 87–119.

2. For the impact of these deportations on Armenians, see Edmund Herzig, "The Deportation of the Armenians in 1604–05 and Europe's Myth of Shah Abbas I," in *Persian and Islamic Studies in Honor of P. W. Avery,* ed. Charles Melville (Cambridge: Cambridge University Center for Middle Eastern Studies, 1991), 59–71.

3. Rebecca Ruth Gould, "Sweetening the Heavy Georgian Tongue: Jāmī in the Georgian-Persianate Ecumene," in *A Worldwide Literature: Jāmī (1414–1492) in the Dār al-Islām and Beyond,* ed. Thibaut d'Hubert and Alexandre Papas (Leiden: Brill, 2019), 802–832.

4. For Georgian slavery at the Safavid court, see Kathryn Babayan, Sussan Babaie, Ina Baghdiantz-McCabe, and Massumeh Farhad, *Slaves of the Shah: New Elites of Safavid Iran* (London: I. B. Tauris, 2004).

5. Said Amir Arjomand, "The Salience of Political Ethic in the Spread of Persianate Islam," *Journal of Persianate Studies* 1, 1 (2008): 5.

6. Rudi Matthee, "The Decline of Safavid Iran in Comparative Perspective," *Journal of Persianate Studies* 8 (2015): 298.

7. Ibid., 295.

8. For a classic account of this print culture, see Edward G. Browne, *The Press and Poetry of Modern Persia* (Cambridge, Cambridge University Press, 1914), with a list of the major Persian journals on 1–153. More recently, see Yaḥya Aryanpur, *Az Saba ta Nima: Tarikh-i 150 Sal-i Adab-i Farsi*, 3 vols. (Tehran: Intisharat-i Zawwar, 1972–95; 2008–9), 2: 40–60.

9. Hasan Javadi, "Molla Nasreddin II. Political and Social Weekly," *Encyclopædia Iranica*, www.iranicaonline.org/articles/molla-nasreddin-ii-political-and-social-weekly.

10. Nile Green, "Paper Modernity? Notes on an Iranian Industrial Tour, 1818," *Iran: Journal of Persian Studies* 46 (2008): 277–84.

11. Scholarship on Jadidism is rapidly evolving, making it difficult to offer a definitive citation, but Adeeb Khalid's *The Politics of Muslim Cultural Reform: Jadidism in Central Asia* (Berkeley: University of California Press, 1999) may still be regarded as a standard text.

12. Adeeb Khalid, "Printing, Publishing, and Reform in Tsarist Central Asia," *International Journal of Middle East Studies* 26, 2 (1994): 188.

13. See Paolo Sartori, "It Was a Dark and Stagnant Night ('til the Jadids Brought the Light): Clichés, Biases, and False Dichotomies in the Intellectual History of Central Asia," 37–92; id., "*Ijtihād* in Bukhara: Central Asian Jadidism and Local Genealogies of Cultural Change," 193–236; and other contributions to *Beyond Modernism: Rethinking Islam in Russia, Central Asia and Western China (19th–20th Centuries)*, special issue on Jadidism, *Journal of the Economic and Social History of the Orient* 59, 1–2 (2016).

14. For a typology of the different elements that informed the thinking of this class of intellectuals, see Ali Gheissari, "Iran's Dialectic of the Enlightenment: Notes on Constitutional Experience and Conflicting Narratives of Modernity," in *Iran's Constitutional Revolution of 1906 and Narratives of the Enlightenment*, ed. Ali Ansari (London: Gingko Library, 2017).

15. Ali Ansari, "Introduction," in *Iran's Constitutional Revolution*, ed. id. Similarly highlighting the need for greater research focused on Iranian interactions with the Russian empire, Fariba Zarinebaf writes: "The opening of the Russian archives will shed light on a very important player in the constitutional revolution. That history is still to be written." See Fariba Zarinebaf, "From Istanbul to Tabriz: Modernity and Constitutionalism in the Ottoman Empire and Iran," *Comparative Studies of South Asia, Africa and the Middle East* 28, 1 (2008), 154n2.

16. Hassan Hakimian, "Wage Labor and Migration: Persian Workers in Southern Russia, 1880–1914," *International Journal of Middle East Studies* 17, 4 (1985): 443–62.

17. Moritz Deutschmann, "Cultures of Statehood, Cultures of Revolution: Caucasian Revolutionaries in the Iranian Constitutional Movement, 1906–1911," *Ab Imperio* 2 (2013): 170

18. See Hakimian, "Wage Labor and Migration," 445, table 1.

19. Rebecca Ruth Gould, "The Persianate Cosmology of Historical Inquiry in the Caucasus: 'Abbās Qulī Āghā Bākīkhānūf's Cosmological Cosmopolitanism," *Comparative Literature* 71, 3 (forthcoming).

20. Yahya Dawlatabadi, *Tarikh-i Mu'asir, ya Hayat-i Yahya* (Tehran: Kitabkhana-yi Ibn Sina, 1950–58), 112–14.

21. Iraj Afshar, *Zindagi-yi Tufani: Khatirat-i Sayyid Hasan Taqizada* (Costa Mesa, CA: Mazda, 1990), 26.

22. Yahya Aryanpur, *Az Saba ta Nima: Tarikh-i 150 Sal-i Adab-i Farsi* (Tehran: Intisharat-i Zawwar, 2008–9), 1: 287.

23. Iraj Parsinijad, "Talibuf-i Tabrizi," *Iranshinasi* 7, 3 (1990): 40.

24. For further details on Talibuf's biography, see M. Qazwini, "Talibuf Tabrizi," *Majala-yi Yadigar* 4, 5 (1327/1949): 86; Aryanpur, *Az Saba ta Nima*, vol. 1; and P.M. Alibekova, "Zhanrovye i idejno-khudozhestvennye osobennosti romana Abdurrahima Talibova 'Puti pravednyh'" (Kandidatskaia diss., Makhachkala, 1998).

25. See "Central Boulevard, Temir Khan Shura" and "Bazaar, Temir Khan Shura," Slavic and East European Collections, New York Public Library, Digital Collections 187.

26. For a detailed history of Temir Khan Shura, see B. I. Gadzhiev, *Temir-Khan-Shura* (Makhachkala, Dagestan, Russian Federation: Izd. Dom 'Dagestan, 2014).

27. Many of these volumes are catalogued in Milena Nurieva Osmanova, *Arabskaia pechatnaia kniga v Dagestane v kontse XIX–nachale XX veka* (Makhachkala, Dagestan, Russian Federation: Nauka Plius, 2006). Another Daghestan publisher who worked primarily with lithographs and used the *nast'aliq* script, Isma'il of Shulani (1867–1930), corresponded with Talibuf.

28. For the relation between different scripts and the new print culture, see K. K. Walther, "Die lithographische Vervielfaltigung von Texten in den Landern des Vorderen und Mittleren Orients," *Gutenberg-Jahrbuch* 65 (1990): 223–36.

29. Khalid, "Printing, Publishing, and Reform," 192.

30. Hasan al-Alqadari, *Diwan al-Mamnun* (Temir Khan Shura: al-Matba'a al-Islamiyya li Muhammad Mirza Mawrayuf, 1913), 189–91, 199–201.

31. Ibid., 189.

32. *Abusuf'ian Akaev: ėpokha, zhizn', deiatel'nost': Sbornik statei, perevodov i materialov*, ed. G. M.-R. Orazaev (Makhachkala, Dagestan, Russian Federation: Dagestanskoe knizhnoe izd-vo, 2012), 172

33. Kh. A. Omarov and G. M.-R. Orazaev, "Dokumenty i materialy o zhizni i tvorchestve A. Akaeva," in *Literaturnoe i nauchnoe nasledie Abusufyana Akaeva (Sbornik statei i materialov)*, ed. Orazaev (Makhachkala, Dagestan, Russian Federation: Institut istorii, iazyka i literatury im. G. Tsadasy, 1992), 108.

34. Mehran Mazinani, "On Liberty in Talebof's Thought," *Iranian Studies* 49, 3 (2015): 383–404.

35. For a still unsurpassed biography, see Hamid Algar, *Mirza Malkum Khan: A Biographical Study in Iranian Modernism* (Berkeley: University of California Press, 1973).

36. Rebecca Ruth Gould, "The Critique of Religion as Political Critique: Mīrzā FatḥʿAlī Ākhūndzāda's Pre-Islamic Xenology," *Intellectual History Review* 26, 2 (2016): 172.

37. Such patterns are chronicled in Iraj Parsinejad, *A History of Literary Criticism in Iran (1866–1951): Literary Criticism in the Works of Enlightened Thinkers of Iran: Akhundzadeh, Kermani, Malkom, Talebof, Maraghe'i, Kasravi and Hedayat* (Bethesda, MD: Ibex, 2003).

38. Aryanpur, , *Az Saba ta Nima*, 1: 289.

39. Talibuf, *Masalik al-Muhsinin* (Cairo: Matba'a-yi Hindiyya, 1323/1905), 4.

40. Talibuf, *Nukhba-i Sipihri* (Istanbul: n.p., 1310/1892), Talibov, *Istoriia Proroka Mukhameda* (Grozny, Chechen Republic, Russian Federation: Groznenskogo Tovarishhestva pechatnogo i izdatel'skogo dela, 1904).

41. Camille Flammarion, *Risala-yi Hayat-i Jadid* (Istanbul: n.p., 1312/1893–94).

42. Marku Awril [Marcus Aurelius], *Pand-nama-yi Markus, Qaysar-i Rum: Tafakkurat-i Marku Awril* (Istanbul: n.p., 1894).

43. Ahmad Kasrawi, *Tarikh-i Mashruta-yi Iran* (Tehran: Zawwar, 1340/1961), 43–46.

44. Talibov, "Predislovie," *Istoriia Proroka Muxameda* (Grozny: n.p., , 1904), i.

45. Talibuf, *Masalik al-Muhsinin*, 4–8.

46. Gould, "Critique of Religion," 172.

47. Talibuf, *Masa'il al-Hayat* (Tbilisi: n.p., 1906), 138–51. See also the discussion in Mana Kia, "Moral Refinement and Manhood in Persian," in *Civilizing Emotions: Concepts in Nineteenth Century Asia and Europe*, ed. Margrit Pernau, Christian Bailey, Einar Wigen, and Angelika C. Messner (Oxford: Oxford University Press, 2015), 158.

48. Ḥusayn ʿAli Tajir Shirazi, *Mikadu-nama* (Calcutta: Mattba'a-yi Ḥabl al-Matin, 1325/1907). See also Abbas Amanat's chapter 12 in this volume on Adib Pishawari.

49. Bernd Martin, *Japan and Germany in the Modern World* (Oxford: Berghahn Books, 2005), 17–78.

50. Talibuf, *Masa'il al-Hayat*, 115.

51. Shiva Balaghi, "Constitutionalism and Islamic Law in Nineteenth-Century Iran: Mirza Malkum Khan and Qanun," *Human Rights with Modesty: The Problem of Universalism,* ed. András Sajó (New York: Springer, 2005), 327348.

52. Talibuf, *Siyasat-i Talibi,* 7 and 5 respectively.

53. Deutschmann, "Cultures of Statehood," 188.

54. Stephanie Cronin, *The Army and Creation of the Pahlavi State in Iran, 1921–1926* (London: I. B. Tauris, 1997), 61.

55. Iago Gocheleishvili, "Georgian Sources on the Iranian Constitutional Revolution (1905–1911): Sergo Gamdlishvili's Memoirs of the Gilan Resistance," *Iranian Studies* 40, 1 (2007): 59 and 85.

56. Deutschmann, "Cultures of Statehood," 178.

12

From Peshawar to Tehran

An Anti-imperialist Poet of the Late Persianate Milieu

Abbas Amanat

Colonial experiences in South and West Asia in the eighteenth and nineteenth centuries, followed by the rise of nationalist postcolonial ideologies in the twentieth century, bore a heavy cultural baggage of identity politics. Whatever their advantages, these experiences helped to shrink the forlorn milieu we now identify as the Persianate world, a once thriving sociocultural sphere that stretched from Khotan to Sarajevo and from Tbilisi to Mysore.[1] As probably the last Indo-Persian scholar-poet to cross not only the geographical but also the sectarian divides between the Sunni Indo-Afghan world and Shi'i Iran, Adib Pishawari (ca. 1844–1930) is an insightful case study of the retracting Persianate world on the cusp of the eras of colonialism and nationalism.

Adib's journey from India to Iran was only possible because he was the product of a rich and still vibrant Persianate Sufi heritage with a Shi'i affiliation, as well as being a recipient of the rich tradition of classical Perso-Arabic *adab* (literary humanism), which he mastered over decades of travel and trouble. Raised in Peshawar, he journeyed as a young man to Kabul and Mashhad and eventually Tehran, where he spent the remaining half century of his long life and died on May 30, 1930. His haphazard, almost subliminal, striving for a cultural revival relied primarily on the classical Persian literary heritage of the tenth and eleventh centuries, but also on the literary and philosophical heritage of Sufism and on the classical Arabic tradition. Yet he was more than a literary figure, an *adib*, as the surname he chose for himself suggests. In addition to the poetic, lexicographical, and Sufi dimensions of his character, Adib held strong anticolonial views, rooted in his unhappy personal history.

This was a potent combination and would have been ideal for the making of a modern Persianate activist—had it not been negated by his arcane literary orientation and reclusive personality. Adib's poetry was scarcely appreciated beyond the small circle of late Qajar and early Pahlavi literati who patronized and sustained him in Iran. Moreover, his anticolonial message never got off the ground, wrapped as it was in unfamiliar poetic imagery that was unfathomable to the distinctly modern Iranian readers of the early twentieth century. Adib's career nonetheless traces the retraction of the formerly far-flung Persianate world.

ORIGINS AND EDUCATION

Adib was born Sayyid Ahmad Rizawi around 1844, most likely into a Shi'i family in a village in Kunar in the Sarhad region.[2] His birthplace was located 130 kilo-meters northeast of Jalalabad and 230 kilometers north of Peshawar in what soon came to be known as the North West Frontier Province of British India. While he was very young, his family moved to the city of Peshawar, presumably because of intertribal clashes in the region. He came from a family of sayyids known as Ojaq (or Ajaq, meaning "hearth"), a term of tribal kinship. Both his father Shihab al-Din (known as Sayyid Baba) and his grandfather Sayyid 'Abd al-Razzaq were Sufi masters with followings in and around Peshawar. According to Adib's devo-tee and biographer 'Ali 'Abd al-Rasuli (1879–1943), the family was attached to the Suhrawardi Sufi order. In the latter part of the nineteenth century, there were no Suhrawardi khanaqahs in the region,[3] Adib's family nonetheless became known for its Sufi remembrance of God (zikr), and the people of the Peshawar and its surroundings paid homage to it, perhaps an indication that their Sufi network in Peshawar also reached to the Kunar, Waziristan, and Khyber regions.[4]

In his Qaysar-nama (Book of the Kaiser, composed around 1917), where he de-voted a short passage to his early life, Adib paid homage to his father for his early education:

> He entrusted [my education] to the care of a well-versed ascetic,
> At the start of each month he paid off the tuition.[5]

Beyond private tuition, Adib's study of "preliminaries" (muqadimat) in the ma-drasa, and his interest in literature and philosophy, seem to have all followed the classical Perso-Arabic curriculum. There is no mention in his poetry of knowledge of Pashto or even Urdu, suggesting that at the time Persian was still the language of high culture in Peshawar.

At some stage in his youth, Adib's father and most of his male paternal and maternal relatives were killed fighting British Indian forces, perhaps in the 1863 Ambela Campaign against the Pashtuns of the North West Frontier, which re-sulted in a thousand British casualties and the deaths of an unknown number of Pashtun fighters. According to British records, the colonial army did not engage the local population of Peshawar in that campaign,[6] but Sufi masters (pirs), such as the members of the Adib's family, were natural leaders of a jihad against the British and may well have fought alongside the rural Pashtuns of the neighboring region. According to Adib, his elderly maternal grandfather Sayyid 'Abd al-Samad carried the banner onto the battlefield before being cut to pieces by the British forces. His father, uncles, cousins, and other members of his family also fought and died. Adib himself sustained two serious wounds, which left him bedridden for eleven months.[7]

Anticolonial resistance had a long history in the region, and no doubt in the living memory of Adib's family. Six years earlier, during the "Indian Mutiny" of 1857–58, after the British had crushed the sepoy mutineers in Punjab, they staged a public execution of rebellious Muslim sepoys in Peshawar, presumably to remind the local population of the grave consequences of putting up any resistance. The Peshawar garrison surrendered without resistance. In 1860, the British victory parade—the so-called Grand Durbar through the streets of Peshawar, with a row of elephants carrying the British viceroy and his court—conveyed a similar message to the bewildered public, who continued nurse anti-British resentment.

A revealing incident, which offers a clue to the young Adib's state of mind, occurred (presumably shortly after 1858) when he was thirteen years old. Many years later, he recalled that in the Peshawar bazaar he had heard a wandering dervish reciting a story from Rumi's *Masnawi* about the Prophet Muhammad and the peace of Hudaybiyya, a well-known episode in which in year six of the Hijra (that is, 628 CE), Muhammad made peace with the infidels of the Quraysh. At one point in his recitation, the dervish came to the verse:

> Suddenly descended upon that light of the prophets,
> The drumbeats of good fortune: "We Conquered!"[8]

On hearing this, the youthful Adib was so moved—presumably in frustration over peace with the British infidels—that he hit his head against a wall until blood ran all over his face.[9] The event, a variant on a familiar trope in Sufi biographies, apparently inspired his lifelong engagement with the *Masnawi*.[10] Soon afterwards, another incident (presumably shortly after 1863) hastened his departure from Peshawar. An argument with a British missionary in the local bazaar led to a brawl in which Adib slapped the missionary's face. This subsequently led to Adib's arrest and detention for nine days. Upon his release, a council of the family's women headed by Adib's mother, Mahd 'Ulya, persuaded him to leave Peshawar for Kabul in the hope that his education as a cleric (*'alim*) might "provide for a group of desperate women."[11]

Under the Afghan ruler Dust Muhammad Khan (r. 1826–39, 1845–63), then an ally of the British, Kabul was nonetheless a haven for Sufi families driven out of the North West Frontier Province. Several of the Sufi families who settled there received pensions and land assignments. We may therefore surmise that in dispatching Adib to Kabul, his mother (herself the offspring of Husayni sayyid Sufi nobility) hoped that he would benefit from Dust Muhammad Khan's patronage. But for reasons unknown, Adib does not seem to have succeeded in this. His family's Shi'i affinity was far from welcome in Kabul, especially after the short-lived Qajar capture of Herat in 1856 led to Dust Muhammad's falling out with Qajar Iran during the Anglo-Persian

War of 1856-57. With British support, Dust Muhammad then expanded his control over Herat, making a great leap toward the unification of Afghanistan.[12]

Even without royal patronage, residence in Kabul offered Adib a chance to further his education. For two years, he studied in a local madrasa there. Then, moving south to Ghazni, where he resided at the tomb of the celebrated Persian poet Sana'i Ghaznawi (d. 1131), and later at the nearby tomb of Sultan Mahmud Ghazna (r. 998–1030) in a cemetery known as Bagh-i Fayruzi. There, for eighteen months, he studied philosophy (*hikmat*) and the literary sciences (*adab*) under a mullah named Sa'd al-Din. This appears to have been his first serious engagement with *adab* literature. From Ghazni, he moved on to Herat, where he stayed for another fourteen months, and thence to Turbat-i Jam in Iranian Khurasan, where he stayed for another eighteen months in the shrine of the celebrated Shaykh Ahmad-i Jam (d. 1141).

By the time he arrived in Mashhad, around 1869, he seems to have undergone the typical training of an itinerant Sufi in the middle decades of the nineteenth century: classical Persian and Arabic language and literature, with some mystical philosophy, perhaps a mix of Avicennan philosophy and Neoplatonic *ishraq* (illuminationism). It is difficult to believe that there were substantial libraries in the Sufi shrines in which he resided, but there must have been enough books to afford him a degree of erudition. Oral traditions of learning must have played an important part in his education as well. This especially seems to be the case in view of his famed memory and capacity to learn by heart a vast body of poetry in Persian and Arabic, as well as his ease in repeating long and complex passages of poetry after merely hearing them once. He belonged to an oral culture that survived, especially in the format of verse (*nazm*), for at least a millennium. That as a habit later in life he listened and memorized a great deal, and borrowed books to read and memorize rather than acquiring a large book collection of his own, similarly points to the place of oral learning in the Persianate world before print culture became dominant. Difficult though it is, much of his own poetry also reveals aspects of this orality, for example, through greater emphasis on the rhythm and sonority of words and phrases rather than on their substance. His was a species of poetic wizardry that was soon to become extinct in the face of modern print-based knowledge.

Life in Mashhad therefore did not fundamentally change Adib's approach to learning. But it did draw him more into the study of philosophy, the rational sciences (*'ulum-i 'aqliyya*), especially mathematics, and poetics and stylistics (*'ulum-i adabiyya*). Although we might imagine that studying under three teachers in Mashhad converted him into a methodic textual scholar, very little of that appears in the small body of scholarly prose writing he left behind. It is as if he never cast off the orality of his earlier years. However, Mashhad did bring out more of his affinity with Shi'ism. Crossing the essentially Sunni zone of Afghanistan into Shi'i Iran gave him the chance to appreciate, and be appreciated, as a *sayyid,* a descendant of the Prophet who composed lengthy panegyrics (*qasidas*) in honor of the families of the Prophet and the Twelfth Imam. That he was a *sayyid* of Razawi descent on his paternal side, as well as of Husayni descent on the maternal side, must have been a special source of pride in a city that housed the tomb of the Eighth Shi'i Imam, Musa al-Riza (d. 818), the progenitor of the Razawi *sayyids*. Yet study in Mashhad did not turn him into a Shi'i jurist (*mujtahid*), nor, as far as we know, did it result in his engagement with jurisprudence and the *naqliyya* (transmitted) Shi'i religious sciences.

Adib's personal proclivities aside, his interest in the '*aqliyya* (rationalist sciences) was in great part due to the fact that, even in the latter part of the nineteenth century, something of the old Khurasani cultural milieu still existed in Mashhad. Despite being home to some jurists, Mashhad's teaching circles resisted the Najaf-oriented Usuli legalism that came to dominate Isfahan and other centers of Shi'i learning in Qajar Iran. Remarkably, one of his teachers of philosophy and the rational sciences in Mashhad was Mulla Ghulam-Husayn Shaykh al-Islam, presumably the chief judge of the city. He may in turn have been instrumental in Adib's next move, in 1871, to Sabzawar, to study with Haji Mulla Hadi Sabzawari (d. 1873), then the most prominent representative of the school of philosophy founded by Mulla Sadra (d. 1640). As the author of the famous *Manzuma,* a long poem in Arabic covering a whole gamut of logic and Islamic theosophical philosophy, Mulla Hadi had preferred the seclusion of his hometown to madrasas in larger cities such as Mashhad or Isfahan. According to Arthur de Gobineau, who showed some interest in the study of philosophy in Iran in the middle decades of the nineteenth century, Mulla Hadi's fame attracted students not only from eastern Khurasan but from Central Asia, Arabia, and even as far away as Tibet.[13] Adib studied for two years under Mulla Hadi's son, Mulla Muhammad, and perhaps also under Mulla Hadi himself toward the end of the latter's life.

After Mulla Hadi's death in 1873, Adib returned to Mashhad. But this did not set him on a conventional madrasa path, even though he was by then gaining some fame under what would become his lasting sobriquet "Adib-i Hindi" (Indian [literary] scholar). The title of *adib* (scholar) rather than "mullah," the usual term for members of the '*ulama,* and by extension for anyone who had some form of traditional Shari'a-based education, clearly differentiated him. Adib's scholarly orientation was perhaps too unorthodox to allow him to establish a teaching circle in the style of the madrasa-based Shi'i jurists. According to his biographer, while living in Mashhad, he would wander for days on end on the outskirts of the city, loudly reciting passages from Rumi's *Masnawi* till he reached the state of ecstasy.[14] He had by now reportedly memorized all six books of the *Masnawi* and his recitation style, in a low voice, resembled the incantations (*zikr*) of the Sufis. This behavior was in tune with that of the wandering dervishes, especially the so-called entranced (*majzub*) Sufis who were more common in the Sufi-dominated eastern Persianate world, particularly India. Adib's recitations in the wilderness got so out of hand that, fearing for his own sanity, he had to force himself to give up the practice.

Restored to sobriety, he placed greater emphasis on literary erudition, as he mustered a repository of Perso-Arabic poetic and lexicographic knowledge. Memorize long, complex verse passages, including numerous classical qasidas from pre-Islamic Arabic poetry and from the Persian poetry of the Khurasan school, made him a noted mnemonist. Residing in the Mirza Ja'far madrasa, adjacent to the shrine of Imam Riza, he occasionally hosted a literary circle (anjuman) devoted to poetry and literary debate. His circle, a novel kind of gathering perhaps, was significant enough to come to the attention of Mirza Sa'id Khan Ansari Garmrudi Maw'taman al-Mulk, who earlier served for two decades as minister of foreign affairs under Nasir al-Din Shah (r. 1848–96). However, at the time when he came to know Adib, between 1873 and 1879, Sa'id Khan was serving as the custodian (mutawalli) of the shrine of Imam Riza in honorable exile.¹⁵ A man of literary sophistication, well versed in Persian and Arabic poetry, Sa'id Khan was the first to recognize the accomplishments of Adib-i Hindi and act as his informal patron. Apparently, it was Sa'id Khan who, after his return to office in 1879, persuaded Adib to move from Mashhad to Tehran in 1882, possibly with an eye to establishing a literary anjuman in the Qajar capital.¹⁶ Mirza Sa'id was no doubt aware of the Anjuman-i Khaqan (Royal Society) of the era of Fath 'Ali Shah (r. 1797–1834), and it is quite possible that he was attempting to create something equivalent for the Nasiri era.

AN INDIAN *ADIB* IN QAJAR TEHRAN

Adib lived the life of a virtually homeless dervish, detached from his surroundings and on the brink of seclusion, during his half-century in Tehran. If he was brought to Tehran to be part of a cultural project, he produced little written work so far as his record shows. For nearly fifteen years, up to 1897, he was a "scholar in residence" in the house of Mirza Muhammad 'Ali Mu'awin al-Mulk (later known as Qawam al-Dawla), where he practically lived in the library. Mu'awin al-Mulk was a high-ranking, affluent state accountant (mastawfi) in the Qajar administration whose father, Mirza 'Abbas Qawam al-Mulk, was a colleague and friend of Mirza Sa'id, who had brought Adib to Tehran. Mu'awin himself had held various high offices under Nasir al-Din Shah. Yet judging by the dearth of available evidence, Mu'awin al-Mulk was not entirely a man of the establishment. Presumably well educated and with a large library, he had twice travelled to Europe, once in the retinue of Nasir al-Din Shah and once on his own. He seems to have been in the camp of Mirza 'Ali Khan Amin al-Dawla (1843–1904), a well-known reform-minded senior statesman of the Nasiri era, who also served briefly as the chief minister of Muzaffar al-Din Shah (r. 1896–1907). When Amin al-Dawla was dismissed in disgrace in 1901, Mu'awin al-Mulk was also accused of taking part in a plot against Muzaffar al-Din Shah, arrested, disgraced, and sent into exile.

So Adib had to look for a new patron. He continued to live as a guest in the houses of other members of the Qajar cultural elite, men of affluence who had literary or Sufi affinities. Though his hosts seem to have taken care of him, he apparently was not a recipient of a state pension or any other regular source of income. In his later years, he was said to routinely frequent a bookstore in the capital, where he would sit for long, lonely hours reading newly published books. Nor did he hold regular teaching sessions, though he did occasionally read Sufi or literary texts with promising students, among them the famous scholar Muhammad Qazwini (1874–1949) and, later in his life, the leading literary critic Badi' al-Zaman Furuzanfar (1903–70). Over time, despite being solitary, aloof, and ill tempered, Adib came to be recognized as the star of Tehran's literary circles. As was often reported, his command of literature and lexicography, improved over decades by access to significant manuscripts and printed collections in Mashhad and Tehran, lent him an impressive presence.

A wide range of celebrated Qajar poets, scholars, statesmen, Sufis, and literary and artistic personalities attended the literary circle presided over by Sayyid Muhammad Baqa Ashraf al-Kuttab (later known as Sharaf al-Ma'ali, 1841–1913), who was known as a poet, calligrapher, and Sufi adept.[17] Held in Baqa's house, this was the first literary society (anjuman) in Qajar Iran known to be in session on a weekly basis, which went on for a quarter of a century from around 1886 to 1913. Adib became its principal figure, even though he apparently did not attend regularly. His close affiliation with Baqa, an influential Ni'matullahi Sufi, was a crucial conduit for his introduction to the late Qajar cultural elite. Baqa even arranged for Adib to have an audience with Nasir al-Din Shah. In his later years, during the early Pahlavi era, Adib continued to appear in a literary circle that seems to have revived Baqa's anjuman. It included some of early twentieth-century Iran's most influential statesmen and literary figures.[18]

The sobriquet adib, a somewhat rare title for a learned man of his time, should not therefore be seen as a mere hyperbole. Rather, it was a signifier of a new form of erudition, distinct from religious (and more specifically Shari'a-based and jurist-dominated) scholarship. To the extent that can be determined, it was applied to masters of both Arabic and Persian as early as eleventh century, a time when Persian literature first emerged in the eastern Islamic world.[19] By the Qajar era, and even more so in the post-Constitutional period after 1906, adib implied similar Perso-Arabic mastery, as well as a certain continuity with the classical era of Persian literature. This was important, because some of the early Qajar poets, historians and statesmen who were involved in the literary movement known as the "School of Return" (maktab-i bazgasht) sought to revive

FIGURE 15. The end of an Indo-Persian era: portrait of Adib Pishawari during his last years in Tehran. Undated photograph by unknown photographer in Pishawari, *Diwan-i Adib-i Pishawari*, ed. ʿAli ʿAbd al-Rasuli (Tehran, 2000), unnumbered plate.

the Persian classical past, especially the Khurasan school of the tenth and eleventh centuries.[20]

In the Qajar era, *adib* first seems to have been bestowed as a title on Mirza Hasan Taliqani (1848–1919), a contemporary of Adib Pishawari's. In the early 1870s, Taliqani was among the original authors of the incomplete multivolume biographical dictionary *Nama-yi Danishwaran-i Nasiri*, begun shortly before Adib's arrival in Tehran. Both the title *Adib al-'Ulama*, given to Taliqani by Nasir al-Din Shah, and his association with the encyclopedic project under prince I'tizad al-Saltana recalled the classical concepts of *adab* and *adib*.[21] Another holder of the title and near contemporary of Adib Pishawari's was Adib Nishaburi, who was also from Khurasan and in many respects mirrored Adib Pishawari's literary erudition.[22] Muhammad Husayn Zuka' al-Mulk Furughi, a celebrated literary figure of the late Nasiri era and a friend and colleague of Adib's, also chose *adib* as his poetic pen name. He collaborated with Adib in the first published edition of Abu al-Fazl Bayhaqi's famous *Tarikh-i Mas'udi* (better known as *Tarikh-i Bayhaqi*), which was published in Tehran in 1889. In his preface, Furughi praised Adib Pishawari in no uncertain terms for his in-depth, all-embracing command of language and his piercing editorial judgment.[23] Adib was responsible for reviving a forgotten text, at that point unknown and unappreciated, Furughi pointed out.

The phenomenon of the *adib,* of which Pishawari was one of the most prominent representatives, should therefore be seen as a late stage in a century-long process of Persian cultural identity formation in the age of proto-nationalism. Yet despite its reliance on the rich heritage of the classical past, Qajar *adab* had limited capacity to shape the predominant discourse of cultural modernity of its time. This is even more evident when we consider the anti-imperialist themes in Adib's poetry.

THE POETRY OF ADIB PISHAWARI

Given Adib Pishawari's literary reputation, his written output is unimpressive, even poor, both in volume and, despite the approbation of his contemporaries, perhaps also in quality. Moreover, his attempt to address the realities of the world around him and the major upheavals of his time in his poetry (World War I in particular) is disappointing. He failed to employ the classical style and model as a means of creating poetry with a sociopolitical message. In the published edition, his *Diwan* comprises about 4,200 Persian verses and 370 Arabic verses, consisting of 37 very long "odes" (*qasida*) of 100 verses on average; 30 lyrical poems (*ghazal*); and some miscellaneous pieces. The *qasida*s are in an arcane and verbose style reminiscent of the most complex odes of the medieval Khurasani poets, such as the relatively obscure twelfth-century poet 'Usman Mukhtari Ghaznawi, who was known for his highly complex (and tedious) panegyrics.[24] Like 'Usman's poems, and the relative simplicity of the writings of many of the

Khurasani poets of the tenth and eleventh centuries, Adib's *qasida*s are replete with obscure words, impenetrable imagery, curious allusions, challenging meters, and tiresome didactics. His goal was more to impress the reader with his lexicographic command than to share poetic sentiments, or even convey a coherent message. Many lines of barren lexical wizardry go by before the reader can detect a glimmer of substance.

A case in point is a *qasida* entitled *Shikwa'iya dar Ma'ani-yi Jang-i 'Umumi* (Eulogy on the Realities of the Great War). Consisting of about 280 verses composed in the style of the famous *khamriyat* (wine-praising) poems of the eleventh-century panegyrist Manuchihri Damghani (d. 1040). It starts

> O cup-bearer! Give [me] a heavy jug of wine cultivated by the squire [*dihqan*],
> A wine that the *dihqan* of the wine jar breeds like soul in the human body.[25]

Yet, despite its great promise, the *qasida* contains barely a single verse that is pertinent to the title. The closest is an allusion to an obscure villain in the *Shah-nama*:

> With much ado, Pilsam rose from among the Turks.
> Bring forward Rustam's Rakhsh! So he can secure victory over Turan.[26]

Even the most substantive of Adib's *qasida*s are often devoid of a concise and clear message. Of the total of thirty-seven panegyrics in his *Diwan*, seven pay homage to the Creator, the Prophet, his son-in-law 'Ali ibn Abi-Talib, and the Lord of the Age (i.e., the Mahdi), which were all predictable topics for a Shi'i poet. Another five are didactic. But the most significant group, comprising some twenty five poems, are meant to have some political bearing. Of these, thirteen are in praise of Kaiser Wilhelm II and the German exploits during World War I, while another twelve are reflections on the misfortunes that had befallen on Iran, India, Afghanistan, and Egypt at the hands of the British Empire.

This group of political *qasida*s sounds a clearer, more consistent voice of protest. Invariably, the anti-British theme—expressed in the strongest of terms—complements an almost messianic aspiration for German success in the war that is often addressed to the person of Wilhelm II, Adib's wartime hero. Most, if not all, of these poems were composed in a brief span of time, roughly between 1916 and 1919, and barely make reference to any other political or social topic. Indeed, there are very few surviving poems by Adib of earlier or later years, and virtually none contain other historical references. It is as if Germany's entry into World War I, rather than any other major events in his long life, motivated him in this endeavor. This is particularly striking given the array of major upheavals Adib must have witnessed during his decades of residence in Iran, not to mention his earlier years. In the two decades of the late nineteenth and early twentieth centuries, he must have seen the Regie Protest (1891–92), the assassination of Nasir al-Din Shah (1896), the Constitutional Revolution and its aftermath (1905–11), and later the coup of 1921, the rise of Riza Khan, and eventually the demise of the Qajar dynasty in 1925. None of these events seems to have moved Adib, at least not to the extent of triggering his poetic inspiration. Among his Arabic *qasida*s there is a poem on the execution in 1909 of Shaykh Fazlullah Nuri, a prominent anti-Constitutional jurist (*mujtahid*) in Tehran. This may well be taken as further evidence of Adib's anti-Constitutional stance.[27] If so, his rather facile anticolonialism was devoid of any democratic dimension.

That in a period of three years he inflexibly composed thirteen *qasida*s, most of them terse and unreadable, in unreserved praise of Kaiser Wilhelm, one of the most despised political figures of the early twentieth century, is all the more a proof of Adib's skewed worldview and misplaced hopes. At best, he can be seen as a naïve poet blinded by Germany's military glitter and at worst as an admirer of an authoritarian warmonger who happened to be anti-British. Even if, as his biographer would led us believe, Adib was a master of all twelve branches of classical knowledge, his poetry reveals no awareness of Germany's own colonialist exploits, which among other crimes led to the first genocide in the twentieth century against the Herero and Namaqua peoples in south-western Africa (today's Namibia) in 1903–4. Nor does he seem to have been aware of the Kaiser's racist views, or even his close, if vexed, relations with the British crown.[28]

Adib's imagined *Qaysar* (the Persian term for Kaiser), the valiant smasher of the British Empire, was about as related to the reality of the German Kaiser Wilhelm as Adib's ode was celebrated beyond his limited circle. None of these *qasida*s were published in his lifetime, or even distributed beyond a very small group of friends and admirers. Even if they had been, it is highly unlikely that the majority of his readers would have made much sense of them. In that respect, the propaganda value of his Germanophilia was probably close to zero. Yet Adib did not seek a wide audience. Once 'Abd al-Rasuli humbly pointed out that a passage in one of Adib's *qasida*s describing a rifle was so complex that "out of a thousand [people], perhaps one can understand it." Adib responded: "I composed this poem for the sake of that one person."[29]

In addition to his pro-German *qasida*s, Adib also composed a long epic poem titled *Qaysar-nama* (Book of the Kaiser) in further praise of Wilhelm II. Originally comprising around 14,000 verses (of which only around 4,000 have survived), it was, predictably, in the style of Firdawsi's *Shah-nama,* to which it made frequent allusions.[30] Despite Adib's conscious effort to write unhindered Persian verse in the style of the *Shah-nama,* here too his style is arduous and substantially inaccessible. *Qaysar-nama* is not entirely devoid of vivid passages, however, such as those wishing the downfall of the British Empire or complaining of the misfortunes that had befallen his homeland and his host country, or expressing his own emotional pain. Ideology aside, the poem reads as if a classical Khurasani poet of the eleventh century had composed it. The opening passage in one version of *Qaysar-nama* clearly demonstrates Adib's mastery of the epic genre:

Because of the poets the world is worthwhile,
For the world is alive because of the poets.
The word is the eye and the poet is the eye's creator,
Look at the entire universe through that eye.[31]

Yet beyond this opening, with its profound mystical undertones, the poem largely
lacks coherence. Wherever Adib tried to inject narrative, as in his description of
the German invasion of Romania—a minor affair in late 1916 that Adib portrayed
as a resounding German victory—his efforts border on the surreal, if not farcical.
Qaysar-nama betrays the suppressed aspirations of a pained but timid soul who
could wage a wishful war against the British Empire, his existential nemesis, only
in the solitude of his own niche.

Like his odes in praise of the Kaiser, his *Qaysar-nama* was a by-product of the
intense Germanophilia (known as *almandusti)* that swept Iran and the neighboring lands throughout World War I. Praise for a powerful rival to the imperial powers surrounding Iran was not limited to the German emperor. Another example
is seen in Mirza Husayn-'Ali Tajir Shirazi's *Mikadu-nama* (Book of the Mikado),
which praised the Japanese emperor and people in the aftermath of Japan's victory
in the Russo-Japanese War of 1904–5.[32] *Mikadu-nama* was one of several turn-of-
the-century epics in the style of the *Shah-nama* that served as a literary backdrop
to what Adib would go on to produce in 1916 in his *Qaysar-nama.*

As in the Ottoman Empire under the Young Turks and Afghanistan under
Habibullah Khan (r. 1901–19), in Iran, German propaganda during World War
I raised hopes of deliverance from the British and Russian imperial yoke. At the
outbreak of the war, a small but active clique of pro-German Iranian journalists
and poets composed poems and published articles in defiance of the British threat
and in admiration of the German rise to power. The majority of Iranian nationalists, disillusioned with the sour outcome of their own Constitutional Revolution
of 1906, were resentful of the neighboring powers and their mischief, especially
the 1907 Anglo-Russian Agreement that divided Iran into two zones of influence.
They welcomed the ascendance of Germany just as much as they welcomed the
war as a long-awaited moment of deliverance.[33]

The poet and journalist Wahid Dastgirdi, a well-known Germanophile, was
imaginative enough to distribute his poems in praise of Germany via the wandering dervishes who were still traversing a sections of the Persianate world. His
Darwish-i Shurishi (Rebellious Dervish), a long poem recited in the bazaars and
public gatherings of Isfahan, included such verses as:

The iron fist of imperial Germany,
Suffocates Russia and Britain.

and

Iran and Germany are united in race,
In the battlefield both fight like Rustam and Shirzad.[34]

Composed at the height of this pro-German period, Adib's *Qaysar-nama* should be seen in the polarized political milieu of its time. According to one source, Adib's fame persuaded the German ambassador in Tehran to pay the reclusive poet a visit and to propose the publication of his *Qaysar-nama*. Adib reportedly turned down the offer on the grounds that he composed it not out of "love for Germany but out of hatred for Britain [*na az ru-yi dusti-i Alman wali dushmani-yi Ingilis*]."[35] Given the complexity of Adib's style, it seems more plausible that the German diplomat approached Adib for reasons of prestige than propaganda. By 1918, in any case, growing uncertainty about the fortunes of the war seems to have persuaded Adib to abandon the project. For the same reason, he wanted his *Qaysar-nama* to remain unpublished during his lifetime.[36]

Irrespective of the success or failure of this particular poetic enterprise, Adib's fascination with the *Shah-nama* should be attributed to more than either Firdawsi's masterful narration or the suitability of the epic meter he had employed. As with many of his predecessors and contemporaries, Adib's efforts to replicate the Persian classical legend should also be attributed to the *Shah-nama*'s mytho-historical narrative, particularly its legendary parts. Firdawsi's old Persian legends appealed to Adib, as to many before him, not only for their capacity to glorify political and military might, but also because they engendered messianic hopes for the advent of a Faridun-like savior to rise up against the Zahhak-like powers of latter days. Or, alternatively, for a Rustam-like restorer of stability and glory against the ever-present threat of a Turani other.

PERSIAN POETRY IN THE WAKE OF WORLD WAR I

At the close of the war, Adib's enthusiasm turned into frustration. His "intense interest in politics"—which often made him "discuss politics with everyone" and consider "love for the homeland and independence [*istiqlal*] his religion and inner self"—now saw "gravitation toward foreigners and betraying one's country as the gravest sin." But in a brief period of poetic activity that followed the end of the war, his disillusionment with Germany's defeat was intertwined with new hope of Iran's deliverance. In a *qasida* of 142 verses entitled "Politics and Upheavals in Iran," composed most likely in mid-1918, he demonstrated both poetic command and depth of emotion.[37] This was despite his usual complexity of imagery and countless references to the literary heritage of the past, with which he was as keenly enthralled as ever. The poem opens with the following verse:

> There rose from Mount Alborz a cloud dark as a woman of Zanzibar,
> Pregnant with sedition and barren of [moral] shackles.[38]

Aside from the misogynistic, even racist, imagery that runs through the poem, and which becomes even more explicit in later verses, the *qasida* mourned the doomed fortune of Iran at a critical juncture in its history. The "dark cloud" and other scornful attributes were references to British colonialism and, in a milder fashion, to President Woodrow Wilson and the Americans who had entered the war on the side of the Allies in early 1918. The *qasida*'s other context was the aftermath of the 1917 Bolshevik Revolution and end of Russia's occupation of Iran, when the British North Persia Force came to occupy the entire country from the Persian Gulf to the Caspian.

This was an unexpected and unnerving experience for Adib. Now he condemned Britain for "spreading seeds of anxiety all over the earth" and for "uprooting trees of calm and safety." Britain was a power that spread "the dust of misfortune" and "insecurity" over Iran and turned it into a "puppet in the hands of demons," "a grazing land for wild beasts." Only the annihilation of London could allow such barren gardens as the land of Iran to thrive again. Were it not for the vagaries of destiny, he proclaimed, the "German King" would have been able to "crush the head of this evil witch [*pityara*]." If destiny had not brought Wilson's Americans into the war, "the hand of the [Anglo-]Saxons would have been severed from the earth" and for every slain Iranian "a hundred Georges and a couple of [Lord] Curzons would have been slain." In a double entendre, the name George alluded not only to King George V but also to Britain's wartime prime minister, David Lloyd George.

It was at this point in the poem that Adib turned his attention to his birthplace, India. He voiced his wish that the "Peacock of India" (*Tawus-i Hind*) would turn into a scavenging vulture and "wipe out all the sneaks and rats" from his homeland. He further called on Iranians to rise up to support the Afghans and Arabs so that everyone could be saved from the hellfire of British sedition and rest instead in the garden of security. He then warned Iranians not to "harvest with a sickle" (an allusion no doubt to the hammer and sickle of the Bolshevik Revolution) but instead to look at the enslaved Irish as a model of patriotic honor. After much elaboration, Adib concluded the *qasida* with the following lines in praise of his own poetry:

> As long as a soul is in my body, it will not rest from this agony,
> So if I am long-winded, there is an obvious excuse.
> Know that my every verse is a piercing arrow aimed at the enemy,
> So as to cut through even armor of Indian steel.[39]

Another extensive *qasida*, presumably composed at the conclusion of the 1919 Anglo-Persian Agreement, condemned Britain in the strongest terms for its imperialist designs that had now extended beyond India, Egypt and Afghanistan and were casting their ominous shadow over Iran. He nevertheless expressed his hope that, if not India and Egypt, then at least Iran might eventually produce a savior like the mythical Faridun or the more historical Nadir Shah (r. 1736–47):

> O felicitous Faridun! Rise up and shine,
> For the "return of the types" is not implausible among the wise . . .
> By necessity after each torment there will be relief,
> It is not implausible that another Nadir will rise again in Iran.[40]

Albeit from an unexpected quarter, Adib's hopes for another Nadir were soon to be fulfilled with the rise of Riza Khan. In 1921, at the onset of Pahlavi rule, portrayals of Riza Khan as a second Nadir were not unusual in the literature of the time. Nor were hopes that, as Adib predicted, Iran would move away from what he called "the path of ignorance and decay."[41] It is worth noting that similar voices from other parts of the Persianate world had been audible as early as the time of Hazin Lahiji (d. 1766) and Mir 'Abd al-Latif Shushatri (d. 1805), who at the outset of British rule in India cautioned the neighboring Iranians about the threat of colonial domination and hoped for the advent of a champion to save their country.

THE QUESTION OF A PERSIANATE LEGACY

Despite his anticolonial utterances, Adib essentially remained a poet-scholar with a premodern outlook who strived, perhaps unsuccessfully, to engage in modern anticolonial discourse. Unlike his younger Indian and Iranian contemporaries, Muhammad Iqbal (1877–1938) and Muhammad-Taqi Bahar (1884–1951), who both employed the language of popular modernity through poetry and prose, journalism and politics, Adib continued to operate in a Sufi Persianate mode. Despite his later sedentary life, he remained a frontier dervish, a warrior from the borderlands fighting with words who restlessly inhabited the Iranian capital while his heart throbbed for his childhood homeland. Although he believed he was breaking new poetic ground, in reality Adib was an anomaly who stood in contrast to the poetic trends of the Constitutional and post-Constitutional eras, characterized by such poets as Bahar, Iraj, 'Arif, and 'Ishqi. Though passionately anticolonial, Adib's political message also failed to draw a serious following. This was in contrast to the nationalist narrative formulated by the likes of Hasan Taqizada (1878–1970), another writer of Persian from the frontier, in his case, Tabriz. Though Taqizada was ultimately unable to deploy his German connections to negotiate the stormy political waters of the time, he and his colleagues in Berlin were more successful in framing a nationalist message for Iran and, through their journal *Kavih,* better equipped to convey it. Named after another mythical hero of the *Shah-nama,* the journal was another example of the preoccupation with Firdawsi and his paradigm of the hero Faridun.

On the other hand, one may argue that the Persianate erudition in which Adib was so well-versed could no longer function as a cross-regional medium. In the face of nationalist ideologies, and their cultural demands on the citizens of newly emerging nations, Persian higher learning could no longer serve as the impetus for a literary revival based on the *adab* humanism of the classical past. Vernaculars in India, Central Asia, and the Caucasus—and even in Iran, Afghanistan, and what soon became Tajikistan—defined boundaries of learning that were no longer welcoming to the movement of ideas, images, and poets along the well-trodden Persianate path that Adib had travelled as late as the close of the nineteenth century.

Under Riza Shah in Iran, policies of cultural homogenization soon persuaded many among the cultural elite of the Constitutional and post-Constitutional eras (including figures like Taqizada and Bahar, both former Germanophiles) to conform to the state's nationalist project. In such a climate, Adib could still be revered as a repository of classical learning and hermetic detachment, but he could not be emulated. His literary language and style were outmoded and could be of scant interest to the nationalist print culture or state-imposed curricula of the new schools. Likewise, his Sufi ethos could at best arouse nostalgic admiration in a milieu that was now wedded to Western modernity and the positivist ideology then in vogue. Nor could the literary societies (*anjumans*) of former decades function as venues for an emerging public sphere in a way that was equivalent to European salons. In short, the new literary establishment, striving to create a national culture, could only view Adib with nostalgia for a form of erudition that was fast disappearing.

Adib was appreciated by a literary establishment that ranged from scholars such as Muhammad Qazwini, and elder statesmen such as Hasan Wusuq al-Dawla, to influential Pahlavi ministers such as 'Abd al-Husayn Taymurtash and major poets such as Bahar and Iraj Mirza. Yet this was an establishment largely coopted by Pahlavi authority. In 1942, Bahar's *Sabk-shinasi* (Stylistics), an influential work defining the history and boundaries of Persian prose, was produced when, after bearing the brunt of Riza Shah's autocracy, its author accepted an academic post at Tehran University and became its most distinguished professor of Persian. Likewise, 'Ali Akbar Dihkhuda (1879–1956), who had long ago bid farewell to his career as revolutionary satirist, excelled in the Pahlavi era as a brilliant folklorist and lexicographer whose *Lughat-nama* (Dictionary) was supported by special legislation of the Iranian Majlis and went on, with such state support, to have lasting influence on modern Persian. As the second president of the Farhangistan-i Iran (Iranian Academy) during its most active period between 1935 and 1938, Hasan Wusuq al-Dawla played an important part in laying the foundation of the Pahlavi era's language reforms. At least six of the Farhangistan's founding members had earlier been in Adib's circle.[42]

Even so, none of these scholars truly carried Adib's legacy into the new era. The closest anyone came to doing so was perhaps Muhammad Qazwini, whose preoccupation with textual accuracy and "correct" usage and vocabulary, at times deliberately complex prose style, and mastery of the classical *adab* literature were reminiscent of Adib. And like Adib, Qazwini did not leave behind a written corpus of scholarly work. It was not without reason that in an autobiographical essay, Qazwini praised Adib in the highest terms. In his youth, sometime between 1890s and the early 1900s, Qazwini had "effusively benefited" from Adib, and discussed him as only second among his early teachers, after the enlightened and crypto-Babi *mujtahid* of Tehran, Shaykh Hadi Najmabadi (d. 1902). Qazwini's description opens a window on Adib's oral mode of transmitting knowledge as it survived in the late Qajar era:

For a few years, it was [Adib's] habit in the summer to come to the shrine of Imam-
zada Salih in Tajrish [in the summer resort of Shimiran, to the north of Tehran] and
to sit for couple of hours in a corner of the courtyard. Mindful of his short temper,
I had to come up with various strategies and invent excuses so as to broach conversation with him and, little by little and every now and then, ask some questions, then
quickly memorize his all-encompassing answers or jot them down in my pocket-
book. His command of Arabic and Persian literature and his extraordinary ability to
memorize Arabic poetry were truly astonishing.[43]

Qazwini went on to compare Adib to the eighth-century Hammad al-Rawiya,
who had memorized as many as 2,900 Arabic *qasidas*. Though of Persian origin,
Hammad was the first scholar to systematically collect and study Arabic poetry,
becoming one of the founders of the *adab* genre of the early 'Abbasid era. Qazwini
then drew another comparison, this time with the great 'Abbasid-era agnostic poet
and philosopher of the Arabic language, Abu al-'Ala al-Ma'arri (d. 1057):

In my mind, I often compared [Adib's] extensive memory and vast knowledge of literature, poetry, and lexicography, as well as his philosophical orientation [*mashrab-i
falsafih*], detachment from the world, hermetic lifestyle, and other temperaments
and behaviors, to those of al-Ma 'arri. But there was one difference: Abu al-'Ala was
uniquely [gifted] in Arabic literature, whereas Adib was a bilingual genius in both
Arabic and Persian.

CONCLUSIONS

In spite of some continuity from one generation to the next, Qazwini differed
from Adib in several important ways, differences that indicate the changing
cultural milieu of the early twentieth century. For Qazwini was not a poet but
primarily a textual scholar. Moreover, like many in his generation, Qazwini en-
thusiastically embraced the Orientalist scholarship of early twentieth-century
Europe, expanded its knowledge base and benefited from its approach to Persian,
Arabic, and Islamic sources through the modern methodology of textual editing. By contrast, Adib and his generation remained adamantly loyal to the older
itinerant Persianate mode of learning and apparently refused to engage in Western scholarly discourse. Even in the late nineteenth century, there were still vast
private manuscript collections available all over Iran and Afghanistan to which,
if they had links to the cultured nobility, scholars of Adib's generation had access. The important libraries belonging to 'Ali-Quli Mirza I'tizad al-Saltana (now
partially in the library of the Madrasa Sipahsalar) and Farhad Mirza Mu'tamid
al-Dawla, as well as those of Mu'awin al-Mulk and Yahya Khan I'timad al-Dawla
Qaraguzlu, which served as Adib's virtual shelter, were only a few of the many
private libraries of the Qajar era.

Despite such wide access to manuscripts, as well as printed sources, by this
period, Adib's mode of scholarship resisted Western modernity. For him, literary

erudition served a purely personal purpose, a wellspring that could only quench a personal thirst for learning. Rather than a methodical engagement with texts, learning was an acquired experience. Though it had survived for many centuries in Sufi convents and clerical madrasas, this was a breed of learning that could no longer cross the new geographical and cultural boundaries of a world of nation-states. Adib's approach to knowledge may to some extent also explain his naïve hope that the Kaiser and imperial Germany would liberate his Indian homeland. The *qasida* written in his memory by Wusuq al-Dawla perhaps alludes to this passing of the age to which Adib had belonged:

> It is the time of the foxes,
> Now that lions have rested in their den.
> Now is the lot of the crows, now that nightingales are silent.
> Who can any longer differentiate the shell from the nut?
> Who but him can set apart the dim from the bright?
> Where is the wise man of Tus [i.e., Firdawsi], where the master of Balkh [i.e., Rumi]
> To witness what he judged as sound and unsound?
> He has joined his friends; woe on us survivors!
> For we are destined to live away from our friend . . . .
> Wusuq heard about this loss and paid homage:
> "Alas and pity for Adib's loss," he said.[44]

Beyond the tropes of verse eulogies, Wusuq's words ultimately acknowledged Adib as a man of the Khurasan of a bygone era, a man who belonged more to the time of Firdawsi and Rumi than to the present age of foxes and crows.

NOTES

* My thanks are due to Mohsen Ashtiyani, Oliver Bast, Ali Gheissari, Nile Green, Farhad Taheri, Farzin Vejdani and Waleed Ziad.

1. Transnational Persianate culture was revived as a concept by the American historian Marshall Hodgson (1922–68) in his rethinking of the traditional boundaries of the Eurasian world.

2. Muhammad Shafi' Sabir, *Shaykhsiyat-i Sarhad* (Peshawar: University Book Agency, 2010), 893–94. I thank Waleed Ziad for this source.

3. One may speculate that at some stage Adib's ancestors had immigrated to Kunar (or to Peshawar) from Sindh or Multan, where the Suhrawardi order held sway. Adib himself was silent on this subject. According to a well-known biographical dictionary of Peshawar's Sufis, a Suhrawardi Sufi called Sayyid 'Abd al-Razzaq, also known as Sayyid-i Makki, with ancestors from the Shi'i stronghold of Sabzawar in Iranian Khurasan, came to Peshawar from Ghazni in the early eighteenth century. This 'Abd al-Razzaq may have been among the émigrés fleeing Iran after the fall of the Safavids. After establishing himself in Peshawar for several years, he moved on to the Mughal court in Delhi, where he became a disciple of a Suhrawardi Sufi luminary called Miran Muhammad Shah. He died there around 1735. See Ghulam Sarwar Lahawri, *Khazinat al-Asfiya* (Kanpur: Nawwal Kishur, 1902). 'Abd al-Razzaq's itinerary resembles Adib's and he may well have been Adib's ancestor. I thank Waleed Ziad for this biographical detail.

4. 'Ali 'Abd al-Rasuli, Introduction to *Diwan-i Adib-i Pishawari*, ed. 'Abd al-Rasuli (Tehran, 1933; repr., Tehran: Ma, 2000), 2. This *diwan* does not seem to include all of Adib's literary production, and

the editor acknowledges that Adib's earlier *qasidas* have not survived. Moreover, in his obituary of Adib, Muhammad Qazwini recalled having seen a manuscript copy of Adib's *diwan* in Paris in the possession of Firuz Mirza Nusrat al-Dawla, which Qazwini regretted had not been published. See Muhammad Qazwini, *Yadgar* 3, 3 (1946): 33–34 (where Qazwini does not cite the 1933 edition).

5. *Diwan-i Adib-i Pishawari*, ed. 'Abd al-Rasuli, 2. The Persian reads:
Bih yik purhunar parsayam sipurd,
Chu mah gasht naw, mahiyana shimurd.

6. There is some confusion as to the date of Adib's family's confrontation with the British forces. 'Abd al-Rasuli merely refers to the British having engaged in "skirmishes with the local population" without providing any date. See *Diwan-i Adib-i Pishawari*, ed. 'Abd al-Rasuli, 3. Other sources suggest or imply 1857–58, but, given the available evidence, 1863 seems to be the most plausible year. In his old age, Adib seems to have had only a vague memory of the exact date and gave inconsistent dates.

7. Shaykh al-Mulk Awrang, "Adib Pishawari," *Armaghan* 31, 1 (1341/1962): 13–17 (15).

8. The Persian reads:
nagahan dar haqq an sham' rusul
dawlat-i "inna fatahna" zad duhul.

9. 'Abd al-Rasuli, Introduction to Pishawari, *Diwan*, 2.

10. The verse from the *Masnawi* in question cites part of a well-known Quranic verse (48:1): "inna fatahna laka fathan mubinan" (We have destined an obvious victory for you). Peace with the infidels, the theme running throughout the sura, must have moved the young Adib.

11. Awrang, "Adib," 15. In 1932, Fazullah Subhi, another admirer of Adib, noted that Adib departed for Kabul at the age of eighteen, which corresponds to the war of 1863. See Fazullah Subhi, "Adab Chist wa Adib Kist?" in *Nama-yi Nik-Khwah* (Tehran: Baqirzada, 1932). I thank Ali Gheissari for this source.

12. See, among other sources, Abbas Amanat, "Herat Question," in *Encyclopædia Iranica*, ed. Ehsan Yarshater (London: Routledge & Kegan Paul, 1982–), 12, fasc. 2: 219–24.

13. Arthur de Gobineau, *Les Religions et les philosophies dan l'Asie centrale* (Paris: Didier, 1866), 99–102. Mulla Hadi had devised a seven-year course of philosophical study with prerequisites in intellectual sciences and logic.

14. 'Abd al-Rasuli, Introduction to Pishawari, *Diwan*, 5.

15. On Mirza Sa'id, see Mihdi Bamdad, *Tarikh-i Rijal-i Iran* (Tehran: Zawwar, 1968), 2: 66–70.

16. There is some confusion about the date of Adib's departure for Tehran. After the dismissal of Mirza Husayn Khan Mushir al-Dawla as minister of foreign affairs in 1879, Mirza Sa'id Khan, a member of the conservative officialdom, resumed his earlier post, which he held till his death in 1885. It is very likely that Mirza Sa'id summoned Adib to the capital during his second tenure.

17. See N. Kasimi, "Sayyid Muhammad Baqa Sharaf al-Ma'ali, Muassis-i Nakhustin Anjuman-i Adabi dar Qarn-i Akhir," *Gawhar* 44 (November 1976): 691–94.

18. For a list of attendants see Parsa Tuysirkani, "Khatirat-i Adabi," *Khatirat-i Wahid*, n.s., 2, 9 (Tehran: Wahid, 1971), 130–31. Tuysikani counts ten major personalities of the time, though a larger aggregate list based on various other sources exceeds twenty. The best known among them are Mirza Husayn Furughi Zuka al-Mulk I; his son Muhammad 'Ali Furughi Zuka al-Mulk II; Mihdi-Quli Khan Hidayat Mukhbir al-Saltana; Hasan Isfandiyari Muhtashim al-Saltana; 'Abd al-Husayn Taymurtash; Nusrat al-Dawla Firuz; Ahmad Qawam al-Saltana (Qawam); Hasan Wusuq al-Dawla; Muhammad Taqi Malik al-Shu'ara Bahar; Shaykh al-Ra'is Afsar; Shaykh al-Mulk Awrang; and Muhammad Qazwini.

19. The poet and linguist Adib Natanzi was apparently the first to be recognized as such. As a *dhu al-lisanayn* (bilingual), he was known for his command of Arabic and Persian lexicographical and literary techniques. Together with Adib Tirmizi, a twelfth-century poet from the secretarial class of the Saljuq period, Adib Natanzi belonged to an era of cultural transition in eastern Islamic lands. See D. Safa, "Adib Saber," in *Encyclopædia Iranica*, ed. Yarshater, vol. 1, fasc. 5: 460–61.

20. They were mostly men of the *diwan* class and were loosely organized in the *Anjuman-i Khaqan*, a royal society of the kind patronized by Fath 'Ali Shah. Like Adib Pishawari and a few others known as

adib, the poets of the "Return School," like Fath 'Ali Khan Saba, were informed by the Khurasan school of the tenth and eleventh centuries and looked to the poetry of Firdawsi and his contemporaries as their literary role model.

21. Later, because of his Babi-Baha'i affiliation, Adib Taliqani was dismissed from his post as one of the original editors. See M. Momen, "Adib Taleqani," in *Encyclopædia Iranica,* ed. Yarshater, vol. 1, fasc. 5: 461. *Nama-yi Danishwaran-i Nasiri* was published in seven volumes (Tehran, 1878–1907) up to letter *shin* but remained incomplete. The editor of the last two volumes, Ghiyath al-Din Kashani, refers to his own title, and to the title of his colleague, Muhammad Mihdi 'Abd al-Rababadi Shams al-'Ulama, as *adib.* See also Abbas Amanat, "E'tezad al-Saltaneh," in *Encyclopædia Iranica ,* vol. 8, fasc. 6: 662–66.

22. J. Matini, "Adib Nishaburi," in *Encyclopædia Iranica,* ed. Yarshater , vol. 1, fasc. 5: 460.

23. Muhammad Husayn Furughi, epilogue in Abu al-Fazl Bayhaqi, *Tarikh-i Bayhaqi* (Tehran: Mirza Habibullah, 1307/1889).

24. Pizhman Bakhtiyari, Preface to *Diwan-i Wusuq* (Tehran: n.p., 1343/1964), 8.

25. *Diwan-i Adib-i Pishawari,* ed. 'Abd al-Rasuli, 37–48. The Persian original reads:
Saqi bidih ratl-i giran z-an may ki dihqan parwarad,
Dihqansh andar khum chu jan dar jism-i insan parwarad

26. Ibid., 44, line 19. The Persian original reads:
Amad burun ba bad u dam az khayl-i Turkan Pilsam
Pish-ar Rakhsh-i Rustam ta fath-i Turan parwarad.

27. Ibid., 190–91. The title specifies "at the time of his [i.e. Shaykh Fazlullah Nuri's] crucifixion [*hin-i salb*]," i.e., 1909. This is the only *qasida* that can be dated before 1915. That Adib composed it in a highly impenetrable Arabic may be attributed to his fear of the prevailing Constitutionalists.

28. The Kaiser was the eldest grandson of Queen Victoria and hence first cousin to both King George V of Britain and Tsar Nicholas II of Russia.

29. *Diwan-i Adib-i Pishawari,* ed. 'Abd al-Rasuli, 12.

30. It is not yet published in its entirety. For the first part, see Adib Pishawari, *Masnawi-yi Qaysar-nama,* vol. 1, ed. A. Puyandihpur and S. Sami' (Qum: Intisharat-i Iram, 2015). Note that this is a private publication. The title of *Qaysar-nama* was apparently proposed by 'Abd al-Rasuli and approved by Adib.

31. Pishawari, *Masnawi-yi Qaysar-nama,* 131–32. The Persian original reads:
Bi guyandih giti barazandih ast/ ki giti zi guyandigan zindih ast
Sukhan chashm u guyandih chashm afarin/ sarapa-yi giti bidin chasm bin.

32. *Mikadu-nama* was published by Mu'ayyid al-Islam as Mirza Husayn-'Ali Tajir Shirazi, *Mikadu-nama* (Calcutta: Habl al-Matin, 1907). There is a summary with an introduction by 'A. Mir-Ansari in Supplement 9 *Ayina-yi Miras* 4 (Tehran, 2006), 128–32. For a discussion of the text, see Roxanne Haag-Higuchi, "A Topos and Its Dissolution: Japan in Some 20th-Century Iranian Texts," *Iranian Studies* 29, 1–2 (1996): 71–83, and Siamak Adhami, "The Conversion of the Japanese Emperor to Islam: A Study of Central Asian Eschatology," *Central Asiatic Journal* 43, 1 (1999): 1–9.

33. On German activities in Iran before and during World War I, see Oliver Bast, "Germany: I "German-Persian Diplomatic Relations," in *Encyclopædia Iranica ,* ed. Yarshater, vol. 10, fasc. 5: 506–19; id., "Germany IX: Germans in Persia," ibid., fasc. 6: 567–72.

34. Yahya Aryanpur, *Az Saba ta Nima,* 2 vols. (Tehran: Shirkat-i Sahami-yi Kitabha-yi Jibi, 1350/1971), 2: 322–23. For other Germanophiles, including Muhammad Taqi Bahar (Malik al-Shu'ara), see ibid., 322–32 and 341.

35. Tuysirkani, "Khatirat-i Adabi," 131–32. The diplomat in question most likely was Wilhelm Litten, the German consul in Tabriz in 1914 and later the German minister in Tehran. He seems to have sponsored pro-German propaganda among the Iranian intelligentsia. On him, see reference in Bast, "Germany IX" and the sources cited therein.

36. Tuysirkani, "Khatirat-i Adabi," 132.

37. *Diwan-i Adib-i Pishawari,* ed. 'Abd al-Rasuli,, 129–35.

38. Ibid., 129, line 1. The Persian original reads:

Bar shud az Alburz abr-i tirih chun zangi zani,
Az fitan abistani wa-z imini istarwani
39. Ibid., 135, lines 14–15. The Persian original reads:
Ta kih janam hast dar tan zin afghan asudih nist,
War kunam itnab bari hast uzr-i bayyini.
Tir nawak dan pay-i dushman tu har bayt-i mara,
Ta bidarrad bar tan az pulad-i hindi juwshani
40. Ibid., "Grieved over the upheavals in lands of Islam and India," 136–49, esp.149, lines 21 and 24.
The Persian original reads:
Ay Faridun-i mubarak-pay brun ay zankih nist,
Raj'at-i amsal nazd 'aqilan mustankari . . .
Bil-zarurih az pay-i har shiddati bashad faraj,
Nist nadir gar zi Iran baz khizad Nadiri
41. Ibid., line 25.
42. These were Muhammad 'Ali Furughi; 'Ali Akbar Dihkhuda; Malik al-Shu'ara Bahar; Muhammad Qazwini; Badi' al-Zaman Furuzanfar; and Rashid Yasimi.
43. Mirza Muhammad Khan Qazwini, *Bist Maqala* (Tehran: Matba 'a-yi Majlis, 1313/1934), 2: 9–10.
44. Hasan Wusuq (Wusuq al-Dawla), *Diwan*. Also cited in *Diwan-i Adib-i Pishawari*, ed. 'Abd al-Rasuli, 17.

Epilogue

The Persianate Millennium

Brian Spooner

THE PROBLEM

Persian, the national language of modern Iran, has played a unique role in world history. In the ninth century, less than two hundred years after the Arab-Islamic conquest, it became the standard language for all public affairs—government, administration, commerce, literature, even religious commentary—spreading beyond its home territory throughout the eastern part of the Islamic world, from Iraq to China, from the Central Asian steppe to southern India. This development resulted not from any property of the language itself, but from the cultural merging of a number of historical factors in the wake of the Arab conquest. Persian continued in this role for a thousand years. No other language before the adoption of printing, not even the Greek koine of the Hellenistic world, ever acquired a similar status, as the common language, over such a large area for so long. Finally, in the nineteenth century, as a result of intrusions from outside the Islamic world, the ecumene it had formed was broken up into separate bounded territories, and lost its integrity.[1] The Persian koine was largely replaced by vernaculars. But although Persian is now known only as a national language, the heritage of its medieval millennium underlies the historical shaping of the modern world and today's currents of globalizing urbanization.

Persian had made its first appearance over a thousand years earlier in the Achaemenian Empire (the largest empire up to that time), in the form of Old Persian, a highly inflected language written in cuneiform on clay tablets. When the Achaemenians were overcome by Alexander the Great in the late fourth century BCE, Persian was displaced by the Greek koine. But it reemerged under the Parthians, the second Persian empire, in the second half of the third century BCE, as Middle Persian, written on papyrus in a simplified form of the Aramaic script, having lost most of its inflections (as had Greek also by that time). Middle Persian continued to be used for administration and religious writing under the third Persian empire, the Sasanian, which succeeded the Parthians in 224 CE. The most important contribution of the Persian empires to later history was the professionalization of a literate administrative class and the culture of the royal court, both of which were elaborations of what had gone before.

Following another brief eclipse, after the Arabs conquered the Sasanians in the middle of the seventh century, Persian reemerged a second time, as New Persian, strengthened by adoption of the more cursive Arabic script and a new source of vocabulary in the language of Islam's scripture. As the Arabs established the new Islamic empire, the switch from horse to camel (which traveled at an average of no more than two miles an hour for some twelve hours a day) had reduced the speed of communication, but the new arrival of paper from China greatly facilitated the production and distribution of written materials. As the empire grew, it drew as much on the imperial heritage of the Persian empires for its organization and administration as on Islam and the language and culture of the Arabs. Persian was well placed to become the koine of the eastern half of the Islamic world.

As the Islamic world continued to expand, its center in Baghdad, the caliphate, became more symbolic than imperial, and the old cities of the earlier empires reemerged as centers of power. Their model was the Sasanian royal court, and their language was Persian, which was known not as the language of a particular community or people (like Hellenika, Turki, or English), but as Dari, "the language of the court," or Farsi (Arabicized from Parsi), the language of Pars (from which our English word "Persian," through the Greek of Herodotus), in the south of the Iranian Plateau, which had been a central location in the Persian empires. Adapted to the new Islamic environment, Persian easily outgrew the boundaries of its earlier use. There were no political boundaries, and as the power of one urban government after another rose and fell over the following centuries Persian provided the cultural glue. At its greatest extent it reached from its pre-Islamic homeland on the Iranian Plateau to the Balkans in southeastern Europe (under the Ottoman Empire), to central China (under the Mongol Yuan Dynasty), and to south-central India (under the regional sultanates and, later, the Mughal Empire), creating an historical ecumene of unprecedented geographical and demographic proportions, and a new Persian identity. Despite the diplomatic efforts of Riza Shah in 1935 to replace "Persia" with "Iran" in international usage, the Iranian identity of the Achaemenians down to the Islamic Republic of Iran is traceable not by blood but by language, which (except for the recent nationalistic name changes—back to Dari in Afghanistan and to Tajiki in Tajikistan) continues to be known as Farsi.

All of these developments are easier to understand by starting from earlier history and looking forward, than from the present looking back. Greek was not the first koine, in the sense of a language adopted in its written form as the language of administration of an empire that then became the standard for speech as well as writing far beyond the community in which its spoken form had developed. The first, Akkadian, which had emerged in the early cities of Mesopotamia (now Iraq), had been followed by Aramaic in the eight century BCE, which continued to be an important language to the west of the Iranian Plateau until the modern period. A koine possesses a vocabulary and a repertoire of closely related speech habits and writing protocols, which generate an accompanying cultural standard. The culture that accompanied the Persian koine was known as *adab* (from Arabic). Over the course of the Persianate millennium, *adab* was the public culture of the Persianate ecumene.

The formation of this ecumene was an early but major step in the long-term historical process of globalization. Despite the political and economic changes of the next thousand years, nothing happened to break it up until the nineteenth century, although the glue that held it together had begun to be weakened by vernacularization. First, the Ottomans replaced Persian with Osmanlıca (Ottoman Turkish), a highly Persianized form of Turkish, for their imperial administration. Then Urdu, a highly Persianized form of the main North Indian language, began to spread in India, and was finally used by the British to replace Persian for their administration, as a partner to English. The written forms of Pashto, Sindhi, and Uzbek also began to gain ground in the seventeenth century. But the process was gradual. What finally brought the Persianate millennium to an end was the expansion of the British, Chinese, and Russian empires, followed by the conversion of the British and Russian colonial territories into "nation"-states on the Western model, beginning in the second half of the nineteenth century and reaching completion in the second half of the twentieth.

Before then, in its heyday, Persian had been the informal equivalent of an official language for a larger part of the world and a larger contiguous population than any other language in world history. The historical questions it raises are not linguistic, but social, cultural, and political. However, they have linguistic implications, and they raise other interesting questions—about the role of language in general, and especially of literacy, in world history. The most interesting and productive human achievements have always come from the largest arenas of social interaction, where the largest number of minds were working together. The spread of Persian in the Persianate millennium created the largest arena before the modern period. The purpose of this Epilogue is to set the historical role of Persian in a larger context, relating, not only to world history, but also to the cultural background of the modern world.

CITIES, TRADE, TRIBES, AND WRITING

Late antiquity was a period of accelerating social change. No society has ever been without change. Culture is the order that enables us to know what to expect in our social lives, which we negotiate over time. But the people we interact with have staggered life cycles, and our relationships are always changing. Our communities grow and decline. If the change is not too fast, we can accommodate it. But accelerating change and fundamental change resulting from an invasive factor are disruptive, changing the social landscape, putting vested interests on the defensive, and shattering the cultural order. Disruption can open a new age. The greater the disruption, the further we need to look back in time to understand all the factors that surface as the new age develops.

Although Islam began in Arabia, and one of the five pillars (*arkan*) of Islam, the pilgrimage (*hajj*), requires Muslims to visit its place of origin, Mecca, once in their lifetime, Arabia has not been the center of Islamic history. After the Prophet Muhammad's death in 632 CE, Islam spread north to Syria and Mesopotamia, and west to Egypt, but also east through Central Asia, the middle of the world's largest landmass. Within eighty years, the new Islamic order had reached Spain in the west, China in the east, and India in the south. Unlike earlier empires, Islam had expanded along trade routes, following the network that had developed from city to city since the beginning of civilization.

This was where history had begun. Ten to fifteen thousand years ago, as the glaciers receded at the end of the last Ice Age, the resulting profusion of vegetation in Mesopotamia made it no longer necessary to be continually on the move to find food. People settled. Settled life favored larger families. Fertility rates rose, and population growth increased. Food collectors became food producers, increasing the carrying capacity of the land. Settlements became villages. When farmers could produce more food than they needed for themselves, some provided services for others. Villages became towns. The number of people living and working together increased. Property accumulated, and society became more complex—in terms of the diversity of livelihoods and relative wealth, power, and social status.

The climate continued to change. As it became more arid, people moved down to the rivers, in order to irrigate. Towns became cities. More minds working together, each with different life experience, increased collective learning, the ability to organize, the rate of innovation, and the adoption of new technologies.[2] A larger proportion of each community became free to develop new skills for the production of commodities. Cities looked for trade with other cities, and long-distance trade developed from city to city through the arid zone of the Northern Hemisphere.

But change was uneven. Unlike most of Europe, in the temperate zone, where there was sufficient soil and rainfall for people eventually to settle and farm almost anywhere, in the arid zone, where civilization began, farming required irrigation, and irrigation required organized labor and investment. As population continued to grow, some were always left out of the urban economies, continuing to survive on the unimproved land, without the increased food supply that that would allow the organization of labor, without investment. They remained nomadic, exploiting any resource they could find, including raiding trade caravans and even cities. After what Andrew Sherratt calls the "secondary products revolution" in the fourth millennium, they adopted pastoralism as their main resource, and supplied meat and milk to the urban economies.[3] But since they could not accumulate property, they remained tribal, recognizing each other not in urban terms of comparative wealth, occupation, and social class, but rather in terms only of the information carried in their genealogies: descent, affinity (marriage connections), and relative seniority.

To begin with, rivers and occasional springs had been the only source of water for irrigation. But the Achaemenians were able to promote investment in a new technology that made it possible to increase the area under irrigation by tapping groundwater. The *kariz* (recently added to UNESCO's World Heritage List under the more common Arabic term *qanat*) was an excavated underground channel that brought water by gravity flow from the underground water table at the head of a valley out on to cultivable soil lower down in the plain, often tens of kilometers away.⁴ Investment in *qanat* construction spread east and west from the Iranian Plateau, enabling each city to greatly expand its agricultural hinterland and include a larger percentage of the population in the agricultural economy. But some were always left out, and nomadic tribal communities have been an important factor in Islamic and Persianate history down to the present.

The society that became Islamic and Persianate in the arid zone was therefore very different from the society that became Christian in the temperate zone, or Buddhist in the tropics, because it was divided between an urban majority based on the organization of labor, investment and interurban trade, and the tribal minority that controlled the territory between the cities through which their trade had to pass. When the urban economies boomed, they were a source of extra labor. When they bust, multiresource nomadism remained an alternative.⁵

The development of the interurban trade network, from the cities on the Euphrates and Tigris to the Nile and further west in North Africa, and east to the Helmand, Oxus, and Jaxartes, and so on to the Yellow River, and then on smaller rivers, with the intermediary territory controlled by nomadic tribes, was the final stage of prehistory. History began toward the end of the fourth millennium, when writing was adopted to facilitate trade by recording transactions and contracts. The Asian trade network generated interaction among larger numbers of people over a larger geographical area than any other part of the world from then until the development of maritime trade toward the end of the mediaeval period and the beginning of transatlantic trade a little later. It became the historically most important route for the movement of cultigens as well as commodities, and everything else conveyed by human interaction, such as language (Persian) and culture (*adab*), between China and the Mediterranean—the beginning of what in the nineteenth century was named the Silk Route.⁶ However, although the association with silk (which was not a major commodity until much later) gave it a brand, it was a distraction from the route's real historical significance. More important than any particular commodity was the adoption of writing, which (despite low rates of literacy) expanded the arenas of social interaction.

From 3000 BCE until the fifteenth century, writing by hand was the only means of communication, organization, or control beyond the face-to-face community, and written language continues to be essential in the digital world of the twenty-first century. Since it was a tool of government, it became a qualification for an elite social class. In the third millennium, writers provided the bureaucracies that

enabled city-states to become empires, and empires to expand. The historical role
of Persian and the thousand-year stability of the Persianate ecumene were rooted
in Persian in its written form. Persian was adopted as a koine not only because it
was the language of the Sasanian model of government, but because it was the tool
of the writing class that was left over from the previous empires, and for which
the Arabs had no replacement. Without both writing and the writing class, there
would have been no koine, no ecumene, and no Persianate millennium. That this
degree of linguistic and cultural homogenization should have developed here before in other parts of the world is not surprising, since apart from being where settlement and civilization, long-distance trade, and writing had all begun, bringing
more people in contact with each other and producing a greater rate of collective
learning than anywhere else, it was the center of the global ecumene.

The Persians had created the last three in the historical succession of empires,
each larger than the one before, that had grown out of Mesopotamia starting in
the third millennium BCE as a result of the new ability of city-states to exercise
remote control by means of writing. The bureaucracy for each new empire was recruited from the one before. The Achaemenians had recruited from the Elamites.
But within a generation or two, the writers had switched from Elamite to Persian.
The third Achaemenian shah, Darius the Great (r. 522–486 BCE), expanded the
use of writing further by establishing the Royal Road, on which relays of couriers
on horseback provided rapid communication with written missives throughout
the empire.

The association of writing with power suggested that any important message
must be written. How could that not apply to a prophet's revelation? By the end of
the Axial Age (800–200 BCE), when the related processes of population growth,
urbanization, trade, and the adoption of writing had generated a new stage of social complexity and human capability, the teachings of Zoroaster, Confucius, the
Buddha, Socrates, and the Torah had all taken written form.[7] The age of scripture
had begun, and when the final revelation was delivered to Muhammad half a millennium later, the original was assumed to have been written, which as the word
of God was eventually rationalized as being "uncreated."

From 821 CE, when the Tahirid dynasty broke away from the 'Abbasid Caliphate
to claim political independence in Nishapur, to the early sixteenth century, when
Islamic civilization became divided into the three large polities of the Mughals,
Ottomans, and Safavids (which Hodgson called the "Gunpowder Empires"), the
political organization of the Islamic world was in continuous flux.[8] Each power
center had a function, formally recognized by the Shari'a, to provide the security
that would allow people to carry out their religious duties as Muslims, but no specific legitimacy. The political flux inhibited the formation of boundaries, helping
to maintain the cultural unity of the ecumene.

As a result, in 1326, at the age of twenty-two, Muhammad ibn Battuta was
able to make his way from Mecca across Arabia to Najaf, Isfahan, Shiraz, Tabriz,

Mardin, and Sinjar. Later, after a trip to Yemen, Somalia, and the East African coast, he travelled via Oman and Hormuz to Delhi. Then, after a trip into Ottoman territory—Crimea, Astrakhan, and (Christian) Constantinople—he went east to Bukhara and Samarqand, then south over the Hindu Kush and across the Indus to Delhi. From Delhi he went back to Sindh, and Gujarat, down to Calicut and southern India, crossing the Indian Ocean to the Maldives, Sri Lanka, up to Chittagong and Assam, and down again to Sumatra, Malacca, Vietnam, and finally through China up to Beijing before returning in 1346 by a similar route. This type of networked travel was much easier during the Persianate millennium than at any other time in world history. It was made possible by urbanization, trade, and the cultural standardization of a widespread *written* language, which (under the informal control of a writing class) carried the urban culture of literature, cuisine, and architectural and textile design that had grown out of the Persian empires, and is now the cultural heritage of Iran. Yet it would not have spread over such a large area without the contribution of the Arabs.

ISLAM AND THE ARABS

The urbanization that began in Mesopotamia in the seventh and sixth millennia BCE and expanded under the Persian empires in the first millennium, continued to expand in the seventh century CE under Islam through the eastern Islamicate world of the Asian arid zone. The citied society of what was to become the Persianate ecumene was a trading network of urban investment centers, which had raised the carrying capacity of the steppe and accelerated population growth.[9] The Arab-Islamic conquest of the Sasanian Empire made two contributions to this situation that facilitated the conversion of the cultural heritage of the Persian empires into the Islamicate empire of the Persianate millennium. The first was the legal formulation of a social template for the whole community, the Islamic *umma*, that was independent of political models and favored trade. The second was the Arabian version of the tribal paradigm.

Islam's Prophet had been socialized in a mercantile family on the Hijaz trade route from Yemen to Syria. But the larger context of his career was neither urban nor mercantile. The population in the arid country outside the Hijaz was mostly tribal, with the typical tribal dependence on a mixed economy with a pastoral emphasis. The social differences between urban and tribal populations generate different expectations with regard to power and authority. Initial support for the Prophet's mission came mainly from the trading communities of the Hijaz towns, which though not large were socially complex enough to appreciate some form of exogenous legitimization of authority, such as a single god with a revealed law. In the more egalitarian tribal communities outside the towns, where political decision making was managed by negotiation and consensus building, people were naturally suspicious of absolute authority, and were less welcoming to proselytizers.

The record of Muhammad's life and his revelation reflect this social conditioning. It is perhaps not surprising that his teaching favored trade but opposed what he saw as the divisive loyalties of tribal life.

When Muhammad died, he left no clear provision for the future of the community he had created and managed. His Companions (those closely associated with him during his lifetime) had to work out a way to manage, not only the preservation of his record, but the continuation of his composite role as (a) leader of an expanding community, and (b) interpreter of his divine revelation in the changing social conditions. Not only the history of Islamic civilization, but the Persianate millennium, were products of the solutions to these problems developed over the next two centuries.

In the tribal leadership model, the Companions, who were senior members of the leading lineages, met together and agreed on which one of them should take on the role of consensus builder. The person thus chosen became the caliph (successor or steward) for the day-to-day management of the *umma*, but without either the religious legitimacy or the political authority of the Prophet. The form of Islam that spread north out of the Arabian Peninsula in the following decades, later known as Sunni or orthodox Islam, was organized according to this Arab model. To begin with, it was centered in the city of Medina (in the Hijaz) where the Prophet had spent the last ten years of his life, till 656, when the fourth orthodox caliph, 'Ali, moved it to Kufa in Mesopotamia (now southern Iraq).

The urban populations of the Persian empires in Syria and Mesopotamia had different expectations of authority. They were stratified according to occupation and relative wealth. Authority could not be negotiated. They needed the security of absolute authority with some sort of legitimation, such as they had known under the Persian shahs, who had ruled by Zoroastrian Divine Right, a concept that had already influenced the Roman emperors and through them would influence the Christian Church and the medieval European monarchies. At the beginning of the seventh century, the Sasanian shah had been the absolute authority, from his center in Istakhr (now in southern Iran) east into Central Asia, west as far as Egypt, and south around the Arabian Peninsula to Oman and Yemen. His rule was continuing to expand to the northwest at the expense of the Byzantine Empire. When the Umayyads took over the caliphate in 661, moved it to Damascus, and established a dynasty, they were satisfying these expectations in a way that resembled the Roman model: absolute authority based on the qualifications of the founder, in this case the record of Mu'awiya's as a Companion of the Prophet, and brother of the second orthodox caliph. The same model was continued by their successor dynasty, the 'Abbasids, who moved the caliphate to Baghdad a century later.

But besides a political model more suitable for a citied society, in order to function in a larger urban society, the caliphate needed a more sophisticated administrative apparatus. Unlike all the previous empires since the second millennium, the caliphate had no professional scribes that could provide a bureaucracy to administer its enormous empire. In its efforts to develop an Islamic bureaucracy, it had no option but to turn to the Sasanian professional class it had displaced. Although the Umayyads attempted to convert them to Arabic, and they did change their script, and contributed to the development of written Arabic, the language they used for administration continued to be Persian.

The use of Arabic barely expanded beyond the needs of the religion. A standard version of the Prophet's revelation was compiled and accepted as the Quran (Recitation) within just twenty years of the Prophet's demise—the first item of Islamic scripture, conserved according to the models of the Judaic Torah (Instruction) and the Christian Bible (Book), of which it was considered to be the replacement. Standard versions of supporting items, the hadith (what was remembered of the Prophet's interpretative teaching, both explicit and implicit) and the Sunna (the model of his life), which together with the Quran were the basic sources for the formulation of the Shari'a (Islamic Law), took longer.

The major emphases of the Law were, first, the organization of society, especially gender relations, family life, and the relationship between private and public life, for which marriage and the family are not only central but constitute the only legitimate form of social grouping. All other forms of organization are considered divisive, and therefore a distraction from the basic principle that distinguishes Islam from other religions: *tawhid,* the focus on God's oneness. This emphasis inhibited the development of political boundaries within the Islamic world. The second emphasis was contract, which promoted trade. Although the sources came from the Arabian Peninsula, the Law was formulated in the citied society of the pre-Islamic empires, where the earliest version of the law from which it was descended had been codified under Hammurabi in the first Babylonian dynasty two and a half millennia earlier. It was a template that facilitated the acceptance and expansion of Islam east and west through the established interurban trading networks, and provided the social order that was necessary for the further development of trade. The Law has been Islam's major strength, distinguishing it from its rivals, Judaism and Christianity (and Buddhism).

Starting at the end of the Axial Age, when religions began to be rooted in scripture, and to spread beyond local communities, religious identity became more important than local or ethnic identity. Buddhism began to spread out of India in Pali in the second century BCE; Christianity from the Levant in the first century CE, first in Greek, then Latin; and Islam in Arabic from the Hijaz in the seventh century. Religion with a basis in written language continued to be an important factor of identity throughout the mediaeval period into the early modern period, when the rise in literacy that came with the adoption of printing in the Christian world after the Reformation led finally to the adoption of national identities rooted in national languages.[10] But despite the idea of nationhood as common descent and the introduction a century ago of the concept of subnational "ethnic" identities, language in its written form has continued to be an important factor in identity down to the current digital age. In the Islamic world, the Law is an additional factor in social identity and the culture of the Persianate ecumene.

The tribal models the Prophet had disapproved of did not disappear. Despite the failure of the caliphate to survive down to the present in its original "orthodox" form (or even its later dynastic form), the Arab tribal model of consensus building continued to underlie the formal interpretation of the scripture by religious scholars in the majority Sunni version of Islam, which was similar to the Judaic model of a synod of scholars.[11] The urban movement to establish an absolute authority in the line of descent through ʿAli, as the Prophet's supreme successor, was successful only in the religious role—until the Islamic revolution of 1979. The division between the Arab (tribal, Sunni) and Persian (urban, Shiʿi) heritage over the problem of authority has divided Islam to varying degrees from the death of the Prophet down to the current twenty-first century sectarianism between Sunni and Shiʿa, and the modern political crisis between Arabia and Iran (though ironically the former is now a kingdom and the latter an Islamic Republic). In Islam, unlike its predecessors, the leadership problem was not how to maintain the distinction between "church" and state, but how to maintain their unity.

THE OPENING AND CLOSING OF THE MILLENNIUM

The Arab-Islamic expansion in the seventh century caused not only a massive disruption of the vested interests that had shaped society over the past thousand years; it was also a revolution, designed to establish an entirely new sway of life as well as a new religion. Revolutions are followed by periods of routinization as people accommodate to a new order. The spread of Persian, beginning in the ninth century, completed the process of routinization. Comparative examples abound in world history, and provide useful context. The Arab conquest of the Sasanian Empire followed on the heels of the collapse of the western Roman Empire in the face of Germanic invaders, which was followed by the rise and spread of Western Christianity in the form that characterized medieval Europe in the following millennium. Why should two such similar cultural and political shifts have occurred so close to each other in space and in time, with no discernable connection? But there are similarities. In both cases the established civilization was exhausted from long periods of warfare, and in both cases the exhaustion was exacerbated by an outbreak of plague, the first pandemic of *Yersinia pestis*, which spread from Egypt through the Mediterranean and into southwest Asia in the late sixth century, and continued to recur till the mid-eighth century.

The European routinization began in the fifth century, with the language and religion of the Romans, and the social forms of the Germans, and took over three centuries till the beginning of the ninth. The Persianate process began in the seventh century, and was completed later in the ninth, with the language and culture of the conquered, the Persians, and the legal template of the invaders. Half a millennium later European society underwent another period of revolutionary change, of similar duration, in which the same plague, this time known as the Black Death, was the primary factor. Starting in the mid-fourteenth century, killing the rich as well as the poor, it removed the vested interests of mediaeval society and opened up land and other opportunities for the survivors. The result was the Reformation, the adoption of printing and the beginning of modern science, as well as eventual political reform and the opening of the modern world.

The Chinese political system, however, which began with the Xia Dynasty in the third millennium BCE, evolved with gradually increasing complexity but no disruptive change of its social and political structure, into the twentieth century. Neither the Chinese establishment of the Republic in 1912, nor the establishment of the People's Republic after the revolution in 1949, disrupted the age-old structure of Chinese society. Only Mao's Cultural Revolution in 1966 finally removed the vested interests of centuries, making possible the fundamental reorganization of Chinese society in the second half of the twentieth century, and the entry of China into the industrialized world.

The Islamic empire had expanded according to a different dynamic from its predecessors, following trade routes, rather than commandeering resources. In addition to melding the cultural heritage of the Persian empires and the Arabian tribes, it formalized and intensified the interaction between the civilizations of east and west in a vast empire with no political center, based on interurban trade that financed urban investment. Its integrity was symbolized by Islam and the Shari'a, but managed by a Persian bureaucratic class operating out of each major city, in the service of competing Sasanian-style royal courts in selected cities. Each of these courts sought to expand their area of control, but with no expectation that the whole of Islamic society should be under one authority, or that there should not be freedom of movement between the territories of different cities.

The trade network provided paths for the spread of Islam's major strength, the Law. The cultural framework of the Law strengthened the trade network. Persian followed it from urban court to urban court, strengthening the cultural glue that formed its identity. Persian returned as the language, not only of administration, but of eulogizing poetry in each of the royal courts. As discussed in the introduction to this volume, these included the Tahirids in Nishapur (821–91), who were followed by the Saffarids in Zaranj (861–1003), the Samanids in Bukhara (875–999), the Ziyarids in Isfahan (931–1090), and the Buyids in Shiraz (934–1062). When the Turks arrived later in the tenth century, they followed the same model: the Ghaznavids in Ghazni (975–1186), and so on down to the Saljuqs (1040–). In the fourteenth century, as the Persianate ecumene continued to expand, the pattern began to change to a threefold subdivision between the Turkic Ottomans (1299–1922), the Safavids (1501–1736), who were of ethnically mixed extraction, and the Turko-Mongol Mughals (1526–1857), establishing the political and cultural basis for the modern division between Sunni Turkey, Shi'i Iran, and the importance of Sunni Islam in South Asia.

Why should Persian, the language of the conquered empire, have become the standard language of more than half of Islamic civilization, rather than Arabic, the language of the conquerors, and of the new religion and the Law, or Turkish, which in one or another of its forms (mostly mutually intelligible), was soon to become the most widely *spoken* language throughout the region? The reason that Arabic did not become the koine of the whole Islamic world is that neither the Quran nor the hadith included any political models or a political philosophy for the enforcement of the Islamic law in the absence of the Prophet himself, and there was no professional class of Arabic writers with the vocabulary for it. The reason Turkish did not supersede Persian is different. By the eleventh century, Turkish had begun to be heard in most places where Persian was heard, and even beyond. Was Turkish a rival koine? The comparison is interesting and useful. As a koine, Persian was rooted in its *written* form. Since the written form was used for remote interaction, by the writing class and the royal courts, its standard form was protected by professional interests. The development of Persian literature was also a factor, related not only to the pomp and circumstance of the court culture in political centers, but to the rise and spread of Sufism. Turkish could not become a koine in that sense, since it was not rooted in a written form. It was, however, a lingua franca, a language in common use throughout the ecumene for local oral interaction between people with different vernacular backgrounds. This use of "Turki" was still expanding in Iran in the mid-twentieth century. Apart from the Qashqai in Fars, it could be heard from Azerbaijan to Qazvin and through the villages of the Alborz mountains to the boundaries of Semnan Province, in northern Khorasan, in Mashhad, and among the staff of the national railway system. But before the Islamic revolution, it was never used in print except for a column in street Turki in the satirical weekly *Tawfiq* (which was discontinued in 1974). Unlike Persian, Turkish was never a source of models for correct speech or correct behavior. It provided no path for social advancement, but simply a medium of communication between individuals with different vernaculars, whatever their place in society, in informal, and intimate, but not public, and formal situations.

The Persianate millennium finally ended in the way it had begun, as a result of severe social disruption. Nothing similar to the Arab-Islamic invasion had happened for over a thousand years—not the arrival of the Turks, beginning in the tenth century, not even the Mongol cataclysm in the thirteenth century. The Turks had assimilated to the Persianate structure. Even the Mongols, despite the destruction and carnage they perpetrated, did not change the structure, language or culture of Persianate society, but effectively strengthened it by imposing the Pax Mongolica. The gradual shift from written Persian to the writing of vernacular languages that began with Ottoman Turkish in the fifteenth century and continued with Urdu, Sindhi, and Pashto was not disruptive. But eventually, at a time when the ecumene was in economic decline because the development of maritime trade between the Persian Gulf, India, and China had eliminated its trading advantage, three external empires, one of which (the British) was based on the new maritime trading network, began to encroach on it. First, in the eighteenth century, the Chinese created Xinjiang (the "New Frontier") in the Tarim Basin and Djungaria, establishing their border with the Russian Empire, which had been moving east since Russia expelled the Mongols in 1480. But more significantly, in the nineteenth century, the British began moving north from India to protect their northwest frontier, in response to the Russians moving south into Central Asia. The competition between the British and the Russians, known as the Great Game, caused the final eclipse of the Persianate millennium, breaking up the ecumene into colonial territories that eventually became nation-states on the Western model. The socioeconomic dynamism that had created the paths for the spread of Islam and the Persian language had lost its driving force, and its cultural unity was divided by political boundaries.

Once the boundaries were drawn, the standards in each country began to diverge. The process was slowest in Iran, which apart from being the largest country with the least outside interference was also the country where identity was most closely linked to the Persian language. When the Islamic revolution in 1979 finally reshaped what had remained of Iran's premodern social structure under the final Pahlavi dynasty, the century-long half-life of the Persianate millennium was over, and the rate of social change accelerated.

HISTORICAL SIGNIFICANCE

Within a century after the Arab-Islamic conquest, Persian reemerged in the Arabic script with Arabic vocabulary. Islam spread along the interurban trade networks, but Arabic spread with Islam only as the language of Islamic scripture, not as that of empire. Gradually in the course of the next century and a half, the Sasanian heritage filled the gaps that appeared in the new system as it grew from its small-town and tribal origins in Arabia to the complex urban society of the earlier empires. The Persianate millennium was the product of the convergence of three major historical components: the legal system that favored trade, the governmental model and administrative class inherited from the Persian empire, and the interurban trade network. Its stability depended equally on each component. The Law could not be changed because it was based on the eternal word of the Quran. The correctness of written Persian was protected by the professional class, and its association with power and privilege made it the unchanging source of standard cultural models. But the trade networks were beyond the control of any internal factors. Their decline began with the development of maritime trade toward the end of the medieval period, which facilitated the further spread of Islam from Arabia and the Persian Gulf to southeast Asia. Later the growth of maritime trade from the West, with its associated political interests, finally closed the millennium in the nineteenth century. It had already been weakened by vernacularization, as the Ottomans became more interested in Europe than Central Asia, though Osmanlıca continued to rely on the vocabulary and idiomatic usage of the Persian koine. Similarly, the British switch from Persian to Urdu (because the maritime trade they controlled was more important to them than the land routes beyond their control to the north) did not cut off their relationship with Persian. But the creation of new "national" boundaries broke up the ecumene and put an end to the ability of the professional class of writers to maintain the standardization of Persian throughout the ecumene.

Nevertheless, Persianate *adab* still lingers in the twenty-first century. The everyday life of the modern countries of Asia south of Russia (Azerbaijan, Afghanistan, Armenia, Bosnia, Georgia, Iraq, Iran, Kazakhstan, Kirghizstan, Pakistan, Tajikistan, Turkey, Turkmenistan, Uzbekistan, much of India, and even to some extent China, even beyond Xinjiang, and some parts of the Arab world—approaching a quarter of the global population, distributed around the geographical center of the global ecumene) all to varying degrees carry the Persianate cultural heritage.

Writing had changed the scale of history. It had been a dominant factor in social change since its adoption began some five thousand years ago, but it had not been seriously studied. Attention turned to it finally in the middle of the last century, when Claude Lévi-Strauss argued (briefly, but with interesting examples) that its importance is not so much as a reliable extension of memory, or a deepening of our awareness and understanding of the past, as is commonly claimed, but rather as a vehicle of social differentiation and organization. He wrote:

> Writing is a strange thing. . . . The one phenomenon which has invariably accompanied [writing] is the formation of cities and empires: the integration into a political system . . . of a considerable number of individuals, and the distribution of those individuals into a hierarchy of castes and classes. Such is, at any rate, the type of development which we find, from Egypt right across to China, at the moment when writing makes its debuts; it seems to favor rather the exploitation than the enlightenment of mankind.[12]

The ensuing discussion, which intensified in the following decades, missed these social points: that the most significant function of literacy had been to open new ways to expand the arenas of social life and to organize society. Writing has shaped history, not so much by increasing knowledge, but by making it possible to organize access to it. Literacy rates were managed. Since most people not only had no one to teach them, but were not aware of anything they needed to read, literacy produced social stratification and subordination. The Persianate case is perhaps the most interesting historical example, because it was associated, not with an ethnic or dynastic empire, but with trade networks that were governed impersonally by a religiously ordained legal system.

Literacy rates in the Persianate world began to change when the vested interests of the writing classes were disrupted—by the Soviet regime in the "-stans," starting in the late 1920s, and in Iran by the "white revolution" of 1963, and more so since the Islamic revolution of 1979. The change was slower in Afghanistan and Pakistan, which had not achieved the same degree of national integration. But the relationship between written and spoken language is now changing everywhere.

Until the middle of the twentieth century, the study of language was philology, which focused on the history of written language, as an academic extension of the study of Latin and ancient Greek. Speech was implicitly regarded as a representation of the written language, that might be careless and incorrect. Linguistics (which had grown out of the anthropological study of the spoken languages of nonliterate communities outside the world's historical civilizations, beginning in the late nineteenth century) gradually replaced philology in the curriculum in the 1950s. The tables were turned. Where the study of written languages had focused on the history of Rome, Greece, the Levant, India, and China, the study of spoken languages was (like anthropology) global in orientation, focusing on the language of each community, irrespective of writing. Gradually, written language came to be regarded simply as a derivative of the spoken. Any attempt to explain the differences tended to fall under the heading of the newly introduced term "diglossia," coined by a linguist, apparently unaware of the five-thousand-year evolving relationship between spoken and written language, for a much more limited type of distinction.[13]

As with Greek and Latin, what was written in Persian in the past continues today to play an important role in the culture of a much larger arena than that of its current usage. But Latin is no longer spoken, and modern Greek is very different now from its classical form. Despite the historical significance of ancient Greek, Greeks today have problems with their language similar to those of the English, who can mostly read Shakespeare without too much difficulty, but Chaucer? Modern Persians, on the other hand, can read their literature from a thousand years ago.

CONCLUSIONS

The development of Persian as a koine, its spread through the ecumene, and its standardization and stability for a full millennium would not have been possible without the social history of its use as a written language, expanding the domains of what Nile Green has called "Persographia." Even though it is no longer recognized, Persian is one of the five or so most important modern languages, not only in terms of its place in world history, but in the culture of today's globalizing world. Apart from continuing as the official language of two modern countries, Iran and Tajikistan, and one of two official languages in another, Afghanistan, Persian continues to be spoken by local communities in several others, and serves as a classical language throughout the region. No other language, not Greek or Latin, not Chinese, can compete with this record. Although Chinese and Greek also have unbroken records in writing as well as speech from the ancient world down to the modern period, the case of Persian covers a larger area, is more international, without being related to any single particular center. Awareness of its past significance faded in the nineteenth-century late Qajar period, but it has been reemerging with the rise of postcolonial nationalism in modern Iran, and is likely to continue to play a role in the future. As a result of its past, it now has a quality of its own, in terms of vocabulary, structure, expressiveness, and textual and literary repertoire. Unfortunately, however, unlike Greek (which continues to hold a central place in the Western curriculum), premodern Persian is known in the West only through the writing of Herodotus (484–425 BCE) and Xenophon (430–354 BCE), and to a lesser extent the poets such as ʿUmar Khayyam (1048–1131) with whom British colonial officials became conversant while working with the elite of Mughal India. It holds a place in the curriculum now only as a modern national language. However, even when the ecumene lost its internal integrity everything that encroached upon it became a vehicle for spreading its cultural influence. We in the West wear "pyjamas," sit on "verandahs" and "balconies," hoping for "serendipity" and eating "candy," and the French term for the customs checkpoint we pass through when we fly to Paris is *la douane*—all words that came to us in various ways through Persian, mostly (if not entirely) via colonial India.

NOTES

1. Said Amir Arjomand, "Unity of the Persianate World under Turko-Mongolian Domination and Divergent Development of Imperial Autocracies in the Sixteenth Century," *Journal of Persianate Studies* 9, no. 1 (2016): 1–18.

2. David Christian, *Maps of Time: An Introduction to Big History* (Berkeley: University of California Press, 2004), 146–48.

3. Andrew Sherratt, "Plough and Pastoralism: Aspects of the Secondary Products Revolution," in *Pattern of the Past: Studies in Honour of David Clarke,* ed. I. Hodder, G. Isaac, and N. Hammond (Cambridge University Press: Cambridge 1981), 261–305.

4. Brian Spooner, "Abyari," in *Encyclopædia Iranica,* ed. Ehsan Yarshater (London: Routledge, 1982–), 1, fasc. 4: 405–11.

5. P. Salzman, "Multi-resource Nomadism in Iranian Baluchistan," in *Perspectives in Nomadism,* ed. W. Irons and N. Dyson-Hudson (Leiden: Brill, 1972), 60–68.

6. Brian Spooner, introduction to *Ancient Iran through Chinese Records,* by Berthold Laufer (London: I. B. Tauris, 2016; reprint of *Sino-Iranica,* Chicago: Field Museum of Natural History, 1919, 1934).

7. Karl Jaspers, *The Origin and Goal of History,* trans. Michael Bullock (New Haven, CT: Yale University Press, 1953).

8. Marshall Hodgson, *The Venture of Islam,* 3 vols. (Chicago: University of Chicago Press, 1974), vol. 3.

9. Ibid., 1: 50.

10. Benedict Anderson, *Imagined Communities: Reflections on the Origin and Spread of Nationalism* (London: Verso, 1983).

11. Hodgson, *Venture of Islam,* 1: 316–17.

12. Claude Lévi-Strauss, *A World on the Wane* (London: Hutchinson, 1961), 291–92.

13. Charles Ferguson, "Diglossia," *Word* 15 (1959): 325–40.

GLOSSARY

Though used in Persian and Persianate texts, the following terms are ultimately of Arabic origin, except for those appended with (P) for Persian.

Adab	Literary sciences; alternatively, politeness and urbanity
Adib	Literary scholar; alternatively, polite and learned
'Ajam	Persia or the Persians; alternatively, barbarians or persons other than Arabs
'Alim (pl. *'ulama*)	Learned one; trained in and Arabic-based religious disciplines
Dabir (P)	Secretary or notary
Darwish (P)	Mendicant or itinerant Sufi; a dervish
Dastan (P)	Tale or romance; name of a prose genre in Persian and Persianate literatures
Diwan	Compendium of shorter poems by a single author; alternatively, a secretary, minister, or court
Fiqh	Islamic jurisprudence based on interpretation of the Quran and *Sunna* (q.v.)
Ghazal	Short poem of between five and fifteen couplets and frequently on themes of love, both mystical and mundane; name of a poetic genre in Persian and Persianate literatures
Hikayat	Story or romance, typically on historic or heroic topics; name of a prose genre in Persian and Persianate literatures
'Ilm (pl. *'ulum*)	Field of learning or science; alternatively, religious learning, particularly of Quran and Hadith
Insha	Ornate prose, belles-lettres; style and composition, particularly of letters

Khanaqah (P)	Sufi lodge, often comprising places for instruction, residence, and worship
Kitab	Book, a text written in Arabic, Persian or Persianate languages
Madrasa	Place of study; a college for the study of the Islamic sciences
Majlis	Gathering salon of poets or meeting of students, usually around a patron or teacher
Masnawi	Long poem in rhyming couplets, often didactic or narrative; name of a poetic genre
Munshi	Secretary, scribe or author; alternatively, a language tutor
Nast'aliq	Form of Arabic-script calligraphy developed around the fourteenth century and used for Persian and Persianate languages
Qasida	Ode or panegyric; name of a poetic genre in Persian and Persianate literatures
Risala	Treatise; prose text or epistle on learned or doctrinal matters
Shari'a	Islamic law, formulated through interpretation of the Quran and Hadith
Shaykh	an elder; title of respect for a Sufi master or senior *'alim* (q.v.)
Siyaq	Numeration by means of the Arabic alphabet; letter-based system of recording and calculating numbers
Sunna	Traditions handed down in Arabic describing the words and deeds of Muhammad
Tarassul	Art of letter-writing, epistolography; writing exercises
Tazkira	Anthology of poetry; alternatively, a hagiography
'Ulama	Learned Ones; the social group trained in Arabic-based religious disciplines

ABBAS AMANAT is professor of history and international studies and director of the Program in Iranian Studies at Yale. His many works include *Resurrection and Renewal: Making of the Babi Movement in Iran* (Cornell University Press, 1989); *Pivot of the Universe: Nasir al-Din Shah Qajar and the Iranian Monarchy* (University of California Press, 1997); and *Apocalyptic Islam and Iranian Shi'ism* (I. B. Tauris, 2009). Professor Amanat also co-edited *Iran Facing Others: Identity Boundaries in a Historical Perspective* (Palgrave Macmillan, 2012) and co-authored *Az Tehran ta 'Akka: Babiyan wa Baha'iayan dar Asnad-i Dawran-i Qajar* (Nashr-i Ashkar, 2016). His most recent book is *Iran: A Modern History* (Yale University Press, 2017).

DAVID BROPHY is a senior lecturer in the Department of History at the University of Sydney. He holds a PhD from Harvard University and teaches modern Chinese and Russian history. Along with numerous articles, he is the author of *Uyghur Nation: Reform and Revolution on the Russia-China Frontier* (Harvard University Press, 2016). He currently holds an Australian Research Council Discovery Early Career Research Fellowship for the project "Empire and Religion in Early Modern Inner Asia."

ALFRID K. BUSTANOV is professor of Islamic Studies at the European University in Saint Petersburg. He graduated with honors from the History Department at Omsk State University and twice interned at the Institute of Oriental Manuscripts of the Russian Academy of Sciences (2008, 2009) before defending his doctoral dissertation at the University of Amsterdam. He has published extensively on Russian Orientalism and the manuscript culture of the Siberian Muslims, and about the Muslims of imperial Russia more generally. His many publications include *Knizhnaia Kul'tura Sibirskikh Musul'man* (The Book Culture of Siberian Muslims) (Mardjani Publishing House, 2012).

DEVIN DEWEESE is a professor in the Department of Central Eurasian Studies at Indiana University. He has held fellowships from the NEH, ACLS, Guggenheim Foundation, and the Carnegie Scholar program. His research on the religious history of Islamic Central Asia focuses chiefly on problems of Islamization, on the social and political roles of

Sufi communities, and on Sufi literature and hagiography in Persian and Chaghatai Turkic. His many publications include *Islamization and Native Religion in the Golden Horde: Baba Tükles and Conversion to Islam in Historical and Epic Tradition* (Pennsylvania State University Press, 1994).

PURNIMA DHAVAN is an associate professor in the Department of History at the University of Washington, Seattle. Her publications include *When Sparrows Became Hawks: The Making of the Sikh Warrior Tradition, 1699–1799* (Oxford University Press, 2011) and essays on Mughal and Sikh history. She is currently working on a new monograph exploring the ways in which literary networks created new identities and notions of public good in Mughal India, *The Lords of the Pen: Self-Fashioning and Literary Networks in Mughal India.*

THIBAUT D'HUBERT is associate professor in the Department of South Asian Languages and Civilizations at the University of Chicago. His teaching covers Bengali language and literature. He has published several articles in various periodicals and collective volumes and a book *In the Shade of the Golden Palace: Ālāol and Middle Bengali Poetics in Arakan* (Oxford University Press, 2018). His research covers Middle Bengali literature and Indo-Persian culture in Bengal, as well as the encounter of Persian, Sanskrit and vernacular poetics in the kingdom of Arakan (modern Bangladesh/Myanmar).

MICHAEL H. FISHER is Emeritus Danforth Professor of History at Oberlin College. He has published extensively about interactions between people from India and from Europe as they occurred in both India and Europe. His most recent books are *A Short History of the Mughal Empire* (I. B. Tauris, 2015); *Migration: A World History* (Oxford University Press, 2013); and *The Inordinately Strange Life of Dyce Sombre: Victorian Anglo Indian MP and Chancery "Lunatic"* (Columbia University Press, 2010).

GRAEME FORD holds a PhD in Chinese Studies from Macquarie University, Australia. He previously studied Latin, Chinese, and other languages at Sydney University and now teaches Chinese and English translation at Sydney Technical College. His research interests include Mongolian and Chinese history and philology, in particular the status of Persian in Ming imperial administration.

REBECCA RUTH GOULD is professor and professorial research fellow in Islamic World and Comparative Literature, at the University of Birmingham. She is the author of *Writers and Rebels: The Literature of Insurgency in the Caucasus* (Yale University Press, 2016), which was awarded the University of Southern California Book Prize in Literary and Cultural Studies. She is also the translator of *After Tomorrow the Days Disappear: Ghazals and Other Poems* by Hasan Sijzi of Delhi (Northwestern University Press, 2016) and *The Prose of the Mountains: Tales of the Caucasus* (Central European University Press, 2015). She is principal investigator from 2018 to 2023 for the ERC-funded project "Global Literary Theory: Caucasus Literatures Compared."

NILE GREEN is professor of history and Ibn Khaldun Endowed Chair in World History at UCLA. Between 2007 and 2016, he served as founding director of the UCLA Program on Central Asia. He is the author of seven monographs, including *Terrains of Exchange: Religious Economies of Global Islam* (Oxford University Press, 2014) and *The Love of Strangers: What Six Muslim Students Learned in Jane Austen's London* (Princeton University Press, 2016). His edited works include *Writing Travel in Central Asian History* (Indiana University

Press, 2014) and *Afghan History through Afghan Eyes* (Oxford University Press, 2016). He has held fellowships from the ACLS and Guggenheim Foundation.

MURAT UMUT INAN is assistant professor of Ottoman and Turkish Studies at the Social Sciences University of Ankara, Turkey. He received his doctoral degree in Near and Middle Eastern Studies from the University of Washington, Seattle. His research and teaching interests focus on literary and cultural histories of the premodern Islamic world. He is completing a book on the reception of Persian literary culture in the Ottoman Empire between 1400 and 1600.

ALEXANDRE PAPAS is a senior research fellow at the National Center for Scientific Research (CNRS) in Paris. He is a historian of Islamic mysticism in Central Asia, Western China, and Northern India. His main publications include *Soufisme et politique entre Chine, Tibet et Turkestan: Étude sur les Khwâjas naqshbandis du Turkestan oriental* (Maisonneuve, 2005); *Mystiques et vagabonds en islam: Portraits de trois soufis qalandar* (Cerf, 2010); *Ainsi parlait le derviche: Les marginaux de l'islam en Asie centrale (XVe–XXe siècle)* (Paris, 2018).

BRIAN SPOONER is professor of anthropology and museum curator for Near Eastern Ethnology at the University of Pennsylvania. He holds degrees from Oxford University and has conducted ethnographic research in Afghanistan, India, Iran, Pakistan, and Tajikistan. He is author or editor of eleven books and a hundred articles and book chapters on subjects relating to the anthropology and languages of the Middle East and to globalization. Together with William L. Hanaway, he co-edited *Literacy in the Persianate World: Writing and the Social Order* (University of Pennsylvania Press, 2012).

MARC TOUTANT is a member of the National Centre for Scientific Research (CNRS) in Paris. His research focuses on Turko-Iranian interactions and their contributions to Central Asian history and culture. He is the author of *Un empire de mots: Pouvoir, culture et soufisme à l'époque des derniers Timourides au miroir de la* Khamsa *de Mīr 'Alī Shīr Nawā'ī* (Leuven, Belgium, 2017), and co-editor with Gulnara Aitpaeva of *Littérature et société en Asie centrale: Nouvelles sources pour l'étude des relations entre culture et pouvoir du XVe siècle jusqu'à nos jours / Literature and Society in Central Asia: New Sources for the Study of Culture and Power from the Fifteenth Century to the Present* (Cahiers d'Asie centrale 24, 2015).

INDEX

Mansur ibn Nuh, Samanid ruler, 14
Mantiq al-Tayr, by Farid al-Din 'Attar, 85
Maqsad-i Aqsa by 'Aziz al-Nasafi (d. 1263), 33
Marathi language, 22, 32, 36, 41, 49
al-Mardjani, Shihab al-Din (1818–89), 197
maritime dimensions of Persographia, 24, 27,
    29, 39
Masa'il al-Hayat, by Mirza 'Abd al-Rahim
    Talibuf, 272
Masalik al-Muhsinin, by Mirza 'Abd al-Rahim
    Talibuf, 271, 272
Mashtots, Mesrop (362–440), 19
Maslak al-Muttaqin, by Allahyar, 146
*masnawi-khwan (masnawi-*reciters), 210
Masnawi, by Isma'il Ankaravi, 87
Ma'sum, Muhammad, *Maktubat,* 145
Matlab al-Talibin, 143
Mavraev (Mawrayuf), Muhammad Mirza
    (1878–1964), 268, 269
Mawarannahr (Transoxiana), 135–37, 148, 150, 185
Mawlawi Sufi order, 77, 83, 86–87
al-Mayhani, Muhammad, *Dastur-i Dabari,* 17
Mecca, 38, 46, 96, 100, 124, 179, 202, 2304, 306
Meditations by Marcus Aurelius, 271
Mehmed Beg, 62n
Mehmed/Mehmet I, Ottoman emperor
    (r. 1413–21), 81
Mehmed/Mehmet II, Ottoman emperor
    (r. 1451–81), 24, 76, 77, 78, 79, 80, 82
Merv, 23
Mesopotamia, 302, 304, 306, 307–08
Miandian (Burmese), 115
Miandianguan ke, 123
Middle Persian (Pahlavi), 10, 13, 15, 19, 38
Miftah al-Talibin by Mahmud Ghijduwani, 248
Mikadu-nama, by Mirza Husayn-'Ali Tajir
    Shirazi, 272, 290
Ming dynasty of China (1368–1644), 24, 33, 177;
    communication with the Timurid Empire,
    116–18; historiography in Persian, 137; use
    of Persian and translation practices, 51–53,
    113–25, 175–76, 177–79; Qing, transition,
    175–89; Veritable Records, 114, 116, 117
Ming dynasty of Khoqand (1710–1876), 244, 254
Minhaj al-Talab, 182
mint technology, 44
Mir Hajji, 119
Mirkhwand, 134; *Rawzat al-Safa,* 143, 248
Mirsad al- 'Ibad, by Najm al-Din Razi, 33
Mkhedruli script (Georgian), 19, 21
Mongol Empire (1206–1368), Mongols, 5, 23–25,
    116, 134, 178, 259, 302, 312, 313; breakup, 50

Mongolia, 24
Mongolian language, 22, 27, 43, 47, 115, 118,
    122, 179, 180, 207; as an administrative
    language, 24
Moretti, Franco, 25–26, 50
Mrauk U, Buddhist-ruled kingdom, 32
Mroveli, Leonti: *Kartlis Tskhovreba,* 19
Mu'awiya, 308
Mubarak 'Ali Khan Bahadur (r. 1824–38),
    Nawab of Bengal, 234
Müfredat by Ahmed-i Da'i, 81–82
Mughal bureaucracy, 36
Mughal Empire, 5, 7, 14, 16, 29, 30, 33, 34, 36, 38,
    42, 51–52, 114, 225–26, 238, 262, 302, 306; and
    the British Empire, transition in India, 53–54;
    collapse of, 41, 227; conquest of Bengal, 93;
    persecution of the Sikh gurus, 37; Persian
    learning, 52; Persian, role in state administra-
    tion and language of cultural elite, 41, 159–71;
    Persian scholarly networks in Punab, 159–71;
    rulers of Turfan, 124
Muginov, Abdulladzhan: *Opisanie uigurskikh
    rukopisei Instituta Narodov Azii,* 208
Muğla, 83
Muhammad 'Ali Khan, 267
Muhammad Amin Khan, ruler of Khiva
    (r. 1845–55), 139, 248
Muhammad Khan, Sayyid (r. 1856–64), 249
Muhammad Ma'sum, 145
Muhammad, Prophet, 10, 102–104, 147, 207,
    209, 214, 271, 281, 293, 288, 304, 306,
    307–310, 312
Muhammad Rahim Khan, ruler of Khiva
    (r. 1806–25), 246, 248, 252
Muhammad Rahim Khan II, , ruler of Khiva
    (r. 1864–1910), 46, 246, 248, 250, 251–52
Muhammad Rahim Quli, ruler of Khiva
    (r. 1842–46), 245
Muhammad Shah, Mirza, 233
Mujaddidi/ Mujaddidiyya. *See* Sufi
Mukhtar al-Ikhtiyar, 30
Mukhtasar al-Wiqaya, 248
al-Mulk, Mirza Muhammad 'Ali Mu'awin al-
    (Qawam al-Dawla), 284, 285, 295
al-Mulk, Mirza Sa'id Khan Ansari Garmrudi
    Mawtaman, 284
Mulla Nasr al-Din (1906–31), 262, 268
Multani, 'Abd al-Majid, 160
multilingualism, 4, 6, 18, 168
Munir Lahawri, Abu al-Barakat (1610–44),
    160, 161–66, 169, 170–71; *Kar-nama,* 161–63,
    165–66; *Nawbada,* 165

CPSIA information can be obtained
at www.ICGtesting.com
Printed in the USA
LVHW011945120519
617567LV00003B/3